THE RAJAS OF THE PUNJAB

THE RAJAS OF THE PUNJAB

Bring

The History of the Principal States in the Punjab

and

Their Political Relations with the British Government

Second Edition

BY

LEPEL H. GRIFFIN

GYAN

Published by

GYAN

Gyan Publishing House
5, Ansari Road
Daryaganj, New Delhi-110002
Phone: 011-47034999, 9811692060
E-mail: books@gyanbooks.com

Distribution Network
gyanbooks.com
India, USA, Canada, UK, Australia, France

ISBN : 978-81-212-1289-2 (PB)
First Published, 1873

2nd Impression 2021

Printed at: Gyan Press, Delhi.

The Rajas of the Punjab
Author: Lepel H. Griffin

THE

RAJAS OF THE PUNJAB

BEING

THE HISTORY OF THE PRINCIPAL STATES IN THE PUNJAB

AND

THEIR POLITICAL RELATIONS WITH THE BRITISH GOVERNMENT

Second Edition

BY

LEPEL H. GRIFFIN

BENGAL CIVIL SERVICE, ACTING SECRETARY TO THE GOVERNMENT OF THE PUNJAB

Author of "The Punjab Chiefs," "The Law of Inheritance to Chiefships"

LONDON

TRÜBNER & CO., 57 & 59 LUDGATE HILL

1873

PREFACE TO THE FIRST EDITION.

THE title of the present work may perhaps be open to objection as too comprehensive, seeing that there are many Chiefs in the territories administered by the Punjab Government, bearing the title of Raja, whose histories have not been here included. But my object has not been to record the biographies of reigning families so much as to give a connected account of the political relations of the British Government with the Independent States of the Punjab from the commencement of the present century.

With Kashmir and Bahawalpur, now its greatest feudatories in North India, the Government had nothing whatever to do until the first Sikh war. The history of the former province is full of interest, and will richly repay the most patient and laborious inquiry; but it was not till the defeats of the Satlej had shaken to its fall the corrupt monarchy of Lahore, that Kashmir was known to English Statesmen as more than the name of a distant valley which romance and poetry had delighted to paint with their most brilliant colours. Bahawalpur was even less known than Kashmir, till the campaign of 1848 brought its Chief as an ally to the side of the British; and even after the annexation of the Punjab, its internal politics were the subject of no interference on the part of the Government, until anarchy and civil war threatened to reduce the country to its original desert, when the Paramount Power was compelled to interpose in the interests of the people, whom tyranny had driven into rebellion and crime.

Among the hills from which the Satlej and the Ravi flow are Chiefs who bear the name of Raja, mostly of Rajput descent, and whose pedigrees stretch back in unbroken succession for several thousand years. But their history has little more than an antiquarian interest. At the time when the Gurkhas attempted the conquest of the Punjab hills, these petty Chiefs appear for a moment in the light of history, but the wave of invasion having been beaten back, they again disappear and are no more seen.

With the powerful Sikh Chiefs of the Cis- and Trans-Satlej the case is very different. Their rule is not sacred by antiquity. Whatever the origin of the race to which they belong, the Sikh Chiefs are, nevertheless, Autochthones, Earth-born, and their ancestors, but a few generations ago, were themselves driving the plough over the very lands which they to-day rule as independent Chiefs. But their history is a most important part of the general history of India. Their fierce enthusiasm, in the days when Sikhism was a living faith, enabled them to conquer the Punjab and defy the enmity of the Muhammadan Empire. It was their faith that made them strong, as it was the absence of all religious enthusiasm in the Muhammadans of India which proved their weakness, and ultimately their ruin.

With the British Government the relations of the Cis-Satlej States have been more or less intimate from the time of the conquest of Dehli by Lord Lake in 1803; and it is the history of these relations, and the policy which the British Government has adopted towards its feudatories, which it is here chiefly desired to record.

This history has been written in considerable detail and without reserve, except with reference to events of recent date, regarding which, obvious political and personal reasons forbid the expression of opinion or detail in relation. As far as I am aware, no chapter of Indian history has ever been written so unreservedly or with so much detail as the present volume, and on this account I would desire to call attention to a conclusion which may fairly be drawn from its pages.

The time may perhaps have passed, though of this I am by no means certain, when educated Englishmen, regarding with some degree of pride the conquest and possession of India, yet believed that the country was won by the most unjustifiable means, that each new province added to British India signified new crimes, and that the conquerors were only successful because they were unscrupulous. If this belief has been generally abandoned by educated men, it is still retained by those who have neither the means nor the inclination to inform themselves of the truth. It is encouraged and stimulated at the present day by writers in England, some of them men of ability, who either find it profitable to abuse their country, or who are so unfortunate as to be able to find nothing but national shame and incapacity where others would find monuments of national energy and glory.

A sufficient answer to hostile criticisms on the Government of India is found in the political history of the Cis-Satlej States for the last sixty-five years. These States form but a small portion of India, but they are, and always have been, considered a most important portion ;

in their control many principles of the highest moment were involved, and it may fairly be assumed that the policy which the Government adopted towards them was the same policy which it maintained towards the rest of India. It is unreasonable to assume that an administration which was just and generous in one province was tyrannical and rapacious in another. The Government of India has had one policy, and one alone, whether the Punjab, or Oude, or Bengal, was concerned; and if its policy has been unscrupulous, traces of its want of principle will most assuredly be found in its relations with the Cis-Satlej States. On this point let the facts which I have recorded bear their own witness. My personal opinion is valueless; like that of any other individual, it may be prejudiced, by association, by tradition, by interest; but facts are uninfluenced by prejudice. The conclusion at which I am convinced that any honest mind will arrive after reading this history, in which the single endeavour has been to record the truth, is, that the policy of the British Government, so far as the Sikh States are concerned, has been uniformly liberal, enlightened, and just; that in no single instance has it abused its strength to oppress its weaker neighbours; but that, on the contrary, it has taken less than its undoubted right, and has decided disputed questions with a generosity and disinterestedness which will be looked for in vain in the administration of any other country.

Absolute power is a dangerous, and often a fatal gift, which few have been able to use wisely; but the time will assuredly come when the enlightened policy of England in the East will be acknowledged by the world as her highest title to respect and honour.

It was but a short time ago that inquiries were instituted in India as to the opinion entertained by the people of the British Government; and on this subject many educated native gentlemen and high English officials recorded their views. The inquiry was chiefly remarkable as proving the excellence of the intentions of a Government which invited such open discussion, and as illustrating the curious tendency of Englishmen to criticise unfavourably whatever belongs to their own race or country. But seriously to compare the British administration with those which preceded it, or with the majority of those which exist side by side with it to-day in India, is an insult to the intelligence. There have been, it is true, Muhammadan and Hindu Princes who have ruled with strength and justice, and whose names are still held in honour. But these have been very few. Native rule in India, in former days, signified oppression of the most terrible kind, insecurity of life and property, luxury and debauchery in the Prince, misery and want in the people; and although much has been written regarding the preference of the people for the rule of their hereditary Chiefs, the simple fact remains that whenever an opportunity has been afforded them, the people have accepted British rule with the most unfeigned satisfaction.

The Punjab proper, during the time of Maharaja Ranjit Singh, was certainly a favourable specimen of a Native State. Yet the revenue system of Ranjit Singh was but an organised system of pillage, and the country was farmed to contractors, who were bound to pay a certain sum into the State treasury, and were permitted to collect as much more as was possible for themselves.

In the Trans-Indus districts, which are now so tranquil that the raid of a few marauders across the border is an event of importance, the revenue, twenty-five years ago, was collected by an army whose march down the frontier could be traced by the smoke of burning villages. Where the people were less warlike the revenue officers were not less cruel; as Kashmir, ground to powder by Sirdar Hari Singh, Nalwa, and the Jalandhar Doab, squeezed dry by the Shaikh tax-gatherers, will surely prove. If there be any feeling of nationality in India whatever, it may be most fairly looked for among the Sikhs. But in no part of India was British rule accepted more gladly by the people; and that they have not had reason to regret the change is shown by the uninterrupted peace and prosperity of the country, and by the willingness with which Sikhs and Muhammadans fought, in 1857, to maintain the British power.

Many Native States in India at the present time are ruled well; and in the Punjab territories, Pattiala, Jhind, and Kapurthalla enjoy an administration as substantially just as that of the British provinces. But this is alone due to English example, as the rulers of these States readily admit. They have voluntarily adopted the English revenue system, in some cases the English codes of law, and, in a modified form, the procedure of the English courts; they encourage education and introduce into their territories roads and canals. English example has done much, but its work is not yet complete; and, were its influence withdrawn, India would soon relapse into the anarchy and misery from which the British Government has rescued it. The education and civilisation of a nation are not achieved in fifty or a hundred years, and the work is both more difficult and more tedious when, as in India, chiefs and people have so much to unlearn before they can understand the new lessons we desire to teach them.

I believe that if the criticisms on the British administration of India are carefully considered, it will be found that they almost invariably turn on the unsympathetic nature of the Government and of the English character generally. So far as these criticisms attempt to assert an obvious fact, they are unobjectionable; but they become harmful when they attempt to go further, and to prove that the want of sympathy between the English and the natives is a grave danger to the Empire. The English are not a demonstrative or sympathetic race, and if there be a danger in such a national characteristic, it must be accepted with equanimity, for it is inevitable. But the natives of India are far less sympathetic and demonstrative than the English; they do not ask for our sympathy, and if it were offered to them, they would decline it.

A Hindu family lives very much alone; its joys and sorrows are nothing to its neighbours, and the social life of India at the present day is altogether undeveloped. Patriotism and nationality, as we understand the terms, have little meaning in India; from time immemorial the country has been ruled by foreigners, sometimes well, sometimes ill; the people have borne the burden of the incapacity and the vices of their rulers patiently, without complaint; they have accepted good government as they welcome the sunlight and the summer rains, with a quiet gladness, but with no feeling of thankfulness, for they knew not and cared not whence good government came.

The heart of the people in India is deep, and if we endeavour to find there any affection for ourselves, we shall most surely seek in vain. But esteem is stronger and better than love, and it will last unchanged when love has passed through its stages of passion, indifference, and disgust. For the English Government the people of India entertain a sincere esteem. They may not like all its ways, or its eager, fretful love of change and progress; but they know it to be just, they know themselves secure in person and property, while they are year by year increasing in wealth under the protection of a Government which demands little more than half of what they have been compelled to pay to the most liberal Government which has preceded that of the English.

If any certain augury of the future can be drawn from the events of the past, a popular rising in India against the Government may be pronounced impossible, so long as the administration of the country is based upon just and enlightened principles.

The delay which has taken place in the publication of the present work is owing to the enormous mass of materials in the shape of official correspondence which it was necessary to examine. The political records of Government, and of the Agencies of Dehli, Ambala, and Ludhiana, from the commencement of the present century, are exceedingly voluminous, and it has literally been the labour of years to index them and master their contents. The difficulties in the way of obtaining full and authentic information of the history of the States previous to their connection with the British Government have also been very great, although the Chiefs concerned have placed their whole family and State records at my disposal, and have facilitated my inquiries in every possible way.

The history of the Mandi State would more appropriately have found a place in a volume which I had hoped and still hope to publish on the Rajput Chiefs, the materials for which have been in a great measure collected. But, considering the length of time over which the preparation of the present work has extended, I have thought it better to include Mandi as the most important, and as, in some way, a representative specimen of the Rajput Hill Chiefs, rather than leave its history to form a fragment of a future work, which I may neither live nor have leisure to complete.

LEPEL GRIFFIN,
Under-Secretary to Government Punjab.

LAHORE, *November 9th,* 1870.

CONTENTS.

THE HISTORY

OF THE

PATTIALA STATE.

THE family of Pattiala belongs to the Sidhu Jat clan, whose villages are widely scattered over the tract of country lying between the Rávi and the Jamna. North of the Satlej the clan has lost its importance, and the war of 1849, and the annexation of the Punjab, broke, for ever, the power of the last great Sidhu family of Attári, one member of which, Raja Sher Singh, commanded the Sikh troops at Chilianwala, where the incapacity of an English General and the gallantry of the Sikhs almost drew upon the British army a calamity as crushing as that which had befallen it, eight years before, in Afghanistan. The Sidhu Jat tribe.

The only other Sidhu families, Trans-Satlej, whose names have any historical interest, are those of Attáriwala, Sidhu, Bhílowál, and Sowrian, but these are now poor, and of no political importance.[1]

---

[1] The Sidhus Trans-Satlej have descended from ancestors who seem to have returned to Rajputana, and re-emigrated to the Punjab in the sixteenth century.

South of the Satlej, however, the Sidhus are more powerful than ever; and among them are numbered the independent Princes of Pattiala, Nabha, Jhind, and Farídkot; the Sirdars of Bhadour, Malod, and Badrukhan; the Bhais of Kythal and Arnowli, and many other chiefs of less note.

The founder of the clan.

Like almost all the Jat tribes, the Sidhus are of Rajput origin, and trace their ancestry to Jesal or Jesaljí, a Bhatti Rajput, and founder of the state and city of Jesalmir, who was driven from his kingdom by a successful rebellion in A.D. 1180; and wandered northwards where Pirthi Ráj was then King of Ajmír and Dehli and the most powerful monarch in Hindostan. Near Hissar, Jesal determined to settle, and here four sons were born to him, Salváhan, Kalán, Hemhel, and Pem. The third of these, Hemhel, sacked the town of Hissar, seized a number of villages in its neighbourhood, and overran the country up to the walls of Dehli. He was driven back by Shamsuddín Altamas, the third Tartar King of Dehli, but was afterwards received into favour and made Governor of the Sirsa and Battinda country in A.D. 1212. He built the town of Hansar, where he died in 1214, and was succeeded by his son Jandra, who was only remarkable as the father of twenty-one sons, from whom as many clans have descended; Batera being the ancestor of the Sidhus. Manjalráb, son of Batera, rebelled against the Dehli Government, and was captured and beheaded at Jesalmir. He left one son, Undra, commonly known as Anand Rai, who was the father of Khiwa, the last pure Rajput of the family. Khiwa first married a Rajputni, but she bore him no children, and he then took, as a second wife, the daughter of one Basir, a Jat zamindar of Neli.

This marriage was considered a disgrace by his Rajput kinsmen, and Khiwa was ever afterwards known as "*Kot,*" which signifies in the Punjabi dialect, an alloy of metals, or any inferior and degrading admixture.

Khiwa, however, obtained what he desired, an heir; but the first wife, jealous of her rival, bribed the midwife to substitute a girl for the boy, whom she took into the jungle and threw into a dry water-course. Shortly afterwards a man passing by, saw the infant, and having no children of his own, imagined that it had been sent by Heaven to console him, so he took it home and adopted it as his son. But the midwife was unable to keep the secret; the Rajputni wife was compelled to confess her guilt, and, after a long search, the boy was found and restored to his father. He was named Sidhu, and from him the Sidhu tribe has derived its name.[1] The birth of Sidhu.

Sidhu, who was, according to Rajput custom, reckoned as of the caste of his mother, a Jat, had four sons, Dhar, sometimes called Debi, Búr, Súr, and Rupach. From the first has descended the families of Kythal, Jhumba, Arnowli, and Sadhowál; and from the second the Phulkian chiefs. Súr, the third, has no family of any note among his descendants, who, however, are numerous in Battinda and Firozpur; while those of Rupach, the youngest, reside at Pír-ki-kot and Ratrya in the Firozpur district. Bír, the son of Búr, had two sons, the eldest of whom, Sidtilkara, did not marry but became an ascetic. Sitrah, the younger, had two sons, Jertha and Lakumba, from the second of whom the family of Attári, in the Amritsar district, has sprung. The descendants of Sidhu.

---

[1] A similar tradition exists regarding the founder of the Shergil Jat tribe.—*Vide* "Punjab Chiefs," pp. 352, 452.

His son Harí, gave his name to Harïkí on the Satlej, near the spot where the battle of Sobraon was fought, and also founded the villages of Bhatta and Ghima. Jertha had one son, Mahi or Maho, and from him descended, in successive generations, Gala, Mehra, Hambir, and Burár, who gave his name to the Burár tribe. He was a brave and a successful man, and waged continual warfare with the Jaid and Dhaliwal Jats, and the Muhammadan Bhattis of Sirsa, who had sprung from the same original stock as himself; also with the Chattarsál Rajputs, against whom he fought at Fakarsar, Theri, and Kot Ladhoha, at which last place it is said that two thousand fell on the side of Burár, and a still larger number on that of the Rajputs, while the Fort of Ladhoha passed into the possession of the conqueror. Burár had two sons, Paur and Dhul, the younger of whom is the ancestor of the Raja of Farídkot, and of the Burár tribe, which holds almost the whole of the districts of Márí, Mudki, and Muktsar, Buchan, Mehraj, Sultan Khan, and Bhadour in the Firozpur district, the whole of Farídkot, and many villages in Pattiala, Nabha, Jhumba, and Malod.

The rise of the family

The two brothers quarrelled, and the elder, Paur, being worsted, fell into great poverty, in which his family remained for several generations, till Sanghar restored their fortunes. When the Emperor Bábar invaded India in 1524, Sanghar waited on him at Lahore and entered his army with a few followers; but soon afterwards he was killed at the battle of Pánipat, on the 21st April 1526, when Bábar defeated Ibrahim Lodi, with great slaughter, and gained the Empire of Dehli. This victory did not, however, lead him to forget the services of Sanghar, to whose son Bariám he gave the Chaudhríyat[1] of the waste country to the south-west of Dehli, which office was confirmed to him by Humayun, the son and successor of Bábar, in 1554. The name of Bariám is the only one by which this chief is historically known, but it was not his original name, and was given him by the Emperor in honour of his bravery, and signifies brave, "Buhádar." He lived for the most part at Neli, the village of Sidhu's maternal relations, and also rebuilt Bhidowal, which had become deserted. He was killed about the year 1560, fighting with the Bhattis, and with him fell his grandson Suttoh. He left two sons, Mehraj (commonly known as Maharaj), who succeeded to the Chaudhríyat, and Garaj, whose descendants people five villages in the Firozpur district. The only son of Mehraj had been killed in his father's lifetime, and Pukko, the grandson, succeeded, but he was soon after killed in a skirmish with the Bhattis at Bhidowal. He had two brothers, Lukho and Chaho; the descendants of the first live in Jakepal; and of the second at the village of Chaho, some eight miles distant from Bhadour in the Ludhiana district. His sons were Habbal and Mohan, the latter of whom was confirmed as Chaudhrí; but he fell into arrears with the Government, and finding himself unable to pay what was due, and also being much harassed by his hereditary foes the Bhattis, he fled to Hansi and Hissar, where his relations were numerous, and, collecting a considerable force, returned home and defeated the Bhattis near Bhidowal. By the advice of Guru Har Govind, the sixth of the

---

1 "A Chaudhri" was, in the time of the Empire, the head-man in a certain district, for the revenue collection of which he was responsible, receiving a percentage on the collections. His office was termed "Chaudhríyat."

Sikh prophets, he founded the village of Mehraj or Maharaj, naming it after his great-grandfather.

The founding of Mehraj.

From this village twenty-two others have been peopled, known as the *Bâis Maharajkian;* and the jagirdars inhabiting them, known as the Maharajkian Sikhs, are now upwards of seven thousand in number.

Mohan, with his eldest son Rup Chand, was killed, according to the custom of his family, in a fight with the Bhattis, about the year 1618, and Kála, the next surviving son, succeeded to the Chaudhríyat and the guardianship of his deceased brother's sons, Phul and Sandáli. The three other sons of Mohan helped to found Mehraj, where their descendants still live. Soon after Mohan's death, Har Govind again visited Bhidowal, and Kála, who had faith in the Guru's power and blessing, told his nephews that when they should see the saint, they were to place their hands on their stomachs, as if suffering from hunger. This they did; and Har Govind asking the reason, was told by Kála that the boys were starving. "What," said the Guru, "matters the hunger of one belly, when these boys shall satisfy the hunger of thousands." He then asked the name of the children; and on hearing that of Phul (blossom), he said, "The name shall be a true omen, and he shall bear many blossoms."

The great ancestor of the Phulkan chiefs.

Phul was the second son of Rup Chand, by Mai Umbi, a Jitáni Jat woman. He was educated by a celebrated fakir named Samerpuri, who taught him the art of feigning death by stopping his breath,[1] an accomplishment

[1] This art is mentioned several times in the Shastras, and in the Sikh Granth, under the name of पुरानयामं puranayam or stopping breath, and in Persian حبس دم habs-i-dam, or retention of the breath. The Hindus believed the breath was drawn up into the brain, which was supposed to be the seat of life.

which had for him a most tragical result. In the year 1627, Phul left Mehraj and founded a village five miles distant, which he called after his own name. He received a *firman* or deed of grant from the Emperor Shah Jehan, confirming to him the office which had been for so many years held by his family. The prophecy of Guru Har Govind was fulfilled, and Phul had seven children from whom have descended many noble families. By his first wife, Bali, the daughter of a zamindar of Dilami in Nabha, he had three sons, Tilokha, Ráma, and Rughu, and one daughter, Rámi Rám Kour or Fatoh, whom he married to a Sirdar of Ram Das, giving her as a dowry the village of Bugar, which her descendants still possess. From Tilokha have descended the houses of Nabha, Jhind, and Badrukhan; from Rama the houses of Bhadour, Pattiala, and Malod; and from Rughu, the Sikhs of Jiundan. By his second wife, Rajji, of Sidhani, he had also three sons, Channu, Jhandhu, and Takht Mal. The second of these died without issue; and the descendants of Channu and Takht Mal, known as the "Laudhgharian" Sikhs, are jagirdars of the village of Gumti.

The death of Phul is said to have happened in the following manner. The Governor of Sirhind had thrown him into prison on failure to make good his revenue collections; and Phul, seeing no other way to escape, practised the accomplishment he had learned from Samerpuri, and, suspending his breath and showing no sign of vitality, was supposed by his guardians to be dead, and his body was given for cremation to his friends, the Pathans of Maler Kotla, who conveyed it to his home. It so happened that his first wife, Bali, alone knew the mysterious power possessed by her husband, and she was

The death of Phul.

absent on a visit to her father. The younger wife, believing her husband dead, placed his body on the funeral pile and burnt him in the orthodox manner. Shortly afterwards Bali arrived, and, hearing of what had taken place, declared that Phul had been burnt alive. Rajji was so disconcerted by her mistake, that she abandoned the village and went to live with her brother-in-law, Sukhan Nand, a Burár, while Bali and her children continued to reside at the village of Phul.

The sacred pool of Ganga.

Previous to the death of Phul, which took place in 1652, the dates of the decease of members of the family are not known with any accuracy; and the reason is said to be that it was not customary with this tribe to convey the ashes of their dead to Hardwar, where Brahmans keep up registers of the deaths of those whose final ceremonies they perform, but to cast them into a sacred pool at the village of Ganga, in the Moga division of the Firozpur district. This pool acquired sanctity through a fakir named Kalunath, a Dhaliwal Jat, who, when importuned to accompany a body of pilgrims to the Ganges at Hardwar, declined, but sent as a substitute his staff and gourd, which he directed should be thrown into the sacred river. On the return of his friends, he inquired if they had complied with his directions, and they replied that they had; but on visiting the pool outside the village, both gourd and staff were found floating on the surface of the water. Thenceforward the pool was considered holy; pilgrimages were made to it, and into it the ashes of the dead were thrown. It has now lost much of its old sanctity; and although a fair is held at Ganga annually, at the Baisakhi, it is only the Jhán Jats of the Cis-Satlej and the Ramána Dhaliwal Jats, who hold it in respect.

The genealogy of the family, from the date of the flight of Jesal from his capital till the death of Phul, including twenty-nine generations, is as below :— Genealogy of the family.

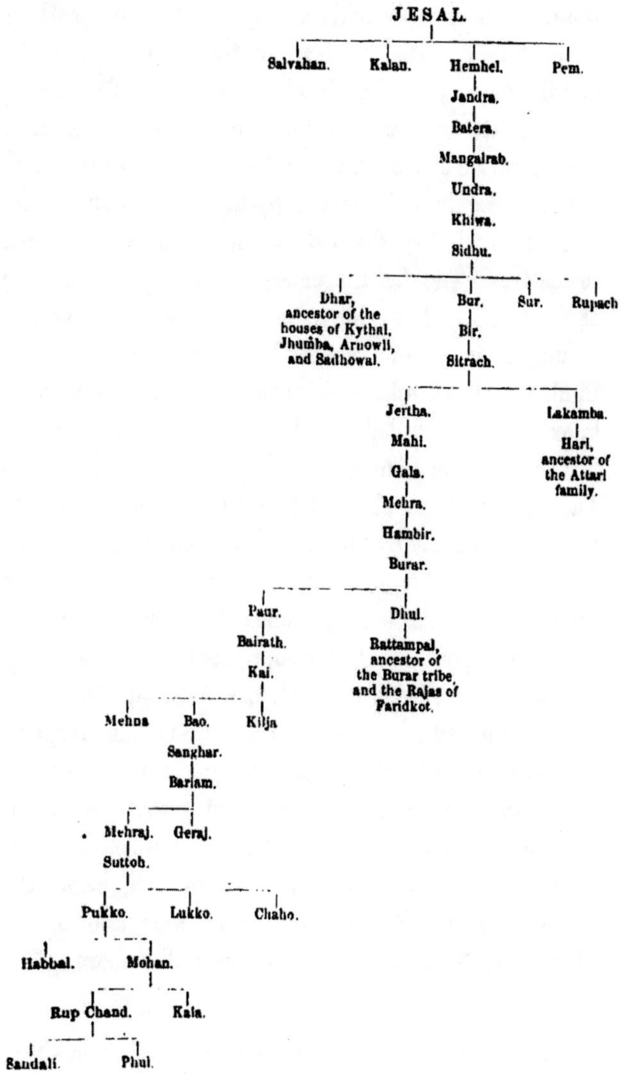

The sons of Chaudhri Phul and their descendants.

From Tilokha, the eldest son of Chaudhri Phul, have descended, as has before been said, the families of Nabha and Jhind. Ráma, the ancestor of the Pattiala family, was the second son of Phul. These brothers, the sons of the Chaudhri's first marriage, appear, after his death, to have at once taken the lead in the family. They induced their four half-brothers, sons of the second marriage, to give up all claim to the estates of their father, on the ground that they were unable to pay their quota of the dues demanded by the imperial authorities at Dehli, and they divided the ancestral land between themselves; Tilokha, the elder, succeeding to the office of Chaudhri. The village of Gumti was assigned to Chanu, Jhandu, and Takht Mal, the younger sons of Phul, and is still inhabited by their descendants, who are known as the Laudhgharian[1] Sirdars.

The founding of the village of Bhai Rupa.

The village of Bhai Rupa was founded by the brothers Tilokha and Rama, about the year 1680, and, being held to the present day by the Phulkian chiefs in equal shares, is the best possible proof of the original equality of the houses of Pattiala, Jhind, Nabha, Bhadour, and Malod. When the question of the supremacy of Pattiala over Bhadour was pending in 1854, the Maharaja stated that his ancestor had given Bhadour a share in this village to strengthen himself against the probable encroachments of Nabha and Jhind; the real truth being that Rama and Tilokha shared equally, and their sons inherited their shares according to custom and Hindu law, before the names of Nabha, Pattiala, and Jhind were known, and while their feuds and rivalries were still unborn. The

---

[1] Laudh signifies "small" in the Punjabi dialect; ghar, "house," and "Laudhgharia," consequently signifies the younger branch.

village of Bhai Rupa is situated in Nabha territory, and about eight miles to the north of the town of Phul.

Rughu, the sixth and last son, settled in the village of Jiundan, about eight miles to the south-west of Phul. From this village he had taken his wife, and his descendants still own its lands.[1]

The following is the Pattiala genealogy :— The Pattiala genealogy.

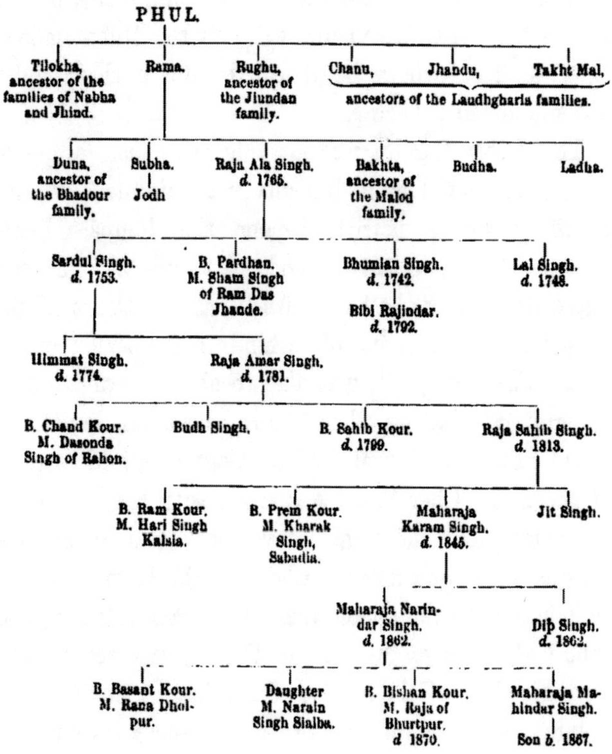

Ráma, or Rám Chand, is said to have first distinguished himself by attacking and dispersing a large body of marauders who were passing the village of Phul

Ráma the founder of the Pattiala family.

---

[1] The descendants of Rughu are mere zamindars. They are thirty-two in number, and their holding is worth Rs. 2079 per annum.

laden with plunder; and obtaining by his success some considerable wealth, he founded the village of Rampur, and began, after the example of the robbers he had despoiled, to attack such of his neighbours as were less powerful than himself. He made a raid into the Bhatti country, and defeated Hassan Khan, one of the old enemies of his family, with much loss, near the village of Chandah, and carried off much spoil, money, horses, and cattle. His next victory was over the Muhammadan chief of Kot, whom he defeated after a sharp fight, and plundered his camp.

He obtains the Collectorship of the jungle iláka.

The Dehli Empire was at this time fast falling to decay, and could with difficulty maintain its authority in the outlying districts beyond the Jamna. Ráma thought the opportunity a good one to increase his own authority; and as he had a friend at the Court of the Muhammadan Governor of Sirhind, in the person of his cousin Chen Singh, he was able to obtain permission to superintend what was then known as the jungle iláka or waste district, on promise of payment of all his arrears of revenue. Chen Singh was to act with him as Joint-Governor; but, as might have been anticipated, the cousins soon quarrelled. Chen Singh, through whose influence alone the appointment had been obtained, and who had access to the Sirhind Darbár, was not content with his share of the income of the district, and tried to obtain a reversal of this order in Rama's favour, and obtain the whole district for himself. Hearing of this intrigue, Rama lost no time in taking action to maintain his authority, and caused his cousin Chen Singh to be murdered in the Faridkot territory, whither he had gone on business.

His murder of his cousin.

And death.

This crime was never punished, nor even investigated,

by the Dehli Government, which had enough to do to take care of itself; but it did not go unavenged, for Bíru and Ugar Sen, the sons of Chen Singh, watching their opportunity, killed Rama at Kotla, in the year 1714.

At the time of his death Rama was not far from his eightieth year. He was a follower of Guru Govind Singh, although neither he nor his sons, with the exception of Ala Singh and Ram Singh, took the name of Singh as an affix to their own. He married Sábi, the daughter of a Bhuttar zamindar of Nánun, who bore him six sons, Duna, Subha, Ala Singh, Bakhta, Ladha, and Dudha. The first of these was the founder of the Bhadour family. Subha, the second son, died in 1729, and his only son, Jodh, the same year; and Hodiana, which he had conquered and made his residence, came into the possession of his brother Ala Singh. Bakhta, the fourth son, was the ancestor of the Malod family, while of the last two brothers, Budha and Ladha, who took the name of Ram Singh, no descendants are now living.

The sons of Rama.

A detailed account will hereafter be given of the families of Bhadour and Malod, which were soon overshadowed by the more powerful Pattiala house. But there seems no truth whatever in the statement made by Pattiala that, from the time of the death of his father, Ala Singh claimed supremacy over his brothers and that they rendered him service as the head of the house. Each brother was absolutely independent; and if two or more joined in a common enterprise, it was on terms of perfect equality. Ala Singh was not, moreover, the eldest son of Rama, as Pattiala authorities would wish to prove, but the third son; and Duna, the Bhadour ancestor, would have been the head of the family, had

The families Bhadour and Malod.

The Phulkian families originally equal and independent of each other.

primogeniture been then the rule. But it was only after the time of Ala Singh, the founder of the chiefship of Pattiala, that primogeniture was adopted as the rule of that family; if indeed it was formally adopted, for the Rajas denied or asserted it as seemed most convenient to themselves. At any rate, before Ala Singh's death, the rule which prevailed in the Phulkian family, as among the Jat Sikhs generally, was that of equal division between the sons; and, among the smaller Phulkian families, this custom, more or less modified, obtains to the present day. Nabha, Jhind, and Pattiala alone of the thirteen Phulkian houses assert the rule of primogeniture, and even these have, more than once, endeavoured to set it aside.

Ala Singh the third son of Rama.

Ala Singh was twenty-three years of age when his father was murdered, and his first thought was to avenge him. For sometime no opportunity occurred, but about two years after Rama's death, his assassins, Kamola, Biru, and Ugarsen, with a small body of attendants, paid a visit to Gumti, information of which having reached Ala Singh and his brother Subha, they hastily collected a few horsemen, surrounded the village, and attacked them. Kamola and his followers made a gallant defence, but were overpowered, and Biru, Kamola, and eighteen of their attendants, were slain. Ugarsen, escaping, fled to Semeke, which was at once attacked and pillaged, and Ugarsen had again to seek safety in flight.

He avenges his father's death.

Soon after this Ala Singh established a Thana or police station in Sangirah, at the request, it is said, of the people of that place, who suffered from the oppression of the chiefs of Kot and Jagráon, and he held the village, though its former owners tried their best to oust him.

In 1718 he left Bhadour to his elder brother Duna, and rebuilt Barnála, which had fallen into ruins, and where he took up his residence. Here one of Ala Singh's most powerful and troublesome neighbours was Sohnde Khan, a Muhammadan of Rajput origin, who owned the village of Nima, but whose occupation was rather robbery than husbandry; and who, besides three hundred horsemen of his own, could count on the assistance of Rai Kalha, the chief of Kot, his relation, who was too powerful for Ala Singh to care to offend him. Sohnde Khan died in 1731, and his adopted son, Nigáhi Khan, disgusted at being refused a share with the two sons of the deceased, took service with Ala Singh, and persuaded Sardul Singh, the son of the latter, to join him in an attack upon the village of Nima, which they captured and destroyed.

He leaves Bhadour to his brother Duna.

When the Rai of Kot, who was then a powerful chief, heard of this, he determined to punish the audacious Sikh, and collected a large force, led by Dalel Khan of Halwárah, Kutbuddin Khan of Mulsian, and other Rajputs of Thattar and Talwandi of the same caste as Sohnde Khan; Jamál Khan, chief of Maler Kotla, and Nawab Syad Asad Ali Khan, the imperial general of the Jalandhar Doab. Outside the walls of Barnala a battle was fought, in which fortune declared on the side of Ala Singh, for Asad Ali Khan having fallen early in the day, his troops became disheartened and withdrew from the field. The Maler Kotla and Kot troops followed the example, and the retreat soon became a rout, in which the Sikhs took many prisoners and the greater part of the enemy's baggage.

He is attacked by Rai Kalka of Kot but holds his own.

And the imperial general is slain.

This brilliant success at once made a great improvement in the position of Ala Singh. He was looked upon as one of the most rising chiefs, under whom both glory

The fame of Ala Singh increases.

and plunder might be won; and many a zamindar from across the Satlej came to Barnala to take service, sometimes alone, sometimes with two or three horsemen behind him. All that a Sikh chief asked, in these days, from a follower, was a horse and a matchlock. All that a follower asked was protection and permission to plunder in the name of God and the Guru, under the banner of the chief.

The qualities necessary for a chief.

There was little question of pay. All Sikhs were theoretically equal; their religion in its first youth was too pure a theocracy to allow distinctions of rank among its adherents; and he who, like Amar Singh Majithia, could pierce a tree through with an arrow, or, like Hari Singh Nalwa, could kill a tiger with a blow of his sword, might soon ride with followers behind him, and call himself a Sirdar. The time came when, like the Jews, the Sikhs took a king, and, in some degree, forgot the dream of equality which had been so dear to them.[1] But all the great families north and south of the Satlej have the same origin: the law of force, the keen sword and the strong hand, were the foundations upon which Sikh society, as indeed every other society in the world, was reared. Thus to attract followers by his power and success was the main desire of every Sikh; who they were or what were their antecedents was a matter of little consequence, if only they could fight and ride; and this almost every Sikh could do, as the English discovered in 1845 and 1849.

---

[1] Ranjit Singh never forgot to humour the democratic feeling, or, rather, the theocratic feeling of the Sikhs. He professed to rule "by the grace of God" like any Christian king; the name of the Guru was on his coins, and he was no more than chosen leader of the people, with whom he was always popular, though the chiefs had little love for him.

In these days every village became a fort, built on a high mound to overlook the plain country, with but one entrance and narrow lanes in which two men could hardly walk abreast. A neighbour was synonymous with an enemy, and the husbandmen ploughed their fields with their matchlocks by their side. No man could consider his land, his horse, or his wife his own unless he was strong enough to defend them; for, although the Sikh leaders were best pleased with the spoil of Muhammadans or the capture of an Imperial convoy, they were more robbers than patriots, and plundered with much impartiality. One thing in their favour must be said, which raises them far above the Pindaris of Central India or the Dacoits of Bengal: they fought and plundered like men, and not like demons. There are few stories in Sikh history of outrage to women and torture to men such as stain the pages of South Indian history with cruelty and blood. Many a pretty Jatni girl was, it is true, carried off in a foray, but she was generally a willing captive. She had been taught to consider courage and strength the only qualities to desire in a husband, and was quite ready to yield herself a prize to the man who had won her in fair fight, and who would make her his lawful wife, though he had killed her brothers and burned their village. Yet, while the Sikhs were undoubted robbers, and though cattle lifting was the one honourable profession amongst them, as on the Scottish border a few hundred years ago, their enthusiasm for their faith, their hatred to the Muhammadans who had so long trampled them under foot, who had killed their prophets and thrown down their altars, gave them a certain dignity, and to their objects and expeditions an almost national interest.

Sikh life in A.D. 1760.

The Sikhs were never a cruel race.

The Sikhs were never a united people.

But they were at no time a united people. During the eighteenth century each leader was absolutely independent, conquering and plundering on his own account, and only joining other chiefs to make an attack on the common enemy, the Muhammadan. Ranjit Singh contrived to make a compact kingdom out of the Punjab proper, north of the Bias, but he did not unite the Sikh people generally under his rule. At the time of his greatest power, in 1830, there may have been 1,250,000 Sikhs in the whole Punjab. But of these 500,000 lived to the south of the Satlej, under the rule of chiefs who looked upon Ranjit Singh as an upstart, and hated him even more than they feared him, if indeed this were possible. The Sikhs of the Cis-Satlej States had, indeed, a secret sympathy with their northern co-religionists, as was very evident during the Satlej campaign; but they had never united with them for any common object during the nineteenth century. Even the Sikhs of the Jalandhar Doab were only partially under the rule of Ranjit Singh. Their leader was the Ahluwalia Chief, who claimed to be the equal of the Maharaja; and although he was compelled to send a contingent to every campaign, and often to attend himself, yet he hated the Lahore Government fully as much as the Cis-Satlej Chiefs, and always looked for protection and countenance to the English, who, had they chosen, might have moved their boundary to the Bias thirty-five years earlier than they did, and have maintained themselves there without a struggle. But it was thought politic to leave a barrier of independent chiefs between British territory and that of Lahore; a policy intelligible enough, and perhaps wise, but denied or forgotten on the only occasions when it should have been remembered.

The victory of Ala Singh over the Afghans was gained in 1731, and he then again attacked his hereditary foes the Bhattis, the Chief of whom was Muhammad Amír Khan, son of Hassan Khan of Bhatner; with his followers and relatives Allahdad Khan of Buhái, Wiláyat Khan and Ináyat Khan of Hariau. The Bhatti country was, however, a very difficult one to conquer, with little forage and less water, while the inhabitants were as warlike as the Sikhs. Ala Singh made no impression upon them worthy of record, though, for ten years, a desultory warfare was carried on, with varying results.

Ala Singh makes war on the Bhattis.

About this time Ala Singh made friends with Ali Muhammad Khan, a Hindu convert of Rampur in Rohilkand, who had been adopted by a Muhammadan officer, and who founded a Rohilla State in the country between the upper Ganges and the hills. In 1741, however, Ali Muhammad was a servant of the Empire, and had charge of the sub-division of Sirhind. Ala Singh accompanied him on several expeditions, one of them against Rai Kalha of Kot, who was defeated and fled to Pákpattan, his brother, Mokham Khan, being killed. But the Sikh Chief was too independent to be long on good terms with any Imperial officer; and he soon saw that his residence at the Court of Ali Muhammad would be dangerous, and asked for his dismissal.

He allies himself with the Rohillas.

This the Governor refused, arrested him, and threw him into prison, where he might have perished but for the devotion of one of his followers, who had no very good reason to love him. This was Karma, one of the relations of Chen Singh, who, it will be remembered, was murdered by Ala Singh's father. He had entered the Pattiala service, but knew that he was thought not to have forgotten the family feud, and to be consequently

His imprisonment and escape

a dangerous character. To prove his devotion to his leader, he made his way at night to the place where Ala Singh was imprisoned, and, changing clothes with him, allowed him to make his escape. This fidelity was not unrewarded: Karma became the most trusted of Ala Singh's followers, and the family of Chen Singh was allowed to return to their home and rebuild their deserted village.

He reduces refractory villages.

Soon after this, Ali Muhammad left Sirhind for Rohilkand, so that the quarrel between him and Ala Singh ended, and the latter had leisure to reduce to submission several refractory villages, which had been induced by Sirdar Jodh Singh of Battinda to throw off his authority, and this work he successfully accomplished in about five months.

And builds the Fort of Bhawánigarh.

In the year 1749, Sirdar Ala Singh commenced to build the Fort of Bhawánigarh; but the progress of the work was interrupted by a petty Rajput Chieftain of the neighbourhood, named Farid Khan, who fancied that his own independence would be in danger by a fort so near his village. Not being able himself to storm the building he set out for Sirhind to invoke the aid of the Imperial Governor. But Ala Singh had heard of his intention, and, intercepting him, routed his party with considerable loss, and seized all his land, about one-fourth of the Samána parganah.

He conquers Sanáwar and founds Pattiala.

Three years later the district of Sanáwar was conquered for Ala Singh by one of his Sirdars, Gurbaksh Singh Káleka. The district was known as Chaurási (eighty-four), from the number of its villages, one of which was Pattiala, now the capital of the territory, where Ala Singh, in the year 1753, built a mud fort in order to overawe his new possessions, and left Sirdar

Gurbaksh Singh in charge. Diwan Lachman Narain, one of the officers of Samand Khan or Abul Samad Khan of Sirhind, fled to this Chief for protection, and his surrender was at once demanded by his master, who, being refused, marched to Sanáwar to enforce his demand. Sirdar Gurbaksh Singh then sent the Diwan to Pattiala, as being a place of greater security, and, joining the force of Ala Singh, they together attacked Abul Samad Khan and defeated him, securing a large quantity of plunder.

In company of Bhai Gurbaksh Singh he attacks Battinda.

The next expedition of the Chief was against Jodh or Jodh Singh, a Sirdar who possessed the district of Battinda, and against whom Bhai Gurbaksh Singh, the founder of the Bhaikian family of Kythal, had asked assistance. Ala Singh sent a considerable force, but his troops were repulsed, and he then called to his aid the Sikhs from the north of the Satlej, who were only too glad to assist in any expedition where plunder was to be obtained. They overran and pillaged the country, and then recrossed the Satlej, leaving Bhai Gurbaksh Singh in possession.[1] Ala Singh then turned his arms against Ináyat Khan and Wiláyat Khan, the Rajput Chiefs of Buhái and Buloda, who were somewhat troublesome neighbours. They called to their aid the Bhatti Chiefs, Hassan Khan and Muhammad Amin Khan, but these were unwilling to interfere, and the Rajputs were compelled to fight alone, which they did gallantly, being themselves killed in the field with several hundred of their followers. The Pattiala Chief lost almost as many men, but he seized the district of Buloda, which he soon afterwards surrendered to Bhai Gurbaksh Singh. The district of Múng was next added to the Pattiala terri-

[1] An account of the Kythal family is given later.

The district of Múng conquered by Sirdar Lal Singh.

tory, by Lal Singh, son of Sirdar Ala Singh. This young man was brave and energetic, and begged his father to make over to him some territory to manage. Ala Singh told him to win it for himself. He took counsel with Sirdar Khan, the original proprietor of Múng, who had been expelled by the Bhatti Chiefs, Abu Khan and Salím Khan, and his assistance was readily given, for he hoped, if not to recover the district for himself, to avenge himself upon those who had dispossessed him. While the Bhatti Chiefs were absent, Sirdar Khan made his way into the fort with a few followers, and signalled his success to Lal Singh, who brought up the main body of the troops and took possession of the village and adjoining district, which has been held by Pattiala ever since.

Ala Singh again attacks the Bhattis.

Sirdar Lal Singh and his father then overran the district of Sohána, Jamálpur, Dharsúl, and Shikárpur, belonging to Muhammad Amín Khan and Muhammad Hassan Khan, Bhattis. These Chiefs invited the Imperial Governor of Hissar to help them, and he sent a detachment; but in the engagement which followed, at Khodal, near Akalghar, the Bhattis were defeated; nor was their second venture more fortunate, for, after three days' skirmishing, Ala Singh made a night attack on the Bhatti camp, which was completely successful, and Muhammad Amin escaped with difficulty, and fled to Hissar. He then, to insure cordial assistance from Nawab Nasír Khan, the Governor, gave him his daughter in marriage, and set to work to raise as large a force as possible, hoping to retrieve his past defeats. The Sikhs and the Bhattis, supported by the Imperial troops, met at Dharsúl, but neither party cared to risk a general engagement. For seven or eight days the hostile forces lay opposite each other, skirmishing and fighting in a desultory manner; and it was more the chance of the death of Nasír Khan, the Governor, which gave the victory to the Sikhs, for the Imperial troops, disheartened by the loss of their leader, left the field, and the Bhattis were then at once attacked by Ala Singh with all his troops, and put to flight with great loss. This engagement, which did much to consolidate Ala Singh's power and increase his reputation, was fought in 1757. And defeats them with great loss, A.D. 1757.

The invasions of Ahmad Shah, Duráni of Kabul.

For ten years previous to this time, the Duráni monarch of Afghanistan, Ahmad Shah, had made almost annual expeditions into Hindostan, and, in 1748, 1756, and 1761, had marched as far south as Sirhind and Dehli. The conduct of the Prince towards the Sikhs was generally conciliatory, and he would have been glad to enlist them on his side, first against the Dehli Government, and then against the Mahrattas, whom he defeated in turn. But the Sikhs, although they hated the Dehli Government, bore no love to the Afghans. They had no wish to aid in building up at Dehli an empire stronger than that which preceded it, and to bind the yoke more firmly on their own necks. They were hoping for a Sikh republic, and a time when all Northern India would be the heritage of the Khalsa; when all hostile creeds should have fallen before the sword of the Guru. Besides this, they were unable to resist the temptation to plunder which the presence of a large army, with an immense train of baggage and innumerable camp-followers, implied; and they hovered about the Afghan line of march, cutting off supplies, and doing what damage they could, but never making a direct attack, for their own discipline was so slight that they entertained a reasonable dread of regular troops.

Ahmad Shah had, in 1761, appointed Zín Khan as

The Sikhs attack Zín Khan, the Afghan Governor of Sirhind.

the Governor at Sirhind, and the moment the Duráni monarch had turned his face homewards, the Sikhs attacked his Lieutenant, and it would have been difficult for Zín Khan to hold his own, had it not been for the aid of several Muhammadan Chiefs in the neighbourhood, among them Jamál Khan of Maler Kotla and Rai Kalha of Raikot. The next year Ahmad Shah again invaded India, and determined to punish the Sikhs for their audacity in attacking Sirhind. All the Phulkian Chiefs, the Singhpurias, the Faizullapurias, the Bhais of Kythal, Jassa Singh Ahluwalia, and many others, had collected to oppose the passage of the Shah, near Barnala, which was then the chief town of the Pattiala territory. The Sikhs, for the first time, met the Afghans in the open field, and the result was the most crushing defeat that they had ever received, their loss being estimated at 20,000 men, though this is probably an exaggeration. The Afghan troops then took possession of Barnala, and plundered it. Ala Singh was captured and taken before Ahmad Shah, and a ransom of four lakhs of rupees was demanded for his life. This the Chief with some difficulty paid, and Ahmad Shah, who was a man of great sagacity, thinking it would be wiser to conciliate the Sikhs after having given them, in their late defeat, so convincing a proof of his power, embraced Ala Singh, and gave him a dress of honour, with the title of Raja.

Ahmad Shah returns, and the Sikhs collect to oppose him, but are utterly defeated.

Ala Singh taken prisoner, but pardoned and created a Raja.

The consequences of good fortune.

It was in March 1762, that Ala Singh obtained this title, and the jealousy and indignation of the other Chiefs was very great. They declared that he had betrayed them, and that the title was the price of his treachery; and that it was unworthy for a Sikh to bear a title conferred by a Muhammadan, a foreigner, and an enemy. The Sikhs were ready to turn upon Ala Singh and avenge upon him their defeat, had it not been for Sirdar Jassa Singh Ahluwalia, who was at this time far more influential than Ala Singh himself, and who took his side in the dispute. Matters were at length smoothed over, but it was necessary for Ala Singh to prove by his actions that he was not a servant of the Duráni King. No sooner had Ahmad Shah returned to Kabul, than the Sikhs began to recover their courage and to coalesce against the Muhammadans. The confederacies, both north and south of the Satlej, for once laid aside their feuds and jealousies, and united to make one great effort against Sirhind, which the Sikhs especially hated, as it was there that the two sons of Guru Govind Singh had been put to death by the Muhammadans. Ala Singh joined with ardour in the expedition, for he had to clear his character in the eyes of his countrymen. The Sikh confederacies from the north of the Satlej assembled in great numbers in the neighbourhood of Sirhind, after having taken possession of the town and fort of Kussur, below Lahore; and Ala Singh, with several of the other Phulkian Chiefs, joined them, till the army, almost entirely horse, numbered 23,000 men. Zín Khan, the Governor of Sirhind, trusting to that dread of regular troops which the Sikhs had ever shown, came without the town to give them battle; but he was killed, and his force utterly routed. The Sikhs immediately took possession of the town, which they almost completely destroyed, to avenge the murder of the children of their prophet, and the province of Sirhind was divided among the conquerors. The town and its neighbourhood was made over to Raja Ala Singh, chiefly through the influence of Sirdar Gurbaksh Singh, his friend, and a nephew of the great Singhpuria Chief, Kapur Singh,

The Sikhs again attack Sirhind, and capture it, December 1763.

The town made over to Ala Singh

and other portions became the property of the Chamkor, Rupar, Sialba, Buria, Kythal, and Shahabad Chiefs, and are in part held by them to the present day. Ala Singh made no attempt to rebuild the city of Sirhind, which is still considered accursed by the Sikhs, but removed the greater number of the inhabitants to his new town of Pattiala, where he soon afterwards built a masonry fort from the proceeds of the custom duties collected at Sirhind, which was on the high road between Kabul and Dehli, a position to which the misfortune of its being thrice sacked was in a great measure attributable.

Ahmad Shah makes no attempt to recover Sirhind.

The next year the Duráni monarch again invaded India, but he was too wise to attempt the experiment of placing another Governor in Sirhind to succeed and share the fate of the unfortunate Zín Khan. He received Ala Singh with an appearance of cordiality, and granted him the Chiefship of the *chalka* or district, on his agreeing to pay three and a half lakhs of rupees a year, as revenue. A portion of this was paid at once; and Ala Singh promised to remit the remainder to Kabul, but of the fulfilment of this promise there is no record. His grand-daughter, Bibi Rajinda, the only child of his son Bhumian Singh, who had died in 1742, offered indeed to pay the balance for him; but this offer Ala Singh did not accept, pleading the Hindu rule which prohibits a man from borrowing or being under an obligation to his sister or his daughter. He probably thought, and with justice, that Ahmad Shah at Kabul would be a creditor more easy to evade than Bibi Rajinda at Pattiala.

The death of Ala Singh, A.D. 1765.

Raja Ala Singh accompanied Ahmad Shah on his return journey as far as Lahore, and then returned to Pattiala, where he died in August 1765.

Among the Sikh Chiefs of his day, Ala Singh was certainly one of the most distinguished. He was gallant, and at the same time prudent, and laid strongly the foundations of the most important of the Cis-Satlej States. It is not easy to determine his exact relative position with reference to other Chiefs, for the number of troops which each could bring into the field is either exaggerated or unknown, but he was probably the most powerful Chief south of the Satlej; although the Kythal family soon became dangerous rivals, and not less so that they were related to the Phulkian house. Of Jassa Singh Ahluwalia, the Pattiala Chief always showed great jealousy, which the remembrance of his good offices with the Sikhs, after the obnoxious title of Raja had been conferred by Ahmad Shah, did not dispel. Indeed, after the conquest of Sirhind, and when Jassa Singh had re-crossed the Satlej, Ala Singh seized his share of the plunder, eight villages, and held them in spite of protests and force. His character.

Ala Singh only married one wife, Fattoh, the daughter of Chowdhrí Khána, a Subhrán zamindar of Kaleke. A story was told of her, that at her birth, her mother, disappointed at having a daughter when she had earnestly desired a son, put the new-born child in an earthen vessel and buried it in the ground. A wandering mendicant of the name of Devi Dass happening to pass, and seeing the mother in tears, inquired the cause of her grief. She confessed to him what she had done, and the mendicant told her to disinter the child, for of her would be born a famous race, which should rule all the neighbouring country. The child was taken out of the ground unhurt, and eventually became the wife of Ala Singh, bearing him three sons, Sardul Singh, Bumian Singh, His family.

and Lal Singh, all of whom died in the lifetime of their father; and a daughter, Bibi Pardhan, who was married to a zamindar of small consideration, and nothing is known of her descendants.

Sardul Singh, his eldest son.

Sardul Singh, the eldest son, married as his first wife the daughter of a Sirdar at Bhíkhe, who became the mother of Maharaja Amar Singh. His second wife was the widow of his first cousin Jodh, whom he married according to Sikh custom, by *karewa* or *chaddar dálna*, a simple and unorthodox rite, always used in the marriages of widows. Little is known of Sardul Singh, who died in 1753. He was a brave soldier, but most of the Sikhs were brave; and he died from hard drinking, a virtue as common as bravery among his countrymen.

The second son, Bhumian Singh.

Bhumian Singh, the second son, left one daughter, Bibi Rajinda, who has before been mentioned. She was married to Tilok Chand, Chaudhrí of Bhagwara, who died before her, and she succeeded to her husband's property, according to Sikh custom. The succession to the property on her death was claimed by her grandson Jodh Singh, a daughter's son. According to Sikh custom, no estate can descend in the female line, and the sons of daughters are not counted among the legal heirs. Chuhar Mal, the brother of Rajinda's husband, consequently ejected Jodh Singh and put him to death, and the family of the latter have now become extinct, though a son, Sahib Singh by name, was living in 1820.

Lal Singh, the youngest son.

The youngest son, Lal Singh, died childless, and from the same cause as his brother, excessive drinking. He added Múng to the Pattiala territory. His widow, Bibi Bhagan, survived him many years.

The succession to Raja Ala Singh.

When Raja Ala Singh died, there were two claimants for the Chiefship, Himmat Singh and Amar Singh, the sons of Sardul Singh and the grandsons of the late Raja. Of these, Himmat Singh was the elder by several years, but he was the issue of an irregular marriage, his mother, as has before been mentioned, having been the widow of Jodh, the first cousin of Sardul Singh.

The Chaddar dálna marriage.

The custom of *chaddar dálna* (throwing the sheet), or *karewa*, marriage, was universal among the Sikhs, and the children of such marriages were often considered inferior in position to those of the regular marriage (*shádi* or *vyáh*), contracted with a virgin, and with all the ceremonies customary among the Hindus. The most common, as well as the most highly respected form of *karewa*, is where a widow is taken to wife by her husband's brother, a custom which seems to have formerly prevailed among the Jews. If a widow chose to refuse this new alliance, she was at liberty to do so, but in that case her life was as miserable and austere as that of the ordinary Hindu widow; and few Sikh women, consequently, refused to remarry, though they generally chose the younger brother of their husband, in preference to the elder, whom strict custom assigned to them.

The marriage of a widow with the cousin of her husband, as was the case with the mother of Himmat Singh, was considered less reputable, and there was some doubt as to the legitimacy of the issue. Still less respectable were marriages with widows unconnected with the family, or women of strange clan and caste, which were considered altogether irregular, little better than concubinage, and the issue had no right to succeed to the property, real or personal, of the father, and could only claim a bare maintenance.

Raja Amar Singh succeeds his father.

Amar Singh, the second son of Sardul Singh, was born in 1747, and was consequently eighteen years old when his grandfather died. He and his grandmother, Rani Fattoh, had been residing at Anáhadgarh or Barnala, fifty miles to the westward of Pattiala. When they heard the unexpected news of Ala Singh's death, they left in all haste for the capital, and the Rani, who was a woman of great ability, as many of the ladies of the Pattiala family have been, placed her grandson on the vacant "*gaddi*,"[1] and declared that he was by right, and by the proclaimed wish of Ala Singh, his successor in the Chiefship. The ministers and officials, whatever they may really have thought of the claims of Himmat Singh, did not attempt any diversion in his favour. The action of Rani Fattoh had been so prompt, and her influence was so great, that there was no opposition; and, in full Durbar, all the Chiefs and Officers of Pattiala presented their offerings (*nazr*) to Amar Singh as the new Raja.

The rebellion of Himmat Singh.

Himmat Singh was not a man to lose a principality without an effort. He hastened from Hariana, where he had been employed with troops, to Pattiala, and asserted his claim to the Chiefship, taking possession of a great part of the town of Pattiala and the neighbouring country. The Sirdars of Jhind and Nabha, however, with the Kythal Chief, exerted their influence in favour of the younger brother; and Himmat Singh was compelled to retire. He then seized the district of Bhawanighar, and captured a portion of the country belonging to the Afghans of Maler Kotla. Amar Singh marched against him, and besieged the town of Bhawanighar, but

[1] The term "gaddi," literally "cushion," is used among Indians as "throne" among other races. For the English expression, "mounted the throne," "gaddi nishin"—"seated on the cushion"—is used in Hindustani, and "takht nishin"—"seated on the throne"—in Persian.

Rani Fattoh persuaded the brothers to make friends, and Himmat Singh was left in possession.

Amar Singh captures Páyal and Isru.

The year after his accession, in 1766, Amar Singh captured the town of Páyal, near Ludhiana, from the Kotla Afghans, with the aid of Jassa Singh Ahluwalia and other of the Trans-Satlej Sikhs; and, after that, Isru, belonging to the same proprietors, Jassa Singh taking one-fourth of the revenue of the town; but later, by an arrangement with Amar Singh, he became possessed of the whole of the Isru district. Sirdar Jassa Singh had given the young Chief the *Páhal*, or baptism, always a bond of affection among the Sikhs, and there was more sincere friendship between them than had existed in the time of Ala Singh.

Ahmad Shah's last invasion of India, and his kindness to Amar Singh.

In 1767, Ahmad Shah for the last time invaded India, but he advanced no further than Ludhiana. Here he was met by Amar Singh, who was cordially received, and the title of Raja, which had been granted to his grandfather, was continued to him with additional honour, as "Rája-i-Rájgán Buhádar."[1] Valuable presents on this occasion were also given him, with a flag and a drum, insignia of an independent prince. In honour of this reception, Amar Singh spent a lakh of rupees in ransoming the captives who had been taken by the Dehli Emperor in the neighbourhood of Mathra and Saharanpur, gaining for himself the popular title of "Bandi Chhor," or "Releaser of captives."

War with the Afghans of Maler Kotla.

Soon after Ahmad Shah had left India for the last time, Raja Amar Singh renewed the old quarrel of his

[1] Cunningham, in his History of the Sikhs, states that on this occasion Amar Singh received the title of Maharaja. But this was granted later, by Akbar II., in 1810, on the recommendation of General Ochterlony. The sanad is still in possession of the family.

family with the Afghans of Maler Kotla. Jamál Khan, the Chief who had done most injury to Pattiala by persuading Ahmad Shah to sack Barnala, had been killed in battle, and the family had become divided—Ata-ulla Khan being the most influential of Jamál Khan's sons. This Chief, after the Raja had taken Tibba, one of his villages, by assault, found that he was unable to resist so powerful an enemy successfully, and made peace, which for many years remained unbroken.

With the Chief of Manimajra.

Amar Singh then sent a thousand men against Gharíb Dás of Manimajra,[1] who, during the confusion which followed the death of Ala Singh, had managed to take possession of the fort and district of Pinjor, an ancient Hindu town, in the low hills above Ambala; and where the Pattiala Chief has now a favourite summer residence and gardens, which are celebrated for their beauty over all Northern India. The place was very strong, and Bakhshí Lakhna, a Dogra General whom the Raja sent

[1] Gharib Dás was the founder of the Manimajra family. After the death of Zín Khan, the Governor of Sirhind, and the break up of the Imperial power, he took possession of 84 villages, which his father Ganga Ram had held as a revenue officer for the Empire, and further extended his territory by seizing the fort of Pinjor. Here the Raja of Náhan attacked him, but without success; and placing his father in charge, Gharib Dás left intent on fresh conquest. It was during this absence that the Raja of Náhan, having obtained aid from Pattiala, attacked the fort as described in the text, and captured it, Ganga Ram being slain. Gharib Dás hastened back, but was not strong enough to attempt to recapture the fort. He, however, expelled the Náhan Raja from Chandangarh, which he had captured shortly before.

Gharib Dás died in 1783, leaving two sons, Gopal Singh and Pargash Chand. The elder of these did excellent service in 1809, and again in the Gurkha campaign of 1814. Sir D. Ochterlony was about to recommend him for a new jagir, but he requested instead the title of Raja, which was given to him. He died in 1816, and was succeeded by Hamir Singh, who only survived his father a few years. Goverdhan Singh, his son, was loyal in 1845, and gave a detachment which was engaged at Mudki and elsewhere. He died in 1847, and was succeeded by Gurbaksh Singh, who died in 1866, when his younger brother Bhagwan Singh, now 22 years of age, inherited the estate of 77 villages, worth Rs. 38,453 a year.

with a thousand men to reduce it, aided by the Rajas of Hindúr, and Kahlur, and Náhan, had a month and a half of hard fighting. But they were at last successful, and Gharib Das allied himself with the Chiefs of Sialba and Rupar,[1] in order to attack the Raja of Náhan,[2] to whom the Raja of Pattiala had left the fort, and with whom he had contracted a strong friendship, exchanging turbans with him at Banaur. The Pattiala force lost three hundred men in this attack on Pinjor.

The attack on Kot Kapura.

One hundred miles due west of Pattiala, and near the town of Faridkot, was the fort of Kot Kapura, belonging to a Burár Chief named Jodh Singh.[3] One of this Sirdar's followers had stolen from the fort of Phul a horse and a mare, which he presented to his master, who was not in the least degree averse to receiving stolen property. It was reported to Raja Amar Singh that the Kapura chief

[1] The founder of the Sialba family was Sirdar Hari Singh, who, about 1763, when the Sikhs became powerful, took possession of a large part of the country at the fort of the hills, both Cis and Trans-Satlej, the principal districts of which were Sialba, Rupar, Khizabad, and Kurali. He had several sons, but only two survived him, Charrat Singh and Dewa Singh, to the former of whom he gave the Rupar ilaka, worth about Rs. 80,000 a year; and to the latter Sialba, with the other estates Trans and Cis-Satlej, worth nearly two lakhs. This partition was made in 1792, the year before his death. Rupar has lapsed, and of the Sialba estate, the present Chief only retains villages worth about Rs. 30,000 a year.

[2] Náhan is a very ancient Rajput principality, about 40 miles due south of Simla. The territory of the Raja, worth about a lakh per annum, was confirmed to him after the Gurkha campaign of 1814, in perpetuity, by a Sanad dated 21st September 1815.

[3] The Kot Kapura family were of the same stock as the Phulkians. Ballan was the founder of the family, and, under the Emperor Akbar, was appointed Chaudhri of the Burár tribe. His son Kapura built the fort which bears his name, and became an independent Chief. He died in 1711. His eldest son, Sukha, succeeded him. Jodh Singh, the Chief mentioned in the text, was the eldest son; and Hamir Singh, the second son, whose quarrel with his brother and report of the insult offered to the memory of Raja Ala Singh, in naming the horse after him, occasioned the death of Jodh Singh, was the founder of the house of Faridkot, the history of which is recorded later.

had been audacious enough to name the horse Ala, and the mare Fattoh, after the names of the Raja's grandfather and grandmother. Amar Singh was much offended, and sent to demand the surrender of the horses. Jodh, confident in his strength, tore the Pattiala letter in pieces, and sent no reply.

And the death of its Chief, Jod Singh.

On this Amar Singh marched against Kot Kapura, and encamped five miles from the fort. Jodh, with one of his sons and an attendant, mounted a chariot, and went out to reconnoitre, but fell into an ambuscade laid by the Pattiala force, and was surrounded and slain, after having killed several of the enemy with his bow and arrows, in the use of which he was very expert. Jit Singh, his son, who had accompanied him, was so severely wounded that he died three days afterwards. Jodh's head was cut off and carried to Amar Singh, who was much distressed, as he had no wish to take the chief's life. He gave up all intention of besieging the fort, and returned to Pattiala.

Another Bhatti expedition.

The Raja then turned his arms against the Bhattis, and subdued Aharma and Singha; but the Bhatti chiefs attacked his camp at night, and occasioned great loss and confusion. After this he left the campaign, which, from the nature of the country, was of a most difficult character, to be conducted by Sirdar Hamir Singh of Nabha. While at Rori, a small town on the border of the present Sirsa district, two men, Gajjai Singh and Jit Singh, paid a visit to the Raja, and begged him to help them to avenge an insult one of their women had received at the hands of Sukhchen Singh, a Sabo zamindar of great repute, owner of the strong fort of Govindgarh, which commanded the town of Battinda. Only too glad of an opportunity for interference, Amar Singh sent a force against Sukhchen Singh, and followed quickly himself. He gained possession of the town of Govindgarh, but the fort was too strong to take by assault, and he had no artillery of sufficient power to reduce it. He was compelled to try and starve Sukhchen Singh out, and for a whole year the fort was besieged without success, till the owner, tired of his resistance, proposed to surrender if the Raja would raise the siege and promise him safety. Amar Singh agreed to this, but before drawing off his troops and returning to Pattiala, he insisted that Kapur Singh, son of the Chief, with four or five of his principal officers, should be given him as hostages. The siege was then raised, but Sukhchen did not give up the fort, and it was not till four months later that he visited Pattiala, accompanied by Sodhi Bharpur Singh, a man whose sanctity was so generally respected by the Sikhs, that Sukhchen thought his company of more value than any safe conduct from the Raja. Arriving at Pattiala, he asked for the release of the hostages, agreeing to remain himself in confinement until the fort was surrendered. To this the Raja consented, and Kapur Singh, with the other hostages, returned to Govindghar, and at once began to strengthen the defences and increase the garrison. On the news of this reaching the Raja, he sent orders to assault the fort without delay, and treated Sukhchen Singh with great severity, to the indignation of Sodhi Bharpur Singh, who protested against such treatment of a man who had been persuaded to come to Pattiala under his solemn assurance of safety. At length Sukhchen, weary of his rigorous imprisonment, sent an order to his son to make over the fort to the Pattiala officials, which was done, and Sukhchen released. This acquisition was

The siege of Govindgarh A.D 1771.

made in 1771, and the Battinda district has been held by Pattiala ever since.

The Mahrattas march northwards.

Soon after this, a Mahratta general, Janko Rao, marched in the direction of Pattiala, to the consternation of Amar Singh, who sent off all his treasure and family jewels to Bhattinda, which, lying amidst sandy wastes, was not likely to be attacked. But, after all, the Mahratta did not visit Pattiala, coming no farther north than Pihoa, sixteen miles beyond Thanesar, and a famous place of pilgrimage, situated on the Sûrsati, the Sanskrit Saraswatí.[1] Here he remained for a short time, and then returned.

Himmat Singh again rebels.

Relieved from his fear of being himself plundered, as he had so often plundered others, Raja Amar Singh set out to punish some refractory zamindars in the neighbourhood of Battinda. Sirdar Himmat Singh considered the absence of the Raja so far from the capital a good opportunity to recover the rights of which he considered himself to have been unjustly deprived, went with all speed to Pattiala, and professing himself to have none but the most loyal intentions, was admitted with his followers into the fort by Sirdar Sukhdas Singh Kaleka, who had been left in charge. He then threw off all disguise, seized the fort, and proclaimed himself the rightful chief, and Amar Singh a usurper. On receipt of this terrible news, the Raja hurried back to Pattiala, and encamped at Samana to take council with his friends, for the reduction of the fort by assault was a difficult and doubtful opera-

Seizes the Pattiala fort.

[1] The Saraswatí is mentioned in some of the most ancient Sanskrit writings, and was a stream of great sanctity. Saraswatí was the wife of Brahma, and the Goddess of Wisdom. Wandering one day in the deserts about Thanesar, she was surrounded by demons, and to escape them, changed herself into the stream which bears her name. The Saraswatí is supposed to have an underground connection with the Ganges.

tion. To this place he invited all the Sirhind chiefs, and a large number responded to his call: Sirdar Tara Singh, the chief of Rahon; the Afghan Nawab of Maler Kotla; the Rais of Kot; Sirdar Hamír Singh of Nabha; Raja Gajpat Singh of Jhind; Bhais Dhanna Singh and Sukha Singh, of Kythal; and Bhai Desu Singh, the father of the famous Lal Singh whose power later became too formidable to Pattiala. There were, moreover, Manjha Chiefs and Jassa Singh Ahluwalia; while Kirat Parkash, the Raja of Náhan, remembering that Amar Singh had helped him in his difficulties, came with his troops without waiting for an invitation at all.

But his friends stands aloof.

Himmat Singh perceived that he could not long resist the large force which had assembled to attack him, and was altogether disappointed at the result of his attempt. He had fancied that the neighbouring chiefs, even those of Phulkian blood, who were jealous of the increasing predominance of Pattiala, would be only too glad to encourage any project which might divide or destroy the power of the State; and there is no doubt that any calamity which might happen to Pattiala would be hailed with a certain satisfaction. But Himmat Singh had been too hasty in his action, and declared against his brother before he had made sure of allies. The name of Amar Singh was now dreaded: he had been a successful general, and it was well understood that any attack upon him, that failed to crush him he would most certainly avenge.

He is compelled to surrender.

So it happened that Himmat Singh remained shut up in the fort without any of his declared friends, Bhai Desu Singh of Kythal, the Rajas of Jhind and Nabha, or the Rai of Kot, who had exchanged turbans with him, offering their help; and at last, seeing preparations made for assaulting the fort, he was easily persuaded by the chiefs above named to surrender. Amar Singh had no wish to proceed to extremities, and readily consented to allow his brother life and liberty, and he even, with the vain hope of rendering him content, increased his jagirs by the grant of several villages from the district of Darbah. But Himmat Singh was not disposed to abandon intrigue; his claim he considered good, for he was an elder brother, and, although by a *karewa* marriage, his mother had been lawfully married according to the custom of the Jats, and he could not rightfully be held to be illegitimate. Even supposing that he had forfeited the title to succeed to the Chiefship, yet equal division among sons was the almost universal rule, and he was entitled to a half-share of the territory which his grandfather Ala Singh had won. Thinking as he did, and with much right on his side, it was not to be expected that Himmat Singh would ever live as a loyal subject, and it was fortunate for the peace of the territory that, in 1774, two years after his attack on Pattiala, he died from excessive drinking at Langowal, and his estates, Bhawanigarh, Darbah, and Dhodrah, were resumed by Amar Singh, who married the widow by *chaddar dálna*. The same year, Amar Singh's first wife, Rani Raj Kour, gave birth to a son, Sahib Singh, who afterwards became Maharaja.

And soon after dies.

The birth of Sahib Singh, A.D. 1774.

The quarrel between Jhind and Nabha.

During the spring of 1774 a fierce quarrel arose between the Chiefs of Jhind and Nabha, the dispute having its origin during the marriage festivities of Sirdar Máhan Singh Sukarchakia with the daughter of the Raja of Jhind. An account of this quarrel, which had unfortunate consequences for Nabha, will be found elsewhere. The Raja of Pattiala, who was invited to make peace between the Chiefs, in reality encouraged the continuance of the quarrel; for although quite ready to join the other Phulkian families in repulsing any attack which might be made against their common safety from without, he was not sorry to see Jhind and Nabha exhausting themselves in a contest from which nothing but increased influence could result to himself.

Only four miles to the north-east of Pattiala was a strong fort, which had been built by Nawab Sef Khan, and called Sefabad after his own name. Its nearness to the town was a sufficient reason for Amar Singh to desire to capture it, and this reason was strengthened by the death of Sef Khan, leaving two young sons under the guardianship of Gul Khan, his principal follower. Without, then, the pretence of a quarrel to justify his violence, Raja Amar Singh invested the fort, and after a seven days' siege so battered the walls that Gul Khan was compelled to surrender, and the Raja took possession. He behaved with consideration to the children of Sef Khan, giving them the village of Chhota Rasulpur for their support, while to Gul Khan he made an allowance of 7 rupees a day, which he enjoyed till his death. **The capture of Sefabad.**

In this attack on Sefabad, the Raja of Náhan had assisted his friend Amar Singh, and after its successful conclusion he retired to his hills, where he soon after died, leaving a son, Jagat Parkash, who was unable to maintain order in his territory, and Raja Amar Singh accordingly visited Náhan, and aided him to reduce the rebellious chiefs to obedience. **Raja Amar Singh visits Náhan.** He then prepared for a campaign on an extensive scale against the Bhatti country to the south of Pattiala, and, in the winter of 1774, marched to Begran, a strong fort now in the Hissar **Marches against the Bhattis.**

district, which he invested. The Bhatti Chiefs made an effort to relieve it, and a sharp fight took place beneath the walls, in which Amar Singh was victorious, losing about one hundred killed and four hundred wounded: one of his generals, Sirdar Natha Singh Kaleka, being among the slain. The loss of the Bhattis was still heavier, and the Raja gained possession of the fort. He then took possession of Fatahabad and Sirsa, and invested Rannia, then a strong fort some eight miles west of Sirsa, held by Muhammad Amin Khan Bhatti. While before Rannia, news arrived that Rahimdád Khan, the Governor of Hansi, had, by the orders of the Dehli Emperor, attacked Jhind, and was then besieging Raja Gajpat Singh in his capital. All the Phulkian chiefs were summoned to aid their kinsman, and leaving Sukhdás Singh to carry on the siege of Rannia, the Raja marched to Fatahabad, from whence he sent a strong detachment to Jhind, under Diwan Nánun Mal. This General successfully effected a junction with the Kythal and Jhind troops, and a joint attack was made upon the enemy, who were defeated with great slaughter. After this, the Diwan, in company with Raja Gajpat Singh, overran the Hansi and Hissar districts, establishing the authority of his master, while Gajpat Singh took possession of parts of Kohána and Rohtak.

Seizes Fatahabad and Sirsa.

The Imperial troops repulsed before Jhind.

When Amar Singh heard of the defeat of Rahimdád Khan before Jhind, he marched from Fatahabad to Hansi; and after having collected the revenue, which was the same thing as plundering as extensively as he was able, he returned to Pattiala, where, four months later, he had the satisfaction of hearing from Sukhdás Singh of the fall of Rannia. On this he again marched southwards, and

Rannia is captured, and the whole of the Sirsa country is conquered.

the whole of what is now the Sirsa district being under his authority he was able to collect a large sum of money as revenue. He thought of attacking the fortress of Bhatner; but its position in the desert, where no supplies could be obtained, and its reputed strength, induced him to abandon the intention, and leave the Bhatti chiefs, Muhammad Amin Khan and Muhammad Hassan Khan, in quiet possession.[1]

The fort of Bhatner.

The Dehli Empire had fallen into confusion and decay from the weakness and inefficiency of its rulers. Had it possessed, at this time, able ministers and competent generals, it might have recovered all the authority that it had lost. The Mahratta power had been broken by the crushing defeat of Panipat in January 1761, when its army had been almost totally destroyed, and Ahmad Shah Durani was dead, leaving a son, Timur Shah, who had little of his father's ambition, and made no determined effort to reconquer Northern India. It seemed that in Najaf Khan the Empire had at last found a minister of the ability necessary to retrieve its fortunes. This Chief determined to recover the districts which the Sikhs had annexed after the defeat of Rahimdád Khan at Jhind, and, heading the Imperial troops, he recovered Karnal and part of Rohtak. The name of the Empire was still a word of power with the undisciplined Sikhs, who knew their inability to stand against regular troops in the field,

The condition of the Dehli Empire, A.D. 1775.

[1] The town of Bhatner is situated a few miles from the western border of the Sirsa district, on the banks of the Gaggar, a fierce and deep torrent near the hills, but here a mere thread of water, or altogether dry, except in the rainy season. The Gaggar was a fruitful source of dispute among the Chiefs whose territories lay on its bank. The obtaining its water was prosperity and good harvests; its diversion was barrenness and famine; and volume after volume of the old official records are filled with correspondence relating to the just distribution of the water, and the settlement of disputes regarding it.

and they sought the aid of Zabitah Khan, the son of the Rohilla Chief Najíbullah, who, in the time of Ahmad Shah, had possessed so much influence at the Court of Dehli. With this accession of strength, which had been duly paid for, Raja Amar Singh was in a position to treat with the Imperial minister, and a meeting was arranged at Jhind. Here the Raja consented to surrender the districts of Hansi, Hissar, and Rohtak, and was allowed to retain Fatahabad, Rannia, and Sirsa, promising to pay on their account a fixed revenue to the Dehli Treasury. The Raja of Jhind was also permitted to retain the seven villages from the territory he had seized. This compromise, so dishonorable to the Dehli Government, was said to have been brought about by the treachery of Najaf Khan, and his second in command, Najab Goli Khan, who were heavily bribed by the Sikhs. The story is probably true; for there was no other reason to induce the minister to surrender districts which had been taken violent possession of by rebels, and which he had the power to recover. The Dehli officials were notoriously corrupt, and if Najaf Khan was known to be open to bribes, there were certainly no scruples on the part of the Sikh Chiefs about offering them.

The compromise with the Dehli minister.

Faridkot territory overrun, A.D. 1777.

In the year 1777, the Raja of Pattiala sent a force under Chaudhri Singh Daya, to overrun the Faridkot and Kot Kapura districts, but no attempt was made to take formal possession of them; and the Raja had, moreover, plenty on his hands in keeping the people of his newly-acquired territories in order. They were wild, lawless, and had never known what it was to pay tribute or revenue, and one fortified village after another took long to reduce, while its reduction was of little advantage.

Raja Amar Singh had not forgotten the doubtful contest, in 1768, with Gharib Dás of Manimajra and Sirdar Hari Singh of Sialba and Rupar, and, in 1778, he determined to reduce these Chiefs under his authority. The estates of the first named were in the plain, where the river Gaggar debouches from the hills, and the Pattiala force, before Gharib Dás had time to summon his friends to his assistance, had overrun the country and forced him to shut himself up in his fort. For three months he held out bravely, but seeing no prospect of release from his position, he offered a large sum of money to the Pattiala Chief to retire and leave him in undisturbed possession of his estate. This was accepted, and Amar Singh then marched against Sialba, sixteen miles to the north-west of Manimajra. But Sirdar Hari Singh had heard of the Raja's intentions, and, as he was both rich and well connected, he had called to defend him many of the most famous fighting Sirdars, Jassa Singh Ramgharia;[1] Gurdit Singh and Diwan Singh Laudawala; Karam Singh Shahid, of Shahzadpur;[2] Gurbaksh Singh

The Chief of Manimajra again attacked.

Sirdar Hari Singh of Sialba attacked.

[1] Sirdar Jassah Singh Ramgharia was the most distinguished leader of the confederacy of that name. He first fortified the village of Amritsar, now the principal village in the Punjab, and took possession of almost all the northern portion of the Bari Doab, the country between the Rivers Bias and Ravi. A confederacy of Chiefs was formed against him, the Bhangis, Kanheyas, and Sukarchakias, headed by Jassa Singh Ahluwalia, and he was expelled from the Doab and fled to Sirsa and Harriana, where he supported himself by plunder and by selling his services to whoever would buy them, as on the above occasion to Hari Singh Sialba. In 1783 Sirdar Jassa Singh returned to Amritsar, and recovered a large part of his possessions. They were, however, confiscated by Maharaja Ranjit Singh, on the death of his son Jodh Singh, in 1816. The present representative of the family is Sirdar Mangal Singh, in charge of the Golden Temple at Amritsar.

[2] The Shahid misl was one of the smaller Sikh confederacies, and obtained its name (*shahid*, martyr) and origin in the following manner :—

Guru Govind Singh, flying from his enemies in the time of the Emperor Aurangzeb, took refuge in the little village of Talwandí, in the jungle to the south of Bhattinda. Here he remained ten days; and, after the Guru's

Ambala, and a number of the smaller Chiefs, who only fought for pay and plunder, and were indifferent as to the side on which they fought.

But defeats the Pattiala force.

The force of the Raja of Pattiala marched to Sialba, where Hari Singh came out to meet it with his mercenaries. The Pattiala general had no idea of the number that would be opposed to him, but he had no option but to fight, for it was too late to retreat; and was utterly routed with the loss of several hundred men, among whom was Bakshi Lokhna. Diwan Nanun Mal was also wounded, and Sirdars Chandu Singh and Mahan Singh were taken prisoners.

Raja Amar Singh determines on revenge.

Raja Amar Singh was much distressed at this defeat, and, determining to avenge it, sent messengers to his kinsmen and friends to assemble at Pattiala with all their forces. First among his relations came his cousin,

death, a temple was raised in Talwandi to his memory, and the name changed to Damdama, which signifies "a breathing place." The first *mahant* or priest put in charge of the shrine was Dip Singh, who was killed in action with the Governor of Lahore, and became a shahid, or martyr. Sudda Singh, his *chela*, or disciple, succeeded him at the shrine. He, however, like his predecessor, was fonder of fighting than praying, and attacked the Muhammadan Governor of Jalandhar, and at Adhkola was killed in a skirmish, his head being severed from his body. He is said to have neither fallen from his horse nor to have given up fighting, and he galloped a long distance and cut down many of the enemy before he died. Hence the family, or rather the followers of the Mahant of Damdama took the name of "the martyrs."

Karm Singh, mentioned in the text, succeeded Sudda Singh, and took possession of the country about Rannia and Damdama, Khari, Jaroli, and Faizullapur. He was the real founder of the *family*, for he was the first to marry, and left, on his death in 1784, two sons, Gulab Singh and Mehtab Singh, the former of whom succeeded him, and was one of the first Chiefs to offer assistance to the British, as a Sanad of Sir D. Ochterlony, dated 4th January 1804, proves. Sirdar Gulab Singh died in 1844, and Shiv Kirpal Singh, then only six years old, succeeded. He has estates worth Rs. 30,000 a year, and is still the guardian of the Damdama shrine, which brings in about Rs. 1000 a year in offerings. Dharm Singh, the brother of Karam Singh, had a share in the original territory, but he died without issue, and his widow was married by his brother.

Bibi Rajindar of Phagwára, a rich widow, as fond of fighting as any of the Pattiala men, who marched with three thousand followers through the territory of the Chiefs who had fought on the side of Hari Singh, harrying and pillaging, till she arrived at Pattiala. Then came the Kythal brothers, Dhanna Singh and Sukha Singh, although Bhai Desu Singh, the most influential of the three, was, in heart, a friend of the Sialba Chief; and the Chiefs of Nabha and Jhind, with the Maler Kotla Nawabs, now allies of Pattiala after their long hostility; a detachment of Náhan troops under Mian Kishan Singh; Jai Singh of Lidhran;[1] Tara Singh Dallehwala,[2] and his follower, Saunda Singh Khannah;[3]

[1] Jai Singh was a Manjha Jat, who, about 1763, having joined the Nishánwala confederacy, obtained 27 villages of Lidhran and 7 of Khar. After the great defeat of the Sikhs by Ahmad Shah, he fled to the hills and found on his return that the Raja of Pattiala had seized his Khar villages. A long dispute was the result, not ending for many years. A compromise was at last effected by which Pattiala kept three villages and Lidhran four. Jai Singh died in 1773, and was succeeded by his son Charat Singh, who was one of the Chiefs who accepted British protection in 1809. On the death of the latter, the estate was divided by General Ochterlony, by "chundaband," *i.e.*, according to the number of the wives, of whom there were three. Sirdar Budh Singh is now the head of the family, enjoying as his share of the jagir, Rs. 4571 a year; but the number of slaves has increased to eleven, and, from continual sub-divisions; the Lidhran estates will soon be undistinguishable. Their total value is at the present time Rs. 23,558.

[2] The Dállehwala confederacy took its name from the village of Sirdar Tara Singh, who was its principal leader, and who, with his followers, took possession of a great portion of the upper Jalandhar Doab, and the northern part of the Ambala and Ludhiana districts. In Firozpur he seized Dharamkot and Fatahabad. Tara Singh was killed at the siege of Narain Garh in 1807; and Maharàja Ranjit Singh seized his large possessions and distributed them among his generals, Diwan Mokham Chand receiving the lion's share.

[3] Saunda Singh was one of the followers of Tara Singh Gheba. He was not a man of any distinction. He left one son, Dya Singh, who died without male issue, and the estate of Rs. 30,000 eventually came into possession of Dya Kour, daughter of Saunda Singh, and widow of Hari Singh, the nephew of Raja Bhag Singh, of Jhind. At her death it lapsed to the Jhind State.

Budh Singh Faizullapuria,[1] and others of less note. The command of the Pattiala troops was given to Sirdar Chuhr Singh Malod, while the contingents of the Chiefs marched under their own leaders. Arrived before Sialba, one or two skirmishes took place with the mercenaries collected by Hari Singh, but the Pattiala leader determined to leave as little as possible to chance, and offered a rupee a day to those of the opposite party who would join him. The effect was immediate, and the force of the Sialba Chief day by day wasted away, and some of the Chiefs who had promised him their assistance began to desert him; among others, Sirdars Karm Singh and Dharam Singh Shahid, and the Buria Sirdars, Rai Singh and Bhag Singh.[2] At last Sirdar Hari Singh found

[1] Sirdar Budh Singh Faizullapuria owned the north-western corner of the Ambala district, on the bend of the Satlej, from near Keritpur to Machiwara. A portion of this territory, the illaka of Bhurtpur, descended to his grandson, Amar Singh, who died in 1847. Subha Kour, the widow of his son, Kirpa Singh, was allowed the four villages of Kot Bala, Aspur, Himatpur, and Bhurtpur Khas for her life.

[2] The Buria Chiefship was formerly of considerable importance. Its founders were Nánun Singh, a Jat of Jhawal Mandan in the Manjha and Bhag Singh and Rai Singh, brothers, all Bhangi Sikhs, who, in 1764, seized the fort of Buria, which the year before had been abandoned by Lachmi Narain, an officer of Zín Khan, the Muhammadan Governor of Sirhind, and had been taken quiet possession of by a few Narwária Sikhs. They were not allowed to keep their conquest without opposition, and the Afghans of Aurangabad, coalescing with the Narwárias, enticed Nánun Singh and Bhag Singh to the Aurangabad fort, and put them to death. Rai Singh and Bhag Singh, the adopted son of the murdered Nánun Singh, avenged their relatives; and seized more territory, in all 204 villages, which they divided; Rai Singh taking 84 villages, forming his estate of Jugadri and Dyalghar; and Bhag Singh, 120, the estate of Buria. Bhag Singh died in 1785, and his son Sher Singh was killed in an engagement with the British at Saharanpur in 1804. After his death a long dispute arose between the widows and the sons of the late Sirdar Jaimal Singh and Gulab Singh, which ended in the estate being divided between the sons; and on the death of Jaimal Singh, in 1817, Gulab Singh succeeded to the whole. He died in 1844, and his son Jiun Singh is the present Chief. Buria ranks third among the minor Chiefships, with a revenue of Rs. 42,000. The present Chief is a Jagirdar magistrate, and is very highly respected. His sister, Karm Kour, married the late Maharaja Narindar Singh, of Pattiala.

himself left almost alone, and had no option but to make such terms for himself as he best could. He accordingly submitted, presented a *nazr* in token of obedience to the Raja of Pattiala, who withdrew his troops without attempting to retain possession of any of the Sialba territories.

The Raja quarrels with Bhai Desu Singh.

After the return from Sialba, Raja Amar Singh sent a force against Bhai Desu Singh of Kythal, who had not assisted him in the late campaign, his sympathies being notoriously on the side of Sirdar Hari Singh; but Bhais Dhanna Singh, Sukha Singh, and Takht Singh, the brothers of Desu Singh, arranged matters between the parties and prevented any contest, which indeed the Raja was glad to avoid, as the hostile attitude of the Dehli Government now gave him full employment.

The new minister at Dehli, and his campaign, A.D. 1779.

Nawab Majd-ud-doulah Abd-ul-ahd was now minister at Dehli. He was an ambitious and covetous man and was not destitute of ability; but he had little courage, and it was audacity alone which, in the last days of the Empire, could command success. He determined, however, to make an effort to recover the Málwa country from the Sikhs, and set out from Dehli, in November 1779, with a considerable force and accompanied by Prince Farkhunda Bakht. He reached Karnal without meeting any resistance, and here was joined by Sirdar Bhagel Singh Krora Singhia;[1] Sahib Singh Khundawala

[1] The Krora Singhia confederacy was founded by Krora Singh, with two companions, Mastán Singh and Karam Singh. Sham Singh, who succeeded Mastán Singh, gave his name to a minor confederacy. The Kalsias were the most powerful of this misl, whose principal possessions lay between the Jamna and the Makanda rivers, bounded on the south by the Buria territory.

Sirdar Bhagel Singh was one of the principal Chiefs of the Krora Singhias. His headquarters were Chiloundi. The family is extinct. After the death of Bhagel Singh, his widows, Ranis Ram Kour and Raj Kour, held Chiloundi for many years and when they died the estate lapsed to the British Government.

Bhai Desu Singh fined.

and Karam Singh Shahid. The envoys of Bhai Desu Singh Kythal had accompanied the Nawab from Dehli, and there is little doubt that this Chief hoped, by early submission, to gain the favour of the Imperial party and obtain an advantage over his rival, Amar Singh of Pattiala, whom he would have been delighted to crush. But in this he was totally disappointed. The Nawab much wished to reconquer the Málwa territory, but he wanted more; and Bhai Desu Singh was reputed to be rich. On a charge of not having paid his arrears of revenue he was seized, and four lakhs of rupees were demanded from him as a fine. Of this he contrived to pay three lakhs; and for the payment of the balance, he gave his son Lal Singh as a hostage.[1]

[1] The Kythal family was of so much importance in the Cis-Satlej States, and their history is so closely connected with that of Pattiala, that a sketch of it is essential here. The genealogy of the family is as follows:—

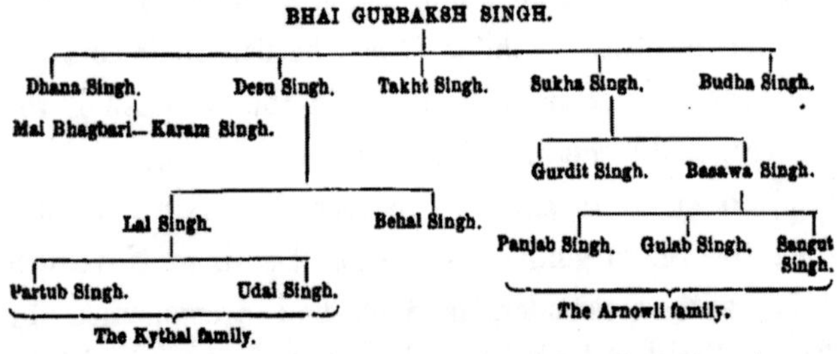

The Kythal family have the same origin as the Phulkian. Gurbaksh Singh, the founder of the Chiefship, was the son of Bhai Ramdyal, who had a great reputation as a saint. The son was a fine soldier and an able man, but he had little of the saint about him, and thought more of annexing territory than of religion. He was a great friend of Raja Ala Singh, of Pattiala, and they made many expeditions together, and he helped the Raja out of more than one difficulty. The possessions of Gurbaksh Singh were divided among his sons; but they soon increased them. Desu Singh captured Kythal from some Afghans, Bhikh Baksh Khan and Nihmat Khan, and, with his brother, Budha Singh, seized Thanesar, though the town and fort were afterwards taken from them by Sirdar Bhanga Singh, the fiercest and most feared of all the Cis-Satlej chiefs. When Desu Singh died in 1871, Lal Singh was in confinement as a rebel against his father, and Behal Singh,

In the meantime the Sikh Chiefs had not been idle, but had sent in all directions to summon the Khálsa to oppose the Muhammadan inroad. But the Nawab marched on, believing he should meet with no opposition, and at the village of Gharám, about 16 miles from Pattiala, he was met by Diwan Nanun Mal, whom the Raja had sent to express his devotion to the Empire generally and the Nawab in particular. But the Khálsa force was marching from the other direction towards Pattiala; the Kanheya Sirdars, Jai Singh and Hakikat Singh[1]; Jassa Singh Ramgharia; Tara Singh Gheba; Jodh Singh[2] of Wazirabad, and many others; while, at Pattiala, the Phulkian Chiefs Jhind, Nabha, Bhadour, and Malod had collected all their troops. The Nawab, who had expected unresisting submission, was terrified when he heard of this gathering of the clans. He knew how keenly these wild warriors scented plunder and blood, and that in a few days fifty thousand horsemen could assemble on the plains of Sirhind. His

Raja Amar Sing and the Sikhs promise obedience.

But secretly collect the forces of the Khálsa for battle.

the elder son, did all he could to keep his brother in prison; but he contrived to escape, killed his elder brother, and took possession of all the estates of his father, which he much enlarged by new acquisition. Lal Singh was, at the the time of the British advance northwards, in 1809, the most powerful Cis-Satlej Chief, after the Raja of Pattiala. He was a very able man, though utterly untrustworthy, and so violent and unscrupulous that the English authorities had the greatest difficulty in persuading him to maintain anything like order. In 1819, the Government allowed him to succeed to the share of the estate held by Mai Bhagbari, the widow of his first cousin, Karam Singh. Partab Singh, the elder son, and then the younger son, Udái, succeeded, but on the death of the latter without issue in 1843, the whole of the Kythal estate lapsed to the Government, with the exception of that portion which had been acquired by the founder of the family, Bhai Gurbaksh Singh, and to which the collaterals of the Arnowli branch were permitted to succeed.

[1] Sirdars Jai Singh and Hakikat Singh were rival leaders of two sections of the great Kanheya confederacy. Their history is given at length in "The Punjab Chiefs," pp. 315-338.

[2] Jodh Singh Wazirabadia was the most powerful Chief in the Rechna Doab, and was much dreaded by even Maharaja Ranjit Singh. His history will be found in "The Punjab Chiefs," pp. 409-413.

And the Nawab makes a hasty retreat.

only thought was of retreat, and, according to Sikh tradition, he gave the Chiefs, by the interested advice of Bhagel Singh Krora Singhia, the greater portion of the three lakhs of rupees which he had extracted from Bhai Desu Singh, on their agreeing not to molest his retreat. The Muhammadans say, on the other hand, that the Sikhs bribed the Nawab to retire, and this is perhaps more probable. At any rate, Lal Singh, the son of Bhai Desu Singh, was carried a prisoner to Dehli, and there tortured, as his father had not paid the balance of the tribute claimed from him.

The death of Raja Amar Singh, A.D. 1781.

In February 1781, Raja Amar Singh, who was only thirty-five years of age, died of dropsy brought on by excessive drinking. During the last year of his life little had occurred worthy of notice. Three months before his death, there had been born, at Gujránwala, forty miles north of Lahore, a child nearly related to himself, who wasdestined to shake the power of the Phulkian house to its foundation, and build up in the Punjab a military Empire as formidable as any yet founded in Hindustan, strong both for defence and for aggression. If Raja Amar Singh had lived, or had been succeeded by rulers as able as himself, the Cis-Satlej States might have been welded into one kingdom and their independence might have been preserved, both against the Lahore monarchy on the one hand and the British Government on the other. But, after his death, the leadership of the Cis-Satlej Sikhs passed from the feeble hands of Pattiala. For many years the only persons in that family who possessed wisdom, energy, or courage, were women; and the power and influence which had been won, with so much labour, by Ala Singh, Lal Singh and Amar Singh, day by day diminished, till no one cared to follow Pattiala in

The birth of Maharaja Ranjit Singh.

The decay of Pattiala power

council or the field, and the only safety of its Chief against an adventurer of his own creed and blood was found in imploring the protection of a foreign power and trusting to the swords of others for defence. Raja Amar Singh would have found a nobler way of saving his kingdom; and it was a misfortune for Pattiala that he died before he had consolidated his conquests, leaving to his child-successor the dangerous legacy of his victories and his fame, with the envy of the more powerful Chiefs, Jhind, Nabha, Kalsia, and Kythal, who strove to undermine and destroy the hated supremacy of Pattiala.

The character of Amar Singh.

Amar Singh was not altogether a character to admire, and he had a fair share of the vices and faults of his age, but he made Pattiala the most powerful State between the Jamna and the Satlej. He formed a successful coalition against the Muhammadan power, which possessed, indeed, only the shadow of its former greatness, but at the name of which India had learned to tremble, and it needed a brave heart and a bold hand to drag away the imperial robes and show the world that the place of the giant had been filled by a tottering scare-crow which a push might overthrow. The conquests of Amar Singh were unscrupulous and often without the shadow of excuse or provocation; but princes can only be judged by success and by the use which they have made of their opportunities. It is true that the ambition of Amar Singh was personal, and he cannot be classed with those statesmen who have no policy but the glory and prosperity of their country, and to whom infamy itself is welcome if they can leave their country more strong and more respected. He was but a fine specimen of a barbarian—rude, courageous, impulsive, generous, and ignorant. He had a quick intelligence and a strong arm, and his success was well deserved; though whether success entitles a man to praise and admiration, is a point on which the world and its teachers have agreed to differ.

Raja Sahib Singh's accession.

Raja Sahib Singh, the new Chief of the Pattiala State, was a child six years of age. It would have been a hard task for a man, however able, to maintain order in a country so lately conquered, inhabited by warlike and independent races, and to ward off the attacks of powerful neighbours and rivals. For a child, surrounded by greedy and unscrupulous servants, who found their own profit in his weakness and inexperience, there could be little hope of a successful or happy reign. Through the influence of Rani Hukmán, the grandmother of the young Chief, Diwan Nanun Mal was appointed Prime Minister, and no better choice could have been made. The Diwan, an Aggarwal Bannia of Sunám, was a man of great experience and honesty. He had served Raja Amar Singh well, both in the council and in the field, and his principal fault was an undisguised contempt for the rude Sikh Sirdars, which may not have been undeserved but which they repaid with hatred and suspicion.

Diwan Nanun Mal.

The rebellion of the Governor of Bhawanigarh.

No sooner had the young Chief taken his seat on the masnad than rebellion broke out in all quarters. The first to throw off the Chief's authority was the Governor of Bhawanigarh, Sirdar Mahan Singh, the brother of Mai Deso, step-mother of Raja Sahib Singh, and the widow of Himmat Singh, on whose death she had been married by the late Raja. Immediately on hearing of the Governor's revolt, Diwan Nanun Mal summoned the Phulkian contingents and marched against Bhawanigarh, which he invested. Mahan Singh was assisted by Sirdar Tara Singh Gheba and held out for more than three months; until his ally was induced to desert him, when he surrendered. It would have been well if an example could have been made of this rebel, but Nanun Mal did not feel himself strong enough to put to death so powerful a Chief, and one so nearly connected with the reigning family, and the only punishment inflicted was degradation from his office as Governor of Bhawanigarh.

Before this affair was settled, another outbreak occurred at Kot Sumer, headed by Rajo, the widow of Sirdar Baksho Singh of Saboka. The fort held by this lady was very strong, and, before the Diwan was able to reduce it, he was summoned away to quell a still more serious revolt at Bhikhe, which Sirdar Ala Singh, the brother of Rani Khem Kour, one of Raja Amar Singh's widows, had seized, with the aid of the zamindars of the neighbourhood, expelling the Pattiala Governor, Thamman Singh, from the town and fort. **Rebellion at Kot Sumer.**

The Ranis and their relations had, at this time, great power in Pattiala. They all, with the exception of Rani Hukman, hated Nanun Mal for his efforts to maintain economy and to restrain their extravagance within due bounds; and the Diwan found himself opposed and thwarted in every possible way. He, however, mustered a large force composed of Pattiala, Jhind, Nabha, Maler Kotla, Bhadour, and Ramgharia troops, and, accompanied by Rani Hukman, marched against Bhikhe and invested the village. After a few days' skirmishing, Ala Singh, seeing further resistance hopeless, escaped from Bhikhe by night, and fled to his home at Talwandi, whither he was pursued by the Diwan and captured. He was imprisoned at Pattiala for a time, but, on the intercession of Sodhi Nahr Singh of Anandpur, a man of great sanctity, he was at length released, on payment of a heavy fine, and allowed Dhámon and other villages for his support. **The revolt of Sirdar Ala Singh at Bhikhe.**

The great famine of 1783.

To add to the difficulties of the Pattiala administration, the year 1783 was one of famine as terrible as any that has ever devastated Northern India.[1] The year previous had been dry and the harvest poor; but, in 1783, it entirely failed. The country was depopulated; the peasants abandoning their villages and dying in thousands of disease and want; but little revenue could be collected; the country swarmed with bands of robbers and dacoits, and the state of anarchy was almost inconceivable. The neighbouring Chiefs began to seize for themselves the Pattiala villages, and all who dared threw off Pattiala authority and declared themselves independent.

The action of the Diwan.

Diwan Nanun Mal did not lose heart. He was a man of extraordinary resource, and his powers appeared to rise with danger. He sent to Lucknow for trained gunners and officers who could discipline his troops after the European fashion, and set to work to reduce the insurgents to order and recover the Pattiala territory which had been lost. First he marched against Sardul Singh, the Governor of Mulepur, a relation of Rani Khem Kour, who, after the unfortunate rebellion of her brother, had sent to Sardul Singh for safety all her money and jewels. The Diwan had besieged the town for twenty days, when one of his own officers, named Karam Beg, bribed, it is supposed, by Sardul Singh, attempted to assassinate him. The murderer was cut down by the attendants, but the Diwan received a severe sword wound and was carried to the neighbouring village of Anandpur Kesoké where he lay in great danger.

Severely wounded by an assassin.

The death of Rani Hukman, and the imprisonment of Nanun Mal.

Rani Hukman, who had come to Mulepur to visit the Diwan, died at this time from an illness caused, in great

[1] Known as the "Chália" the year being, according to Hindu computation, 1840 A. V. (forty "*Chális.*")

part, by anxiety; and Nanun Mal lost in her the best and most influential of his friends. She seems to have thoroughly understood that he was the only man who could restore the State to prosperity, and gave him her warm support. On her death, the Diwan's enemies, Rani Khem Kour, Soman Singh Dhali, Bibi Pardhán, great-aunt of the Raja, and others, gathered courage, arrested him as he was lying wounded at Anandpur, and sent him a prisoner into Pattiala.

Fortunately for Nanun Mal and the country there was another woman of sense and courage in the Pattiala family. This was Rani Rajindar of Phagwára, a first cousin of Raja Amar Singh, and who had helped him in former difficulties. Hearing of the state of affairs, she assembled a force, and, heading it herself, marched to Pattiala, released Diwan Nanun Mal, and re-instated him in his place as minister. She had not arrived a day too soon; for, no sooner had the Diwan been imprisoned, than the neighbouring Sirdars renewed their encroachments, and Pattiala itself was in imminent danger of being sacked by some of the hostile confederacies of Sikhs.

Rani Rajindar of Phagwára.

Marches to Pattiala and reinstates the Diwan.

Nanun Mal, finding that he could not count upon the support or sympathy of any of the Pattiala nobles in his attempt to restore order, opened negotiations with Dhára Rao, a Mahratta leader, who had been for some time in the country about Dehli, where several of the more powerful Sikh Chiefs, who held estates between the Satlej and Jamna, had joined him. Among these were Bhagel Singh Krora Singhia; Diwan Singh Laudah; Bhanga Singh and Mehtab Singh of Thanesar.[1] Sirdar Bhagel

Nanun Mal coalesces with the Mahrattas.

[1] The founder of the Thanesar family was Mith Singh, a Jat of Sirháli, near Patti, in the Manjha, and received the Páhal from Gurdial Singh, who obtained for him the post of personal attendant (*garwa bardar*, a servant who carries a drinking vessel and water) to Tara Singh Gheba. Mith Singh,

Singh, who had then great influence to the south of the Satlej, arranged matters with the Mahratta, who consented to assist Nanun Mal for a consideration of two lakhs of rupees; and straightway marched from Karnal to Thanesar, where Sirdar Bhanga Singh had his fort, and where he was joined by the Diwan, Rani Rajindar, and Raja Gajpat Singh, of Jhind, who, before their departure from Pattiala, had seized and imprisoned Sirdar Somán Singh, fearing lest he might give trouble during their absence. Having joined forces, they marched against some of the neighbouring Chiefs, the Mahratta receiving tribute from the Bhais of Kythal and recovering Kot and other Pattiala villages from the Sirdars of Ambala. During this march, Raja Gajpat Singh fell ill, and, returning to his residence of Sufidun, died there at the close of 1789.

The siege of Banúr

The Diwan then, in company with Dhára Rao, marched

in 1765, offended with the conduct of his master, induced 200 of his troopers to desert, and set up for himself. Being absolutely without means, he determined on a bold stroke, and attacked Thanesar, where were two forts, one in possession of the Shaikhs, and the other belonging to Bhai Desu Singh, of Kythal. That belonging to the Shaikhs was captured, and the other, after the death of Mith Singh, was gained by bribing the Commandant, and the surrounding country was taken possession of by his nephews Bhag Singh and Bhanga Singh, who divided it between them, the latter obtaining the larger share. Bhanga Singh, who died in 1815, joined the British force when, under Lord Lake, it came north of the Jamna, and was rewarded with additional territory. He was, however, of a most savage and untamable character, and gave a great deal of trouble. Bhag Singh died twenty-four years before his brother, leaving four sons, who were, if possible, more audacious and violent than their uncle, Bhanga Singh. In 1806, Bhanga Singh, with the aid of the Ladwa Chief, seized Dhowa, which he held till his death. He left a son, Fatah Singh, and a daughter, Karam Kour, who was married to Maharaja Karm Singh, of Pattiala. There was also an illegitimate son, Sahib Singh, born of a slave girl, who was not allowed to succeed to a share with Fatah Singh, though maintenance was given him. Fatah Singh died in 1819, leaving two widows, who succeeded him, although the mother managed the estate, which, in 1850, escheated to Government.

Only one of the sons of Bhag Singh left issue, Jamiyat Singh, who died in 1834, when the estate lapsed.

against Banúr. This town, which is of some importance, is situated about 12 miles to the north-west of Ambala, and was defended by two forts, an old imperial one, called Zulmgarh, and another of more recent date. This town, with the neighbouring villages, had been conquered by the Singhpuria Sirdars.[1] But Raja Amar Singh, who had assisted in its conquest, obtained a half share of the revenue. During the troubles which followed the death of Amar Singh, Sirdar Khushhal Singh Singhpuria had seized the whole district. He was, however, able to make but faint resistance to the force brought against him, and the Diwan was able to recover the Pattiala share of the town. After this success, Nanun Mal, by means of forced

[1] The Singhpuria was a very powerful family, and its founder, Kapur Singh, was undoubtedly the most distinguished of the Sikh leaders before the days of Jassa Singh Ahluwalia, and Ala Singh, of Pattiala. He was known as "Nawab;" almost the only instance of a Sikh taking a Muhammadan title; and conquered the village and country about Faizullapur, near Amritsar, from Faizulla Khan, and gave it the name of Singhpura, from which the family take its name, though it is as frequently known as Faizullapuria. Nawab Kapur Singh died at Amritsar in 1753, giving what command over the Khalsa army any one Chief could in those days be said to possess, to Sirdar Jassa Sing Ahluwalia. His territory, however, descended to his nephew, Khushhal Singh, who equalled his father's reputation, and obtained possession of a large tract of country, worth about 4 lakhs of rupees a year, both Cis and Trans-Sutlej, including Jalandhar, Bulandgarh, Singhpuria, Patti, Nurpur, Behrampur, Ghanoli, and Bhartgarh. He was one of the most active against the Muhammadans, and it was one of his troopers who killed the Afghan Governor, Zin Khan in 1763. After this he seized Ludhiana and Banur, with the assistance of Pattiala, which State afterwards received a half share of the latter district. Khushhal Singh had two sons, of whom one, Sudh Singh, died in his father's life-time, and the second, Budh Singh, succeeded to the estate in 1795. All the Jalandhar territory was seized by Maharaja Ranjit Singh, and the Sirdar had to take up his residence, Cis-Satlej, under British protection, where, in 1815, he held estates worth Rs. 54,000 a year. Budh Singh died in 1816, and his estate was divided among his sons, seven in number, by "chundaband," *i.e.*, in shares according to the number of wives.

At the present time there are four distinct branches of the Singhpuria family, the Chief of which is represented by Sirdar Jai Singh, of Manoli, who holds half of the ancestral estates. The remainder is divided among the branches of Ghanoli, Bungah, and Kandola.

Dhára Rao retires to Karnal.

contributions from Chiefs and zamindars, contrived to pay the Mahratta the two lakhs as agreed, and to induce him to leave for Karnal. Sirdar Bhagel Singh Krora Singhia remained behind to assist in reducing refractory subjects and to obtain what the Diwan had promised him for his services in negotiating with the Mahrattas.

The Diwan's campaign of 1786.

From Banúr, the Diwan marched southwards, collecting fines and contributions from Kythal, Makiran, and Serai Doráha, where he was repulsed from the fort by the Sikhs. He aided Sirdar Dalel Singh Malod to recover the village of Sehnke, of which his younger brother Bagh Singh had taken forcible possession; and then attacked Kot Kapura, on which he was able to make no impression, but he built a mud fort about three miles distant, at Dholan, to overawe the place, and then marched against the Bhattis, who had recovered all the territory of which Raja Amar Singh had deprived them. He overran the country and collected some arrears of revenue due from Sangah, Chandah, and Bhinah, but had only indifferent success elsewhere, and, being quite unable to hold the country he had ravaged, returned to Pattiala, where Sirdar Bhagel Singh was dismissed with the promised money.

The marriage of Raja Sahib Singh to a Bhangi lady, A.D. 1787.

In 1787, Raja Sahib Singh was married to Rattan Kour, daughter of Sirdar Ganda Singh Bhangi,[1] who had long been dead, but his grandson Gulab Singh still held, though with diminished authority, the city of Amritsar and its neighbourhood, and was a powerful Chief, and the marriage was performed with proportionate splendour.

The dispute between Sirdar Chuhr Singh of Bhadour and Maler Kotla.

About this time Ata-ulla Khan, the Chief of Maler Kotla, asked for the help of Pattiala against Sirdar Chuhr Singh Bhadouria who had seized several of his villages.

[1] For an account of Sirdar Ganda Singh Bhangi, *vide* "Punjab Chiefs," pp. 385-389.

The Maler Kotla Nawab had become a fast friend of Pattiala and it was necessary to assist him; but Chuhr Singh was now too powerful to be attacked with impunity, so an arrangement was made by which the latter gave up the villages he had seized, in return for others of the same value from Pattiala territory.

The invasion of Amba Rao Mahratta.

The expedition of Dhára Rao to Pattiala had taught the Mahrattas that the country to the north of the Jamna was a good field for plunder, and, in the spring of 1788, another Chief, named Amba Rao, determined to try his fortunes in that direction. He persuaded Ghulam Kadir Khan, the son of Zabita Khan Rohilla, who had died three years before, to join him; and, at Karnal, Sirdar Bhagel Singh Krora Singhia made his submission, for the Chief was generally the first to welcome an invader and follow him as a jackal the lion, to obtain a share of the prey, however insignificant. The Pattiala Diwan met the invaders at a village in the Kythal territory, where the Mahratta levied a contribution which Pattiala assisted to pay on the mortgage of seven villages which Bhai Lal subsequently released. Amba Rao did not make much by his expedition. The Rohilla Chief, Ghulam Kadir, either quarrelled with him or was bribed by the Sikhs, and retired towards Dehli, which he soon afterwards took by storm, disgracing himself by permitting every kind of atrocity and putting out the eyes of the Emperor Shah Alam with his own hand. After Ghulam Kadir's departure, Amba Rao could make little impression on the Sikh Chiefs who were profuse in promises which they had no intention to fulfil; and, much disappointed with the result of his expedition, he recrossed the Jamna.

Who retires with but little plunder.

Dawin Nanun Mal again attacks the Singhpuria Chief, but without success.

Diwan Nanun Mal was now induced by Sirdar Hari Singh of Sialbah to make another attack upon Khushhal

Singh Singhpuria, who had taken Awankot and other villages of the Sialbah territory. Their joint forces first attacked Kotlah, a small fort held by Man Singh, son-in-law of the Singhpuria Chief, and reduced it without much difficulty. Thence they went to Awankot and invested the place, but Budh Singh, son of Sirdar Khushhal Singh with Tara Singh Gheba, Rai Singh Bhangi,[1] and other Chiefs, came to the rescue and compelled the raising of the siege. Nanun Mal sent to Pattiala for reinforcements, and Ata-ullah Khan of Maler Kotla, Rai Muhamad of Rai Kot,[2] with some Nabha and Kythal troops soon joined him, but the fighting, which was little more than skirmishing, was indecisive, and it was thought advisable to abandon any further attempt on Awankot. The campaign of Diwan Nanun Mal had been successful on the whole. He had reduced to submission a great number of refractory villages and collected arrears of revenue of which the State treasury was much in need, for war, famine, and the exactions of the Mahrattas had effectually

[1] This was the Chief of Jagadri.

[2] The Chiefs of Rai Kot, who, at the beginning of the century, possessed considerable territory, were Muhammadan Rajputs, immigrants from Jasalmir, which Tulsi Das, their great ancestor, left in 1323 A.D.; settling at Mogal, afterwards Faridkot, and adopting the Muhammadan faith. His second son, Gopal, founded Shahjahanpur in the Ludhiana district, and Rai Kalha, another of his descendants, the town of Talwandi, in A.D. 1478. The family became of some importance, and, about 1620, obtained possession of the town of Ludhiana, which had been founded 140 years before by Yusaf and Nihang, two Lodi Chiefs, whence the name of the town. From Ludhiana the Rai Kot Chiefs were expelled by Sahib Singh Bedi, but they afterwards recovered it; and, at the end of the 18th century, owned Rai Kot, Talwandi, Jhandiala, Jagraon, Baddowala, Ludhiana, Basia, and other districts. Rai Alyas, the last Chief, died in 1802, and his mother, Nur-ul-nisad, succeeded him. Maharaja Ranjit Singh, in 1806, seized the whole territory and divided it between his allies, Raja Bhag Singh, of Jhind, Raja Jaswant Singh, of Nabha, Sirdar Gurdit Singh, Ladwa and Diwan Mokham Chand. A few villages alone were left, which have descended to Rai Imám Baksh, the present representative of the family.

emptied it. He had, moreover, recovered much of the territory which the neighbouring Chiefs had seized during the troubles which followed Amar Singh's death, and had shown himself to be not only brave but far-seeing and anxious for the good of the State.

But the Diwan was too honest to be successful. In a Native State, during a long minority, the general rule of practice is corruption of the grossest and most unblushing kind; and should chance place an honest man in power, he is at once assailed by the crowd of parasites and slaves who hate a character which is a perpetual menace and reproach to themselves; and he must be strong as well as honest to defy his enemies, who include in their ranks every man in the State except himself. Nanun Mal besides was of so proud a disposition that he did not care whom he offended. He had given many of the most lucrative offices of the State to his sons and relatives, and excited the greatest dislike by his custom of smoking his *hukka* in Durbar, when giving audience to Sikh Chiefs, tobacco being odious to them and forbidden by their creed. The unpopularity of the Diwan.

Raja Sahib Singh was now fourteen years old. It is difficult to say what was his natural disposition, for the chief object of his ministers was to confine his attention to pleasure, nautches, hunting, and elephant fights, that he might be disposed to leave State affairs to their management. Against the Diwan they poisoned his mind, hinting that it was his intention to seize the power for himself and with this object was intriguing with the Mahrattas, while even if he designed to leave the Raja nominal authority, all real power would be taken away. It was easy to induce the boy to believe stories such as these, to which the pride of the Diwan and his family gave some The dislike of the Raja to him.

colour, and he began to hate Nanun Mal as bitterly as his courtiers did.

New dangers to Pattiala.

Other dangers were now impending. The crimes of the infamous Ghulam Kadir Khan Rohilla and the misfortunes of the tortured and insulted Emperor had been well avenged by Sindhia Mahdaji, the great Mahratta leader, who drove the Rohilla from Dehli, pursued and captured him at Mehrat, and put him to death with tortures. The Emperor Shah Alam was again placed, with all honour, on the throne of Dehli, and Sindhia set himself to reduce to obedience the country north of the Jamna in the name of the Emperor.

Another Mahratta invasion.

The Mahratta force marched northwards, commanded by Rane Khan Dadaji and Ali Buhadar Peshwa. At Thanesar they halted some time, and the Pattiala Durbar began to hope that this might be the limit of the expedition; but Bhanga Singh of Thanesar annoyed the Mahrattas so much by plundering their baggage and intercepting their convoys, that they marched to Ajrára, eight miles nearer to Pattiala. At the capital there was great dismay. The treasury had been drained by the late war, and it was not the Mahratta custom to retire from before a town with empty hands, and what was not freely given they were quite prepared to take. In this emergency Diwan Nanun Mal did not know where to turn for aid. He visited the ladies at the palace, and advised them to leave Pattiala for Múng or Bhattinda, where they would be in greater safety, till the storm had blown over. Rani Rajindar, who now began to distrust the Diwan's loyalty, and who did not know what fear was, refused to leave Pattiala; and told Nanun Mal that it was his duty as Prime Minister to make arrangements with the invaders, and, if necessary, to buy them off.

The Diwan felt that in the Rani he was losing his only friend, and, knowing that he was suspected, formed the design of leaving Pattiala for ever. But he determined to make an effort to raise some money, and calling together the subordinate Chiefs, visited the Mahratta camp where he made himself very useful to Rane Khan, introducing the different Chiefs, and giving information as to the amount of *nazrana* which each could pay.

The enemy demand tribute.

The Pattiala contribution was at last demanded. The Diwan, being either really unable to find money, or more probably wishing to punish the coolness with which he had been treated by Rani Rajindar, sent her news of what was demanded and begged her to take measures for the payment, without delay, as, in default of payment, the city of Pattiala would certainly be attacked. But the Rani was as proud as the Diwan, and as brave as she was proud, and returned answer that Nanun Mal was Minister and must pay the Mahratta fine himself. Convinced as she was of the Diwan's treachery, she determined to take immediate action to counteract it, and sent an officer to seize Devi Ditta, the Diwan's son, whom she placed in confinement as a guarantee for the father's good conduct. This hasty action had deplorable results. The Diwan, seeing that all hope of reconciliation with the Rani was lost, and that his only chance of regaining power was in Mahratta interference, at once persuaded Dadaji to march to Pattiala with 30,000 men.

Difficult negotiations.

The Mahratta army appears before the city of Pattiala.

The force encamped at Sohlar, about two miles from the town, whence a message was sent to the Rani directing her to deliver up the Diwan's son, for until he was released Nanun Mal refused to take any steps towards obtaining the *nazrana*. The Rani was prepared to defend the city; but she gave up Devi Ditta, thinking it unadvisable to press matters to extremities. Several of the neighbouring Chiefs tried to arrange terms, and, notably, Sirdar Bhagel Singh Krora Singhia, who was compelled to meddle in the business of every one between the Satlej and Dehli; but Rani Rajindar declined to pay a single rupee. She made several visits to the Mahratta camp, following the example of Mai Deso, the mother of Raja Jaswant Singh of Nabha, who had been fortunate enough to secure good terms for her son. But Diwan Nanun Mal and Rani Rajindar were able to settle nothing, each declaring that the other was the proper person to pay the fine; the truth being that the treasury was empty; the Chiefs and the people had been ground down by exactions till they could give nothing more, and whoever satisfied the Mahratta demands would have to do so from private means, which, in the case of both the Rani and the Diwan, were very large.

And takes possession of the fort of Sefabad as security for the fine demanded.

The Mahrattas, at last, tired of waiting, insisted upon the fort of Sefabad, situated a few miles north-east of the city and known as Buhádargarh, being placed in their hands. To this the Diwan consented, though Rani Rajindar opposed it. No sooner had the Mahrattas obtained the fort, than they thought to hasten the payment of the *nazrana* by a display of force; and for a month and a half skirmishes were frequent between the Sikhs and the Mahrattas, though the leaders on either side were unwilling to come to a complete rupture. Rani Rajindar still refused to pay and declared herself willing to march with the Mahrattas to Mathra, where she would arrange matters with Sindhia himself. To this Rane Khan Dadaji was compelled to consent, and the Rani, with a strong force, marched southwards, the Mahrattas insisting on Diwan Nanun Mal accompanying them; but, at Karnal, he induced them, on consideration of his services, to release him, and take his son Devi Ditta with them instead.

Raja Sahib Singh confiscates the Diwan's property.

No sooner had the Mahratta army disappeared, than Raja Sahib Singh, who had taken shelter at a distance from the capital, marched to Dhodan or Bhawanigarh, where, instigated by his followers, who were determined on the ruin of the Diwan, he confiscated much of Nanun Mal's property, and thence to Barnala, where he seized and imprisoned Narinda Rai, one of the Diwan's sons, and collector of the districts of Hodiana and Barnala. From this town he marched southwards to Mong (Monak or Akalghar), of which Ditta Mal, the third son of the Diwan, was commandant, and who, at first, refused to surrender the fort. But his troops, knowing the Diwan's fortunes were on the ebb, refused to act against the Pattiala forces, the fort was given up, and four lakhs of rupees plundered. The Raja found that spoliation was an easy way of raising money, and after a hurried visit to Pattiala, he left for Ghanor, and besieged the fort which was defended by Zugi Mal and Diwan Mal, nephews of the Minister.

The Diwan takes refuge at Shahabad.

Nanun Mal was on his road back from Karnal when he heard of all that his enemies had accomplished against him. Understanding that, till fortune changed, it would be madness to return to Pattiala, where he could only expect imprisonment or death, he took refuge with Sirdar Karm Singh of Shahabad.[1]

[1] Karm Singh was an immigrant from the Manjha, in 1759. The Shahabad district had been seized by several Chiefs of the Nishania confederacy, the widow of one of whom, Himat Singh, gave to Karm Singh five villages. In return for this kindness, Karm Singh obtained a grant of her whole estate from Dehli and ousted her from all but the village of Islamabad. This conduct scarcely agreed with his agnomen of "Nirmala," or

The treachery of the Chief of Shahabad.

This Chief promised him not only protection, but assistance to recover his power in Pattiala; but treacherously wrote to Raja Sahib Singh, telling him of the arrival of the fugitive, and urging him to take Ghanor before the Diwan could raise troops and come to the help of his relatives. Nanun Mal with difficulty collected a small force and marched to the relief of the fort; but on the road he heard of its capture, his men deserted, and he was obliged to seek a new asylum in the Kythal territory, where he took up his residence at the little village of Chikah, close to the Pattiala frontier. All his estates were confiscated, his property seized, and his relations expelled from office or placed in confinement.

The fall of the Diwan and his family.

Rani Rajindar returns to Pattiala.

In the meantime Rani Rajindar had paid her visit to Sindhia at Mathra, and had been well received, arranging for the payment of the *nuzrana*, and leaving Devi Ditta Mal as a guarantee for the fulfilment of the stipulated conditions. On returning to Pattiala, she found the arts which had been so effectual against the Minister had been employed with equal success against herself, and that the foolish Raja had been persuaded to fear her power as too great for his safety and dignity, and to believe her in alliance with Nanun Mal to restore the old order of things, and reduce the Chief to the mere cypher for which his intellect and vices so eminently fitted him. She made several

spotless. He died in 1808, leaving four sons, Ranjit Singh, Sher Singh, Kharak Singh, and Kahn Singh, who divided the estate equally between them in 1811. Kharak Singh died without issue, in 1831, and his share was allotted to his full brother, Sher Singh. The latter died in 1861, and his only son, Kesra Singh, a year and a half later, when the estate, valued at Rs. 11,500 was resumed by Government. The other shares are still held by Sirdars Dharm Singh, Kishan Singh, and Partab Singh. The two former are the sons of Sirdar Ranjit Singh, and their estate is worth Rs. 5237 per annum; while that of Partab Singh, the son of Kahn Singh, is worth Rs. 3632.

attempts to see Sahib Singh, but he persistently avoided her; and, at last, wearied out and mortified at the ingratitude which repaid the most devoted service with suspicion and insult, she took to her bed and died at Pattiala, after a short illness.

Her death, A.D. 1791.

Her character.

Rani Rajindar was one of the most remarkable women of her age. She possessed all the virtues which men pretend are their own—courage, perseverance, and sagacity—without any mixture of the weakness which men attribute to women; and, remembering her history and that of Ranis Sahib Kour and Aus Kour, who, some years later, conducted, with so much ability, the affairs of the Pattiala State, it would almost appear that the Phulkian Chiefs excluded, by direct enactment, all women from any share of power, from the suspicion that they were able to use it far more wisely than themselves.

Nanun Mal's last effort for power.

Diwan Nanun Mal had ruled so long in Pattiala that he was unable to resign all hope of regaining his authority without another struggle, and looked about for some powerful and discontented Chief whom he might use to obtain his object. He found a suitable instrument in Ata-ulla Khan, the Nawab of Maler Kotla, from whom Pattiala had taken many villages at different times, considerably reducing the Afghan Chief's territory. The Diwan assured him that his opportunity to recover his lost lands was now come; that the Pattiala treasury was empty and the people oppressed and discontented, while the Raja was entirely in the hands of men without courage or energy, who would be unable to help him in any serious emergency. This was all true enough; but the Diwan had overrated the influence that he still possessed in Pattiala. He was almost universally disliked, and his immediate relations, who alone desired his success, had fallen with his fall, and were unable to assist him. Ata-ulla Khan collected his troops and marched as far as Khanpur, some fourteen miles from Pattiala, in company with Nanun Mal. Here he was met by the Pattiala force, headed by Sirdar Chuhr Singh Bhadour and Dalel Singh Malod, and after several trifling engagements, in which the Maler Kotla troops were invariably worsted, he discovered that the advice of the Diwan had been evil; that no Pattiala feudatories came to join him; and Its failure. he wisely made his submission, which, being accepted, he returned to his own territory.

The death of Nanun Mal, A.D. 1792. Diwan Nanun Mal did not long survive this failure of all his hopes, and died at Maler Kotla in 1792, deserted by his old friends, and despised by his new ones whom he His character. had counselled so unwisely. An estimate of his character is difficult, as Pattiala records are almost the only source of information, and that Court cannot look with favour on a Minister who directly rebelled against his Chief. But for his rebellion there were many excuses, while his great services to the State were indisputable. He alone saved Pattiala from utter collapse after the death of Raja Amar Singh, when every neighbouring Chief was ready to dismember it, and when feudatories and subjects were in open revolt. That he oppressed the people, is true, but he was compelled to find money for necessary war. He also insulted and alienated the Chiefs, and their hostility was the cause of his downfall. His conduct at the time of the Mahratta invasion is open to grave suspicion; and Rani Rajindar, who was remarkably acute, was convinced of his dishonesty. But, although he doubtless desired to benefit himself, for he was avaricious in the extreme, there is no proof that he did not do his best for the State. Ministers at Native Courts are not to be judged by the standard which European morality has set up, and even were they so judged, there are many instances in European countries, of statesmen and generals who have rendered conspicuous services to their country, and whose names are justly remembered with gratitude, who have yet made use of their opportunities to enrich themselves and their families. Rebellion against his Chief cannot be justified; but all the excuse which is ever possible for rebellion he certainly had. Sahib Singh was a mere puppet in the hands of greedy and unscrupulous men, who had no thought except for themselves, and whose intrigues against the Minister were prompted by no other motives than jealousy and a desire to obtain the power of helping themselves from the State Treasury. It was rather against these creatures than against the miserable child who was called Raja, that the Diwan took up arms. His fate was that which generally awaits ministers of ability and honesty in Native States; and the intrigues which overthrew him are the very proof of his capacity and devotion to the interests of his country.

The successors of the Diwan and their fate.

The successors of Nanun Mal in the favour of Raja Sahib Singh were Syad Mír Ilahi Baksh and Kesar Mal, a Khatrí, whose influence soon became as distasteful to the Sikhs as that of the old Minister had been; and Sirdar Albel Singh Kaleka, Fatah Singh Mihrmah, and Munshi Ramdyal, who had before been favourites, but who were now neglected, determined to get rid of them. Accordingly, in open Durbar, and in the very presence of the Raja himself, these ruffians assassinated the Syad, Dyal Singh Rorah and Sukha Singh Dhillon being the actual murderers. Diwan Kishan Chand, one of the Syad's party, was also severely wounded, and escaped with difficulty.

A new ministry, A.D. 1793.

Raja Sahib Singh fled to his private apartments, but he could only reward the men who had murdered his friends, and Albel Singh was created Minister, and Ramdyal Chief Munshi. This was in 1793. The Raja was unable to trust the men whom he had raised to power; and believed, with some justice, that they might some day serve him in the same way that they had served Ilahi Baksh; but the only person in whom he could trust was his sister, Sahib Kour, who had married Sirdar Jaimal Singh Kanheya,[1] the master of a great part of the Bari Doab, above Dínanagar. To her he sent, begging her to pay him a visit at Pattiala; and when she arrived, he proclaimed her his Chief Minister, with Tara Singh, one of her own people, as Deputy; and Diwan Singh, the nephew of Nanun Mal, was again taken into favour and made Finance Minister or Diwan. She had not been long at Pattiala, when she heard that her husband, at this time a young man of twenty-one, was in difficulties and hard pressed by his cousin Fatah Singh. She accordingly begged a force from her brother, which he willingly granted, and, heading it herself, she marched to Fatahgarh and rescued her husband, who had been captured by Fatah Singh, returning soon after this exploit to Pattiala in triumph.

Rani Sahib Kour becomes Chief Minister of Pattiala.

The Cis-Satlej States invaded by Anta Rao Mahratta.

In 1794, a large Mahratta force, under the command of Anta Rao and Lachhman Rao, crossed the Jamna and marched in the direction of Pattiala, the smaller Chiefs making their submission, and even the larger ones, Jhind and Kythal, sending agents to make their compliments and express their devotion. But the lady who now ruled the feeble Pattiala Chief was as courageous as

[1] For the history of this family, *vide* "Punjab Chiefs," pp. 322-338.

her cousin Rani Rajindar, and was not inclined to yield to the invaders without a struggle. Raja Bhag Singh of Jhind; Jodh Singh Kalsia;[1] Bhanga Singh and Mehtab Singh of Thanesur, and the Bhadour Sirdars, Dip Singh and Bir Singh, agreed to join her, while Sirdar Tara Singh Gheba sent a detachment, and the whole force, numbering together about 7000 men, marched to meet the enemy near Murdanpur, a few miles from Amballa, where a brisk engagement took place; but the Sikhs, who were far inferior in discipline and numbers to the Mahrattas, began to give way. Retreat would have soon turned to flight had not Bibi Sahib Kour, who had come herself with the troops, leaving her brother in his *zanána* at Pattiala, stepped down from her chariot (*Rath*), and, drawing her sword, declared that the Sikhs would be for ever disgraced if they allowed her, a woman

Preparations for resistance.

The gallantry of Sahib Kour.

[1] The Chief of Kalsia takes rank above all Cis-Satlej Chiefs, except Pattiala, Jhind, Nabha, Maler Kotla, and Faridkot. The founder of the family was Sirdar Gurbuksh Singh of Kalsia in the Manjha, one of the Krora Singhia confederacy, and a companion of Sirdar Bhagel Singh of Chiloundi. He was not a man of much note, but his son, Jodh Singh, born in 1751, possessed great ability, took possession of the district of Chichrowli, and, on the death of Sirdar Bhagel Singh, was acknowledged as the head of the Krora Singhia confederacy. He conquered Dehra and Bassi from Sirdar Khazan Singh; Lotal and Achrak; and encroached upon Pattiala and Nabha territory; but Raja Sahib Singh gave to Hari Singh, son of Jodh Singh, his daughter Karm Kour as wife, in 1803, and thus quieted a most dangerous neighbour. In 1807 he fought under Maharaja Ranjit Singh at the siege of Nariangurh, and was rewarded with estates at Budala, Kaneri, and Chubbal. At the time of the treaty of 1809, the Kalsia territory was worth two lakhs and a half per annum. Jodh Singh gave a great deal of trouble to his neighbours and to the British Agent, and no one was sorry when he died at Multan, where he had been left in command of a detachment after the siege of 1818. Only the elder son, Sobha Singh, survived him, and held the estate till 1858. Both he and his son Lehna Singh did good service in the mutinies, and supplied a contingent of twenty foot and four sowars. The latter received a sanad conferring the right of adoption in March 1862. Sirdar Lehna Singh has lately died, and his only son, Bishan Singh, aged 16, is now Chief of Kalsia. The estate is worth about Rs. 130,000 a year, with a population of 62,000.

and the sister of their Chief, to be slain, for she was determined never to retreat. This gallantry so shamed and encouraged the soldiers, that they returned with renewed fury to the fight, which they maintained, though with considerable loss, till nightfall, neither side being able to claim the victory. The Sikh Chiefs now wished the lady to return to Pattiala while she was able, as the next day must bring with it their defeat, but she refused; and their case being desperate, proposed a night attack on the Mahratta camp. The very audacity of the proposal contained its best chance of success; the troops were immediately put under arms and, just before daybreak, attacked the Mahrattas, who were taken completely by surprise. The Sikhs did little more than gallop through the camp, cutting down those of the enemy they met, and the Mahrattas suffered no great loss; but the confusion caused was very great, and the next day, Anta Rao, hearing that large Sikh reinforcements were approaching, retired towards Karnal.

Night attack on the Mahratta camp.

The enemy retire.

In 1794, a man, half fanatic and half impostor, and as dangerous, greedy, and unscrupulous as such characters usually are, appeared to disturb the Cis-Satlej States. This was Bedi Sahib Singh, the lineal descendant of Baba Nanak, the first and most revered of the Sikh Gurus. His father, Jit Singh, was a quiet man, who had never left his village of Unah, where a pious disciple had given the grandfather, Kala Dharia, a little farm; but Sahib Singh, knowing the fanatical and superstitious character of the Sikhs, thought it would not be difficult to influence them to his own advantage. Accordingly, he proclaimed a religious war against the Maler Kotla Afghans, whom he accused of killing cows, as great an offence in the eyes

A religious war proclaimed by Bedi Sahib Singh, A.D. 1794.

of a Sikh as of any other Hindu.[1] He induced Sirdars Tara Sing Gheba, Bhagel Singh, Bhanga Singh Thanesar, and several other Chiefs, to join him, all men who thought little of religion and a great deal of plunder, and who considered a religious cry as good as any other, so long as they could kill and pillage.

He attacks the Afghans of Maler Kotla.

The unfortunate Maler Kotla Afghans, who were probably as innocent of the charge brought against them as most other victims of religious enthusiasm, prepared for defence. Ata-ulla Khan was still the head of the house, and, with his four nephews, Wazir Khan, Fatah Khan, Himmat Khan, and Dalel Khan, made a short resistance, but they were overpowered and defeated, and fled to Kotla, which the Bedi immediately invested. Ata-ulla Khan sent off messengers to Raja Sahib Singh begging for assistance, and as a Pattiala force, under Bakshi Seda and Sirdar Chen Singh, was encamped close by at Amargarh, it soon reached the town. Bedi Sahib Singh was a sacred character, and the Sikh soldiers were unwilling to fight against him; but after paying him a sum of money and threatening the Sirdars who accompanied him with the future vengeance of Pattiala, the Bedi was induced to withdraw across the Satlej.

Pattiala buys off the invader.

The Bedi makes another raid in 1798, and attacks Rai Kot.

Four years later, in 1798, the Bedi preached, at Amritsar, a second religious war against the Afghans of Rai

[1] Another reason given in the "Gosha-i-Punjab" for the enmity of Sahib Singh to the Afghans of Maler Kotla, was that Sher Muhammad Khan, the grandfather of Ata-ulla Khan, had eloped with a woman of the family of Guru Govind Singh, and induced her to accept Muhammadanism. It was to avenge this insult, and to recover the bones of the lady, that Sahib Singh attacked Kotla. But a Bedi, descendant of Nanak, would have no object in avenging an insult offered to Govind Singh, a Sodhi, of which family there were many members to defend its honour. Sahib Singh only made religion an excuse to loot a comparatively defenceless town.

Kot, on the same pretext as the last. These infidels, he declared, had killed kine, and their lands should be taken away and given to him. The Sikhs again crossed the Satlej, about 7000 in number, and overran the Rai Kot district, which included Jagraon, Rai Kot, Ludhiana, and the neighbouring country. The Chief, Rai Alyas, was only fifteen years of age; but his principal officer, Roshan Khan, made a gallant stand at the village of Jodh, and, although outnumbered four to one, fought the whole day, and would have repulsed the Sikhs had he not been killed by a musket shot, when his troops, disheartened, took to flight. Rai Alyas sent to his neighbours for help, and the Chiefs of Pattiala and Jhind, with Bhai Lal Singh of Kythal, and Jodh Singh Kalsia, collected their forces and marched towards Ludhiana, driving the Sikhs before them, and recovering the villages which the Bedi had seized. Karm Singh, of Shahabad, and Budh Singh Faizullahpuria, who had been active supporters of the Bedi, deserted him and went over to the other side. The Phulkian Chiefs were not disinterested in their action, and Pattiala annexed Badowal, a few miles south of Ludhiana, and three other forts, as the price of her assistance, while the fort at Wakha was mortgaged to Bhai Lal Singh.[1]

The Bhai driven out of the Rai Kot villages.

Driven out of some villages, Bedi Sahib Singh seized others. To Mansur he was invited by the zamindars, weary of the tyranny of Sher Khan, the Collector of Rai Alyas; and the Naobat fort came into his possession, while he built a new one in the village of Doghari. The Hindus

1 Pattiala records speak of the help given to Maler Kotla, Rai Kot, and other Chiefs, as given to her feudatories or "*Zaildars*," whom it was the duty of the paramount to aid. This is of course untrue. Rai Kot and Maler Kotla, though less powerful, were quite as independent as Pattiala herself, and would have laughed at the idea of being her zaildars.

and Sikhs of the town of Ludhiana then invited him there, and he surprised the town by night, and besieged the fort which was defended by Hassan Khan. The Bedi built a mud fort on the spot where the "*Suthhri-ki-Dharamsal*" is now situated, and prepared for a regular siege. Rai Alyas did not know where to look for help. He induced the Chiefs of Philor, Sudha Singh and Kour Singh, to come into the fort; but their assistance was not of much value, and he at length sent to George Thomas, an English adventurer, who had become very powerful, and who ruled the country about Hansi and Hissar. Thomas, who was rapidly extending his territory, was only too glad of an opportunity of interference in the affairs of any of the Cis-Satlej States, and at once left Hansi with a strong force. The Bedi, hearing of his near approach, raised the siege of Ludhiana, and retired across the Satlej; while Thomas, having no further excuse for interference, returned to Hansi.

He attacks Ludhiana.

The Chief asks the assistance of George Thomas of Hansi.

And the Bedi retires.

Between the first and second visits of Bedi Sahib Singh to the Cis-Satlej country, a Pattiala expedition had been sent to Náhan, to assist the Raja, who had, as usual, got into difficulties with his people, who were in open rebellion. Rani Sahib Kour was at the head of the force, and remained at Náhan for three months, settling the affairs of the little State, and reducing the insurgents to obedience.

Expedition to Náhan, A.D 1796.

George Thomas,[1] who had come to the assistance of the Rai Kot Chief, was an Englishman of some tact and courage, who had come to India in the year 1781, and had

The rise of George Thomas.

[1] The history of George Thomas has been written, and no more of it will consequently be noticed here than is necessary to explain his connection with Pattiala history from 1798 to 1802. The work is now, however, very rare—"The Military Memoirs of George Thomas," 4to, by W. Franklin, Calcutta, 1803.

He enters the service of Zebun Nissa.

wandered about the country seeking his fortune for several years, till he was taken into the service of the famous Zebun Nissa, more commonly known as the Begum Samru. In 1792, for some misconduct, he was reduced in rank, and left her service in disgust for that of Apa Khandi Rao, a Mahratta Chief, relative of Madhaji Sindhia, and master of the Jhajjar, Dadri, and Narnol territory. Thomas raised troops for the Mahrattas, and instructed them as well as he was able in the European system of drill; and, in return, the district of Jhajjar was assigned him in jagir. Here he built a fort which he named "Georgegarh," but which, by the people, was corrupted into "Jaházgarh." When Báwa Rao, the nephew of Apa Khandi Rao, succeeded his uncle, Thomas became independent, and, taking possession of Hansi and Hissar, began to encroach on the neighbouring States. He had a force of eight regiments of foot, a thousand horsemen, and about fifty guns; and he strengthened the old fort of Hansi, which he made his capital. In 1797, he made overtures to the principal Sikh Chiefs, inviting them to join him in a combined resistance to the Mahrattas, and in the conquest of Northern India; but they regarded him with suspicion, for his selfish aims were barely concealed, and they thought that to help him would only be to resign their own independence.

Leaves her for the Mahrattas.

He sets up for himself.

Thomas, unable to cajole the Sikhs, determined on subduing them, and taking advantage of the absence of the principal Chiefs at Lahore, in 1798, to oppose the invasion of Shah Zamán Duráni, of Kabul, he laid siege to Jhind, the nearest Sikh town, being not more than twenty miles north-east of Hansi. Hearing of this danger the Phulkian Chiefs hurried back and assembled their forces for the relief of Jhind. The Kythal troops were under

And attacks the town of Jhind.

The combination against him.

the command of Sirdars Sawan Singh, Saman Singh, and Diwan Ramdyal; while Gurdit Singh of Ladwa, and the Thanesar Chiefs, Bhanga Singh and Mehtab Singh, were induced to join by considerable presents. They had not yet fallen so low as to fight for honour or for a friend, without the hope of some personal gain. The combined force marched to Jhind, but in several skirmishes that took place the Sikhs were worsted, till a large detachment of Pattiala troops arrived, commanded by the gallant lady, Sahib Kour. The force of the allies cannot have numbered less than 25,000 men, and is estimated, in some traditions, at 40,000. After some further skirmishing, Thomas, seeing that he was overmatched, raised the siege and retired to Mehm, whither Raja Bhag Singh pursued him, pillaging several villages of the Hansi district. But Thomas' retreat was only a blind; and at night he attacked the Sikh camp with two thousand men, at Narawind, twelve miles to the south of Jhind. The Sikhs had kept no watch, and were carousing after their imaginary triumph of the day before, when Thomas' horsemen galloped through the camp. The Sikhs took to flight in all directions, losing a large number of men and much baggage. The allied army after this defeat became completely demoralised. The jealousies between the Chiefs were so fierce that no disaster could happen without it being attributed to treachery; and, on this occasion, Pattiala declared that Sirdar Jaswant Singh of Nabha had planned the night attack in concert with Thomas, to avenge a scornful speech of Bibi Sahib Kour, who had said that the Nabha soldiers, in comparison with those of Pattiala, were no better than sweepers (Chumárs). In proof of this treachery, it was observed that, although the Jhind and Pattiala troops had suffered most severely

Thomas raises the siege, but defeats the Sikhs in a night attack.

The quarrels among the Sikh leaders.

in this night attack, the Nabha contingent had lost neither men nor baggage. It is impossible to say how far this story of treachery is true; and the probability is, that it was invented to account for a discreditable defeat, as the myth of Raja Tej Singh's treachery was invented to excuse the defeats of Fiorshahr and Sobraon. Karm Singh, "the spotless" (Nirmala), was also accused of having accepted Rs. 5000, from Thomas to set the example of running away. Bribed or not, he certainly ran away with the greatest alacrity.

The Sikhs make peace with Thomas.

After this defeat, the Phulkian Chiefs were content to make peace with Thomas, who, on his part, had so many enemies, that he was delighted to make friends with the Sikhs, who were his only possible allies in the event of a rupture with the Mahrattas, which he saw was sooner or later inevitable.

Raja Sahib Singh quarrels with his sister.

No sooner had danger from without ceased, than dissensions were renewed within; and the weak-minded Sahib Singh, influenced by his favourites, who were jealous of Rani Sahib Kour's power, began to treat his sister with great coldness. There was, moreover, a new element of discord in the person of Rani Aus Kour, daughter of Sirdar Gurdus Singh, of Chattah, whom the Raja had married in 1792, and who, in 1797, bore him a son and heir, who was named Karm Singh. This lady, both clever and ambitious, thought the influence possessed by Bibi Sahib Kour over the Raja belonged legitimately to her, and coalesced with his Court officials against Sahib Kour, who was accused to her brother of many imaginary offences. Of these, the first asserted that she had herself kept the elephant given by the Raja of Náhan as a return for the services rendered in restoring order in his State. As Rani Sahib Kour had performed all the work at Náhan,

The new cause of family discord.

The charges brought against Rani Sahib Kour.

while her brother was squandering health and money among pimps and prostitutes at Pattiala, she might well have pleaded her right to keep the present. It was also alleged, as a crime, that she had built, in 1795, a fort near Sunam, in her jagir, without her brother's permission, and had changed the name of the village of Bhirian to Ubhowal, which it still retains. When the Rani saw that the evil advice of his favourites had more weight with the Raja than all her services, she left Pattiala in disgust for Bhirian, where her new fort stood. This conduct seemed to confirm the Raja's suspicions, and he ordered her to leave Bhirian and return to her husband at Fatahgarh. The Rani had been so long accustomed to command that she was not disposed to obey, and took no notice of this order; on which the Raja himself marched against the fort, and was making preparations to reduce it, when Bhai Dal Singh and other mutual friends succeeded in persuading him that it would not be for his fame to commence his military career by fighting with his sister, and in inducing the Rani to submit and return to Pattiala. On the road, however, suspicious, with very good reason, of the intentions of her brother, she escaped and returned to Bhirian, when all the negotiations had to be commenced afresh. At last, on promises of safety, she consented a second time to return to Pattiala; but when the Raja had conveyed her as far as Dhodan, or Bhawanigarh, he placed her in confinement in the fort. She soon contrived to escape, changing clothes with one of her servants, and returned to Bhirian, where she lived without further molestation for some time, but died in 1799, the unjust treatment that she had received having probably shortened her life.

Her flight from Pattiala.

The Raja's first military expedition.

The treatment of Sahib Kour.

Her death, A.D. 1799.

The peace which George Thomas had made with Jhind

George Thomas again attacks the Sikhs.

was not of long duration. He had a large force which he was only able to pay by expeditions against neighbouring States, and the Jhind and Kythal villages were nearest at hand and most defenceless. In 1799, he renewed his attacks, and the Phulkian Chiefs, with Bhai Lal Singh, of Kythal, again coalesced to resist him. A fight took place between Thomas and Bhadour troops at Dirbah, in which the former was victorious, and he then marched northwards and pillaged the town of Bhawanigarh, though he did not attempt to attack the fort. Thence he proceeded to Ghanor, half way between Ambala and Pattiala, where he was met by Diwan Singh, but it was not Thomas's desire to fight, and he marched back to Sunam, plundering the villages and devastating the country. Near Narangwal, the Jhind forces, with Sirdar Tara Singh Gheba, came up with him, and an undecided engagement took place, in which both parties lost many men. Thomas now pretended to be anxious for peace, and remained quiet for some time, sending proposals for a settlement of their differences to the Phulkian camp. But he suddenly broke off negotiations and disappeared, and was next heard of plundering the village of Rajwánah. The Pattiala troops pursued, Thomas retiring as they advanced, and at length he left the Pattiala territory, where he had done great damage, and entered that of Kythal.

Thomas ravages the Pattiala territory.

Invades Kythal.

Bhai Lal Singh had now taken to defend his own possessions, while the Pattiala troops remained at Akalgarh, prepared to march if their assistance was required; and Raja Bhag Singh returned to Jhind, which promised to be the next object of attack. So it happened to be; for having plundered with impunity many Kythal villages, and having been vainly pursued by the Sikhs, he marched southwards, and attacked Sufidon, in Jhind territory, defended by a weak garrison. Raja Bhag Singh went at once to its relief, but, before his arrival, the fort, which was old and half in ruins, had fallen into the invader's hands. It was useless for Thomas to remain shut up in a fort, so he gave battle to Raja Bhag Singh beneath the walls of the town. His good fortune had, on this occasion, deserted him, and the Jhind Raja was victorious, and Thomas forced to retire with all haste, having lost about 500 men, and recover himself at Kalwah in Kythal territory.

And attacks and captures Sufidon.

But is defeated in an engagement without the town.

This desultory fighting had now lasted a very long time, and both parties were thoroughly exhausted, especially the Sikhs, who had most to lose. Their towns and villages were sacked, and the harvest destroyed, while the rapidity of the enemy's movements made it almost impossible to overtake him; and the discipline he maintained made an attack upon him, even with far superior numbers, a proceeding of doubtful wisdom. In their extremity they determined to make peace on any terms, and, when they had once induced Thomas to retire, to invoke against him the aid of the French General who was commanding, with much brilliancy and success, the northern division of the Mahratta army, and whose disciplined troops would be able to meet Thomas on equal or superior terms.

Peace is concluded between Thomas and the Sikhs, A.D. 1801.

Thomas was anxious for rest, and as his expedition had been rich in plunder, he was not difficult to satisfy, and, abandoning the territories of the allies, he returned to his fort of Hansi, early in the year 1801.

General Perron Commander of the Mahratta army of North India.

The principal Cis-Satlej Chiefs, Pattiala, Jhind, Nabha, and Kythal, then resolved to send a joint embassy to General Perron, at Dehli, and ask his assistance. This officer had succeeded the Comte de Boigne, a Savoyard, who had entered the service of Sindhia about the year 1785, and had, by his energy and knowledge of military science, made the Mahratta army the most formidable owned by any native prince in India. He left India in 1796, and was succeeded by General Perron, also a man of conspicuous ability, who extended the Mahratta authority northwards beyond the Jamna, and commanded a powerful and highly trained army. It was to this officer that Raja Bhag Singh of Jhind, Bhai Lal Singh of Kythal, and two Sirdars, Chen Singh and Hamir Singh, on the part of Pattiala, addressed themselves. The General was willing to assist them, for the increasing power of George Thomas had excited both his jealousy and alarm; and he saw in this adventurer a rival whose influence, unless checked in time, might endanger his own. He accordingly received the deputation with great consideration, and despatched a force under one of his Lieutenants, Louis Bourquin, to act with the Sikh troops against Thomas. No Pattiala troops joined in the expedition, but Jhind and Kythal detachments, with the Mahratta force under Bourquin, marched to Chinargarh, and thence to Bedi, where they came up with Thomas, and an engagement was fought in which the advantage remained with the latter, Bourquin losing so many men that he was compelled to wait for reinforcements from General Perron. When these arrived he again assumed the offensive, and compelled Thomas to retire to Hansi. Here he was surrounded, and after an obstiate defence surrendered, and abandoning all his conquests, retired into British territory, never again disturbing the peace of the Cis-Satlej States.[1]

He resolves to assist the Sikhs.

Bourquin sent against Thomas.

Thomas defeated and compelled to abandon Hansi.

[1] George Thomas died about a year after this. His career shows not so much what a determined and clever man can do among races inferior in energy and knowledge, but how complete was the anarchy and confusion

But a power was now rising before which Mogals, Mahrattas, and Sikhs had alike to yield. Year by year the red line which marked the British possessions was advanced further to the north. Bengal, Benares, Oude, Allahabad, Cawnpur, Farrukhabad, had in turn fallen; till, on the 11th of September 1803, General Lake defeated the Mahratta army commanded by Bourquin, beneath the walls of Dehli; and four days later entered the capital of Hindostan as a conqueror. On the 1st of November the battle of Laswari was fought, when the Mahrattas were again defeated with great loss; and Sindhia, by the treaty of Sirji Anjengaom, ceded Sirsa, Hissar, Rohtuk, Dehli, Gurgaon, and Agra, to the British Government. The three first named districts were not, however, taken under British administration till the year 1809.

The rise of the British power.

The capture of Dehli, A.D. 1803.

The Cis-Satlej Chiefs miscalculated the strength of the English. They had besides made friends with the Mahrattas; Bourquin had just overthrown their most dangerous enemy; and for these reasons they fought on the side of the Mahrattas at Dehli against the English. Among those present in this battle were Gurdit Singh Ladwa, Bhanga Singh of Thansesar, and many minor Chiefs, though it does not appear that the Phulkian Chiefs, or the Bhai of Kythal, were present or sent a contingent.

The Sikh estimate of the English.

During the whole of the year 1804, the Sikhs, in the

in India at the close of the last century. Thomas was an able man in some respects, but his ability was in no way remarkable. But, when he obtained power, at the time of the disintegration of the Dehli monarchy, and while the Mahratta power was now threatening to become predominant and now appearing about to crumble into ruins, India was in perhaps a more anarchical state than at any other period of her history, and any adventurer, untroubled with scruples and of ordinary capacity, might have carved out for himself a kingdom.

The English attack and rout the Sikhs.

neighbourhood of the Jamna, incited by Amir Khan, the Rohilla Chief, and Jaswant Rao Holkar, Mahratta, continued to be hostile, and large parties constantly crossed the river, and ravaged the country.[1] On the 18th of December 1804, Colonel Burn, leaving his camp standing, made a forced march of twenty miles, and surprised and completely routed the Sikhs; and Raja Bhag Singh, and Bhai Lal Singh, wise in their generation, joined the English army with their forces on the 26th January 1805, bearing letters from Colonel Ochterlony to Colonel Burn, who bestowed presents upon them and treated them with politeness.[2] The hostile Sikhs, some 6000 in number, were at this time encamped at Mulánah, some twenty miles to the south-east of Panipat, but retired when the British force marched against them, and their movements were so rapid that they were not overtaken; but after having been driven for two months from one place to another, they thought it expedient to recross the Jamna into the own territory.

An amnesty proclaimed by the English General, A.D. 1805.

An amnesty was proclaimed in the month of March 1805, by the Commander-in-Chief, to all those Sikhs who would agree to observe peace and abstain from operations against the English; and, in a short time, this was accepted by Rai Singh, of Jagadri, whose brother Sher Singh had been mortally wounded in the engagement with the English of the preceding year, and by all the Chiefs in arms, with the exception of Sirdar Gurdit Singh Ladwa, who was expressly excluded from its provisions, although he had not been so active against the

[1] Lord Lake to Colonel Ochterlony, 2d February 1804. Colonel Burn to Colonel Ochterlony, 4th March, 28th March, 6th June, 8th June, 28th November, 30th November, and 2d December 1804.

[2] Colonel Burn to Colonel Ochterlony, 20th December 1804, 30th January 1805.

English as the Jagadri Chiefs; and his fort of Karnal, which Raja Bhag Singh had lost some years before, was captured by the English in April.[1]

Jaswant Rai Holkar takes refuge in the Punjab.

In October 1804, Jaswant Rai Holkar, who had just gained a great triumph over the brigade of Colonel Monson, laid siege to Dehli with 20,000 men, but was repulsed by General Ochterlony and Colonel Burn, after a most gallant defence which lasted nine days. Two months later, at Fatahgarh and Deeg, Generals Lake and Frazer utterly routed the Mahrattas, inflicting on them immense loss, while their leader, Holkar, left without an army, and after vain attempts to create a new one south of the Jamna, went northwards to seek among the Sikh Chieftains more reliable, if not more efficient aid, than he could obtain from Sindhia, who hated him while he was compelled to appear his friend. He remained for some months at Pattiala, and obtained large contributions from both Raja Sahib Singh and Rani Aus Kour, between whom there was a violent quarrel; but he was not able to induce the Raja to give him much active

[1] Colonel Burn to Colonel Ochterlony, 29th March, 31st March, 2d, 5th, 7th, 8th, 9th, 10th, 11th, of April 1805. Sirdars Sahib Singh and Gurdit Singh of Ladwa were members of the Krora Singhia confederacy. They were Sansi Jats of the village of Bain Poin, ten miles south of Amritsar, and joined the troop of Mit Sind Rohela about 1758. After the defeat of Zin Khan, Governor of Sirhind, in 1763, they seized Bahein, Shamghar, and Ladwa. The last-named district fell to the share of Gurdit Singh. In a skirmish with Agha Shafih, near Karnal, Sahib Singh was killed, and Gurdit Singh took the whole estate, with the exception of Shamghar, given to the brother of Sahib Singh's widow, and twelve villages given to Bhagwan Singh, the adopted son of the deceased. Gurdit Singh was granted the district of Badowal by Ranjit Singh. He was succeeded by his son Ajit Singh, who built a bridge over the Sirsuti, or Saraswati, at Thanesar, and obtained the title of Raja. He rebelled in 1845; his estates were confiscated, and he was imprisoned at Allahabad. He contrived to escape, after killing his keeper, and after long wanderings is supposed to have died in Kashmir. His children are still living in the North-west Provinces.

assistance; and when General Lake had seriously taken the field against him, in October 1805, and entered the Punjab in pursuit, he was compelled to take flight to Amritsar, where, on the 11th of January 1806, a treaty was concluded between Holkar and the British Government, by which the former gave up all possessions in North India; while Sirdar Ranjit Singh, of Lahore, agreed to give the Mahratta no assistance.

The disputes at Pattiala between Raja Sahib Singh and the Rani.

It is now necessary to return to Pattiala, where the disputes between the Raja and Rani Aus Kour had grown more bitter than ever, and their unfortunate results were seen in all the neighbouring States. The Rani turned her arms against Jaswant Singh of Nabha, and Raja Bhag Singh of Jhind, having for her allies Bhai Lal Singh of Kythal, and Sirdar Bhanga Singh of Thanesar.

The mediation of Ranjit Singh of Lahore requested.

The contest continued for some time with varying success and much bloodshed, till, at length, Raja Bagh Singh, desirous of putting an end to it in a manner favourable to himself and his ally of Nabha, requested the aid of his nephew Ranjit Singh of Lahore. Raja Jaswant Singh of Nabha joined in his request, for he had just been defeated by the Pattiala Chief at Mirwana, and was eager for revenge. Ranjit Singh was only too glad of an opportunity of interference, and, on the 26th of July 1806, crossed the Satlej with a force which was estimated at 30,000 horse, though half this number would be nearer the truth, accompanied by Sirdar Fatah Singh Ahluwalia, Gurdit Singh Ladwa, and other Chiefs. On the 28th he took possession of Doladhi, a town belonging to the Raja of Pattiala, and the subject of dispute between him and Nabha, and some twenty-two miles to the north of the capital; and the following day he reached Nabha.[1]

The English mistrust the motives of the Lahore Chief.

It does not appear that the British authorities had been requested to decide the dispute between Nabha and Pattiala; and although they desired to believe the friendly professions of Ranjit Singh, yet they viewed his approach with some distrust and anxiety. Raja Bhag Singh indeed wrote, assuring the Resident at Dehli that the only object of his nephew's visit was to settle the disputes which had arisen at Pattiala itself and among the petty Chieftains in the neighbourhood; but it was still considered advisable to strengthen the Karnal garrison in case Ranjit Singh should enter the district in force. But he had no wish to offend the English, and there was abundant territory which he could seize without rousing their jealousy. He proceeded no further south than Ambala and Thanesar, and then retired northward, having done little to restore friendship between the Pattiala Raja and his wife, but receiving from both large sums of money to secure his good-will. The position of his uncle Raja Bhag Singh he considerably strengthened, giving to him the town of Ludhiana and its surrounding villages, which he had taken from the Mussalman Rajputs of Raikot, who had held it for about two hundred years.[2]

The conquests of Maharaja Ranjit Singh in 1806.

This unfortunate family was completely despoiled to reward the friends and allies of Ranjit Singh. The chief representatives were, at this time, two women, Nur-un-nisa, widow of Rai Alyas Khan, and Lachmi; but

[1] Circular of Resident Dehli to all Residents, Magistrates, &c., dated 1st November 1806. Captain Murray to Sir E. Colebrooke, dated 12th April and 11th May 1828.

[2] President Dehli to Officer Commanding at Karnal, dated 10th November 1806. Officers Commanding at Meerut, Karnal, Rewari, and Saharunpur to Resident Dehli, dated 3d, 4th, 5th, 10th of November 1806.

Ranjit Singh had no generosity, and preferred despoiling a widow to attacking a Chief who was better able to resist. From the plunder of this family Raja Bhag Singh received the districts of Ludhiana, Jhandála, Kot, Jagraon, and Basia, including 54 villages, of an annual rent of Rs. 23,260; Sirdar Gurdit Singh of Ladwa, the districts of Baddowal, with portions of Jagraon, 32 villages, worth Rs. 23,540; Raja Jaswant Singh of Nabha, portions of Kot Basia, Talwandi, and Jagraon, 31 villages, worth Rs. 26,690; Sirdar Fatah Singh Ahluwalia, portions of Dhaka, Kot, Basia, Jagraon, and Talwandi, 106 villages, worth Rs. 40,505; Diwan Mokham Chand, portions of Ghilla, Kot, Jagraon, and Talwandi, 71 villages, worth Rs. 33,945; Sirdar Bassawa Singh, 10 villages, in Kot and Jagraon, worth Rs. 5714; and Sirdar Bhanga Singh, one village in Talwandi, worth Rs. 400. The only other conquest of Ranjit Singh, during this campaign, was the district of Ghumgrana from Gujar Singh, Jat Singh, and Kabil Khan, which he divided between Sirdar Gurdit Singh Ladwa and Raja Jaswant Singh, the former taking 5 villages, worth Rs. 23,550, and the latter 7, worth Rs. 3350.[1]

The departure of the Raja of Lahore was the signal for a renewal of the conflict between Sahib Singh and Rani Aus Kour. The confusion into which the administration fell was inconceivable; the officials taking one side or the other as they fancied their own fortunes would be better furthered, and perpetual fights and bloodshed being the result. It became unsafe for strangers to enter the territory; and Lieutenant White, employed by the British

[1] *Vide* Appendix A.—Statement of the conquests of Maharaja Ranjit Singh during the years 1806, 1807, 1808, and History of Diwan Mokham Chund in "Punjab Chiefs," p. 552

Government on a survey of the frontier, was fired upon at Khoralah, a town held by the friends of the Rani, compelled to retrace his steps, and abandon his survey for the time, although furnished with full authority under the Raja's hand and seal.[1]

Ranjit Singh again invited to Pattiala, A.D. 1807.

The Pattiala Sirdars, and the Rajas of Jhind and Nabha, who had benefited so much by the late visit of Ranjit Singh, again invited his assistance, which he very willingly promised. He collected a large body of horse, under the command of his famous General Diwan Mokham Chand, and Sirdars Fatah Singh Ahluwalia and Gharba Singh;[2] and in September 1807, he appeared before Pattiala, where the intrigues of the former year were repeated in order to induce him to espouse the cause of one party or the other. It was a mere question of money, and the Rani bribed highest. Besides money and diamonds, she gave Ranjit Singh a brass gun named Khuri Khan, afterwards taken by the English during the Satlej campaign; and by his influence and that of the Rajas of Jhind and Nabha, Sirdar Bhanga Singh of Thanesar, and Bhai Lal Singh, a compromise was at last effected, by which an estate of Rs. 50,000, consisting of the districts of Banur, Manimajra, Sunour, Surali Bissoli, and Minarthal, was settled upon Rani Aus Kour for the maintenance of herself and her son Kour Karm Singh.[3]

The compromise effected.

The conquests of Ranjit Singh during 1807-8.

After this arrangement, Ranjit Singh marched by way of Ambala to Naraingarh, a strong fort held by Kour Kishan Singh, which he invested. For nearly three

[1] Lieutenant White to Resident Dehli, 18th and 28th July 1807. Resident Dehli to Lieutenant White, 25th May 1807.

[2] Resident of Dehli to Major-General Commanding Mathra, dated 20th August 1807.

[3] A copy of this document accompanies the letter of Captain Ross, D. Superintendent to Agent to Governor-General Dehli, dated 5th February 1823.

weeks it held out, and in one of the assaults, Sirdar Fatah Singh, Kalianwala, one of Ranjit Singh's bravest Generals, was mortally wounded. After the capture of the place, it was conferred, with its surrounding villages, on Sirdar Fatah Singh Ahluwalia, the estate being valued at Rs. 12,580 a year. The same Chief received 3 villages of Jat Mal Singh, of Raipur, worth Rs. 1200; and 3 villages in Ghumgrána, captured from the same Chief, and worth Rs. 2255, were given to Raja Bhag Singh, of Jhind, with the estate of Morinda, in Sirhind, taken from the sons of Dharam Singh, who refused to pay a *nazrána* to the invader. This estate consisted of 27 villages, and was worth Rs. 17,000. The Nabha Chief only received one village from the Ghumgrána estate; while Diwan Mokham Chand, who was fast rising to favour, obtained the district of Zira, now in the Firozpur district, taken from the widow of Sirdar Mohr Singh of Nishánwala, and comprising 12 villages, worth Rs. 7500; Kot Kapura in the same district, held by Jaggat Singh of Buria, with 77 villages, worth Rs. 61,400; and 12 villages from Dharam Kot, being part of the estate of Sirdar Tara Singh Gheba, who had lately died. The remainder of this estate, with the exception of a few villages, was given in jagir to Gharba Singh, whose share consisted of 62 villages, worth Rs. 22,634. The remainder of the Ghumgrána district, 36 villages, worth Rs. 23,415, was conferred on Sirdar Karam Singh of Nagla.[1]

[1] *Vide* Appendix A.

The fort of Ghumgrána, with these villages, belonged to Sirdar Tara Singh Gheba. Soon after his death, the Rajas of Pattiala, Nabha, Jhind, Bhai Lal Singh of Kythal and Gurdit Singh of Ladwa, joined forces and besieged it. The fort was defended by Gujar Singh, son of Sirdar Tara Singh, for some time with success; till at length Ranjit Singh raised the siege by a message to the confederated Chiefs, ordering them to desist; and, in spite of their disgust, they obeyed the order. Was it then possible that the

During this same campaign the district of Wadni, in Firozpur, was conquered by Diwan Mokham Chand, and later in the year was given by the Maharaja to his mother-in-law, Mai Sada Kour, whose family lived in Raoki, a Wadni village.[1]

The Cis-Satlej Chiefs ask British protection, but can obtain no promise.

The Cis-Satlej Chiefs now began to perceive that unless they united among themselves, or invited foreign assistance, they would, one by one, be destroyed by the Lahore Raja, whose power their own divisions had so much increased. In March 1808, Raja Bhag Singh of Jhind, Bha Lal Singh of Kythal, and Sirdar Chen Singh, the confidential Agent of the Raja of Pattiala, visited Mr Seton, the Resident at Dehli, to sound him as to the extent and kind of protection which the British Government might be willing to afford them.[2]

Maharaja, for once in his life, should protect the weak against the strong, and do an action which might be called generous? The motive was easily found. He sent an army to seize the fort and estate for himself; and the unfortunate Gujar Singh, unable to resist, fled to Pattiala.

[1] Diwan Mokham Chand, in March 1808, captured Patoki and fifteen villages of the Wadni district from Mian Noudan. In September the Maharaja, when encamped at Maler Kotla, made an unconditional grant oi the whole district to Sada Kour, who paid for it Rs. 15,000. She was put in possession of the fort of Patoki and the villages seized by Mokham Chand, but she did not obtain possession of Wadni and Himatpur till 1817, when she crossed the Satlej in person, and took both the forts by force ot arms from Amar Singh, son of Mian Noudan, who had died some time before. Her right did not, however, arise from this action of hers, but from the grant of Ranjit Singh, for Mian Noudan had from the date of the grant been recognised as her zamindar; and Sir D. Ochterlony, in a decree dated 21st November 1811, gave her full authority to employ troops against him. The expedition against Amar Singh was, on the same grounds, permitted by Sir D. Ochterlony, who authorised her to eject Amar Singh from his villages in a precept dated 20th July 1816.

Vide also Sir D. Ochterlony to Captain Ross, dated 7th November 1821, and Captain Murray to Sir E. Colebrooke, dated 19th February 1828.

The estate of Wadni has lately been the subject of a political claim, in the course of which it has been affirmed that the district was conquered by Sada Kour in the first instance, and also that it was inherited by her. Both assertions are utterly untrue.

[2] Resident Dehli to Mr C. Metcalfe, 2d April 1808.

The Government was disposed to protect them, but had not determined how to act; and the Chiefs then proceeded to Hurdwar, hoping to make some amicable arrangement with Ranjit Singh, who meditated a visit to the sacred city; but, at the last moment, after all had been prepared for his reception, he changed his mind and remained at Lahore. One reason for this was that he had heard of the intrigues of the Pattiala Raja with the English, and desired an interview with that Chief on Sikh soil rather than on British, where he could not use force if he were unable to persuade. He accordingly proposed a meeting with Raja Sahib Singh at Laknour, south of the Satlej. The Raja was most unwilling to accept the invitation, and evaded compliance for some time, but at last he consented from sheer terror, and the meeting took place on the 24th November 1808, when Maharaja Ranjit Singh appeared at the head of his army, which he had been employing in the reduction of Faridkot Saniwal, Jhandbar, Bairampur, Dhari, and Chandpur, all of which, worth some Rs. 50,000 a year, he had granted to his favourite Mohkam Chand. He received Raja Sahib Singh with the utmost kindness; swore to remain always his friend; to have no enemies but his enemies, no friends but his friends; and, as a token of eternal brotherhood, the Chiefs exchanged turbans, a ceremony which had in it something of a sacred nature, but in which neither were sincere, nor were any of those who witnessed the engagements persuaded that they were made otherwise than for temporary convenience.[1] After this farce had been played out, Ranjit Singh marched

Ranjit Singh arranges a visit with the Raja of Pattiala at Laknour.

[1] Letter of Resident Dehli, to Secretary to Government, dated 7th December 1808, and of Mr C. Metcalfe, Envoy to Lahore to Resident Dehli, dated December 9, 1808.

northwards, accompanied by Raja Bhang Singh of Jhind, to the Satlej, which he crossed on the 2d December, leaving a garrison of nearly ten thousand men behind him in Ambala, which he had taken from Rani Dya Kour, widow of Sirdar Gurbaksh Singh, who had died in 1783.[1] Raja Sahib Singh made no secret of his sentiments, which may be best seen from a letter which he addressed to the Resident of Dehli, who, on the approach of the Maharaja of Lahore, had written to Sahib Singh, without waiting for distinct orders from Calcutta, and had promised him protection. This comforting letter Sahib Singh did not, however, receive till after the dreaded interview was over. His own narrative of what occurred is as follows :—"Having marched from Kotlah to this quarter, he (Ranjit Singh) expressed a desire that a meeting between us should take place. He himself advanced to the neighbourhood of Pattiala, and fixed his camp at Ambala, which he took possession of; moreover, in consequence of Sirdar Bhanga Singh having come to Pattiala through friendship for me, and joined my party, he ordered Dumah and other places belonging to the said Sirdar to be given up,

Ranjit Singh's return to the Punjab, December 1808.

The account given by Sahib Singh of the Maharaja's visit

[1] Sirdar Gurbaksh Singh had himself obtained Ambala by violence and fraud. The town and district were first conquered by Sangat Singh, who made them over to his brother-in-law Dhyan Singh, and went to Singhwala in Firozpur, where he died. Dhyan Singh also went away, leaving Gurbaksh Singh and Lal Singh as Thanadars in charge; but, after five years absence, he found they had taken possession for themselves, and refused to give up the town. Lal Singh then built a fort called Jamiyatgarh, on the Pattiala border, rousing the jealousy of Raja Amar Singh, who attacked him in company with the Raja of Jhind and the Rai of Kot, but was unable to prevent the building of the fort. After the death of Lal Singh, his colleague, Gurbaksh Singh, became sole Sirdar. He died childless, and his widow, Dya Kour, succeeded in 1783. She was temporarily ejected by Ranjit Singh, but was restored by General Ochterlony; and held the estate till 1823, when it lapsed to Government. She was an excellent ruler, and her estate was one of the best managed in the protected territory.

and placed them in charge of Sahib Singh Balik, who had united with the Chiefs of Aluah. He then encamped at Shahabad. The kind conduct [used ironically] which he observed towards the family of the late Karm Singh, a relative of mine, is well known. Although after such conduct on his part I should have declined a meeting, yet upon his reaching Shahabad he sent Raja Bhang Singh, Chen Singh, my agent, and his own agent, Mast Singh, to Pattiala, for the purpose of expressing his wish to meet me. Still, however, four or five days were taken up in discussing the matter on my part, but at length all the Chiefs gave it as their opinion that since Mr Metcalfe had been sent on the part of the Governor-General to wait on the Singh Sahib (Ranjit Singh), and establish the relations of friendship, my objecting and opposing singly would be of no avail. Having no choice, I followed the advice of the Chiefs, and, marching from Pattiala, I encamped at Laknour, where Baba Sahib Bedi Sahib Singhji, the revered descendant of Baba Nanak, was already encamped. The second day after my arrival the Singh Sahib (Ranjit Singh) left Shahabad, and repaired to the same place, and we met in the presence of Baba Sahib. Four or five days after this, no further intercourse taking place, I sent for Mast Singh, the agent to the Singh Sahib, and asked the reason for the discontinuance of our intercourse. He replied that the wish of the Singh Sahib was to bring about that complete and precise friendship which is testified by an exchange of turbans; adding that, in the event of my objecting, although, in consequence of the presence of Baba Sahib, nothing hostile to me might be manifested, yet, after my departure for Pattiala, the real intentions of the Singh Sahib would be evident.

"My friend; after repeated delays, I became at length completely hopeless, and seeing that the mind of the Singh Sahib was inclined to violence, I was induced, by the advice of all the Sirdars, to consent to his desire. Had your kind letter arrived at Pattiala two or three days before my departure, notwithstanding the number of his troops then in my country, I would have replied to him in the language of defiance."

The reply of the Resident to Pattiala and Jhind, December 1808.

The letter is interesting, both as giving a true account of the facts and a striking picture of the feebleness of the Raja of Pattiala. The Resident at Dehli returned a friendly and encouraging answer, as also to a letter from Raja Bhag Singh of Jhind, directly asking for British protection for Pattiala, Nabha, and Jhind; but the Resident was not in a position to give full assurances of protection.[1] Sahib Singh then urged his case in stronger terms, assuring the Resident that "he considered the officers of the English Government his superiors, patrons, and protectors," without whose aid he had no hope of safety.[2]

The policy of the English Government towards Ranjit Singh and the Cis-Satlej States.

It is now necessary to go back in the narration a few months, to show the intentions of the British Government towards the Cis-Satlej States, and the modifications which circumstances effected in those intentions.

In 1808, when the European Napoleon was at the height of his power, the Governor-General received intelligence that the French, who, for some time, had been endeavouring to establish themselves in Persia, designed also the conquest of Kabul and the Punjab. The Government accordingly determined to despatch Envoys

[1] Resident to Raja Sahib Singh, dated 3d December 1808, and to Raja Bhag Singh, of the 4th December. Letter of Raja Bhag Singh to Resident, received 3d December 1808.

[2] Raja Sahib Singh to Resident, dated 4th December 1808.

to both Lahore and Kabul, who might persuade the rulers of those countries that their interests and those of England were identical, and that their wisest policy was to unite for the destruction of the common enemy.

Envoys despatched to Lahore and Kabul.

Mr C. T. Metcalfe was selected to conduct the Lahore negotiations, and Mr Elphinstone those with Kabul; and in August 1808, the former started on his mission.

The position of Maharaja Ranjit Singh in 1808, and his feeling regarding the Cis-Satlej States and the British Government.

At the time of the mission to Lahore, Ranjit Singh had conquered a large portion of the Punjab proper between the Jhelam and the Bias. Those Chiefs, like Jodh Singh Ramgharia and Fatah Singh Ahluwalia, who still held a large extent of territory, were, in reality, subject to his authority, and attended him on all his expeditions with large contingents of troops. The north-west portion of the Punjab was held by the Afghans; the province of Maultan by Muzaffar Khan; and the hill country by Raja Sansar Chand, Katoch; but all these were beginning to respect the power and the fortune of the Maharaja, and to calculate the time when his arms would be turned against them. His great ambition was to be ruler of the whole Sikh nation, and from this design he was not to be turned except by finding opposed to him a power greater than his own. Already, in the campaigns of 1806, 1807, 1808, he had made considerable progress in reducing the country between the Satlej and the Jamna, aided not more by his own energy and determination than by the apathy of the Cis-Satlej Chiefs, who had no union among themselves, whose interests were mostly conflicting, and who seemed to wait, with despair, their certain absorption, unless the British Government should take them under its strong protection; and of this they had now little hope. They still continued, and with some success, to impress upon the Maharaja that the

His ambition and conquests.

British Government was prepared to defend them against his attacks; but after the discouraging reception which the principal Chiefs had experienced from the Resident at Dehli, in March, they were disposed to trust more to the clemency of the Maharaja than the protection of the English. Soon after this interview, the whole party, with the exception of Sirdar Bhagwan Singh of Jagadri, went to Lahore, and were still there in attendance on the Maharaja, when the British Envoy reached Kassur, in September.[1] The Chiefs with him, at that time, were Raja Bhag Singh of Jhind; Raja Jaswant Singh of Nabha; Bhai Lal Singh of Kythal; and Gurdit Singh of Ladwa; while the Raja of Pattiala, the Chiefs of Thanesar, Basia, and others, were represented by their agents. Some of these Chiefs, as has before been shown, had acknowledged the supremacy of Ranjit Singh by aiding him in the field and by accepting estates from the conquered territory, which they held on jagir tenure, subject to him.

The despair of the Cis-Satlej Chiefs, who resolve to make terms with Lahore.

Little was, indeed, wanting to extend his authority over all the Cis-Satlej States; and the fear of English interference, which had hitherto influenced him, was growing weaker and weaker as he perceived that his successive encroachments met with no opposition.

This dream of a Sikh monarchy uniting the whole nation under his rule, having for the Maharaja so great an attraction, it was to be supposed that any opposition to its realisation from the British Government would be sufficient to change him from a suspicious ally into a secret enemy, or, indeed, into an active and open one, should any opportunity occur, when, by alliance with a foreign power, he might hope to avenge himself upon the

Ranjit Singh had no reason to love the British Government.

[1] Letter of Mr Metcalfe to Government of India, dated 1st October 1808.

Government that had thwarted him. Over the whole territory that he had conquered his power was absolute; for his policy was to remove to new jagirs the families he had reduced, and to entrust their possessions to such of his dependants whose devotion he could surely trust. Although in the army there was much disaffection, yet he was implicitly obeyed; and every private soldier was taught to look to the Maharaja as his master, although he might be serving under the banner of his own hereditary Chief. By the Sirdars he was hated, for he had destroyed their power; and he treated them with a hauteur which showed his determination to make no distinction between them and the common people so far as absolute subservience to himself was concerned. The Envoy to Lahore remarked that the Cis-Satlej Rajas and Chiefs in the Maharaja's Camp were as submissive as if they had long been used to his authority, and showed no sign of independence whatever.

He was hated by the Chiefs of the Punjab proper.

His jealousy of the English.

Towards the British Government the Maharaja, at this time, had no sincere good-will; and it was commonly reported that he intended to try his strength with the English, and had, with this design, made a secret alliance with Holkar and the Raja of Bhurtpur. Though this was unfounded, and although the Maharaja was too wise to wish for a rupture with the British Government, yet he, like all ambitious princes, looked with the greatest jealousy, if not hatred, upon any power stronger than his own; especially one whose interests he knew were adverse to his, and whom he suspected of an intention to thwart his most cherished schemes. He had not yet learnt the strength and resources of the British Government, and his unvarying success, and the flattery of his courtiers, had half persuaded him that he was invincible.

Such being the position and the sentiments of Ranjit Singh, it was hardly to be supposed that he, to whom the French Emperor was a very doubtful danger and a possible ally, should have entered with any enthusiasm into the designs of the Governor-General, without seeking to obtain some real and tangible advantage for himself.

The British Embassy leaves Karnal, August 1808.

Mr Metcalfe left Karnal in the middle of August 1808, and on the 22d arrived at Pattiala, and was received by Raja Sahib Singh with the greatest politeness. At the first public reception, the Raja tried to induce the Envoy to accept the keys of the town, and to restore them as a gift on the part of the British Government, saying, in the strongest language, that he threw himself on its protection, and that, without it, his Government and life would end together. Mr Metcalfe declined the ceremony, understanding that the Raja desired to thus obtain the appearance of a guarantee from the British Government for the integrity of his State, and, assuring him of the good-will which the Government entertained for him, remarked that the keys of Pattiala had for long been secure in his hands, and that there was every hope of their long remaining so.[1]

Reaches Pattiala.

The terror of Raja Sahib Singh.

The Raja had, nevertheless, good reason for alarm. It was given out publicly, at Lahore, that Ranjit Singh was about to march against Farídkot, adjoining the Pattiala territory, and intended to deprive Sahib Singh of all his possessions; and after the departure of the mission, the Raja hastily began to strengthen Pattiala and his other forts, though his weakness and indecision were such that it was most unlikely he would offer any resistance to the Maharaja, should he appear as an enemy.

As the Envoy approached the capital of the Lahore

[1] Mr Metcalfe to Government of India, 24th August 1808.

Ranjit Singh marches to Kassur.

State, the Maharaja marched into camp at Kassur, with the double object of being prepared for the expedition beyond the Satlej, which he had definitely determined, and of preventing the British Envoy from seeing his principal cities of Lahore and Amritsar. Mr Metcalfe reached Kassur on the 11th of September, and was courteously received,[1] but it was difficult to induce Ranjit Singh to enter upon the subject of the negotiations with which Mr Metcalfe was entrusted. Meeting after meeting took place, at which all reference to business was studiously avoided, the Raja seeming to desire to cross the Satlej and commence his campaign without waiting to hear the propositions of the Envoy at all.

The opening of the negotiations.

Proposals and counter-proposals.

At length, at a private Durbar, Mr Metcalfe was invited to explain the wishes of the British Government, which he accordingly did, pointing out the danger threatened by a French invasion; that the Maharaja and the English were both deeply interested in preventing it; and that an alliance of the two States, for mutual defence, would be the highest wisdom. The Maharaja and his advisers expressed the greatest satisfaction at the prospect of an alliance with the English, and an entire concurrence in the Governor-General's wishes.[2] This alliance, it was said, would put to shame those who spoke of hostility between the two States; and it would be materially strengthened by the agreement of the Envoy to certain propositions which the Maharaja had laid before the Governor-General, and which, it was presumed, the Envoy had authority to answer. The chief point was the acknowledgment of Ranjit Singh's sovereignty over

[1] Mr Metcalfe to Government of India, dated 2d, 4th, 5th, and 13th of September 1808.

[2] Mr Metcalfe to Government of India, dated 15th, 17th, 18th, and 20th September 1808.

all the Sikh Chiefs and territories, after which the treaty could be signed and the alliance with England remain firm for ever. Mr Metcalfe urged that in the defensive treaty against France the advantage to both the English Government and the Maharaja was apparent, and that it was not fitting to turn from this common basis to propositions which only concerned the advantage of one party. The Sikh ministers, however, pressed for a reply to their demands, and it was decided that both parties should put their propositions in writing for further consideration.[1] The next day, after another conference with his ministers, in which the Envoy had held out little hope of his claims over the Cis-Satlej States being allowed, Ranjit Singh struck his camp, and, inviting the Envoy to follow him, marched to the Satlej, and the next day crossed the river and encamped at Khai, a village some ten miles inland.[2] His jealousy was now fully roused: the mission to Kabul he desired to stop, as he believed that an alliance with that Court, hostile to himself, was projected; and the mission to his own Court he determined to get rid of as soon as possible. Mr Metcalfe was justly displeased at the discourtesy with which he was treated, but he followed the Maharaja to Khai and had another interview, which did not much advance the negotiations.[3] But the question was, in a way, settling itself. Faridkot surrendered to Ranjit Singh without offering any resistance, on the 1st of October, and the Chief prepared for further conquests, though he had promised to remain at Khai for sufficient time to enable the negotiations to be concluded. On the 4th of

The Maharaja crosses the Satlej, and determines to break off negotiations.

He captures Faridkot.

[1] Mr Metcalfe to Government of India, 23d and 24th September 1808.

[2] Mr Metcalfe to Government of India, 25th and 26th September 1808.

[3] Mr Metcalfe to Government of India, dated 30th September 1808.

October, in spite of the protests of the Envoy, who urged that he had no authority to accompany the army on a campaign, he marched to Faridkot to inspect his new acquisition.[1] The Envoy felt himself constrained to follow, as he had already submitted a draft treaty, and was awaiting the Maharaja's reply.[2]

The draft treaty of the Envoy.

The draft treaty of the Maharaja.

The draft treaty of the British Envoy only referred to an alliance against France; but the Maharaja, who considered that the present was the time to obtain concessions from the English Government, submitted, on the 8th October, the draft of a second treaty, also consisting of three propositions: the first asking for non-interference in his disputes with the sovereign of Kabul; the second, concluding a perpetual alliance between him and the English; and the third, declaring his right of sovereignty over the whole Sikh country. It required, moreover, this right to be acknowledged with an engagement that no Chief should be defended by the English; but that the whole country should be left to his management without any interference whatever.

The Envoy again stated that he had no authority from his Government to make any promise or sign any treaty regarding Ranjit Singh's connection with Kabul or the Cis-Satlej States, but agreed to refer the propositions to Calcutta for the decision of the Governor-General. It was finally decided that two treaties should be drawn up, one containing the propositions of the Maharaja; the other

[1] Mr Metcalfe to Government of India, of 1st, 5th, and 15th October.

[2] The treaty only consisted of three propositions:—

1. A defensive alliance between the two States against France in case of any invasion.

2. Free passage and assistance to an English army, should it be necessary to meet the enemy beyond the Indus or in Afghanistan.

3. The maintenance of a line of communication with Kabul, the messengers and runners to be especially protected by the Maharaja.

those of the Envoy, and that both should be forwarded to Calcutta for ratification.[1]

Who marches against Maler Kotla.

The Maharaja, the day after this decision, marched from Faridkot to Maler Kotla, seventy miles to the eastward, where Ata-ulla Khan was still Chief. At Faridkot he had not made up his mind whom to attack. He had no enemies in the Cis-Satlej States upon whom specially to avenge himself; to him all were enemies who were independent of him, or who possessed wealth which it was possible for him to seize. The Rajas of Pattiala, Nabha, and Jhind had promised him a large sum of money if he would put them in possession of Batner, Sirsa, and Fatahabad, the three principal forts of the Bhatti country; but Ranjit Singh was too cautious to risk an expedition into a country so ill-supplied with water and grass; and he possibly may have suspected the real motive of his advisers, who desired to engage him in a difficult contest with the Bhattis, in which his power might be broken, or in which he might give offence to the British Government, by invading territory which was theirs by conquest, though they had not yet taken formal possession. So he chose the policy of plundering Chiefs who were unable to resist, and demanded from Maler Kotla a tribute of a lakh of Rupees, part of which, after some protest, was paid, as the seizure of the whole estate would have been the result of a refusal, and for the remainder the Phulkian Chiefs gave their security.

The Afghan Chief implores British protection.

The Maler Kotla Chief, on the day of Mr Metcalfe's arrival in camp, sent an agent to implore his assistance, and to claim the protection of the British Government; but the Envoy

[1] Mr Metcalfe to Government of India, dated 20th October 1808. With this, the draft treaties were forwarded, and the notes of the 9th, 11th, and 14th of October, of the Maharaja and Envoy.

could only tell him that he was unable to interfere, though the Government had no sympathy with this act of oppression, and that the presence of the mission in the Maharaja's camp gave no sanction to the Cis-Satlej expedition.[1]

The policy of Maharaja Ranjit Singh eminently wise.

It was, indeed, high time to give such assurances, for the presence of the Envoy with the Maharaja could not but be misunderstood. However insincere the conduct of Ranjit Singh may have been, there was something of genius in his policy, which deserved success. When the Envoy first commenced his negotiations, the Maharaja at once perceived that an opportunity had arrived for demanding an acknowledgment of his right to sovereignty over the Cis-Satlej States, the first desire of his heart. It is true that he had absolutely no right to such sovereignty, and had himself proposed to Lord Lake that the Satlej should be the frontier line of the two States. But since that time his strength had infinitely increased, and his ambition had grown with his strength. Besides, he fancied, perhaps erroneously, but still with some reason, that the British Government were somewhat in his power. France to him was a name and nothing more: he neither loved nor hated it, or its Emperor; and he clearly perceived that the Envoy's assurances that the Governor-General desired this defensive treaty against France out of a sincere regard for the interests of Lahore, and that the Punjab, and not British India, was the State that would benefit by the alliance, were absurd—for England, and not Lahore, was the enemy of France; and if the love of the British Government for him was so great, why had they so long kept it a profound secret? Yet if they were sincere; if they truly thought first of him and

The defensive treaty proposed by the Government gave advantage to them alone.

[1] Mr Metcalfe to Government of India, 25th October 1808.

his interests, rather than of their own, and had no desire to persuade him into an alliance which might be fatal to his rule, let them prove their sincerity by admitting his supremacy over the Cis-Satlej States. So the Maharaja argued, and it is difficult to say that he was wrong. For these reasons he determined to make the acceptance of his terms the condition of his signing the treaty; he resolved to protract the negotiations as long as possible, so as to allow him time to seize as much of the Cis-Satlej territory as he could before the negotiations were completed, for he would thus have in possession the best of arguments, while, if he could only entice the British Envoy to join his camp, he would have almost an authority to continue his conquests; and the Cis-Satlej Chiefs would be deprived of all heart for resistance when they saw the Envoy of the power to which they looked for protection in the very camp of the enemy.

He required concessions advantageous to him.

With designs such as these, Ranjit Singh, by persuasion and promises and trickery, drew the Envoy to the Satlej, to Khai, to Faridkot, and lastly to Maler Kotla. Here Mr Metcalfe determined to make a stand. He perceived that he had been used as a tool to work out the Maharaja's ends; and when it was proposed that he should proceed to Ambala, in the vicinity of those very Chiefs who had solicited the protection of the Government, where the negotiations should be concluded, he resolved to refuse any longer to approve, by his presence, the subjugation of the entire country. He accordingly communicated his absolute objection to proceed further with the army, and desired some place to be assigned at which the mission might wait until the campaign was over.[1]

He tricked the Envoy.

Who at last resolved to resist, and refused to accompany the camp.

Ranjit Singh now determined to make a last effort to

[1] Mr Metcalfe to Government of India, 26th October 1808.

shake the Envoy's resolution, and to obtain from him a declaration that he, the Maharaja, had full authority over the Cis-Satlej States, and that the British Government would not interfere to protect them. Mr Metcalfe has left a most interesting account of this passage of arms, in which Ranjit Singh himself took part with his principal ministers, Diwan Mokham Chand, Bhowani Das, Misr Prab Dyal, Fakirs Azizuddin and Imamuddin, and Sirdar Mith Singh Padhania. The subject of the conversation had been often discussed before, and the Envoy had nothing new to say. It was urged that the Governor-General had referred this very question of the Cis-Satlej States to his decision: the Envoy could only reply that the Governor-General would no doubt wish from him full information on this subject, and that this would be furnished; but that no authority had been granted him to complete the arrangement, and that without such authority no action would be valid. One passage from the Envoy's description of the interview may be here quoted:[1]—

A passage of arms.

"Reverting to the object of his wishes, the Raja said that the only little doubt that remained in his mind proceeded from his not being able to conceive why the Governor-General should hesitate to grant such a trifling request. He did not, he said, ask any country from the British Government; he only wanted to be left to carry on his concerns with the people of his own nation, his brethren, without interference. That they all acknowledged his supremacy, and that he merely wanted the Governor-General to say that he would not dispute what was acknowledged by all. That the British Government had given away territories yielding large revenues

The Envoy's letter.

[1] Mr Metcalfe to Government of India, 30th October 1808.

on many occasions, and was known to make great sacrifices for its friends; and that he was not able to account for the hesitation in complying with his small request. I remarked, upon this, that if the object of his request was trifling, the earnestness with which he pursued it was surprising; and that, if it was important, he ought not to wonder that a certain degree of deliberation should take place upon it."

Neither party would give way.

The Envoy finally declined any declaration such as that desired without a reference to his Government, nor would he engage to do more than submit the whole matter for the consideration of the Governor-General. After this, the hope of the negotiations being brought to a speedy or even a satisfactory termination seemed very remote. The Maharaja appeared determined to make his adhesion to the treaty dependent upon the acceptance of his propositions by the British Government, and after vainly attempting to persuade the Envoy to accompany him to Ambala, he assigned the town of Fatahabad for the residence of the mission, and started from Maler Kotla with his army on the 1st November 1808,[1] having despatched to the Governor-General a letter in which were reiterated the arguments which had failed to make any impression on the Envoy.

The mission halts at Fatahabad.

The progress of the campaign.

His campaign, after parting with the mission, was of the briefest. As has been before stated, he seized Ambala from the widow of the late Chief, and, not content with the land, he converted to his own use the money and jewels of this unfortunate lady. Shahabad he took from the sons of Sirdar Karm Singh, but restored it on the payment of a fine, for the payment of which the Raja of Pattiala became security.

[1] Mr Metcalfe to Government of India, 1st November 1808.

The only Chiefs who had not submitted to the supremacy of the Maharaja, a submission extorted by violence, fraud, and the prospect of imminent danger, were Sirdar Bhanga Singh of Thanesar and the Raja of Pattiala; and towards the capital of the latter he marched the third week in November. Bhanga Singh joined Raja Sahib Singh at this place, and their united forces would have been able to offer a serious resistance to the Maharaja. But he was ever more of a diplomatist than a warrior. He preferred to attack those who were unable to defend themselves; and throughout his march he had scrupulously avoided injuring the territory of Raja Sahib Singh. In the same way, although he took several places from Sirdar Bhanga Singh of Thanesar, a very powerful Chief, yet he restored them again without any apparent cause. His infantry and artillery were at Thanesar several days, but were recalled without any attempt to injure the place. The meeting between him and Raja Sahib Singh has been described, and there can be no doubt but that Ranjit Singh felt as much hesitation regarding it as Sahib Singh himself. He would have liked to attack the Raja and annex his country, but he dared not do so; and he instead swore eternal friendship, with the intention of breaking the oath on the first suitable opportunity. After this he returned to Amritsar by forced marches, arriving there on the 4th December, and was joined by Mr Metcalfe, the British Envoy, on the 10th of the same month.

Ranjit Singh marches to Pattiala.

The meeting between the Chiefs of Lahore and Pattiala, November 1808.

Ranjit Singh returns to Amritsar.

The ultimatum of the Governor-General.

The storm which had been long impending over the Maharaja now broke; and the Envoy's first duty was to give him a letter from the Governor-General, rebuking him for his discourteous treatment of the mission, and emphatically declaring the Cis-Satlej Chiefs under the protection of the English Government.[1] From the note of the Envoy of the 12th December,[2] may be learnt the

The protection of the Cis-Satlej territory declared.

[1] *Vide* instructions of Government to Mr Metcalfe, dated 31st October 1808.

[2] Note of Mr Metcalfe of 12th December 1808, transmitted to the Raja of Lahore :—

"His Lordship has learnt with great surprise and concern, that the Maharaja aims at the subjection of Chiefs who have long been considered under the protection of the power ruling in the north of Hindoostan, and is more especially astonished to find that the Maharaja requires the assent of the British Government to the execution of his design.

"By the issue of a war with the Mahrattas the British Government became possessed of the power and right formerly exercised by that nation in the north of Hindoostan.

"At the time the Maharaja had no claim on the country between the Satlej and the Jamna. In an early period of that contest, a communication was received from the Maharaja, by the late Lord Lake, which proposed to fix the Satlej as the boundary between the British Government and his; which is a clear proof that the Maharaja in those days was well aware that the country in question was dependent on the power paramount in the north of Hindoostan.

"Since the British Government has come into this situation, it has relieved the Chiefs between the Satlej and Jamna from tribute, and that degree of subserviency which they were used to pay to the Mahrattas, and has allowed them to carry on their own concerns without interference or control. But this liberality on the part of the British Government was meant for the benefit of those Chiefs, not for their injury. It was never intended that the forbearance of the British Government should be taken advantage of by another power, to oppress and subjugate those whom the British Government wished to protect and relieve.

"In reply, therefore, to the Maharaja's requisition, it is hereby declared that the British Government cannot consent that these Chiefs should be subjugated by the Maharaja, or any other power; and it is hereby announced that those Chiefs, according to established custom, are, and will remain, under the protection of the British Government.

"Exclusive of these considerations, which are sufficient to demonstrate the just principles by which the determination of the British Government is swayed, there are circumstances in the conduct of the Maharaja in bringing forward his proposal, which would, in any case, make it impossible to comply with.

"The British Government sent an Envoy to the Maharaja to give him information of a great danger, and to offer the assistance of the British Government to repel it, and made certain propositions to the Maharaja which were particularly calculated to promote his interest. The Maharaja, for reasons which are not discernible, did not receive those propositions with the same confidence and cordiality with which they were made, but in reply brought forward a demand for the assent of the British Government for the subjugation of the Chiefs connected with it, and made a compliance with that

considerations which induced this decision of the Government; but other reasons, which it was then inconvenient

demand the condition of his assent to the friendly propositions of the Governor-General. It would be unworthy of the dignity of the British Government to comply with any demand so brought forward."

"Besides this the Maharaja, in making a reference to the British Government on this subject, instead of waiting for a reply, proceeded to execute his intention of subjugating the Chiefs, taking the country, which were the objects of the reference, thus apparently endeavouring to secure his object, whether the reply should be favourable or not.

"In making the reference, the Maharaja showed that he well knew that, without the consent of the British Government, he had no right to invade the country between the Satlej and the Jamna; for if this had not been the case, there would not have been any necessity to make the reference. It was therefore, peculiarly inconsistent with the respect due to the British Government and an improper return for the friendly confidence which that Government had reposed in the Maharaja, to proceed to seize the object of his requisition, without so much as waiting for a reply.

"This is quite contrary to the established practice amongst States, which requires that when one power makes a reference to another, it should await the result of that reference. This principle is so clear, and according to the rules of common respect so indispensable, that it is surprising that the Maharaja should not have attended to it. I have repeatedly endeavoured to impress it on the Maharaja's mind, but without success.

"Moreover, the Maharaja proceeded to execute his plans without giving any notice to me, and although he carried his arms close to the confines of the British territories, never made any candid communication to me of his designs, but sometimes even assigned a different intention from that which afterwards appeared.

"In addition to those circumstances, the Maharaja's behaviour towards me, the representative of the British Government, was in other points neither consistent with the respect due to a great State, nor with the confidence due to a friendly State. The Maharaja will find in his own breast an explanation of this observation, and his recollection will point it to the facts which have caused it. It is unnecessary in this place to particularise them; suffice it to say, that they constituted a violation of the rules established for the intercourse between States.

"Under all these circumstances, even if the Maharaja's demand had been in itself unexceptionable, it would have been impossible to comply with it.

"I am directed by the Right Honourable the Governor-General to protest against the invasion of the country between the Satlej and Jamna in the name of the British Government; and further to declare, that the British Government cannot acknowledge any right in the Maharaja to any territories that he may have taken possession of, situated between the Satlej and Jamua, since the first reference of this question to the British Government.

"Moreover, the Governor-General feels himself authorised to expect, and entertains no doubt, that the Maharaja will restore all the places that he has taken possession of since that period to the former possessors, and will conto state openly, had their weight. A French invasion was beginning to be believed the impossibility it really was; and the desire for a defensive alliance against France was growing naturally weaker. The British Government was not, at any rate, disposed to allow its northern frontier to be in a chronic state of invasion or disturbance in order to obtain a treaty which would probably be worthless when obtained. For, in the first place, a French invasion was most unlikely; and, in the second place, were the treaty concluded, it was still more unlikely that Ranjit Singh would respect it, should an invasion take place. The Government argued that as the Maharaja systematically broke every engagement, however solemn, formed with his own Chiefs and friends, he would not be likely to treat a foreign power with more honesty, should it be to his advantage to betray it.

The true reasons for the determination of the British Government.

The check given by the letter here quoted, was quite unexpected by the Maharaja; but he pretended to treat the declaration of the Governor-General as not final, and to be altered by negotiation; though the Envoy assured him that the decision was unalterable, and pressed for an

Ranjit Singh unwilling to accept the declaration as final.

fine his army to the right bank of the Satlej, since he can have no object in maintaining it on the left bank, except to overawe and subjugate the Chiefs situated between that river and the Jamna, who are now declared to be under the protection of the British Government.

"In expressing these sentiments, I am directed to inform the Maharaja, that the British Government is desirous of maintaining the most amicable relations with his Government, and wishes that the friendship subsisting between the two States may daily improve and increase. The British Government desires no country for itself. It has enough, and its only ambition is to improve the territories of which it is possessed, and to promote the happiness of its subjects. It wishes to live in amity with all mankind. It cannot consent to the subjugation of Chiefs who are closely connected with it, and have claims on it for protection.

"At the same time, it entertains the most friendly designs towards the Maharaja; with whom, notwithstanding the just causes of complaint which the Maharaja's conduct has afforded, it is anxious to cultivate the relations of intimate friendship."

immediate reply to the demands of the Government.[1] But this was precisely what Ranjit Singh desired to avoid. Afraid to defy the English Government, and refuse compliance with its demands, he yet could not find it in his heart to resign the new and valuable possessions, Ambala, Faridkot, and Saniwal, which he had won so triumphantly, and under the Envoy's very eyes. So he delayed the negotiations by a thousand artifices. Now Prabdyal, the Kapurthalla Agent, was essential to the consultation and must be summoned; now it was Mith Singh Padhania, for whose arrival everything must wait; disturbances broke out in Amritsar, and he must leave for Lahore; at Lahore, similar disturbances prevented him from thinking of other matters. He promised compliance, yet made no effort to carry out his promises; and he complained bitterly of the change of policy of the British Government, whose Envoy had arrived with the expressed object of increasing the friendship between the two States and concluding a treaty against France. Yet the only friendship shown was in thwarting his schemes and his policy, which was neither new nor strange, while the original object of the treaty was altogether forgotten.[2]

The negotiation delayed.

Complaints of the Maharaja not unreasonable.

[1] Mr Metcalfe to Government, dated 14th, 15th, and 18th December.

[2] Mr Metcalfe to the Government, dated 20th and 22nd December 1808; and 3d and 4th of January 1809; and notes of Mr Metcalfe and Ranjit Singh, dated 25th, 26th, 29th of December and 4th January.

It is impossible to deny that there was some truth in the complaint of Ranjit Singh, and the following extract from Colonel Ochterlony's instructions is not without significance :—

"As the intelligence lately received of the favourable change in the aspect of affairs on the continent of Europe justifies a conviction that the project of France against the British possessions in India must, if not entirely abandoned, at least be so far suspended as to render any extraordinary and immediate preparations for defence unnecessary, the views and intentions of Government, under which your instructions of the 29th ultimo were framed, are materially altered."—Government to Colonel Ochterlony, 30th January 1809.

Ranjit Singh determines on war with the English.

At this time the Maharaja had all but decided upon war with the English. The movement of British troops to the Satlej seemed to him to prophesy a no-distant day when his dominions would fall into the hands of strangers; and he was inclined to prefer a struggle, in which success seemed to him not impossible, to relinquishing his most cherished design, the subjugation of the whole country betwe n the Satlej and the Jamna. He accordingly carried on his military preparations with the utmost activity. Troops were called in from all quarters; ammunition and military stores were collected; the new fort of Govindgarh at Amritsar was prepared for defence, and guns were mounted and provisions laid in for a siege. Diwan Mohkam Chand, the best of the Sikh Generals, and a bitter enemy of the English, who, with a large force, had been sent to Kangra to assist Raja Sansar Chand in expelling the Gurkhas, was hastily re-called, and marched to Philor Ghat, on the Satlej, opposite the town of Ludhiana, where he encamped.[1] But the Maharaja had no sooner formed his design than he abandoned it; and although it was openly reported in Lahore that Mohkam Chand was about to cross the Satlej and join the Ambala garrison,[2] the troops, with the exception of four companies of infantry, were withdrawn from Ambala on the 12th of January. They determined, however, to be unpleasantly remembered by Raja Sahib Singh, and on their return march, devastated Niamalpur and Jaiswah, about 20 miles from Pattiala.[3]

Preparations for war.

Changes his mind and withdraws from Ambulla.

[1] Mr Metcalfe to Government, 12th January 1809, and notes of Mr Metcalfe and the Maharaja of the 4th, 6th, 7th, and 8th January.

[2] News letter Lahore, 12th of January, and Resident of Dehli to Government of India, dated 18th January 1809.

[3] Resident of Dehli to Government of India, 17th January 1809, and news writer at Pattiala to Resident of the same date.

British troops march to the Satlej, January 1809.

The detachment of British troops, which the Government had decided to station on the Satlej, as a check to any further extention of Ranjit Singh's power to the south, and as a guarantee of efficient protection to the Cis-Satlej Chiefs, crossed the Jamma on the 16th January 1809. It was under the charge of Lieutenant-Colonel D. Ochterlony, who had been specially selected by Government for the service, as possessing, in addition to the highest intelligence and energy, an accurate acquaintance with the politics of the north-western frontier.[1] Colonel Ochterlony's instructions left a good deal to his discretion. He was to watch the movements of the Maharaja; to obtain information regarding his power, resources, and the disposition of the Chiefs subordinate to him; to be careful to bind the Government by no promises to the Maharaja; and, on the other hand, to close with no offers of assistance or demands for protection from disaffected Chiefs in the Punjab proper; though he was to allow them to understand that, at some future time, their services might be acceptable. The compulsory engagements made by the Maharaja with the Pattiala and other Chiefs were not to be considered binding, and it was to be his especial care to reconcile the Cis-Satlej Chiefs to British protection by showing them that it was essential to their very existence; while the only advantage the Government could derive from its connection with them would be to have, in time of difficulty, a confederacy of grateful Chiefs, bound to it by ties of interest and affection. The protection was at first to be general but would be defined later. No subsidy would be asked from

Colonel Ochterlony's character.

His instructions.

[1] Government to Colonel Ochterlony, dated 14th and 18th November 1808. Colonel Ochterlony to Resident Dehli, dated 16th and 17th January 1809.

them; but hereafter they would have to contribute towards the expense of their own defence. It was also intimated to Colonel Ochterlony, that the detachment under his command would be eventually employed in resuming the conquests made by Ranjit Singh during his last campaign.[1]

The Raja of Pattiala summoned to Lahore

On the 14th of January 1809, Bhai Gurbaksh Singh, an agent of the Maharaja's, arrived at Pattiala, for the purpose of desiring Raja Sahib Singh or his minister Chen Singh, with the Rajas of Nabha and Jhind, to wait upon his master at Amritsar. Sahib Singh, who knew that the English were preparing to cross the Jamna, refused to send any one to Amritsar. He said that Jaswant Singh of Nabha could go or not as he chose; and expressed his satisfaction that Raja Bhag Singh of Jhind had already, in accordance with the advice of the Resident at Dehli, joined Colonel Ochterlony.[2]

His refusal.

Colonel Ochterlony arrives at Pattiala.

This officer arrived at Pattiala on the 1st February. He had been received, on his march, with evident satisfaction, by the Chiefs through whose territory he passed, and Rani Dya Kour of Ambala came in person to thank the representative of the British Government for the restoration of her territory. Raja Sahib Singh welcomed him with a joy almost childish, so great was his relief at being freed from all apprehension of the Maharaja of Lahore.[3] On the 5th of February the detachment marched to Nabha,

The joy of the Raja.

[1] Government of India to Colonel Ochterlony, dated 29th December 1808, and Government of India to Resident Dehli, dated 26th December.

[2] Resident Dehli to Government, dated 15th, 19th, and 25th January. Colonel Ochterlony to Resident Dehli of 20th January.

[3] To give some insight into Sahib Singh's character, it may be stated that, although the interview with Colonel Ochterlony had been fixed for an early hour, it was not till past noon that it was granted; many hours having been spent by the Chiefs in persuading the Raja to allow his son, a boy of twelve years of age, to be present at the interview.

where Colonel Ochterlony was received by Raja Jaswant Singh with equal though more decorous satisfaction.[1] He then proceeded to Maler Kotla and reinstated the Pathan Chief in his former authority; for it will be remembered that Ranjit Singh had demanded a contribution of a lakh of rupees from this little State, compelling the Raja of Pattiala and other Chiefs, whose police stations and collectors were all over the territory, to become securities for its payment.[2]

The Maler Kotla Chief reinstated.

The Lahore negotiations.

The negotiations at Lahore were not advancing favorably. The Maharaja talked of joining his army on the Satlej, which would have been equivalent to a declaration of war.

Ranjit Singh refuses to relinquish.

He would not consent to relinquish Faridkot and other territory to the south of the Satlej; the troops recalled from Ambala had not yet recrossed that river; the army continued to collect at Philor, and all preparations for war were continued; while Diwan Mohkam Chand stopped the Envoy's post and acted in so offensive a manner that Mr Metcalfe considered he would be compelled to leave Amritsar and break off all further negociations. He expressed his conviction that Ranjit Singh was determined upon war, and recommended to the Commander-in-Chief, the invasion of the Punjab, as the best means of breaking the Maharaja's power and ensuring a satisfactory peace.[3] The general disaffection in the Punjab was what Mr Metcalfe counted upon to secure success to the English. He believed that every

Envoy recommends war.

[1] Colonel Ochterlony to Government, 4th February 1809.

[2] Colonel Ochterlony to Government, 9th February 1809.

[3] Mr Metcalfe to Government of India, dated 13th, 18th, 21st, 26th January. Resident Dehli to Government, 5th February.

Mr Seton, the Resident at Dehli, recommended a more cautious policy, believing that Ranjit Singh would never rush into war unless rendered desperate.

principal Chief would gladly throw off the Maharaja's yoke, which was almost too heavy to bear. Ranjit Singh knew his danger and made extravagant promises to his followers. His mother-in-law, Mai Sada Kour, he petted and coaxed, for she was the head of the great Ramgharia confederacy, and he knew she had been intriguing with the English. He again cohabited with her daughter Mehtab Kour, his first wife, whom he had long discarded, and he acknowledged as his own, Sher Singh and Tara Singh, two children called her sons, but with whose existence neither he nor Mehtab Kour had anything to do, and whom he had till now disowned.[1]

The effect of the advance of the British army.

The Maharaja could not, however, fail to perceive that the advance of the British army under General St Leger and the detachment under Colonel Ochterlony was productive of considerable effect on the Satlej Chiefs, who, fearing to compromise themselves with the English, withdrew one by one; their contingents followed their example, and had it not been for a considerable reinforcement from Lahore the army of Diwan Mohkam Chand would have disappeared. At length, Ranjit Singh awoke to the fact that the British Government was not to be turned from its resolution by his opposition; and he determined, though somewhat late, to persuade the world that he was a consenting party. He, accordingly, sent to Colonel Ochterlony, Sirdar Sada Singh and Nizamuddin Khan, to see if the new Englishman was more practicable than Mr Metcalfe.[2]

A Sikh embassy to Colonel Ochterlony.

These men arrived at Colonel Ochterlony's camp on the 13th February. They were full of complaints of

[1] Government of India to Mr Metcalfe, 23d January 1809; and Mr Metcalfe to Government of India of 29th January and 3d February.

[2] Mr Metcalfe of 6th, 12th, and 15th February to Government.

Which induces him to delay his march.

Mr Metcalfe's reserve, and the Maharaja's pacific and generous spirit; and after having obtained all the information regarding the intentions of the Government they were able to extract, they persuaded the Colonel to halt for a few days until some reply should be received from the Maharaja.[1]

His action disapproved by Government.

The conduct of Colonel Ochterlony, in this instance, was disapproved by the Government. He was told that he would have acted more prudently in refusing to allow any representation of the Maharaja's agents to delay the advance of the detachment; that by listening to remonstances founded on an impeachment of the candour and sincerity of the Envoy he had exposed to risk the dignity of the British Governement; and the more manifest the hostility of the Maharaja the more the honour and interest of the Government demanded his unhesitating advance.[2]

The change of policy of the Governor-General.

The policy of the Governor-General had been greatly changed by circumstances. Seeing no longer any danger from France he had thought it advisable to give up the idea of a military post at Ludhiana or at some other place on the Satlej, and establish it rather at Karnal, where its presence would give no offence to Ranjit Singh.[3] But the representations of the Commander-in-Chief, of the Resident at Dehli, and Colonel Ochterlony caused Ludhiana to be finally selected, though only as a temporary measure.[4] The change of policy of the Government simply amounted to this. A French invasion being now a remote contingency, there was less objection to a treaty of amity with Ranjit Singh and less necessity to limit

[1] Colonel Ochterlony to Government, 14th February 1809. General Ochterlony to Major-General St Leger, 10th February 1809.

[2] Government to Colonel Ochterlony of 13th March 1809.

[3] Government to Colonel Ochterlony of 30th January 1809.

[4] Ludhiana has remained a military station ever since 1809.

his power. Having steadily refused to conclude any treaty of amity until the Maharaja should accede to the demands made upon him, it was for the honour of Government to meet him with a sincere friendship now that he showed willingness to comply with those demands. Two draft treaties were accordingly sent to Mr Metcalfe. The restitution of the late conquests was to be complete; the older conquests would not be interfered with: but Ranjit Singh was not to claim allegiance from the Cis-Satlej Chiefs, even for territory which he himself had given them.[1]

Ochterlony reaches Ludhiana.

Colonel Ochterlony, who reached Ludhiana on the 20th of February, resigned his command on the arrival of the reprimand from Government; but, while his resignation was accepted, his services and zeal were so warmly commended that he was induced to recall it, and remained in political and military charge of Ludhiana.[2]

The negotiations at Lahore were now drawing to a satisfactory termination. A circumstance which showed Ranjit Singh the power which discipline gave to the British army is said to have strengthened his desire to keep on good terms with the British Government.

The attack on the Envoy's escort at Amritsar.

This was an attack made on Mr Metcalfe's escort at Amritsar, by the fanatical Akâlís[3] of the Golden Temple, who were enraged with the Muhammadan soldiers belonging to the British camp for celebrating the festival of the Muharam in the neighbourhood of the sacred city. These men, whose courage and military qualities were notorious, headed by one Phula Singh, afterwards well known in

[1] Government of India to Mr Metcalfe, dated 13th March 1809.
Government of India to His Excellency the Commander-in-Chief of the same date.

[2] Colonel Ochterlony to Government of 15th April and 4th May.
Government to Colonel Ochterlony of 20th April and 13th June.

[3] "*Akâlís*"—immortals. The military priests of Sikhism.

Punjab history, were completely routed by the few British Sepoys upon whom the undisciplined valour of the Akâlís could make no impression.[1] The outrage had no political significance nor had the Maharaja any share in it. It was an outburst of Sikh fanaticism, from which the Maharaja himself had suffered more than once;[2] and his power, which rested very much on opinion and on the respect paid by the Sikhs to the representative of the Gurus and the head of the Khalsa, was not sufficient to punish men whose only offence was too great a zeal in the service of religion.

The repulse by the British troops.

Faridkot surrendered.

The surrender of Faridkot, held by Diwan Mohkam Chand, was the most difficult concession to obtain from the Maharaja, and every possible delay was made and every artifice employed to avoid it, so much so that the British Envoy again thought that war was inevitable.[3] But at length, on the 2d of April, the place was evacuated by the Lahore troops and made over to its rightful owner.[4] The conclusion of the treaty now became easy, and the second draft forwarded from Calcutta being accepted by Ranjit Singh in its integrity, it was signed at Lahore, on the 25th of April, and received the confirmation of the Governor-General in Council.[5]

And the treaty concluded, April 1809

[1] Mr Metcalfe to Government, 26th February and 7th March.

[2] Only two months before this, Lahore and Amritsar had been in a state of revolt, because Moran, the mistress then in favour with the Maharaja, had persuaded one of her friends to turn Muhammadan for her love. The Hindus and Sikhs were furious, and demanded that she should be given up to them. Ranjit Singh refused: but with a generosity as rare as it was just, he offered them instead her brother, whom they might put to death.

[3] Mr Metcalfe to Government, 22d March 1809. Resident Dehli to Military Secretary to Commander-in-Chief, 1st April.

[4] Colonel Ochterlony to Government of India, 6th April 1809.

[5] TREATY BETWEEN THE BRITISH GOVERNMENT AND THE RAJA OF LAHORE.

Whereas certain differences which had arisen between the British Government and the Raja of Lahore have been happily and amicably adjusted, and

By this treaty Maharaja Ranjit Singh resigned for ever all supremacy over the Cis-Satlej Chiefs, and all claims to the Cis-Satlej territory which came under the protection of the British Government. Nor did the Maharaja, at any future period, seek to evade its provisions, which destroyed his most cherished ambition and to which he Its results.

both parties being anxious to maintain the relation of perfect amity and concord, the following Articles of Treaty, which shall be binding on the heirs and successors of the two parties, have been concluded by Raja Ranjit Singh, on his own part, and by the agency of Charles Theophilus Metcalfe, Esquire, on the part of the British Government.

ARTICLE 1.—Perpetual friendship shall subsist between the British Government and the State of Lahore. The latter shall be considered, with respect to the former, to be on the footing of the most favoured powers; and the British Government will have no concern with the territories and subjects of the Raja to the northward of the river Satlej.

ARTICLE 2.—The Raja will never maintain, in the territory occupied by him and his dependents on the left bank of the river Satlej, more troops than are necessary for the internal duties of that territory, nor commit or suffer any encroachment on the possessions or rights of the Chiefs in its vicinity.

ARTICLE 3.—In the event of a violation of any of the preceding Articles, or of a departure from the rules of friendship on the part of either State, this Treaty shall be considered to be null and void.

ARTICLE 4.—This Treaty, consisting of our Articles, having been settled and concluded at Amritsar, on the 25th day of April 1809, Mr Charles Theophilus Metcalfe has delivered to the Raja of Lahore a copy of the same, in English and Persian, under his seal and signature, and the said Raja has delivered another copy of the same under his seal and signature; and Mr Charles Theophilus Metcalfe engages to procure, within the space of two months, a copy of the same duly ratified by the Right Hon'ble the Governor-General in Council, on the receipt of which by the Raja the present Treaty shall be deemed complete and binding on both parties, and the copy of it now delivered to the Raja shall be returned.

Seal and Signature of	*Signature and Seal of*
C. T. METCALFE.	RAJA RANJIT SINGH.

(Signed) MINTO.

Ratified by the Governor-General in Council on the 30th May 1809.

Letters of Government to Mr Metcalfe of 3d June 1809, to Colonel Ochterlony of 11th and 20th June, and to Maharaja Ranjit Singh of 3d June.

had agreed with so much reluctance. Had it not been for the tact, patience, and diplomatic ability of Mr Metcalfe, the British Envoy at Lahore, the treaty would never have been concluded at all, or only as a concession extorted after a successful campaign.[1]

From 1809 the history of the Cis-Satlej States is altogether separate from that of Lahore.

From this time, till the year 1845, the history of the

[1] As a supplement to the treaty, a Proclamation of protection against Lahore was issued to the Cis-Satlej Chiefs, of which the following is a translation:—

"It is clearer than the sun, and better proved than the existence of yesterday, that the detachment of British troops to this side of the Satlej was entirely in acquiescence with the application and earnest entreaty of the Chiefs, and originated solely through friendly considerations in the British to preserve the Chiefs in their possessions and independence. A treaty having been concluded on the 5th April 1809, between Mr Metcalfe, on the part of British Government, and Maharaja Ranjit Singh, agreeably to the orders of the Right Honorable the Governor-General in Council, I have the pleasure of publishing, for the satisfaction of the Chiefs of the country of Malwa and Sirhind, the pleasure and resolutions of Government contained in the seven following Articles:—

"Article 1.—The country of the Chiefs of Malwa and Sirhind having entered under the protection of the British Government, in future it shall be secured from the authority and control of Maharaja Ranjit Singh, conformably to the terms of the Treaty.

"Article 2.—The country of the Chiefs thus taken under protection shall be exempted from all pecuniary tribute to the British Government.

"Article 3.—The Chiefs shall remain in the exercise of the same rights and authority within their own possession which they enjoyed before they were taken under the British protection.

"Article 4.—Whenever a British force, for purposes connected with the general welfare, shall be judged necessary to march through the country of the said Chiefs, every Chief shall within his own possessions assist and furnish the British force, to the full of his power, with supplies of grain and other necessaries which may be demanded.

"Article 5.—Should an enemy approach from any quarter for the purpose of conquering this country, friendship and mutual interest require that the Chiefs join the British army with their forces, and, exerting themselves in expelling the enemy, act under discipline and obedience.

"Article 6.—Any European articles brought by merchants from the eastern districts for the use of the army shall be allowed to pass by the thanadars and sirdars of the several districts belonging to the Chiefs without molestation or the demand of duty.

"Article 7.—All horses purchased for the use of the cavalry regiments, whether in Sirhind or elsewhere, the bringers of which being furnished with sealed rahdarees from the Resident at Dehli or officer commanding of Sirhind, the several Chiefs shall allow such horses to pass without molestation or the demand of duty."

Cis-Satlej States is, for the most part, distinct from that of the kingdom of Lahore. The protected Chiefs were too well aware of the certain danger they had escaped to intrigue with the Maharaja against the English, and were too contented to have any cause for intrigue; while Ranjit Singh himself, shrewd enough to understand the strength of the British Government and wise enough to accept the inevitable, found abundant work for his restless ambition in the conquest of Kashmir, Peshawur, Multan, and the Derajat.

The satisfaction of Pattiala at the result.

No one of the Cis-Satlej Chiefs was more rejoiced at the new order of things, than the Raja of Pattiala. Possessing a character whose weakness bordered on imbecility, he felt that he was unable to resist Ranjit Singh; and, indeed, it was with the utmost difficulty that he could hold his own against Rani Hus Kour, his ambitious and clever wife, who, not content with the estate granted her, demanded also a share in the administration of the State.

The outrage on Captain White.

It was not long before the weakness of the Raja was shown in a desperate outrage committed in his territories on Captain White, employed in surveying the boundary line, who, it will be remembered, was compelled, two years before, to suspend operations owing to the disturbed state of the Pattiala territory. This gentleman, who had with him about 80 native troopers as an escort, was attacked at the village of Chowki, by a large body of horse and foot under the command of the Akâlí Phula Singh, the same man that had attacked Mr Metcalfe's escort at Amritsar. The number of the enemy was soon increased by contributions from the neighbouring villages to upwards of a thousand men, and, after a retreat in which all the tents and baggage were lost, the little British force only found safety by storming the hostile village of

Patoki, which they held gallantly till the arrival of Ram Singh, nephew of Raja Jaswant Singh of Nabha, and fresh reinforcements restored tranquillity and forced the enemy to disperse. In the skirmish six of Captain White's party were killed and nineteen wounded.[1]

Representations were made to the Resident at Dehli that the outrage had been caused by the conduct of some of Captain White's escort; but this was clearly proved to be false, and strenuous efforts were made to punish those concerned in the attack. The Rajas of Nabha and Jhind and Bhai Lal Singh promised their cordial assistance, as did the Raja of Pattiala, but his imbecility was such that nothing could be hoped from him. Phula Singh who resided at Damdama, near Battinda, owned allegiance to no Chief, and his sacred character as an *Akâli* was his protection on this occasion, as it had been at Amritsar. Finding the British Government determined to punish him he crossed the Satlej and returned to Amritsar, from which place he defied the power of Ranjit Singh to remove him.[2] Much pressure was put upon the Maharaja to compel the surrender of the criminal, but Phula Singh had great influence, and, although he was banished for a time, he was later taken into favour and became the leader of the *Akâli* troops in the Maharaja's service.[3]

The disorder in the Pattiala State.

The mismanagement of the Pattiala State became now

[1] Captain White to Resident Dehli, 24th and 25th December 1809, and Lieutenant Marshall to Captain White of 25th December 1809.

[2] Resident Dehli to Colonel Ochterlony, of 24th and 27th January, and 22d and 23d February and 26th April 1810. Resident Dehli to Adjutant General 2d February 1810.

Resident Dehli to Secretary to Government of 7th and 11th May.

[3] The history of this man is most romantic. He was killed, after having distinguished himself in many battles, at Teri on the Kabul river, where the Afghans were defeated chiefly through his courage and devotion. Curiously enough he offered his services to Mr Moorcroft at Lahore in 1820.—*Travels in the Himalayan Provinces*, vol. i. 110; also *vide Carmichael Smyth.*

so gross, owing to the growing imbecility of the Raja and the rapacity of his advisers, that Colonel Ochterlony was compelled to interfere, although the proclamation of the 3d of May 1809 had reserved to the Chiefs the right of perfect liberty in their internal affairs. But the other great Chiefs of the Phulkian house, the Rajas of Nabha and Jhind and their friend and connection Bhai Lal Singh were most anxious that the agent should use his influence to restore some order to the administration. The Raja was completely in the hands of unworthy favourities, whose ascendancy was used to aggrandise and enrich themselves. His wife, Rani Aus Kour, was too able and independent to be in favour with the Raja's advisers, who wished to retain all power themselves, and the Raja had been taught to look upon her with suspicion and dislike.

The British Agent visits Pattiala, A.D. 1811.

On the 9th January 1811, at the invitation of Raja Sahib Singh and the Rajas of Nabha and Jhind, Colonel Ochterlony visited Pattiala. The Raja appeared most desirous that some satisfactory arrangement should be made by which order might be restored. He wished, however, to place the administration in the hands of Rani Khem Kour, his step-mother, whose interests were distinct from his own and from those of the heir to the throne, and whose rapacity was as great as that of any of the ministers. Although Colonel Ochterlony would have desired to see Rani Aus Kour at the head of affairs, a wish that was shared by the Rajas of Jhind and Nabha, he would not consent that any one should be appointed in opposition to the wish of the Raja; at any rate, till such time as the instructions of the Governor-General should be received.

Certain reforms agreed upon and effected.

It was agreed by the Rajas and Bhai Lal Singh that certain reforms should be made without delay; that the extravagant grants of land should be resumed, and new ones made with reference to the just claims of the grantees; and that jagirdars should be compelled to keep their contingents ready for service. Colonel Ochterlony recommended to Government that Rajas Jaswant Singh and Bhag Singh should be authorised to place, in case of necessity, the *Diwâni*, or general administration, in the hands of Rani Aus Kour, who was admittedly the only person competent to undertake it; subject to the condition that all business should be conducted in the name of Raja Sahib Singh, and that the Rani should soften any refusal by referring to the Rajas of Nabha and Jhind, who should decide what was expedient to grant or reject.[1]

And others recommended.

The Supreme Government unwilling to interfere.

The Government of India, while entertaining a favourable opinion of the measures proposed by Colonel Ochterlony, was averse, on general principles of policy, to take any direct participation in their adoption. This was the first occasion, since the Cis-Satlej States had been taken under British protection, that the direct interference of Government had been requested, and the reason for its determination was that it considered an adherence to the principle, which had been so often and so solemnly professed, of abstaining from all interference in the internal administration of the Cis-Satlej States of more importance than the attainment of the benefits which a deviation from that principle might be expected to produce in an individual case; that even if the interference was with consent of the Chief and his friends most directly interested, yet still the credit of the public professions of the Government would be lessened; that the interference of a powerful State in the affairs of a weaker was necessarily progressive, with relation not only to the latter but

Its reasons.

[1] Colonel Ochterlony to Government, dated 9th March 1811.

to others contiguous; that such interference involved the guarantee of the arrangements which it was employed to introduce; and placed the interposing power in connection with some local interest and in opposition to others; while, by the natural effects of action and re-action, the Government which employed its influence for the adjustment of these foreign concerns would be ultimately compelled to become the arbiter and controller of the local administration in all its branches, and to identify the rights and interests of the protected State with its own. On these grounds the Government desired its Agent to limit his interference to advice and recommendation on points that might be submitted to his judgment.[1]

The British Government was not, however, long in discovering that, with every wish to abstain from interference with the affairs of the Chiefs, these latter were likely, if left to themselves, to destroy each other as effectually as if their ruin had been left to Maharaja Ranjit Singh. Believing that their mutual aggressions would not be checked, the larger and more powerful Chiefs prepared to absorb the smaller; and it was found necessary to address to them a second proclamation, warning them of the penalties to which violence and disturbance would render them liable.[2] **The proclamation of the 22d August 1811.**

[1] Government of India to Colonel Ochterlony of 5th April 1811.

[2] Colonel Ochterlony to Government, 18th and 30th of July. Mr Metcalfe to Colonel Marshall, Commander 3d Division Field Army, dated 21st May 1811. Government to Colonel Ochterlony, dated 5th July; to Mr Metcalfe of the same date.

"PROCLAMATION OF PROTECTION TO CIS-SATLEJ STATES AGAINST ONE ANOTHER, 22D AUGUST 1811.

"For the information and assurance of the Protected Chiefs of the plains between the Satlej and Jamna.

"On the 3d of May 1809, a proclamation comprised of seven Articles, was issued by the orders of the British Government, purporting that the country of the Sirdars of Sirhind and Malwa, having come under their protection, Raja Ranjit Singh, agreeably to treaty, had no concern with the possessions

Rani Aus Kour placed at the head of the administration.

After the departure of Colonel Ochterlony from Pattiala, affairs appeared to promise well. The Raja, actuated

of the above Sirdars; that the British Government had no intention of claiming tribute or fine, and that they should continue in the full control and enjoyment of their respective possessions. The publication of the above Proclamation was intended to afford every confidence to the Sirdars that they had no intention of control, and that those having possession should remain in full and quiet enjoyment thereof.

"Whereas several zemindars and other subjects of the Chiefs of this country have preferred complaints to the officers of the British Government, who, having a view to the tenor of the above Proclamation, have not attended and will not in future pay attention to them; for instance, on the 15th June 1811, Dellawar Ali Khan of Samana, complained to the Resident at Dehli against the officers of Raja Sahib Singh, for jewels and other property said to have been seized by them; who in reply observed 'that the village of Samna being in the territory of Raja Sahib Singh, this complaint should be made to him;' and also on the 12th July 1811, Dussownda Singh and Gurmook Singh complained to Colonel Ochterlony, Agent to the Governor-General, against Sirdar Churrut Singh, for their shares of property, &c., and in reply, it was written on the back of the petition, that, 'since during the period of three years, no claim was preferred against Churrut Singh by any of his brothers, nor even the name of any co-partner mentioned, and since it was advertised in the Proclamation, delivered to the Sirdars, that every Chief should remain in the quiet and full possession of his domains, their petition could not be attended to.' The insertion of these answers to complaints is intended as examples, and also, that it may be impressed on the minds of every zemindar and other subjects that the attainment of justice is to be expected from their respective Chiefs only, that they may not in the smallest degree swerve from the observance of subordination. It is therefore highly incumbent upon the Rajas and other Sirdars on this side of the river Satlej that they explain this to their respective subjects and court their confidence, that it may be clear to them that complaints to the officers of the British Government will be of no avail, and that they consider their respective Sirdars as the source of justice, and that of their free will and accord they observe uniform obedience.

"And whereas, according to the first Proclamation, it is not the intention of the British Government to interfere in the possessions of the Sirdars of this country, it is, nevertheless, for the purpose of ameliorating the condition of the community, particularly necessary to give general information that several Sirdars have, since the last incursion of Raja Ranjit Singh, wrested the estates of others, and deprived them of their lawful possessions, and that in the restoration they have used delays until detachments from the British army have enforced restitution, as in the case of the Ranee of Zeera, the Sikhs of Cholian, the talooks of Karowley and Chehloundy, and village of Cheeba; and the reason of such delays and evasions can only be attributed to the temporary enjoyment of the revenues, and subjecting the owners to irremediable losses. It is therefore, by order of the British Government, hereby proclaimed that, if any of the Sirdars or others have forcibly taken possession

perhaps by caprice, accepted the advice that had been offered him, placing Rani Aus Kour at the head of the administration, and it was not long before a marked improvement was apparent.[1] When she obtained power every department was in the utmost disorder, and the Raja could not even raise 250 horse for the service of the British Government; but, by the end of the year, all was changed. Villages which had not paid revenue for years were reduced to obedience and compelled to liquidate their long-standing balances; and the jagirdars were compelled to supply contingents proportionate to the lands they held, so that, in December 1811, the Raja had 2000 horse and 2000 foot in arms, enforcing arrears due from refractory zamindars, while, in place of being burthened with debt, he had a lakh of rupees in his treasury.

The immediate improvement resulting from the change.

But the evil advisers of the Raja were not disposed to allow the Rani to retain power without an effort to overthrow her. The two most prominent members of the opposition were Albel Singh and Gujar Singh. The first of these held a grant of all the Bángar country, adjoining that of the Bhattis, and he was bound to keep up a sufficient force to maintain order, and to remit Rs. 7000 a year to the treasury. When the British Government assumed the adjoining district, and order was re-estab-

The intrigues against the Rani.

Albel Singh Governor on the Bhatti frontier.

of the estates of others, or otherwise injured the lawful owners, it is necessary that, before the occurrence of any complaint, the proprietor should be satisfied, and by no means to defer the restoration of the property; in which, however, should delays be made, and the interference of the British authority become requisite, the revenues of the estate, from the date of the ejection of the lawful proprietor, together with whatever other losses the inhabitants of that place may sustain from the march of troops, shall, without scruple, be demanded from the offending party; and for disobedience of the present orders, a penalty, according to the circumstances of the case and of the offender, shall be levied, agreeably to the decision of the British Government."

[1] Raja Sahib Singh to Colonel Ochterlony of 14th, 23d, and 25th March. Colonel Ochterlony to Raja of 15th, 24th, and 28th March.

lished, the Rani demanded Rs. 14,000 a year instead of Rs. 7000, on which Albel Singh sent in his resignation, hoping that she would be unable to collect the revenue. But when, contrary to his expectations, she realised large collections, he began to fear that his extortions would be claimed from him and plotted for the Rani's downfall.

The hostility of Gujar Singh.

Gujar Singh's reasons for hostility were equally clear. The district of Pinjor, which he held at a rental of Rs. 500 was resumed, and given in farm at its proper value of Rs. 14,000 a year.

With these men was allied the whole army of corrupt officials who made their harvest out of the plunder of the State. As they had persuaded the Raja that his sister Sahib Kour was a danger to his independence, so now they persuaded him that his wife desired to be independent, and was arranging to place him under restraint. He believed everything told him, and, in a fit of rage and fear, ordered her arrest and imprisonment, with that of her son, the heir-apparent, and her Diwan, Misr Noudha, a man of the highest capacity and honesty. But the Raja was as cowardly as he was imbecile, and no sooner had he imprisoned the Rani than he began to fear the consequences of his act. The administration, too, fell forthwith into disorder; the troops dispersed; and the officials in every department disobeyed his orders. The Rani was consequently released and requested again to undertake the management of affairs. She consented to this, for although her influence had been so injured that she could not hope to recover it without a guarantee that she should not a second time be exposed to disgrace and removal, and although she knew that the Raja's next caprice might endanger her very life, yet she was too ambitious to willingly resign power which she could by any means retain.

The intrigues succeed temporarily, and the Rani is imprisoned.

The confusion which resulted, and her restoration.

She addressed Colonel Ochterlony, begging him to visit Pattiala and arrange matters; and although he dissuaded her from again placing herself in so dangerous a position as head of the administration, he requested permission from Government to interfere and obtain a solemn pledge from the Raja that, so long as no offence was proved against the Rani, she should not be molested.[1]

She appeals to the British Agent for support.

The Government, perceiving that the Pattiala State would be ruined unless some support was afforded to the cause of order, permitted Colonel Ochterlony to make such arrangements as he considered indispensable, and on the 6th of April 1812 he arrived at Pattiala, taking with him an escort sufficiently large to compel attention to his advice.[2]

Which the Government permits to be given.

The insanity of the Raja increased every day; "God knows," said Sirdar Albel Singh, who was one of his favourites, "whether the Raja is an *avatár* (incarnation of a deity), or what he is; but though at times he is a fool and at others a madman, he yet sometimes possesses uncommon quickness, and whatever he determines on himself he pursues with uncommon obstinacy; and he often acts himself when he is supposed to be governed by others, and when, in fact, we dare not oppose him, lest he should suppose us inimical, and rob us of our heads. The admitted loss or gain of lakhs, or the ruin or prosperity of his country, are of no consideration in competition with his will or humour." If to this friendly portrait, which is true enough, hypocrisy and deceit are added, it will be tolerably complete. The Raja would break up a council

The character of Raja Sahib Singh painted by a friend.

[1] Colonel Ochterlony to Government, 19th January 1812. His letters to Raja Sahib Singh of the 27th, 28th, 29th, and 30th December 1811, and 16th January 1812.

[2] Government to Colonel Ochterlony, without date, received 1st April 1812. Colonel Ochterlony to Government dated 1st and 27th April.

in which with apparent shrewdness he was discussing affairs of State, and retire to his palace, where, with a drawn sword, at the head of a band of children, he would load and fire small guns with the utmost satisfaction; and in no civilised country in the world would he have been permitted to retain even nominal authority.[1]

The difficulty of negotiations.

Negotiations with a man of this disposition were difficult, as the British Agent soon experienced. He had hoped to have found Rani Aus Kour reinstated in power, and that his own duty would have been simply to declare, under sanction of the British Government, that she should not be again liable to disgrace and dismissal. But the news of the approach of the Agent was the signal for all the evil advisers of the Raja to intrigue against a reconciliation with the Rani, which would, at all events, be their ruin; while they had persuaded their imbecile master that Colonel Ochterlony had designs against his freedom, and, at his first interview,

The Raja's suspicions and duplicity.

he showed his suspicions by a crowd of armed retainers and every sign of fear in his manner and conversation. A few days later, the Agent forwarded certain propositions which he urged the Raja to accept, by which the authority of the Rani would be restored and the ministers then in power displaced. The Raja replied by counter-propositions, in which the superintendence of the Rani was assented to, but refusing to pledge its continuance in writing; meaning that so soon as the Agent

[1] Two corps of boys were maintained by this madman, at a rupee each a day, and dressed in regular uniform. Two parties of these he drew up opposite each other, as representatives of the British army and that of Ranjit Singh, and having caused their miniature guns to be loaded with pieces of lead and iron, commanded them to fire. This was actually done, and two boys, seriously wounded, were carried off the field of action. The Raja himself, always fearful of danger, looked on from an upper window whilst the children were to butcher each other. Letter of Colonel Ochterlony, 8th May 1812.

should have returned to Ludhiana, or at any other suitable opportunity, the same treatment which she had before experienced would be repeated. On the receipt of this reply, Colonel Ochterlony sent for an additional force of both cavalry and infantry to support his authority, and induce the Raja to abandon the interested advice of his counsellors, who had several times proposed to attack the little British force. The approach of two regiments from Ludhiana had the effect anticipated, and the Raja promised to bring the Rani back with all honour to Pattiala, and invest her with the conduct of affairs. But the advice of his Diwan Gurdial, who had plundered the Treasury in the most shameless manner ever since the Rani's retirement, again induced the Raja to waver, and it was only Colonel Ochterlony's threat to go himself and bring the Rani to Pattiala that compelled the fulfilment of the promise.

The Agent determines to compel assent to his propositions.

The Rani was now nominally reinstated, but the party of Gurdial had not yet lost their power. No orders were issued for the officials to attend the Rani's Durbars; the customary offerings were not presented; and the policy of the opposition was to induce Colonel Ochterlony to return to Ludhiana, and the Raja to leave the capital for one of his country seats, when, as one article of the agreement provided that everything should be done by mutual consultation, the whole business of the State would necessarily be brought to a stand-still.[1] The disposition of the Raja strengthened the policy of the opposition. He was fully sensible of the advantage to be derived from the Rani's management; but no sooner did he perceive that the British Government was anxious

The intrigues of Gurdial against the Rani.

[1] Colonel Ochterlony to Government, dated 27th April 1812, and voluminous documents accompanying.

for her reinstatement than his native obstinacy was aroused, and he became jealous and tenacious of the authority which all his life he had been accustomed to leave in the hands of Mai Khem Kour, Sahib Kour, Chen Singh, or others of his favourites. Every delay and evasion was practised—every slight cast upon the Rani; and the Chief's greatest pleasure seemed to be in thwarting all her measures, his greatest desire the departure of the British Agent whom he had so earnestly entreated a short time before to visit Pattiala and settle satisfactorily the existing disputes. It was several times proposed to place him under restraint; or, at least, to confine his authority to his own personal estates; but however beneficial to the country, it was considered, not unreasonably, that such a procedure might be viewed with suspicion by the Cis-Satlej Chiefs, although they might perceive its justice and necessity. A coalition with the opposition was next attempted, as the Rani's party did not seem able to hold their ground alone; and Diwan Gurdial and Albel Singh were associated with the Rani and Misr Noudha in the Government.[1] But this arrangement was found ineffective, and was marred by the deceit and jealousy of the Raja, whose insanity, from excessive intemperance, assumed each day a more violent form.

A coalition with the opposition was attempted, but soon failed.

It is wearisome to relate the story of this madman's conduct throughout the negotiations; but it is also necessary to show how complete a justification it afforded for the subsequent action of the British Government. Pretending to acquiesce in the instructions of Colonel Ochterlony, he yet sent positive orders to Diwan Gurdial to throw every possible obstacle in the way of any

The opposition of the Raja to any arrangement.

[1] Colonel Ochterlony to Government, dated 5th May 1812, with inclosures.

investigation into the state of the finances, and discontinued the sittings of the law court and the transaction of routine business. The Agent now perceived that there was no hope of any radical reform without such an authoritative interference with internal details as he had not contemplated when he arrived at Pattiala, and the investment of the Rani with absolute authority. He, accordingly, recommended that the British Government should acknowledge her as virtual Regent; while the Raja, without being actually deposed, would yet be unable to bring the Pattiala State to bankruptcy and ruin. He urged, moreover, that recent events had opened his eyes to the real feeling of the Cis-Satlej Chiefs in the matter; that they were thoroughly convinced that the establishment of the supreme authority of the Rani, by the British Government, was absolutely necessary; and that such action would be received with their general and unqualified approval.[1]

A proposal to give the Rani absolute authority.

Some of the ruffians who surrounded the Raja, and by whose evil counsels he chose to be governed, now formed a plot against the life of Colonel Ochterlony. It was fortunately detected in time, and it is doubtful whether the Raja himself had not a knowledge of it. If the design was not confided to him, it was simply because his insanity might have revealed it; and not from any idea that he would have withheld his consent if a murder could have saved him from the hateful superintendence of his wife.

A plot formed to assassinate Col. Ochterlony.

The Raja at length pretended to agree to a reduction in his expenditure and in the allowances granted to the hungry dependants who were ruining him; and, under

The Raja agrees to important reductions

[1] Colonel Ochterlony to Government of India, dated 8th and 17th of May.

his own directions, a list was prepared, which, without treating any individual with harshness, or altogether depriving him of his usual maintenance, effected a saving of upwards of Rs. 50,000 a year. When this was ready for signature, his whole determination changed, and, under the influence of some of the lowest and most contemptible of his menial servants, he refused absolutely to sign; he declared that he saw the drift of the whole affair, which was to annihilate his authority; that the reduction in the allowances was but to deprive him of his friends, and the reduction in the troops was only to supply the vacancies with partisans of his wife. He then gave orders for an additional guard to be placed on an upper room in the palace to which he retired for security, as he pretended to believe that his life and liberty were in danger.

But changes his mind and refuses to make any reform.

Colonel Ochterlony now saw that further forbearance might be misconstrued as weakness and timidity, and that there was no hope of the Raja himself becoming the ostensible agent in the reforms which had been determined upon. He, accordingly, sent to Colonel Reade for three companies and two guns to join him, and to General Marshall, to send him, from Karnal, a battalion with its guns and two eighteen pounders.[1]

An additional force summoned from Karnal.

The Rani in fear of her life.

Rani Aus Kour had, for some time, been in terror of her life. The apprehensions of the Raja for his safety, which induced him to fill the fort with wild Rohillas and fanatical Akalis, gave her just cause for alarm; and the Raja refused her permission to leave the fort and retire to Sanour, where she might be in safety in a fort of her own. Her danger, however, was at an end when the British force arrived on the 3d and 4th of June. She

[1] Colonel Ochterlony to Government, of 31st May 1812, with inclosures.

then left the fort before daybreak, disguised as a servant in a palanquin carried by only two bearers, and took refuge at the house of her brother, where she was immediately joined by 200 men, according to a preconcerted arrangement. Colonel Ochterlony, at the same time, issued a proclamation, stating that the British Government had only interfered in the interest of the Pattiala State, and on account of the folly and deceit of the Raja, and that henceforth the sole authority would be vested in Rani Aus Kour.

She escapes from the fort,

Is proclaimed Regent,

The Raja could offer no opposition, and his advisers saw that they had at length succeeded in ruining both him and themselves. He first proceeded to the house of the Rani, who declined to receive him; and then, by the advice of Raja Bhag Singh and Bhai Lal Singh, visited Colonel Ochterlony and made over to him the keys of the fort. The Rohilla troops were ordered to evacuate, and British sepoys took possession of the outer gate, while the interior was held by the soldiers of Sodi Surjan Singh, one of the Rani's friends, until such time as a satisfactory arrangement could be effected between the Raja and his wife. The next day, the *guru mukhi*, or private seal, was delivered to the Rani, and directions were issued to all commandants of forts to make over their charge to whomsoever she might appoint. This was done at once at Sefabad and several small places near Pattiala; and the troops were about to be ordered to their several cantonments when the duplicity of the Raja, and the intrigues of one of his wives, Rani Parbab Kour, again brought about a complication which might have had disastrous results, had the example set been followed by the military officers of the State.

And assumes all authority.

One of the strongest forts in the Pattiala territory was

New complications.

Dhodan, into which the commandant positively refused, when summoned, to admit the troops of the Rani. The Raja solemnly declared that the commandant was acting in disobedience to his orders, and ostensibly reiterated commands to deliver the fort according to his agreement; but private and peremptory orders were also sent that he should on no account deliver the fort to Rani Aus Kour's people, nor even to the British troops should they appear before it. A detachment from the British force was then despatched against the place, and it was only after a severe cannonade, and after the walls had been much damaged, that the commandant surrendered, declaring that his resistance had been only in accordance with the most positive instructions.

The fort of Dhodan given up.

The British force leaves Pattiala, June 1812.

The British troops then left Pattiala, and Colonel Ochterlony followed on the 15th of June. Previous to his departure he informed the Raja that the estate of Chamkoian had been bestowed on his son; he enjoined on the Rani a careful administration of the trust conferred on her; and to all the civil and military officers he gave a precept, purporting that the Rani would protect and maintain them in their jagirs if they did not forfeit them by disobedience or misconduct.[1]

The estate of Chamkoian.

With regard to the estate of Chamkoian, given to Prince Karm Singh, there are no English records extant between the years 1809 and 1815, but from Persian documents in the office of the Agent at Ambala, it appears that, in August 1809, the Raja of Pattiala complained to General Ochterlony of the infamous character of Nand Singh, the Chamkoian Chief, and his attacks upon friends and feudatories of Pattiala; and

[1] Colonel Ochterlony to Government, dated 7th and 19th of June 1812. Government of India to Colonel Ochterlony, dated 4th July.

stated that, in consequence, he had seized his fort. General Ochterlony ordered it to be restored and the property plundered from Nand Singh, by the Bhadour and Behr Chiefs, to be given back, referring to the proclamation of 1809, which guaranteed all the Chiefs their respective possessions. Pattiala objected, urging that Nand Singh was one of her own feudatories; but General Ochterlony, making further inquiries, and ascertaining that he was not so, but a dependant of the Nishanwala Chief, insisted on the restoration of the fort, which was given up in 1810. The next year, however, in consequence of fresh aggressions on the part of Nand Singh, his lands and fort were transferred to Pattiala, in deposit, and on 12th of June 1812, the Supreme Government not approving of the Chamkoian villages being mixed up with Pattiala, in consequence of Raja Sahib Singh having mismanaged them, the estate was granted in jagir to Prince Karm Singh.[1]

The position of the Rani a very difficult one.

The position of Rani Aus Kour, now Regent, was by no means an enviable one, and from a generous desire to leave the Raja every possible liberty and indulgence, too great power for evil was also left to him. He had been allowed to retain the uncontrolled disposal of the proceeds

[1] In 1832, twenty years after the estate had been assigned in jagir, the Chamkoian Sikhs presented a petition to Mr William Fraser, Resident at Dehli, complaining that Pattiala had usurped twelve other villages besides those given in jagir; but that as Prince Karm Singh had become Maharaja, the estate should be released, or their possessions, including the twelve usurped villages, restored to them. No notice of their request was taken; and they continued to petition till 1835, when Mr T. Metcalfe, after investigating the claim, rejected it, observing, with reference to the villages which they asserted had been seized, that, having kept silent for so many years, any right which they might have possessed had lapsed; and no order was necessary with reference to the jagir granted to Prince Karm Singh. The whole estate was subsequently included in the general grant in perpetuity to Pattiala under the Sanad granted to the Maharaja on the 22d September 1847.

of his personal estates, amounting to upwards of a lakh of rupees, and also of on quarter of the revenue of the whole country, and it was moreover directed that, on any emergent necessity, he should be permitted to dispose of a second quarter of the revenue. Every indulgence allowed him was turned to the worst use of which it was susceptible. He expressed a wish that he had the power to annihilate every acre of his territory, that nothing might remain to his heir; and, as this was impossible, he endeavoured to injure him, as far as he could, by disposing of all the valuable personal property in jewels and State ornaments, which should have descended, as heir-looms, in the family. Rani Partab Kour was the ill-adviser who encouraged his prodigality and hatred to Rani Aus Kour; and it was her friends and favourites who were enriched by the imbecile Chief. He at last refused to take the air, or leave the house, and it was no secret that he had the insane intention of flying from Pattiala and exciting disturbances in remote parts of his territory; or of seeking assistance from the Gurkhas to regain his lost power.

The Raja thinks of flight.

The allowances of the Raja reduced.

Under these circumstances a further limitation of his power for evil became necessary, and, with the sanction of the Governor-General, the Treasury and *Toshakhana* (Private Royal Treasury) were put in charge of the Rani; the monthly stipend of the Raja was reduced to Rs. 12,000 for his private expenses and amusements, and he was given to understand that any improper conduct would reduce his allowance still further, and subject him to personal restraint.[1]

The Rani's power was now increased, but, as may be supposed, intrigues were carried on as uninterruptedly as ever.

[1] Colonel Ochterlony to Government, of 5th July 1812. Government to Colonel Ochterlony, of 7th August 1812.

Her chief adviser was a Brahman, named Misr Noudha, who was as unpopular as Diwan Nanun Mal had been; sharing the dislike felt by his class to the Jats, and hardly caring to veil his contempt for their rascality and fraud. Forgetting that the disorders of thirty years were not to be removed in a few months, he set to work at reform with an energy and unsparing vigour which all but brought upon him the usual fate of reformers. His enemies first insinuated that he carried on an intrigue with the Rani, and brought him into some discredit until the absolute falseness of the charge was proved. Finding this assault unsuccessful, they determined upon his assassination and that of some nine of his more obnoxious subordinates. The Raja had no opposition to make, and it appears certain that the young and inexperienced Prince was made a party to the conspiracy, foolishly hoping that he would be at once placed on the throne; while Sahib Singh and his confederates merely desired to make a tool of him for their own purposes. The murder of the Misr would undoubtedly have taken place, had it not been for the scruples of Dal Singh, brother of Rani Partab Kour, through whose instrumentality the plot came to light.[1]

Misr Noudha Chief Minister.

The intrigues against his reputation,

And life.

The plot discovered.

But while Raja Sahib Singh was preparing death for others, he fell suddenly ill himself, and died on the 26th March 1813. In such a den of intrigue and wickedness as Pattiala, poison was at once suspected to have been the cause of his death; but there is no reason to believe that this was the case. The party of the Rani could not desire a death which would probably terminate

The death of Raja Sahib Singh, March 1813.

[1] Colonel Ochterlony to Government, of 15th February and 4th and 26th March 1813. Government of India to Colonel Ochterlony, dated 5th March and 23d April 1813.

her administration, while the party opposed to her lost in the Raja the support and object of their intrigues. The probable cause of his death is found in his intemperate habits. Formerly taking much exercise, he had, since the reinstatement of the Rani, remained entirely secluded; while he drank more deeply than ever. A few days previous to his death he had, in consequence of a dream, abandoned the use of wine or spirits altogether, in spite of the advice of his physicians, who had recommended him rather to diminish gradually its quantity; and the want of the accustomed stimulant may have had a fatal effect on a frame exhausted by debauchery.[1]

The cause of his death.

The political situation at Pattiala.

The aspect of affairs at Pattiala was now gloomy in the extreme. Karam Singh, the heir-apparent, had, in the late proceedings, appeared in far from a pleasant light; and the interference of the British Government, however well and generously meant, could only be pronounced a failure. The jealous and ignorant Sikh Chiefs of the Cis-Satlej States threw upon the Rani and the British Government the odium of the Raja's voluntary seclusion, and this was the very result which he desired; the Rani's most judicious measures had been thwarted; the troops, though better and more regularly paid than ever, were discontented and mutinous; while murder was actually plotted in the very Durbar, and the forbearance of the British Government openly claimed as an immunity for the grossest crimes.

The unfortunate results of the interference of the British Government.

This interference withdrawn entirely.

The policy of the British Government, on the death of Raja Sahib Singh, underwent a necessary change. Although it appeared certain that Rani Aus Kour and Misr Noudha would lose power, and the Pattiala State

[1] Colonel Ochterlony to Government, dated 27th March and 2d April. Government of India to Colonel Ochterlony, dated 30th April.

again become a prey to anarchy, yet there were no longer any reasons sufficient to justify any authoritative interference. Raja Sahib Singh had been an imbecile, and the exercise of the influence of the British Government had been earnestly solicited by the well-wishers of the Pattiala State. The character of his successor, whatever it might be, gave no occasion for interference; and the British Government accordingly withdrew from all concern in the internal affairs of Pattiala, and cancelled the guarantee it had given to support the Rani's authority.[1]

The policy of the new Raja.

The young Raja was naturally influenced by his mother, and he showed a disposition to leave the administration in her hands and in that of Misr Noudha, in whom he professed to have entire confidence, though a short time before he had agreed to his death. The old Rani Khem Kour, a widow of Raja Amar Singh, was much disappointed with the turn affairs were taking, and busied herself with stirring up fresh disturbances, in the hope of obtaining some share of power by placing on the throne Ajit Singh, a younger son of the late Raja. This was the woman who was the originator of the plot against the life of Misr Noudha, and there can be little doubt but that it was she who employed the assassin to murder Colonel Ochterlony. Her intrigues were not without powerful support. Raja Jaswant Singh of Nabha, one of the ablest Chiefs in the Protected States, was a man of the most unscrupulous character, who, for an acre of fresh territory, would sacrifice truth and honour without a thought. He had married the niece of Rani Khem Kour, and, partly from this connection, partly from a jealousy of the power of Pattiala, but chiefly from a desire to see that State divided and in the hands of a minor, who would nominally

The intrigues of Rani Khem Kour,

Aided by Raja Jaswant Singh of Nabha.

[1] Secretary to Government to Colonel Ochterlony, 30th April 1813.

be under the guidance and guardianship of Rani Khem Kour, but, in reality, of himself, aided her scheme as far as was in his power. But these intrigues seemed destined to be disappointed. Colonel Ochterlony was present at the installation of the young Raja on the 30th June, and, on that occasion, at the Raja's special request and in open Durbar, the Agent conferred a valuable khillat upon Misr Noudha, as a sign of the Raja's satisfaction and determination to retain him in office.[1]

The installation of Raja Karam Singh.

The Gurkha war of 1814.

On the 1st November 1814, the Government of India were compelled to declare war against the Gurkhas, who had for years been encroaching on British territory at the foot of the hills, and whose Government had refused either redress or apology. The briefest notice is, in this place, required of this war, which only so far affected Pattiala as to gain for the Raja, in return for zealous co-operation with the British army, a large increase of territory.

Amar Singh Thappa at Arki.

The Gurkha conquests in the Punjab hills.

The story of the Gurkha conquests in the Punjab hills will be found in the histories of the Kangra and Simla Chiefs. Driven from Kangra by the superior power of Ranjit Singh, Amar Singh Thappa, the Gurkha leader, had established himself at Arki, in the little State of Bhagal, the Rana of which he had driven into exile. When war was declared the Gurkha conquests, between the Satlej and the Jamna, included Náhan, otherwise known as Sirmur; Hindoor; Kahlur, also known as Bilaspur; a large portion of Bassahir; twelve smaller States[2] (Tha-

[1] Colonel Ochterlony to Government, dated 16th April, 23d April, 20th June, and 1st July. Government of India to Colonel Ochterlony, 15th May 1813, and 24th June.

[2] Keonthal, Mylog, Bhaji, Bhâgal, Bhagât, Kotbar, Konhîâr, Dhâmi, Júbal, Balsan, Mangal, and Kamarsen. Government to Colonel Ochterlony, dated 30th September and 1st October 1814.

Colonel Ochterlony's Report of 29th August.

kori) and the Thakoris dependent on Sirmur, the revenue of which amounted to Rs. 3,81,500 per annum. The Gurkha troops occupying this territory were estimated at 5250 men, of whom 1600 were in Náhan, and 2000 with Amar Singh at Arki.

The encroachments of the Gurkhas had been indifferently directed against British territory, independent and protected States; and the Raja of Pattiala had more than once, before the declaration of war, been engaged in repelling these encroachments, under the direction of the Governor-General's Agent at Ludhiana,[1] and it was to Pattiala troops that the villages of Mundlai and Berowli, which had been unjustly seized, were given up.

Their encroachments on British and Pattiala territory.

In October 1814, Colonel Ochterlony marched into the hills by way of Rupar; captured Nalagarh and Taragarh on the 5th and 8th of November, and, after a long and desperate defence, took possession of Rangarh, the strongest position of the enemy, on the 11th February 1815. On the 15th of April he completely defeated Amar Singh and compelled him to retire to the fort of Malawa, where, reduced to extremity, he at length surrendered, and was allowed to retire with his whole garrison, with their arms, giving up all the forts between the Satlej and the Jamna, and completely evacuating the whole of that territory.[2]

Colonel Ochterlony opens the campaign.

Completely defeats Amar Singh, April 1815.

And evacuation of the country by the Gurkhas.

During this campaign, the infantry of the Pattiala Raja had been with Colonel Ochterlony's force, and a portion of his cavalry had been employed in guarding

Pattiala services.

[1] Colonel Ochterlony to Government, 17th April, 23d July, 16th September, 28th October 1813.

[2] Voluminous correspondence of the years 1814, 1815, and 1816. The final treaty of Segowli, of the 2d December 1815, was delivered by Colonel Ochterlony to the Nipal Agent at Makwanpur, 4th March 1816. Aitchison's Treaties, vol. II., No. XLIX.

the plain country at the foot of the hills. In recognition of his services, the British Government conferred upon him, at the close of the war, sixteen purgunnahs, of which the detail is given in the annexed Sanads.[1]

[1] Sanad to Raja Karam Singh of Pattiala for Purgunnahs Mahili under the Seal and Signature of His Excellency the Governor-General in Council :—

"Whereas all the hill country has come into the possession of the British Government, and whereas Raja Karam Singh was forward to afford the co-operation of his troops during the late contest, therefore the present Sanad is granted, conferring on the said Raja Karam Singh, and on his heirs for ever, the purgunnahs of Waheelee, Kuljoun, Buntheera, Koosalla, Chubrote, Kehmullee, Baddayheer, Saugur, Toorasutgowa, Jubub, and Pollakotee, together with the saeer duties of the same, and all the rights and appurtenances belonging to them, in exchange for a nuzurana of the sum of one lakh and fifty thousand rupees; and the said sum having been paid into the Company's treasury by kists, as agreed upon, nothing further shall ever be demanded on this account. The British Government will always protect and support the said Raja and his heirs in the possession of this territory. The Raja, considering this Sanad a legal and valid instrument, will immediately take possession of the aforesaid lands, but he must not encroach on any lands beyond the acknowledged limits of the purgunnahs enumerated. In case of war, the Raja must, on the requisition of the British authorities, furnish armed men and Begarees to join the detachment of British troops which may be stationed for the protection of the country. He will omit no exertion to do justice, and to promote the welfare and happiness of the ryots; while they, on their part, considering the said Raja as their true and rightful lord, must obey him accordingly, and pay their revenue punctually, and be always zealous to promote the cultivation of their lands, and to testify their loyalty and obedience."

Dated 20th October 1815.

Sanad to Raja Karam Singh of Pattiala for the Thakooree of Bughat and Juggutgurh, under the Seal and Signature of His Excellency the Governor-General in Council :—

"Whereas all the hill country has come into the possession of the British Government, and whereas Raja Karam Singh was forward in affording the co-operation of his troops during the late contest. Whereas by order of the Right Honourable the Governor-General the present Sanad is granted to said Raja, conferring on him and on his heirs for ever—

"1st. The Purgunnah of Bughat and the city of Taksal, with the first fort at Sookchinpoor, and the second fort at the end of the Bazar of Taksal, and the fort of Tharoogurh; and Purgunnah Parleekhar with the fort of Ajeergurh, and Purgunnah Keeateen with the fort of Rajgurh, and Purgunnah Luchherany, and Purgunnah Berowlee; and together with these purgunnahs and the five forts specified, saeer collections amounting to one thousand eight hundred rupees, the whole forming a portion of the Thakooraee of Bughat; also

For some time the Pattiala administration was carried on with more regularity and success than for many years previously. The Rani and the Misr remained in power, and no more grave disputes arose between neighbouring States, than an old standing quarrel with Manimajra regarding the distribution of the waters of the Gaggar nallah, an important question in a dry and sandy country ;[1] the reduction of the fort of Kunori, belonging to the contumacious Chalians ;[2] and the rightful ownership of certain Purgunnahs in Hariana, which Mr Fraser, the Assistant Resident at Dehli, claimed for the British Government,[3] and the detailed history of which dispute will be given hereafter.

Karam Singh assumes the authority of Raja.

But Raja Karam Singh again fell into the hands of bad advisers, and determined to remove Misr Noudha and the Rani from power. The Misr himself believed that his life was in danger, and accused both the Raja and

"2d. The fort of Juggutgurh with the Purgunnah of Juggutgurh and its dependencies, forming a portion of Sirmore, together with all the rights and appurtenances belonging thereto, in exchange for the sum of Rs.1,30,000, and the said sum having been paid at the Company's treasury, no further demand will ever be made on the Raja on this account. The British Government will always protect and support the said Raja in possession of the said lands, and the Raja taking possession of the aforesaid lands shall not encroach on the possessions of another. In case of war, the troops stationed by the Raja for the protection of the said lands shall be sent to join the British Forces. The Raja will promote the welfare of his ryots ; on their part, &c. (as in preceding Sanad)."

Dated 20th October 1815.

The purgunnahs mentioned in these two Sanads were taken from the Ranas of Keonthal and Bhagat for their hesitating and unfriendly conduct during the war.

Colonel Ochterlony to Government dated 28th July, 9th August, and 23d September 1815. Government of India to Sir D. Ochterlony, 20th October 1815.

[1] Captain Birch to Resident Dehli, 31st May 1818.

[2] Captain Birch to Sir D. Ochterlony, of 21st March and 4th April 1818.

[3] Sir D. Ochterlony to Resident Dehli of 5th November 1816, 25th April, 15th June, and 4th October 1817.

Resident Dehli to Captain Birch, 14th June 1818.

Bhai Lal Singh of having designs against him; but this was not likely, though the Misr's former experience made his apprehensions natural. But he was able to make no objection to the Raja taking, after two months, the whole power into his own hands, and the latter having extorted this promise, visited his mother, who seeing that opposition was useless and desiring to make a virtue of necessity, told him that if he desired power there was no need to wait two months, but that he might assume it at once. He, accordingly, retaining Misr Noudha as Chief Minister, appointed several of his own friends to important offices, and assumed charge of the Treasury, Household, and Revenue Departments. The English authorities, by direction of the Governor-General, informed the Raja that he would best promote his own interests by allowing his administration to remain as before, and by upholding the authority of his able Minister; but no other interference was advisable, the more especially as the partial abdication of the Rani had been voluntary, and as the arrangement by which the Raja acquired power was, sooner or later, inevitable.[1]

Retaining Misr Noudha as Minister.

Death of the Minister, October 1818. His character.

Misr Noudha died soon after this, in October 1818, returning from a pilgrimage to Joala Mukhi. No State had ever been better served than Pattiala had been by him. He, in consort with Rani Aus Kour, saved the country from anarchy and restored it to prosperity; while no charge was ever advanced against his honesty, even by his enemies. He seems to have been as clever as Diwan Nanun Mal, though perhaps more cautious and timid. Rani Aus Kour, after the death of her adviser, continued to lose influence and power, but no open

1 Captain Birch to Resident Dehli, dated 10th June and 10th July 1818. Resident Dehli to Captain G. Birch, 3d July, 12th July. Secretary to Government of India to Resident, 31st July 1818.

dispute took place between her and her son until the beginning of 1821.

His successor.

The Raja had appointed as Chief Minister in the room of Misr Noudha, one Barkat Ali Khan, a native of Oude, who had long been in the service of Sir David Ochterlony. The Rani had retained in her charge the *Toshakhana*, with the Treasury, Jewel House, &c., and she had increased the jagir of Rs. 50,000, which had been granted, in 1807, for the maintenance of her and her son, to nearly two lakhs of rupees, which she held in sole possession. This determination to strengthen herself at his expense naturally irritated the Raja, and a quarrel arising between Wazir Khan, a Pathan leader in favour with the Rani, and Barkat Ali Khan, the Minister, in which a few wounds were given and received by the partisans of either, the Raja believed or professed to believe that his mother desired to raise a revolt against him and to resume charge of the administration. He begged the British Political Officer at Karnal to visit him and make some satisfactory arrangement with the Rani, the result of which was that the Raja was declared to possess sole and absolute power, and the Rani agreed to retire to her estate at Sunour and abstain from all interference in public affairs.[1]

The rupture between the Raja and his mother.

She retires from Pattiala to Sunour.

There seemed a probability of peace, but two important points were still unsettled: first, the enormous amount of territory claimed by the Rani as her jagir; and, secondly, the custody of the *Toshakhana* which the Rani had carried away with her to Sunour. With regard to the jagir, Sir D. Ochterlony held that, although the Rani had no right to the whole estate of Rs. 50,000,

The jagir of the Rani.

[1] Captain Birch to Sir D. Ochterlony, dated 12th February and 9th March 1821.

which had been granted not only for her own maintenance but also for that of the Prince, yet it would be generous and becoming in the Raja to interpret the grants in her favour; but to the enormous additions which she had made to the estate while she possessed full power, during the late reign, she had absolutely no claim whatever, and the Raja would do well to resume them all.

The private treasury kept by the Rani, who refuses to give accounts.

The *Toshakhana*, which was supposed to contain in money, jewels, and gold and silver plate, fifty lakhs of treasure, Captain Birch, the Assistant Agent, had allowed the Rani to take with her to Sunour, believing that the Raja was not averse to this arrangement, and that the treasure would be safe with the Rani, who would be responsible for its custody, and who promised to send a correct list of its contents to her son. But this she would not do: she sent indeed a memorandum which was so imperfect as to be worthless, and refused a more detailed account.[1]

The departure of Sir D. Ochterlony from Dehli, A.D. 1821.

Such was the unsatisfactory state of affairs when Sir D. Ochterlony left Dehli, and the Raja hesitated to take any decided action, uncertain whether any change of policy was signified by Sir David's departure. But the rejection by the Rani of all friendly overtures; her determination to retain both land and treasure; and the belief entertained by the Raja of the misappropriation of some of the most valuable property in his mother's possession, decided him, early in 1823, to take further and immediate action.

[1] The only memorandum she submitted was "Five lakhs of rupees with other articles in chests and coffers."

Captain Birch to Sir D. Ochterlony, 30th July and 8th, 14th, and 16th August 1821.

Sir D. Ochterlony to Captain Birch, 29th May, 1st, 5th, 10th, and 17th August 1821.

The complaints of the Raja against his mother.

The whole matter was finally referred to Captain Ross, the Deputy Superintendent of the Cis-Satlej States. The Raja complained that his mother did not observe the seclusion which was becoming and consistent with the family honour; that she had falsified the *Sanads* by which she held her estates; that the most valuable effects of the *Toshakhana* were misappropriated; that, by holding a separate Court, she impaired his legitimate authority; and, lastly, that her officers interfered in the administration. He added that the strength and resources of the State were so much injured, that he would probably be unable to furnish the required contingents, and be condemned as having failed in his duty to the British Government.

His proposal to restrain the power of the Rani.

The Raja proposed, as a remedy for these evils, that his mother should return to Pattiala and reside there, and that her income should be Rs. 50,000 per annum, the amount of the original jagir; while the newly acquired estate should be resumed, also that the *Toshakhana* should be brought to Pattiala, and only allowed to remain in the Rani's custody if complete lists were given of its contents, and if it should be proved that, hitherto, no part of it had been misappropriated.

The proposals the Raja just, b difficult of accomplishment.

The proposals of the Raja were just, and the provision promised to his mother liberal, being more than twice as large as any Dowager Rani of Pattiala had ever before received after the accession of her son; and there was no reason for the British Government to interfere to prevent the Raja taking whatever steps he chose to enforce his wishes; except that the Rani possessed so large a territory and so many troops, having also at her disposal all the accumulated treasure of the family, that it appeared probable that should the Raja attempt to coerce her, she would oppose him by force, and appear at the head of a revolt against her son as, sixteen years before, she had headed a revolt against her husband.[1]

The interference of the British Government again asked and given.

The British Government thus again interfered in the internal affairs of Pattiala, at the urgent request of the Raja, and to save his territory from the horrors of civil war. In October 1823, Captain Murray was sent with a detachment to assist the Raja in enforcing his legitimate wishes—namely, the possession of the State treasure, and the resumption of such jagirs as the Rani had newly acquired; also to compel her to resign the fort of Sunour, only two miles from Pattiala, since her residence so near the capital was a fruitful source of intrigue and dispute.

British troops at Pattiala.

When the British officer made his demands to Diwan Rup Chund, the Rani's agent, that official burst into tears, and declared he could not carry them to his mistress, who would probably commit suicide. At length he consented, and soon brought a reply from the Rani, offering Captain Murray a lakh of rupees to allow the existing arrangement to continue, and to forward to Calcutta a report which she would prepare, as she had not yet been heard in her defence. If this was refused, she declared that she would spend the remainder of her life in retirement by the Ganges, and accept neither jagir nor provision from her son. But a prompt acquiescence in the demands of the Government being insisted upon, she made over the fort to the Raja's troops, and came herself into camp, where she was treated with every respect. But for several days she refused all amicable settlement of the dispute. She refused to live at Amargarh, her old jagir, and declared that unless she was permitted to

The opposition of the Rani to the demands of her son.

[1] Captain Ross, Deputy Superintendent, 4th February 1823. Government of India to Mr Elliott of 31st July 1823.

retain Sunour, she would go in person to Calcutta and appeal to the Governor-General against the cruelty of her son. She had, of course, no real ground for complaint; for the Raja was most anxious to treat his mother with all consideration, and had included in her jagir the best lands, the strongest fort, and richest town in his territory, and would have placed his treasure at her sole disposal; but her servants, who thought more of their own advantage than of that of their mistress, encouraged her in a useless opposition, and on the 14th October, she left for Ambala, refusing all terms unless Sunour was granted to her. The Raja was in despair: the honour of his family was ruined should his mother wander about the world a supplicant seeking for redress against her son, who only demanded his rights, and was ready to concede to her every point not absolutely essential. Much as he disliked to yield, he gave up to her the town and fort of Sunour, and she, knowing this victory was all she could expect, returned there, and, before the end of October, was put in possession of her estate of Rs. 50,000, and consented to make friends with her son.[1]

She leaves Pattiala for Ambala.

She is persuaded to return.

Here ended the political life of Rani Aus Kour. She was a woman of great ability, and her wise administration of the Pattiala State, during part of her husband's reign and during the minority of her son, was the admiration of the neighbouring States, and was warmly praised by the British Government. Her ambition may easily be forgiven, and it was no more than natural that she should be unwilling to part with the power she had held so long and used so wisely.

The close of the political career of Rani Aus Kour, A.D. 1823.

[1] Captain Murray to Mr W. C. Elliott, dated 9th, 10th, 11th, 12th, 14th, 15th, 16th, 18th, and 28th of October 1823. Mr Elliott to Captain Murray, dated 18th September and 29th September. General Reynell to Agent to Governor-General, Dehli, dated 30th September 1823. Government of India to Mr Elliott, 21st November 1823.

The claim of Pattiala to the Bilaspur estate, A.D. 1819.

A few incidents of rather earlier date in Pattiala history should behere recorded. In 1819 died Rani Dya Kour, widow of Sirdar Sher Singh of Kalsia, and the owner of the Bilaspur estate. To this inheritance the Raja of Pattiala advanced a claim, as his sister had married Sirdar Hari Singh, second son of Jodh Singh, the head of the Kalsia family. Hari Singh was dead, and the Pattiala claim was utterly preposterous and invalid according to Sikh law, and the estate was offered to Sobha Singh, the eldest son of Jodh Singh, on terms that he did not care to accept, and in consequence it lapsed to the British Government.[1]

The ill-feeling between Nabha and Pattiala.

In the same year, 1819, the ill-feeling between Nabha and Pattiala, which had for long existed, became so great as to threaten hostilities between the two States. One of its causes was a dispute between the zamindars of Kowlasherí, a village belonging to Pattiala, and those of Phulisherí, a Nabha village. Raja Jaswant Singh complained of the encroachments of the Pattiala zamindars, and the matter was referred to arbitration and decided in favour of Nabha. Raja Karam Singh then sent sepoys to Kowlasherí, under the pretence of protecting it against the rival village; but their presence had its natural effect in disturbances in which lives were lost on both sides.

The Kowlasherí dispute.

The Bhadour and Kangar disputes.

There was a similar case between the villages of Bhadour and Kangar, in which the Pattiala Raja was also in the wrong; and, lastly, a fierce dispute regarding the Hariana lands, which was settled in a summary manner by the British Government taking possession of the subject of dispute.[2] This last question will more

The Hariana boundary.

[1] Ambala Settlement, Report Southern Purgunnahs, pp. 15–28.
Captain Birch to Agent to Governor-General, 27th, 28th, 29th April and 27th May 1820. Captain R. Ross to Resident, Dehli, 14th January, 3d April, and 20th August 1822.

[2] Captain Birch to Resident, 22d November, 17th November 1820, and 27th January 1821.

conveniently be considered later, as the case was not finally decided till 1856.

Raja Karam Singh had not freed himself from the tyranny of his mother when he was subjected to the extravagant claims and pretensions of his half-brother Kour Ajit Singh. This was the youth whom, it may be remembered, the Raja's grandmother, Rani Khem Kour, had intrigued to place on the throne ten years before. This lady died in June 1821; but many others, especially his chief adviser Gopal Singh, continued to encourage the pretensions of the young Prince, and sow discord between him and his brother. In 1820, he left Pattiala with his mother, refusing to live on her jagir of twelve villages, and went to reside at Dehli, where his extravagance soon loaded him with debt; and, in 1823, he usurped the title which belonged of right to the reigning representative of the family, and had engraved on his seal Mahárája Rájagán Máhárája Ajit Singh Mohindar, Báhádar.

The pretensions of Prince Ajit Singh.

He assumes the title of Maharaja.

This title of Raja had been granted to Ala Singh of Pattiala by Ahmed Shah Abdáli, and the higher title of Maharaja by the Emperor Akbar II. of Dehli, in 1810, on the recommendation of General Ochterlony.

The Prince had no right whatever to adopt either one title or the other, for no one of the Pattiala family, except the one on the throne, had ever received a title higher than that of Kour or Prince. Raja Karam Singh was most anxious to make friends with his brother, and to remove all cause of complaint. He sent his Minister, Barkat Ali Khan, to Captain Murray, with a *carte blanche* to that officer to propose and conclude any arrangement which might satisfy the Prince, with a list of twenty-one towns and forts, any one of which he might choose for a residence. The absurd pretensions of Ajit Singh

His ridiculous demands.

and his friends made negotiation difficult. He desired the territory to be divided and a great portion of the revenue alienated for his benefit, although he knew that the rule of primogeniture was in force in the Pattiala family. Then he demanded either the towns of Sefabad, Sunam, or the strong fort of Batinda to be given to him. The first of these, only three miles from Pattiala, was a favourite hunting-place of the Raja; the second was the retreat in the rainy season, and contained the houses of the chief officers of the Court; the third was the strongest fort in the Pattiala territory. Finding that these demands were not likely to be granted, he applied for a fort with an adjacent town, such as Dhode and Mansurpur, or Hariana and Burnala. The Raja replied that he could not consent to alienate so much of his territory as would create a dangerous precedent, and allow his children in after years to demand an equal independent provision. He offered, however, to give one of the four places mentioned, or two of less importance. The Kour then declared his fixed determination of accepting no less than the districts which had lately been resumed from Rani Aus Kour and incorporated with Pattiala, worth about two lakhs of rupees. This declaration necessarily brought the negotiations to an end for the time.

Which are resisted by the Raja.

Ajit Singh now perceived that the British Government would not support his claims, and that unless he accepted his brother's terms, he might receive nothing. Yet such was his pride, that after he had agreed to accept an estate *(jaidâd)* of Rs. 30,000 and a personal allowance of Rs. 5000 in addition to the jagir of Rs. 15,000, then held by him and his mother, he, at the last moment, refused the provision, and returned with his mother to Dehli.

He finally agrees to accept Rs. 50,000 a year.

Here he lived till 1828, when, having grown wiser as he grew older, he became reconciled to his brother, accepted the provision made for him, and went to live at Pattiala, where his marriage was celebrated with great splendour in June of the following year.[1]

His marriage, A.D. 1829.

Raja Karam Singh showed his loyalty and good-will to the British Government by coming forward at a time of some financial difficulty and subscribing 20 lakhs of rupees (£200,000) to the 5 per cent. loan of 1827. This money was paid without any limitation as to the period of repayment and in spite of the sneers of the neighbouring Chiefs at his thus parting with his family treasure.[2]

The Raja subscribes 20 lakhs to the Government loan.

In the year 1828 a boundary dispute between Nabha and Pattiala was arranged, which deserves mention, not only from the length of time that it had continued, and from the importance attached to it by the Chiefs concerned, but also from its being an immediate cause of Maharaja Ranjit Singh's first invasion of the country to the south of the Satlej.

Boundary dispute between Pattiala and Nabha.

Two miles from the city of Nabha is the little village of Doladhi, which, in 1807, was settled and ploughed by Bhai Tara Singh, an *Ahlkâr* (official) of the Pattiala State. Rajah Jaswant Singh of Nabha was indignant at this encroachment on his town land, and remonstrated; but, receiving no redress, he occupied the land by force and the Bhai was slain in the skirmish that ensued. Raja Sahib Singh of Pattiala, furious at the loss of a

The origin of the village of Doladhi, A.D. 1807.

Bhai Tara Singh slain.

[1] Captain Murray to Agent to Governor-General, 9th and 17th May 1823, 18th January and 23d February 1824. Agent to Governor-General to Captain Murray, 21st January, 21st February 1824. Captain Murray to Sir E. Colebrooke, 19th January 1828. Sir E. Colebrooke to Captain Murray, 15th June 1829. Mr Metcalfe to Sir D. Ochterlony, dated 30th September 1820.

[2] Deputy Secretary to Government to Captain Murray, 28th May. From Assistant Resident, Dehli, dated 10th June and 14th September 1827. From Captain Murray to Sir E. Colebrooke, 12th January 1828.

favourite officer, marched to Nabha and defeated Jaswant Singh at Nirwana, who shut himself in his capital, and sent his friend Raja Bhag Singh of Jhind to ask help from Lahore. Ranjit Singh, on his arrival, besieged Sahib Singh in Mansurpur, and destroyed the wells of Doladhi, which he made over to the Pattiala Chief, forbidding the wells to be repaired or a strip of waste land, which he pointed out, to be ever cultivated. For twenty-one years the neutral land of Doladhi remained untilled, and if either Pattiala or Nabha atttempted to cultivate it, the greatest jealousy and ill-will was the immediate result. In 1827 the old quarrel was revived, Nabha accusing the Doladhi villagers of encroaching on the disputed land, and Pattiala retorting. The Chiefs refused to appoint arbitrators, and Captain Murray, the Political Agent, was himself compelled to visit the spot and draw the boundary line.

The arbitration of Maharaja Ranjit Singh.

The quarrel revived in 1827.

The point was a difficult one to decide. The decree of Maharaja Ranjit Singh, given in 1807, could not be held valid, for the proclamation of the British Government of 1809 only guaranteed the maintenance of the States at that time; and in 1809 Nabha had become more powerful than Pattiala, which had not been able to recover the land for which Bhai Tara Singh had fought and died. But Captain Murray was successful in fixing a boundary line which pleased neither party. The Raja of Nabha was only partially discontented; but the Pattiala Chief was entirely so, and the case was referred for orders to Dehli.

Captain Murray attempts to decide the case,

And fails to satisfy either party.

[1] Captain Murray to Sir E. Colebrooke, 12th April; and Sir E. Colebrooke to Captain Murray, dated 11th May and 18th June 1828.

Sir E. Colebrooke to Captain Murray dated 25th July, 30th September, 2d and 13th October. Captain Murray to Sir E. Colebrooke, 30th July, 4th, 5th, and 21st October 1828.

The agents of the Kythal and Jhind Chiefs, together with the British officials, were then sent to fix a new boundary line between the wells of Doladhi and the city of Nabha, to remove the pillars fixed by Captain Murray, and to destroy all cultivation on the disputed land. The new decision was favourable to Pattiala, and the Raja of Nabha became eager to preserve the boundary pillars which he had before been so anxious to destroy. But his remonstrances were unavailing; the cultivation was destroyed by the cattle of Nabha and Doladhi; the pillars, which the Nabha officials refused to remove, were thrown down, and the new line marked out.

A new decision in favour of Pattiala.

The Raja of Nabha appealed against this decision, which only injured him inasmuch as it was a triumph for Pattiala; and daily complaints were made of encroachments and quarrels, until the direct injunction of the Resident at Dehli compelled the boundary, fixed under sanction of the British Government, to be respected.[1]

Nabha appeals against it,

The Raja of Nabha was still dissatisfied, and directly charged Sir E. Colebrooke with having been unduly influenced by the Pattiala authorities; and a commission was appointed to sit at Dehli and investigate the case. The conclusion of the Committee was thus expressed in a note by Mr Trevelyan, Assistant to the Resident at Dehli: "I will conclude by remarking that the proceedings afford strong grounds for confirming Captain Murray's decision; and the proceedings held before the Special Commissioners, by evincing the motives which induced Sir E. Colebrooke to set it aside, afford still stronger. Should it please His Lordship in Council to

And Captain Murray's decision is confirmed by the Supreme Government.

[1] Captain Murray to Sir E. Colebrooke, 13th December 1828; and letters to Maharaja of Pattiala and Raja of Nabha.

confirm Captain Murray's decision on the Doladhi case, in consideration of the unlawful means that were taken to set it aside, a memorable example will be afforded to all Hindostan, which will have more effect in checking these illicit practices than the punishment of many delinquents."

The Governor-General, agreeing with the opinion of the Commissioners, authorised the Resident at Dehli, if he thought fit, to set aside Sir E. Colebrooke's decision, and to confirm that of Captain Murray; which was done; and the boundary pillars set up by the last-named officer were restored.[1] To this Doladhi quarrel, trivial as was its origin, and worthless as was the subject in dispute, may, more distinctly than to anything else, be traced the ill feeling which has existed between Pattiala and Nabha for sixty years, which beyond all doubt had a considerable influence over the Nabha policy during the first Sikh war, and which has not, even to this day, entirely disappeared.

The grave results of this dispute.

The Maharájkian Sikhs had formed another constant subject of dispute between the Phulkian Chiefs, Pattiala, Nabha, and Jhind, each claiming supremacy over them. These jagirdars were of Phulkian origin, and, in 1833, were estimated at between forty to fifty thousand souls, inhabiting twenty-two large villages, the total area of which was about forty thousand acres.

Supremacy over the Mahárajkian Sikhs.

Their customs were peculiar; each individual claimed to be absolutely independent, and neither son nor brother remained in subjection after he was able to

Their peculiar customs and character.

1 F. Hawkins, Esquire, officiating Resident, to Secretary to Government of India, 12th January 1830, with note by Mr C. Trevelyan. Government of India to officiating Resident, dated 29th January. Officiating Resident to Colonel Murray, dated 6th March, and to Secretary Government 12th December 1830. Letter of Raja of Nabha to officiating Resident, dated 13th November 1830.

cultivate his share of the land. The soil they owned was unirrigated, yet it nevertheless yielded abundant harvests. But although no more than simple agriculturists, the Maharájkians had given up none of their warlike habits. Each man carried arms, which he never laid aside, even at the plough; for the whole community was of so turbulent a character, that no one was safe from the encroachment of his neighbour. Such being the case, it may seem strange that these men had been so long able to preserve their independence, were they not always ready to unite against any common enemy; and their strength, bravery, and warlike habits, caused them to be respected. They had scarcely any sort of municipal government, and their only law was of equal division of inheritance.

The causes which led to the interference of the Phulkian Chiefs with the Maharájkians;

During Muhammadan days the Maharájkians had paid tribute to Dehli, and, when the empire fell, they naturally referred to the neighbouring Chiefs to arbitrate in their disputes; some going to Nabha, some to Jhind, and others to Pattiala; and as these States had Police and Revenue posts on the boundary, they were always ready to send troops into the Maharájkian territory whenever their help was asked. This state of things led to the usual results. The Chiefs whose assistance was asked gave it with the sole object of strengthening their own personal influence and power: rival factions called in rival Chiefs, and the people gained very little benefit from the foreign interference; while jealousies and feuds continually increased. Weary, at last, of perpetual disorder, the Maharájkians solicited the help of the British Government. The case was a very difficult one to decide: Pattiala, Nabha, and Jhind, each claimed superiority, but to this they had no title, nor could they show that, at any time,

Who, at last, solicit the protection of the British Government.

they had received from the Maharjákians any kind of acknowledgment of such superiority. But the people were so wild and lawless that some strong hand was necessary to control them. The idea of divided authority exercised by the three Phulkian houses was felt to be impracticable, and at length the Government decided to make over the villages, for a term of years, to Pattiala, as being the strongest and the most likely to keep its troublesome neighbours in order. Certain conditions were however appended to the grant, to which the Maharaja of Pattiala would not accede, and persisted in maintaining exclusive rights of unconditional jurisdiction; rights which had been repeatedly denied by the British Government. The result was that the Maharájkians, in August 1833, were brought under direct British superintendence, and the Phulkian Chiefs were warned not to interfere in the affairs of the community, which became peaceful and well-behaved, as soon as the rival influences of Nabha and Pattiala ceased to agitate it.[1]

They are taken under direct British administration.

The immediate change in their character for the better.

This change in the character of the Maharájkians for the better was very marked, and was apparent immediately they had come under British control. No harsh rules or unintelligible procedure were prescribed for them, but simple village courts were formed, in which the elders were to decide upon most disputed cases. The result was that in a few years the bloodshed and affrays which were before so frequent, became almost unknown, and

[1] Resident Dehli to Political Agent, 6th May 1826, 16th February 1829, 23d March 1831, 5th May and 19th September 1831, 21st July 1832. Political Agent to Resident, 27th January 1829, 13th April, 4th May, and 3d September 1831; 29th January, 17th June 1832; 23d July 1833. Agent to Governor-General, 12th December 1832, and 16th September 1833.

Secretary to Government 5th November 1832, and 22d August 1833.

the confidence of the people in the intentions of the British Government was such that they begged that a Thanah or Police Station might be placed in their midst, though they had always refused to admit any such post belonging to the neighbouring Chiefs, and would have resisted such an encroachment to the death. They gave up almost entirely the practice of female infanticide, which had been before universal. Their excuse for the prevalence of this crime was singular enough. When told that it was expressly forbidden in the precepts of their Guru, Govind Singh, they replied that it had been impossible for them, during the times of anarchy that had prevailed since they had adopted Sikhism, to find leisure to become acquainted with the doctrines of their Scripture; and that the first notice that they had ever received of infanticide being an offence against their religion was in an injunction issued some years before by the Rajas of Pattiala and Nabha. They, however, engaged to suppress the crime, and they were both sincere and successful; the punishment of forfeiture of his estate being ordained for any one who should commit it.[1]

Their confidence in the Government,

And social reforms.

In 1834, several cases occurred, requiring no special mention, between Pattiala and the British Government relative to boundary disputes; trespass of Pattiala troops in the Hissar district, and encroachments of Pattiala zamindars on British territory, but these were all easily and satisfactorily arranged. One dispute, before alluded to, must be now related with some detail,[2] for

The great Hariana boundary dispute.

[1] Agent to Governor-General to Political Agent, 28th April 1836. Political Agent to Agent to Governor-General, 31st August 1836.

[2] Agent to Governor-General, Dehli, to Political Agent, Ambala, 11th January, 7th February, 3d and 19th April, 30th June, 23d August, 3d September. Political Agent to Agent to Governor-General, 12th March, 3d and 12th May 1834.

it gave more trouble to the English Government than any other with Pattiala, and remained a fruitful source of jealousy and suspicion for upwards of twenty years. This was the case regarding the Harriana and the Bhatti districts, conquered respectively from the Mahrattas and the Bhattis in 1803 and 1818.

The Bhatti country conquered from the Mahrattas.

After the victory of Dehli in 1803, the British Government succeeded to all the possessions of Sindhia north of Agra, including the Gangetic Provinces and the Dehli territory west of the Jamna. To the north lay the States of Pattiala, Kythal, and Jhind, but between them and the inhabited portion of Dehli territory, was a strip of waste land, now known as the Sirsa and Hissar districts. This country consists of vast plains covered with grass and a scrubby brushwood, while the only elevations which break the monotonous level are sand hills, which seem to speak of a time when the tract was a wilderness of drifting sand. But Bhattiana had once been more prosperous than it was in 1803. Just twenty years before, a terrible famine had desolated the land; the mountain streams, to whose water the people trusted for their scanty cultivation, had dried up; no rain had fallen; and the vast herds of cattle, for which Bhattiana had been renowned for many hundred years, died. The villages were deserted, and, to this day, the country has not recovered the fatal famine of 1783.

The nature of the country.

The famine of 1783.

The character of the Bhattis.

The inhabitants of this country were a pastoral race, fierce and restless in their habits and impatient of any control. They lived for the most part in open villages, or wandered about with their flocks in search of pasture. A few towns, or rather fortified villages, were scattered through the waste, which the Bhatti tribes made their rendezvous on the approach of a common danger. These were

Fatahabad, Sirsa, Rania, and Ubohar. The Bhatti race was little more than a band of robbers, and it was their boldness, the rapidity of their movements, and the savage character of their country, which had saved them from being crushed by powerful neighbours whom they had continually irritated by their raids.

The campaigns of Raja Amar Singh only had a temporary effect.

Raja Amar Singh of Pattiala had more than once, it is true, invaded the Bhatti country, stormed the strongholds of the robbers, and exacted from them a reluctant submission. But his influence lasted for little longer than the time that his army was in the country; and, after his death, the Bhattis completely recovered their independence; his son Sahib Singh, being a child, and the Pattiala State in too great confusion to waste much time and money on a region so unproductive as Bhattiana.

The Bhatti conquest of Thomas, A.D. 1795.

Between 1795 and 1799, George Thomas extended his authority over all the Hissar, Hansi, and Sirsa territory.[1] He fell before the Mahrattas in 1802, who, in their turn, were overthrown by the English in the following year.[2]

The English obtain the country A.D. 1803.

The new masters of the country were either ignorant of the amount and value of inheritance they had gained from the Mahrattas, or were too apathetic to attempt to secure it, and, from 1803 to 1818, no steps were taken to define the boundary of the Sikh States. The right of the British Government to the territory had not, however, been allowed to lapse. In the year 1810, an expedition was sent against Khan Bahadar Khan, a Bhatti Chief, whose raids into British territory had been frequent. He was overpowered and expelled the country, while the tract of Fatahabad, which he had held in possession, now

Expedition against the Bhattis, A.D. 1810.

[1] *Vide ante*, p. 75. [2] *Vide ante*, p. 83.

included in the district of Hissar, was formally annexed to the British territory.

The second expedition of 1818.

But of the country to the west, from Sirsa to the Bahawalpur deserts and the Satlej, the Bhattis retained the undisturbed possession until 1818, when another of their leaders, Zabta Khan, roused by his forays the wrath of the British Government, as Khan Bahadar Khan had done. A force was sent against him, and the territory, now known as the district of Sirsa, came under the English rule.

The action of the Sikh Chiefs during these years.

During these fifteen years, while the English had paid no attention whatever to the state of the border, the Sikh Chiefs had not been idle. They had understood that the wild country, then almost depopulated, would, under good management, become valuable, and in anticipation of the time when the Government would understand its value, they steadily laboured at manufacturing the strongest possible claims to as large a portion of it as they could annex without opposition.

The constant and systematic encroachments of Pattiala on the frontier.

From the accession of Raja Sahib Singh till their overthrow by the English, the Bhattis had remained the real masters of the country, with the exception of the short interval of the rule of George Thomas, who, however, made no attempt to interfere directly with the authority of the Bhatti Chiefs over their respective clans. They had successfully resisted all attempts of Pattiala to subdue them, and had done much to prevent the encroachments which, from 1803, Pattiala was constantly making; advancing her villages further and further into the waste, and bringing cultivators from her own settled territory to found new hamlets in Bhattiana.

The defeat of the Bhattis an advantage to Pattiala.

The overthrow of the Bhattis by the English removed the last barrier to Pattiala encroachments; and that

State immediately made the most of the opportunity. In 1821, passing over the belt of waste land, she planted an outpost of twenty soldiers in the village of Gudhah, within fourteen miles of the British police post at Sirsa, and waited to see if this audacity would be noticed. No remark was made, and, the next year, the post was further strengthened by a detachment of forty horse; and, in 1823, cultivators were brought from the interior of Pattiala and induced by large rewards to appropriate and cultivate the surrounding waste. Similarly, in 1827, the Maharaja of Pattiala took possession of Ubohar, sixty miles to the north-west of Gudhah, repaired the fortifications, and began to found villages and occupy all the neighbouring country.

The attention of the English authorities aroused.

Mr William Fraser, the District Officer, had, in 1818, called the attention of Government to the unsettled state of the frontier, but no notice was taken of the report. Subsequently, the Honourable R. Gardner and Mr S. Brown, successively in charge of the district, had reported to the same effect; but it was not till 1835, when Sir Charles Metcalfe was Lieutenant-Governor of the North-Western Provinces, and Mr William Fraser Resident at Dehli, both gentlemen most intimately acquainted with the case, that it was determined to bring the matter to a satisfactory settlement. Mr Ross Bell, the Acting Collector of Hissar, was selected for the duty, and, for his guidance, certain principles were laid down which were to be closely and invariably followed.

Mr Bell appointed to report on the question, A.D. 1836.

The principles which were to guide him.

These principles were that whatever belonged to Pattiala at the time of the British conquest of Harriana in 1803, should be adjudged to that State; and whatever belonged to the Government which the English had superseded, should be adjudged to the latter. With regard to the district of Fatahabad and the portions of the Bhatti country conquered in 1810, and to the remaining portion of that country conquered in 1818, the same principle was to hold good, and the *status* of those years to be maintained.[1]

The conclusion at which he arrived.

Mr Bell, who was appointed to investigate the whole question, submitted an able and voluminous report, of which the following conclusions were accepted by the Government. The first tract of country was Harriana. When George Thomas was finally defeated by the Mahrattas in 1802, nineteen districts fell into their hand: Bheri, Rohtak, Mahem, Hansi, Hissar, Agroha, Burwala, Siwani, Buhal, Ahurwan, Fatahabad, Sirsa, Rania, Bhatner, Sufidun, Dhatrat, Jamalpur, Tohana, and Kassuhan. Of these, the first thirteen were placed immediately under Sindhia's officers, and, with the exception of Bhatner, were subsequently annexed to the British dominions. Sufidun and Dhatrat were transferred to Raja Bhag Singh of Jhind, and the last three districts, with the forts of Badsikri and Kanhouri, alone remained in dispute.

The district of Kassuhan.

Kassuhan consisted of 16 villages, originally belonging to Pattiala. It had been conquered by George Thomas in 1798, and again wrested from him by Louis Bourquin, the lieutenant of General Perron, who made it over to the charge of Bhai Lal Singh of Kythal, by whom it was, on the cessation of hostilities, re-transferred to Pattiala, with whom it had remained ever since. This district, with its intervening villages, was adjudged to the Raja of Pattiala.

The district of Gorakpur.

Another strip of land called the Ilaka Gorakpur, and consisting of 15 villages, had been in turn held by

[1] Secretary to Government, Agra, to T. T. Metcalfe, Agent to Governor-General, 11th July 1835.

Thomas and Bourquin, and, on the defeat of Sindhia, had been granted to three Chiefs by the British Government, but, in 1809, had been annexed to British territory. The Raja's claim to this tract was based upon four letters addressed by General Perron and Bourquin to Captain Manuel Deremao, directing him to make over the district to the Raja, and Lord Lake's order guaranteeing all lands in the Raja's possession at the time of Sindhia's overthrow. There was, however, no evidence to show that the Raja had ever possession, and the district was adjudged to the British Government.

The forts of Badsikri and Kanhouri.

The circumstances of the fort of Badsikri were precisely similar to those of Kassuhan, and the claims of the Chief were acknowledged, as also in the case of the fort of Kanhouri, originally belonging to Kythal, wrested from that Chief by Thomas, but recovered previous to 1803.

The districts of Jamalpur and Tohana.

The last Harriana districts for consideration were Jamalpur and Tohana. From 1750 to 1777, they had been overrun by Bhatti and Sikh marauders, and, in the last-named year, were seized by Raja Amar Singh of Pattiala. From 1798 to 1802 they were held by Thomas, and at the time of the Mahratta overthrow by General Perron. The Pattiala Chief certainly did not obtain possession till 1809, for the intervening land was owned by the Bhattis and the right of the British Government was clear. It may be mentioned, to show what peace and security had done for the Cis-Satlej States, that whereas, in 1803, there were in these districts only 11 inhabited estates, in 1836 there were no less than 122. These districts allotted to the English Government were the last affected by the conquests of 1803.

The district of Fatahabad.

The district affected by the conquest of 1809 was Fatahabad, consisting of 46 villages, 25 in possession of

Pattiala, and 21 in possession of Kythal. Raja Amar Singh conquered Fatahabad, Rania, and Sirsa, holding them himself, with the exception of a few villages made over to Nabha and Kythal. In 1783 the country was laid waste by famine, and the next year the Bhattis regained possession and held it till 1811, two years after the annexation of Fatahabad to the British territory. The Sikh Chiefs, having ceased to hold the district in 1783, had no right, and Fatahabad was anew declared British territory.

The district of Sirsa.

Sirsa, in the same way, was in possession of the Bhattis till 1818, when their revolt took place, and the claim of the Sikh Chiefs was disallowed, except to four villages: one of which, Panchiari, was gained by Nabha in 1812, and Singha, Udarthana, and Jhanda, by Pattiala in 1814. Of the remaining 24 villages, 14 were in 1836 in possession of Pattiala, 6 of Kythal, and 3 of Nabha.

The district of Rania.

The Pargannah of Rania was the last for consideration. It was of considerable extent, with 109 inhabited villages, of which 77 were in possession of Pattiala, and the remainder held by Kythal, Nabha, Jhumbah, Arnowli, and Shahzadpur. The claims of these States were absolutely rejected. The district was conquered by the Sikhs under Raja Amar Singh. At his death in 1780, the Bhattis recovered the greater portion of the territory; and, three years after, aided by the great famine, made themselves masters of the remainder, from which time till 1821, three years after the annexation of the Bhatti country to British territory, the Sikhs had held no portion of Rania whatever.[1]

[1] Mr T. Metcalfe to Government, North-Western Provinces, dated 15th September 1836. Government, North-Western Provinces, to Mr Metcalfe, 29th October 1836.

Resident Dehli to Colonel Ochterlony of 9th May 1814, and 14th Novem-

The Government generally admitting these conclusions as correct and final, was yet anxious not to exert its power to obtain anything not justly its due; declared itself willing to take a liberal view of any points that might be really doubtful; and directed the Agent at Ambala to submit any such points for further orders.

The conclusions of Mr Bell generally admitted by Government.

The Home Government, which naturally knew less than the Indian Government of the character of the Sikh Chiefs, was still more anxious to guard what were curiously described as their rights. The Directors' despatch of the 11th February 1838, admitted the principles which had been laid down to regulate the decision of the case as just; but asserted that it was a matter for compromise, and not for arbitrary assertion of right; that if the Sikhs could really prove that General Perron had agreed to give up to them certain districts, to which at that time they asserted their right, and which they were expecting to receive when the country came into possession of the English, then that Lord Lake's guarantee of their actual possessions would be too strictly construed by affirming that the accident of their not having actually received possession cancelled all equitable claim on their part; and, secondly, that any right founded upon the sort of possession which a roving tribe like the Bhattis could be considered to maintain over any country, was not such as would be creditable to English liberality to assert

The scruples of the Home Government, and the principles they asserted.

ber 1816. Sir D. Ochterlony to Resident, 18th May 1814, 17th November 1816, 27th April, 15th June, and 13th September 1817.

Captain Birch to Sir D. Ochterlony, 11th August 1820, and 27th January 1821.

Agent to Governor-General to Mr Clerk, Political Agent, 30th March and 11th May 1836.

Mr Clerk to Agent to Governor-General, 3d May 1836.

Mr Bell's Report, with Agent to Governor-General's letter, dated 15th September. This report, with annexures, fills several volumes.

without qualifications, after allowing the other claimants, without official remonstrance, to expend money in bringing the country into cultivation.

The view of the case taken by the Home Government was a very generous one.

It was no doubt for the Government itself to decide which of their just claims they would resign; but if an officer of Government had acted, without specific orders, in the sense of this despatch, he would have justly deserved censure. Any right which the Sikhs could possess through a promise of General Perron's was as valid as if, previous to the battle of Waterloo, the Emperor Napoleon had promised to give Belgium to Italy. After the complete overthrow of the Emperor, the European powers would hardly have insisted on fulfilling his promise. The Mahrattas held Hissar and Sirsa in 1803, after the overthrow of Thomas, and had given no single acre of it to the Sikhs. It was easy enough to forge letters and papers proving such promise, but it was not pretended that the promise was ever carried with action. No one could say that Perron ever intended to fulfil it. But for the English, the enemies and the conquerors of the Mahrattas, to consider it a point of honour to carry out their promises, was an extravagance of sensitiveness of which, fortunately, very few traces are found in our foreign policy.

The argument might be used more justly in favour of the Bhattis than the Sikhs.

The argument which was used in favour of the Sikh Chiefs, whose audacity was their only title to consideration, might have been employed more logically on behalf of the Bhattis; yet any right of possession which a tribe like the Bhattis could assert was questioned. The Bhattis were certainly a pastoral rather than an agricultural race, but they possessed towns and villages, and the tradition of possession of the very same soil for hundreds of years. If the argument against their claim to possession, drawn from their roving habits, was correct, very few people would be able to maintain their right to the lands of their forefathers, unless strong enough to defy attack.

The conduct of the Maharaja not deserving of consideration.

The outcry made by the Maharaja of Pattiala was loud enough, but it was utterly unreasonable. This Chief had throughout the whole inquiry acted himself, and instigated the other Sikh Chiefs concerned to act in the most contumacious manner. He had refused to acknowledge the right of Mr Ross Bell to make inquiries; he had forbidden the cultivators of the disputed villages to give any information of the time at which they were settled; he had thrown every obstacle in Mr Ross's way, and had thwarted him to the best of his power. The reasons which induced Pattiala to act thus were clear, and were certainly not deserving of the consideration shown to him by the Home Government. The Maharaja was in possession of the whole of the disputed land, and would only lose by the inquiry. For the last twenty years, ever since Mr Fraser had first brought the question of the boundary to the notice of Government, Pattiala had on various pleas and pretexts opposed the settlement of the question, and while the British Government was patiently considering her objections, she was making still further encroachments, and only desired delay in order to strengthen her fraudulent claims. The Pattiala Chief finally refused to arbitrate at all, hoping thus to postpone the settlement of the case indefinitely; but Mr Ross Bell was ordered to decide according to the evidence accumulated, and the result was, as has before been detailed, that a vast tract of land, more than a hundred miles long, and from ten to twenty miles broad, was transferred from the Maharaja of Pattiala to the British Government.

His reasons for opposition to the inquiry.

The reasons against re-opening the case.

There was then no reason for re-opening the case, and many reasons for allowing Mr Ross Bell's decision to remain final. It was hopeless to expect that officers of such knowledge and experience could be found to deal with the case a second time. Before the inquiry was ended, Mr William Fraser had been murdered at Dehli, Sir Charles Metcalfe in 1837 left India for ever, and Mr Ross Bell was sent as Political Officer to Sind, where he soon after died. To re-open the case, decided by officers so distinguished and so complete masters of the subject, was to insure a less just and satisfactory decision. Moreover, if the Maharaja of Pattiala had suffered in any way by the result, he had himself alone to blame. He had done everything in his power to prevent the success of the inquiry, and he richly deserved to suffer for his litigious and dishonest conduct.

Mr Conolly appointed to reconsider the case, A.D. 1840.

The remonstrances of Pattiala had however their effect, and on 1st January 1840, instructions were issued to Mr Conolly to effect some sort of compromise; not in any way surrendering the principle which had been originally laid down, but pressing it against the Sikhs less rigorously. Accordingly, in May 1840 he submitted his report, which was more in favour of the Sikhs than the report of Mr Ross Bell had been adverse to them. He proposed to give up the most valuable portion of the Hissar district, and his conclusions were accepted by the North-Western Provinces Government; and from the report of the Collector of Hissar, the following tabular statement is taken, which shows the financial result of Mr Conolly's decision, so far as the Hissar district was concerned.[1]

His report on the Hissar boundary.

[1] Mr Conolly's Reports, dated 5th December 1839, and 23d May 1840. Secretary to Government of India to North-Western Provinces Govern-

	No.	Cultivation in Acres.	Total Area in Acres.	Approximate Value.
				Rs.
Villages to be restored	119	99,403	272,415	90,000
Villages to be retained	147	68,788	255,623	60,000
TOTAL, . .	266	168,191	528,038	1,50,000

After Mr Bell's decision had given so large a tract of country to the British Government, Sirsa, Rania, and Ubohar were separated from Hissar and formed into a new district under the name of Sirsa. On this frontier, Mr Conolly also reported. He was inclined to give up forty or fifty villages, but the want of an accurate map prevented him from making definite proposals.

No definite proposals submitted with reference to Sirsa.

The Maharaja of Pattiala, although he had obtained so much when he had right to nothing, still held out with characteristic obstinacy, and asserted his right to the whole of the tract. He drew upon himself a just rebuke from Government, and was directed either to accept the decision or reject it, in which case the whole tract would be at once resumed by Government.[1]

The Maharaja still discontented.

This language brought him to his senses, and he consented to take over the villages assigned to him on the Hissar frontier, and was paid their revenue, less 20 per cent. for the cost of management, from the time that they had been in English possession. This final transfer was made in April 1842, since which time perfect tranquillity has existed on the Hissar frontier.

The Hissar boundary finally settled, April 1842.

The proposals of Mr Conolly with regard to the Bhattiana frontier, through not precise as to the number or

The Bhattiana frontier still undecided.

ment 7th January 1840. Resolution of North-Western Provinces Government, dated August 1840. Collector of Hissar to Government, North-Western Provinces, 23d September 1840.

[1] Secretary to Government, North-Western Provinces, dated 11th April and 7th August 1841, to Political Agent, Ambala.

names of villages, for want of sufficient information, included the cession to Pattiala of the waste land adjoining her border villages. He assumed that the inhabitants of these villages must have made some use of the waste land for grazing, and proposed to surrender all that was within the ordinary range of occupation from Sikh villages.

Mr Conolly's opinion.

His principle accepted by the North-Western Provinces Government.

The Government of North-Western Provinces, while remarking on the indistinctness of the proposal, adopted and confirmed the principle, on Mr Conolly's assurance that it was capable of being practically worked out; and Captain William Brown was directed to survey the country, and Captain Robinson, the Superintendent of Hissar, to decide on the villages to be ceded. The survey was completed in 1842, and Captain Robinson sent his results to Mr Conolly, at Rai Bareilly, for approval, who replied that the proposed line of border was in exact accordance with the principles he had suggested in his report of the 6th August 1840.

The Sirsa country surveyed, A.D. 1842.

The Report of the Superintendent of Hissar.

The report of Captain Robinson mentioned 42 villages to be restored to Pattiala, and 102 to be retained.[1] But on this report no action was taken. The Maharaja was himself to blame for much of the delay. He refused to negotiate with Mr Conolly, as he had before refused to negotiate with Mr Bell; and in April 1841, it was intimated to him that he must accept this compromise, or the Government would decline to give him anything at all. He obstructed the officers engaged in the survey of the tract,[2] and in 1844, Colonel Richmond, writing to the North-Western Provinces Government,[3] states that the Maharaja still continued to brood over what he considered

[1] Report, dated 23d March 1843.
[2] Do. para. 91.
[3] No. 162, dated 9th September 1844.

a deprivation of territory. Lastly, Colonel H. Lawrence, in 1846, informed the Governor-General[1] that the Maharaja had again revived the boundary dispute "in a very disrespectful *critique* on the orders of Government, and especially on the amended judgment given by Mr Conolly;" and finally recommended that he should be rebuked for his litigious spirit, and given a month to finally make up his mind.

Reasons for delay in the settlement of the question.

The Sikh war then broke out, and prevented the disposal of the case, which was transferred from Agra to Lahore; then the second Sikh war and the annexation of the Punjab, and it was not till 1850-51, that Mr Edmonstone, Commissioner, Cis-Satlej States, attempted to settle the dispute; but he could not find leisure to dispose of it, and Mr G. Barnes, his successor, finally reported on it in 1855.[2]

The final report of Mr G. Barnes.

His proposals were unfavourable to the Maharaja. He considered that, although Pattiala was really entitled to nothing, yet that the principle asserted by Government having been approved, something must be given. No details were, however, sanctioned, and it was for the Government to give what they thought expedient and just. He accordingly proposed to give twenty villages, or, if this was considered insufficient, seven more, specially selected with reference to the configuration of the frontier, and the necessity of preserving the customs line which had been established with great labour and expense. All the villages inconveniently near the customs line Mr Barnes proposed to retain.

The Chief Commissioner of the Punjab did not agree

[1] No. 205, dated 26th September 1846.
[2] Commissioner, Cis-Satlej States, to Punjab Government, No. 219, dated 22d September 1855.

The opinion of the Punjab Government.

with these proposals. He admitted that Colonel Richmond's letters and the Maharaja's replies[1] proved that the latter had not agreed to the decision made by Mr Conolly, and that the Lieutenant-Governor of the North-Western Provinces, with the sanction of the Supreme Government, had intimated that if Pattiala did not accept the terms, the offer would be cancelled.[2]

But this threat had never been formally carried into effect: the discussion on the question had been several times renewed, and the Maharaja had been permitted to urge his claims again and again. Some delay moreover was due to the action of the British Government, and the revenue of the tract made over to Pattiala might fairly be paid her from 1843. As to the number of villages to be ceded, although the Government was not strictly bound by the arrangements of 1845, no orders having been issued on Captain Robinson's report, yet there was no doubt that by the spirit of Mr Conolly's award, which had been approved by the Government, Pattiala should receive the forty-one villages proposed by him, or their fair equivalent if inconvenience would arise from the customs line passing through foreign territory.[3]

The final orders in the case, A.D. 1856.

The Supreme Government made no secret of their regret that the question, after its decision by Mr Ross Bell, had been re-opened; but this step having been taken, and the Government having accepted Mr Conolly's award, it was necessary to abide by it. The Government accordingly approved of the villages suggested by the

[1] Letters from Maharaja, Pattiala, to Agent to Governor-General, dated 29th February 1841, 26th April 1842, 27th April 1844, 8th April 1848. Colonel Richmond to Maharaja, 17th February 1844, 15th April 1844.

[2] To Agent to Governor-General, Ambala, 7th September 1841.

[3] Chief Commissioner to Government of India, No. 9, dated 7th January 1856.

Commissioner, Cis-Satlej States, and others, making 41 in all, as originally proposed, being given to the Maharaja, with arrears of revenue from 1843 to 1st May 1856.[1]

There was some difficulty in arranging the transfer of villages, and the North-Western Provinces Government objected to several being given up on account of the existing arrangements of the customs line; but, eventually, this objection was withdrawn. Twenty-six villages were made over by the Superintendent of Bhattiana, and, for the balance of revenue still due, Rs. 4131, the Bhadour Sirdars transferred to the Maharaja the 5 villages of Aspal, Mandehar, Suhoki, Baini, and Bhadra, worth Rs. 4120 per annum; being compensated by an assignment on the revenues of Government villages to a like amount.[2] The transfer of villages.

This long dispute, the origin of which was in 1803, and the conclusion in 1856, has deserved attention from the great intricacy of the questions involved, the large interests at stake, and the obstinacy with which every inch of ground was contested by the Maharaja of Pattiala. If so much importunity and obstinacy were successful, they almost deserved success; and if the British The importance of the case.

[1] Supreme Government to Government, Punjab, No. 1251, dated 28th February 1856.

[2] Commissioner, Cis-Satlej States, to Government, Punjab, No. 159, dated 16th June; and Government, Punjab, to Commissioner, Cis-Satlej States, No. 547, dated 8th July 1856.

Government, North-Western Provinces, to Government of India, No. 2218, dated 31st March 1856. Government of India to Government North-Western Provinces, No. 2274, dated 25th April. Officiating Commissioner, Customs, North-Western Provinces, to Government, North-Western Provinces, No. 45, dated 10th March. Secretary to Government, Punjab, to Government, North-Western Provinces, 11th January and 12th April. Government, North-Western Provinces, to Government of India, No. 3102, dated 29th May. Government of India to Government, Punjab, No. 3412, dated 20th June.

Government, in the final decision, obtained far less than was its clear right, it could, at least, afford to be magnanimous.

It is now necessary to go back in the history of Pattiala, and allude to its connection with the Kythal State. Bhai Udey Singh, the last Chief, was bedridden for some years before his death, and unable to keep his State in order. This indeed he was always too weak and debauched to do; but, in 1838 and 1839, the disorder and affrays on the Kythal and Pattiala frontier became so serious, that trade was interrupted, and the peace of the whole country disturbed.[1] In the time of Bhai Lal Singh the two States had been firm friends, but now they secretly encouraged acts of plunder and aggression on each other's villages. Bands of armed men, 300 or 400 in number, would openly assemble, cross the border, plunder and burn villages, and kill the inhabitants, till all the smaller villages in the neighbourhood were deserted. This state of things was only partially stopped by a strong remonstrance addressed by the British authorities to the several Chiefs, insisting upon their putting an end to disorder, which not only injured their own territory, but that of the British Government.[2]

The Kythal State and its Pattiala frontier, A.D. 1838.

The disorder which prevailed.

The death of Bhai Udey Singh, March 1843, and the lapse of the Kythal territory.

Bhai Udey Singh of Kythal died on the 15th of March 1843, and the Chiefship, with territory to the amount of one lakh of rupees per annum, devolved upon Bhai

[1] Despatch of Court of Directors, dated 13th February 1838, to Government of India.

Government of India to Agent to Governor-General, Dehli, 28th July 1838.

[2] Mr S. S. Brown, Magistrate, Western Division, Dehli Frontier, to Agent to Governor-General, 18th September 1839.

Agent to Governor-General to Political Agent, Ambala, dated 26th September 1839.

Gulab Singh of Arnowli, while the remaining territory, including Kythal, and worth about four lakhs of rupees per annum, escheated to the British Government. To the Rajas of Pattiala, Nabha, and Jhind, this lapse was odious. They were connected with the Bhais of Kythal, and they wished to retain the whole of their large possessions in the family; and they also imagined that the precedent was one which might be, at some future day, employed against themselves. The Pattiala Raja had other and more personal motives. Bhai Udey Singh had lent to Ajit Singh, the spendthrift brother of Raja Karam Singh, large sums of money, and he feared that the British Government might exact payment of the bonds from him. He therefore prepared to oppose, as far as was safe, the resumption of the estate; and his agents, with those of the other Rajas, went to Kythal, where Mr Greathed had arrived on a special mission to enforce immediate compliance with the demands of Government. The Kythal ministers would not give any definite answer to these demands, and the Envoy addressed the Phulkian Rajas, desiring them to withdraw their deputies from the Kythal Council, as otherwise they would incur the imputation of supporting the contumacy displayed. At first some disposition was shown to disregard this request; but, on a serious warning being addressed to the Rajas, they withdrew their special agents, and directed those ordinarily in attendance to confine their communications with Kythal to the forms of condolence and to admonitions against disobedience of the orders of Government.[1]

The Phulkian Chiefs prepared to resist the British occupation of Kythal.

[1] Mr Clerk, Envoy to Court of Lahore, to Government of India, 16th March 1843; to Mr Greathed, 13th March; to Raja of Pattiala, 17th, 27th, 30th March. Mr Greathed to Envoy to Lahore, 25th and 27th March, and 8th April; to Raja of Pattiala, 24th March.

The result of their intrigues.

But their intrigues had already produced sufficient mischief, and, on the 10th April, an insurrection broke out at Kythal, which soon became general, and which the force with Mr Greathed was not strong enough to repress. Reinforcements, however, quickly arrived, and the town and fort of Kythal were soon in possession of the British. The Maharaja of Pattiala now thought it time to show his loyalty, and, with 1000 horse and two guns, surrounded the party of Teg Singh, the leader of the insurgents, who had fled from Kythal, and after a short skirmish, in which a few men were killed and wounded on either side, took him prisoner. Several other leaders of less note he also intercepted and captured. With Teg Singh were taken four elephants, two brass guns, one lakh and a half of rupees, and a considerable quantity of other property, all of which the Raja forwarded to Mr G. Clerk at Ambala.[1]

The insurrection of Kythal suppressed. The action of Pattiala.

The Chiefs still dissatisfied, and attempt to prevent the resumption, which is effected in 1844.

The insurrection was crushed as speedily as it had broken out, but the Rajas were no better pleased than before at seeing the Kythal estate pass out of the hands of the then representative of the family. The British Government had ruled that only the acquisitions of Bhai Gurbaksh Singh, the great-grandfather of the chief recently deceased, and of his second cousin Gulab Singh, the new claimant, should be inherited by the latter, and the amount of these acquisitions it was most difficult to determine. The Rajas, who alone could give accurate information, at first declared ignorance of the matter; and, at last, only replied in general terms, urging the claims of the nearest of kin or of the widow to the whole

1 Mr Clerk to Government of India, 11th, 17th, and 25th April; to Raja of Pattiala, 11th, 12th, and 14th April 1843. Mr Greathed to Mr Clerk, 10th April. Rajah of Pattiala to Mr Clerk, 13th, 15th, and 16th April 1843.

of the territory. Their objections were, however, set aside, and the case finally settled at the close of 1844.[1]

The feeling of the Cis-Satlej Chiefs in 1845 unfriendly to the English Government.

The beginning of the year 1845 did not find any of the great Sikh Chiefs south of the Satlej well disposed towards the English Government. The disastrous campaign in Afghanistan had produced upon them an effect even more powerful than on the Lahore Court, which, presided over by a series of adventurers and debauchees, whose only thought was of personal advantage and degrading pleasures, allowed the country to drift helplessly into the war, which was in one sense its ruin, and in another its salvation. But the Cis-Satlej Chiefs had abundant leisure to observe the signs of the times. From Sir David Ochterlony's first advent till the Afghan campaign they had been governed with a strong hand. They had understood that it was the British power alone which had saved them from absorption by Maharaja Ranjit Singh; and they had believed that this power was invincible, since they had never seen it successfully opposed. But the result of the Kabul expedition dispelled this belief. Seeing that their resources, in money and supplies, were required for the English armies, they began to think that they were necessary to the existence of the British power, not that it was essential to their own. All fear of the Lahore Monarchy was now over; there was no longer a strong and sagacious ruler like Ranjit Singh, who made British protection sound pleasantly in the ears of neighbouring princes; and this protection now seemed little more than a restraint, without which each Chief

[1] Colonel Richmond, Agent to Governor-General, to Government of India, 14th October 1844. Maharaja of Pattiala to Agent to Governor-General, 29th September. Secretary to Government, North-Western Provinces, to Major Broadfoot, Agent to Governor-General, 28th December 1844. Court of Directors' Despatch, No. 33, dated 25th October 1843.

fancied that he himself might play the part which, under similar circumstances, the Raja of Lahore had played with so much brilliancy and success.

The jealousy between Pattiala, Jhind, and Nabha.

There were, however, certain indications that, in any conflict with the Sikhs which might be approaching, and which some knew to be inevitable, the Phulkian Chiefs would take different sides. The Pattiala and Jhind Rajas felt a bitter and inveterate hostility to the Raja of Nabha, whose imbecilities and their punishment have been detailed elsewhere. Raja Devindar Singh of Nabha was the natural head of the Phulkian house, the representative of the elder branch of the family, and the hereditary "chaudhrí:" a title which the Chiefs had held when they were still zamindars, and which they were proud to retain.

The absurd claims of the Nabha Raja.

Of Pattiala, which possessed five times his income and territory, he had always been jealous, and his great desire was to obtain from the British Government the title of Maharaja, and precedence of Pattiala, the Chief of which he would never permit to be named in his presence by a higher title than Raja. The Jhind Chief he treated with contempt, affecting to consider him not entitled to the rank of Raja at all, being only collaterally related to the former Chiefs. Both these States were thus inclined to oppose any cause which the Raja of Nabha favoured, and one reason of the latter's hostility during the war was the hope that the Sikhs would allow him to assert the supremacy over Pattiala, which was the first desire of his heart.

The loyalty of Pattiala in 1845.

When hostilities with the Lahore Government became certain, at the close of 1845, Maharaja Karam Singh declared his loyalty and devotion to the British Government, and his readiness to furnish all necessary supplies for the army, and a contingent for active service. But he was at this time dangerously ill, and, anxiety completing what disease had begun, he died on the 23d of December, the day after the battle of Firushahr, and was succeeded by his son Narindar Singh, then twenty-three years of age.

Death of Maharaja Karam Singh, A.D. 1845.

The new Chief was even better disposed towards the British Government than his father had been; but it would be idle to assert that in him or in any Sikh Chief south of the Satlej, there existed, at this time, an active spirit of loyalty, such as, in 1857, induced this very Prince to strain every nerve, and enlist every available man to fight for the English; or which led the Rajas of Jhind and Kapurthalla to head their troops and help Englishmen to capture Dehli and reconquer Oude. In 1845 the feeling south of the Satlej was strongly in favour of the Khalsa; and although the Chiefs of Pattiala and Jhind knew that their interests were bound up with those of the English, their sympathies were with Lahore. No information was given to the British authorities of the intention of the Sikh army to cross the Satlej on the 11th of December; although this intention was well known to every Chief south of that river, where every Jat village contained soldiers of the Lahore army, regular or irregular, by whom a constant communication was kept up with the "Panches," or Committees, of the army, and to whom the intention to invade British territory was universally confided.

Maharaja Narindar Singh succeeds.

The sympathies of the Pattiala Chiefs with Lahore.

No information of the intention of the Sikh army to cross the Satlej given to the English authorities.

Yet, in comparison with other States, Pattiala did good service, as Major Mackeson, Captain Mills, and Mr Cust have testified. From the first, supplies and carriage were freely given, and the conduct of the contingent only proved that the authorities at Pattiala were not always

Pattiala furnished supplies and behaved fairly, though unable to keep her troops steady.

able to control troops whose sympathies were with the Lahore army. At the investment of Gongrana the contingent behaved well, though it was unsuccessful in intercepting the garrison when they vacated the fort; but a detachment of the same contingent, consisting of 200 horse, had, on a previous occasion, when garrisoning Badhowal for the English, given up that post without a struggle to an overwhelming force of Sikhs, which the contingent joined in a body, a desertion at the time highly prejudicial to the English cause.[1]

The Maharaja rewarded for his services.

At the conclusion of the war the Maharaja of Pattiala was rewarded for his services by the grant of a *Sanad* expressing the high sense which the Government entertained of his loyalty,[2] and of certain estates resumed from

[1] From Major Mackeson, Commissioner, Cis-Satlej States, to Agent to Governor-General, of 27th July 1846. Agent to Governor-General to Government of India, 18th September 1846. Mr R. Cust, Assistant-Agent to Governor-General, to Commissioner, Cis-Satlej States, of 7th March 1846.

Captain Mills, Assistant-Agent to Governor-General, to Commissioner, Cis-Satlej States, 1st February 1846.

Parwanas from the office of Agent to Governor-General to Pattiala authorities, of 27th December 1845, 9th, 13th, 14th, 15th, 17th January, and 13th February 1846. Major Broadfoot, Agent to Governor-General, to Government of India, 26th April 1845.

[2] Sanad to the Maharaja of Pattiala, dated 22d September 1847 :—

"The Right Honourable the Governor-General having resolved to bestow certain lands on the Raja of Pattiala, as a mark of consideration for his attachment and services to the British during the late war with the Lahore State, and the Raja of Pattiala having requested that he may at the same time receive a renewed assurance of protection and guarantee of his rights in his former possessions, the Governor-General is pleased to confer this assurance in the form of a Sanad or grant as follows, in order that the Maharaja, and his successors after him, may, with perfect confidence, continue to exercise the same rights and authority in his possessions as heretofore.

"The Maharaja's ancient hereditary estates, according to annexed schedule, shall continue for ever in the possession of himself and his successors, with all Government rights thereto belonging of police jurisdiction and collection of revenue as heretofore. The Maharaja's chaharumians, feudatories, adherents, and dependants, will continue bound in their adherence and obligations to the Raja as heretofore. His Highness will exert himself to do justice and to promote the welfare and happiness of his subjects, while

the Raja of Nabha. Lands to the value of a lakh of rupees per annum, belonging to this Chief, were confiscated; of which Rs. 22,766, were taken by the British Government as commutation for the service of horse, and the remainder, Rs. 71,224, divided equally between Pattiala and Faridkot. The Maharaja also received a gift of a house belonging to the rebel Raja of Ladwa, situated at Hardwar.[1]

The change effected by the Sikh war in the relations of the British Government with the Cis-Satlej States.

The services, the ingratitude, the rewards, and the punishments of the great Cis-Satlej Chiefs, will be recorded in detail in their family histories; but, as Pat-

they, on their part, considering the Raja as their true and rightful lord, must obey him and his successors accordingly, and pay the revenue punctually, and be always zealous to promote the cultivation of their lands, and to testify their loyalty and obedience. The Maharaja has relinquished for himself and his successors for ever all right to levy excise and transit duties, which have been abolished throughout the Pattiala territory. His Highness also binds himself and his successors to the suppression of suttee, infanticide, and slave dealings within his territories. If, unknown to the Maharaja's authorities, any person should be guilty of these acts, the Maharaja's authorities will, on conviction, punish them with such severity as to deter others. The British Government will never demand from the Maharaja and his successors and their dependants above-named anything in the way of tribute or revenue or commutation in lieu of troops or otherwise, for the reason that his Highness will ever continue as heretofore sincerely devoted to the service and interests of the British. The British authorities will not entertain complaints of the Maharaja's subjects or dependants, or interfere with the Maharaja's authority. Should an enemy approach from any quarter to this side the Beas or Satlej for the purpose of conquering this country, the Raja will join the British army with his forces, and exert himself in expelling the enemy, and act under discipline and obedience; and in time of war place the resources of his country at the disposal of the British Government. His Highness engages to have made and to keep in repairs, through his own officers, the military roads through his territory, for the passage of British troops from Umballa and other stations to Ferozpore, of a width and elevation to be determined on by the engineer officer charged with the duty of laying down the roads. His Highness will also appoint encamping grounds for British troops at the different stages, which shall be marked off, so that there be no claims made hereafter on account of damaged crops."

[1] Government of India to Agent to Governor-General, 1st May 1846.

Agent to Governor-General to Commissioner, Cis-Satlej States, 9th May 1846.

Agent to Governor-General to Government of India, 18th September 1846.

tiala is the representative and head of all, it is necessary to explain here the effect which the Sikh war had upon the general relations of the British Government with the States, small and large, south of the Satlej. It has been seen that from the year 1809, when the Chiefs were taken under British protection, till 1845, their relations with the Government had undergone no change. Protected by the proclamation of 1809 against the ambition of Lahore, and by that of 1811 from one another, the Cis-Satlej Chiefs had enjoyed thirty-six years of absolute peace and security. No tribute was demanded from them, though they were required to aid the Government with all their force in the event of war; but no special contingent had been fixed, and through all these years no occasion had arisen to test their fidelity and their gratitude. They were allowed absolute civil, criminal, and fiscal jurisdiction within their respective territories, subject to the general authority of the Governor-General's Agent, while the Government most scrupulously abstained from any interference with their internal and domestic affairs. To the Cis-Satlej Chiefs the British Government had been an unmixed good. Under its strong protection, which asked for no return save good conduct and loyalty, they had greatly prospered. To the north of that river which had been fixed as the boundary of Ranjit Singh's ambition, there was, in 1845, no independent Chief whatever, with the exception of Nihal Singh Ahluwalia, whose existence, always precarious, was only due to the indirect action of the British Government. Every one else had fallen before the strong, shrewd, faithless ruler of Lahore. The great Katoch family of Kangar, which had ruled in the hills through all historic time, had been driven as exiles from the Pun-

The advantages which British protection had given the Chiefs.

The contrast between their position, and that of the country north of the Satlej.

jab; Mandi and Suket were Sikh provinces; the ancient tribes of the north, the Ghakkars, the Awâns, the Janjoahs, who had held their own against the Emperors of Dehli, were now tenants on the lands which they had once ruled as lords; the Afghans had been driven beyond the Khyber; and the whole frontier side, after a thousand fights, had been compelled to acknowledge Lahore as supreme: Kashmir had been conquered, and the chivalrous ruler of Multan had been slain with his sons in the hopeless defence of his capital.

South of the Satlej there had been neither war nor conquest. With the exception of a few estates which had lapsed from failure of heirs, the descendants of the Chiefs who had welcomed Sir David Ochterlony in 1809 still ruled over the territory which they at that time possessed.

The ingratitude of the Chiefs and their punishment.

Their prosperity had been so great; the benefits which British protection had conferred on them were so undeniable, and ingratitude for benefits conferred is so certain, that it was no matter for surprise when at the first opportunity certain Chiefs turned against the power which had befriended them, and openly or secretly joined the ranks of its enemies. But the British Government was still strong to punish. The Raja of Nabha was deposed, and one-fourth of his territories confiscated and divided among the faithful allies of the English. All the Cis-Satlej possessions of the Raja of Kapurthalla were forfeited; the Chiefs of Ladwa and Rupar were removed as prisoners from the province, and the whole of their estates confiscated, as was that of the Sodhis of Anandpur.

The relations of Government and the Chiefs undergo a change.

But the time had arrived when an entire change in the character of the relations of the Government with the

Chiefs had become necessary. There was nothing whatever to admire in the internal management or administration of their States, and there was certainly no sign that the people preferred native rule—the rule of their own hereditary Chiefs—to that of the English. The history of every State proves that the reverse was the case, and that it was with the universal satisfaction of the peasants that any estate came under the direct management of the British Government. Thirty-six years of peace had somewhat tamed the barbarous Sikh barons; but their civilisation was still imperfect, and their progress had not been such as to wipe out the memory of the days when their administration was but an organised system of rapacity and oppression; when each one did what seemed most advantageous to himself, without any thought of the rights or wrongs of others; when fraud of the grossest kind, debauchery the most degrading, and an entire absence of any principle of truth and honour, were the characteristics of almost every Sikh State south of the Satlej.

Their mal-administration.

Nor had the majority of the Chiefs shown their loyalty in 1845 in any more conspicuous manner than in not joining the enemy. Gratitude they did not understand, and to show them any special consideration at the close of the campaign was unnecessary. Several most important measures were then adopted by the Government. The first was the abolition of all police jurisdiction in most of the States; for the existing system was so favourable to crime that, in the midst of half a hundred conflicting authorities, the capture of a criminal was well nigh impossible. The second measure was the abolition of transit and custom duties, which were as injurious to trade as the police system was fatal to justice; and

Several important reforms introduced.

the last was to accept a commutation for the personal service of the Chief and his contingent.

The following are extracts from the despatch of the Governor-General of the 17th November 1846, giving his views at length, and the resolution at which he had arrived :—

1. "It is impossible to read the reports drawn up by Lieutenant-Colonel Lawrence, C.B., and Major Mackeson, C.B., and to examine the documents by which their proposals are supported, without coming to the conclusion that it is the duty of the Government of India to correct the inefficiency and danger inherent in the present system of our relations with the Sikh Protected States, provided the remedies to be applied can be reconciled with justice and good faith.

The views of the Governor-General on the sentiments of the Chiefs and people of the Cis-Satlej in 1845, and the policy necessary to adopt towards them.

2. "This system has lasted for nearly forty years, during which period, judging from the experience of the last campaign, no progress has been made in gaining the attachment of the Sikh population under British protection. The people seldom have any opportunity of feeling the benefits of British rule, being in all their internal affairs governed by their own native Chiefs. Although of warlike and predatory habits, they were never taken into our service, whilst their own national and religious feelings disposed them to consider the Sikh army, into whose ranks they were admitted by thousands, as composed of friends and relations. The Panchayat system—good pay and loose discipline—was infinitely more agreeable to their habits than the stricter system of our regular system.

3. "Our protection was felt by the Chiefs during Ranjit Singh's career of conquest, but as regards the people of these States, our intercourse was not of a

nature, by the benefits we could confer, to secure their attachment.

4. "Every village had some relations in the Sikh ranks, and if questioned by our officers to what regiment he belonged, the soldier usually replied in a tone of defiance that he was a soldier of the Khalsa army on furlough at his native home. On the breaking out of the war, these men came over to their villages as emissaries, and whenever the hostile feeling against the British Government could be prudently exerted, no occasion was omitted for so doing by intercepting stragglers and plundering baggage. Even in the case of the troops of the Maharaja of Pattiala, the most faithful of our adherents, when the affair of Buddeewal was going against us and the baggage was sent off from the main body, the whole of the Pattiala cavalry, about 200 in number, went over bodily to the enemy, and the villagers in the rear cut up our sick and plundered the camp-followers. This force employed at Loodiana conveyed daily information to the enemy. I notice these facts because this contingent was esteemed to be the most trustworthy, in consequence of the fidelity of their Chief to the British cause.

5. "It is scarcely necessary to dwell upon the fact that the hearts of the Sikh population in our protected States were with the men of their own tribe and sect, and decidedly averse to the British Government.

6. "The disaffection to the British power, which for years had protected them, may be said to have been almost universal from the Jamna to the Satlej, with the exception of a few villages which for years had been administered by British officers.

7. "The great majority of the petty Chiefs, some of

whom held offices at Lahore, and to many of whom the Lahore service held out the prospect of making their fortunes, were as adverse as their own ryots to the British Government; in fact, neither these petty Chiefs nor their ryots derive any direct and manifest advantages from British protection. The door for employment with us is closed against them; with the Lahore Government it was open.

8. "Throughout the Lahore districts and the Aloowala estates, now about to be brought under the direct superintendence of British officers, the case will be different. Liberal assessments and strict justice over the Sikh States ceded to us, will, I should hope, in a short time create a feeling very favourable to British rule, as contrasted with that of the native Chiefs. The estates now belonging to the East India Company will comprise about one-half of the territory between the Jamna and the Satlej.

9. "But these papers demonstrate that the hostility was not confined to the less wealthy Chiefs.

10. "The Raja of Ladwa, with an estate of £10,000 a year, almost openly avowed his treason, and, after a time, went over to the enemy with all his troops and artillery.

11. "The Raja of Nabha, with an estate of £40,000 a year, did not hesitate openly to defy the British Authorities by a total disregard of the orders he received.

12. "At the time when this hostile feeling was so unequivocally expressed, the British army had been successful in capturing 100 pieces of the enemy's artillery, and in compelling the Sikh army to cross the Satlej.

13. "There can be no doubt, if we had suffered reverses, that, as in the case of the Pattiala troops at Buddeewal, the contingents would have joined the enemy,

and we should have had a general rising of the population in our rear as far east as Kurnal, cutting off our supplies and our small detachments, and making war upon us to the knife.

14. "When the war suddenly broke out I felt, notwithstanding this hostile feeling on the part of the population, that it was quite impossible to apply a military remedy by detachments in sufficient strength to keep up our communication with the rear. This could only be partially and occasionally done by the regiments marching up to the south; no detached forces could be afforded of sufficient strength. It was absolutely necessary to concentrate every man where the battle was to be fought, against a well-appointed and well-drilled army, inferior to none in Asia for its courage and its national pride, and superior to every other native army except our own, from its European system of discipline.

15. "Minor points were risked by bringing away 5000 men and 12 field guns from Loodiana; the same measure was adopted at Ferozepur on the 21st December; and my deliberate conviction is, that if the British army had concentrated its forces on Ambala, allowing the Sikh army to advance through the protected States to meet us, that the whole population would have risen in arms against us.

16. "I state this conviction in reference to the policy of the questions now before me in these reports.

17. "There can be no doubt that the security of this part of the country demands a modification of the existing system, as far as it can be effected, consistently with good faith and an adherence to treaty.

18. "These papers incontrovertibly show the existence of a disaffected feeling on the part of the Chiefs

and the people, either by overt acts, or by neglecting to obey orders, which they were lawfully bound to fulfil.

19. "The refusal to obey the orders given to afford supplies, and to join the British army with their contingents, is clearly established by proof. The evidence is ample to justify the general measures proposed of no longer permitting these States to raise contingents of their own, but to pay to the British Government a ratable annual sum in lieu of personal service. These contingents were not forthcoming when wanted: the disobedience was wilful and almost universal, and by the 4th and 5th Articles of the Declaration of Protection, these obligations are laid down in the most precise terms—*viz.*, that the contingents are bound to join the British forces in war, and their Chiefs to provide supplies. This betrayal of their duty did not arise from any want of power to fulfil the requisitions made on them. Supplies came in most abundantly as soon as the struggle was decided, and not before.

20. "The delay was persisted in for the purpose of impeding the operations of the British army at a most important crisis, by crippling our means of movement; and after the experience of the past, it can never be tolerated that the territories under British protection, who pay no taxes and contribute nothing to the State, shall furnish from 10,000 to 15,000 soldiers to the ranks of a neighbouring power, and shall, in time of war, evade, with impunity, to fulfil the very moderate demands which the paramount power has thought it right to exact.

21. "These States have, in reality (with very few exceptions), forfeited their privileges by their repeated acts of disaffection and disobedience during the war; they have shown that their contingents are not to be depended upon; they cannot be distinguished from the

enemy; they are neither an efficient nor a faithful force; and are worse than useless, for they are positively dangerous.

22. "To abolish the existing practice of each petty Chief furnishing his contingent for the service of the paramount power, and substituting in lieu of it local corps, commanded by our European officers, recruited from the Sikh population, and paid by the Sikh Chiefs indirectly, will, to a certain extent, remedy the mischief of the present system.

23. "I therefore, without hesitation, sanction the proposition, that the moderate rate proposed shall be taken in commutation of personal service, making the exceptions recommended by the Political Agent, and including the Chief of Mamdot in the number of the excepted Chiefs.

24. "I also sanction, on the same ground—*viz.*, that these States have forfeited their privileges by their disobedience—the abolition of all transit and custom duties, which, levied through so many independent small States, is a system most ruinous to the trade of the country, and ought to be, as it has been in our Provinces, abolished. I approve of the exceptions to be made in favour of the Chiefs who conducted themselves with loyalty to the British Government, and I trust the equivalents for their loss by the abolition will be given so as to afford satisfaction.

25. "I also entirely approve of the proposal to take this opportunity of settling the rules of succession to property, by a recorded declaration of what the rule is to be for the future in the families of the landholders.

27. "With regard to paras. 16 and 17, proposing to resume all the Sikh Protected States, and then granting new Sanads from the Government, I consider the same ends will be obtained by carrying out the proposals of

the Political Agent, as detailed in the preceding paras. to 16 and 17 which I have sanctioned. A general measure of resumption would create alarm, and must be preceded by a public declaration of the disloyalty of the largest portion of the Sikh Protected States, explaining the grounds of forfeiture, which general measure, not being absolutely necessary, had better be avoided. The object in view seems to be as well obtained without it.

28. "I therefore prefer to apply the remedies proposed, as being justified by the misconduct of the Chiefs during the late war, without proclaiming that misconduct to all India.

29. "The preceding observations apply to the general measure proposed."

The States exempted from the operation of the reforms.

The only States exempted from the action of these reforms were Pattiala, Jhind, Faridkot, Maler Kotla, Chichrowli, (Kalsia) Raikot, Buria, and Mamdot.[1] Nabha was treated exceptionally, and part of its punishment was the abolition of all transit duties, with the exception of the customs of the town of Nabha itself.[2] Every care was taken that the changes thus effected should not needlessly offend the susceptibility of the Chiefs, and their persons were exempted from police jurisdiction, except under the direct orders of the Commissioner.

Changes in legal procedure.

These arrangements were completed in March 1847, and a few months later it was ruled that the Chiefs and their subjects were amenable to the British Judicial Courts, if the defendant resided within jurisdiction of these Courts, or if the cause of action arose there. But if the de-

[1] The States of Raikot and Buria have since lapsed: Mamdot was annexed in 1855 for the gross mis-government of the Chief, but on his death in 1863 was restored to his brother, who, however, has no fiscal jurisdiction.

[2] Secretary to Government to Agent to Governor-General, 17th November 1846.

fendant was a subject of an independent State, and the cause of action arose in such State, the case was not cognisable by the British Courts. Nor could any authority be exercised over the person or property of a foreign subject amenable to the Courts, when he was beyond its jurisdiction. In that case a notice was directed to be served on the defendant, though the agency of the Political Officer; and should he not appear, an *ex parte* judgment would be given, and the decree, if granted againt the defendant, would be executed against any property he might possess within the jurisdiction of the Court, or against his person if found therein.[1]

The abolition of police jurisdiction somewhat inconvenient.

After a short trial it was found that, when their police jurisdiction was gone, the Chiefs were unable to collect their revenue, and the Commissioner proposed the execution of a regular Settlement to protect the interests of the Chiefs and the people alike. The time for this might perhaps be considered to have not yet arrived, in which case papers might be drawn up for every village, defining the rights and obligations of both parties.

The insurrection of 1848, and the annexation of the Punjab.

But the circumstances of the case again changed before the Government was able to reply to these recommendations. The Sikh army had again taken arms to expel the foreigners who were loyally doing their best to make a Sikh Government possible, and the result was the annexation of the Punjab. From Calcutta to Peshawar the whole country was in the hands of the British, and there were no political reasons, save those arising from considerations of good faith and equity, which could influence the Government in its determination of the amount of power to be left to the Cis-Satlej Chiefs. Accordingly, in June

[1] Chief Commissioner, Punjab, to Commissioner, Cis-Satlej States, dated 9th and 13th June 1848.

1849, it was declared that, with the exception of the nine States before mentioned, all the Chiefs would cease to hold sovereign powers; would lose all civil, criminal, and fiscal jurisdiction; and would be considered as no more than ordinary subjects of the British Government in possession of certain exceptional privileges. The political power of the district officers was abolished, and the Commissioner of Ambala appointed the only referee in disputes between the Chiefs. The zamindars were declared to have the power of claiming an assessment in money or grain, or a regular settlement, and records of rights were directed to be prepared; where the British Government held any shares of the estate, no option was permitted, and the whole was to be measured and assessed; and such an estate was to be brought under British jurisdiction in police and revenue matters, even though a sovereign Prince might be a co-sharer; but exchanges of such co-parcenary tenures were permitted to be effected. Regular settlement operations were also to be carried on in estates under the police jurisdiction of the British Government; in those from which an appeal lay to Government, or in the concerns of which the Governor-General's Agent had ever authoritatively interfered; also in those estates which would escheat to Government on failure of heirs, or those held by the sovereign Princes with concurrent police jurisdiction.[1]

Civil, criminal, and fiscal jurisdiction abolished in all the States, save those before mentioned.

With this decision of the British Government fell, for ever, the power of the petty Cis-Satlej Chiefs, who had

The result.

[1] Mr Erskine to Chief Commissioner, Punjab, 7th February 1849. Board of Administration to Commissioner, 8th June 1849. Board to Commissioner, 3d May, 29th June, and 18th October 1849.

For the whole question of escheats and the rights of collaterals, reference must be made to "The Law of Inheritance to Chiefships," by the author of the present work.

too long been permitted to play at independence, which for them had no nobler significance than the right to do evil without restraint, and to oppress the people who were so unfortunate as to be their subjects. It was with a satisfaction, too enthusiastic to be insincere, that the people of these States came under the direct administration of the British Government; while their loyal and peaceable conduct since that time proves that they have not yet found cause to regret the change.

The case of the Chahárumi Sikhs.

The necessary result of the British Government assuming the direct management of so large a portion of the Cis-Satlej territory was the re-adjustment of the relations of those petty Chiefs who were half subject to, and half independent of, the larger States. The most intricate and tedious of the cases which thus arose, related to what were known as *Chahárumi*[1] villages, in which the Maharaja of Pattiala and various petty Sikh Chiefs were co-sharers. Colonel Mackeson had, in 1850,[2] reported to the Board of Administration, with regard to the majority of these villages, declaring them to have rights independent of Pattiala, and, consequently, to be entitled to a separation from her should they so desire. This separation was desired by them, and the Board of Administration reported at length on the subject to the Government of India, which issued orders to at once take up and dispose of the case.[3] The Singhpuria Sirdars

[1] A "Chahárumi" is a sharer entitled to a quarter (*Chahâram*—fourth) of the *gross produce* of the village; two shares, or a half, going to the cultivator, and a quarter to each of the lords of the estate. This is the definition accepted in the Punjab, and by the Chiefs themselves in their depositions before Sir D. Ochterlony in 1816. In the course of the present case, however, Pattiala tried to maintain that the Sikh co-sharers, the Chahárumis, were only entitled to a quarter of the *revenue*.

[2] Colonel Mackeson's Report, No. 16, dated 8th January 1850.

[3] Board of Administration to Government of India, No. 21, dated 6th January 1852.

and the Lidhrán Chiefs had not originally been included by Colonel Mackeson in his Report, but were subsequently added. The *Chahárumi* villages, ninety-seven in number, were grouped into several distinct estates, and the shares held by the Sikhs and by Pattiala had been fixed at the time of their first conquest, when the several Chiefs were stronger and Pattiala weaker, and unable to claim the lion's share of the new territory. In the division of these petty baronies, or co-seigniories, it was directed that the villages should be assigned to the different claimants with regard both to shares and to topographical considerations; that, in those allotted to Pattiala, she would collect the revenue and exercise full jurisdiction, while the Sikh co-sharers would collect the revenue in the villages allotted to them, but in every other respect would be under British jurisdiction.

The principle of division.

The estates affected were the following:—

The estates affected.

	VILLAGES.
Shill,	9
Gurángan,	10
Gudherah,	7
Burás,	4
Todar Májra,	8
Chuni Machhli,	39
Singhpúrah (Banúr),	15
Lidhrán,	5
TOTAL,	97

On these estates, Mr Melvill, Settlement Officer of Ambala, was directed to report, which he did at great length in 1853.[1] The inquiry into the rights of the claimants was one of extreme difficulty. It was necessary to understand in what proportion the shares were

Mr Melville's Report on the case.

Government of India to Board, No. 399, dated 27th February 1852; and Commissioner, Cis-Satlej States, to Settlement Officer, Ambala, No. 1484, dated 5th August 1852.

[1] P. S. Melvill, Esq., No. 128, dated 25th May 1853, to Commissioner, Cis-Satlej States.

held at the first acquisition of the villages; what encroachments had been made; and whether these encroachments had been so recent, or so persistently resisted, as to give the injured party a claim to redress.

Pattiala unscrupulous in her encroachments.

The Pattiala State, as has been several times shown in its history, has felt no scruples in possessing itself of the territories of its weaker neighbours, nor regarding the means of obtaining such possession. Previous to 1809, violence, without any shadow of excuse, was the usual means employed, while, subsequent to that time, fraud, corruption, and intimidation were used, too often with success; for the agents of the British Government could only judge from such evidence as was put before them, and Pattiala evidence was mostly bought, and reference to arbitration was merely reference to persons whose opinions had been, for sufficiently strong reasons, formed in favour of Pattiala, entirely independent of the merits of the case, and indeed before the case had been submitted for their decision.

The final recommendations.

The final recommendations of the Settlement Officer were as follows:—

Designation of Chahárumis.	Pattiala's Share.		Chahárumis' Share.		Excess given to the Chahárumis.	Deficiency given to the Chahárumis.
	No. of Villages.	Jama.	No. of Villages.	Jama.		
Shill, ...	5	2,416	4	3,011	297	...
Gurángan, . . .	2	4,278	8	3,485	...	381
Burás, ...	4	1,662	2	1,325	...	86
Todar Májra, . .	4	1,112	4	2,351	231	...
Chuni Machhli, .	20	12,006	19	11,991	...	7
Banur, ...	9	10,310	6	2,124	...	4163
Lidhrán, . . .	...	...	5	2,335	1165	...
Khas Pattiala, .	...	...	4	2,954	2954	...
Gudherah, . . .	...	...	...	...	...	...
Total, . . .	44	35,377	52	31,932	4647	4772

The four khás villages, Budali, Budiala, Tolah Majra, and Moti Majra, were the property of Pattiala; but being surrounded by estates under British jurisdiction, were proposed for exchange with two others, Naya Shahr and Badálah, which the Maharaja had some wish to retain, as he had lately located some traders in the former village. The two villages assigned to Sirdar Khan Singh of Burás belonged to Pattiala, and were allowed him as a matter of convenience, with regard to residence and the boundary line, instead of assigning him a share in the four Burás villages.

Pattiala objects to the decision, and claims more than a half share.

The arrangement, after much discussion and some modifications, was laid before Government,[1] and the Pattiala officials were allowed to urge any further objections they might have to the scheme. With reference to the estates of Todar Majra and Lidhran, no objection whatever was made; but in the Shill, Gurángan, and Gudhera estates, which had been divided in equal shares between the Chahárumis and Pattiala, and to which division and the allotment of villages the latter had advanced no objection whatever before the local officers, the Maharaja, before the Chief Commissioner, claimed more than a half share. A proceeding of Mr Clerk, the Governor-General's Agent at Ambala, of the year 1842, was produced in support of this claim, by which it certainly appeared that Pattiala had, in these estates, been accustomed to collect on certain kinds of crops about five-eighths, and the Chahárumis three-eighths only: while the village account-books produced by Pattiala were to the effect that the

And produces proofs in support of her assertion.

[1] Commissioner, Cis-Satlej States, to Financial Commissioner, No. 111, dated 3d April 1854.

Memorandum by G. F. Edmonstone, Esq., late Financial Commissioner, dated 21st April 1854. Financial Commissioner to Government, Punjab, No. 221, dated 17th June 1854.

Pattiala collections, for many years past, had been in excess of those of the Chahárumi Sikhs to the amount of Rs. 863 per annum, to which amount Pattiala required to be further reimbursed.

The shares of Pattiala and the Chahárumis were originally equal.

The question really at issue was, whether the original share of Pattiala was larger than that of the Sikhs, and, if not larger, whether the Sikhs had accepted the encroachments by Pattiala on their right, or had resisted them. It was evident that the shares were originally equal, the villages having been conquered by the Sikhs and Pattiala conjointly, and a half share conferred on Raja Amir Singh by Ahmad Shah Durani. The encroachments of Pattiala had been continuous, violence and fraud being alike used to increase her own rights at the expense of the Sikhs; but the latter had never acquiesced in this state of things. Between 1830 and 1844 they had given in some three hundred petitions praying for protection and redress. In these they constantly reiterated their claim to a full half share. Even after the *Dastúr-ul-amal*, or rules of practice, had been drawn up by Mr Clerk in 1842, the Sikhs continued to remonstrate against its terms; declaring that the papers on which it was formed were false and fraudulent. There is little doubt that this was the case: the village accountants and headmen who compiled the annual accounts were in complete subordination to Pattiala, and dared not express any view opposed to her; and there was nothing to show that in the document finally framed, the arguments of the Sikhs had been fairly considered, or their long and persistent opposition to Pattiala claims taken into account. The Government accordingly ruled, with reference to their former instructions, that the estates should be equally divided, an aggressor not being permitted to

The Chahárumis had always resisted Pattiala encroachments.

The proofs produced by Pattiala were unworthy of credit.

profit by encroachments which had been continuously resisted.[1]

The Banur estate.

Pattiala gained an advantage in the Banur estate, shared with the Singhpuria Sirdars, in the possession of the town of Banur, the second in importance in the whole territory. To compensate the Chiefs for this, a somewhat larger moiety of the income than their proper share was allowed them, the village of Baddali, formerly in Pattiala, having by this distribution been assigned to the Singhpurias and then annexed to British territory, a payment of Rs. 10 per cent. on the value of the share was allowed to the Maharaja to compensate him for the loss of the remote and contingent interest in the succession to lapsed sharers.

The Burhas estate.

With reference to the State of Burhas, which was so isolated that it was considered better to make over the four villages to Pattiala, and allot the Sirdar villages elsewhere, the Maharaja objected to the proposed payment of 10 per cent. on the revenue to compensate the Sirdar for the inconvenience of moving; and the Government allowed this objection, considering that although the Chief of Burhas was entitled to compensation, it should be paid by the British Government, and not by Pattiala, who had nothing to do with his compulsory removal.

The Chuni Machhli estate.

The last case was that of Chuni Machhli. Here the dispute had reference to the important village of Barwala, which both Pattiala and Sirdar Jaswant Singh,

[1] Punjab Government, No. 59, dated 27th January 1855, to Commissioner, Cis-Satlej States. Nos. 41 and 139, dated 10th February and 9th May, from Deputy-Commissioner, Ambala, to Commissioner, Cis-Satlej States; and Nos. 42 and 138, dated 23d February and 22d June, to Government, Punjab. Government, Punjab, No. 533, dated 18th July, to Government of India, and Government of India's No. 3799, dated 26th October 1855, to Government, Punjab.

the co-sharer, desired to retain. The Maharaja's claim was based chiefly on the alleged possession of a fort and certain family cenotaphs in the village; but, on inquiry, it appeared that the fort was nothing more than a defensible house, while the cenotaphs were admitted to be in Barnála, a totally distinct village; it apparently being hoped, as was nearly the case, that the difference of a letter in the name would be overlooked. It appeared, however, that the possession of the village of Barwala, was far more necessary to Sirdar Jaswant Singh than to Pattiala, and it was included in his share of the estate.[1]

The termination of the case.

Thus terminated, with some approach to equal justice, a conflict which had been going on between Pattiala and the Chahárumi Sikhs ever since the British connection with the Cis-Satlej territory. If justice was at length done, it was owing to the long, painful, and patient inquiry of British officers, and owed nothing to the sense of generosity or justice of Pattiala. Neither in this case nor in any of a similar nature does the conduct of Pattiala appear to advantage. Unwilling to yield to the British Government, to whose protection she owed her existence, the rights which every paramount power necessarily claims, and jealous of every advantage gained by a neighbour, she abused the patience with which the Government attended to her every remonstrance, and investigated her every claim, to press claims the most extravagant and unfounded, to support them with fraudulent evidence, and to prevent, in every possible manner, the British officers, whose duty was suffi-

The uniformly litigious and ungenerous conduct of Pattiala.

[1] Punjab Government to Government of India; No. 553, dated 18th July; and Government of India to Government, Punjab, No. 3799, dated 26th October 1855.

ciently arduous without her wilfully adding to its difficulty, from obtaining a fair view of the case. Justice, in the eyes of Pattiala, consisted in the British Government surrendering everything to her, and she considered herself treated with exceptional harshness if their undoubted rights were accorded to her weaker neighbours. Every neighbour was for Pattiala a rival, and every rival an enemy against whom all arms were legitimate. It would be unfair to assert that in this conduct Pattiala was singular. What is considered unfair and dishonourable in English politics, is the ordinary practice of most native States. Founded upon violence, they ruled and increased their dominions by force, so long as this was possible. A stronger power than themselves has now insisted upon peace; and they attempt to win by fraud what they are unable to gain by force.

The case of the village of Bugar.

There were several other Pattiala cases, besides that of the Chahárumi Sikhs, difficult to settle, a brief account of which is necessary here. The first of these relates to the village of Bugar, and the case is chiefly interesting from a ruling of the Supreme Government with reference to the investigation of rights which had accrued previous to 1809. This village, which must not be confounded with one granted to Pattiala in 1855, had been originally given by Rama and Tilokha, the sons of Phúl, to their sister Fatoh, whose descendants still own it. Both Pattiala and Nabha, the descendants of the original grantees, claimed jurisdiction over Bugar; and the jagirdars were divided into two parties, favouring the claim of the respective States, while the cultivators of the village asserted that both Nabha and Pattiala exercised jurisdiction and inflicted fines. The Commissioner, Cis-Satlej States, held that neither had a right to the village, which

Granted to Bibe Fatoh by her brothers Rama and Tilokha.

Dispute as to Pattiala or Nabha supremacy.

had been granted when the ancestors of the Pattiala and Nabha Chiefs were mere zamindars, subjects of the Dehli Emperor, who received the Imperial share of the revenue of Bugar as of other villages, and that the British Government, in taking the place of that of Dehli, had succeeded to its jurisdiction also. It was, besides, unjust to the people to make them over to either State, for partisans of the one would be, in any case, oppressed by the triumphant partisans of the other; while to continue the joint jurisdiction of both in a single village was impossible.

Or the supremacy of the British Government,

Which declines to assert any claim.

The Government of India declined to take this view of the case. The argument drawn from the status at the time of the grant was asserted to be fallacious, for the proclamations of Sir D. Ochterlony, in 1809 and 1811, had absolutely shut the door against the investigations of anterior rights, and guaranteed the Chiefs of the Cis-Satlej States in the exercise of the same rights and authority, within their possessions, which they enjoyed before they were taken under British protection. As the village, at the date of the proclamation, was under the jurisdiction of either Pattiala or Nabha, it would be a breach of the agreement then made to extend the British authority over the village. The inconvenience to the people by giving Bugar to either State might be great, but this, though matter of regret, did not, in any way, affect the merits of the question, or render a breach of the distinct understanding on which the Government assumed the protection of the Cis-Satlej States any less objectionable. It was manifest that the Government could not interfere in favour of the rights of all the people of India, to whomsoever they might happen to be subject; and it was ordered that the village should be given to Pattiala or Nabha, as appeared the most appropriate.

The village assigned to Nabha.

After some further discussion the village was assigned to the Raja of Nabha, the Maharaja of Pattiala acquiescing in the decision.[1]

The Khumánun estate.

The second case referred to the estate of Khumánun, consisting of fifty-eight villages, and situated a few miles north of Sirhind. Pattiala had in it no proprietary rights, but, in 1815, it was entrusted to her by Sir D. Ochterlony, for administrative purposes; and the Pattiala Chief was empowered to exercise criminal jurisdiction and exact service. When the English first took the Cis-Satlej territory under their protection, they seem to have fancied that the whole was under the jurisdiction of a few great Chiefs, and it was only gradually that it was discovered how numerous were the small communities claiming virtual independence. The Government at length sought to lighten its own labours by making the principal Chiefs responsible for the conduct of their weaker neighbours, authorising them to hear and decide their disputes, and this course, though it gave a power to some States which was not unfrequently abused, on the whole worked well. In 1815, the Sikhs of Khumánun, a large coparcenary body, were so transferred to Pattiala jurisdiction. The next year the Sikhs of Panjokra, Syadpur, Dhanori, Lakhnour, Khumbra, and Barail; and, in 1821, the Chahárumis, co-sharers with

Transferred to Pattiala jurisdiction in 1815.

[1] Commissioner Cis-Satlej States to Government Punjab, No. 184, dated 16th August 1855. Government Punjab to Government of India, No. 630, dated 29th August. Government of India to Government Punjab, No. 643, dated 15th October 1855.

Commissioner Cis-Satlej States to Government Punjab, No. 106, dated 4th May 1857. Government Punjab to Commissioner, No. 400, dated 25th April, and to Government of India, No. 624, dated 4th September 1857. Government of India, No. 4641, dated 19th November 1857.

Pattiala, were referred to her for general control and, in 1823, the Sikhs of Tullakour.[1]

The arrangement allowed to continue in 1847.

Colonel Mackeson, in his report of 1847, suggested that the Khumánun Sikhs might be permitted to select whether they would remain under Pattiala or come under British jurisdiction; but the Government of India, while admitting that it would be desirable to assume the direct control of the estate, declared that it was not desired to alter the position or limit the authority of the Pattiala Chief, as exercised before the Satlej campaign, but rather to improve and increase them, in consideration of the excellent service then rendered by him, and declined to alter the arrangement, which would be reconsidered at the death of the Maharaja.[2]

Difficulty of maintaining the rights of Government.

In 1855, when the Chahárumi tenures came under consideration, that of Khumánun was also discussed. The British Government had not given up its rights as paramount over the estate. It exacted a commutation of Rs. 4128 a year, and claimed all escheats. But there was much difficulty in discovering what escheats lapsed, and their real value, of which it was evidently not the interest of Pattiala to inform the Government. To obviate this, it was ruled by Mr Edmonstone, when Commissioner Cis-Satlej States, that inquiries into escheats should not be made on the ordinary basis—*viz.*, the year of protection, 1809—but that existing possession should be made the foundation for regulating rights of the British Government to future escheats, while the

[1] Of these the Khumánun, Tullakour, Dhanori, and Lakhnour Sikhs are still under Pattiala jurisdiction for life of the Maharaja, paying commutation tax in lieu of service to Government.

[2] Commissioner Cis-Satlej States to Secretary to Government of India, No. 125, dated 9th June 1847.

Government of India, No. 2352, dated 5th October 1847, to Commissioner Cis-Satlej States.

Maharaja was to file papers showing the approximate value of the share, the amount of which would be added to the annual amount of commutation paid by Pattiala.[1]

This rule had worked badly, and it was then proposed either to request the Maharaja to prepare a complete rent-roll of the whole estate, with the value of each share, or to make a regular settlement of all the villages. But the Government was unwilling to adopt the latter course, as it was thought likely to give umbrage to the Maharaja, the estate having been so long under his sole jurisdiction; and it was finally determined to leave the existing arrangements as they were during the lifetime of Maharaja Narindar Singh.[2]

Which were not however resigned.

Some doubt was, after this, expressed as to the intention of Government to relinquish all claims to escheated shares, and it was found necessary to intimate to the Maharaja that the just claims of Government were in no way abandoned. He was directed to file, within three months, a list of sharers and their collateral descendants, showing the shares held by them, and the ancestor from whom they derived their right; and his acquiescence in this was a condition on which his jurisdiction over the Khumánun estate was continued. The rules of succession of 1851 were applicable to this estate, according to which collaterals claiming from a common ancestor would succeed to so much of the estate as was in possession of that

[1] Mr Melvill to Commissioner Cis-Satlej States, No. 102, dated 30th December 1852. Commissioner Cis-Satlej States to Mr Melvill, No 35, dated 11th January 1853.

[2] Commissioner Cis-Satlej States to Government Punjab, No. 204, dated 5th September 1855. Government Punjab to Government of India, No. 762, dated 11th October. Government of India, No. 3894, dated 2d November 1853; Government Punjab to Commissioner Cis-Satlej States, No. 983, dated 14th November 1855.

ancestor in 1809.[1] The Maharaja nevertheless delayed the required report till the 7th May 1857. The number of lapses were only two, amounting to Rs. 1650 per annum, which was very small considering that the number of sharers was 225. This amount was charged against the Maharaja from the date of the lapses.[2] Two years later the Khumánun estate was transferred to Pattiala in perpetuity.

The proposed visit of the Maharaja to England.

Maharaja Narindar Singh had always expressed a great desire to visit England. The Sikhs are not a race much addicted to travelling, and no Sikh Chief of any consequence had ever left India, and very few had travelled as far as Calcutta. In 1854 he formally asked permission to visit England, and that an English officer might be appointed to accompany him. The consent of Government was given on the condition that satisfactory arrangements were made for the administration of the

Arrangements during his absence.

Pattiala State during his absence. A council of Regency was appointed, consisting of three officers, who were to have full powers, and in case of difference of opinion, the majority was to decide; and, in compliance with the suggestion of the Government of India, the Maharaja abandoned his intention of taking with him a suite of 500 persons in favour of a smaller number. All arrange-

[1] Commissioner Cis-Satlej States to Government Punjab, No. 282 dated 19th December 1855. Government Punjab to Government of India, No. 934, dated 27th December. Government of India to Government Punjab, No. 837, dated 13th February 1856. Government Punjab to Commissioner Cis-Satlej States, No. 134, dated 21st February 1856.

[2] Government of India to Government Punjab, No. 2131, dated 11th June 1858. Government Punjab to Commissioner Cis-Satlej States, No. 421, dated 23d June. Commissioner Cis-Satlej States to Government Punjab, No. 197, dated 9th July. Commissioner Cis-Satlej Statesto Deputy Commissioner Ambala, No. 601, dated 20th April 1857; and Deputy-Commissioner Ambala to Commissioner Cis-Satlej States, No. 204, dated 5th July 1858.

ments were completed, but the Maharaja at the last moment postponed his departure, and before he had again made up his mind to start, the mutiny broke out, and his presence was necessary in his own State.[1]

The design abandoned.

After the mutiny, Narindar Singh again determined to visit England. His services during 1857 had been so brilliant, and the acknowledgments of the Government so warm, that he believed that in England he would receive a very flattering reception. His expectation would no doubt have been realised, but unfortunately a second time domestic affairs and political questions forced him to abandon the intention, after all arrangements had been completed, and an English officer, Major R. Lawrence, Military Secretary to the Chief Commissioner, had been selected to accompany him.[2]

The design a second time formed,

And again abandoned.

The mutiny put on its trial the great experiment which the British Government had been laboriously working out since 1809 with regard to the Cis-Satlej States; and it indisputably proved that the Sikh Chiefs knew that they had been treated with generosity and consideration by the paramount power.

The mutiny of 1857.

During the disturbances of 1857–58, no prince in India showed greater loyalty or rendered more conspicuous service to the British Government than the Maharaja of Pattiala. He was the acknowledged head of the Sikhs, and his hesitation or disloyalty would have been attended with the most disastrous results, while his

The influence of the Maharaja.

[1] Commissioner Cis-Satlej States, Nos. 154 and 205, dated 13th July and 23d August 1854, with enclosures. Government Punjab to Government of India, Nos. 642 and 717, dated 19th July and 6th September. Government of India's Nos. 3648, 800, and 885, dated 18th August, 25th September, and 15th November 1854.

[2] Commissioner Cis-Satlej States to Government Punjab, No. 289, dated 16th October 1858. Government Punjab to Government of India, No. 791, dated 30th October.

ability, character, and high position would have made him a most formidable leader against the Government. But following the honourable impulses of gratitude and loyalty, he unhesitatingly placed his whole power, resources, and influence at the absolute command of the English, and during the darkest and most doubtful days of the mutiny, he never for a moment wavered in his loyalty, but, on the contrary, redoubled his exertions when less sincere friends thought it politic to relax theirs.

His conspicuous loyalty.

His immediate action on the side of the British Government.

When the news reached Pattiala of the mutinies at Dehli and Meerat, and the doubtful attitude of the native troops at Ambala, the Maharaja placed himself at the head of all his available troops, and marched the same night to Jesomli, a village close to Ambala, sending at the same time his elephants, camels, and other carriage, to Kalka, for the transport of European troops to Ambala from the hill stations of Kussowli, Dagshai, and Sabathu. From Jesomli he marched to Thanesar, and placed there a force of 1300 men with four guns, for the protection of the district.

The opinion of the Commissioner of Ambala.

"This straightforward and loyal conduct," wrote the Commissioner of the Cis-Satlej States, "was of infinite importance to our cause at that time. People's minds were agitated with various rumours about the cartridges, about the adulteration of flour, and other subtle designs to destroy their caste. When the Maharaja placed himself boldly and heartily on our side, these mischievous reports began to be discredited. The Maharaja was an orthodox Hindoo, whose position and career alike commanded respect. His support at such a crisis was worth a brigade of English troops to us, and served more to tranquillise the people than a hundred official disclaimers would have done."

Thanesar, Karnal, and the station of Ambala, were held by Pattiala troops, who also guarded the Grand Trunk Road from Karnal to Phillor. The Maharaja constantly expressed his earnest wish to lead a contingent to Dehli, but, both by the Commander-in-Chief and the Civil Authorities, he was dissuaded from this, as his presence in the Cis-Satlej States was considered of the highest importance. He sent, however, 500 horse and foot, under the command of Sirdar Partab Singh, and these troops did good service during the siege and at the assault of Dehli, and the assistance rendered by Pattiala was warmly acknowledged by General Wilson in his despatch of the 22d September 1857.

His services at Ambala, Thanesar, and Dehli;

At the commencement of the disturbances, the Maharaja received a letter from the King of Dehli, urging him to come over to his side, and promising him rewards for so doing. This letter the Maharaja gave to the English authorities.

Besides troops at Dehli, Karnal, Thanesar, and Ambala, the Pattiala Chief sent a detachment with General Van-Cortlandt, and materially aided in restoring order in Sirsa, Rohtak, and Hissar; another detachment was employed at Saharunpur and Jagadri, and was twice engaged with the mutineers: on the revolt of the 10th Cavalry at Fírozpur, his troops followed them up, and in a skirmish that took place, several of his men were killed and wounded.

In Sirsa, Rohtak, and Hissar.

The Maharaja, in his own territories, furnished supplies and carriage, and kept the roads clear for all Government troops passing through from the Punjab to Dehli; and all refugees from Sirsa, Rohtak, and Hissar, who came into Pattiala were received with kindness, and supplied with everything they required.

He furnishes carriage and supplies.

And subscribes to the Government loan.

He also gave a loan of five lakhs of rupees to Government, and expressed his willingness to double this amount, but no more was required of him.

The number of his troops employed.

The Pattiala contingent employed in the British cause during 1857, consisted of 8 guns, 2156 horse, 2846 infantry, with 156 officers, the most distinguished of whom were Sirdar Partab Singh and Syad Muhammad Hassain, who commanded the detachment at Dehli; Kour Dip Singh at Thanesar; Sirdars Híra Singh and Hazara Singh at Ambala; Sirdars Karam and Kahan Singh at Hissar; Sirdars Dal Singh and Fatah Singh at Hansi; and Sirdar Jiun Sing at Firozepur.[1]

The services of the Maharaja in 1858, at Dholepur and Gwalior.

Most of the services of the Maharaja in 1858 were rendered at Dholepur, a small Rajput State, between Agra and Gwalior, the Chief of which, Rana Bhagwant Singh, had married his daughter. Early in September 1857, the combined insurgent forces of Indore and Gwalior entered the Dholepur State. Most of the Rana's troops and officials joined the rebels, who ravaged the district, defied the Chief's authority, and even threatened his life until he consented to their demands. At length they left Dholepur, taking with them the Rana's guns, for Agra, where they were totally defeated by the Agra garrison and the Dehli column under General Greathed, on the 10th of October. But Dholepur remained in a state of anarchy, and the Chief was unable to restore order; till, with the consent of the North-West and Punjab Autho-

[1] No. 77, from the Commissioner Cis-Satlej States to Chief Commissioner Punjab, 9th March 1858, enclosing statement of the Maharaja's services. No. 34 of 13th April 1858 from Chief Commissioner Punjab to Government of India.

Commissioner Cis-Satlej States, Nos. 8, 133, 150, 200, 352, dated 8th January, 12th May, 21st May, 12th July, 12th November 1858. Commissioner Hissar's, Nos. 38, 44, 140, dated 15th June, 22d June, 30th October 1858. Commissioner Dehli's No. 31, dated 4th November 1857.

rities, the Maharaja of Pattiala sent there a force of 2000 men and two guns, under the command of Nihal Chand and Diwan Jagdesh Singh Motando, two of his ablest officials.[1] Although Dholepur was tranquillised, the neighbouring States were in so disturbed a condition, that the Pattiala troops were directed to remain there. Gwalior, which had already been the scene of rebellion and bloodshed, was again attacked by the rebels, and, for a time, held by them. The Maharaja Sindiah fled to Dholepur on the 2d of June, and was supplied with an escort of Pattiala troops to Agra. A British force then marched against the rebel army at Gwalior, and the Pattiala Chief increased his force at Dholepur by every available man. He guarded all the ferries on the Chumbal river, collected supplies for the British army, and a detachment of 500 of his troops served under General Napier in the action at Alipur, on the 19th of June, when the rebels, who had been defeated before Gwalior, were again attacked and routed.

A month later, at the requisition of Sir R. Hamilton, a Pattiala detachment of 600 infantry and 300 horse was moved from Dholepur to Gwalior, where it remained, doing excellent service, reducing rebellious villages, and acting as guards and escorts.

In February 1858, the Maharaja, at the request of the Chief Commissioner, sent a force of 600 foot and 200 horse, afterwards doubled in strength, to Jhajjar, where they were employed during the whole year under the

At Jhajjar and in Oude.

[1] Letter of Colonel Riddell, commanding Dholepur force, to Diwan Nihal Chand, dated 2d February 1858.

No. 784, of 27th July 1858, from General G. Lawrence, Agent Governor-General Rajputana, to Government of India. No. 6, of 10th February 1858, from Major Macpherson, Political Agent, Gwalior, to Agent Governor-General for Central India.

civil authorities, in maintaining the order of the district. Two months later the Chief Commissioner of Oude applied for a regiment fully equipped for service in that province. Although all his regular troops were employed at this time on active service, the Maharaja raised 820 infantry and 203 sowars, and despatched them to Oude without delay, where their services were most useful.[1]

The rewards given to the Maharaja for his service.

The Pattiala Chief was splendidly rewarded for his services by the Government.

Firstly, The Narnoul division of the Jhajjar territory, the ruler of which had rebelled, valued at Rs. 2,00,000 a year, was granted to him on condition of good behaviour and service, military and political, at any time of general danger or disturbance.

Secondly, The jurisdiction over Bhadour, long the subject of dispute, was ceded to him, with the right of escheats, the reversion to lapsed estates therein, and the annual commutation tax, amounting to Rs. 5265.

Thirdly, The confiscated house in Dehli, formerly belonging to the Begam Zenat Mahal, and valued at Rs. 10,000, was granted to him, and his honorary titles were increased.[2]

[1] No. 53, from Commissioner Cis-Satlej States to Secretary to Government, Punjab, dated 16th February 1859. Government Punjab, to Government of India, No. 161, dated 23d February. No. 2216, from Government of India to Government Punjab, dated 23d April 1859. Kharita addressed to Maharaja of Pattiala by his Excellency the Viceroy, dated 21st April 1859.

[2] The titles of the Maharaja in 1857 were :—

Maháràja Dhiráj Rájeshar Maháràja Rájagán Narindar Singh Mohindar Buhádar.

They were increased in 1858 as follows :—

Farzand Khás, Dowlat-i-Inglisia, Mansúr Zamán, Amír-úl-Umra, Mahárája Dhiráj, Rajeshar Srí Mahárája Rájagán Narindar Singh Mohindar Buhádar.

No. 34, from Secretary to Government Punjab to Government of India, dated 13th May 1858.

No. 1549, from Government of India to Chief Commissioner, Punjab, dated 2d June 1858.

It had been first proposed to give the Maharaja territory adjoining his own State, to the value of Rs. 50,000 a year, but this idea was abandoned; for it was undesirable to transfer territory which had been for many years under British rule, the more especially as there was new territory which had been only recently annexed, that of the rebel Nawab of Jhajjar, which was not too far from the Pattiala territory to prevent the Maharaja exercising over it an efficient control. It was, moreover, an advantage to have a Sikh Chief, whose loyalty had been so well tried, located in the midst of the turbulent and, at that time, disaffected Muhammadan population of the Jhajjar territory, and interposed as a barrier towards the independent States of Alwar and Jaipur, with its feudatories of Shaikhawatí and Ketrí, whose army and population had shown themselves unfriendly during the mutinies. The Narnoul division of the Jhajjar territory which was granted to the Maharaja, was the frontier division adjoining the above-named States. The revenue of Narnoul was estimated at two lakhs of rupees, on the faith of the assessment fixed by the Nawab of Jhajjar, which was in excess of that sum. It did not, at any rate on its first acquisition by the Maharaja, yield more than Rs. 1,70,000, inclusive of fines and miscellaneous revenue, and this was made the ground for a request for further grants to complete the two lakhs of territory which had been assigned to the Maharaja. But the Government had made no promise, and given no guarantee, that the territory would yield as much as two lakhs of rupees, nor was there any

The reason for granting Jhajjar territory to Pattiala.

The territory was not as valuable as was supposed.

The term "Dowlat-i-Inglisia," meaning "of the British Government," was inserted later. "Farzand Khás," signifying "choicest son," and requiring some after qualification to show *whose* son the Chief was.

Commissioner, Cis-Satlej States, No. 337, dated 30th December 1859. Government of India, No. 8, dated 4th January 1860.

means of ascertaining its income, except from the assessment of its late owner, which was in excess of two lakhs; and it was reasonably supposed that under another native ruler it would yield at least as much. The Government were thus under no obligation whatever to make up to the Maharaja the amount deficient; for, although he had been told the approximate rental, he was quite aware that the territory would yield somewhat less, and that it was made over to him for no specific revenue, but simply for what it was worth.[1]

But the Government had given no guarantee of its value.

The claims of the Maharaja received every consideration, and in September 1859 the Commissioner, Cis-Satlej States, made a further and full inquiry into them.[2]

But the Government, unable to admit any claim to compensation on account of an alleged deficiency in the income of the grant, was yet willing to make a further grant of territory to the Maharaja in acknowledgment of the good service he had done, and a proposal was submitted by the Commissioner, Cis-Satlej States, to transfer to Pattiala portions of the pargannah of Kanoudh and Budwana, in the Jhajjar territory, with an income of about a lakh of rupees per annum, the Pattiala Chief giving a *nazarána* equivalent to twenty years' revenue.[3]

The districts of Kanoudh and Budwana assigned to Pattiala.

These pargannahs were the southernmost portion of the confiscated territory of Jhajjar, and it would have been inconvenient for the Government to retain them, as

[1] No. 53, dated 16th February 1859, from Commissioner Cis-Satlej States to Secretary to Government Punjab. No. 161, dated 23d February 1859, from Secretary to Government Punjab to Secretary to Government of India. No. 2216, of 23d April 1859, from Secretary to Government of India to Secretary to Government Punjab.

[2] Commissioner Cis-Satlej States Nos. 264 and 274, dated 27th September and 1st October 1859 to Government Punjab.

[3] Memorandum by Commissioner Cis-Satlej States, dated 22d December 1859, and Memorandum by Lieutenant-Governor, Punjab, 31st December 1859.

it would entail the maintenance of a separate judicial and revenue establishment. The Chiefs of Pattiala, Jhind, and Nabha were, on the other hand, most anxious to acquire this territory, which lay adjacent to that conferred upon them in 1858. There was, besides, an advantage to Government in clearing off the large debts which were due to Pattiala and Nabha for loans advanced in 1848 and 1857. These amounted, in 1860, to the following sums:— The Pattiala and Nabha loans.

Pattiala, 5 per cent. loan of 1848, ...	Rs. 16,96,000 [1]
Do. 6 per cent. loan of 1857, ...	2,36,000
Total, ...	Rs. 19,32,000

Nabha, 5 per cent. loan of 1848, ...	Rs. 7,00,000
Do. 6 per cent. loan of 1857, ...	2,50,000
Total, ...	Rs. 9,50,000

There was also a large sum due to Pattiala for interest which had not been drawn since 1857, which was separately considered. The Raja of Jhind had never had any pecuniary transactions with the British Government, but, considering the great services he had rendered during the mutiny, and his desire to acquire additional territory, it was determined to give him a share with the other States. To Pattiala were assigned villages of Kanoudh, with the town and fort, worth Rs. 98,000 a year; to Nabha, villages worth Rs. 48,000; and to Jhind, villages worth Rs. 21,000. Twenty years purchase of the share allotted to Pattiala would be more than the principal of his debt, but the balance was deducted from the interest still due; in the same way with the Nabha grant; while the Raja of Jhind

[1] The sum lent by Pattiala in 1848–49, was Rs. 30,00,000, and in 1857 Rs. 5,00,000.

paid for his new territory a *nazarána* of Rs. 4,20,000. The remainder of the district of Jhajjar was then absorbed into the Rohtak district.[1]

The estate of Khumánun granted in lieu of interest due,

There still remained a balance of interest due to Pattiala, amounting to Rs. 3,10,666, principally on the 5 per cent. loan. To reduce this the district of Khumánun, which has been before described, was made over to Pattiala, the Government giving up the commutation tax of Rs. 4128 per annum, and the right to escheats, estimated at 10 per cent. on the gross rental of the estate, which was worth Rs. 48,000. Four out of seven villages, shared with the British Government, Chiri, Phuror, Lakhanpur, and Amargarh, were also made over to Pattiala, and the value of the estates and rights ceded to him amounted to Rs. 1,76,360. On the 30th of June 1860, the balance due to Pattiala was Rs. 93,767-15-10, which was paid to him in cash and the transactions closed.[2] Sanads were granted to the several Chiefs for their new territory, and complimentary letters addressed to them by the Governor General.[3]

And the accounts finally closed.

Sanads granted for the new territory.

[1] Commissioner Cis-Satlej States to Government Punjab, No. 87, dated 23d May 1860. Government Punjab to Government of India, No. 347, dated 4th June. Government of India to Government Punjab, No. 1977, dated 14th June 1860. Despatch of Secretary of State, No. 12, dated 30th January 1861.

[2] Commissioner Cis-Satlej States to Punjab Government No. 109, dated 14th June 1860. Punjab Government to Government of India, No. 423, dated 3d July. Government of India to Government Punjab, No. 2779, dated 18th July 1860. Despatch of Secretary of State for India, No. 12, dated 30th January 1861.

Commissioner Cis-Satlej States to Government Punjab, No. 187, dated 22d September 1860.

[3] Translation of Sanad or grant of portions of the Pargannahs of Kanoudh and Budwana, district Jhajjar, and of Ilaquah Khumanan, district Ambala, bestowed upon His Highness the Maharaja of Pattiala by His Excellency Earl Canning, G.C.B., Viceroy and Governor-General of India :—

PREAMBLE.—Whereas the devotion and loyalty of His Highness the

There were other privileges and concessions granted to the Maharaja of Pattiala and the Rajas of Nabha and Jhind, of the greatest value, and of a character which changed materially the nature of their relations with the British Government. In 1858, these Chiefs had united in soliciting certain concessions which were referred to the Secretary of State, and some granted at once; others, including the most desired of all, the right of adoption guaranteeing the perpetuity of their rule, a little later.

Other valuable concessions granted to the principal Phulkian Chiefs.

The first request related to the power of inflicting capital punishment. This had been taken from the Chiefs after the first Sikh war, although no allusion had been made to it in the granted Sanads, for reasons given by the Secretary in his letter conveying the Government

The power of inflicting capital punishment.

Maharaja of Pattiala and of his ancestors have always been conspicuous since the establishment of British supremacy in India, His Excellency the Viceroy and Governor-General being desirous of marking his high appreciation of those qualities, has been pleased to bestow upon the Maharaja portions of Pargannahs Kanoudh and Budwana, of the district of Jhajjar, containing one hundred and ten villages (110) according to vernacular list annexed, assessed at a yearly revenue of ninety-six thousand nine hundred and forty rupees (96,940), and to accept from His Highness a "Nuzzuranah" of nineteen lakhs thirty-eight thousand and eight hundred rupees (19,38,800). Further, His Excellency has been pleased in like manner to bestow upon the Maharaja the Ilaquah of Khumánun, district Amballa, with the service commutation tax, and the right to escheats, and to accept from His Highness a Nuzzuranah of one lakh seventy-six thousand three hundred and sixty rupees (1,76,360).

It is accordingly ordained as follows :—

"ARTICLE 1.—The territories above-mentioned are conferred upon His Highness the Maharaja of Pattiala and his heirs for ever.

"ARTICLE 2.—The Maharaja and his successors will exercise the same rights, privileges, and prerogative in these newly-acquired territories as His Highness at present enjoys in his ancestral possessions, according to the term of the Sanad, dated 5th May 1860, and signed by His Excellency Earl Canning, Viceroy and Governor-General of India.

"ARTICLE 3.—The Maharaja and his successors will continue to maintain the same loyal relations with the British Government, and to fulfil the same obligations with regard to these newly-acquired territories, as were imposed upon His Highness by the terms of the Sanad dated 5th May 1860, relating to His Highness' ancestral possessions."

orders :[1]—"You must impress upon the Maharaja and upon the other protected Chiefs under your jurisdiction, that no mutilation will be allowed within their respective territories, and that in no case can they be permitted to execute the extreme sentence of the law and deprive of life, without the approval and consent of the Agent, to whom each case considered deserving of capital punishment must be submitted, after receiving the final orders of the local authorities. No stipulations to this effect have been inserted in the Sanad, in consequence of the desire expressed by the Raja of Jhind that such might be omitted; but you will require both His Highness and the Maharaja of Pattiala to conform implicitly to the above instructions of Government, as if the stipulations were formally entered in the Sanad."

This deprivation of the power of inflicting capital punishment was regarded by the Chiefs as limiting their independence more than any other of the regulations which were issued after the Satlej campaign. The Maharaja of Pattiala would never apply for sanction to inflict it, and the practical result of the order was abolition of capital punishment in his territory. Indeed, between 1847 and 1856, only three applications for sanction were made to the Agent, two from the Raja of Jhind, and one from the Raja of Faridkot.[2]

The three Phulkian Chiefs, accordingly, solicited, in 1858, that the power of life and death might be again restored to them. During the mutiny, indeed, it had been restored, for, without it, they could never have

[1] Para. 19 of No. 2352, dated 5th October 1847, from Secretary to Government of India to Commissioner Cis-Satlej States.

[2] Commissioner Cis-Satlej States to Secretary to Government Punjab, No. 13, dated 16th January 1856; and No. 39, dated 21st January, from Secretary to Government Punjab to Commissioner Cis-Satlej States.

maintained order in their territories, and they were then specially authorised to execute heinous offenders without reference to the Commissioner; and the Government, in 1858, granted them the right fully and absolutely, as they desired, considering that they might with safety be entrusted with the power; that they would, as a rule, be more sparing of its exercise than European officers would be; and that, under the existing system, the Commissioner could exert no real check, except a moral one, which would not be lessened by conferring the power. If the moral check should fail, there remained the power of sequestration or absolute deprivation of powers which had been abused, which, in 1856, the Government had used against the Nawab of Mamdot.

The arrangement with regard to the appointment of a Council of Regency.

The second request of the Chiefs was, that in case of a minority in any one of the three houses, a Council of Regency, formed of three of the old and trusted servants of the State, should be appointed by the British Agent and the other two Phulkian Chiefs, while, from this Council, strangers and the relatives of the minor should be excluded. The Government agreed to this request.

The right of adoption.

The third and fourth clauses of the memorial of the Chiefs asked for the right of adoption, in default of male issue, from among the members of the Phulkian family; and, in case of the death of a Chief without male issue and without having adopted an heir, that the two remaining Chiefs should have power to elect a successor from the same family.

By custom and law the adopted son had no right to succeed.

The privilege of adoption was one which the Chiefs desired with the greatest earnestness. Hitherto, among the Sikhs, Cis and Trans-Satlej, adoption, though carrying with it all the right of succession to private property enjoyed by the son of the body, had never been acknowledged as conferring any right of succession to a Chiefship. In the Punjab proper, the Maharaja of Lahore, and, south of the Satlej, the British Government, claimed, as paramount, the right of inheriting all estates to which there were no near male heirs, among whom the adopted son had no place; and the families of Ambala, Firozpur, Bilaspur, Ruper, and many others, had vainly endeavoured to secure for adopted children a share at least in the estate.

The policy of the Government with regard to collaterals.

The British Government, too, had, in 1837, excluded females from the succession to the Phulkian States; and although allowing the right of collaterals, had only admitted their right to such property as had been held by the common ancestor from whom they derived their claim.

The Chiefs feared the extinction of their families and the lapse of their estates.

The Cis-Satlej Chiefs thus lived in a perpetual fear that one portion of their possessions, in the event of their dying childless, would pass to distant kinsmen with whom they were at constant feud, while the most ancient and dearest loved portion would become an escheat of the British Government, which threatened in course of time to absorb them all. Nor was this fear at all unreasonable. The number of lapses that had fallen to the Government from the time of its first connection with the country north of Dehli was very great; and Chiefship after Chiefship had been absorbed in the British territories. The debauched lives of the Sikhs, and their addiction to intoxicating spirits of the fiercest quality, were all in favour of the paramount power, if the policy of that power was annexation. Vainly did a Sikh Chief marry a succession of wives; his excesses had brought their curse with them, and no son was born to inherit his wide estates. It was, then, with a keen desire, that

Their debauched lives made their fear reasonable.

the Chiefs solicited the privilege of adoption. To them, as to all Hindus, the adopted son was as dear and as much their own as one born of their body; and Hindu law and custom had ever held him as such. It was in succession to Chiefships alone that the right of adoption was denied, and the Rajas asked themselves whether the English protection had not been bought at too dear a cost, and whether the policy which had given to the British Government the fairest portion of the territories won by the Khalsa in the days of its first triumphs, had been so disinterested as that Government had always declared. It is not that they would have fared better with Ranjit Singh: he asserted the rights of a sovereign more jealously than ever the British Government had done, and neither allowed the claims of adopted sons nor of the nearest collaterals. But his conquests and annexations were made in the name of the Sikh nation, and for the glory of a religion of which its professors had not yet had time to grow weary. So it happened that, at the time of the campaign on the Satlej, many of the Chiefs thought that if it were their fate to be absorbed, it were better to become a portion of the monarchy whose seat was at Lahore, than of that which ruled them from Calcutta, not unkindly nor unjustly, but with which they had little sympathy; which sternly repressed anarchy and confusion; and forbade them to increase their possessions at the expense of their neighbours.

Ranjit Singh had, like the British Government, denied the right of adoption.

The British Government saw at once the significance of the request made by the Chiefs. To allow it, was to change the policy which had been sanctioned by long usage, and which had been, to a certain extent, successful. It was at least difficult to prove that any of the dangers which had, from time to time, gathered thick

The great importance of the question.

around the Government, were due to the sense of insecurity in the permanence of their rule, felt by the native princes of India. Were the right of adoption granted, the Government must give up all hope of future escheats; for so long as one male of the Phulkian race existed, he would unite under himself all the possessions of the family. In 1858, there were thirty-four males of this family living, and as time progressed the family might be expected to multiply. Yet the Government had begun to doubt the wisdom of the policy which, till 1857, it had followed. The mutiny had taught it some lessons, and had disposed it to try experiments which were opposed before, because they were new. In open Durbar, the right of adoption had been conferred on the Raja of Chirkarí, the Maharaja of Rewah, the Maharaja of Gwalior, and the Maharaja of Jaipur; and the Phulkian Chiefs had thus reason to hope that it would not be denied to them. In this, however, they were at first disappointed.

The policy of the Government had changed since 1857.

The Governor-General declined the request,

The Governor-General stated that the right of adoption, and, on failure of adoption, the right of electing a successor from among the descendants of Phul, were important innovations on the custom which had always prevailed among the Chiefs of the Cis-Satlej territories, and could not be sanctioned.

Which was granted by the Home Government.

But the Home Government took a view of the case more favourable to the wishes of the Chiefs. "The request," wrote the Secretary of State, "preferred by the Maharaja of Pattiala, and the Rajas of Jhind and Nabha, to be permitted, in all cases of failure of male issue, to adopt an heir from among the descendants of their common progenitor Phul, and in case of such heir by adoption not being named before the decease of any one of the three, for permission to the surviving Rajas to elect a successor from the same stock, has not been complied with by your Lordship's Government. But, adverting again to the very great services rendered by these Chiefs; to their long tried loyalty and fidelity to the British Crown; and to the great anxiety which they evince to obtain this boon, Her Majesty's Government are of opinion that you might expediently, as a special case, concede to them the desired privilege; and to request, therefore, that you will take steps to communicate, with as little delay as possible, this decision to the Chiefs concerned; and request them to supply you with an authenticated list of the existing descendants of Phul, to be periodically revised by them. Her Majesty's Government are, however, of opinion that, in consideration of this concession, you should levy a *nazarâna* of a year's revenue on the occasion of every case of adoption or election in the manner above described. It should be distinctly made known to them that, in no case of direct lineal descent, will any *nazarâna* be demanded."[1]

The happy results of the concession.

The concession thus granted was valued by the Chiefs more highly than the new territory, the reward for their loyalty; and later it was extended to other Chiefs in the Punjab—Sikh, Rajput, and Muhammadan. Till now these Chiefs had believed, and with justice, that the British Government, while it would neither use violence nor fraud to obtain their territories, would, nevertheless, gladly annex them to its own dominion should misfortune leave them without male heirs. They had at last learned that it was possible to be strong and yet generous, and that a Government like the British, before which organised

[1] No. 104, from Chief Commissioner Punjab to Government of India, of 16th June 1858. No. 3047, from Government of India to Government Punjab, of 25th May 1859. Secretary of State to Government of India, of 1st December 1859.

opposition was hopeless, and against which surprise had been tried in vain, might be content to trust rather to the affection and confidence of its feudatories than to their weakness or their destruction.

The exclusion of women from political affairs.

The fifth request made by the Phulkian Rajas was, that no women should have admission into the Council of Regency, or have any participation in affairs of State, either on the ground of the youth of the Chief, or on any other pretext whatever; and that no complaints of any sort, preferred by women of their family, should be received by the British Government.

The Government agreed to the exclusion of women from participation in affairs of State, considering that nothing but evil could accrue from the supremacy of women, uneducated and secluded, as is the custom in Hindostan.[1] It refused, however, to promise never to interfere in case of complaints on the part of female relatives of the Chiefs. The Government had not been accustomed, as a rule, to interfere in such cases, but it was impossible to surrender the right to do so when its protection was especially invoked, as in a case that had recently occurred, where the Raja of Faridkot kept his two sisters-in-law in confinement until the interference of Government compelled their release.

Interference of Government on behalf of dependants.

The Chiefs, moreover, requested that the British Government should bind itself not to interfere on behalf of relatives, connections, or dependants of the family. The Government would not pledge itself to such a promise, though its interference never had been, nor would be great.

[1] It was not the custom for women to be secluded in early Sikh days. In Pattiala the custom was introduced so late as the reign of Raja Karam Singh; and, as has been shown, the ladies of the family have shown quite as much or more political ability than the men.

The request for Sanads under the hand and seal of Her Majesty, and for exemption from the jurisdiction of the Civil Courts, refused.

Seventhly. The Chiefs asked for *Sanads*, guaranteeing to them their hereditary possessions in perpetuity, under the hand and seal of Her Majesty the Queen.

This request was submitted for the consideration of the Secretary of State for India, but, on the recommendation of the Governor-General, it was not complied with. Such a concession was considered unnecessary, as the fullest powers had been conferred on Her Majesty's representative in India, and *Sanads* would acquire no additional force or sanctity by execution in England; while such execution would be both inconvenient and impolitic, as all *Sanads* formerly granted would require renewal, or a suspicion of their validity might be raised; and not only *Sanads*, but treaties would be affected, to the renewal of which there are two parties, and some of which, still in force, were of such a nature that it would be most impolitic to cast loose the obligations of the engagement.

The last request was, that no claims against subjects of the Chiefs should be entertained in British Civil Courts. Previous to 1853, all suits against foreign subjects had been referred to the tribunals of the territory in which the defendant ordinarily resided; since that time,[1] if the cause of action arose in British territories, or the defendant possessed property therein, the suit could be heard and determined in the ordinary way. Although this system had not worked altogether well, yet it was fair, seeing that foreign subjects ordinarily used the British Courts to prosecute claims against parties resident in British territory; and to insure reciprocity for British subjects it was necessary to maintain it. This request, upon which the Chiefs did not lay much stress, was accordingly refused.[2]

[1] Board of Administration, 13th October 1849.

[2] No. 84, from Government of India to Secretary of State, dated 3d June 1859. No. 149, from Commissioner Cis-Satlej States to Chief Commis-

Lord Canning's Durbar at Ambala in January 1860.

In January, 1860, Lord Canning, the Viceroy and Governor-General, visited the Punjab, and on the 18th of that month he held a private Durbar at Ambala, for the reception of the Chiefs of the Cis-Satlej States and the Simla Hills, at which the Maharaja of Pattiala, the Rajas of Jhind, Nabha, Bilaspur, and Keonthal, the Nawab of Maler Kotla, and the Sirdar of Bassi, had audiences. The next day an open Durbar was held, at which were present all the Rajas, Chiefs, Sirdars, and native gentlemen of the Cis-Satlej States and the neighbouring districts. In investing the Maharaja with his khillat, the Viceroy addressed him in the following terms:—

"MAHARAJA OF PATTIALA,—

"It is very agreeable to me to have this opportunity of thanking you, personally and in public, for the valuable services you have rendered to the State. I esteem them, not more for the effective aid which they gave to the forces of the Government, than for the promptness with which they were offered, and for the example of hearty and unhesitating loyalty which you thereby set before the Queen's subjects in Upper India from the very beginning of the strife.

"I need not recount those services; they are well known to every one here present, and the history of them is recorded in the history of the operations by which the British troops sustained and asserted the power of England in this part of Her Majesty's dominions. There is no fear, therefore, of their being forgotten.

sioner Punjab, dated 20th May 1858. No. 104, from Chief Commissioner Punjab to Government of India, dated 16th June 1858. No. 3047, from Government of India to Government Punjab, dated 25th May 1859. No. 64, from Secretary of State to Government of India, dated 1st December 1859. No. 9, from Governor-General of India to Secretary of State, dated 28th January 1860.

"But I desire to assure you, before this Durbar, of the satisfaction which the Queen's Government has had in augmenting your honour and possessions, and of the wish which it entertains that these may long remain under the rule of descendants of your own—brave and loyal as yourself.

"I have directed that a grant be prepared confirming your title to these possessions, and to all the privileges attached to them. I have also directed that it be recorded, that if, unhappily, lineal heirs should fail you, your adoption of a successor from the ancient Phulkian house, of which your family forms a part, will be recognised and respected."[1]

The Sanad of adoption.

The grant referred to in this speech, confirming to the Maharaja all his territories, ancestral and acquired; conferring the right of adoption on failure of male issue, and of election of a successor under certain circumstances set forth, was given to the Maharaja by the Viceroy on the 5th of May 1860.[2]

[1] Notification, No. 172 A, dated 20th January 1860.

[2] Translation of the *Sanad* of the 5th of May 1860:—

Since the establishment of British authority in India, His Highness the present Maharaja of Pattiala, and his predecessors, have always been steady in their allegiance. They have frequently received rewards for their fidelity in the accession of fresh honours, dignity, and territory. More recently, His Highness, the present ruler of Pattiala, has surpassed the former achievements of his race, by the constancy and courage he evinced during the mutiny of 1857-58. In memory of his unswerving and conspicuous loyalty, his Excellency the Viceroy and Governor-General of India has conferred additional honours and territory upon the Maharaja for himself and his heirs for ever, and has graciously acceded to His Highness's desire to receive a Sanad or grant under the hand and seal of the Viceroy, guaranteeing to the Maharaja the free and unreserved possession of his ancient territories, as well as of those tracts bestowed on His Highness and his predecessors at various times by the British Government. It is accordingly ordained as follows:—

Clause I.—His Highness the Maharaja and his heirs for ever will exercise full sovereignty over his ancestral and acquired domains according to the annexed list. All the rights, privileges, and prerogatives which his Highness enjoys in his hereditary territories, he will equally enjoy in his acquired

The Maharaja invested with the order of the Star of India.

On the 1st November 1861, Maharaja Narindar Singh was invested with the Most Exalted Order of the Star of India, at Allahabad; and, about the same time, he was appointed a member of the Governor-General's Council for making Laws and Regulations. The Maharaja accordingly left for Calcutta, arriving there in time for the opening of the session, on the 15th January 1862.

Appointed member of the Legislative Council.

During the absence of the Maharaja, the Commissioner

territories. All feudatories and dependants of every degree will be bound to render obedience to him throughout his dominions.

Clause II.—Except as provided in Clause III., the British Government will never demand from His Highness, or any of his successors, or from any of his feudatories, relations, or dependants, any tribute on account of revenue service, or on any other plea.

Clause III.—The British Government cordially desires to see the noble house of Pattiala perpetuated, and in this spirit confers upon His Highness and his heirs for ever, whenever male issue may fail, the right of adopting a successor from among the descendants of the Phulkian family. If, however, at any time, any Maharaja of Pattiala should die without male issue, and without adopting a successor, it will still be open to the Rajas of Nabha and Jhind, in concert with the Commissioner or Political Agent of the British Government, to select a successor from among the Phulkian family, but in that case a *nazardna* or fine equal to one-third of the gross annual revenue of the Pattiala State shall be paid to the British Government.

Clause IV.—In 1847 the British Government empowered the Maharaja to inflict capital punishment after reference to the Commissioner. It now removes the restriction imposed by this reference, and invests His Highness with absolute power of life and death over his own subjects. With regard to British subjects committing crime, and apprehended in his territory, the Maharaja will be guided by the rules contained in the Despatch of the Honourable Court of Directors to the Madras Government, No. 3, dated 1st June 1836. The Maharaja will exert himself to execute justice, and to promote the happiness and welfare of his people. He engages to prohibit Sati, Slavery, and Female Infanticide throughout his territories, and to punish with the utmost rigour those who are found guilty of any of these crimes.

Clause V.—The Maharaja will never fail in his loyalty and devotion to the Sovereign of Great Britain.

Clause VI.—If any force hostile to the British Government should appear in this neighbourhood, the Maharaja will co-operate with the British Government and oppose the enemy. He will exert himself to the utmost of his resources in providing carriage and supplies for the British troops, according to requisitions he may receive.

Clause VII.—The British Government will not receive any complaints from any of the subjects of the Maharaja, whether mafidars, jagirdars, relatives, dependants, servants, or other classes.

of the Cis-Satlej States, at the request of the Chief, was directed to exercise a general supervision over the affairs of the Pattiala State, aiding with his counsel the officers who had been appointed to conduct the administration of the country, and taking care that the wishes of the Maharaja were loyally carried out.[1]

The Pattiala Chief remained in Calcutta the whole time that the Legislative Council sat, and, on the

Clause VIII.—The British Government will respect the household and family arrangements of the Maharaja, and abstain from any interference therein.

Clause IX.—His Highness the Maharaja will, as heretofore, furnish, at current rates, through the agency of his own officers, the necessary materials required for the construction of railroads, railway stations, and imperial roads and bridges. He will also freely give the land required for the construction of railroads and imperial lines of road.

Clause X.—The Maharaja and his successors, &c., will always pursue the same course of fidelity and devotion to the British Government, and the Government will always be ready to uphold the honour and dignity of the Maharaja and his house.

SCHEDULE OF TERRITORIES BELONGING TO THE MAHARAJA OF PATTIALA.

Ancestral.—Parganah Pattiala Khas and Sanour.

Ilakas Murdanpur, Ghanour, Ranimazra, Amargarh, Chinarthal, Sonam, Rajpura, Anahadgarh or Barnala, Sherpur, Bhiki, Banur, Bhawanigarh urf Doda, Boha Surdulgarh urf Dodhal, Akalgarh or Manak, Karmghar or Kulbanun Dirha, Bangarh or Narwana, Pinjor, Govindgarh or Batindah, Ramgarh or Ghuram, Sahibgarh or Pael, Fatahgarh or Sirhind, Alamgarh or Nandpur Kalour.

Acquired Territories.—Ilaka Umralah. The Hill district of Bughal, the Hill district of Keonthal, Ilaka Chamkorian, Parganahs Bassai Mulk Hydar, Fatah Jhuneri, Muhla, and Narnoul.

List of Feudatories.—Sikhs of Lunda, Lohari, Bhet Kot, Gunar, Chakia, Rara, Kotila, Bulara Bulari, Budadi Bhai, Bir Singh Rampur, Kot Duna, The Jagirdars of Badour and Jiundan.

The Jagirdars of Khumanun, Tullakour, Dhanouri and Lukhnour, are at present under the jurisdiction for life of the Maharaja of Pattiala, but paying commutation-tax in lieu of service to the British Government.

Ilaka Bhai Rupa shared with Nabha and Jhind.

[1] Government of India to Government Punjab, No. 210, dated 27th December 1861. Letter from Secretary to Government of India to Maharaja, dated 10th December 1860; and No. 188, the same date, to Commissioner Cis-Satlej States.

approach of summer, returned to his capital, where everything had gone on satisfactorily.

In March 1862, the right of adoption granted in 1860 was confirmed by a special Sanad.[1]

The death of Maharaja Narindar Singh, November 1862.

It was a calamity for Pattiala that the life of the most enlightened ruler she had ever possessed was destined to be short. In the beginning of November 1862, the Maharaja fell ill of fever, and though his illness was not at first considered serious, he was unable to regain his strength, and died on the 13th November, aged thirty-nine, after a reign of nearly seventeen years.[2]

His character.

The character of Narindar Singh has been shown in the preceding pages. He inherited from his father and grandfather a jealousy of the English Government, and a disposition to assert his own dignity, rights, and pretensions in a factious and litigious spirit, which turned into

[1] SANAD OF ADOPTION.

Dated 5th March 1862.

"Her Majesty being desirous that the Governments of the several Princes and Chiefs of India who now govern their own territories should be perpetuated, and that the representation and dignity of their houses should be continued, I hereby, in fulfilment of this desire, repeat to you the assurance which I communicated to you in the Sanad under my signature, dated 5th May 1860, that, on failure of natural heirs, the adoption by yourself and the future rulers of your State of a successor, from the ancient Phulkian House, of which your family forms a part, will be recognised and confirmed; and that if at any time any Maharaja of Pattiala should die without male issue, and without adopting a successor, it will still be open to the Rajas of Jhind and Nabha, in concert with the Commissioner or Political Agent of the British Government, to select a successor from among the Phulkian family, but in that case a nazârana or fine, equal to one-third of the gross annual revenue of the Pattiala State, shall be paid to the British Government.

"Be assured that nothing shall disturb the engagement thus made to you so long as your house is loyal to the Crown and faithful to the conditions of the treaties, grants, or engagements which record its obligations to the British Government."

[2] Commissioner Cis-Satlej States to Punjab Government, No. 852, dated 14th November 1862. Deputy-Commissioner Ambala, No. 852, dated 14th November.

a conflict every inquiry which the Government were compelled to make, and which they desired to conduct with the utmost delicacy and consideration for Pattiala. The events of 1857-58 changed the disposition of the Maharaja altogether. He was wise enough to understand what the inevitable result would be; and, like a brave soldier as he was, his sympathies were all with the few Englishmen, holding gallantly their own throughout India against tremendous odds. The generous manner in which he was rewarded by Government after the mutiny, and the grant of the right of adoption, with its assurance that the British Government did not desire the ruin of the Cis-Satlej Chiefs, but their continued prosperity, removed all mistrust from his mind; and, had he lived, Narindar Singh would have been one of the most valuable friends of the British Government in Northern India.

The Punjab Government issued a Gazette Extraordinary on receiving the news of his death, the terms of which will show the estimation in which he was held:—

The Gazette Order announcing his death.

"The Hon'ble the Lieutenant-Governor has received, with the deepest regret, intelligence of the demise, on the 13th instant, of His Highness the Maharaja of Pattiala.

"His Honour, in announcing the melancholy event, laments the removal, in the prime of life and usefulness, of a Feudatory Prince, who, at the time of the mutiny of the Native Army in 1857, performed the most eminent services to the Crown, and who administered the Government of his territories with exemplary wisdom, firmness, and benevolence."

Dip Singh, the brother of the deceased Chief.

Maharaja Narindar Singh had a half-brother, Dip Singh, who died, without issue, a short time before him, in 1862, aged thirty-five. He was not a man of any note. He enjoyed for life the income of the district of Karhali, about Rs. 25,000 a-year; but generally lived in Pattiala. Some suspicion of his loyalty was entertained at the time of the mutiny, but there is no reason to believe that he was in any way implicated.

The family of the Maharaja.

Narindar Singh married seven wives, who bore him one son and three daughters. The eldest of these was Basant Kour, born in 1845, and married to the Rana of Dholepur. The second daughter is now dead: she married Sirdar Narain Singh, son of Sirdar Dewa Singh of Sialba. The third was Bishan Kour, born in 1849, and married, in 1859, to Maharaja Jaswant Singh of Bhartpur. From this last marriage the happiest political results were hoped, which unfortunately have not been realised. The wedding ceremonies were conducted on a scale of great splendour, though the Maharaja of Bhartpur was induced to depart from the custom of distributing large sums of money among the congregated multitude of mendicants, vagabonds, and thieves. Among the Chiefs assembled at the ceremony were the Rajas of Jhind and Nabha, Raja Jowahir Singh, Raja Gurbaksh Singh of Manímajra; Sirdar Jiun Singh Buria; the Nawab of Maler Kotla; Sirdar Dewa Singh of Kalsia; the Nawabs of Loharu and Karnal. Presents were given, amounting in cash to Rs. 62,608, thirteen jewelled ornaments, 404 articles of ladies' dress, 94 horses (18 of them with gold trappings), two elephants, and two pairs of Kashmír shawls. The Maharaja of Kashmír sent a present of Rs. 21,000; the Raja of Kapurthalla, Rs. 1100, thirty-one articles of dress, and two horses; and the Maharaja of Jodhpur, Rs. 500 and an elephant. The British Government gave a marriage gift (*neotá*) of Rs. 5000.[1]

[1] Government Punjab to Government of India, No. 860, dated 28th

Mahindar Singh

Mahindar Singh, the only son of the Maharaja, was born on the 16th September 1852, though his birth was not announced to Government till the 14th January 1853 He was consequently only ten years old at the time of his father's death, and it was necessary to make immediate arrangements for carrying on the administration.

A Council of Regency provided for in 1858.

It will be remembered that in June 1858 a paper of requests from the Phulkian Chiefs was submitted for Government sanction, one of the paragraphs of which proposed that in the event of the death of any one of the three Chiefs, leaving an infant heir, "a Council of Regency, consisting of three of the old and trusty and most capable Ministers of the State may be selected by the British Agent, acting with the advice of the other two Chiefs, and that no stranger be introduced into the Council of Regency except with the consent of these two Chiefs, and in the event of misconduct on the part of any one of the Council, a successor to the Regency be appointed by the same means; in no case should any relatives of the infant heir be admitted to the Regency."

The dying commands of Narindar Singh.

This request was sanctioned by the Government of India. When Maharaja Narindar Singh felt himself to be dying, he called to him the Chief Officers of the State and gave them his last commands, which were to

December 1859. Government of India to Government Punjab, No. 76, dated 9th January 1860. Commissioner Cis-Satlej States to Government Punjab, No. 28, dated 29th February 1860. Despatch of Secretary of State, No. 45, of 1860, dated 31st May.

A "Neotâ," or wedding present, has occasionally been given by Government as a mark of special favour; but it is not necessary, nor warranted by precedent. The only instances are, that in the text; the marriage of the Maharaja himself, 5th March 1865, a like amount, Rs. 5000; the marriage of Prince Randhir Singh, Ahluwalia, 21st February 1848, Rs. 1100; the marriage of his brother Prince Bikrama Singh, 16th February 1849, a like amount; and, lastly, the marriage of the third brother, Suchet Singh, 5th February 1852, Rs. 1100; the father, Raja Nihal Singh giving a return present of jewels of equal value.

adhere to the British Government as he had done, to teach his son to follow in his steps, and in the administration of the State, to maintain the arrangements which he had made. The Maharaja must be considered to have referred to the agreement between the Chiefs and the British Government, as to the measures to be adopted in the case of a Regency; but a later paper was produced, a *Dastur-al-amal*, or Rules of Practice, drawn up on the 13th October 1860 for the guidance of the Ministers in the event of a Regency. This paper was not in any way in supersession of the agreement sanctioned by Government in 1858; it entered much more into details, and made no mention whatever of the number of the Council of Regency, or the assistance in their selection to be given by the British Agent or the Chiefs of Jhind and Nabha. The Pattiala Ministers tried to show that this document virtually superseded the agreement of 1858, and declared that the Raja's last wish that the arrangements he had made should be maintained signified that the Ministers then in power should continue to hold office, and that no Council of Regency consisting of three members should be appointed. Such a Council, they urged, would be injurious to the best interests of Pattiala. The members composing it would obtain too much power, and discord and jealousy would be introduced into the State, while the new appointments would cause additional expense and necessitate inferior men being nominated to their former appointments. All the chief officers of Pattiala were in favour of the administration being left as before in the hands of Diwan Kulwant Rai, Financial Minister; Abdul Navi Khan, Munshi or Secretary; Bakshi Bassawa Singh, Military Minister; and Syad Muhamad Hassan, *Adálati*, or

A later document produced, which the Ministers consider of superior validity to the former agreement.

The objections of the Ministers to the Council.

Their proposals.

Judicial Minister; with perhaps the addition of the tutor of the young Prince, an office not then filled up.

The opinion of the Rajas of Nabha and Jhind.

The Agent Cis-Satlej States addressed the Rajas of Jhind and Nabha on the subject of the Pattiala administration, inquiring their views and asking why the purport of the *Dastur-ul-amal*, or Code of Rules, had not been communicated to Government. These Chiefs approved of the continuance of the existing Ministry at Pattiala, and politely represented that, under the terms of the Sanads granted them by Lord Canning, the late Maharaja was not under any necessity of stating his intention to the Agent, as full independence had been granted to him, and full power to make any arrangements which might seem to him appropriate for the administration of his territory.[1]

The interpretation of the Sanad.

A simple, but at the same time a most important, question was thus raised as to the interpretation of the Sanad of the 5th of May 1860. The first clause of this agreement, similar to that made with the Rajas of Jhind and Nabha, contained these words: "His Highness the Maharaja and his heirs for ever will exercise full sovereignty over his ancestral and acquired domains." It is true that this Sanad was granted subsequently to the sanction accorded to the "Requests" of the Chiefs, containing the Regency arrangement; but did it give to the Maharaja any such powers as to set aside a solemn agreement sanctioned by the British Government at the request of the Chiefs? Of what nature was the "full

[1] From Commissioner Cis-Satlej States to Punjab Government, Nos. 278 and B, and 292, dated 21st and 25th November, and 26th December 1862. Original *Dastur-ul-amal*, of thirty-one Articles, dated 2d Asoj Badi 1917 Sumbat (13th October 1860). Letters ofRajas of Jhind and Nabha to Agent to Governor-General, dated 21st and 20th December 1862. Secretary to Government of India, No. 1213, dated 30th December 1862.

sovereignty" accorded to the Maharaja? The original Sanad contained the Persian words, "*hasb-i-dastúr-i-kadím hukmrán báshand*," signifying that the "full sovereignty" was such as had been enjoyed according to ancient custom. This undoubtedly meant that it was the intention of Government to acknowledge the independent sovereignty of the Chiefs in the manner allowed in 1809 and 1811, and restore the power of capital punishment withdrawn in 1847, but in no way to preclude the exercise of all interference in matters of extraordinary importance by Government.

The first clause only restored the powers which the Chiefs had lost.

The eighth clause did not prohibit control in extraordinary matters.

Clause VIII. of the Sanad, by which the Government promised to respect the household and family [1] arrangements of the Maharaja, and abstain from any interference therein, did not prohibit interference in a matter of the highest political and public importance, such as the formation of a Regency, the arrangements for which had been sanctioned on the formal request of the Chiefs themselves.

The term "full sovereignty" was a loose rendering of the original version, which the Chiefs had clearly understood as restoring to them the power they lost after the Satlej war. The interpretation of treaties is no difficult matter if the intention of the contracting parties is known and former treaties exist to explain the meaning. One Sanad does not cancel another unless this is specially provided, nor had any Chief the power, by a document to which no sanction had been accorded, to cancel a solemn engagement into which he had entered with the British Government. If "full sovereignty" meant a power such as this, the rights of the British Government, as paramount, would altogether disappear. "Full sovereignty," as far as Sanads are concerned, is a conven-

"Full Sovereignty" has a conventional meaning.

[1] "*Intizám-i-andarúní*"—internal arrangements.

tional term, and signifies such independence as is compatible with the claim which the British Government asserts to general control, active loyalty, and regard to all engagements which have not been expressly modified or cancelled.

Maharaja Naritdar Singh had u wish to set the agreement of 1858 aside.

There is no reason to believe that Maharaja Narindar Singh had any thought of setting the Code of Rules which he had framed in opposition to the agreement of 1858 regarding the Regency. Indeed, this document expressly declared that it was executed for the purpose of supporting the paper of Requests which contained the agreement. The Maharaja looked confidently to the British Government as his best friend, although he had, perhaps, more than any Chief in North India, a high regard for his own dignity; and when he left for Calcutta as a member of the Legislative Council, it was at his particular request that the Commissioner of Ambala was enjoined to generally supervise the affairs of the Pattiala State.

The Council of Regency appointed.

The Government held that the agreement of 1858 must be assumed to remain in force, and directed that a Council of Regency, consisting of three members, should be appointed. This was done, and the members selected, with the approbation of the Rajas of Nabha and Jhind, were Sirdar Jagdeo Singh, Bakshi Rahim Baksh, and Bakshi Udeh Singh.[1]

No detailed account of the Regency desirable.

It is undesirable, for obvious reasons, to give any detailed account of the administration of the Pattiala State since the formation of the Council of Regency. Like every native State in a similar position, with the

[1] Government Punjab to Government of India, No. 49, dated 24th January 1863. Government of India, No. 126, dated 13th March 1863. Despatch of the Secretary of State, No. 60, dated 15th August 1863.

Chief a minor and the interference of Government limited by engagements which it had no desire to infringe, the atmosphere of Pattiala has been, for some years, one of intrigue, in which a few have laboured for the advantage of their Prince and the country, while the majority have thought more of creating confusion in every department of the State to conceal their own inefficiency and dishonesty. But it must be left to another hand, at a future time, when the strong feelings which now exist with regard to Pattiala affairs have subsided or are forgotten, to write the story of these unhappy days.

Changes in the Council of Regency.

Bakshi Udeh Singh died on the 26th September 1863, and, in January of the next year, Bassawa Singh, who had been first on the Ministry proposed by the Pattiala Court, was appointed in his place, with the approval of the Rajas of Nabha and Jhind.[1] His tenure of office was very short, for he died in 1866, as did Bakshi Rahim Baksh.

New appointments.

On the visit of the young Maharaja to Simla in the autumn of 1866, the Viceroy confirmed the appointments of Moulvi Muhummad Hassan and Sirdar Fatah Singh, as members of Council, in the room of those deceased. The former was at the head of the Department of Criminal Justice, and the latter Governor of the district of Narnoul.

Diwan Kulwant Rai banished.

In December 1867, Diwan Kulwant Rai, the head of the Revenue office, and Bakshi Bir Singh, Commandant of the Forces, with some of their adherents, were banished from Pattiala. The Council, which had for some time been very unanimous, soon after this split into two parties,

[1] Commissioner Cis-Satlej States to Government, No. 3, dated 4th January. Government Punjab to Government of India, No. 17, dated 8th January; and Government of India, No. 84, dated 28th February 1864.

and in June 1868, the Agent of the Lieutenant-Governor appointed Abdul Naví Khan, Keeper of the Seal, an Extraordinary Member of the Council. Affairs in Pattiala did not, however, progress more smoothly than before, and in February 1870, the Maharaja was invested with full powers, and the Council of Regency was dissolved.

Full powers are bestowed on Maharaja Mahindar Singh in February 1870.

Character of the young Prince.

Maharaja Mahindar Singh is now eighteen years of age. His education has been carefully conducted by Ram Chandar, an eminent mathematician of Dehli, who long performed delicate and difficult duties at Pattiala with singular courage and honesty. His labours appear to have been successful. The young Maharaja is well educated for a native Prince, knowing English, Persian, and Gurmukhi. Possessed of great natural intelligence and force of character, there can be little doubt that Mahindar Singh will choose to rule his territory himself, and not surrender his power to unworthy subordinates. The troubles of the Regency have taught him many lessons, which will not be quickly forgotten. He, at any rate, will not begin his reign as his father did, with any suspicion of the intentions of the British Government: he knows well that its only wish is to see him prosperous and contented; while education has taught him that no Prince can be distinguished or worthy of honour who does not rule for the benefit of his people.

The Lieutenant-Governor visits Pattiala, 1867.

There remain a few incidents worthy of record in Pattiala history. First may be mentioned the visit of the Lieutenant-Governor of the Punjab to Pattiala in January 1867.[1] In March 1869, Maharaja Mahindar

[1] It may be interesting to give the programme of this visit as a picture of the ceremonies which custom enjoins in meetings with Native Princes. A similar ceremonial would be followed in the case of the Nawab of Bahawalpur, who is of equal rank with Pattiala :—

Singh attended the Durbar held at Ambala in honour of Amir Sher Ali Khan of Kabul, and, in February 1870, visited Lahore, to meet His Royal Highness the Duke of Edinburgh, when the usual ceremonial visits were exchanged between the Prince and the Maharaja.

The Sirhind Canal.

During the present year, 1870, a scheme of great importance to the Pattiala territory has been finally decided, which had been for many years under discussion. This is a canal from the Satlej near Rupar to irrigate the Pattiala and Ambala districts.

Programme of Proceedings on the occasion of the Visit of the Honourable the Lieutenant-Governor of the Punjab to His Highness the Maharaja of Pattiala.

The Honourable the Lieutenant-Governor will leave his camp at 7 o'clock, A.M.

Two Ministers of State of the first class will come out two miles from the city to meet the Lieutenant-Governor.

His Honour will be met by His Highness the Maharaja and his retinue at the village of Chourah.

At this place the Lieutenant-Governor will mount the Maharaja's elephant, and proceed to the camp, sitting on the Maharaja's right.

The Maharaja will have a suitable guard of honour drawn up in the vicinity of the town of Pattiala, who will salute the Lieutenant-Governor as he passes.

A salute of nineteen guns will be fired, as the cortège proceeds, from the walls of the town, and on the Lieutenant-Governor reaching his tents.

The Maharaja will accompany the Lieutenant-Governor to his tents, and there take leave.

Two Ministers of the State of the first rank will come from the Maharaja to inquire after the Lieutenant-Governor's health.

His Highness the Maharaja's Visit.

In the evening, at 4·30 P.M., the Maharaja will pay a visit to the Lieutenant-Governor. In the absence of the Deputy Commissioner, the Deputy Inspector General of Police will proceed on an elephant to accompany the Maharaja. The Military Secretary, Private Secretary, and Aide-de-Camp will go half-way on elephants to meet him; the Agent and Secretary to Government will receive him on alighting. The Lieutenant-Governor will come forward two or three paces beyond the edge of the carpet to meet the Maharaja.

The Agent will sit on the Maharaja's right, and the Maharaja's retinue on the right of him.

On the Lieutenant-Governor's left will sit the Secretary to Government and the staff of the Lieutenant-Governor.

In February 1861, the late Maharaja Narindar Singh, at an interview with the Lieutenant-Governor at Pinjor, expressed a desire to construct, at his own expense, a canal from Rupar, on the Satlej, into his own territory. He had some time before formed this intention, but the then Commissioner Cis-Satlej States considered the work impossible, and his idea was temporarily abandoned; however, in 1861, he again took it up and applied for the services of an engineer officer to survey the line. An officer of experience reported that the

First suggested by the late Maharaja in 1861.

The Maharaja's officials will then present the usual nuzzars.

Khilluts will then be brought in for the Maharaja and the Officials of the Pattiala State; and after the ceremony of *uttur* and *pan* the ceremony will conclude.

The ceremony of taking the Maharaja back will be the same as those for bringing him reversed.

A salute of seventeen guns will be fired on the Maharaja's coming and going, and the troops present in the Lieutenant-Governor's camp will present arms.

RETURN VISIT.

On the following day, at 4·30 P.M., four Ministers of State of the first rank will come to fetch the Lieutenant-Governor, and the Maharaja himself will come half-way to meet His Honour; and on meeting, the Lieutenant-Governor will take the Maharaja up with him on the elephant.

At the gate the troops will present arms.

In the Durbar, the Lieutenant-Governor will sit on the right of the Maharaja, and on his right, the Secretary to Government, and the other officers present. The Agent will sit on the Maharaja's left. State chairs will be provided for the Lieutenant-Governor, the Maharaja, the Agent, and the Secretary to Government; the rest will be plain chairs.

The officers of the Pattiala State will present the usual Nuzzars. The Lieutenant-Governor's Peshkush will then be brought in; after which *uttur* and *pan* will be given by the Maharaja himself to the Lieutenant-Governor, the Agent, and the Secretary to Government, and by the Council to the other officers; and the Lieutenant-Governor will take leave and return. The ceremonies on return will be those of coming reversed.

A salute of nineteen guns will be fired on the arrival and departure of the Lieutenant-Governor.

On the morning of the 26th instant, the Lieutenant-Governor will leave Pattiala for Bazidpore; on his departure a salute of nineteen guns will be fired.

The ceremonies of Ziafat, &c., will be carried out by the Maharaja, in communication with the Agent of the Lieutenant-Governor.

country was well adapted for irrigation and greatly in want of it, and the Government expressed a strong desire to give every encouragement possible to a work so useful.[1]

The scheme delayed.

The sudden death of the Maharaja prevented the realisation of the project, and it was not till July 1867, that, on the motion of the Government of India, it was again revived, and Sirdar Jagdeo Singh, Member of the Pattiala Council, and Abdul Navi Khan, Foreign Minister, deputed to discuss its details at Simla. Owing to the fierce dissension in the Pattiala Council, great delay took place in the negotiations as to the terms on which that State should join in the work of constructing the canal; but, in December 1869, the Pattiala Government assented to all the stipulations of Government, and the terms were finally determined in March 1870. The execution and supervision of the work is to be entirely in the hands of the British Government, whose officers are to have control over the water supply in the main channel, leaving the distribution from the smaller channels with the Pattiala Government. The cost of the canal is to be borne by both Governments in proportion to the amount of water taken by their respective territories; a certain seigniorage being paid, in addition, to the British Government, for the use of the water of the Satlej, a river in British territory. The works of this canal have been already commenced at Rupar, and its completion will prove of the greatest benefit to Pattiala, and largely increase its revenue.[2]

The conditions finally determined upon, A.D. 1870.

[1] Commissioner Cis-Satlej States, No. 108, dated 6th May 1861. Letter of Maharaja of Pattiala to Commissioner Cis-Satlej States. Memo. by Secretary to Government Punjab, Public Works Department, dated 14th May. Government of India to Government Punjab, Public Works Department, No. 1843, dated 30th May 1861.

[2] Government of India, No. 220, dated 12th July 1867, to Government

The Maharaja, in May 1870, presented to the University College of Lahore the sum of Rs. 70,000, of which Rs. 20,000 was intended to found a scholarship in honour of the Duke of Edinburgh, and to commemorate his visit to the Punjab.[1]

Donation to the University College.

Rani Basant Kour, sister of the Maharaja, had married the Raja of Bhartpur, and, early in 1869, after a long correspondence, she was allowed to visit her home at Pattiala, bringing with her the heir to the Bhartpur State, her son, only a few years of age. She remained at Pattiala for the rest of the year, but the child fell ill and died on the 4th of December, of inflammation of the lungs. The Rani herself soon after this fell ill of fever, and, after an illness of nearly three months, died on the 17th February 1870, while her brother was at Lahore, during the visit of the Duke of Edinburgh.[2]

The death of the heir to the Bhartpur State at Pattiala, December 1869.

The Rani of Bhartpur dies in February 1870.

Maharaja Mahindar Singh has married three wives. The lady last married, daughter of Mian Mehtab Singh Dhaliwal of Dina, a relative of the Raja of Faridkot, gave birth to a son on the 17th of October 1867.[3]

Birth of a son to the Maharaja, 1867.

Punjab. Commissioner Cis-Satlej States to Government of India, No. 203, dated 13th July. Government of India to Government Punjab, No. 247, dated 7th August, with Memorandum, No. 1867. Government of India to Government Punjab, No. 24, dated 30th November 1869. Government Punjab to Commissioner Cis-Satlej States, No. 1299, dated 10th December. Government Punjab to Government of India, No. 6-14, dated 3d January 1870.

[1] Letter of Maharaja to Agent Lieutenant-Governor, dated 29th March 1870; and No. 228, dated 30th May 1870, from Agent to Government Punjab.

[2] Commissioner Cis-Satlej States, Nos. 341 and 952, dated 7th September 1868, and 9th December 1869. Government Punjab to Commissioner, No. 816, dated 17th September 1868, and 6th October. No. 389 to Government of India, 21st December 1869, and 7th June 1870. Government of India to Government Punjab, No. 1100, dated 29th September 1868, and No. 189, dated 28th January 1870.

[3] Commissioner Cis-Satlej States to Government Punjab, No. 412, dated 3d December 1867. Government of India to Maharaja, dated 31st December 1867.

Appointed to the Order of the Star of India.

In May 1870, the Maharaja was nominated a Knight of the Most Exalted Order of the Star of India.

The area, population, and revenue of Pattiala.

The area of the Pattiala State is 5412 square miles; the population is not accurately known, but is probably about 1,650,000, and the revenue is estimated at Rs. 38,00,000 a year. A military force of 8000 men is maintained, and a contingent of 100 men is furnished by the Maharaja to the British Government for general service.

The Maharaja is entitled to a salute of seventeen guns, and ranks second of the Punjab Chiefs in Viceregal Durbars: the Maharaja of Jammu and Kashmir taking the first place. The following statement of the revenue of the Pattiala State for the year 1868-69 is supplied by the kindness of the Maharaja.

Statement of the Revenue of the Pattiala State for Sumbat 1925, *corresponding with Financial Year* 1868–69.

	Rs. a. p.	Rs. a. p.	Rs. a. p.
ACTUAL REVENUE RECEIPTS.			
1. Land Revenue, with other cesses and imports............	36,05,943 11 3		
2. Miscellaneous Receipts under different heads, such as Law and Justice, &c..................	2,12,365 5 0		
Total.......		...	38,18,309 0 3
LANDS EXCLUDED FROM THE STATE ASSESSMENT.			
3. The Bhadour Jagirs.............	77,779 15 0		
4. The Khamanun and other Sikh Feudatories Jagirs..............	1,20,626 4 0		
Total Revenue of the *Jagirdars'* or *zeldars'* villages..		1,98,406 3 0	
5. Revenue which the State collects, and pays to the Sohdis, Bhaikeans, and others, as *Maafi*............................	30,000 0 0		
6. Villages allowed to Sahds, Sohdis, &c., who collect the Revenue themselves.........	1,32,213 0 0		
Carry forward, .	1,62,213 0 0	1,98,406 3 0	38,18,309 0 3

Statement of the Revenue of the Pattiala State—continued.

	Rs. a. p.	Rs. a. p.	Rs. a. p.
Brought forward, .	1,62,213 0 0	1,98,406 3 0	38,18,309 0 3
7.[1] Minor Revenue Free Grants (a) *Zamindárá*, and (b) Miscellaneous, about.........	1,00,000 0 0		
Total Revenue Free and Religious Grants..................		2,62,213 0 0	
			4,60,619 3 0
Total Revenue of the State....	...	...	42,78,928 3 3
Of the actual Receipts,......	...	38,18,309 0 3	
The following (annual) Allowances being made, *i.e.* :—			
8.[2] Allowances to Headmen.........	2,01,379 0 6		
9.[3] Allowance (Adhkari) of Brahmans, Syads, and Faqirs.....	90,703 3 3		
10.[4] Usual *Panchai*, &c................	10,900 1 6		
11.[5] Maafidars..............................	18,178 12 6		
12.[6] Panchi-i-Mushakhsah (Settlement Allowances)..............	25,338 14 0		
Total,......		3,46,499 15 9	
The nett Income for the year was....................			34,71,809 0 6

[1] The amount of No. 7, Rs. 1,00,000 is only a calculated one, but as the calculations were made carefully, it may be considered to be tolerably correct. The *Zamindárá Maafis* (a), refer to those plots of land (generally two or four ploughs) which have been excluded from the State Assessment, and allowed to Biswádárs, for distinction and maintenance. The second class, *Miscellaneous* (b), includes those Revenue Free Grants which were allowed either for religious reasons or rewards for service.

[2] A percentage is allowed to Biswádárs from the total assessment of a village for distinction and maintenance. This is called "Inám-i-Panchán," and its right descends to the children of the Biswádár. A person receiving this *Inám* is at once acknowledged as a Biswádár. This percentage varies from above Rs. 10 to 9, 8, and less.

[3] *Adhkari* means half. It is an allowance to Brahmans, Syads, and Faqirs, (Hindu or Muhammadan) agriculturists, who only pay half the demand in proportion to others. Thus it will be seen that Rs. 90,703, 3 a. 3 p. were remitted to them in the year. This amount is subject to fluctuation, as such occupants transfer or abandon their holdings.

[4] *Panchai* is a fixed sum, not on the principle of percentage, and is allowed for the distinction and maintenance of certain families. It is not specially allowed to Biswádárs, as No. 8.

[5] Certain persons, though entered as Jagirdars or Maafidars of entire or portions of villages, are not, however, in actual possession of their Jagir or Maafi. The State collects the revenue from such village or portions of villages, and considers it as part of the State *Revenue*, the Maafidar being paid an annual pension equal to the amount of his Maafi.

[6] This Panchai is neither a distinctive nor a permanent one. It is allowed to Lambardars, at the option of the settlement officers during settlement operations, as a reward for services performed.

THE HISTORY

OF THE

BHADOUR CHIEFSHIP.

The Chiefs of Bhadour.

THE Sirdars of Bhadour are now altogether subordinate to the Maharaja of Pattiala, but as this subordination is of recent date, it is necessary to give a brief outline of their history till the year 1858, when the supremacy of Pattiala was allowed by the British Government by favour and not by right. The genealogical tree of the family is as follows :—

- **PHUL**, *d.* 1652.
  - **RAMA**,[1] *d.* 1714.
    - **DUNA**, *d.* 1726.
      - **Bigha Singh**, *d.* 1773.
        - **Gurdas Singh**, *d.* 1748.
        - **Chuhr Singh**, *d.* 1793.
          - **Bir Singh**, *d.* 1823.
            - **Johwair Singh**, *d.* 1827.
              - **B. Attar Kour. M. Prince Nao Nihal Singh of Lahore.**
            - **Jaimal Singh**, *d.* 1808.
              - **Khazan Singh**, *d.* 1831.
                - **Mahan Singh**, *d.* 1858.
                  - **Ishar Singh**, *d.* 1866.
              - **Nidhan Singh**, *d.* 1838.
                - **Kehr Singh**, *b.* 1835.
                  - **Partab Singh**, *b.* 1853.
                  - **Utar Singh**, *b.* 1863.
            - **Jagat Singh**, *d.* 1865.
              - **Gulab Singh**, *d.* 1850.
              - **Basawa Singh**, *d.* 1845.
              - **Khem Singh**, *d.* 1846.
              - **Narain Singh**, *d.* 1865.
              - **Ajepal Singh**, *b.* 1858.
          - **Dip Singh**, *d.* 18[illegible]2.
            - **Kharak Singh**,
              - **Attar Singh**, *b.* 1833.
                - **Bhagwant Singh**, *b.* 1852.
                - **Balwant Singh**, *b.* 1855.
        - **Mohr Singh**, *d.* 1826.
          - **Amrik Singh**, *d.* 1826.
            - **Dewa Singh**, *d.* 1857.
              - **Narain Singh**, *b.* 1852.
          - **Samand Singh**, *d.* 1836.
            - **Achhal Singh**, *b.* 1832.
          - **Sujan Singh**, *d.* 1828.
            - **Uttam Singh**, *d.* 1855.
              - **Attar Singh**, *b.* 1837.
        - **Dal Singh**, *d.* 1793. Ancestor of the Kot Duna Sirdars.
      - **Dao**, *d.* 1723.
      - **Sangu Singh**, *d.* 1744.
      - **Sukhu Singh**, *d.* 1765.
      - **Suma Singh**, *d.* 1772. Ancestor of the Rampuria Sirdars.

---

[1] The imperial Sanads given in the following pages, of Aurangzeb and Timur Shah, do not coincide in date with the recorded time of Chaudhri Rama's death.

The first is dated the fifteenth year of the Emperor Aurangzeb's reign, or A.D. 1673, and is directed to Chaudri Duná. The second is dated A.H. 1131, corresponding with A.D. 1719, and also purports to be a grant of the Emperor Aurangzeb, although that prince died A.H. 1119, corresponding with A.D. 1707, or twelve years before the Sanad assumes to have been issued. The third Sanad, dated 1192 A.H., or 1779 A.D., is of the Emperor Timur Shah, to Sirdar Chuhr Singh.

If the first Sanad be a genuine document, Rama must have been dead at the time of its issue, that is, in A.D. 1673, as the deed is in the name of his son as Chaudhri, in succession to his father deceased. The date given in the margin for the death of Rama, namely, A.D. 1714, would in that case be incorrect. But by comparison of many documents, the date given in the text would appear to be correct. The evidence in favour of its genuineness is stronger, at any rate, than the evidence in favour of the authenticity of the Sanads. That authenticity is further rendered more doubtful, by the curious mistake as to dates occurring in the second Sanad. The genuine-

Chaudhri Duná, the founder of the family.

Duná, the founder of the family, lived at Bhadour, with his brother Ala Singh, until the latter left for Barnála in 1718, when Bhadour came into his sole possession. He was a man of peace, and, not being a Sikh, he did not join his kinsmen in rebellion against the Muhammadan Empire, by which he had been entrusted with authority, as "Chaudhri," over Sangrur, Bhadour and other districts, which his father Ráma had enjoyed according to Sanads of more than doubtful authenticity.[1]

The office of the Chaudhri a dangerous one.

The office of Chaudhri was, in these days, hardly a

ness of the third document cannot be disputed like the other two, from internal evidence, but the three must stand or fall together. They were put forward to suit a certain purpose by the Bhadour Sirdars, and are inserted for what they are worth.

[1] Copy of a Firmán, said to have been granted by the Emperor Aurangzeb to Chaudharí Duná, A.H. 1063, or A.D. 1673:—

"Whereas it has been brought to our notice, that by order of the late Emperor, Taluká of Phul, &c., was granted to Chaudharí Ráman, &c., free, subject to the payment of Rs. 85,000 per annum to the Government. And Chaudharí Duná and others, his (Ráman's) heirs are alive and in possession of the Taluká, and that they request that a Firmán may be issued, therefore the order is issued that the Taluká of Phul, Bhadour, and Tappa, &c., and the Chaudharí thereof, shall be maintained to Chaudharí Duná and the other heirs. The Rs 85,000 which Chaudharí Duná paid to the Government, after the death of his father, he may realize their shares from his brother. At present the Rs. 85,000 are remitted to him.

"He should appreciate this kindness, and pray for the prosperity of the Empire.

"The Officers, Governors, Jagirdars, and Karrís of the present and future times should consider this a constant order, and let the Taluká remain in the possession of the grantee. This tenure will be free from change, and no fresh Sanad should be demanded."

Copy of Firmán, said to have been granted by the Emperor Aurangzeb to Chaudharí Duná, A.H. 1131, or A.D. 1719.

"At this time the Firmán is issued to the effect that Chaudharí Duná, of Bhadour, the son of Raman Phulwala, has always obeyed the Imperial orders, and is in no way opposed to the welfare of all parties, therefore the office of Chaudharí, of the Talukás of Sangrur, Dhanaula, Bhadour, and Hadaya, &c. (dependencies of the Pargana of Tehora), is bestowed upon him. He should esteem this a favour, and pay year by year Rs. 85,000 of current coin to the Hazúr, and endeavour to secure the happiness of the people, and pray for the prosperity of the Empire."

Dated 19th Muharram, 1131 Hijri (1719 A.D.)

desirable one, for it implied collection of the Imperial Revenue, which the people were very rarely willing to pay, and no excuses were of any avail if the money was not forthcoming at the appointed time.

In 1725, the Muhammadan Governor of Lahore demanded the customary payment, and Duná left for the capital, his brothers promising to send their quota after him. This they failed to do, and Duná and his son Dau were thrown into prison, in which the latter died. The intercession of a friend, Shaikh Alayás of Khawáspur, obtained the release of Duná, but the hardships of his imprisonment destroyed his health, and, returning to Bhadour, he died there in the year 1726. He left four sons, of whom Bigha succeeded him; the youngest, Suma Singh, being the ancestor of the Rampuria Sirdars.

He falls into difficulties.

His death, A.D. 1726.

Chaudhri Bigha

Regarding Bigha little of importance is recorded. He, like his father, fell into difficulties about the revenue, and when the Imperial officers arrived to arrest him, he generously proposed to give his eldest son, Gurdás Singh, in his stead. To this the mother of the boy would not consent, and carried him away with her to her father's home; and Bigha was imprisoned till he contrived to pay the amount of his arrears. In the meantime Gurdás Singh had died, and his mother, distracted with grief, poisoned herself. These melancholy events had so much effect upon Bigha, that he resolved to resign his office of Chaudhri, and become a recluse; but the Phulkian Chiefs induced him to abandon this design, and he married a second wife, who bore him Chuhr Singh and Mohr Singh. His third wife was the widow of his brother, Sukhu Singh. She became the mother of Dal Singh, from whom the Sirdars of Kot Duná, a village founded by Chaudhri Duná, have descended.

Chuhr Singh succeeds in 1773.

Bigha was succeeded by his eldest son, Chuhr Singh, in 1773. This Chief was the most famous of all the

His prowess and fame.

Bhadour stock, and his prowess and energy added much to his ancestral possessions, and the fame of "Chuhr Singh ke Bâr;" his victories over the Burars, and his charity to the poor, are still sung in many ballads by the village bards. He was the acknowledged arbiter in all disputes; the people preferred their complaints before him, and he punished offenders severely. For all this, Chuhr Singh was the most notorious robber on the border; cattle-lifting was not named in the code of offences which he punished, and to this very day, his old enemies, the Burars, if an ox or buffalo strays, will call it in the jungle, "*O! Chuhr leia!*" (O! carried away by Chuhr!)

In the year 1799, Chuhr Singh was appointed Chaudhri and collector of revenue in the Pihora and Bhadour districts, by Timur Shah, who in that year had invaded India, desiring to recover some of the authority possessed by his father, Ahmad Shah.[1]

[1] Translation of a Sanad of Timur Shah in the name of Chuhr Singh Phul, dated 11th Rajjab, 1192 A.H., 1779 A.D. :—

"At this time the magnificent mandate is issued, owing to the enhanced kindness of Royalty.

"The old Taluka of Pargana Sihara, together with the Ilaka of Bhadour, which is in your possession, is granted to you as heretofore. You may realise the fees collected by the Phuls, as were heretofore collected by your ancestors. And you should pay obedience to the Raja of Pattiala, and submit whetever you might have to say to the Hazúr through the Raja of Pattiala.

"It has also reached our ears that Hari Singh has raised a tumult in his country. You should ally yourself with the other Rajas and restrain him from injuring the creatures of God; and Muhammad Hussein Khan will be soon deputed in order to take possession of the country of Hari Singh through the Raja of Pattiala, and annex it to the Royal territories.

"As Hari Singh originally came from Multan, his native country, he should return to it.

"All matters connected with yourself have been explained to Muhammad

After the death of Raja Amar Singh of Pattiala, and the succession of the weak-minded Sahib Singh, the Bhadour Chief began to extend his possessions at the expense of the Pattiala State. He seized ninety villages in the neighbourhood of Bhadour, many of which he subsequently lost; attacked the Maler Kotla Afghans, whose villages were redeemed by Pattiala giving certain others in exchange, and even gained for a time possession of the district of Barnála. But, in the midst of his successes, treachery put an end to his life. On his road home from Barnála he remained to rest at the village of Ghanne, and was invited by a Burar of the name of Sujjan to sleep in a small burj, or tower, for the night. Chuhr Singh, who was accompanied by his brother, Dal Singh, suspected nothing; but their deceitful host, having drugged their liquor, and seeing them in a deep sleep, surrounded the tower with armed men, and, piling brushwood against the walls and doors, set it on fire. Awoke by the heat and noise, and finding all exit barred, the two brothers mounted to the roof, from which they shot arrows at their enemies till the roof fell in, and both perished in the flames. This happened in 1793.

His conquests.

Sirdar Chuhr Singh and his brother murdered, A.D. 1793.

The news of their father's murder had no sooner reached his two sons, Bir Singh and Dip Singh, than they determined to avenge it. They set out in search of Sujjan, and surprised him hawking, riding the horse of the mur-

The revenge of his sons.

Hussein Khan; and they will be determined and executed through the Raja of Pattiala.

"You should wait on us, else your country will be taken possession of by the Government.

"Hari Singh had proceeded to the Taluka of Nali. The Raja of Pattiala excluded him from thence. If Hari Singh should now go to the Jungul, let him not enter it.

"As of old you should remain obedient to the Raja of Pattiala, and depend upon the royal favours."

dered Chief. They killed him, and seized Ghanne, with the ten neighbouring villages forming the Ilaka of Malukha. Pattiala troops joined in this expedition under the command of Albel Singh and Bakshí Seda.

The Bhadour estate equally divided between the brothers Bir Singh and Dip Singh.

Bir Sing, the elder son of Chuhr Singh, succeeded to the estate; but in 1813, after the Cis-Satlej States had been taken under British protection, the two brothers divided it equally between them.

On the demarcation of boundaries in 1809, Maharaja Ranjit Singh retained two Bhadour villages, Saidoki and Bhagta. The British Government did not insist on their surrender, but paid to Bhadour Rs. 2000 per annum, as an equivalent, which sum was paid direct to the descendants of Bir Singh and Dip Singh, from 1813 to 1840, when Pattiala, with the design of supporting her unjust claim of supremacy over Bhadour, contrived to obtain its payment through her vakils.[1]

Dip Singh accompanied Raja Bhag Singh of Jhind on his visit to Lahore in 1805, and returned with him the next year, when Ranjit Singh made his expedition against Pattiala; but refused to join against the head of the Phulkian house, and left the camp of Ranjit Singh at Jagraon. This Sirdar died in 1822, and his brother the following year. After the Cis-Satlej States came under British protection, the history of Bhadour is contained in that of Pattiala, and although its Chiefs asserted vigorously their independence, yet they admitted Pattiala to be their head, and had no policy distinct from hers. There is, therefore, little further of interest to record.

The death of Bir Singh and Dip Singh, A.D. 1822

Kharak Singh.

Kharak Singh, the son of Dip Singh, succeeded to his father's share of the estate, and, although a man of considerable character and ability, was more devoted to reli-

[1] Government of India to Sir D. Ochterlony, 2d July 1813.

gion than administration, and built and endowed many temples and charitable institutions. At the time of the Satlej campaign he gave assistance to the British with a contingent, and furnished supplies to the army. After the campaign, when the whole question of the relations of Government to the States, and their relation to each other was discussed and settled, the connection of Pattiala and Bhadour could not but come under review, and since the question was disputed with especial warmth and earnestness, it is necessary to explain the circumstances of the case with some detail.

His service in 1845.

The great dispute regarding supremacy over Bhadour, A.D. 1850.

The proposals of the Board of Administration regarding the joint-estates held by Pattiala and other Sirdars had been formally approved by Government, and, in obedience to their instructions, the estates had been divided and disputed questions regarding them adjusted.[1] But at the date of Colonel Mackeson's report of 1850, no orders had been passed with reference to the territory of Bhadour, comprising fifty-eight villages, and situated on the southern border of the Fírozpur district, and over these villages the Maharaja of Pattiala exercised sovereign jurisdiction, as he did over all joint-estates before the final division above referred to. Colonel Mackeson held that the British Government possessed the right of escheat to heirless shares, but did not determine the exact relations between the Maharaja of Pattiala and the Bhadour Sirdars. Mr Edmonstone, Commissioner of the Cis-Satlej States, had been in favour of admitting the independence of Bhadour. He considered that the Phulkian families had each gained its principality by the sword, and that

The general orders of Government regarding joint-estates.

The number of Bhadour villages.

The opinion of Colonel Mackeson and Mr Edmonstone.

[1] Colonel Mackeson's Report, No. 16, dated 8th January 1850. Proceedings of Financial Commissioner, Nos. 76 to 83, dated 10th January 1852. Government Order, No. 399, dated 27th February 1852; and Financial Commissioner's Proceedings, Nos. 118, 119, dated 13th March 1852.

each, with the exception of Bhadour, was admittedly independent of the other, and there was no reason that Bhadour should be considered an exception.[1]

Mr Barnes reports on the case in 1854.

The question whether Bhadour should remain a feudatory of Pattiala, or be brought under the direct control of the British Government, had been referred for decision in 1850, but no orders were issued, and it remained for Mr Barnes, the Commissioner of the Cis-Satlej States, to report, in 1854, on the case.[2]

The representatives of the family.

At this time, the descendants of Duna, the founder of the Bhadour family,[3] were represented by six separate branches, among whom the estates were divided according to ancestral shares, the Sirdars being Kharak Singh, Jagat Singh, Kehr Singh, Mahan Singh, Dewa Singh, and Uttam Singh, whose relative position will be shown by a reference to the genealogical tree. The estate comprised fifty-eight villages, and was valued at Rs. 60,000 per annum; most of these villages were held entirely by the Bhadour Sirdars, and seventeen in joint-tenure with Pattiala. The Sirdars received, moreover, a pension of Rs. 2000 a year, in lieu of the two villages transferred in 1813, by Sir D. Ochterlony, to Maharaja Ranjit Singh, and this pension they had enjoyed for upwards of forty years.

There were also eight villages in Ludhiana, held in joint-tenure by the rebel Chief of Ladwa and the Bhadour Sirdars, who retained their share when the moiety of Ladwa was confiscated after the first Sikh war.

Pattiala claimed supremacy over Bhadour, and the

[1] Letter, No. 325½, dated 8th June 1850, and Financial Commissioner's Proceedings, Nos. 88 to 92, of 6th July 1850.

[2] No. 21, of 4th February 1854, to Chief Commissioner.

[3] The genealogical tree at the commencement of the Pattiala history, p. 11, will explain the relationship between the families of Pattiala and Bhadour.

right to succeed as paramount to all legitimate escheats. The Maharaja asserted, in support of his claim, that Bhadour had been always subject to Pattiala.[1] Ala Singh, the founder of the Pattiala family, gave Duna, the founder of the Bhadour house, the village of Shahnákí, to be held on a subordinate tenure, and the supremacy of Pattiala had always been acknowledged by Bhadour, which never even contracted a matrimonial alliance with Nabha or Jhind without Pattiala's consent. The Bhadour family never had exercised independent powers, and their estates were not acquired by conquest. Bhadour was founded by Rama, father of both Ala Singh and Duna, and was then the capital of the joint-territory. Ala Singh made it over, after the death of Duna, to his heirs, and founded for himself a new capital at Barnála. So far, then, from this estate being a conquest of Duna's, it was a grant from Pattiala, and only came into the possession of the Bhadour family after his death. Moreover, the Bhadour Sirdars had themselves repeatedly admitted their dependence, and were still most anxious to remain in subordination to Pattiala, which they regarded as their natural head, and to which they were bound by every tie of interest and affection. Pattiala had, on their account, paid tribute to Ahmad Shah Durani, the Mahrattas, and Ranjit Singh; and her right to supremacy had been admitted by successive agents of the British Government, and notably by Mr G. R. Clerk, who authorised the Maharaja to employ force to reduce to order the Bhadour Sirdars; stating, in his letter, that, on all previous occasions, at the instance of the British Government, Pattiala had maintained order in Bhadour.[2] So late as the 28th of August 1852, the Sirdars themselves had addressed the

The arguments of Pattiala in favour of her claim to supremacy.

[1] *Vide* objections filed by Pattiala Vakil in February 1854.
[2] Mr G. Clerk, April 1835, and 1841.

Settlement Officer, who required their attendance at Ludhiana, to the effect that they were then, and always had been, feudatories of Pattiala, and had no desire to deny or change relations from which they had always derived benefit.

The argument on the other side of the question.

Such were the arguments which Pattiala advanced to prove her supremacy. On the other side, it might be urged with great force that the custom of the Phulkian family was not to unite under one selected leader, but that each man of courage and capacity conquered what territory he could for himself, and left it in independent possession to his heirs. Thus had been founded the Chiefships of Pattiala, Nabha, Jhind, and Malod, and thus, it might be presumed, had it been with Bhadour. Pattiala had, it is true, far outstripped her rivals in the race for power, but her wealth and extensive territory had never given her a right to supremacy over the other Chiefs. Duna, the founder of Bhadour, was certainly not a warrior, but he nevertheless acquired a certain number of villages, while his grandson, Chuhr Singh, was one of the most distinguished Chiefs of his day. Even were the acquisitions of Duna made with the assistance of Ala Singh, yet he was nevertheless independent of his brother, and was his equal, not his vassal.

The Bhadour Chiefs desired to come under Pattiala authority in 1854.

It was quite true that, in 1854, the Bhadour Sirdars were desirous of claiming the protection of Pattiala, but their reasons were evident, and were not such as the British Government could allow.

They had always denied Pattiala supremacy before.

There were plenty of old records in the Agency Office which showed that these Chiefs had insisted on their independence, and had rejected the pretensions of Pattiala, proving that a struggle between the States had always been maintained; complaints from Pattiala that Bhadour would not yield allegiance, and protests from the Sirdars against the unjust claims of their powerful neighbour.

The reason for the sudden change in the disposition of the Bhadour Chiefs is found in the change which the Sikh war had made in the relations of the Cis-Satlej States with the British Government. Before the war every State had exercised sovereign powers, and the Sirdars knew that if they were declared independent of Pattiala they would have full authority over their own subjects, and would be practically under no control. For this reason they struggled against the pretensions of Pattiala. But the consequence of the war was the disfranchisement of all but the largest Sikh States. The Bhadour Chiefs would, separated from Pattiala, have sunk to the level of ordinary jagirdars, with no civil or criminal powers, and even their revenue limited at the discretion of Government officers. Under Pattiala they would enjoy far greater power, and, as she was anxious to retain them as feudatories, she was disposed to allow them exceptional privileges and immunities, which the British system was unable or unwilling to grant. These considerations made the Sirdars as ready to acknowledge the supremacy of Pattiala as they had before been to resist it. **The reason for the change in their wishes clear.**

That Bhadour had originally been independent was further proved by the joint possession of estates with the Raja of Ladwa, showing that it was able to ally itself with another Chief, and make conquests on its own account. The large village of Bhai Rupa, in which every Phulkian Chief held a share, was an additional proof; since, if Bhadour was merely a Pattiala feudatory, it would not have become possessed of an equal share in the estate. Lastly, the tenure of the fifty-eight villages of the Bhadour territory, of which seventeen only were **Proofs of Bhadour independence.**

held conjointly with Pattiala, went some way to prove that these seventeen alone were acquired by Ala Singh and Duna together, and that the remainder, in which Pattiala held no share, were the sole and independent acquisition of the latter.

The claims of Pattiala rejected by Government.

The British Government was unwilling to surrender to Pattiala a position which had always been denied, and a supremacy which belonged to itself, the paramount power; or to refuse to the people the improved administration and the diminished assessment which would be the result of the State being brought directly under its own control; and, considering the independence of Bhadour sufficiently proved, directed that British jurisdiction should be extended over the forty-one villages held by Bhadour alone, and that the seventeen villages held in joint tenure by Pattiala and Bhadour should be divided according to the principles which had determined the division of other estates held in co-parcenary.[1]

The Maharaja begs for a re-decision of the case.

The Maharaja of Pattiala was not satisfied with the decision thus given against him, and addressed to the Chief Commissioner a remonstrance pointing out what he considered defective in the arguments which had been adduced to prove the independence of Bhadour. He urged that the order of Government was opposed to the letter of the treaty, which declared that all his zaildars and feudatories should remain unmolested, and the Chief Commissioner directed further inquiries to be made, and the objections of the Maharaja to be, if possible, satisfactorily answered.[2]

[1] Chief Commissioner to Government of India, No. 160, dated 28th February 1854, and Government of India to Chief Commissioner, No. 1013, dated 17th March 1854. Government of India, No. 399, dated 23d February 1852.

[2] Kharitah of the Maharaja to Chief Commissioner, of July 1854. Letter

Pattiala asserted her own right to succeed to heirless shares in Bhadour; but this claim could not be admitted by the British Government, which, ever since its first connection with the Cis-Satlej States, had, as paramount, claimed all such succession. The States were taken under British protection, and their independence and, indeed, their very existence were preserved; neither tribute nor contingent was demanded from them, and the trouble and complications which this connection involved were enormous. Was it to be supposed that, out of mere benevolence, so onerous a charge had been accepted? The British Government never professed to be absolutely disinterested in its motives. In return for protection, it insisted on the rights claimed by every sovereign power, of which the chief and the only profitable one was the right of succession to shares of estates in which the only heirs were distant collaterals.

Pattiala asserts extravagant claims.

The rights of a sovereign power.

A very large number of estates, comprising some of the wealthiest in the Cis-Satlej territory, had thus come into British possession, including among them estates held by feudatories of Pattiala itself, such as Chamkurian, in 1812, and Serai Lashkar Khan, in 1835, the latter decision being confirmed by the Home Government.[1]

Nor had Pattiala itself ever exercised the right of succession to heirless shares; and the instance which the Maharaja adduced of the succession of Sardul Singh to the estate of his cousin Jodh was not a case in point, for that succession was simply through a marriage with his cousin's widow; and if Jodh's estates had lapsed to

of Commissioner Cis-Satlej States to Chief Commissioner, No. 167, dated 28th July 1854, and Chief Commissioner's No. 653, dated 7th August 1854, to Commissioner Cis-Satlej States.

[1] Supreme Government, dated 24th June 1835; Agent Dehli, dated 14th August 1834.

Pattiala as an escheat, Sardul Singh would never have inherited them, seeing that he was at no time Chief of Pattiala, dying in the lifetime of his father, Ala Singh.

The Firmân of Prince Timur Shah.

One of the *firmâns* granted to Chuhr Singh by Prince Timur Shah [1] is said to prove the feudal tenure of Bhadour, and its subordination to Pattiala. This is not the construction, however, which would generally be placed upon it, even were its authenticity certain, instead of being doubtful in the extreme, as has been shown in a previous note. It would rather seem to show that Bhadour was, and had been from the first, independent.

A reference is certainly made to the Raja of Pattiala, who was to be obeyed, and through whom any necessary representations were to be made; but this does not destroy the idea of independence which is created by an Imperial *firmân* being issued to Bhadour at all, and by the direction to form alliance with other Rajas to restrain the violence of Harí Singh. It was, besides, natural for Timur Shah to refer to the Raja of Pattiala as the head of the Cis-Satlej Sikhs, which indeed he was, though without any actual supremacy, since both Rajas Ala Singh and Amar Singh had been ennobled by his father, Ahmad Shah; and though gratitude was a virtue rare among the Sikhs, yet the Pattiala Chief might be expected to entertain it and to be loyal towards Timur Shah, if his interests did not forbid loyalty altogether.

The manner in which Bhadour had been acquired was clear.

It has before been stated that Duna, the ancestor of the Bhadour Sirdars, was a peaceful man, content with the office of Chaudhri, which he received from the Dehli Emperor, possessing none of the ambition of his brother, Ala Singh. But there is nothing to show, as asserted by Pattiala, that Duna was in any way subordinate to his

[1] *Vide ante*, pp. 250, 251.

brother. The Maharaja declared that Bhadour was not a conquest, but founded by Rama, and considered the capital till after the death of Duna, when Ala Singh gave it to his nephews, who had been entrusted to his care, as a mark of high favour, and as a reward for services rendered to him by their father. It is true that Bhadour was not a conquest, and that it remained the joint capital for some time after the death of Rama, its founder; but it came into the hands of Duna by a friendly compromise between the brothers, not as the gift of a superior to an inferior. At the time when Bhadour was transferred, Duna was the head of the family, and Ala Singh had not yet made wealth and fame. What more natural than that he should have left the ancestral village to the head of the family, trusting to conquer an estate for himself elsewhere. That Duna was acknowledged as head of the family is evident from the two Imperial *firmâns* of Aurangzeb[1] by which he is authorised to collect the revenue of Rs. 85,000 from his brothers, including Ala Singh; and it was as the representative of the family that he visited Lahore, where he was imprisoned, and where his son Dau died.

The independence of Duná was also clear.

In 1825, Maharaja Sahib Singh furnished Captain Murray, the Political Agent, with a list of villages over which he had jurisdiction, and he then, with reference to the Bhadour estate, entered, as belonging to the Bhadourias, fifty-three villages, and a share in Bhai Rupa, with seventeen villages bestowed by himself on Chuhr Singh Bhadour, on account of service and bravery in his cause. The distinction drawn between the fifty-three villages acquired by Bhadour apart from Pattiala, and the seventeen villages, being a Pattiala grant, is clear.

The list furnished by Raja Sahib Singh strong proof against Pattiala.

[1] *Vide ante*, p. 254.

Even this grant of the seventeen villages to Chuhr Singh was not such a one as to imply any supremacy, for several of these villages were extorted from the almost imbecile Sahib Singh by his energetic kinsman, while others appear to have been given in exchange for the lands taken by Chuhr Singh from the Maler Kotla Afghans, and which he restored.

The view of the case taken by Mr Clerk.

There would be no advantage in following the arguments of Bhadour and Pattiala step by step, and determining the amount of truth in each. There can be no doubt that Mr Clerk, the Political Agent, who on one occasion did permit the Pattiala Chiefs to coerce the Bhadourias, which permission would have been better withheld, formed later a perfectly just estimate of the connection between the States. Writing to the Maharaja on the 8th of June 1835, he states as follows:—"In truth, the relations between Pattiala and Bhadour are of the following nature. The Sirdars of Bhadour, since the date of protection, have existed on precisely the same footing as all other Chiefs of the Cis-Satlej. The late Maharaja was accustomed to call the Bhadourias his uncles (*chhacha sâhib*), whereas you designate them as dependants and vassals. Your vakil has been the usual channel for presenting applications from the Bhadour Sirdars in pending cases, and therefore Bhadour disputes have generally been referred to you. I and Mr Ross Bell have always counselled you that Pattiala is, as it were, the elder brother, and the Bhadourias younger brothers. The senior has the authority to discipline his younger brethren, and, in this view of your relations, the affairs of Bhadour have been usually consigned to you."[1]

[1] Letter of Mr Clerk to Maharaja Sahib Singh, 8th June 1835. Objections and arguments filed by Pattiala in 1854 and 1855, and Letter No.

That the Bhadour Chiefs acknowledged Pattiala as the head of the Phulkian family is clear. Nabha and Jhind did the same, but Pattiala never claimed to assert over them any supremacy. There is no evidence to show that the Bhadour estate, or any large portion of it, was a Pattiala grant; while there is ample proof that it was an independent acquisition. The British Government, often careless of its rights, and served by men who have not been sufficiently jealous of its prerogatives, had undoubtedly allowed Pattiala to act towards Bhadour in a manner which gave some colour to the claim of supremacy; and in the interval between the death of Bir Singh in 1823, and 1847, the date of the extension of British protection, the power and aggressiveness of Pattiala constantly increased, while the capability of resistance on the part of Bhadour as constantly diminished, for, while the right of primogeniture kept Pattiala compact, the rule of division among the sons had reduced the Bhadour State to a number of petty Chiefships, without any cohesion or power of combined resistance.

Pattiala had always been acknowledged as head of the family.

The wishes of the Chiefs had also changed in 1847, and they preferred the licence which Pattiala promised them, if her supremacy was allowed, to the dulness and compelled moderation of their position as simple jagirdars in British territory. At the present day, with their position assured and the supremacy of Pattiala acknowledged, the Bhadourias have again changed, if not their desire, their mode of expression, and assert their former independence as sturdily as they were wont to do forty years ago, and as obstinately as they denied it in 1847 and 1854.

The many changes in the assertions of the Chiefs.

221, dated 12th September 1855, from Commissioner Cis-Satlej States to Government Punjab.

The claims of Pattiala finally rejected in 1856.

In 1855 the supremacy of Pattiala was refused by the British Government, which declared its final determination to adhere to the former decision of the 17th March 1854, by which British jurisdiction was extended over the villages held by Bhadour, while those held in joint-tenure by Pattiala and Bhadour were to be divided on the principle which regulated the Chahárumi tenures.[1] The Sirdars of Bhadour were, moreover, by a later order, exempted from the jurisdiction of the ordinary tribunals for acts done by them previous to the 27th of April 1855, the date on which the final orders of Government were passed.[2]

The joint estate divided.

There was still some difficulty in settling the terms of the agreement; but at length Pattiala agreed to accept as her share of the assessment, which amounted to Rs. 7676, the villages of Chota and Bara Bazídri, Bawant, Bilaspur Sunda, Gidhari, Mandian, and Jahángirpúr, worth Rs. 7786 per annum.[3]

Certain villages given up to Pattiala.

Of the eleven villages to which Pattiala made specific claims subsequent to the final settlement of the Bhadour dispute, the Maharaja's right to one was allowed, and in other six cases denied. With reference, however, to the four villages of Kot Duna, Bugar,[4] Rampur,

[1] Government Punjab to Government of India, No. 162, dated 9th February 1855; and Government of India to Government Punjab, No. 1524, dated 27th April 1855.

[2] Commissioner Cis-Satlej States to Punjab Government, No. 211, dated 17th September 1855. Punjab Government to Government of India, No. 741, dated 3d October. Government of India to Government Punjab, No. 3729, dated 24th October 1855.

[3] Deputy-Commissioner Firozpur to Commissioner Cis-Satlej States, No. 314, dated 15th November 1855. Commissioner to Deputy-Commissioner, No. 1536, dated 17th November 1855. Commissioner Cis-Satlej States to Government Punjab, No. 5256, dated 10th and 13th March 1856. Government Punjab to Commissioner Cis-Satlej States, Nos. 209 and 210, dated 22d March 1856.

[4] This village must not be confounded with the village of the same name.

and Kotla Kowra, it was recommended that, under the special circumstances of the case, they should, as an act of grace, be surrendered to the Maharaja, although the right of jurisdiction was clearly proved to belong to the British Government.[1] A subsequent recommendation was made in favour of the village of Mán, which was held in equal shares by Pattiala and the Kot Duna branch of the Bhadour family, and lay in the midst of the Pattiala possessions. These five villages were accordingly made over to Pattiala.[2]

The supremacy over Bhadour granted as a reward for service in 1857.

The supremacy for which the Maharaja had struggled with so much pertinacity, but which he was unable to establish as a right, was granted as an act of grace and as a reward for loyal service to the British Government in the year 1858. All the rights of the paramount power were yielded to Pattiala—the jurisdiction over Bhadour, the right of escheats, the reversion of lapsed estates, and the annual commutation tax, amounting to Rs. 5265.[3]

The supremacy of Pattiala having been thus allowed,

regarding which there was a dispute between Pattiala and Nabha, and which, in 1857, was assigned to the latter.

[1] Commissioner Cis-Satlej States, Nos. 155 and 156, dated 10th July 1855. Punjab Government, No. 670, dated 1st August 1855.

[2] Deputy-Commissioner of Firozpur to Commissioner Cis-Satlej States, No. 290, dated 24th October 1855. Commissioner Cis-Satlej States to Government Punjab, Nos. 22 and 281, dated 9th February and 5th September 1857. Government Punjab to Government of India, Nos. 180 and 623, dated 6th March and 9th September 1857. Government of India to Government Punjab, Nos. 1617 and 4600, dated 14th April and 18th November 1857.

[3] Government Punjab to Government of India, No. 34, dated 13th April 1858. Government of India to Government Punjab, No. 1549, dated 2d June 1858. Kharitah of Governor-General to Maharaja of Pattiala of the same date. Some doubt was felt by the Maharaja as to the terms of this grant, and the Government of India subsequently declared that the Bhadour territory was to be held by the Maharaja and his lineal male heirs in perpetuity. Commissioner Cis-Satlej States to Government Punjab, No. 140, dated 20th May 1859. Government Punjab to Government of India, No. 386, dated 1st June; and Government of India to Government Punjab, No. 7712, dated 17th June 1859.

The reasons for dwelling at such length on the case.

it would seem almost unnecessary to have dwelt at so much length on the dispute regarding it, were it not of importance as showing the manner of the rise of the Cis-Satlej States, the nature of their mutual relations, and the motives which influenced the statements of the Chiefs. Much of the difficulty of questions relating to these States is occasioned by the uncertainty which surrounded the law of inheritance—an uncertainty increased by the utter disregard of truth in the statements made by the Chiefs, unless the truth happened to favour the view which they desired to maintain. The more careful the search in the history of these States, the more certain it appears that no statement should be accepted without rigorous inquiry, unless made by a person absolutely devoid of interest in the matter at issue. The idea of preferring truth to his own interests never seems to have occurred to any Sikh Chief.

Sirdar Attar Singh of Bhadour.

Sirdar Attar Singh, who succeeded his father, Kharak Singh, in 1858, is the present head of the Bhadour family, and was born in the year 1833. He was educated at Benares, and there acquired a taste for learning which is very rare among the Sikhs. He has a good library at Bhadour, stocked with valuable MSS.—Sanskrit, Gurmukhi, and Persian—and has founded a school in which these languages are taught free of all charge, the very poor being fed as well as taught. Besides encouraging learning, Attar Singh is himself a good scholar, and composes in a graceful style. In 1870 he was appointed one of the Senate of the Punjab University College. While a jagirdar of the British Government, he did good service in 1857 at Ludhiana and at Firozpur with fifty horsemen, and received the acknowledgments of Government and exemption from payment of six months' commutation.

THE MINOR PHULKIAN FAMILIES.

MALOD—BADRUKHAN—JIUNDAN—LANDGHARIA—DIALPURIA—RAMPURIA—AND KOT DUNA.

THE family of Bhadour is the most important of the smaller Phulkian houses, but there are several others who must receive a brief mention here to render the account of the clan complete.

The chief of these is Malod, descended from Bakhta or Bakht Mal, the fourth son of Chaudhri Rama, and brother of Duna and Ala Singh, the founders of the Bhadour and Pattiala houses. **The family of Malod.**

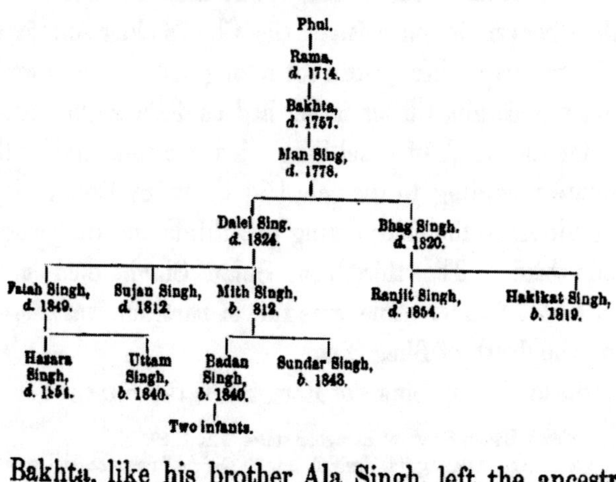

Bakhta, like his brother Ala Singh, left the ancestral village of Bhadour, and founded, eight miles to the eastward, a village which he called after his own name. Nothing further is related of him, but his son Man Singh was a distinguished Chief. His mother was of the Man Jat clan; and a popular tradition in the Punjab makes all of the Man tribe brave and true. He conquered the district of Malod from the Maler Kotla Afghans in 1754,[1] and dying in 1778, left two sons, the elder of whom, Dalel Singh, took the whole estate to the exclusion of his younger brother, Bhag Singh, who complained to Raja Sahib Singh of Pattiala, and begged his interference in his behalf. Sirdar Chuhr Singh of Bhadour was requested to arrange matters, and by his arbitration the elder brother took two-thirds and the younger one-third.

Sirdar Dalel Singh of Malod.

Sirdar Dalel Singh was a Bairagi,[2] and employed as his officials Fakirs and Muhants.[3] He would not allow any one to hunt or shoot in his estate, and fined any one convicted of so doing. In 1806 Maharaja Ranjit Singh, who was marching through the country, summoned him, but he sent answer that he was engaged in devotion and could not come. Ranjit Singh, who thought more of earth than heaven, at once seized the Chief's elder son, forced him to carry a heavy load for a long distance, and would not release him till his father had paid Rs. 22,000 fine.

On the death of Dalel Singh, his two sons divided the estate according to the rule laid down by Chuhr Singh Bhadouria—the elder taking two-thirds and the younger one-third. The third son, Sujan Singh, died in his father's lifetime. The same rule of partition was adopted on the death of Bhag Singh.

Sirdar Uttam Singh of Ramgarh.

Sirdar Uttam Singh of Ramgarh is the present head of

[1] Siruar Uttam Singh of Ramghar states, A.D. 1759.

[2] The term "Bairagi" is derived from "*Bairág*," penance, and signifies an ascetic. It is, however, confined to the followers of Vishnu.

[3] Religious mendicants and heads of religious institutions.

the Malod family. He is the second son of Sirdar Fatah Singh, to whose whole share he succeeded on the death of his elder brother, Hazara Singh, without heirs. He is thirty years of age, and is a man of great intelligence. In 1866[1] he was created a Jagirdar Magistrate in his own estate, which is worth Rs. 34,655 per annum.

Sirdar Mith Singh of Malod is the second in rank of this family. He, with his brother Fatah Singh, did good service during the war of 1845-46, supplying fifty sowars, and fought himself at Mudki and Firushahr. In 1857 he showed conspicuous loyalty, being always ready with men and money, and received, as a reward, the remission of a year's commutation money, while one-sixteenth of the whole sum was for ever excused. He is regarded with great esteem by all who know his character and services. *Sirdar Mith Singh of Malod.*

The younger branch of the Malod family has only one representative—Sirdar Hakikat Singh of Ber. On the death of his brother, Ranjit Singh, he succeeded to the Ber estate, having before held only that of Chime. He is an Honorary Magistrate, and did good service in 1857. *Sirdar Hakikat Singh of Ber.*

The Badrukhan family ranks next among the Phulkians, after Bhadour and Malod. The principal part of the history of this family is given with that of Jhind, of which it was a branch, Sirdar Bhup Singh, the founder, being the son of Raja Gajpat Singh and the brother of Raja Bhag Singh of Jhind. He received his separate estate in 1789, from which time he was always considered independent of Jhind. However, in 1834, the Jhind line being extinct on the death of Raja Sangat Singh, Sarup Singh, the grandson of Sirdar Bhup Singh, was allowed by the British Government to succeed, and *The Badrukhan family.*

[1] Circular order No. 641, dated 26th May 1866.

became the father of the present Raja of Jhind. Basawa Singh, the uncle of Raja Sarup Singh, was the first Chief of Badrukhan, his father having held this estate and that of Bazidpur; and the Phulkian Chiefs assigning Badrukhan and Bamman Bade, the more valuable portion, to the younger son, since he has been obedient to his father, while Karam Singh, the elder, had openly rebelled against him.

Sukha Singh, the elder son of Basawa Singh, who died in 1830, claimed the Jhind Chiefship on the death of Sangat Singh, on the ground that the custom of the Jhind house was for the estate to devolve on the second son, and also that his brother, Karam Singh, had been disinherited for his disobedience; but these claims were disallowed by the British Government.

The Badrukhan genealogy.

The Badrukhan genealogy is as follows:—

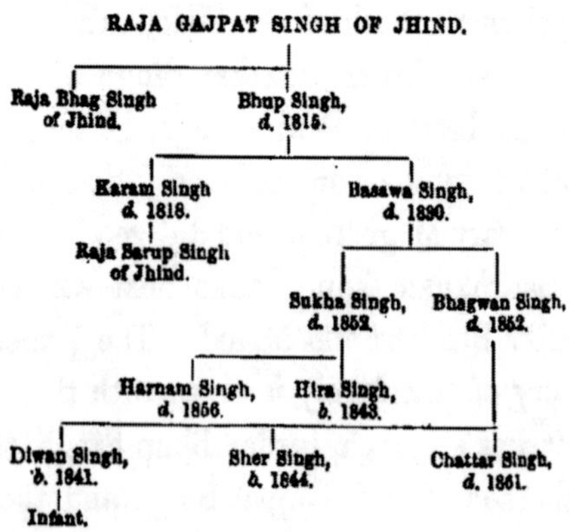

On the death of Sukha Singh, his estate was equally divided between his two sons, but on the death of Harnam Singh in 1856, Hira Singh, the younger, succeeded to the whole. Diwan Singh is the representative of the younger branch of the family. The jurisdiction over the village of Badrukhan was transferred in 1861 to Jhind.

Those of the Phulkian family who have at this day rank and position have now been mentioned. Eleven of the descendants of Phul are entitled to attend the Durbars of the Viceroy, namely :— The Phulkian Chiefs who are entitled to seats in Vice-regal Durbars.

Maharaja Mahindar Singh, Pattiala.
Raja Raghbir Singh, Jhind.
Raja Bhagwan Singh, Nabha.
Sirdar Attar Singh, Bhadour.
Do. Kehr Singh,[1] Bhadour.
Do. Achhal Singh, Bhadour.
Do. Uttam Singh Rampuria, Malod.
Do. Mith Singh, Malod.
Do. Hakikat Singh, Ber, Malod.
Do. Diwan Singh, Badrukhan.
Do. Hira Singh, Badrukhan.

The Bhadour Chiefs sit in Durbar as feudatories of Pattiala; the Badrukhan Chiefs of Jhind, and the Malod Sirdars, as British jagirdars.

There are several other families of the Phulkian stock who are of no political or historical importance, who count no Sirdars among their number, and who are not entitled to be present at any Durbar. But the only difference between them and the great Chiefs is in wealth and power; all the Phulkians are presumed to be socially equal, and their daughters marry into the families of Pattiala, Jhind, and Nabha. The zamindar families of the Phulkian Clan.

These poor relations of the great houses form five families: two descended direct from Phul, the common ancestor; one an offshoot from the Jhind; and the two last offshoots from the Bhadour stock.

[1] In the Vice-regal Durbar of 1864, Ishar Singh, the representative of the elder branch, took Kehr Singh's place, but he died two years later, and that branch is now extinct.

The Sikhs of Jiundan.

First are the Sikhs of Jiundan and Bhagrawal, thirty-two in number, and owning land worth Rs. 2079 a year. They descend from Rughu, the third son of Chaudhri Phul, by his first wife, Bali. He married, in the village of Jiundan, the daughter of "Malkher Bullar," and seems to have had no more distinguished profession than highway robbery. When he became too blind to follow this occupation, he settled in his wife's village of Jiundan, where he died in 1717.

When Pattiala made specific claims to certain Bhadour villages after the general question of jurisdiction had been settled, a separate discussion arose regarding the village of Jiundan. Pattiala asserted that Rughu was killed in a fight with the Burars, and that his widow and children came to settle in her father's village, Jiundan, the Pattiala Raja looking after her interests, bringing up her sons, and still, in 1855, exacting service from their descendants. Nabha also claimed the village, stating that it was close to her village of Phul, and should be under her authority. Jiundan was situated about eight miles south-east of Phul, surrounded on three sides by Nabha villages, while British territory bounded it on the north. The jurisdiction evidently belonged to the British Government, for Rughu lived before Pattiala became a State at all; and, though of the Phulkian clan, there was no reason that his descendants should be considered Pattiala feudatories, rather than any other branch of the Phulkian family. The claim was accordingly disallowed, but permission was given to Pattiala to take Jiundan in lieu of the village of Ramanah, which had been assigned to that State on the ground of its being a grant to Ramdat, the father of one of Raja Amar Singh's wives.[1]

[1] Commissioner Cis-Satlej States to Punjab Government, No. 155, dated

Of the four sons of Rughu, the only one who left issue was Hardas Singh, the ancestor of the present Jiundan Sikhs.

Second in order come the Gumti Sikhs, or, as they are commonly known, the "Laudgharias," a term signifying the "younger branch." These are the descendants of Phul by his second wife, Rajji, who bore him three sons—Channu, Jhandu, and Takht Mal. Jhandu died issueless; Channu had two sons, named Kilas and Masur; and his brother Takht Mal had five—namely, Bir, Lakmir, Bhumia, Dalloh, and Bakhta. These founded the village of Gumti, ten miles north of Phul, and half-way between Dialpur and Bhai Rupa, dividing it into seven shares, which are now held by their respective descendants. The Gumti Sikhs, being weak, attached themselves to whomsoever they thought best able to defend them. Sirdar Chuhr Singh of Bhadour helped them against the Maharajkian Sikhs; and they later accepted the protection of Raja Jaswant Singh of Nabha, to whom they are still bound to furnish fourteen horsemen. In 1868, the Gumti Sikhs numbered 850 souls, and their holding is worth Rs. 2500 per annum. **The Gumti Sikh or "Laudgharias."**

Third among the zamindari Phulkian families is that of Dialpura or Mirza-ka-Dialpura. The founder of this branch was Bulaki Singh, the third son of Sukhchen, and younger brother of Gajpat Singh of Jhind. He first married, at Kot Kapura, Taran, a girl of a Nehre Sanduan family, who bore him a son named Mirza. His second wife, Malan, was the widow of his eldest brother, Alam Singh. She was the mother of Jitu. Bulaki Singh died about the year 1785. The village of Dialpura was founded **The Dialpura or Mirza-ka-Dialpura Sikhs.**

10th July 1855; and Punjab Government to Commissioner Cis-Satlej States, No. 670, dated 1st August 1855.

by Mirza, but both the brothers lived there, and their descendants, fifty-one in number, share it among them. The estate is worth Rs. 4000 a year.

The Rampura Sikhs.

The Rampura family is fourth on the list. It comprises seventy members, descended from Suma or Suma Singh, the fifth and younger son of Chaudhri Duna of Bhadour. Suma married three wives, who bore him five sons—Jassa Singh, Massa Singh, Tek Singh, Charat Singh, and Budh Singh. The eldest, Jassa Singh, died childless, and from the other four have descended the Sikhs of Rampura and Kotla Koura, the former founded by Chaudhri Rama, and the latter by his son Bakhta. These villages, worth Rs. 6500 a year, they hold in proprietary right.

The Sikhs of Kot Duna.

Last of the zamindar Phulkian families are the Sikhs of Kot Duna, a small branch consisting of only six members. It has descended from Dal Singh, the youngest brother of Sirdar Chuhr Singh of Bhadour.

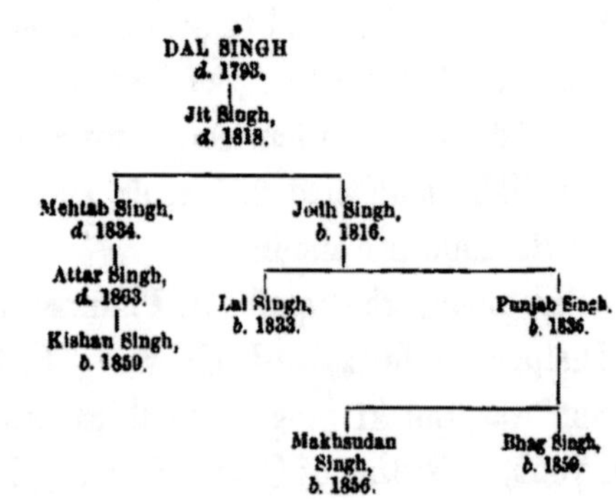

Dal Singh owned three villages, Kot Duna, Bugar, and Man Mibarian. He perished with his half-brother, Chuhr Singh Bhadouria, in 1793, when their enemy, Sajjan of Ghanne, set fire to the house in which they were sleeping. Jit Singh, his son, died of hard drinking in 1818, and the estate was divided between his sons.

Of the elder branch, Kishan Singh, a child of eleven years, alone survives. His grandfather and father died at the early age of thirty-two and thirty-one respectively, having shortened their lives by their excesses. Jodh Singh enjoys the other half of the jagir, which is worth Rs. 5826 a year. The village of Kot Duna is in Pattiala territory, about eleven miles to the south of Dhanowra.

THE HISTORY

OF THE

JHIND STATE.

The origin of the family of Jhind.

UNTIL the time of Chaudhri Phul, the history of the Pattiala and the Jhind families are the same, and there is no occasion to repeat here what has already been recorded regarding it.[1]

Tilokha, the eldest son of Phul, had two sons, Gurditta and Sukhchen, from the elder of whom has descended the Nabha family, and from the younger the Chiefs of Jhind, Badrukhan, and Bazidpur. Tilokha succeeded his father as Chaudhri; but although he thus became the head of the family, he was not a man of any energy, and made no attempt to increase his share of the estate. Sukhchen, the second son, was a simple zamindar, and nothing worthy of record is known of him, except his marriage to Agan, the daughter of Chuhr Singh, a Bhullar Jat of Mandi, who bore him three sons, Alam Singh, Gajpat Singh, and Bulaki Singh. He founded several new villages, one of which, called after his own name, he gave to his youngest son, Bulaki Singh; and a

[1] *Ante*, pp. 2–9.

second, Balanwali, to Alam Singh. After having made this division of his estate, he continued to reside with his second son, Gajpat Singh, at the ancestral village of Phul, where he died, aged seventy-five, in the year 1758.

The following is the genealogy of the Jhind family :— The genealogy.

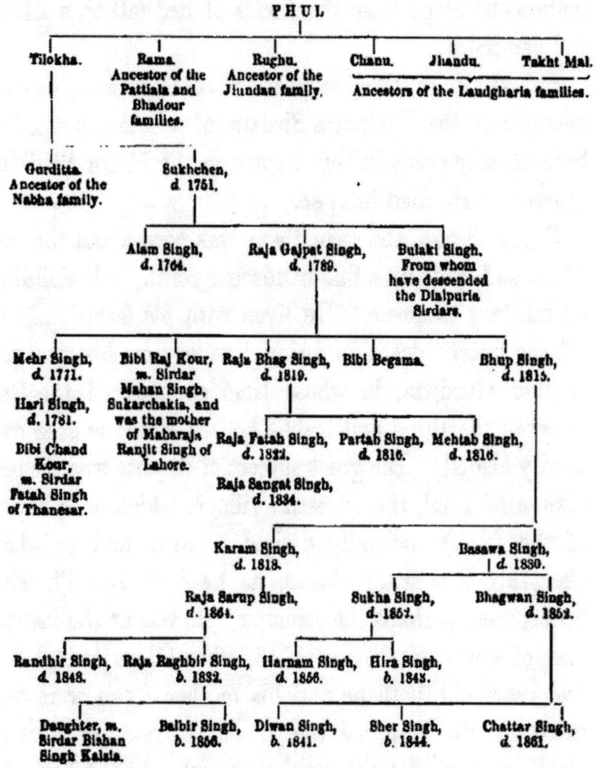

It is with Gajpat Singh that Jhind history is especially concerned, and the briefest notice is required of the other sons of Sukhchen.

Alam Singh, the eldest, was a brave soldier, and distinguished himself in many fights with the Imperial troops. After the conquest of Sirhind, in 1763, he took possession of a considerable tract of country, but was Alam Singh, the eldest son of Sukhchen.

killed the following year by a fall from his horse. He left no children, though he had married three times. His first wife was of a Gill family of Gholia Chubara, his second the daughter of Man zamindar of Maur Saboki, and the last a girl, Mala by name, whom he had induced to elope from the house of her father, a Dhaliwal zamindar.

Bulaki Singh.

Bulaki Singh, the youngest son of Sukhchen, was the ancestor of the Dialpuria Sirdars, of whom a notice has been already given in the chapter on the Minor Phulkian Houses.[1] He died in 1785.

Gajpat Singh.

Gajpat Singh, the second son, was born about the year 1738, and grew up a fine handsome youth, well skilled in all military exercises. He lived with his father at Phul, till the latter's death, assisting him against his rival and brother Gurditta, in whose time commenced the feud between the Jhind and Nabha houses, which is even now hardly healed. The great subject of dispute was the possession of Phul, the ancestral village, which each branch of the family naturally desired to own, and to which Chaudhri Gurditta's claims, as head of the Phulkian house, were perhaps the stronger. It was at the instigation of Gurditta that, in 1743, when Gajpat Singh was five years old, both he and his mother Agan were captured by the Imperial troops and carried prisoners to Dehli as hostages for Sukhchen, who had fallen into arrears with his revenue collections, and who contrived to escape the troops sent to seize him. The mother and child were fortunate enough to escape soon, through the fidelity and courage of one of Agan's slave girls, who disguised her mistress in her own dress, and remained behind in her place in the prison.

[1] *Vide ante*, p. 279.

Gajpat Singh married, in 1754, one of the widows of his brother Alam Singh, and succeeded to his estate of Balanwali. This wife bore him one daughter, Begama. Previous to this he had married the daughter of Kishan Singh of Monshia, of whom were born four children, Mehr Singh, Bhag Singh, Bhup Singh, and a daughter, Raj Kour, who was married to Sirdar Mahan Singh Sukarchakia, and became the mother of Maharaja Ranjit Singh of Lahore. **The family of Gajpat Singh.**

Gajpat Singh joined the Sikh army in 1763, when Zin Khan, the Afghan Governor of Sirhind, was defeated and slain; and he then seized a large tract of country, including the districts of Jhind and Safidon, overrunning Panipat and Karnal, but he was not sufficiently strong to hold them. Yet, in spite of this rebellion, he did not deny altogether the authority of the Dehli Court. He remained, as before, a *Malguzur* of Dehli, paying revenue to the Emperors; and, in 1767, having fallen a lakh and a half into arrears, he was taken prisoner by Najib Khan, the Muhammadan Governor, and carried to Dehli, where he remained a prisoner for three years, only obtaining release by leaving his son, Mehr Singh, as a hostage for the punctual payment of what was due. He then returned to Jhind, where, after great difficulties and delay, collecting three lakhs of rupees, he carried them to Dehli, and not only freed his son, but obtained the title of Raja, under a Royal *Firman*, or grant.[1] From this time Gajpat Singh assumed the style of an independent prince, and coined money in his own capital.[2] **His conquests and misfortunes.** **He obtains the title of Raja, A.D. 1768.**

[1] This *Firman* is dated 25th Sháwal 1185 A.H. (A.D. 1772), under the Seal of the Emperor Shah Alam.

[2] The right of coining is a privilege which belongs to independent Chiefs alone, as the term "independent" is technically used in Indian politics.

The following information regarding the Mints in the three Phulkian

The marriage of Rai Kour to Sirdar Mahan Singh.

In 1774, the marriage of Sirdar Mahan Singh Sukarchakia was celebrated with Raj Kour, the daughter of

States of Pattiala, Nabha, and Jhind, was collected by Major-General R. G. Taylor, C.B., C.S.I., Agent to the Lieutenant-Governor Cis-Satlej States, at the request of the Foreign Secretary to the Government of India. The only other recognised mints in the States in political dependence on the Punjab Government, are in Maler Kotla and Kashmir.

PATTIALA MINT.

I. *Political condition.*—No trace is ascertainable of any communication having been held with this office regarding the Mint. The Pattiala authorities have alluded to an application made, on the occasion of Lord Dalhousie holding a Durbar at Pinjor in 1851, by the Pattiala Government for permission to remodel the Pattiala State Mint. To this the Pattiala Officers say no definite answer was given, and they presume that the record must be in this office, but I have had it searched for without success.

The Mint of Pattiala is said to have been established by the order of Ahmad Shah Durani, when the Pattiala State was ruled by Maharaja Amar Singh. This would have been about 100 years ago; in fact, in another place in the Pattiala reports, Sambat 1820 (A.D. 1763) is mentioned as the year.

II. *The nature, title, and character of the coinage.*—The Pattiala rupee is known as the Rajah Shahi rupee; it is three-fourths of an inch in circumference, and weighs 11¼ mashas: it is of pure silver. The coin is really five ruttees less in weight than the British Government rupee, but the amount of actual silver in each is the same, and consequently the Pattiala rupee fetches the full 16 annas, but is subjected sometimes to arbitrary discount by the shrafhs in British territory, and its value also fluctuates with the value of silver in the markets, fetching in this way sometimes more than the 16 annas.

The Pattiala gold mohur weighs 10¾ mashas, and is of pure gold.

No copper coin is struck in Pattiala.

The inscription on the gold and silver coin is the same: it runs—

> " *Hukm shud az Qadir-i-bechun ba Ahmad Badshah:*
> *Sikka zan bar sim-o-zar az ouj-i-mahi tá ba Mah:*
> *Jalus Meimunut Manus zarb Sirhind.*"

The translation of which is: "The order of God, the peerless, to Ahmad Badshah: Strike coin on silver and gold from earth to heaven" (this is the real meaning of the passage; the actual words are, "from the height of the fishes back to the moon"), "in the presence, favoured of high fortune" (here would follow the date) "the Sirhind coinage."

No alteration has ever been made in the inscription; certain alterations are made in the marks to mark the reign of each Chief.

Thus, Maharaja Amar Singh's rupee is distinguished by the representation of a *Kulgi* (small aigrette plume); Maharaja Sahib Singh's by that of a *Saif* (or two-edged sword); Maharaja Karam Singh's had a *Shamsher* (bent sabre) on his coin; Maharaja Narindar Singh's coin had a *Katta* (or straight sword) as his distinguishing mark.

The present Maharaja's rupee is distinguished by a dagger.

Raja Gajpat Singh, at Bhadra Khan, then the capital of Jhind. The Gujranwala Chief came with a large retinue,

The inscription being long, and the coin small, only a small portion of the inscription falls on each coin.

III. *The annual out-turn of the establishment, and the value of the coinage as compared with that of the British Government.*—The annual out-turn is in fact evidently uncertain; the striking of the coin being only capriciously carried out on special occasions, or when actually wanted.

The officials report that the Pattiala Mint could strike 2000 coins per diem, if necessary; always supposing that there be sufficient grist for the mill.

The value, with reference to British Government coin, has been given above in reply to question No. II.

IV. *The process of manufacture, and any particulars as to the artificers employed.*—The Mint is supervised by a superintendent, a mohurrir, two testers, one weigher, ten blacksmiths, two coiners, four refiners of metal, and one engraver.

The metals are refined carefully, and thus brought up to the standard of the gold and silver kept as specimens in the Mint; the metal is tested and then coined.

The chief implements are anvils, hammers, scales, dies, pincers, vices, &c.

V. *The arrangements for receiving bullion, and the charges (if any) levied for its conversion into coin.*—Metal brought by private individuals is coined at the following rates:—

Silver.—1 rupee 1 anna for 100 coins, of which the State dues amount to 10½ annas, and 6½ go to the establishment.

Gold.—Rs. 24 per 100 coins:—

	Rs.	a.
State, . . .	17	2½
Establishment dues, .	1	2
Miscellaneous expenses, .	5	11½

VI.—The currency is principally confined to the area of the State, but there are a good many Pattiala rupees about in the neighbouring districts, but not probably beyond the limits of the Civil Division.

JHIND.

I. *Political conditions, &c.*—The Jhind Mint would seem to have been established at the same time as that of Pattiala, as the inscription is exactly the same. There does not appear to have been any correspondence with this Agency or the British Government regarding its continuance or conditions.

II. *Nature, title, and character of the coinage.*—The rupee is called the "Jhindia;" it is 11¼ mashas in weight.

The inscription is, as in the case of the Pattiala Raja Shai rupee, viz.:—

"Hukm shud az Kadir-i-bechun ba Ahmad Badshah;
Sikka zan bar sim-o-zar az ouj-i-mahi tá ba Mah."

The third sentence which appears on the Pattiala coin is omitted in the Jhind inscription.

Translation of the inscription has been given above.

III. The out-turn is quite uncertain; on the occasion of marriages large

and all the Phulkian Chiefs were assembled in honour of the occasion. A trifling incident, which occurred during the festivities, was the cause of a serious quarrel between Nabha and Jhind. The Sirdar of the former State, Hamar Singh, had a valuable grass preserve, or "Bir," in the neighbourhood of Bhadra Khan, in which the Baratis, or attendants of the bridegroom, were permitted to cut grass for their horses. But no sooner had they commenced operations than Yakub Khan, the agent of Hamir Singh, more zealous than hospitable, attacked them, and a fight was the result, of which no notice was taken till after the ceremony and departure of the bridegroom. Raja Gajpat Singh then resolved to avenge the insult, and feigning

The quarrel with Nabha.

sums are coined, but otherwise only the actual quantity considered necessary is struck. The value of the coin is said to be about 12 annas, but I have been unable to procure a specimen in Ambala, and the shrafhs in our markets know little about this coin.

IV. *Process of manufacture, &c.*—The only point noted is, that the die is entrusted to the care of the State Treasurer, the process of manufacture and arrangements of the workshops, &c., is not noticed.

V. *The arrangements for the receipt of bullion.*—Bullion has never been tendered for coining at the Jhind Mint, so no rates for conversion have been fixed.

VI. *The general area of currency.*—Only within the State.

NABHA.

I. *Political conditions, &c.*—This Mint appears to have been established under Sikh rule; there has never been any correspondence on the subject with the British Government.

II. *Nature, title, and character of the coinage.*—The rupee is called the "Nabha" rupee; its full weight is 11¼ mashas, of which 10 mashas 4½ ruttees is pure silver. It is thus 5 ruttees in actual weight, and 2¼ ruttees in pure silver less than the British Government rupee.

Gold mohurs are occasionally struck by the Nabha Government for its own use. The weight of the mohur is 9¾ mashas, and it is of pure gold.

The inscription on both coins is the same, viz.:—

"*Deg, tegh-o-fatah nasrat be dirang;*
Yaft az Nanak Guru Govind Singh.
Julus meimunat manus Sirkar Nabha, sambat 1911."

The above may be rendered:—

"Food, sword, and victory were promptly obtained from Nanak by Guru Govind Singh."

to be at the point of death, sent to his cousin of Nabha, requesting him to come and see him before he died. The unsuspecting Sirdar arrived in haste, with Yakub Khan, and to his great surprise was arrested and placed in confinement, while his officer was put to death. The Raja then sent a force against Imloh and Bhadson, two strong places in Nabha territory, and attacked Sangrur, which was defended for four months by Sirdarni Deso, wife of Hamir Singh. At length, seeing her cause desperate, she begged the Raja of Pattiala to interfere. This Chief, who had encouraged the attack in the first place, hoping to weaken both Jhind and Nabha and consequently increase his own power, had no wish to see the former become too powerful, and interposed with other Sikh

In the above, food is expressed in the couplet by the word *deg*, signifying the large cooking-pan in use among the Sikhs; but I have found it very difficult to introduce *pot* or *pan* into the English rendering; the spirit of the expression is "*abundance.*"

III. *The out-turn of the establishment, value, &c.*—The Nabha officials have not noticed the out-turn, but I know that, as in the other States, money is only coined on grand occasions, or when there is supposed to be need of it; so that no rule can be fixed.

The value is exactly 15 annas.

IV. The Mint establishment consists of one superintendent, one tester, one smelter, a silversmith, and a blacksmith.

The silver is carefully refined in presence of the Superintendent, who sees the metal brought up to the proper standard.

V. Silver has often been received from without for coining. Gold has never been tendered.

The mint-duty for coining is 14 annas per 100 rupees, which is distributed as follows :—

To Silversmith, . .	4¾	annas per cent.
„ Smelter, . . .	2	„
„ Blacksmith, . .	0¼	„
„ Tester, . . .	1	„
„ Superintendent, . .	0¾	„
„ State dues, . .	5¼	„
	14	

VI. *General area of the currency.*—These rupees find their way into the neighbouring markets, but not to any great extent.

Sirdars, compelling Raja Gajpat Singh to restore Imloh and Bhadson, and release Hamir Singh. Sangrur was retained, and has ever since been included in the Jhind territory.

Jhind attacked by the Governor of Dehli.

The next year Rahim Dad Khan, Governor of Hansi, was sent against Jhind by the Dehli Governor, Nawab Majad-ul-dowla Abdulahd Khan, and Raja Bhag Singh summoned to his assistance the Phulkian Chiefs. Raja Amar Singh of Pattiala, who sent a force under Diwan Nanun Mal, Sirdar Hamir Singh of Nabha, with the Bhais of Kythal, assembled for its defence, and compelled the Khan to raise the siege and give them battle, in which he was defeated and killed. Trophies of this victory are still preserved at Jhind, and the tomb of the Khan is to be seen within the principal gate. After this, Gajpat Singh, accompanied by the Pattiala detachment, made an expedition against Lalpur, in Rohtak, and obtained, as his share of the conquered country, the district of Kohana. But Zalita Khan, the son of the Rohilla Chief Najib-ud-dowlah (Najib Khan), marched with Ghulam Kadir against the allied Chiefs with so strong a force that they saw it was hopeless to resist, and, at an interview at Jhind, the Raja was compelled to give up a portion of Kohana, though he was allowed to retain certain villages known as Panjgiran, and Pattiala had also to abandon a great part of its conquests in Hissar, Rohtuk, and Karnal.[1]

Conquests to the south.

The relations of the Raja with Pattiala.

Raja Gajpat Singh was a constant ally of the Pattiala Chief, and accompanied him on many of his expeditions. He joined in the attack on Sirdar Hari Singh of Sialba; aided in subduing Prince Himmat Singh, who had risen in revolt against his brother, Raja Amar Singh; and, in 1780, marched with a force composed of Pattiala and

[1] *Vide ante*, p. 42.

Jhind troops to Meerat, where the Sikhs were defeated by Mirza Shafi Beg, Gajpat Singh being taken prisoner, and only released on payment of a heavy ransom.

When Sahib Singh succeeded his father at Pattiala, Raja Gajpat Singh did his best to restore order, and assisted Diwan Nanun Mal to put down the rebellion of Sirdar Mahan Singh, who had proclaimed himself independent at Bhawanigarh. He also in person marched against Ala Singh of Talwandi, who had thrown off the authority of Pattiala. In 1786, while engaged in an expedition against refractory villages in the neighbourhood of Ambala, with Diwan Nanun Mal and Bibi Rajindar, sister of the Raja of Pattiala, he fell ill with fever and was carried to Sufidon, where he died, aged fifty-one. His eldest son, Mehr Singh, died in A.D. 1780, leaving one son, Hari Singh, who was put in possession of Sufidon by Raja Gajpat Singh. But he was of dissipated habits, and in a state of intoxication fell from the roof of his house and was killed. This was in 1791, when he was only eighteen years of age. He left a daughter, Chand Kour, who was married to Fatah Singh, the son of Sirdar Bhanga Singh, the powerful Chief of Thanesar. After her husband's death, she, with his mother, Mai Jiah, and another widow, Rattan Kour, succeeded to the estate, which fell entirely into her possession in 1844, and was held by her in independent right till her death in 1850, when it lapsed to the British Government. The widow of Hari Singh, Dya Kour, retained till her death the district of Khanna, which had been given to her by her father-in-law, when it also lapsed.

Death of Raja Gajpat Singh, and his eldest son, Mehr Singh, with the extinction of this branch of the family.

The town of Jhind was much enlarged by Raja Gajpat Singh, who built a large brick fort on its northern side, but at no time was it a place of much strength.

The fort of Jhind built.

Raja Bhag Singh.

The possessions of Gajpat Singh were divided between his sons, Bhag Singh and Bhup Singh, the latter taking the estate of Badrukhan, and the elder, Jhind and Sufidon, with the title of Raja.

His expeditions and wars.

Bhag Singh was twenty-one years old when he became Chief. Much of his history has been given in the history of Pattiala, with which he was generally allied. In 1786, the districts of Gohana and Khar Khodah, were conferred upon him in jagir by the Emperor Shah Alam, and, in 1794, he joined the Pattiala army under Rani Sahib Kour in the attack on the Mahratta Generals, Anta Rao or Amba Rao, and Lachman Rao, at Rajgarh near Ambala, when a night attack was made on the enemy's camp with great success. In the next year the Raja lost Karnal, which was captured by the Mahrattas and made over to George Thomas, who had been of good service in beating back the Sikhs who had crossed the Jamna in force and threatened Saharanpur.

The war and conquests of Thomas have been related in the history of Pattiala, and the expeditions which he undertook against Jhind and Sufidon in 1798 and 1799.[1] Supported by kinsmen and neighbours, Raja Bhag Singh was fortunate enough to repulse his enemy, and in 1801 he went to Dehli in company with other Chiefs to ask General Perron, commanding the Northern Division of the Mahratta army, for assistance to crush the adventurer whose existence at Hansi, on the southern border of the Jhind State, was a perpetual menace to all the Sikh Chiefs in the neighbourhood.

Thomas expelled from the Punjab.

The expedition against Thomas, in which Raja Bhag Singh personally joined, was successful, and he was driven

[1] *Ante*, pp. 75–82.

from Hansi, and compelled to seek an asylum in British territory.

Raja Bhag Singh makes friends with the British, and joins General Lake, A.D. 1803.

Raja Bagh Singh was the first of all the great Cis-Satlej Chiefs to seek an alliance with the British Government. Immediately after the battle of Dehli, on the 11th September 1803, he made advances to the British General, which were favourably received; he then joined the English camp, and his title to the estate of Gohanah and Khar Khodah, in the neighbourhood of Dehli, was upheld by General Lake, who writes of Bhag Singh as a friend and ally.[1]

Bhai Lal Sindh of Kythal, who had great influence with the Jhind Raja, induced him to declare thus early for the English. He was a remarkably acute man, and saw clearly which would eventually prove the winning side; on this side he determined to be himself, and induced his friend to be equally wise. After having made their submission, they returned to their respective territories, but in January 1805, after the defeat of the hostile Sikhs by Colonel Burn, they thought that active service would prove more advantageous to their interest, and joined the British army with a large detachment. For several months the Raja remained with the General. His services were not important, but his influence had a good effect, and on one occasion he, with Bhai Lal Singh, held Saharanpur while Colonel Ochterlony was in pursuit of the Mahrattas.[2]

[1] A *Sanad* from Lord Lake, dated 26th September 1803, informing the officers of the Shahjahanabad Suba or Division that Pargannah Khar Khodah has been confirmed to Raja Bhag Singh.

A *Sanad* from Lord Lake, dated 7th March 1804, informing the officers of the Shahjahanabad Suba, that Pargannahs Gohana, Faridpur, and Barsat, have been allowed to Bhai Lal Singh and Raja Bhag Singh.

[2] Colonel Burn to Colonel Ochterlony, dated 7th, 18th, and 24th February, and 8th, 18th, and 27th March 1805.

At length the Sikh Chiefs were tired of a fruitless struggle, and accepting a general amnesty, peace was restored on the north-west frontier.

His assistance in the negotiations at Lahore with reference to Holkar, A.D. 1805.

Raja Bagh Singh joined Lord Lake in his pursuit of Jaswant Rai Holkar in 1805, accompanying him as far as the Bias, whence he was deputed to Lahore as an envoy to his nephew, Maharaja Ranjit Singh, to warn him of the approach of the English General, and against espousing the hopless cause of Holkar, who was then in the last extremities. An agent of Bhai Lal Singh accompanied him, and the mission was conducted entirely to the General's satisfaction. It is probable that Bhag Singh was able to exert considerable influence with his nephew in favour of the English, and at any rate the negotiations, which had been commenced, were broken off, and Holkar was compelled to leave the Punjab. Raja Bhag Singh returned with Lord Lake to Dehli, and received the grant of the pargannah of Bawanah, immediately to the south-west of Panipat, as a reward for his services: it was a life-grant in the name of Kour Partab Singh. Hansi had first been given him, but at his own request this district was exchanged for Bawanah. The villages of Mamrezpur and Nihana Kalan were also granted him in jagir.[1]

The grants made to him in reward for service.

The disputes at Pattiala, and the expeditions of Maharaja Ranjit Singh.

The disputes between Pattiala, Nabha, and Jhind, and the struggle for supremacy at the Pattiala Court between

[1] A *Sanad* from Lord Lake, dated 15th March 1806, allowing Pargannah Bawanah to Kour Partab Singh, son of Raja Bhag Singh, on a life tenure.

A *Sanad* from Lord Lake, dated 19th March 1806, allowing the village of Mamrezpur to Raja Bhag Singh, in jagir on a life tenure.

A *Sanad* from Lord Lake at 20th March 1806, informing the officers of Pargannah Khar Khodah that the village of Nihana Kalan, formerly enjoyed by Raja Bhag Singh on payment of Rs. 1200, is granted to him in jagir for life.

the parties of the Raja and his wife, ending in the mediation of Maharaja Ranjit Singh, have been described in the history of Pattiala.[1] Raja Bhag Singh gained in territory by his nephew's visit; and during the expedition of 1806 he received from the Maharaja the following estates: Ludhiana, consisting of twenty-four villages, worth Rs. 15,380 a year; twenty-four villages of Jhandiala *from the same family*, worth Rs. 4370; two villages of Kot, and two of Jagraon, worth Rs. 2000 a year; all taken from the Rani of Rai Alyas of the Muhammadan Rajput family of Raikot; while from the widow of Miah Ghos he acquired two villages of the Basia District. During the expedition of the following year, the Maharaja gave him three villages of Ghumgrana, conquered from Gujar Singh of Raipur, and twenty-seven villages of Morinda in Sirhind, conquered from the son of Dharam Singh, and all together worth Rs. 19,255 a year.[2]

Survey of the Jhind territory.

In April 1807, Raja Bhag Singh readily consented to the survey of his country by Lieutenant F. White, and did all he could to make the expedition successful.[3] A survey in Sikh territory was not then so commonplace a proceeding as at present, for the people were both ignorant and suspicious, and generally imagined that a survey of their country was only a preliminary to its annexation; and two years later, in Pattiala, Lieutenant White's party was attacked and nearly destroyed.[4] But Raja Bhag

[1] *Ante*, pp. 86–97.

[2] Statement of the conquest of Maharaja Ranjit Singh in 1806, 1807, and 1808, prepared by Sir D. Ochterlony, *vide* Appendix A. Archibald Seaton, Resident Dehli, Circular of 1st November 1806. Gosha-i-Punjab, p. 571. Archibald Seaton to General Dickens, 20th August 1807.

[3] Resident at Dehli to Lieutenant White, 26th, 28th of April, 25th of May 1807.

[4] Captain White to Resident Dehli, 24th and 25th December 1809. *Vide ante*, pp. 123, 124.

Singh was not altogether superior to the prejudices of his countrymen. He was well disposed to the English, and a faithful ally, but he had not entire confidence in his new friends, and it was through his advice that Maharaja Ranjit Singh did not trust himself in British territory. This Chief, in the spring of 1808, much wished to visit the sacred fair of Hurdwar, on the Ganges. He sent Sirdar Mohr Singh Lamba and Sirdar Bishan Singh to Dehli to obtain the permission of the Resident, and, at Hurdwar, all arrangements for his reception, including an escort of three thousand followers, were made. But, at the last moment, Raja Bhag Singh dissuaded him from the idea. He declared that the Envoys, Mohr Singh and Bishan Singh, were playing him false; that they were converting all their wealth into notes and Government paper at Dehli, intending to leave the Punjab for Benares; that their declarations of the security with which the Maharaja would make the journey were untrustworthy, and that he could not travel with any safety unless accompanied by his whole army. The design of visiting Hurdwar was consequently abandoned. There is no knowing on what grounds Bhag Singh considered the Maharaja's servants untrustworthy, but there was probably some reason for his belief, since Sirdar Mohr Singh left the Punjab for Benares a year or two later, contrary to the wish and orders of his master.[1]

Bhag Singh's advice to Ranjit Singh.

The Hurdwar Fair.

Raja Bhag Singh himself visited Hurdwar, and, after the fair[2] went to Lahore, where he remained in attendance

[1] Letter of Maharaja Ranjit Singh to Resident Dehli of 6th August 1808. Resident Dehli to Magistrate Saharanpur, 18th and 22d March. Circular of Resident 20th March 1808. To C. Metcalfe, Esq., 22d March, and 2d April 1808. Gosha-i-Punjab, p. 580. Punjab Chiefs, p. 544.

[2] Mr Metcalfe to Resident Dehli, 10th April 1808. An extract from this letter may not be without interest, as this was the first large festival at

on Ranjit Singh, and accompanied him in the Cis-Satlej campaign of 1808, undertaken while Mr Metcalfe, the British Envoy, was with the Sikh camp.[1]

At the beginning of 1808, Raja Bhag Singh, with Bhai Lal Singh, the Nabha Raja, and a Pattiala contingent, attacked the strong fort of Ghumgrana, owned by Gujar Singh, son of the famous Tara Singh Gheba, who had lately died. The siege proceeded for some time, till Ranjit Singh raised it by a message ordering the besiegers to desist. The Maharaja did not take this course in the interests of the owner, but sent a force of his own against the fort, took it without resistance, and gave it to The siege of Ghumgrana.

Hurdwar under the management of the British, and the description is not unlike that given of the Great Fair held sixty years later in March 1867.

"Raja Rajgan Sahib Singh of Pattiala, Raja Bhag Singh, Sirdar Bhai Lal Singh, and Sirdar Gurdit Singh, were the principal Sikh Chieftains that came to the Mela ; and though not charged with any prescribed duty with respect to these, I thought that the nature of my situation called on me to pay them every suitable attention, with particular reference to the distinguished rank of Raja Rajgan Sahib Singh. All the Sikhs, who attended the *mela* in great numbers, behaved with perfect propriety, and the Chiefs did not express any objection to the application to their own followers of the general prohibition against carrying arms into the place when the *mela* was held.

"Amongst the innumerable crowds that were assembled at Hurdwar there did not take place the slightest disturbance, and the perfect good order that was preserved had a surprising effect upon the multitude. It is not within the line of my duty to dwell on this subject, but I cannot refrain from remarking that the conduct of the vast numbers that came from all quarters was most gratifying to the feelings of an Englishman. Their prayers for the prosperity of the British Government were most fervent ; the respect shown to an Englishman whenever he appeared struck us all as far exceeding anything that we had met with before ; their expressions of admiration at the whole arrangement of the *mela* were unbounded, and they repaid the care bestowed for their comfort with an evidently heartfelt gratitude. I am afraid to attempt to describe what at the place was manifest to all, lest you should suspect that the gratification excited by the universal joy might be carrying me into fields of romance; but I am satisfied that the loud praises and thanksgiving of the honest multitude proceeded from the sincere effusions of their hearts ; and I am confident that the reports which they will carry to their distant homes will considerably extend the fame and reputation of the British Government."

[1] C. Metcalfe, Esq., to Resident at Dehli, 1st October 1808.

one of his favourites, Karam Singh of Nagla. Rája Bhag Singh still retained some of the villages which he had seized in its neighbourhood, and though Karam Singh represented to the Maharaja that they were necessary to the completeness of his jagir, yet the latter did not like to compel his uncle to restore villages to which, when all were robbers, he had as good a right as any one else.

And its results.

A bitter feud between Raja Bhag Singh and Sirdar Karam Singh was the consequence, and perpetual fighting and bloodshed between the rivals took place around Ghumgrana. The British Envoy had himself an opportunity of observing the state of affairs, for, on one occasion, when he was taking his evening ride in the vicinity of the fort, he was fired upon from one of Bhag Singh's villages, whose defenders believed his escort to be their enemies.[1]

The ransom of Maler Kotla.

Raja Bhag Singh was one of the Chiefs who were securities for the ransom of Maler Kotla, from which, in October 1808, Ranjit Singh demanded the tribute of a lakh of rupees. Only Rs. 27,000 were at once forthcoming, and for the balance, Pattiala, Nabha, Jhind, and Kythal became security, receiving from Maler Kotla Jamalpura and other territory in pledge. By the treaty of Lahore the conquests of Ranjit Singh during his last campaign to the south of the Satlej had to be restored, and Jhind, with the other Chiefs, was compelled to resign the lands given by Maler Kotla, and the Maharaja, after some negotiation, absolved them from the necessity of paying the sum for which they had become sureties.[2]

[1] Envoy to Lahore to Secretary to Government, 20th November 1808.

[2] Mr C. Metcalfe to Government of India, 26th October 1808, and Resident Dehli to Government, 10th August and 16th August 1809.

Raja Bhag Singh's confidence in the moderation of his nephew was very much shaken by the unprovoked attack on Maler Kotla, and he perceived that his own possessions would be safe only so long as they were not coveted by his dangerous relation. He accordingly turned to his friends, the English, with whom he had maintained the most amicable relations, prompted by his adviser, Bhai Lal Singh. The Resident at Dehli had addressed, on the 21st November, a letter to the Raja, informing him that although the British Government was not prepared actively to interfere, yet that the Governor-General had written to Maharaja Ranjit Singh, and expressed a hope that the Cis-Satlej Chiefs, the friends and allies of the English, would be left unmolested by him. In reply, the Raja declared his unalterable feelings of friendship for the British Government, and his confidence that, under its protection, his power and honour would be secure. The Resident again wrote in general terms, for the idea of a protectorate of the Cis-Satlej States was not yet matured, that the Government had no wish save the perpetuity of the rule of the Sikh Chiefs, and had full confidence in their assurances of good-will.[1]

The feelings of Raja Bhag Singh towards the Chief of Lahore, and his intrigues.

The Raja continued to address the Resident and solicit his good offices in his favour, and a translation of a portion of one of his letters will show the mistrust which the Chiefs had begun to entertain of Ranjit Singh.

His letter to the Resident at Dehli.

"I have lately received two letters from you, containing assurances of kindness and friendship, and calculated to tranquillise my mind. The perusal of these letters has inspired me with confidence, and filled me with gratitude: may the Almighty reward you.

[1] Letter of Raja Bhag Singh to Resident of 3d December, and reply of Resident, 4th December 1808.

"The state of matters in this quarter is as follows:—Previously to the receipt of your letters, Raja Sahib Singh had, with a view to his own safety, made an arrangement for meeting Maharaja Ranjit Singh, and he accordingly proceeded, by successive marches, to the camp of the Maharaja, and a meeting took place. In conformity to the custom of interchanging turbans, which is established among Sikh Chiefs, the Maharaja and Raja Sahib Singh exchanged theirs, and seemingly settled everything. But in truth, we four Sirdars[1] are inwardly the same as ever, and adhere to the same sentiments towards the British Government which we felt and expressed on the first day of our being dependent upon it, and which all repeated to you when we visited you, and explained the particulars of our situation. This will doubtless be present to your recollection. Under every circumstance, we trust that it is the intention of the British Government to secure and protect us four Sirdars. As Sirdar Ranjit Singh is now preparing to cross the Satlej, it is probable that he will soon cross that river. Raja Sahib Singh will take leave at Laknow and return to Pattiala, and Bhai Lal Singh and myself, after accompanying Ranjit Singh to the other side of the Satlej, will return to Pattiala, and after consulting together with respect to everything, we will communicate the whole of the result to you in detail."

Bhag Singh visits Mr Seton, the Resident.

The next month, Maharaja Ranjit Singh having returned to Lahore, Raja Bhag Singh set out for Dehli, to have an interview with Mr Seton, the Resident. He reached Karnal, and from thence he wrote announcing his arrival and requesting permission to proceed. But at this time General Ochterlony was advancing with a strong force to the Satlej, to strengthen, by his propin-

[1] Raja Sahib Singh, Raja Bhag Singh, Sirdar Jaswant Singh, and himself.

quity, the arguments of Mr Metcalfe, the Envoy at Lahore, whose tedious negotiations seemed still far from any satisfactory conclusion; and the Resident, thinking Bhag Singh's presence with the English force would have a good effect, advised him to join it, which he at once did with his troops, overtaking the General at Buria.[1]

His desire to avoid an interview with the Maharaja

The reason which induced this action on the part of Bhag Singh, was that he had heard that an agent of the Lahore Maharaja was on his way to Pattiala, to summon him, Jaswant Singh of Nabha, and Cheyn Singh, the confidential agent of the Pattiala Chief, to Lahore. To a journey to Lahore Bhag Singh had, at this time, a strong and natural objection. He was an independent Chief, and at liberty to make such friends as pleased him; but his conscience told him that his conduct to Ranjit Singh, who had always treated him with the greatest consideration, and had much enlarged his territories, was somewhat questionable, and he had no wish at present to meet him. The Lahore agent accordingly, on his arrival at Pattiala, found Bhag Singh absent, and this was an excuse for Maharaja Sahib Singh to decline to send his own agent, an excuse of which he was ready enough to avail himself.[2]

He joins General Ochterlony,

Raja Bhag Singh was received by General Ochterlony with great kindness, and the information which he was able to give with regard to the disposition of the several Sikh Chiefs was of much value. All of them were, according to the Raja, disposed to welcome the English

[1] Letters from Raja Bhag Singh to Resident Dehli, 13th and 25th January 1809.

Resident to Raja Bhag Singh, 15th January, and to Government of India, 15th January 1809.

[2] Resident to Government of India, dated 18th and 19th January 1809. *Vide ante*, p. 115.

and joyfully accept their protection, though one or two, like Sirdar Jodh Singh of Kalsia, were under too heavy obligations to Ranjit Singh to come forward at once and declare against him. It was explained to the Raja that the restitution of conquests during the late campaign must in justice be enforced against the friends of the British as against the Maharaja, with which the Raja fully agreed, the more readily that he would by this act of justice lose no more than territory worth Rs. 4000 a year, which had been taken from Rani Dya Kour and conferred upon him.[1]

And marches with him to Ludhiana.

The Raja continued with General Ochterlony till his arrival at Ludhiana, at which place the detachment was ordered to halt, and acted as a mutual friend in the negotiations which were necessary between the General and the Lahore agent. On the 10th of February, at Ghumgrana, he received a confidential message from the General, stating that the following day he would have to march to Ludhiana, which the Lahore troops, in spite of the Maharaja's promises, had not yet evacuated, and asked him, as a friend of both parties, to take such measures as he judged best to prevent the occurrence of hostilities, which would be the result should the Sikhs not cross the river without delay. The Raja urged the General to halt; but this he at first refused, as he had received direct orders to advance, and expressed his belief that Sirdar Gainda Singh, in command at Ludhiana, would evacuate the fort at his approach, in accordance with the promises of the Maharaja. The Lahore agents who were in camp denied that their master had ever made any

He assists in the negotiations.

[1] Resident Dehli to Government, dated 25th January. Raja Bhag Singh to Resident, dated 25th January. Government of India to Resident, dated 13th and 27th February 1809.

Sir D. Ochterlony to Government of India, dated 20th January 1809.

promise of the kind, and the assertion, though evidently made only to delay the advance, so staggered the General, that he consented to march to Sirnawal instead of Ludhiana, and there await further orders from General St Leger, then commanding the army in the field.[1] The conduct of General Ochterlony was severely censured by Government in attending to the Lahore agents rather than to their direct orders; but in the advice given by Raja Bhag Singh, there was nothing of treachery, and only a weak desire to maintain such friendship as was possible with both sides.

The arrival at Ludhiana, A.D. 1809.

The detachment arrived at Ludhiana on the 19th of February. This town, well situated on the river Satlej, and commanding the principal northern road, had been for only two years in possession of Raja Bhag Singh, and was one of the advantages he had gained from his connection with Ranjit Singh. He was not, however, unwilling to give it up to the English, who desired to form there a permanent cantonment, hoping to obtain in exchange the pargannah of Karnal, which had once been in his family. He addressed the Government to this effect, stating that he would not be able to collect the revenues of the forty-one villages round Ludhiana, having lost possession of the fort, and praying that these should be taken by Government, giving him in exchange the pargannah of Karnal, with the right to collect the duties, or if this were impossible, the pargannah of Panipat. If the revenue of the latter should exceed that of Ludhiana, which was Rs. 17,800, he offered the pargannah of Jhandiala in lieu of the excess.[2] General

Raja Bhag Singh willing to exchange it for Karnal.

[1] Colonel Ochterlony to General St Leger, dated 10th February 1809. Government to Colonel Ochterlony, dated 30th January and 30th March 1809. Colonel Ochterlony to Government, dated 14th February 1809, and to Resident Dehli, dated 27th January 1809.

[2] Letter of Raja Bhag Singh to Resident Dehli, 25th February 1809.

General Ochterlony supports his application.

Ochterlony, who had evidently a strong liking for the Raja, strongly supported his application, writing to the following effect :—

"It would be unjust in me were I to withhold on this occasion an expression of the earnest desire I feel to effect the wishes of the Raja, not merely from a conviction that the loss of the fort will occasion a considerable decrease, if not entire loss of the collections of the Taluqa Ludhiana, but because he has in this, and every other instance, acted with an openness and candour which reflects an honour on his character, showing himself grateful for the benefits derived from the British Government. Without affecting to disguise a very warm interest in the fate of his nephew, Raja Ranjit Singh, at the same time manifesting a readiness to comply with every request which could be considered of importance, beyond even my most sanguine expectations—as I certainly was prepared for a little hesitation, if not a request for a short delay, when I informed him that His Excellency the Commander-in-Chief had directed the interior of the fort to be immediately cleared and levelled—it was most satisfactory to me to observe that without hinting at the request he had before personally urged, he gave an immediate and cheerful acquiescence, observing only that he had experienced too much of British liberality to fear any ultimate loss."[1]

The reasons in favour of the exchange.

The Karnal pargannah, which was in a very turbulent condition, and which required strong measures to keep its inhabitants in order, had already been conferred on Muhammad Khan, a Patan of the Mandil tribe. The Government acknowledged the services of Bhag Singh, and would have been glad to restore, by an act of justice, the district of Ludhiana to the family of Rai Alyas; but

[1] General Ochterlony to Resident, 25th February 1809.

considered that there was no obligation to reinstate the latter at the hazard of other political interests. Compensation for the absolute loss sustained by Bhag Singh in the cantonment of British troops at Ludhiana was all that was necessary, for he, commendable as his conduct had been, had sacrificed no interest for which he would not receive an equivalent, while, in common with other Sikh Chiefs, he had derived the solicited benefit of British protection.

The Government declines the propositions.

An obligation to restore Ludhiana to its former Muhammadan owners could be only maintained with great danger and imprudence.

"To pursue the dictates of abstract justice and benevolence," wrote the Governor-General, "by the indiscriminate redress of grievances beyond the admitted limits of our authority and control, would be to adopt a system of conduct of which the political inconvenience and embarrassment would not be compensated by the credit which might attend it."

The Government consequently declined to entertain the Karnal proposal, but allowed Raja Bhag Singh fair compensation, although it was observed that this was the less necessary, as "the occupation of the military post of Ludhiana was only intended to be temporary, and that consequently the fort and the ground at present occupied by the British detachment would revert to that Chief."[1] The military station of Ludhiana has, nevertheless, been retained from that day to this.[2]

[1] Resident Dehli to Government, 24th February and 3d March. Government of India to Colonel Ochterlony, 3d April 1809, and to Resident Dehli of the same date. Resident Dehli to Colonel Ochterlony, 24th February, 4th and 10th March, and 1st April 1809.

[2] Ludhiana is a town of small intrinsic value as a military post, and in 1868 only 300 Native troops were stationed there, with sixty British artillerymen in the fort of Philor on the opposite bank of the Satlej. When the

A second attempt of the Raja to obtain Karnal.

Raja Bhag Singh was not at all pleased with the refusal of the Government to allow him Karnal, which, as an old possession of his father's, he much desired to regain, and the next year made another attempt to possess himself of the coveted territory.

The estate of Dharampur.

Bhara Singh, the jagirdar of Dharampur, or in Karnal, a valuable estate worth Rs. 12,000 a year, died early in 1810, and the Raja at once claimed to resume the property. He pleaded that the whole pargannah had belonged to his father, Gajpat Singh, and that the estate in question had continued in the family, though in the name of Bhara Singh, one of its dependants; and in support of the claim he produced a petition from Bhara Singh to Lord Lake,

English first occupied Ludhiana, Maharaja Ranjit Singh, who seemed to know better than the Government that the occupation would not be temporary, directed his General, Diwan Mokham Chand, to build the fort of Philor on the opposite bank on the site of an Imperial Serai.

That the Government had no intention of retaining Ludhiana as a military station when it was first occupied, is evident from the despatch above quoted, and also from former despatches of the 13th of March 1809, from the Governor-General in Council to Colonel Ochterlony and Lieutenant-General Hewett, the Commander-in-Chief. The right to advance to the Satlej at any time could not, however, be surrendered, and this was one of the reasons that Ranjit Singh was not pressed to relinquish the Cis-Satlej conquests of 1806, 1807.

Ludhiana remained a Political Agency till the close of the first Sikh war, generally in charge of an Assistant Agent; Sir David Ochterlony and Sir C. Wade being the only officers with the full powers of Agents.

1808 to 1815, Sir David Ochterlony.
1815 „ 1816, Captain Brown.
1816 „ 1823, Captain W. Murray.
1823 „ 1838, Sir C. Wade.
1838 „ 1839, Captain E. Robinson.
1839 „ 1840, Lieutenant J. D. Cunningham.
1840 „ 1841, Mr H. Vansittart.
1841 „ 1842, Mr P. Melvill.
1842, Captain C. Mills.
1842 „ 1843, Mr H. Greathed.
1843 „ 1844, Captain C. Mills.
1844, Captain S. Abbott.
1844 „ 1845, Captain C. Mills.
1845 „ 1846, Captain E. Lake.

to the effect that the petitioner had long entertained 50 horse for the service of the rulers of Dehli, in consideration of which he had held in *jaidad*, Moranah and four other villages in Karnal, and had, moreover, enjoyed a pension of Rs. 189, per mensem, for the confirmation of which he solicited a *Sanad*.

This petition was endorsed by Lord Lake as follows :— **The order of Lord Lake.**

" On consideration of service and fidelity, the arrangement which prevailed in the time of M. Perron, is hereby continued."

Now it is evident that Lord Lake could not have bound himself to more than he was cognizant of; and his endorsement could thus be only considered as granting that which was solicited on the face of the petition, *viz.*, the continuance to Bhara Singh of the possession of the estate in question so long as he should furnish the 50 horsemen ; and, indeed, a *jaidad* grant is scarcely capable of any other construction. Besides, Raja Bhag Singh, by subsequent admissions, destroyed his own case. It may have been quite true that Dharampur was held by him after the loss of the rest of Karnal, but he also stated that it had been twice wrested from him by the Mahrattas, and that, after this second occupation, it was restored by George Thomas at the time that he received Karnal in *jaidad*. Now, it is notorious that Thomas received Karnal in 1795, both as a reward for his successful opposition to the Sikhs at Saharanpur and to enable him to maintain a force to act against them in conjunction into the Mahrattas. It is impossible that he should have allowed Raja Bhag Singh to retain the villages, unless he was an ally of the Mahrattas, and he was, on the contrary, in opposition to them. But even admitting that these villages did not revert to the Mahrattas, yet their right to dispose of them was admitted by Bhag **Their interpretation.**

Singh himself, since he did not deny the grant under which Bhara Singh held them, but, on the contrary, identified, by date and description, his own grant with that of Sindhia of the 23d of April 1800, about which time Bhag Singh asserted that he bestowed the villages on Bhara Singh, when George Thomas invested Jhind in 1799. The service of the body of horse, moreover, as specified in the grant, was not due to Bhag Singh, but to the Mahrattas, and the pension was paid by them.

The claims of the Raja rejected.

The Government were satisfied that the Raja possessed no title whatever to the estate, and seeing no reason for alienating it in his favour, directed it to be resumed.[1]

The attitude of the Raja of Pattiala.

During all the troubles which came on the Pattiala family[2] in the imbecility of the Maharaja, the Regency, and the intrigues and quarrels among the young Princes, Raja Bhag Singh showed himself the best friend of the house. He was not a man of ability or force of character sufficient to restore order and save the State from the worst evils of misgovernment and anarchy; but what he could do he did, and was almost the only disinterested adviser Pattiala could consult.[3]

His excesses and their result.

But his health was fast breaking. Like most of the Sikhs Chiefs he was a man of dissipated habits and a hard drinker. Finding that the excesses endangered his life, he was induced to give up drinking for a short time, but the habit was too confirmed to be abandoned, and the result of resuming it was a paralytic stroke, in March 1813, which deprived him of speech, and almost of the power of motion. There was no doubt that his illness would have a fatal termination, and it became necessary

[1] Resident Dehli to Mr Fraser, 28th June. Mr Fraser to Resident, 8th March and 17th April 1810. Resident to Government, 22d August and 10th September. Government to Resident, 18th October 1811.

[2] *Vide ante*, pp. 125–129.

[3] Gen. Ochterlony to Government of India, 12th July 1811, 2d April 1813.

to think of his successor.[1] About a year before, when the Political Agent was at Pattiala, the Raja had given him a draft will, containing the arrangements which he desired to take effect at his death. By this he left to his younger son, Partab Singh, the fort and district of Jhind, and declared him his successor, leaving to the elder son, Fatah Singh, only the districts of Sangrur and Basia, with a request to the British Government that he might continue to hold the jagirs he enjoyed from them for life. When the Raja made this will he was in sound health, both of body and mind, and it was the expression of his deliberate intention and wishes. He had no particular cause of complaint against Prince Fatah Singh, but the younger son was his favourite, the child of a woman to whom he had been much attached, and who had long been dead.

The draft will by which the elder son was dispossessed.

The Agent tried to induce the Raja to change his determination. He pointed out that certain ill-feeling and disputes must be the result between the brothers, and that the State would suffer thereby, while the British Government was strongly in favour of the rule of primogeniture; but the Raja had set his heart on the arrangement. He urged that the father had the right of nominating his own successor, and bequeathing his lands as he pleased. That he was himself a second son, and had been preferred by his father, and that the custom of the Jhind family was not in opposition to the disposition he had made. The contents of the will, which the Raja then made over to Sir D. Ochterlony, he desired to be kept secret, and it was only after his paralytic attack that the Agent forwarded it to the Resident at Dehli for transmission to the Government of India.[2] The secret had now

The evils which would ensue if they were carrie out.

The Raja's argu ments in its favour.

[1] Sir D. Ochterlony to Government, 20th April 1813.
[2] General Ochterlony to Government, 21st April 1813.

become known, and Prince Fatah Singh with Jaishi Ram and Shadi Ram, the very men who had been privy to the will, were now intriguing to set it aside, for Partab Singh was universally disliked, and very few, save his immediate followers and favourites, regarded his succession without apprehension.

The refusal of the Government to sanction the proposed arrangements.

The Governor-General was unwilling to sanction the Raja's will, considering that there was no proved custom in the Jhind family of an elder son being superseded by a younger. "Whatever doubt the Governor-General might entertain," the despatch continued, "with respect to the justice or propriety of opposing the will of Bhag Singh, if there were good reasons to suppose that it was warranted by the laws and usages of his tribe and family, His Lordship in Council can have no hesitation, under the contrary impression which exists in his mind, in refusing to afford the countenance of the British Government to an arrangement which is, in his Lordship's estimation, no less unjust in its principle than likely to be pernicious in its effects. You are authorised, therefore, to declare to the parties concerned, and to the surviving friends of the family, after the death of Bhag Singh, that the succession of Kour Partab Singh cannot be recognised by the British Government. You are authorised, moreover, to employ the influence of the name and authority of Government in support of the claims of the elder son to the Raj, and to the possessions generally of Bhag Singh, or rather to that superior portion of them which, by the terms of the will, has, together with the Raj, been bequeathed to the second son, signifying at the same time, that care will be taken to secure to Partab Singh a suitable provision, as well as to see the bequest to the younger son duly carried into effect. Your own judgment and local knowledge will suggest to you the most

The Despatch of the Governor-General.

proper means of rendering the influence of Government most effectual in sustaining the rights of the eldest son, without invoking the necessity of its authoritative interposition, which the Governor-General in Council will be desirous of avoiding, and which ought on no account to be resorted to without the express sanction of Government; and it will no doubt occur to you that the aid and co-operation of Bhai Lal Singh and other friends of the family, will be profitably employed for the purpose. It may be expected that their discernment will perceive the many advantages attending a fixed and definite rule of succession, and, unless they are misled by some personal interest of their own, that they will be disposed to support the pretensions of the elder son of Bhag Singh, in preference to upholding the provisions of a will which appears to have been dictated only by the caprice or injustice of the testator. It is superfluous to observe that, in communicating on this subject with Bhai Lal Singh and others, it will be proper carefully to avoid anything that can be construed into an admission of their right to interfere in the regulation of the succession or management of the affairs of the family. A just and simple arrangement would be, either to reverse the provisions of the will in favour of the eldest and second son, or to assign to the latter other lands equal in value to those designated in the will as the provision of the elder."[1]

The grants made by the British Government to the Raja.

Regarding the jagirs granted by the British Government to the Raja, and which he desired to be confirmed to his elder son during his life, the Governor-General reserved his opinion.

These grants were four in number: first was Gohana and Faridpur, situated to the south west of Barwanah, and granted, in 1804, to Raja Bhag Singh and Bhai Lal

[1] Government of India to Colonel Ochterlony, 15th May 1813.

Singh jointly, in recognition of their services against the Mahrattas.

Barwanah was granted to Bhag Singh in 1806, in the name of his son Partab Singh; Kharkhoda and Mumrezpur in the Hansi purgannah were granted him in Jagir in March 1806, having formerly been held by him on *istimrari* [1] tenure.

These jagirs, which were situated in the midst of British territory, had been placed under efficient police supervision in 1810, the inhabitants of the Karnal pargannah having at that time a bad reputation for violence and lawlessness. [2]

And the decision of Government concerning them.

It was decided by the Government that these grants were merely life grants, and should be resumed at the death of Bhag Singh; and, moreover, that the provision made for Partab Singh was so ample, that he was not entitled to any new grant either in land or money on account of those resumed. [3]

The estate held in co-parcenary with Bhai Lal Singh.

With regard to the estate held, in co-parcenary with Bhai Lal Singh, it was clear that it was not intended to be granted for their joint lives, with benefit of survivorship, nor indeed, did this appear to be the view of the Chiefs themselves, and the Raja's share was consequently resumed on his death. [4]

The helpless state of Raja Bhag Singh.

Raja Bhag Singh lingered in a paralytic state for many months. His intellect did not appear to suffer very much, but he was practically incapable of business, and it became necessary to make arrangements for carrying on the administration of the State. At this time the family of

The Candidates for a Regency.

the Raja consisted of three sons and two wives. Fatah

[1] On fixed rates.

[2] Resident Dehli to Mr Fraser, 30th January 1810.

[3] Resident Dehli to Government of India, 18th June 1813. Government of India to Resident, 9th July 1813.

[4] Sir D. Ochterlony to Government, 16th July 1817. Government to Sir D. Ochterlony, 9th July 1813.

Singh, the eldest son, was separated from his father who had a dislike to him, and it was thus almost impossible for him to act as Regent during the Raja's illness. The second son, Partab Singh, whom the Raja desired to succeed him, had been declared by the British Government incompetent for succession, and it was manifestly undesirable to entrust him with even temporary power. The third son, Mehtab Singh, was still very young. The objection to the Regency of the eldest son applied equally to that of his mother, who was also disliked by the Raja and lived separate from him on a portion of the territory assigned for her maintenance. The mother of Partab Singh had long been dead, and Rani Sobrahi, the mother of Mehtab Singh, seemed the person against whose appointment as Regent the fewest objections could be urged. The Raja was not opposed to this arrangement and the Ministers desired it.

Rani Sobrahi appointed Regent, A.D. 1814.

This lady was, accordingly, with the sanction of the Government, appointed Regent. She engaged to respect and advance the wishes of the British Government with regard to the succession, and to abstain from any interference with the eldest son or his mother, who were to be permitted to reside on their estates, without molestation, during the remainder of the reign of Raja Bhag Singh.[1] Sir David Ochterlony was directed to proceed to Jhind, and himself superintend the new arrangements.[2] The Rani was installed in the presence of the Raja, Bhai Lal Singh, and all the confidential servants of the State, and the Raja, by most unmistakeable signs, showed his full concurrence in the measure.[3]

[1] Resident to Secretary to Government, 28th November. Resident to Colonel Ochterlony, 29th November. Colonel Ochterlony to Resident, 15th October, and Government to Resident, 23d December 1813.

[2] Resident to Sir D. Ochterlony, 2d February 1814.

[3] Sir D. Ochterlony to Resident, 29th August 1814. Government to Resident, 4th March 1814.

The dissatisfaction of Prince Partab Singh.

But Prince Partab Singh was thoroughly dissatisfied. He had for long believed that on the death of his father the power would become his, and the present arrangements convinced him that he was intended to be excluded. He intrigued against the Regent, raised troops secretly, and, in June 1814, the Rani wrote that there could be no doubt that he meditated rebellion and that her life was no longer safe. The Prince was warned that the consequence of rebellion would be only to lose him the provision which would otherwise be made for him, and that he could not hope successfully to oppose the measures which had been determined on by Government; but he would accept no warning, and, on the 23d of August, took the fort of Jhind by surprise, and put to death the Rani, Munshi Jaishi Ram, her principal adviser, the Commandant of the Fort, and many other persons.[1] The Agent of the Governor-General at once wrote to the Officer in command at Karnal to hold himself in readiness to march at once to Jhind, on receipt of orders from the Resident of Dehli, and the force at Hansi was also directed to move to Jhind, if the Prince, as anticipated, should attempt resistance. Sir Charles Metcalfe, the Resident, took instant action, and issued the following memorandum of instructions for the re-establishment of a legitimate Government at Jhind.[2]

He rebels, captures Jhind, and murders the Regent.

The action of the British authorities.

The memorandum of instruction for the re-establishment of a legitimate Government at Jhind.

"In consequence of the imbecility of Raja Bhag Singh, a provisional Government was lately established at Jhind under the authority of His Excellency the Governor-General in Council.

"The Rani Sobrahi was placed in the management of affairs, though the Government was carried on in the name of the Raja as before.

[1] Sir D. Ochterlony to Government, 3d July 1814, and 24th August 1814.

[2] Sir D. Ochterlony to Lieut.-Colonel Thompson, Commanding at Karnal, 26th August 1814, and to Sir C. Metcalfe of same date.

"This arrangement was at the time judged most advisable for several reasons.

"The Raja's eldest son and lawful successor was not appointed to the management of affairs because he was known to be obnoxious to the Raja. A similar reason operated against the appointment of the Rani, the mother of the eldest son.

"The Raja's second son could not be appointed because it was known that the Raja wished to establish the succession in favour of the second son to the exclusion of the eldest. The same consideration would have prevailed against the Rani, the mother of the second son, had she been living.

"Rani Sobrahi, the mother of a third son, a youth since dead, from whose claims no apprehensions were entertained, was appointed to the Regency, under the idea that this arrangement united a sufficient degree of security for the succession of the eldest son, with a suitable degree of attention to the feelings of the Raja, more than any other that could be adopted.

"The second son, Kour Partab Singh, has now murdered the Rani, and her Chief Minister, and the Commandant of the Fort of Jhind and others. He has obtained possession of the fort, and has usurped the Government.

"The Raja has been an unresisting or a willing instrument in the hands of Kour Partab Singh in these atrocious transactions.

"It is now necessary to subvert the usurped authority of Kour Partab Singh, and to re-establish a legitimate Government under the protection of the British power.

"The following arrangements are therefore to be effected :—

"1st. Kour Fatah Singh, the eldest son of Raja Bhag Singh, to be appointed to the entire management of affairs ; but the Government to be carried on in the name of his father the Raja.

"2d. Suitable arrangements to be made for the

dignity and comfort of the Raja, who, in every respect but the exercise of power, with which he is not to be trusted, is to be considered and treated as heretofore.

"3d. Kour Partab Singh, and the most notorious of his accomplices in the late murders, to be seized and sent in confinement to Dehli to await the orders of His Excellency the Governor-General.

"It is most desirable that these arrangements should be accomplished without opposition, but if opposition be attempted, it must be defeated by the most prompt, decisive and energetic measures.

"Raja Bhag Singh, the eldest son Kour Fatah Singh, and the second son Kour Partab Singh, will be severally desired to wait on Colonel Arnold and Mr Fraser. All the officers of the Jhind Government, Civil and Military, will also be ordered to put themselves under the orders of Colonel Arnold and Mr Fraser. If all these requisitions be complied with, the arrangements prescribed will probably be carried into full effect without resistance.

"Kour Fatah Singh resides on his own estate at a distance from Jhind, and to that circumstance is probably indebted for his safety during the late murders. He will no doubt attend in conformity to the summons, and will also be directed to collect his adherents.

"The conduct of the Raja may probably depend on the will of Partab Singh, and may, therefore, as well as that of Partab Singh's be considered doubtful. Yet if there are about the Raja's person any of those Councillors who have advised him hitherto during his connection with the British Government, it is to be expected that he will comply with the requisition, and submit without resistance to the arrangements prescribed.

"It is even possible that Partab Singh may do the same, though it is perhaps more probable that he will either determine to resist or endeavour to effect his escape.

"In the former case his opposition must be overcome by the most decisive measures, as before mentioned, whether it be supported or disavowed by the Rajah. In the latter case the escape of Partab Singh will facilitate the unresisted accomplishment of the arrangements in view, but every exertion must be made to apprehend him and his accomplices.

"It has already been stated that Kour Fatah Singh is obnoxious to the Raja. It is therefore to be apprehended that the Raja will never be reconciled to the Regency of Fatah Singh. The most desirable arrangement is that the Raja should continue to reside at Jhind; and should be reconciled to the eldest son, and that Fatah Singh should treat the Raja with the utmost respect and attention. If this arrangement be impracticable owing to the Raja's strong aversion for his eldest son, the Raja may in that case be allowed to choose another place of residence, and such arrangements as may be requisite can afterwards be adopted to make the remainder of his life easy and comfortable.

"It will be advisable to recommend Fatah Singh to employ in the transaction of the affairs of his Government the old and faithful servants of his family, accustomed to business, against whom there may not be any objection founded on participation in the recent atrocities.

"The utmost promptitude in the execution of the arrangements proposed is desirable. A detachment should advance as soon as possible to Jhind. No time should be lost in negotiation. But the first appearance of an inclination to resist should be followed on our part by the most decisive measures, consistent with the maxims of military prudence, on which point Colonel Arnold will be the sole judge.

"All the arrangements prescribed are of course to be understood to be subject to the revision of His Excellency the Governor-General."

The Prince tries to implicate the Raja in the murder.

An attempt was made by Partab Singh to persuade the world that the murder of Munshi Jaishi Ram and the Rani had been directed by the Raja himself, and was the punishment for an intrigue which dishonoured the family, but of this there was no shadow of proof, and the fact of so many other persons interested in the continuance of the Regency being murdered at the same time sufficiently explained the reasons for the crime.

Partab Singh flies from Jhind to Balawali.

Prince Fatah Singh now took charge of the administration, and Partab Singh, knowing that British troops were marching from all sides against him, left Jhind and retired to Balawali, a fort in the wild country about Batinda. The zemindars of Balawali were a turbulent race, and Partab Singh had no difficulty in persuading them to adopt his cause. But he was at once followed by several troops of English cavalry who were directed to surround Balawali and prevent Partab Singh's escape, until a force, composed of five companies of infantry and three guns, which marched from Ludhiana on the 30th September, should arrive.

Thence he crossed the Satlej and joins Phula Singh Akali.

The Prince saw that it was dangerous to remain at Balawali, where his capture was certain, and, the day after he had entered the fort, he abandoned it, carrying off fifteen or twenty thousand rupees with other valuables that had been lodged there; and after a long and circuitous march, crossed the Satlej at Makhowal, with forty followers, and joined Phula Singh Akali who was in force on the opposite bank.[1]

With whom he makes an expedition south of the Satlej.

This famous outlaw[2] had taken up his residence at

[1] Sir D. Ochterlony to Resident Dehli, 30th September 1814. Sir G. Clerk to Agent Governor-General, 20th March 1836.

[2] Phula Singh was the leader of the Akalis of the Amritsar temple, who attacked Mr Metcalfe's party in 1809, and also Lieutenant White on survey

Nandpur Makhowal and defied the whole power of the Sikhs to expel him. He had with him about seven hundred horse and two guns. With this man Partab Singh remained for two months, then persuading him to cross the Satlej and actively to assist him at Balawali, which remained in open rebellion against the Raja of Jhind. When it became known that Phula Singh had crossed the Satlej, the Agent at Ludhiana wrote without delay to Raja Jaswant Singh of Nabha and the Khans of Maler Kotla, directing them to combine their forces and attack him, though such was the veneration in which Phula Singh was held by the Sikhs that there appeared little chance of the Nabha troops loyally acting against him, and Maler Kotla was not sufficiently strong to act alone.[1] Balawali, at this time, was invested by Pattiala troops, and was almost prepared to surrender, when its defenders heard of the approach of Phula Singh. They at once broke off negotiations, while Partab Sing went in advance and with a few men threw himself into the fort. Seven hundred of the Pattiala troops marched to intercept Phula

Partab Singh reaches Balawali, but Phula Singh compelled to retire.

duty, and, who, for his numerous crimes, had been outlawed by Ranjit Singh on demand of the British Government.

Vide ante, pp. 128-134.

[1] Phula Singh had, as an Akali (a Sikh ascetic class), great influence with his countrymen. The Maharaja tried for years, with half sincerity to capture him, and the English drove him from place to place, but could never seize him. At this very time, when Partab Singh joined him at Makhowal, the Maharaja had sent the most positive orders for the Philor troops to drive him out of his territories. The garrison was accordingly marched against him, but when they approached, Phula Singh sent to ask them if they would kill their *Guru* (spiritual teacher). The Sikhs would not molest him ; and the whole force was kept out some two months to prevent his plundering, marching where he marched, more like a guard of honour than anything else. Numberless stories of the same kind can be told of Phula Singh, who was a very remarkable man. He was a robber and an outlaw, but he was nevertheless a splendid soldier, and a brave, enthusiastic man. He made friends with Ranjit Singh later, and won for him the great battle of Teri, in which he was killed, in 1823.

Singh, who was unable to relieve the fort, and retired toward the Satlej, taking refuge in a village belonging to two Sirdars, Dip Singh and Bir Singh, who reproached the troops for attempting to offer violence to a poor fakir and their *Guru*. The Pattiala General did not know what to do in this emergency, and wrote to the Political Agent, who warned the Sirdars against protecting an outlaw whom all the Cis-Satlej Chiefs had been ordered to expel from their territories. The Chiefs of Nabha and Kythal were directed to send their forces to Balawali to co-operate with those of Pattiala, as the latter were afraid of the odium that would ever afterwards attach itself to them should they be the only assailants of Prince Partab Singh. The Pattiala authorities wished a British force to be sent to Balawali, but this was unnecessary, for the garrison was reduced to great straits, and the fort surrendered on the 28th of January. Prince Partab Singh was taken prisoner, but was placed under merely nominal restraint, and declared his intention of proceeding to Dehli to throw himself on the protection of the British Government. His ally, Phula Singh, was more fortunate. He marched to Mokatsar, in the Firozpur district, and there levied contributions, and being joined by Sirdar Nihal Singh Attariwala, gave battle to the Philor garrison, which he defeated with a loss of three hundred killed and wounded, the Akali not losing more than fifty men. The Maharaja was much annoyed at this affair, and thinking Phula Singh might be made useful if he took him into his service, invited him to Lahore, where he declined to go, demanding that Mokatsar, which was a sacred place of pilgrimage among the Sikhs, should be given him for his residence.[1]

The fort of Balawali at last surrenders, and Partab Singh is taken prisoner.

Phula Singh escapes, defeating the Philor garrison.

[1] Captain Birch to Secretary to Government, 7th, 11th, 16th, 17th December 1814 and 28th January 1815.

Partab Singh fled to Lahore, but Maharaja Ranjit Singh refused to shelter a murderer, and gave him up to the English authorities, who placed him in confinement at Dehli, where he died in June 1816, and the estate of Barwana, which was granted in his name, lapsed to Government.[1] Partab Singh married two wives, Bhagbari, the daughter of Kirpal Singh of Shamghar, and the daughter of Sadha Singh, Kakar of Philor, but neither bore him any children. His younger brother, Mehtab Singh, died a few months before him, when only sixteen years of age.

Partab Singh seeks an asylum at Lahore in vain.

His death at Dehli, A.D. 1816

Death of Prince Mehtab Singh.

The administration of Jhind was now carried on with tolerable tranquillity, Prince Fatah Singh acting as Regent, and Raja Bhag Singh, having no other son, did not oppose an arrangement which was nevertheless distasteful to him.

Prince Fatah Singh as Regent

In 1817 a case, which gave rise to voluminous correspondence, but which requires only the briefest mention, occurred, regarding the villages of Dabri and Danouli. Twelve years after the British Government had been established at Dehli, and some time after it had taken Hissar from Abdul Samad Khan, Mr Fraser, the Revenue Officer, discovered that two villages, called Dabri and Danouli, were in the ancient register of the pargannah of Muhim. He found them ten miles distant from any other villages of that pargannah, surrounded by Jhind lands, and, on his own authority, placed them under attachment. The Raja pleaded that these villages were his; that they formed part of the conquests of his father Gajpat Singh, which had been maintained and confirmed to him both by the British and the Mahrattas. His zamindars had tilled the lands of these villages; and had always made use of the waste attached to them for the pasturage of their cattle. There was little doubt that the claim of the Raja

The dispute regarding the villages of Dabri and Danouli.

The villages are surrendered to the Raja of Jhind.

[1] Sir D. Ochterlony to Resident Dehli, 31st August 1816.

was good, and that set up for the British Government by a too enthusiastic officer was abandoned.[1]

The death of Raja Bhag Singh, 1819.

Raja Bhag Singh died in 1819, and was succeeded by his son Fatah Singh. He had married three wives: first, Dya Kour, daughter of Bakhsu Singh of Bari Mansa, the mother of Fatah Singh; secondly, Sada Kour, the daughter of Pakhar Singh of Jodhpur Subake, who bore him Partab Singh; and, lastly, Subrahi, from a zamindar family of Kaleki, the mother of Mehtab Singh, and who was murdered by Prince Partab Singh.

His family.

The reign of Fatah Singh uneventful.

The reign of Raja Fatah Singh was very short and quite uneventful. He died on the 3d of February 1822, at his residence of Sangrur, aged thirty-three, leaving one son, Sangat Singh, eleven years of age, the child of his second wife Sahib Kour, daughter of Khushhal Singh of Bournewala. His first wife, Khem Kour, daughter of Sirdar Didar Singh, bore him no children.

His death in A.D. 1822.

No special arrangements were made by the British Government with regard to the Jhind administration, but the officers of that State were directed to carry on the Government in the ordinary manner.[2]

Raja Sangat Singh installed.

The installation of the young Raja took place on the 30th July 1822, at Jhind, in the presence of all the Phulkian Chiefs, and Captain Ross, the Deputy-Superintendent, who presented the usual Khillat of investiture on the part of the British Government.[3] In April 1824, the

[1] Sir D. Ochterlony to Resident Dehli, 27th April 1817. Letter from Resident to Sir D. Ochterlony, enclosing Mr Fraser's report. Captain Birch to General Ochterlony, enclosing letter from Raja Bhag Singh, dated 26th December 1816.

[2] Captain Ross to Secretary to Government, dated 7th February and 2d March 1822; and Secretary to Government to Mr A. Ross, Agent Governor-General, dated 16th March 1822.

[3] Captain Ross to Agent Governor-General, dated 9th August 1822. Agent Governor-General to Captain Ross, 22d May 1822; and Secretary to Government to A. Ross, Esq., dated 4th May 1822.

young Chief was married to Sabha Kour, daughter of Sirdar Ranjit Singh of Shahabad, with great pomp, Maharaja Ranjit Singh, who was not able to attend himself, sending a deputation headed by Sirdar Baisahka Singh, Captain Murray, the Deputy-Superintendent, attending on behalf of the British Government.[1] His marriage.

The confusion into which the Jhind administration fell.

The usual results which a minority produces in Native States, soon began to show themselves in Jhind. The affairs of the Raja fell into the utmost confusion; the territory was ill-managed, the people discontented, and no attention was paid to the remonstrances of the British authorities regarding grievances that he was called upon to redress. To such a point did this recklessness proceed, that the Political Agent at length recommended that the monthly and quarterly cash payments received by the Raja on account of the Ludhiana cantonments, and for the Sayer and Abkari duties thereof, should be suspended until the Raja should satisfy all just claims pending against his territory and subjects.[2]

The Raja visits Amritsar and Lahore.

In 1826, Raja Sangat Singh paid a visit to Maharaja Ranjit Singh. He was met at Amritsar by some Sirdars of the Court, and conducted with honour to Lahore, where the Maharaja received him very kindly, and on the festival of the Holi made his officials present *nazrs* to him. Ranjit Singh invited the Raja to accompany him to Jowala Mukhi, a place of pilgrimage in the Kangra Hills, and

The Khillats presented to Rajas Fatah Singh and Sangat Singh, on their respective installations, were composed of the following articles:—

A string of pearls; a *jigha* (worn in the turban); a Sirpesh (ditto); a pair of shawls; one square shawl; one piece of Kinkhab; one piece of Gulbadan; a turban; two pieces of Srisaf cloth; an elephant; a horse; a jewelled crupper saddle; girths and elephants' trappings.

[1] Captain Murray to C. Elliott, Esq., Agent to Governor-General, April 1824.

[2] Captain Murray to Agent Governor-General, dated 3d October 1824.

he consented to go as far as Dinanagar, where he waited for the Maharaja's return, when he received the grant of a jagir in the Jalandhar Doab. In 1827, he again visited Lahore. Maharaja Ranjit Singh seems to have taken a great liking for him, and gave him many presents, one of which brought him into some trouble with the British Government. Antiana was an estate held by Sirdar Ram Singh, on the south side of the Satlej, claimed by Ranjit Singh as a dependency of Lahore, but the claim to which had not been admitted. This village Raja Sangat Singh suddenly attacked and took from the rightful owner, who complained to the Agent of the Governor-General. The Raja was called upon for an explanation, and, in reply, produced a grant from Ranjit Singh of the village in question, with two others, named Rajnana and Joghal, in exchange for a *nazrana* of Rs. 30,000, a female riding elephant, and a horse. The conduct of Ranjit Singh in granting a village which did not belong to him was not remarkable; but that of Sangat Singh, while under the protection of the British Government, in accepting or purchasing villages from a foreign power, was most reprehensible. He was consequently directed to restore the villages without delay, and received a severe rebuke for entering, without the knowledge or permission of the Government, into negotiations with Lahore. The Raja had no choice but to obey, and surrendered Antiana to Ram Singh, on which he was allowed to retain the other two villages.[1]

A second visit to Lahore in A.D. 1827.

The village of Antiana given to Bhag Singh by the Maharaja,

But the British Government insist on its surrender.

The case of the Trans-Satlej jagirs, which Sangat Singh had received during his visits to Lahore in 1826 and 1827,

The jagir grants of the Maharaja, of 1826, 1827.

[1] Sir E. Colebrooke to Secretary to Government, 12th June 1838. Secretary to Government to Sir E. Colebrooke, 3d July 1828. Sir E. Colebrooke to Captain Murray, 29th July 1828.

was also discussed. The annual revenue derived from these was estimated at Rs. 25,500; from some the owners had been ousted to make way for the new master, and others had been already held by the Maharaja's officers on military tenure. The first was Rai Majara, consisting of twelve villages, worth Rs. 13,000, which was given to Sangat Singh at Dinanagar in 1826; Mahrampur, consisting of six villages, valued at Rs. 6000; Musapur, one village, worth Rs. 4500; and an assignment of Rs. 200 a year from a jagir, Trans-Satlej, held by Sirdar Dewa Singh, all given during Sangat Singh's visit to Lahore in 1827.[1]

The principle laid down by the Government with reference to foreign grants.

The Government did not consider it necessary to enforce the relinquishment of these jagirs on this occasion, but laid down the fundamental principle that the circumstance of the alliance with the protected Chiefs required them to abstain from all connection or intercourse with foreign Princes and Governments, excepting such as should be of a purely complimentary nature, without the knowledge and sanction of the British authorities. The jagirs already granted were not directed to be returned, for the reason that it did not appear that the practice had ever been carried, or was likely to be carried, so far as to cause any practical inconvenience; but should such result, action would at once be taken to compel adherence to the principle which had been laid down.[2]

The Raja again opens negotiations with Lahore.

No sooner had this case been settled, than Raja Sangat Singh again opened negotiations with Lahore without the sanction of Government. The question related to six

[1] Captain C. Wade to Sir E. Colebrooke, 5th August 1828.

[2] Secretary to Government to Sir E. Colebrooke, 18th July 1828. Sir E. Colebrooke to Government, 23d and 24th June 1828. Captain Wade to Sir E. Colebrooke of 14th August; and Sir E. Colebrooke to Captain Wade of 19th August 1828.

villages held in joint proprietorship to the south of the Satlej, by the Maharaja and Sangat Singh, and which the latter desired to possess altogether, farming the Maharaja's share. There was, of course, no particular objection to this proposition in itself. The evils of divided authority were apparent, but it would have been more objectionable and liable to still greater abuse if the Raja should farm the portion of the estate belonging to the Maharaja, and the latter should retain the civil and criminal jurisdiction, which he declined altogether to resign; and under these circumstances Sangat Singh was compelled to abandon the idea of farming the share held by Lahore.[1]

The Cis Satlej Rajas all had agents at the Lahore Court.

It was almost impossible to prevent the Cis-Satlej Chiefs carrying on independent negotiations with Lahore, when almost every one of them had agents and vakils at that Court. Those of the Nabha and Jhind Rajas were generally in attendance, while the Maharaja of Pattiala had a recognised agent residing at Lahore, and it was seriously contemplated to require all those parties who were accustomed to communicate directly with Maharaja Ranjit Singh to recall their agents altogether; but this idea was never carried into execution.

The mismanagement of Jhind increases, and the Raja deserts his capital.

The mismanagement of Jhind continued to increase, and it became, perhaps, the worst of the ill-managed States on the border. The Raja deserted his capital altogether as a residence, and went to live at a town some eighty miles distant, from which he was only recalled by the action of Captain Murray in sending a native official to carry on the Jhind administration. But no sooner

[1] Captain C. Wade to Sir E. Colebrooke, 17th February 1829. Sir E. Colebrooke to Captain Wade of 10th February; and to Captain Murray, 27th March 1829. Captain Murray to Resident, 7th February 1829.

was this officer recalled, than Sangat Singh again left his capital, and did not revisit it for years. Remonstrances were vainly addressed to the Raja, and Diwan Singh, his principal adviser, was able to persuade him that matters could be so arranged as to satisfy the British authorities without any trouble on his own part. Outrages were committed on British subjects for which no redress could be obtained, and the demoralisation of the State was extreme.[1] Nor were the persons of British officers themselves safe; and, in March 1833, Lieutenant Talbot, of the 8th Regiment of Native Infantry, was attacked in Jhind territory by robbers, and subjected to personal outrage, as well as heavy pecuniary loss.[2] Compensation was indeed procured for the loss of property, but the Jhind authorities were unable to bring the offenders to the punishment they deserved.

The detention of British subjects in confinement without just cause by the Jhind authorities was, in 1834, reported to Government by the Governor-General's Agent, and the particular grievances complained of were redressed, but the general inefficiency and oppression of the administration remained the same.[3] A short time afterwards, the Raja left on a visit to Lahore, to be present at the Dusehra festival, to which he had been specially invited by Ranjit Singh, with whom he seemed more anxious to remain on good terms than with the English Government, to whom this visit gave just cause of dissatisfaction, occurring so soon after the censure which had been passed

Raja Sangat Singh visits Lahore in A.D. 1834.

[1] Mr W. Fraser, Agent to Governor-General, to Mr Clerk, 20th April 1832; and Mr G. Clerk to Mr Fraser, dated 28th May 1832.

[2] Political Agent to Agent Governor-General, 22d March 1833; and to Lieutenant Talbot of the same date.

[3] Agent Governor-General to Mr Clerk, 17th July and 23d August. Mr Clerk to Agent Governor-General, 19th August 1834.

on the Raja for his unauthorised negotiations with the Lahore Court.[1]

The sudden death of Raja Sangat Singh, A.D. 1834.

But an unexpected close was brought to Raja Sangat Singh's extravagance and misgovernment. On the 2d of November he was at Basia in perfect health, though intoxicated, as usual, before evening. The next morning he complained of feeling unwell, and, becoming rapidly worse, was advised by his followers to leave Basia and return to Sangrur. He at once set out in his palanquin, but died before he had passed the gate of Basia.[2]

The evil results of minorities in Native States.

At the time of his death, Sangat Singh was only twenty-three years of age. Left, by the death of his father, the heir to a large principality while still a child, he had naturally, and, indeed, necessarily fallen into the hands of men who found their interest in debauching his mind and encouraging his lowest passions and worst extravagances. The history of long minorities in Native States is ever the same. The ministers to whom the administration is confided, think only of themselves and their personal gain and advancement: honesty, loyalty, devotion, and truth are unknown; and the young Prince, who is one day to exercise independent power, and to whom a whole people must look for their only hope of justice, is abandoned to prostitutes, fiddlers, and buffoons; till, at eighteen, with a body enfeebled by debauchery, and incapable of ever giving an heir to his State, with an intellect untrained and neglected, and a morality which would disgrace a brothel, he is useless for any purpose on the earth save to fill the pockets of his greedy favourites, to squander the wealth which his ancestors

[1] Mr G. Clerk to Mr W. Fraser, 25th October 1834.
[2] Mr G. Clerk to Mr W. Fraser, 6th November 1834.

had laboriously amassed by their energy and courage, and to drag in the dirt a name which was once illustrious.

The natural faults of Sangat Singh's character were carefully encouraged by his ministers for their own ends. His father, Fatah Singh, had left a large quantity of treasure, which had been still further increased by Sahib Kour, while Regent for her son. But it was all squandered by Sangat Singh in a thousand extravagances, more especially in his expeditions to Lahore; and for some time before his death, he found the money he required, and for which the legitimate revenue of his country would not suffice, in repeated extortions from all classes of his subjects; administrative duties were altogether neglected; life and property became insecure; while the most faithful servants of the State sought, in British territory, an asylum where they might be secure from the molestations and oppressions of the Raja and his minister Diwan Singh.[1]

The character of Sangat Singh.

Sangat Singh left no son. He had married three times: first, to Subhan Kour, daughter of Sirdar Ranjit Singh of Shahabad; secondly, to Sukhan, daughter of Sirdar Jiun Singh Dhaliwal; and lastly, to Nand Kour, the daughter of Dulla Singh of Tibba.

The extinction of the direct line of Jhind Chiefs.

The nearest relations of the deceased Chief were three second cousins: Sarup Singh, Sukha Singh, and Bhagwan Singh, the Sirdars of Badrukhan and Bazidpur, who had for long been separated from the Jhind branch of the family. The principality, according to Sikh custom, might justly have been treated as an escheat, and have been annexed to the British dominions, for in Sikh States the right of collaterals to succeed did not obtain. But for some time no action was taken, either by Government

The collateral relatives and the law of escheat.

[1] Mr G. Clerk to Mr W. Fraser, 2d November 1832.

or the collateral relations of the deceased Chief, and Mai Sahib Kour, the mother of Sangat Singh, and Regent during his minority, carried on the administration.

The Cis-Satlej Chiefs refuse to pay tribute in exchange for the right of succeeding to heirless estates.

Four years before the death of the Raja, the Political Agent had been directed by the Government to sound the principal Chiefs and ascertain if they were willing to pay tribute, on the understanding that should they not do so, the Government would take advantage of all lapses as the only means of reimbursing itself for the expenses incurred in protecting the States between the Satlej and the Jumna.

The Political Agent accordingly held conversations with the Pattiala, Jhind, Nabha, and Kythal representatives, pointing out to them that although the Chiefs had full liberty to adopt the suggestion or reject it, the consequences of non-payment of tribute might justly cause some apprehension as to the permanency of those estates to which there were no direct heirs. The examples of Jhind and Kythal were, at the time, before the eyes of the Chiefs, who met at Dhodan, a village situated on their common frontiers, to discuss the matter. But no conclusion was arrived at. Two of the Chiefs thought it desirable to revise their relations with the British Government, but they were overruled by others, who, with true Sikh recklessness, preferred the easy terms which they enjoyed in the present, to a more secure future which involved some present sacrifice. The time very shortly came when they bitterly regretted not having accepted the terms offered them, when their power was materially reduced by the lapse of Kythal and the partial lapse of Jhind.

The decision regarding Jhind postponed.

The intention of the British Government at first was undoubtedly to annex the whole State of Jhind. The

Governor-General, in January 1835, directed that as the descendants of Hamir Singh (the Nabha house), and Bhup Singh (the Bazidpur and Badrukhan house), had been separately provided for, they had no claims whatever to the Chiefship; whether the widows of the deceased Raja were entitled to a life-interest was a point reserved for future consideration and report. In the meantime, Rani Sahib Kour was to continue to act as Regent; and, in case the claims set up by the widows were disallowed, the whole State would be sequestered, Maharaja Ranjit Singh of Lahore being directed to advance any claims he might desire for estates conferred by him on Raja Bhag Singh.[1]

The claims of the widows.

The claims of the widows were conflicting and numerous. By ordinary Sikh law the widows of the deceased Chief would succeed to his estates, but there were many reasons which made such a succession, in the case of Jhind, objectionable in the extreme. The three widows of the late Chief—Ranis Subha Kour, Nand Kour, and Sukhan—were all very young, the eldest being only twenty-three years of age. This latter claimed to succeed to the whole estate, as being the senior, while the two younger asserted their claims to an equal partition. But the evils attending female rule were so great and notorious, that it was felt that the entire disorganisation of the State would be the result were it now permitted. In smaller estates, widows of mature age had, on the death of their husbands, succeeded and carried on the administration with credit; but the case was different in the case of a

The inconvenience of allowing their claim, and the evils of female rule.

[1] Mr Fraser, Agent to Governor-General, to Secretary to Government, dated 7th and 9th of November, and 5th December 1834, and 6th January 1835. Secretary to Government to Agent Governor-General, dated 21st January 1835.

large principality like Jhind, which could only with the utmost danger be entrusted to the hands of three young women, little more than children, who would, without doubt, be entirely in the hands of designing favourites, who would use the authority of the Ranis for interested ends, while the honour of the family could not be safe with women whose passions or caprice would be subject to no practical restraint.

The widows of Raja Fatah Singh.

Besides the widows of the late Chief, two of his father's widows also advanced their claims to succession. Sahib Kour was the elder of these, and the mother of Raja Sangat Singh, during whose minority she had carried on the administration with considerable ability. Khem Kour was the junior widow, who claimed an equal share with Sahib Kour, who, on her part, claimed the whole. Neither of these ladies had any legal right whatever.[1]

The claim of Rani Bhagbari, widow of Prince Partab Singh.

Rani Bhagbari was the senior widow of Prince Partab Singh, who put in a claim as being the widow of Raja Bhag Singh's favourite son, in whose favour he had executed a will assigning to him the Raj. But the claim of this lady was quite invalid, as Partab Singh had never succeeded his father, and the widow could have no right to claim through him.[2]

That of the Raja of Nabha.

The Raja of Nabha advanced a claim as the descendant, with the Jhind house, from a common ancestor; but this claim was at once disallowed, for his branch of the family had separated from that of Jhind previous to the founding of the principality by Raja Gajpat Singh.

[1] Mr G. Clerk to Agent Governor-General, dated 20th February, 12th March, and 4th June 1835. Agent Governor-General to Mr Clerk, dated 2d February and 14th May 1838.

[2] Agent Governor-General to Secretary to Government, dated 7th July 1836; and Secretary to Government to Agent Governor-General, dated 27th July 1836.

The Raja advanced in support of his claim the decision of Government, *in re* the Kakrala estate, which had been adjudged to escheat to the Bhai of Kythal in preference to the other branches of the Bhaikian family.[1] He also urged the importance of transferring the charge of so important an estate as that of Jhind to a State possessing the authority and the means requisite to the due administration of such extensive territories, in preference to adopting, as their sovereign, a less influential member of the family, and expressed his readiness to tender a *nazrana* of four lakhs of rupees on the recognition of his title to inherit. But the claims of the Nabha Raja were too mythical to be substantiated by any payment of *nazrana*.[2]

The arguments in favour of his claim.

The only remaining claimants were the Chiefs of Bazidpur and Badrukhan, Sirdars Sarup Singh and Sukha Singh; and to explain their position, it is necessary to trace back a short way the history of this branch of the Jhind family.

The remaining claimants—the Chiefs of Bazidpur and Badrukhan.

Sirdar Bhup Singh was the third son of Raja Gajpat Singh of Jhind. He was a brave man, but not gifted with any particular intelligence, and lost more territory by his imbecility than his courage ever enabled him to gain. Raja Bhag Singh succeeded his father as Chief of Jhind, while the estates of Badrukhan and Bazidpur went to Bhup Singh. The latter had two sons, Karam Singh, by his first wife, the daughter of Arbel Singh of Kaleki; and Basawa Singh, by his second wife, the daughter of Gajju Singh of Ralla. Karam Singh was a man of bad character. He quarrelled with his father;

The founder of the Badrukhan family, Sirdar Bhup Singh.

[1] Secretary to Government to Agent Governor-General, dated 4th April and 4th May 1822.

[2] Political Agent to Agent Governor-General, dated 24th June 1836.

The rebellion of his son, Karam Singh.

and, taking up arms against him, wrested from him the estate of Badrukhan. The dispossessed Chief called to his assistance some of his Phulkian relations and recovered the estate, yet he did not punish his son by entirely disinheriting him, but made over to him, for his maintenance, the village of Muhammadpur. But with this Karam Singh was not content, and seized by force Bazidpur, which he was not able to retain, and, crossing the Satlej, took service with Maharaja Ranjit Singh at Lahore.

The division of the ancestral estate by the Phulkian Chiefs.

On the death of Bhup Singh, his territories were divided between his sons by the Phulkian Rajas, who assigned to the younger son, Basawa Singh, the largest and best estate of Badrukhan, and to the elder, Bazidpur, of far less value, as a punishment for his disobedience and rebellion. Sirdar Bhup Singh received his share in 1789, from which time he was considered as an independent Chief, altogether separate from the Jhind house, and as such he was always treated by the British Government. After his death, his sons Karam Singh and Basawa Singh were similarly treated as independent.[1]

Karam Singh, on his father's death, returned to Bazidpur, where he died in 1818, leaving one son, Sarup Singh, who claimed to succeed to the principality of Jhind.

Sarup Singh had the best *prima facie* claim.

If the right of collateral succession were admitted by Government, the claim of Sarup Singh appeared good. He was the son of Karam Singh, the elder of Bhup Singh's children, and as such had a preferential right to Sukha Singh, who was of the younger branch, the rule

[1] Political Agent, Mr G. Clerk, to Agent Governor-General, dated 6th November 1834 and 23d March 1836. Secretary to Government to Agent Governor-General, dated 6th January 1836.

of primogeniture having been affirmed by Government to prevail in Jhind.[1]

The claim of Sirdar Sukha Singh of Badrukhan, and the objections advanced to Sirdar Sarup Singh's succession.

Sirdar Sukha Singh based his claim mainly on the alleged fact that Karam Singh had been disinherited and disowned by his father, and that consequently he was incompetent to succeed; and, secondly, on an alleged custom in the Jhind family by which the estate ordinarily passed to the second son. This latter objection was of little importance. It will be remembered that Raja Bhag Singh urged the same custom when he desired to obtain sanction for the will he had made in favour of his second son, but the Government declined to acknowledge it, nor had it any real existence. In the case of Sukha Singh, moreover, the argument was peculiarly unfortunate, for he had a younger brother, Bhagwan Singh, whose rights would naturally be stronger than his own.

The disinheritance of Karam Singh.

With regard to the disinheritance of Karam Singh, which his son Sarup Singh denied, there can be no doubt that Sirdar Bhup Singh viewed the unnatural and rebellious conduct of his son with extreme displeasure, and, during the latter years of his life, would never receive him. This feeling was shared by the other members of his family, for, on Karam Singh's death, at Bazidpur, on his return from the Punjab, none of the Phulkian Chiefs paid the usual visit of condolence, a ceremony never omitted among allied houses, while they all sent deputations and paid the highest respect to the family of his brother Sirdar Basawa Singh, on his death, a few years later. This feeling was shown still more strongly in the

[1] The question of the right of collaterals to succeed has been discussed, with special reference to the Jhind case, in a treatise on "The Sikh Law of Inheritance to Chiefships," by the author of the present work.

disposition of the territory after Bhup Singh's death, when the Rajas, believing that the British Government were anxious that it should be equally divided among the sons, endeavoured to give the partition that appearance, while in reality they allotted to the younger son a far more valuable share, that of Badrukhan, of which Karam Singh ever afterwards tried vainly to possess himself.

The funeral rites, which, among Hindus and Sikhs alike, are considered of the utmost importance, were undoubtedly performed by Sirdar Basawa Singh alone, and on this point Sukha Singh laid great stress. Karam Singh, it is true, came to his father's funeral, but was excluded from all participation in the ceremonies. On the death of Raja Sangat Singh of Jhind, Sirdar Sukha Singh again performed the customary rites; but this was easily explained in a case of death so unexpected as that of the Raja's, and in a climate where cremation must take place so soon after death. Sirdar Sarup Singh being at a distance was unable to be present, and, apart from other right, the personal superintendence of the funeral ceremonies could not confer a title to inherit.[1] The claim of Sarup Singh was accordingly held to be good as against that of Sukha Singh, and his disinheritance not to have been complete, for at all events, by the decree of the Phulkian Rajas, he was in possession of a large share of his father's territory.

The right of Sirdar Sarup Singh of Bazidpur having

[1] Petition of Sirdar Sarup Singh. Mr G. Clerk to Agent Governor-General, 15th June, 4th July, 9th December 1836. Petition of Sirdar Sukha Singh with Secretary to Government's letter, 10th April 1839. Mr G. Clerk to Agent Governor-General, 23d October 1835. Petition of Sarup Singh with Secretary to Government's letter to Agent Governor-General, 6th January and 27th July 1836. Agent Governor-General to Mr Clerk, 10th August, 24th October, and 21st November 1836.

been admitted by the British Government, the question arose, what principle should be held to govern the disposition of the several portions of the territory. This territory consisted of three distinct portions: that which was possessed by Raja Gajpat Singh, the founder of the family, through whom Sarup Singh claimed, and which comprised the districts of Jhind and Sufidon, the best portion of the territory; secondly, the grants made by Maharaja Ranjit Singh of Lahore to the Jhind Chief previous to the treaty of 1809, including Ludhiana, Basia, Morinda, &c.; and, lastly, certain grants made by the Maharaja subsequent to that treaty.

The principle on which Jhind territory was to be disposed of.

Sarup Singh urged that his claim to succeed being admitted, he was entitled to inherit the whole territory, including ancient and modern acquisitions, both old and recent grants: he urged this partly on the ground that, as regarded collateral succession, the Phulkian family was different in its position from others, and this was no doubt true, though not in the manner that Sarup Singh intended it.

Sarup Singh asserts his right to the whole territory.

The Rajas of Pattiala, Nabha, and Jhind, and the Bhais of Kythal, were all *malguzars* or tributaries of the Dehli Emperors. They had joined with other Sikhs in predatory incursions into Dehli territory, and had forcibly taken possession of country which the Muhammadan rulers were too feeble to retain; but they, nevertheless, remained nominally, and as far as payment of tribute was concerned, actually the subjects of the Emperors; and when this tribute fell into arrears, they were compelled by force of arms to make it good, in the same way as other contumacious *zamindars*. They were not, and never had been, independent, and the British Government, which had assumed towards them precisely

The nature of the tenure of the Phulkian Chiefs in the days of the Empire.

the same position that the Dehli Government had held, was entitled to the benefit of all escheats in return for its protection, and as a compensation for the non-payment of tribute which it did not demand. Sarup Singh pleaded Hindu law and the authority of the Shastras in support of his claim, but these laws applied to personal and private property alone. Besides, the Sikhs had abandoned the Hindu faith, and with it the system of law which is the basis of that faith, and which was inseparable from it. For a hundred and fifty years they had been governed, as far as Chiefships were concerned, by another code altogether, and it was as reasonable for them to refer to Manu and the Shastras as the source of legal authority, as it would have been for Muhammadans, who had embraced Sikhism, to appeal to the Shara. The Phulkian Chiefs, moreover, had only a few years before the death of Raja Sangat Singh of Jhind, declined the Government proposal to surrender all right to escheats in favour of a fixed tribute.

Hindu law as applied to Sikh inheritance.

They preferred a present to a future good, and would have had no just cause for complaint had the Government decided to treat the whole principality of Jhind as a legitimate escheat. They certainly had no just cause for complaint in the decision which gave to Sirdar Sarup Singh the Chiefship, the title of Raja, and the possessions which had been held by the ancestor from whom he derived his claim, which constituted the most valuable portion of the territory, resuming all later grants and acquisitions, excepting those which had been conferred by the Government of Lahore subsequent to the treaty of 1809, which justly reverted to the original donor. Raja Bhag Singh had conquered no new territory, and everything which he obtained, beyond what he

The principality of Jhind was a legitimate escheat to the Government.

inherited from his father, was by direct grant from the Maharaja of Lahore, or the British Government.[1]

Grants made by the Lahore Government.

With reference to the Lahore grants, Maharaja Ranjit Singh asserted his right to succeed to all the estates which he had granted to Jhind, both previous and subsequent to the treaty, but his right to the former the Government declined to allow. He, like Sarup Singh, fell back upon the Hindu law of inheritance, which he had never respected, but which, had it been in force, would have had no bearing on the question at issue. The Sikh Chiefs who claimed British protection were not, it is true, exempted necessarily from all dependence on the ruler of Lahore. Those who were at that time avowedly dependent upon Ranjit Singh in respect to any portion of the lands in their possession, did not necessarily find their relations with that Chief altered by the treaty, which only provided that the Maharaja should not commit or suffer any encroachment on the possessions or rights of the Chiefs in his vicinity of the territory conferred by him on the left bank of the Satlej; but grants, absolutely ceded without conditions, were held on a different tenure. The Maharaja could not claim, as lord paramount, any escheats south of the Satlej, and neither Hindu nor Sikh law warranted a donor resuming a gift on the death, without heir, of the donee.

[1] Mr G. R. Clerk to Agent Governor-General, 26th February, 23d July 1835. Agent Governor-General to Mr Clerk, 30th December 1835. Secretary to Government of India to Agent Governor-General, 7th July, 9th September, and 16th December 1835. Petitions of Sarup Singh to Governor-General, 21st August and 5th November 1835. Letter of Sarup Singh to Mr Clerk, 6th May 1835. Mr Metcalfe to Captain Murray, 13th January 1826. Mr Secretary Edmonstone to Sir D. Ochterlony, 14th July 1810. Political Agent Ludhiana to Political Agent Ambala, 15th and 25th November 1834. Political Agent Ambala to Mr Fraser, Agent Governor-General, 29th December 1834.

The opinion of the Governor-General as to Lahore grants.

In the letter of the Governor-General to the Maharaja of the 15th of June, he stated: "The jagirs, which were held by the late Raja's family before the treaty of friendship was concluded between yourself and the British Government, through my agency, may, as observed by you, be considered with reference to that treaty, but in respect to those given after the treaty, I agree with you that you have a right to resume them."

Ambiguous language.

The term jagir, used in these letters, was meant to signify such grants as were made by a superior to an inferior on conditions of dependence, and did not refer to unconditional grants. But the term was of a somewhat ambiguous signification, and since the Maharaja had understood, or pretended that he understood it to apply to grants of whatever character they might be, the Governor-General was unwilling to dispute the point.

The grants previous to the treaty of 1803.

In the Maharaja's first communication with the British Government, he had only asserted his claim to the grants made to the Raja of Jhind previous to the treaty of 1809, and it was only subsequently that he claimed all the estates granted both before and after that treaty, even hinting that he was entitled to the entire territory possessed by the late Raja in virtue of the law of inheritance. To this last claim the Agent to the Governor-General, in his letter to the Maharaja of the 1st February 1836, replied: "It is hardly necessary for me to remind your Highness that though you may be distantly allied to the late Chief, yet the succession to principalities is not governed, either in law or usage, by the ordinary rules of inheritance which are applicable to the property of individuals."[1]

[1] Secretary to Government of India to Agent Governor-General, dated 8th July 1835; to Captain Wade, Political Agent, dated 1st February, 11th

The correspondence regarding the Jhind succession was long continued, and the principle was at length laid down that the Maharaja of Lahore should resume the grants made subsequent to the treaty of 1809; that the new Raja should succeed alone to the acquisitions of Raja Gajpat Singh; and that the remaining territory, including Ludhiana, should lapse to the British Government. This decision, which, as far as Sarup Singh and the Lahore Maharaja were concerned, was liberal in the extreme, was conveyed in the following resolution of the Governor-General, dated 10th January 1837.[1] **Those subsequent to that treaty to be resumed by Lahore.**

"3. His Lordship in Council regrets to find that it is almost impracticable to lay down any general rules for succession to property in the Sikh States. The information now furnished, so far from affording any new light on the subject, tends only to confirm the remark contained in Captain Murray's paper on the rules and customs of the Sikhs, to the effect that 'the rules of succession to landed property in the Sikh States are arbitrary, and are variously modified in accordance with the usages, the interests, and prejudices of different families, nor is it practicable to reduce the anomalous system to a fixed and leading principle.' **The final decision of the Government of India.**

"4. I am desired to observe that the Governor-General in Council cannot concur in the opinion expressed by the Agent at Dehli in the 11th paragraph of his letter, dated the 9th ultimo, that the claims of the widows in the case

April, and 4th July 1836. Agent Governor-General to Maharaja Ranjit Singh, dated 8th July 1835. Mr G. Clerk to Agent Governor-General, dated 23d July 1835.

Secretary Government of India to Government North-Western Provinces, dated 4th July 1836.

[1] Agent Governor-General to Mr Clerk, Political Agent, dated 11th February 1837.

of the Jhind succession would appear to be strengthened by the facts recorded in the precedents cited. It is true that in nine of those cases where brothers succeeded, they married the widows of the last possessors; but it by no means follows that the succession was in virtue of such marriage. It by no means follows that the succession would not have taken place without such ceremony, still less that the widows could have succeeded to the prejudice of the male heir, had no such ceremony been performed.

"5. When authorities are so conflicting, and the practice so unsettled, as they appear to be in the tract of country referred to, his Lordship in Council is of opinion that it is proper and expedient that some general principle should, when practicable, be established by the British Government; and every consideration of usage, justice, and policy seems to require that, as regards the four principal Chiefships of Pattiala, Jhind, Kythal, and Nabha, the rule ought to be that the estate should devolve entire to the nearest male heir, according to the Hindu law, and to the exclusion of the females. With regard to all the other Sikh estates, the custom of the family must be ascertained in each instance by the best evidence procurable.

"6. Applying the above principle to the case of Jhind, Sarup Singh would unquestionably appear to have the best claim, but he can have no right to succeed to more than was possessed by his great-grandfather, Gajpat Singh, through whom he derives his title."

The Jhind Raja endeavours to obtain a reconsideration of this order.

With this decision the new Raja was not content, the other Phulkian Chiefs uniting with him in urging that it should be reconsidered, and the whole territory possessed by Raja Bhag Singh surrendered. But the Government declined to reopen the question, and informed the Raja that he had obtained everything that could be considered his due.[1] The disposition of the territory, the estates which were made over to Lahore, those given to Raja Sarup Singh, and those resumed by the British Government, are shown in the following table,[2] which was, however, modified later in one or two particulars :—

STATEMENT OF THE JHIND POSSESSIONS.

To be restored to Sarup Singh.

Pargannahs.	No. of Villages.	Estimated Revenue.	Remarks.
		Rs.	
Jhind Proper, . .	140	1,20,000	The estimated revenue has been taken from Mr Clerk's report of the 10th November 1835.
Sufidon, . . .	25	42,000	Not given in his report of the 29th December 1834; is much below that here shown.
Assowndha, . . .	26		
Salwan, ...	8		
Balawali, . . .	108	20,000	This estimate is shown as comprising only 13 villages in Mr Clerk's report of the 29th December 1834.
Sungrai, . . .	11	50,000	
Jichewal, . . .	1	4,000	This is taken from the report of 29th December 1834.
Bhowki, . . .	1		
Samout, . . .	1		
Mhelun, . . .	1		
Total, . .	322	2,36,000	

To be restored to Maharaja Ranjit Singh.

Pargannahs.	No. of Villages.	Estimated Revenue.	Remarks.
		Rs.	
Hulwara, . .	1	9,000	* Only one-fourth of these estates appears to have been granted by Maharaja Ranjit Singh, agreeably to the translation of the Sanads received with the Agent's letter of the 30th January 1837.
Talwandi, . .	1		
Half Mudkee, . .	*		
Half Gyaspurah, .	*		
Total, . .	...	9,000	

[1] Sir C. Metcalfe to Mr G. Clerk, Political Agent, dated 15th June 1837, and 2d January 1838. Letter from Raja Sarup Singh to Sir C. Metcalfe, 25th November 1837; and Sir C. Metcalfe to Raja, 16th December 1837.

[2] This sketch, which is not altogether accurate, was drawn up in the office of Mr Bushby in February 1837.

To be retained by the British Government.

Pargannahs.	No. of Villages.	Estimated Revenue.	Remarks.
		Rs.	
Bassia, . . .	16	16,000	If any of the places in this list are beyond the Satlej, they are not, of course, to be retained by the British Government.
Ludhiana, . .	77	85,000	
Morinda, . .	36	44,000	
Half Mudki, . .	8	10,000	
Jandhiala, . .	9	11,000	This is a grant from Ranjit Singh, made in 1807. It is not included in Mr Clerk's report of the 10th November 1835.
Total, . .	146	1,66,000	
Chuhal, . . .	...	2,000	It does not appear how these estates were acquired, and by whom. It is doubtful, therefore, whether they are to be retained or restored.
Dialpurah, . .	...	3,000	
Scattered villages, .	...	11,000 *	* These villages are not included in Mr Clerk's report of the 10th November 1835; but are mentioned in the abstract rendered on the 29th December 1834.
Total, . .	...	16,000	

NOTE.—Nine villages have been ordered to be annexed to the Western Division of the Dehli territory—viz., Bumboury, Sundlana, Kaprow, Kharrak, Panihari, Dhab, Bhadour, and Brana Khera Khar Khoda—and of course none of these are to be transferred to Raja Sarup Singh, as they are part of the British Dominions.

(Signed) G. A. BUSHBY, Secretary.

The ruling of the Court of Directors.

In November 1837, the Court of Directors, to whom the final arrangements regarding the Jhind succession had been referred, ruled that all portions of the territory which had been acquired since Gajpat Singh's time, otherwise than by grant from Ranjit Singh or from the British Government or its predecessors, might be considered to belong justly to the new Raja. "If any portion," the despatch went on to say, "was acquired otherwise, as for instance by conquest, we cannot perceive on what grounds it can lapse to Government. Such possessions, we should conceive, ought to pass to the next heir, Sarup Singh, as private property, under similar circumstances, would do;

and the fact that territory may so pass is proved by numerous instances (produced by the agents of the four Phulkian Chiefs) where territory, not derived from the common ancestor, but acquired since his death, has passed to a collateral heir."[1] This ruling did not affect the decision which had placed Sarup Singh in possession of all the territories held by the extinct branch of the family, excepting such as were grants from other powers.[2]

The widows are indignant at the claims of Sarup Singh being preferred to their own.

The mother and widows of the late Chief were naturally indignant that a man whom they considered an interloper, of far inferior rank to the reigning Jhind house, should succeed to the Chiefship, and urged their claims with great pertinacity, though entirely without success. Ranis Subha Kour and Sahib Kour, especially, in many petitions dwelt upon their grievances, and those of the other Ranis. They complained that they were treated with the greatest harshness and indignity; that the privacy of the female apartments was invaded; and the old and faithful servants of the family expelled and their possessions confiscated. They begged that a fresh inquiry might be made into their claims, when the intrigues which had been practised by the allied Rajas, and the injustice which had been done to helpless women, unable from their position to protect themselves, would be brought to light.[3]

The complaints of the Ranis had little foundation, their real object being the revival of their claims to the territory, which were inadmissible, and the Raja was only

[1] Despatch from the Court of Directors, No. 28, of 8th November 1837.

[2] Mr Clerk, Political Agent, to Agent Governor-General, 19th August 1838; Colonel Richmond, 15th February 1844.

[3] Two long petitions from Ranis Sahib Kour and Subha Kour of Jhind to Mr Clerk, Political Agent, 23d August 1837.

assured that the Governor-General would be glad to hear that these ladies had no ground for complaint.[1]

The territory which the Government gained by escheat.

Of the territory acquired by the English as an escheat from Jhind, the district of Ludhiana was the most important, yielding a revenue of about Rs. 85,000, the remaining acquisitions together yielding a like amount.

The installation of Raja Sarup Singh, A.D. 1837.

Raja Sarup Singh was formally installed in the presence of all the Phulkian Chiefs and the British Agent, in April 1837.[2] The long dispute regarding the succession had not been without its evil effects on the more restless and turbulent of the Jhind people. The Balawali ilaqua rose in rebellion early in 1836. The inhabitants of this place, situated near Batinda, about one hundred miles to the west of Ambala, had always been notorious for their wild and independent character; and it was they who, in 1815, when Prince Partab Singh had fled from Hansi, under the pretence of supporting his claims, rebelled against the Jhind Government, and were only reduced to obedience when Sir David Ochterlony had marched against them with a strong force. Under Jhind they had done exactly as they pleased, and had paid no revenue whatever; but after the death of Raja Sangat Singh, the administration of Balawali came into the hands of the British Government, and the people were called upon to pay revenue. They had preferred what they seemed to consider a prescriptive right to a light assessment; and, taking all the circumstances of the case into consideration, it was thought advisable to make only the most moderate demand from them. But this did not

The revolt of Balawali.

[1] Agent Governor-General Dehli to Secretary to Government, dated 16th February 1838, and Secretary Government to Agent Governor-General, 3d March 1838.

[2] Letter of Governor-General to Raja, dated 19th June 1837; and Lieutenant-Governor N.-W. P. to Raja, 31st July 1837.

satisfy them. They attacked Mr Edgeworth, when passing through their country, possibly at the instigation of the Akalis who resorted to Gurusar, a sacred place of pilgrimage of the Sikhs in their immediate neighbourhood, and then rose in revolt, apparently believing that their wild and barren country would secure them from any attack by British troops, whom the authorities would be unwilling to move into camp at the commencement of the hot season. The leader of the insurrection was Gulab Singh, Gil, a resident of Balawali, formerly a Risaldar in the Jhind army; and a large number of Jhind troopers joined the insurgents. These soldiers should long before have been paid up and dismissed, and this course was urged upon Mai Sahib Kour, in September 1835, when Regent; but she refused to take action in the matter, and the consequence was that the country was filled with discontented men, half starving, and with no means of subsistence save violence and robbery. The insurrection was encouraged by Mai Sul Rai, widow of Prince Partab Singh, whose brother Dal Singh was one of its leaders; and the inhabitants of the Bhai-Chakian villages also lent their assistance. Great efforts were made by the insurgents to bring over to their side the Maharajkian Sikhs, as turbulent and independent as those of Balawali, but they were too cautious to join in what they considered a hopeless undertaking. The insurrection was of short duration, for the rebels had no place of any strength in their possession. The fort of Balawali, which was of burnt brick laid in mud, had never been of much strength, and it had not been repaired since the refractory zamindars were expelled from it in 1815. On the night of the 17th of March, the rebels surprised it and the Thannah, but a strong body of troops was sent against them and

The leaders of the rebellion,

And its suppression.

completely routed them. Dal Singh, Lukha Singh, and Mai Sul Rai were taken prisoners, Gulab Singh was killed in action, and Desu Singh, another of the leaders, stabbed himself when about to be apprehended. A number of prisoners were taken and sent to Ambala for trial, and a detachment was stationed at Balawali and retained there until tranquillity was completely restored.[1]

The escheat of Kythal, and the action of the Raja of Jhind.

Raja Sarup Singh did not abandon hope of obtaining the whole of the possessions which had been held by his predecessors, and several times addressed the Government without success. The escheat of Kythal, in March 1843, furnished him with another argument; for although the lapse of this territory was made on the principle which had regulated the Jhind succession—viz., that a collateral descendant should inherit so much only of the territory as was possessed by the ancestor from whom he derived his claim—yet, on a former occasion, the Kakrala estate, which was a portion of Kythal, had been allowed to pass collaterally without regard to any such considerations; and, accordingly, both Raja Sarup Singh and Maharaja Karam Singh of Pattiala tried their best to obtain a recognition of the full right of succession of the second cousin of the late Bhai of Kythal, believing that if this were once allowed, the right of Sarup Singh to the whole of the Jhind territory would be likewise admitted.[2] In this expectation, however, they were disappointed. The Government had made in the Jhind succession case quite as many concessions as they considered just, and on the

[1] Assistant Political Agent to Mr Clerk, 19th March. Mr Clerk to Agent Governor-General Dehli, 20th March, 9th May, and 8th of July 1836. Agent Governor-General Dehli to Political Agent, 6th July 1837. Mr Clerk to Sir C. Metcalfe, 10th November 1835.

[2] Maharaja Karam Singh to Agent Governor-General, 29th September 1844. Raja Sarup Singh to Agent Governor-General, 5th October 1844.

same principle Kythal was resumed. The three Phulkian Rajas intrigued against this decision as long as was possible, and their sympathy and secret advice encouraged a rebellion at Kythal, which was only put down after some bloodshed. Yet, when the insurrection had fairly broken out, they gave every assistance in suppressing it, and their troops captured and dispersed several parties of the rebels.[1]

Jhind obtains a portion of the Kythal territory by exchange.

Of the resumed Kythal territory, a pargannah, Mahala Gabda, was given to the Raja of Jhind, in exchange for a portion of Sufidon, the former consisting of twenty-three villages, worth Rs. 30,042 a year, and the latter consisting of thirty-eight villages, worth Rs. 33,380. The difference was calculated on the eventual lapse of rent-free lands, the quality of soil, and the depth of water, in which particulars Mahala was more fortunate than Sufidon. The village of Sufidon itself was excluded from the transfer, as it was a place of pilgrimage, and a favourite hunting-seat of the Raja of Jhind, containing, moreover, the cenotaphs of the family.[2]

The case of the village of Bains.

One of the villages which had come into the possession of the British Government, with the Jhind territory, was Bains, which Raja Bhag Singh had given to Jamadar Khushhal Singh, one of the most powerful Chiefs of Lahore. The village had been allowed to remain with the Jamadar by Raja Fatah Singh, and was confirmed to him by Raja

[1] Mr Clerk to Government of India, 30th March. Mr Greathed, Secretary of Legation, to Mr Clerk, 27th March, and Raja Sarup Singh, 24th March. Mr Clerk to Government of India, 8th April. Mr Greathed to Mr Clerk, 29th March. Mr Clerk to Government, 25th April. Maharaja of Pattiala to Mr Clerk, 13th April 1843. Raja of Jhind to Governor-General, 5th October 1844.

[2] Major H. Lawrence, Assistant Envoy, to Mr Clerk, 11th May 1843, and 9th July 1843. Colonel Richmond to Government North-Western Provinces, 1st August 1843.

Sangat Singh. In July 1844 the Jamadar died, and the village was resumed. The grant was a special one to the Jamadar; the British Government were not bound to maintain it after his death; and Khushhal Singh had been so much disliked by Raja Hira Singh, the Prime Minister of Lahore, that the greater portion of his jagirs were resumed on his death. But, for all this, the resumption was looked upon by the Lahore Government as an unfriendly act. At this time the Sikhs were in a very excited and suspicious frame of mind, and were particularly jealous of any interference with their presumed possessions. The case of the village of Mourah, in Nabha territory, which had been resumed from Lahore, was of a similar nature; and, in both instances, the Lahore Government considered the action of the English to be inspired by hostile intentions, and to prove a desire to annex more of their territory when a convenient opportunity should offer itself.[1]

The irritable state of the Sikh nation.

The action of the Raja of Jhind during the war of 1845–46.

The attitude of the principal Cis-Satlej Chiefs, immediately previous to the war of 1845, has been described in the Pattiala history.[2] The Jhind Raja was at this time a partisan of Pattiala, and a bitter enemy of Raja Devindar Singh of Nabha, who treated him with studied contempt, affecting to consider him as of an inferior branch of the family, and refusing to allow any title of honour to be accorded him. The conduct of the Jhind Raja had strengthened this ill feeling, for he had gained the support of Devindar Singh to his claim to the Jhind territory by promising to cede to him the district of Sangrur, a promise which he refused to keep after his claims

[1] Agent Governor-General to Secretary to Government, 31st July 1844, and 4th August 1844.

[2] *Vide ante*, pp. 183–186.

had been acknowledged by the Government. It was thus only to be expected that, when war broke out, Pattiala and Jhind should be found on one side, and Nabha on the other.[1]

The feelings toward the English Government.

The Raja of Jhind was undoubtedly well disposed towards the English Government, from whom he had received the most generous treatment, and the recognition of a claim which could hardly be said to have any legal existence. But he was not altogether content. He had received so much that he thought himself entitled to receive all, and never ceased to hope that the course of events would make it possible for him to acquire the whole of the possessions held by former Chiefs. The general feeling of suspicion and dislike to the English, which had been so carefully encouraged by the Lahore Government, and the unfortunate termination of the first Kabul expedition, which had shaken the belief of the natives of India in the fortune of the English, had not been without their effect upon Sarup Singh; and, in 1845, his conduct gave very serious dissatisfaction to the Lieutenant-Governor of the North-Western Provinces when travelling through the Jhind territory, and he also insulted Mr Metcalfe of Dehli in such a manner as to call for a special communication on the subject from the Agent to the Governor-General.[2]

Services during the campaign of 1845-46.

Early in the month of November 1845, Sarup Singh was called upon to send 150 camels for the use of the Sirhind Division; but this, in spite of promises and repeated orders, he neglected to do, and the result was great inconvenience to the troops when called upon to

[1] Agent Governor-General to Secretary to Government, 26th April 1845, Major H. Lawrence to Government of India, 18th September 1846.

[2] Report of Mr R. Cust to Major Mackeson, 7th March 1846.

march. A fine of Rs. 10,000 was levied upon him by Major Broadfoot, which was realised in the following year. After this warning the conduct of the Raja was quite satisfactory. The exertions of his people in providing supplies and carriage were great; his contingent served with the British troops, and a detachment of it, which accompanied the Pattiala contingent to Ghumgrana, under Captain Hay, was highly praised by that officer for its steady conduct and discipline.[1] Still later, a detachment accompanied the expedition to Kashmir, where Imamuddin Khan, the Governor, was in revolt against Maharaja Gulab Singh.

For these services the Governor-General remitted the fine of Rs. 10,000, and sanctioned the grant of lands not exceeding in value Rs. 3000 a year, as a mark of the satisfaction of Government at his conduct; and double allowances were granted to the troops who had served with the Kashmir force.[2]

Sanad granted to the Raja after the war.

After the war, excise and transit duties were abolished in the Jhind territory, the British Government engaging never to demand from the Raja or his successors tribute or revenue, or commutation in lieu of troops, or otherwise; and the Raja, on his part, engaging to aid the Government with all his troops in the event of war, to maintain the military roads, and to suppress *sati*, slave-dealing, and infanticide in his territories. In consideration of the abolition of the transit duties, a further grant of

[1] Major Mackeson to Government, 27th July 1846. Murasilas from Agent Governor-General, dated 11th December 1845, 2d February, and 25th March 1846, complimenting the Raja on the services and discipline of his men.

[2] Government of India, 17th December 1846, to Agent Governor-General; and Agent Governor-General to Government, 11th December 1846. Commissioner Cis-Satlej States to Raja, dated 17th March 1849.

lands, worth Rs. 1000 a year, was given to the Raja from the recent Lahore conquests.[1]

As to the other Phulkian Chiefs, a Sanad was granted after the war to the Raja of Jhind,[2] confirming to him

[1] Letter from the Governor-General to Raja of Jhind, dated 13th February 1847, and from Agent Governor-General, 16th February, informing the Raja that the example he had set in abolishing duties was an excellent one, and should be notified in the Government Gazette.

[2] Sanad to the Raja of Jhind, dated 22d September 1847 :—

"The Right Honourable the Governor-General having resolved to bestow certain lands on the Raja of Jhind, as a mark of consideration for his attachment and services to the British during the late war with the Lahore State, and the Raja of Jhind having requested that he may at the same time receive a renewed assurance of protection and guarantee of his rights in his former possessions, the Governor-General is pleased to confer this assurance in the form of a Sanad or grant as follows, in order that the Maharaja and his successors after him, may, with perfect confidence, continue to exercise the same rights and authority in his possessions as heretofore.

"The Maharaja's ancient hereditary estates, according to annexed Schedule, shall continue for ever in the possession of himself and his successors, with all Government rights thereto belonging of police jurisdiction and collection of revenue as heretofore. The Maharaja's Chaharumians, feudatories, adherents, and dependants, will continue bound in their adherence and obligations to the Raja as heretofore. His Highness will exert himself to do justice, and to promote the welfare and happiness of his subjects, while they, on their part, considering the Raja as their true and rightful lord, must obey him and his successors accordingly, and pay the revenue punctually, and be always zealous to promote the cultivation of their lands, and to testify their loyalty and obedience. The Maharaja has relinquished for himself and his successors for ever all right to levy excise and transit duties, which have been abolished throughout the Jhind territory. His Highness also binds himself and his successors to the suppression of suttee, infanticide, and slave-dealing within his territories. If, unknown to the Maharaja's authorities, any person should be guilty of these acts, the Maharaja's authorities will, on conviction, punish them with such severity as to deter others. The British Government will never demand from the Maharaja and his successors, and their dependants above-named, anything in the way of tribute or revenue or commutation in lieu of troops or otherwise, for the reason that His Highness will ever continue as heretofore sincerely devoted to the service and interests of the British. The British authorities will not entertain complaints of the Maharaja's subjects or dependants, or interfere with the Maharaja's authority. Should an enemy approach from any quarter to this side of Beas or Satlej, for the purpose of conquering this country, the Raja will join the British army with his forces, and exert himself in expelling the enemy, and act under discipline and obedience, and, in time of war, place the resources of his country at the disposal of the

his ancestral possessions, and containing assurances of renewed protection, so long as he might continue to serve the Government loyally.

The second Sikh war of 1849.

When the second Sikh war broke out, Raja Sarup Singh was anxious to prove his devotion to the Government, and offered to lead his troops in person to Lahore, to join the English army. His services were declined, as they were not needed, but he was warmly thanked for the offer, and the loyalty that had prompted it.[1]

Jhind after the annexation of the Punjab.

After the annexation of the Punjab, the Raja of Jhind was one of the few Chiefs permitted to retain independent powers, with the exception of the right of capital punishment, which was conceded to him after the mutiny. He showed himself deserving of the privileges granted him, endeavouring to reform his administration after the English model, and to adopt the English system of revenue and police. Like most reforms, those instituted by the Raja were not altogether popular, especially among the wild tribes on the border. The peasants of

Revolt of border villages.

Sujuarah, a village on the Rohtak boundary, rose in revolt, killing the Tehsildar, who had been sent to measure the cultivated area of villages, with a view to making a settlement and to mark off the surplus waste lands into separate estates. They then called together the villagers of the neighbourhood belonging to the same

British Government. His Highness engages to have made and to keep in repair, through his own officers, the military roads through his territory for the passage of British troops from Ambala and other stations to Firozpur, of a width and elevation to be determined on by the engineer officer charged with the duty of laying down the roads. His Highness will also appoint encamping grounds for British troops at the different stages, which shall be marked off, so that there be no claims made hereafter on account of damaged crops."

[1] Commissioner Ambala to Raja, 5th June 1848. From Mr F. Currie, Resident Lahore, to Raja, dated 31st July and 24th November 1848. Commissioner Ambala to Raja, 1st September 1848.

clan, and threw up entrenchments, arming and provisioning themselves for a siege.

The Raja's energetic action.

The Raja marched against the insurgents with all his available force, but before attacking them, by the advice of the British Government, he issued a proclamation granting a free pardon to all concerned except the leaders of the revolt, if they would retire quietly to their homes. This proclamation, and the presence of a strong force, had the desired effect: the greater majority of the insurgents dispersed; their leaders, finding themselves deserted, fled; and the revolt was brought to an end without the loss of a single life.[1]

The mutiny of 1857.

When the mutiny broke out in May 1857, Raja Sarup Singh was not behind the Maharaja of Pattiala in active loyalty. When news reached him at Sangrur of the revolt at Dehli, he at once collected all his troops, and by forced marches reached Karnal on the 18th, where he undertook the defence of the city and cantonments.[2] His contingent did not exceed 800 men, but it was orderly and well disciplined, and its presence at Karnal gave confidence, and secured that station from plunder. From Karnal the Raja sent a detachment to secure the bridge of boats at Bhagpat, twenty miles north of Dehli, enabling the Meerat force to cross the Jumna and join Sir H. Barnard's column. The town of Panipat, which was in a most excited state, was restored to order, and the Jhind force marched in advance of the British column, the post of honour, recovering Sumbhalka and

[1] Commissioner Cis-Satlej States, Nos. 68 and 90, dated 28th March and 26th April 1854. Government Punjab to Government of India, Nos. 306 and 396, dated 22d April and 20th May. To Commissioner Cis-Satlej States, Nos. 346 and 442, dated 15th April and 13th May 1854.

[2] Commissioner Cis-Satlej States to Raja, 14th May; Mr Montgomery, Judicial Commissioner, dated 16th May. Chief Commissioner, 17th May. Commissioner Cis-Satlej States, dated 19th, 20th, 23d, and 26th May 1857.

Rai, securing the road, and collecting supplies for the army.

Raja Sarup Singh's services in the field.

On the 7th of June, Raja Sarup Singh joined the British camp at Alipur, and the following day the battle of Badli Serai was fought, in which the Jhind troops behaved well, and were complimented on the field by the Commander-in-Chief, who sent one of the captured guns to the Raja as a present. On the 19th of June the Jhind troops aided in repulsing the Nasirabad force which attacked the camp; and, on the 21st, were sent to Bhagpat to repair the bridge of boats, which had been destroyed. In three days the bridge was completed, but had to be again destroyed, as the mutineers attacked the Raja in overwhelming numbers, compelling him to retire. The Raja had now to return to his own territories, where the rebels of the Hansi, Hissar, and Rohtak districts had incited Jhind villages to revolt. The disturbance was soon quelled by the energy of Sarup Singh, who then employed himself in raising recruits and purchasing horses for the British force before Dehli; returning to the camp on the 9th of September. The Jhind force, under Commandant Khan Singh, took a prominent part in the assault of the city, scaling the walls side by side with English troops, and of their number several were killed and wounded.

The assault of Dehli.

Raja Sarup Singh was the only Chief who was present with the army before Dehli. In this he was more fortunate, though not more loyal or courageous, than the Maharaja of Pattiala and the Raja of Kapurthalla, both of whom desired to join the besieging force; but their presence was considered more useful elsewhere.

Rohtak made over to the Raja temporarily.

The administration of the district of Rohtak was made over to the Raja of Jhind during the most disturbed period, and the head men of villages and the zamindars were directed to pay their revenue to him, his receipt being sufficient acknowledgment of payment.[1]

After the fall of Dehli, Sarup Singh returned to Sufidon. He left twenty-five men for service at the Larsowli Tehsil, and the same number at Dehli; sent a detachment of 200 men with General Van Cortlandt to Hansi, and 110 men, under the command of Commandant Khan Singh, to Jhajjar, with Colonel R. Lawrence. Besides these, 250 Jhind troops remained stationed at Rohtak, and 50 at Gohana, about twenty miles to the north.[2]

The services subsequent to the fall of Dehli.

The services of Raja Sarup Singh were thus of the most valuable kind. The Commissary-General, Colonel Thomson, C.B.,[3] declared that but for the timely supplies furnished by him, the quantity of stores would have been, at first, insufficient for the troops. General Wilson, in his despatch of the 22d of September, announcing the fall of Dehli, brings "prominently to notice the admirable service performed by the Jhind Raja and his troops, who are said not only to have discharged harassing duties in the constant escort of convoys, but to have aided the General on more than one occasion in the field; and, finally, to have participated in the capture and assault of Dehli." The Governor-General, in his notification of the 5th November 1857, declared that the steady support of the Raja of Jhind called for the marked thanks of the Government.

The great value of these services.

But Raja Sarup Singh received rewards more substan-

[1] Proclamation of Commissioner Dehli, dated 26th July 1857. Letter to Raja of same date.

[2] Commissioner Cis-Satlej States to Government Punjab, dated 3d March 1858. Government Punjab to Government of India, No. 202, dated 13th April 1858. Chief Commissioner to Raja, 1st June 1857. From Colonel Dunsford, 29th July; from the Viceroy, dated 12th August; Commander-in-Chief, dated 27th September 1857; from the Viceroy, dated 2d June 1858.

[3] No. 51, dated 17th June, from Colonel Thomson, C.B.

His rewards.

tial than mere thanks. It was at first proposed to grant him an estate of about Rs. 50,000 a year near his own territory; but, for the same reason as influenced the grant to Pattiala, it was subsequently thought desirable to assign him a portion of the confiscated Jhajjar territory. This was, however, situated a long way from Jhind, and would have been difficult for the Raja, whose means were limited, to control; and, finally, the Dadri territory, 575 square miles in extent, which had been confiscated on account of the rebellion of its Nawab,[1] was conferred upon him. This territory, situated about twenty miles due south of Jhind, and between the estates of Jhajjar and Loharu, was worth about Rs. 1,03,000 per annum, though it was capable of great improvement, and at the present time brings in a much larger revenue. Thirteen villages in the Kularan sub-district, conveniently situated near Sangrur, and valued at Rs. 13,813 per annum, were also ceded to the Raja in perpetuity. These villages were, Bhaiapura, Alampur, Balamgarh, Kularan, Dodura, Rotli, Rangloi, Dharamgarh, Buzurg, Saipura, Mani, Kakralah, and Shahpur. As a memorial of his services before Dehli, the confiscated house of the rebel Shahzadah Mirza Abu Bakr, situated in that city, and valued at Rs. 6000, was bestowed on the Raja; whose salute was raised to eleven guns; the number of trays of presents presented to him in Viceregal Durbars was increased from eleven to fifteen, and the honorary title, "*Farzand dilband rasikh-ul-itikad Raja Sarup Singh Buhadar wali Jhind,*" was conferred upon him.[2]

The confiscated territory of Dadri given to him.

His salute and honorary title increased.

[1] Chief Commissioner to Government of India, No. 123—12 B., dated 9th April 1858.

[2] Commissioner Cis-Satlej States, No. 65, dated 3d March 1858, to Chief Commissioner. Statement of the Raja of Jhind, dated 15th January 1858. Commissioner Cis-Satlej States to Chief Commissioner, No. 89, dated 20th

Two villages were held by kinsmen of the Raja, Badrukhan and Bumhamwadi, an isolated plot of land near Sangrur, nominally in the Thanesar district, but really eighty miles distant from Thanesar. The Raja had a great desire to become possessed of these villages, which were large and valuable, being worth Rs. 5171 a year. This revenue was enjoyed by jagirdars, the Chiefs of Badrukhan, who were willing to come under Jhind jurisdiction, but there was some objection to the villages being transferred, the Raja having been already amply rewarded. The Badrukhan Sirdars were, however, allowed police jurisdiction in their village, subject to British control.[1]

The villages of Badrukhan and Bumhamwadi.

Two years later, Raja Sarup Singh proposed to purchase the interest of Government in these villages. This only consisted of the commutation-tax of Rs. 643, 14 a., which the Raja was willing to redeem at twenty or twenty-five years' purchase. The transfer, on payment of twenty years' purchase—viz., Rs. 12,877, 8 a.—was permitted by the Government as an exceptional case, and the Badrukhan Chiefs have since 1867 been feudatories of Jhind.[2]

The Raja allowed to purchase Government interest therein.

There were fourteen villages—Chang, Mithathal, Bamla, Naorangabad, Bhund, Rankouli, Aon, Bas, Ranela, Saifal, Khairari, Jawa, Bijna, and Changrour—belonging to the Dadri territory, but scattered in the Rohtak and Jhajjar

Scattered Dadri villages in British territory surrendered

March. Commissioner Dehli to Chief Commissioner, No. 84, dated 17th March. Chief Commissioner to Government of India, No. 32, dated 13th April. Government of India to Chief Commissioner, No. 1549 A., dated 2d June 1858. Government of India to Government Punjab, No. 5260, dated 18th December 1859.

[1] Commissioner Cis-Satlej States, Nos. 89 and 264, dated 20th March and 14th September 1858, to Chief Commissioner. Chief Commissioner to Commissioner Cis-Satlej States, dated 25th September 1858.

[2] Commissioner Cis-Satlej States to Punjab Government, No. 131, dated 23d May 1861. Punjab Government to Government of India, No. 311, dated 30th May. Government of India to Punjab Government, No. 3265, dated 22d June. Despatch of the Secretary of State, No. 122, dated 31st October 1861.

districts. The first nine of these had been administered by the District Officer of Rohtak, both as regarded the collection of revenue and criminal jurisdiction, for varying periods, one village having been so administered since 1858, and three since 1853. The criminal jurisdiction of the ninth village, Saifal, had, since 1845, been vested in the Deputy-Commissioner of Rohtak, though the Nawab of Dadri had collected the revenue, and the four last villages, both in fiscal and criminal administration, had been subordinate to the Nawab.

For the convenience of both States, and to preserve a satisfactory boundary, a transfer was proposed of these villages to the British Government, in exchange for others of equal value in the Budhwara and Kanoudh pargannahs of the Jhajjar district. The revenue of the Dadri villages amounted to Rs. 10,641, and the transferred villages made over to the Raja—viz., Churkli, Nanda, Tiwali, Siswala, Pachobah Kalan, Pachobah Khurd, and Todhi—were worth Rs. 10,850 a year. The Raja was perfectly satisfied with the transfer, which was approved by the Government of India, and carried into effect.[1]

Exchange of Government lands for outlying Jhind lands.

In 1861, several villages of the Jhind territory were exchanged for others of equal value belonging to the Government. There was a district belonging to the Raja, almost surrounded by lands of Hissar, consisting of twelve villages—Banbhori, Bhadakhera, Byanakhera,

[1] Secretary to Government Punjab, No. 1016, dated 28th December 1858, and No. 193, dated 17th February 1859, to Commissioner Cis-Satlej States. Commissioner Hissar to Government Punjab, Nos. 102, 103, and 132, dated 29th June and 13th August 1859.

Government Punjab to Commissioner Hissar, Nos. 895 and 975, dated 8th and 22d August.

Government Punjab to Government of India, No. 601, dated 30th August. Government of India to Government Punjab, No. 5728, dated 10th September 1859.

Panihari, Dhad, Sursanah, Sohnah, Jandlanah, Khurk Punia, Gyanpur, Kapron, and Khurkuri—which were inconvenient to manage, and the exchange of which for others nearer his principal town of Sangrur was much desired by Sarup Singh, while their transfer would render the boundary line more regular. The Government consented, in exchange for these, assessed at Rs. 8366, to give twelve villages of the Kularan pargannah, part of which had been already granted to Jhind after the mutiny. The villages assigned to Jhind from the autumn harvest of 1861 were Nagri, Chupki, Mundawala, Lotki, Dhunela, Osmanpur, Siparheri, Murori, Murdanheri, Murlanwala, and Nunhera, valued at Rs. 8345 a year.[1]

The Raja of Jhind joined with the Maharaja of Patiala and the Raja of Nabha in submitting to Government a paper of requests for regulating the succession to their Chiefships, and soliciting certain favours, a detailed account of which, with the orders of Government thereon, has already been given.[2] The Paper of Requests.

He also received a new Sanad[3] granting him full sovereignty in his new and acquired possessions, embodying the additional privileges which had been conceded to him, and the arrangements which had been made for the The Sanad of May 1860.

[1] Commissioner Cis-Satlej States, No. 57, dated 7th March 1861. Government Punjab to Government of India, No. 172, dated 14th March. Government of India to Government Punjab, No. 1454, dated 28th March 1861.

[2] *Vide ante*, pp. 223-231.

[3] Translation of the Sanad given to the Raja of Jhind by His Excellency the Viceroy and Governor-General, dated Simla, 5th May 1860 :—

Since the establishment of British authority in India, the present Raja of Jhind and his predecessors have always been steady in their allegiance. They have frequently received rewards for their fidelity in the accession of fresh honours, dignity, and territory. More recently the present ruler of Jhind has surpassed the former achievements of his race, by the constancy and courage he evinced during the mutiny of 1857-58. In memory of this unswerving and conspicuous loyalty, His Excellency the Viceroy and Governor-General of India has conferred additional honours and territory

administration of the State in the event of a minority or the death of the Chief without having appointed a successor; and to this Sanad a schedule of the territory belonging to him was annexed.

upon the Raja for himself and his heirs for ever, and has graciously acceded to the Raja's desire to receive a Sanad or Grant under the hand and seal of the Viceroy, guaranteeing to the Raja the free and unreserved possession of his ancient territories, as well as of those tracts bestowed on the Raja and his predecessors at various times by the British Government.

Clause I.—The Raja and his heirs for ever will exercise full sovereignty over his ancestral and acquired dominions according to the annexed list. All the rights, privileges, and prerogatives which the Raja enjoys in his hereditary territories, he will equally enjoy in his acquired territories. All feudatories and dependants of every degree will be bound to render obedience to him throughout his dominions.

Clause II.—Except as provided in Clause III., the British Government will never demand from the Raja, or any of his successors, or from any of his feudatories, relations, or dependants, any tribute on account of revenue, service, or any other plea.

Clause III.—The British Government cordially desires to see the noble house of Jhind perpetuated, and in this spirit confers upon the Raja and his heirs for ever, whenever male issue may fail, the right of adopting a successor from among the descendants of the Phulkian family. If, however, at any time any Raja of Jhind should die without male issue and without adopting a successor, it will still be open to the Maharaja of Pattiala and the Raja of Nabha, in concert with the Commissioner or Political Agent of the British Government, to select a successor from among the Phulkian family; but in that case a nazarana or fine, equal to one-third of the gross annual revenue of the Jhind State, shall be paid to the British Government.

Clause IV.—In 1847 the British Government empowered the Raja to inflict capital punishment after reference to the Commissioner. It now removes the restriction imposed by this reference, and invests the Raja with absolute power of life and death over his own subjects. With regard to British subjects committing crime, and apprehended in his territory, the Raja will be guided by the rules contained in the Despatch of the Honourable the Court of Directors to the Madras Government, No. 3, dated 1st June 1836. The Raja will exert himself to execute justice, and to promote the happiness and welfare of his people. He engages to prohibit suttee, slavery, and female infanticide throughout his territories, and to punish with the utmost rigour those who are found guilty of any of these crimes.

Clause V.—The Raja will never fail in his loyalty and devotion to the Sovereign of Great Britain.

Clause VI.—If any force hostile to the British Government should appear in the neighbourhood, the Raja will co-operate with the British Government and oppose the enemy. He will exert himself to the utmost of his resources in providing carriage and supplies for the British troops, according to the requisitions he may receive.

A special Sanad was moreover granted, confirming, in almost the same terms used in the Sanad granted to Nabha and Pattiala, the right of adoption in case of failure of male heirs.[1] The Sanad of adoption.

Clause VII.—The British Government will not receive any complaints from any of the subjects of the Raja, whether Maafeedars, Jagirdars, relatives, dependants, servants, or other classes.

Clause VIII.—The British Government will respect the household and family arrangements of the Raja, and abstain from any interference therein.

Clause IX.—The Raja, as heretofore, will furnish at current rates, through the agency of his own officers, the necessary materials required for the construction of railroads, railway stations, and imperial roads and bridges. He will also freely give the land required for the construction of railroads and imperial lines of road.

Clause X.—The Raja and his successors, &c., will always pursue the same course of fidelity and devotion to the British Government, and the Government will always be ready to uphold the honour and dignity of the Raja and his house.

SCHEDULE OF THE TERRITORIES BELONGING TO THE RAJA OF JHIND.

Ancestral Possessions.

1. Pargannah Jhind and the villages surnamed the Punjgraon Circle.
2. Pargannah Sufidon.
3. Pargannah Sujwanah.
4. Pargannah Baliwali.
5. Pargannah Sangrur, with the villages Mohlan and Ghabdan.
6. Pargannah Bazidpur, with Mouzah Laloda.
7. A share in the village of Bhai Rupa.

Acquired Possessions.

Mouzah Dolumwalla (now in pargannah Jhind).

Mouzah Borada Mouzah Busseinee Mouzah Khatla	Now in pargannah Sufidon. Granted by Sanad dated 22d September 1847, signed by Viscount Hardinge, Governor-General.
Pargannah Dadree 14 villages of pargannah Koolaram.	By letter from Secretary to Government of India, dated 2d June 1858, No. 1549 A.

Jagheer Feudatories.

Dyalpoora Sikhs.

[1] To Farzand dilband rasikh-ul-itakad Dowlut-i-Englishia Raja Sarup Singh Buhadar of Jhind, dated 5th March 1862:—

"Her Majesty being desirous that the Governments of the several Princes and Chiefs of India who now govern their own territories should be perpetuated, and that the representation and dignity of their Houses should be continued, I hereby, in fulfilment of this desire, repeat to you the assurance which I communicated to you in the Sanad under my signature, dated 5th May 1860, that, on failure of natural heirs, the perpetuation of your family by your adoption of an heir from the Phulkian House will be in accord-

Part of Jhajjar transferred to Jhind.

The circumstances under which a portion of the Jhajjar district was assigned to Raja Sarup Singh has been related.[1] Nineteen villages, adjoining his new estate of Dadri, were assigned to him on payment of a *nazarana* of Rs. 4,20,000, and for these a separate *Sanad* was granted.[2]

ance with the wishes of the paramount power, and will be gladly recognised and confirmed ; and that if at any time any Raja of Jhind should die without male issue, and without adopting a successor, it will still be open to the Maharaja of Pattiala and the Raja of Nabha, in concert with the Commissioner or Political Agent of the British Government, to select a successor from among the Phulkian family, but in that case a nazarana or fine, equal to one-third of the gross annual revenue of the Jhind State, shall be paid to the British Government.

" Be assured that nothing shall disturb the engagement thus made to you, so long as your House is loyal to the Crown and faithful to the conditions of the treaties, grants, or engagements which record its obligation to the British Government."

[1] *Vide ante*, pp. 218–221.

[2] Translation of Sanad or grant of portion of the pargannah of Budwanah, district Jhajjar, bestowed on the Raja of Jhind by His Excellency Earl Canning, G.C.B., Viceroy and Governor-General of India :—

Preamble.—Whereas the devotion and loyalty of the Raja of Jhind and of his ancestors have always been conspicuous since the establishment of British supremacy in India, His Excellency the Viceroy and Governor-General being desirous of marking his high appreciation of these qualities, has been pleased to bestow upon the Raja portions of pargannah Budwanah, of the district of Jhajjar, containing nineteen villages, according to vernacular list annexed, assessed at a yearly revenue of eighteen thousand five hundred and twenty rupees (Rs. 18,520), and to accept from the Raja a "nazarana" of three lakhs seventy thousand and four rupees (Rs. 3,70,004). It is accordingly ordained as follows :—

Article 1.—The territory above-mentioned is conferred upon the Raja of Jhind and his heirs for ever.

Article 2.—The Raja and his successors will exercise the same rights, privileges, and prerogatives in this newly-acquired territory as he at present enjoys in his ancestral possessions, according to the terms of the Sanad dated 5th May 1860, and signed by His Excellency Earl Canning, Viceroy and Governor-General of India.

Article 3.—The Raja and his successors will continue to maintain the same loyal relations with the British Government, and to fulfil the same obligations with regard to this newly-acquired territory, as were imposed on him by the terms of the Sanad, dated 5th May 1860, relating to the Raja's ancestral possessions.

Letter of the Viceroy to the Raja, dated 5th January 1861.

When the Dadri district was made over to the Raja of Jhind, the villages were overlooked, which were not at the time of its confiscation under the direct control of the Nawab. From his not being able to manage them, as well as from many of them having been mixed up with Rohtak villages, their administration, in police and revenue matters, had been conducted by the British authorities, while the revenue was paid to the Nawab. The Raja requested that these villages might be made over to him, or villages of equal value elsewhere. The Government held that although the Raja had obtained land of the full estimated value, yet that it was intended that the Dadri territory should be made over to him in its integrity, without any exact calculation of the value; and that the villages in question had consequently formed part of the grant. But considerations of convenience with reference to district administrative arrangements, made it advisable to give the Raja villages of equal value in Hissar, and this was accordingly arranged to his complete satisfaction.[1]

Exchange of Dadri villages for others in Hissar.

The only question of importance regarding the new territory made over to the Cis-Satlej Chiefs, had reference to their right to resume rent-free grants, or *maafis*, at their pleasure. The question was first raised by the attachment of the jagir of one Hakim Kasim Ali Khan of Jhajjar, situated in the pargannah of Dadri. The Raja of Jhind considered this man a rebel, but several high officials of Government thought this opinion mistaken, and that the Hakim was deserving of protection for services which he had rendered. He owned eleven

The right of the Chiefs to resume rent-free grants in their newly acquired territory.

1 Commissioner Cis-Satlej States, Nos. 166 and 50, dated 14th December 1858 and 10th February 1859. Government Punjab to Commissioner Cis-Satlej States, Nos. 1016, dated 28th December 1858, and 193, dated 17th February 1859.

villages, which were asserted to have been in possession of his family for five generations, long anterior to the advent of the Muhammadan Chiefs now dispossessed by the Sikhs.

The origin of the rights of these freeholders.

In favour of the rights of jagirdars and *maafi* holders, it could be urged that, in the original grants to the Muhammadan rulers of the Jhajjar territory, dated 4th May 1806, the rights of all rent-free tenures were especially exempted from the control of the Chiefs.[1] Unless therefore any special rights had been granted to the Sikh Rajas with the new territory, they could only be presumed to possess the same rights and powers as were enjoyed by their Muhammadan predecessors. There was a precedent for this view in the case of the Raja of Faridkot, to whom certain portions of the old Lahore territory in the Firozpur district were made over; the rights of all holders of rent-free lands being reserved, not only jagirdars holding villages, but the holders of mere patches of land. The rights of all were investigated, and all were taken under British protection.

The argument in favour of the full right of the Rajas to resume,

On the other side of the question was the independence which the Cis-Satlej Rajas enjoyed in hereditary territory, and the right they certainly possessed to resume rent-free grants. When the new territory was granted to them no hint was given that their powers would be more limited in the new territory than in the old, and the presumption was not that the Chiefs merely succeeded to the rights formerly possessed by the Muhammadan Nawabs, who were unable to resume, but that, as the

[1] "There is assigned to you the undermentioned lands as a *jaidad* for a Risaleh, and as a jagir for your support. The undermentioned lands, together with the land revenue and customs, *with an exception to such gardens and ayma jaghiri punarth and rent-free lands as have always been assigned.*"

grants were made without reservation or limitation of power, they had full right to resume at their pleasure. Besides arguments drawn from the manner of the grant, there was the extreme impolicy of interference. Were all the rent-free holdings to be taken under British protection—were appeals from every petty jagirdar to lie to British officers—such an amount of irritation would be felt, and justly felt, by the Rajas, as would go far to neutralise the feelings of gratitude and loyalty which the grants made to them had created. In addition to this, there was no reason for interference: native Governments were far more liberal in the matter of rent-free grants than the British Government had ever been, and there was no reason to believe that the grantees would suffer by being left under their control.

Which is admitted as valid by the Government.

This view of the case was taken by Government, and full powers were allowed to the Chiefs in their newly-acquired territory, and the British authorities were directed to exercise no interference, except in extreme cases, and then only by influence and advice.[1]

The Secretary of State maintains the rights of the freeholders to a perpetual tenure

The Home Government took a somewhat different view of the case from the Government of India, holding that as the original grants to the Muhammadan Nawabs had contained an express stipulation securing the holders of rent-free lands and villages from arbitrary interference, the forfeiture of the territory and its grants to Sikh Chiefs made no difference in the position of freeholders, who had the same claim to have their tenures secured from

[1] Commissioner Hissar to Government, No. 79, dated 14th May; Nos. 129 and 145, 8th and 31st August 1859.

Commissioner Cis-Satlej States to Government, No. 142, dated 23d May. Government Punjab to Government of India, No. 562, dated 18th August. Government of India to Government Punjab, No. 5590, dated 14th September 1859.

arbitrary resumption that was recognised when the jagirs were granted in 1803–1805. The transfer to the Sikh Chiefs made this difference only, that they were not required to proceed for the resumption of invalid tenures in the ordinary Courts, but should, before dispossessing any of the guaranteed freeholders, satisfy the Political Officer of the grounds of their actions.[1]

The Chiefs are dissatisfied with this decision,

The Phulkian Chiefs were much disconcerted by this decision, and the Maharaja of Pattiala and the Rajas of Jhind and Nabha jointly protested against the ruling, and requested its reconsideration.

Which they consider inconsistent with the terms of their Sanads.

The circumstances of the case had much changed since the order of the 14th September 1859 had been passed. The Chiefs had objected to the interference, limited to influence and advice, of the Political Officer; and Lord Canning, in the Sanads granted on the 5th of May 1860, had yielded the point, and had entered a clause to the effect that "the British Government will not receive any complaints from any of the subjects of the Maharaja (or Raja) whether maafidars, jagirdars, relatives, dependants, servants, or other classes." Moreover, in the Sanads granted on the 4th of January 1861, conferring the new Jhajjar territory, it was expressly provided that the Chiefs and their successors should exercise the same rights, privileges, and prerogatives in their newly-acquired possessions as they enjoyed in their ancestral possessions, according to the Sanad dated 5th May 1860.

The Chiefs were thus naturally disturbed when a new restriction was proposed to be inserted in their Sanads. They knew but of one authority, the Viceroy, who, in

[1] Despatch of the Secretary of State, No. 28, dated 15th November 1861. Government of India to Government Punjab, No. 24, dated 11th January 1862. Government Punjab to Commissioner Cis-Satlej States, No. 112 dated 15th February 1862.

the name of Her Majesty, had granted these documents, and they considered that if one condition could be set aside, all might at any time be cancelled. The Sanad of the 5th May 1860 was looked upon by the Chiefs as inviolable—their record of rights, duties, and privileges—and they were naturally anxious when any order of Government seemed to question its sacred character.

The good faith of the Government had been generally pledged to the freeholders.

There can be no doubt that in a certain way the good faith of the British Government had been pledged to the minor jagirdars. The guarantee given them in 1803 had been general, but it had been acted upon till 1858, and there was no reason that their position under the Sikh Rajas should be different than under the Muhammadan Nawabs, except that in the one case it had been guaranteed by express stipulation, and in the other that no stipulation had been recorded. In any case, there was good reason to protect the freeholders in 1803 from the Muhammadan Chiefs of Jhajjar and Dadri, mere adventurers, who came over to Lord Lake during the Mahratta war, and were rewarded for their services with grants of land. There was little or no reason to protect them in 1860 from the Cis-Satlej Rajas, Princes of position and respectability, whose system of administration had been brought into close conformity with that of the British Government, and to whom the protectorate over the freeholders might reasonably be ceded.[1]

But the Sanads having been granted without reservation, the view of the Home Government was not pressed.

The Secretary of State, after a reconsideration of the case, and acknowledging the great importance of maintaining the validity and integrity of Viceregal Sanads,

[1] Letter from Maharaja of Pattiala and Rajas of Jhiud and Nabha, dated 5th June 1862. Commissioner Cis-Satlej States, Nos. 178 and 180, dated 9th and 10th June 1862. Government Punjab to Government of India, No. 430, dated 31st July. Government of India, Nos. 910, dated 30th September 1863, and 174, dated 13th April 1863.

virtually cancelled the order of the 15th November 1861, and the terms of the Sanads of 1860 were upheld in their integrity, though it was considered matter for regret that in the grants to the several Rajas provision had not been made for the maintenance of existing rights in the land.[1]

The precedence of Jhind and Nabha.

When Lord Canning visited the Punjab in 1860, the question of the order of precedence of Jhind and Nabha in Viceregal Durbars, which had long been a subject of dispute, required decision. At the Durbar held by Lord Dalhousie at Pinjor, in 1851, the order of the Chiefs was determined by Mr Edmonstone, the then Commissioner of the Cis-Satlej States: 1. Pattiala, 2. Nabha, 3. Jhind; and this decision was a source of great annoyance to the Raja of the last-named State, and was hardly supported by former precedent.[2]

[1] Despatch of Secretary of State, No. 9, dated 9th February 1863.

Kasim Ali Khan obtained no redress. He had indeed suffered no injury. He had made extravagant claims on the peasants of his jagir, who had bitterly complained, and requested the Raja to fix cash payments, which he had done in a just and satisfactory manner. As to the loyalty of the Hakim, of which he loudly boasted, he was known to have been one of the principal advisers of the rebel Nawab of Jhajjar, and remained with him to the last, till after the fall of Dehli, when the Chief was executed for his treason. Government Punjab to Commissioner Cis-Satlej States, dated 25th February 1861. Government Punjab, No. 539, dated 27th September. Government of India, No. 589, dated 7th October 1864.

[2] The earliest record of Viceregal Durbars is of 1828. In that year the Cis-Satlej Chiefs had an interview with the Governor-General at Manimajra. Pattiala was received first: then the three next Chiefs were received together, named in the following order—

1. Bhai Udey Singh of Kythal;
2. Raja Sangat Singh of Jhind;
3. Raja Jaswant Singh of Nabha.

In 1839, the Chiefs were received at different places by the Governor-General: the Raja of Jhind first, at Dehli; the Maharaja of Pattiala at Burnala; and the Raja of Nabha at Dhanowla, in their respective territories. In 1843, at Sunam, in Pattiala territory, the Maharaja was first received, then the Raja of Jhind, and thirdly Nabha, who was late for the interview.

In 1846, after the battle of Subraon, only the Pattiala and Jhind Chiefs were

With reference to the position of the Chiefs, decision was by no means easy. Both were descended from the same ancestor, were addressed by the same formula, entitled to the same khillat and the same salute, and presented *nazrs* of equal value. The relative claims of the tw Chiefs.

Nabha was the representative of the elder branch, and the office of *Chaudhri* had been hereditary in his branch of the family.

In 1860, Jhind possessed an income of Rs. 3,25,000, and Nabha, Rs. 3,75,000; and, previous to the first Sikh war, the latter had probably a fair claim to take precedence. But in 1845-46, the Raja of Jhind furnished supplies and showed loyalty to Government, and was rewarded with a grant of villages worth Rs. 4000 or Rs. 5000 a year. The Raja of Nabha behaved badly, was deposed, and one-fourth of his territory was confiscated.

In 1857, both Chiefs did equally well, but the Raja of Jhind had greater opportunities of distinction, and served in person at the siege of Dehli. There had, besides, been no break in his loyalty. He was the first of the Cis-Satlej Chiefs to join Lord Lake in 1804, some time before the Nabha Chief made any advances towards the English, and he had been ever since a faithful ally. The Government justly took these good services into consideration, and assigned to the Raja of Jhind precedence in the Durbar of 1860. It was, nevertheless, distinctly stated, that the order was only given as it was necessary for one Chief or the other to take precedence. The two Rajas were The decision in favour of Jhind.

received; the Raja of Nabha being at the time under the displeasure of Government. Lastly came the Durbar at Pinjor in 1851, when Jhind was received after Nabha, though no reasons were given for the order laid down. The precedents appear thus to be of doubtful value, and hardly to support the claim of either Chief so indisputably as to render a decision founded upon them easy.

considered as precisely equal in dignity, and were regarded by Government with equal favour.[1]

The Raja of Nabha remonstrates.

This decision gave considerable dissatisfaction to the Raja of Nabha, and he remonstrated against it. But the Government saw no reason to alter the conclusions at which they had arrived. The Raja then desired to submit a memorial to the Secretary of State, praying for a reconsideration of the case; but, while arrangements were being made with this object, the Raja died, and though his successor desired to continue the agitation, nothing further was done.[2]

[1] Commissioner Cis-Satlej States to Government, No. 2, dated 6th January 1860. Government Punjab to Government of India, No. 29, dated 10th January. Supreme Government to Government Punjab, No. 114, dated 16th January.

[2] Commissioner Cis-Satlej States No. 102, dated 23d April 1862. Government of India to Government Punjab, Nos. 38, 440, and 512, dated 30th January, 10th and 27th May 1862. Government of India, No. 631, dated 21st September 1863 Commissioner Cis-Satlej States to Government, Nos. 239, dated 6th October 1863, and 409, dated 30th November 1865. Government to Commissioner Cis-Satlej States, No. 1100, dated 15th December 1865.

The question of precedence is one which is felt by native gentlemen to be of the highest importance. But several questions are still in doubt as to the relative positions of the Chiefs, principally arising from the fact that they have never all met in one Durbar, while contradictory rulings have been occasionally given. It may be interesting to give what is believed to be a correct list of the order of the Chiefs of the Punjab, showing the population of their territory, their revenue, and the salute to which they are entitled :—

	Names.		*Revenue.*	*Population.*	*Salute.*
1.	Maharaja of Kashmir,	...	64,00,000	1,500,000	19 guns
2.	Ditto Pattiala,	...	40,00,000	1,700,000	17 "
3.	Nawab of Bahawalpur,	...	14,43,174	364,582	17 "
4.	Raja of Jhind, ...	...	7,00,000	311,000	11 "
5.	Ditto Nabha, ...	...	7,00,000	276,000	11 "
6.	Ditto Kapurthalla,	...	5,77,000	212,721	11 "
7.	Ditto Mandi, ...	...	3,00,000	139,259	11 "
8.	Ditto Sirmur (Nahan),	...	1,00,000	75,595	11 "
9.	Ditto Bilaspur (Kahlur),	...	70,000	66,848	11 "
10.	Ditto Bussahir,...	...	70,000	45,025	
11.	Ditto Hindur (Nalagarh),	...	60,000	49,678	
12.	Ditto Keonthal, ...	...	30,000	66,848	

On the 26th January 1864, Raja Sarup Singh died of severe dysentery, from which he had been suffering for several months. He was at the time residing at his country-seat of Bazidpur, near Pattiala, and had been attended occasionally by an English doctor. But the Raja had unfortunately a superstitious belief in the efficacy of the prescriptions of any wandering mendicant, one of whom is said to have administered to him a decoction of copper coin, which nearly caused his death at the time, and in all probability shortened his life. The death of Raja Sarup Singh, A.D. 1864.

Sarup Singh was in his fifty-first year when he died ; His character.

	Names.	*Revenue.*	*Population.*	*Salute.*
13.	Nawab of Malerkotla, ...	2,00,000	46,200	9 guns.
14.	Raja of Faridkot, ...	75,000	51,000	11 „
15.	Ditto Chamba, ...	1,64,000	120,000	11 „
16.	Ditto Suket, ...	80,000	44,552	
17.	Sirdar of Kalsia, ...	1,30,000	62,000	
18.	Nawab of Patodi, ...	92,000	6,600	
19.	Ditto Luharu, ...	60,000	18,000	
20.	Ditto Dujana, ...	10,000	6,390	
21.	Rana of Bhagal, ...	35,000	22,350	
22.	Ditto Jubal, ...	18,000	17,262	
23.	Ditto Kumharsen,... ...	7,000	7,829	
24.	Ditto Bhajji, ...	15,000	9,001	
25.	Ditto Mailog, ...	8,000	7,358	
26.	Ditto Balsan, ...	6,000	4,892	
27.	Ditto Dhami, ...	4,000	2,853	
28.	Ditto Kuthar, ...	5,000	3,990	
29.	Rai of Kunihar, ...	3,000	1,906	
30.	Rana of Mangal, ...	1,000	917	
31.	Thakar of Bija, ...	2,000	981	
32.	Rana of Bhagat, ...	2,000		
33.	Ditto Darkuti, ...	500	612	
34.	Thakar of Taroch, ...	2,500	3,082	

This list cannot be considered conclusive as regards the relative position of the group 8–20, and group 21–34. The latter are the minor Hill Chiefs of Simla, and have never met the former in Durbar. Should they meet, it is not improbable that Bhagal and Jubal might receive a step in rank.

The position of Pattiala and Bahawalpur is that observed at the visit of the Duke of Edinburgh in 1870, the only time that these Chiefs have met on any occasion of State ceremony. But the order then fixed was not intended to be necessarily final. The Nawab of Bahawalpur was a child of ten years of age, and the question of his relative precedence will be con-

and it was both strange and unfortunate that the three great Chiefships of Pattiala, Nabha, and Jhind, should have become vacant almost simultaneously, and the three men who had done such signal service to the British Government, and whose prolonged life would have been of so much benefit to the Punjab, should pass away together. But, of these three Chiefs, the Raja of Jhind was perhaps the most distinguished. In person and presence he was eminently princely, and the stalwart Sikh race could hardly show a taller or stronger man. Clad in armour, as he loved to be, at the head of his troops, there was perhaps no other Prince in India who bore himself so gallantly and looked so true a soldier.

sidered later. On the one hand, his revenue, and the population of his State, is much below that of Pattiala; on the other, his territory is four times as extensive, and his independence has been more complete.

The next State about which any doubt exists is Mandi. A Durbar for certain Hill Chiefs was held at Simla on the 4th May 1847, at which they were introduced in the following order: 1. Nahan, 2. Hindur, 3. Bussahir, 4. Bilaspur, 5. Mandi, 6. Suket.

The order was subsequently altered at Lord Elgin's Durbar, dated 30th May 1863, when the four principal Hill Chiefs were introduced as follows: 1. Nahan, 2. Bilaspur, 3. Bussahir, 4. Hindur. The Raja of Mandi was not present at this Durbar, but his position would probably have been reconsidered. At the time of the first Durbar, Mandi had only just come under British control, being one of the Lahore feudatories taken over with the Jalandhar Doab in 1846, the Mandi Sanad being dated the 24th October of that year. The revenue and population of the State was then imperfectly known, and the order of the Durbar of 1847 appears not to have been intended as final, from the changes subsequently made. By population, revenue, and salute, Mandi would seem entitled to the seventh place, but these considerations alone do not determine precedence, and the position of Mandi in the list must be held as doubtful, should he ever meet the Simla Hill Chiefs in Durbar.

The position of the Simla Hill States given in the foregoing list, is that observed at the Durbar of Lord Canning in May 1860, with the exception of Bhagat, the Rana of which estate does not appear ever to have attended any Durbar. Indeed, in 1851, at the time of Lord Dalhousie's Durbar, and at Lord Canning's in 1860, there was no Chief, the territory having escheated to Government in 1849, and only being restored in 1861. At the date of Lord Elgin's Durbar in 1863, the Rana was only four years old, which accounts for his non-attendance.

In character he was honest and just, and though his pride and restlessness led him to quarrel with his neighbours, yet the British Government has never had an ally more true and loyal in heart than Sarup Singh, who served it from affection and not from fear. He was naturally disappointed at the decision of Government, which allowed him to inherit only a portion of the Jhind territories, yet he never permitted this decision to embitter his feelings or to influence his loyalty.[1]

His nomination to the Star of India.

Raja Sarup Singh had been nominated a Knight Grand Commander of the Star of India in September 1863, but he was too ill to visit Ambala to be invested, and died before the honour to which he had been designated could be bestowed.[2]

Raja Ragbhir Singh, his successor.

Ragbhir Singh, the son and heir of Raja Sarup Singh, was in every way worthy of his father. He was, at this time, about thirty years of age, and had been thoroughly trained in judicial and administrative matters, in which the late Raja was an excellent teacher; for he had kept his territory in excellent order, and had been eminently just in his dealings with his subjects.

The installation.

The installation of the new Chief took place on the 31st of March 1864, in presence of Sir Herbert Edwardes, the Agent of the Lieutenant-Governor, the Maharaja of Pattiala, the Raja of Nabha, the Nawab of Malerkotla, and many other Chiefs.[3]

[1] Commissioner Cis-Satlej States to Government, No. 20, dated 27th January 1864. Government Punjab to Government of India, No. 45, dated 30th January. Government of India to Government Punjab, No. 177, dated 20th February. Despatch of Secretary of State, No. 38, dated 16th July 1864.

[2] Letter of Sir Herbert Edwardes, Commissioner Cis-Satlej States, to Raja, dated 26th September 1863.

[3] Commissioner Cis-Satlej States to Government, Nos. 54 and 84, dated 4th and 31st March 1864.

The revolt of Dadri.

The new Raja had scarcely taken his seat on the *gaddi* than a rebellion broke out in the newly-acquired territory of Dadri, to test his energy and determination.[1]

The administration of the late Nawab of Dadri.

The Nawab of Dadri had been, as a ruler, incompetent and entirely in the hands of his servants. He was accustomed to farm the revenue collections to the headmen of villages, sometimes for Rs. 80,000, sometimes for a lakh of rupees or a little more, while they doubled the amount by extortion and oppression. When the Raja of Jhind took possession, a complete change was wrought in the system, a regular settlement was made after the English method, and the assessment was raised to rather above two lakhs of rupees. Raja Sarup Singh was notoriously fond of money, and the new assessment was not a light one, but it was not oppressive. The British Government has adopted the policy of light assessment—a wise policy if not carried to a point where the revenue is sacrificed to sentimentality—but it cannot be expected that native States will follow the example thus set. There is not a single State in India where the ruler does not take a far larger share of the produce of the land than the British Government, and it is natural that the border villages of native States should make unfavourable comparisons between their own condition and the prosperity enjoyed under British rule. But Sarup Singh, although avaricious, was a wise ruler and popular, except in the neighbourhood of the town of Jhind, where he was much disliked. He esteemed the people of Jhind the worst of his subjects, and lived away from them as much as he could, and often said that, in 1857, they were quite

That of the Raja of Jhind.

1 Commissioner Cis-Satlej States to Government, Nos. 111-868, dated 6th May. Commissioner Hissar to Government, No. 31, dated 2d May. Inspector-General of Police to Government, dated 5th May.

ready to rise against him if they had the opportunity. The assessment of Dadri, though far higher than would have been fixed by British officers, was not oppressive, nor was it as much as the sum really taken from the people under the Nawabs, though it was nominally more heavy.

The real exciters of discontent in Dadri were the head-men of villages, who found all their gains at an end, and themselves reduced to the position of simple lumberdars. Besides these, Hakim Kasim Ali Khan, who has before been mentioned as a malcontent on account of the Raja having made a cash assessment of his jagir, instigated the revolt; the Loharu State was favourable, and help was promised from the Rajput border. **The instigators of the rebellion.**

During the lifetime of Raja Sarup Singh the discontented villages did not dare to stir, but, on his death, above fifty villages broke into open revolt, the police station of Badrah was captured, and the Thanadar placed in confinement, while rude entrenchments were thrown up round some of the villages; arms and ammunition were received from the neighbouring territory of Sheikhawatti, Loharu, and Khetri, and the famous Sheikhawatti robbers were summoned to help on promise of plunder and pay.

The Dadri people had made a great mistake when they fancied that the new Raja was less energetic than his father. Immediately on hearing of the rebellion, he left Jhind with two regiments of infantry, 1500 strong, 350 horse, and 4 guns, and marched to Dadri, which he reached on the 8th of May. He did not ask Pattiala or Nabha for the assistance which they were quite willing to give; and politely declined the presence of a British officer in his camp, as he imagined that it might seem **The energy of the new Raja** that he was unable to meet and overcome the first difficulty which he had experienced after ascending the throne.

He attacks the rebels and destroys their villages,

On the 14th of May the Raja, at daybreak, attacked the village of Charki, about four miles south-west of Dadri, where some 1500 or 2000 of the rebellious Jats had collected and entrenched themselves. They had been repeatedly warned, and several days had been allowed them to come in and make their submission, but they declared their determination to resist the Raja's authority to the last. But when the attack really took place, and the guns opened on the village, the insurgents broke at once, and, in their flight, a good many were overtaken and cut up. The village was then burnt, and the Raja, the same day, marched against another, Mankinas, six miles distant, which was captured and destroyed. The village of Jhanju was the last place at which the rebels made a stand, but it was taken by storm on the 16th of May, with a few casualties on both sides. It shared the fate of the two other villages, and the insurgents, finding their cause hopeless, fled to Rajputana territory, and the rebellion was over. The Raja was as merciful after his success as he had been energetic in action. He only punished the ringleaders of the revolt, permitting the zamindars to return to Dadri territory and rebuild their ruined villages; and order has ever since been maintained in this part of the Jhind dominions.[1]

And restores order.

The family of Raja Ragbhir Singh.

Raja Ragbhir Singh married, as his first wife, the

[1] Agent Lieutenant-Governor Cis-Satlej States, Nos. 113, 115, 121, 126, 127, 129, and 134, dated 9th, 11th, 13th, 18th, 19th, 20th, and 23d of May 1864.

Government Punjab to Agent Cis-Satlej States, No. 360, dated 12th May, and No. 383, dated 23d May. Commissioner Hissar to Commissioner Cis-Satlej States, demi-officials of 16th, 17th, and 19th May 1864.

daughter of Jowahir Singh, Chaudhri of Dadri. She bore him one son and a daughter. The former, Balbir Singh, is now fourteen years of age, and the girl was married to Sirdar Bishan Singh Kalsia in April 1865, when wedding gifts to the value of Rs. 3000 were presented on the part of the British Government.[1]

The Raja married a second time in the family of Dhyan Singh, Gil, of Rajamajra, but there has been no issue of this marriage.

The principal residence of Raja Ragbhir Singh is at Sangrur, but he does not neglect the administration of the distant parts of his estate. He is a man of excellent judgment and great honesty, and during the late minorities in Pattiala and Nabha, his advice has always been good, even if his young relatives have not always cared to follow it. The Raja is a keen sportsman and a brave soldier, and his little army of 1500 men is in a state of great efficiency. **His character.**

The Jhind territory is 1236 square miles in extent, with a population of about 350,000. The revenue has rapidly increased of late years, and is now between six and seven lakhs of rupees a year. **The revenue, area, and population of the Jhind State.**

[1] *Vide ante*, pp. 238, 239.

The "neota" or marriage present is quite optional; there are very few precedents in favour of its being made, and it is only given as a token of the special favour of Government.

Agent Lieutenant-Governor, No. 119, dated 14th April 1865, to Government Punjab. Government Punjab to Agent, No. 425, dated 2d May 1865.

THE HISTORY

OF THE

NABHA STATE.

The Nabha family the eldest branch of the Phulkians.

THE Nabha Chiefs claim precedence over the other Phulkian houses on account of their descent from the eldest branch of the family. The histories of Pattiala and Jhind have contained an account of the common ancestor Phul, and of his two sons, Gurditta and Sukhchen, from the elder of whom the Nabha house has sprung, and from the younger the house of Jhind.

The genealogy.

The Nabha genealogy is as follows :—

PHUL.

- Tilokha, *d.* 1687.
  - Gurditta, *d.* 1754.
    - Suratya, *d.* 1752.
      - Kapur Singh.
      - Hamir Singh, *d.* 1783.
        - Raja Jaswant Singh, *d.* 1840.
          - Ranjit Singh, *d.* 1832
          - Raja Devindar Singh, *d.* 1865.
            - Raja Bharpur Singh, *d.* 1863.
            - Raja Bhagwan Singh, *b.* 1842.
        - Bibi Subha Kour *m* Sirdar Sahib Singh Bhangi.
        - Bibi Sada Kour, *m.* Sirdar Jai Singh.
  - Sukhchen, from whom the Jhind family has descended.
- Rama.
- Rughu.
- Chanu.
- Jhandu
- Takht Mal

On the death of Tilokha in 1687, his estate was divided between his sons. Gurditta married the daughter of Sirdar Sardul Singh Man, of Mauran, who bore him one son, Suratya. He founded the village of Dhanaula or Dhanala, on that portion of the estate of his father that fell to his share, and, subsequently, the town of Sangrur, which remained the headquarters of the Nabha State, till seized by treachery by the Raja of Jhind, and he also took from his neighbours a considerable portion of the surrounding country. He was always on bad terms with his younger brother, Sukhchen, and on more than one occasion their disputes ended in bloodshed. **The division of the estate of Chaudhri Tilokha.**

He died in 1754, and was succeeded by his grandson, Hamir Singh, his only son, Suratya, having died two years earlier, leaving two sons, Hamir Singh and Kapur Singh. Kapur Singh married Raj Kour, the daughter of Sujan Singh Mansahia, but died without issue, and his brother, in accordance with the Sikh custom of *Karewa or chaddardalna*, married the widow, and succeeded to his brother's estate of Kapurgarh and Sangrur, which he had increased by the addition of the villages of Pakho and Badyala. This lady was the only one of Hamir Singh's wives who bore him a son, Jaswant Singh, born in the year 1775. The Chief married, besides, a daughter of Natha Singh, Magharia; Desu, the daughter of Sirdar Makhan Singh of Rori, who gave birth to two daughters, Subha Kour and Sada Kour, the former of whom was married to Sirdar Sahib Singh,[1] the powerful Bhangi Chief, and the latter to Sirdar Jai Singh of Batala. His fourth wife, Raj Kour, the daughter of Sirdar Dhan Singh **The death of Gurditta, and succession of Hamir Singh.**

[1] Translation of replies of the Nabha Ahlkars in the Mowran case, 18th May 1844, and the Bhangi History. It is curious that both the Nabha and Bhadour family histories make Subha Kour the wife of Sirdar Gujar Singh Bhangi, which is quite erroneous.

of Nirhana, had no children. Hamir Singh was a brave and energetic Chief, and added very largely to his possessions. He founded the town of Nabha in the year 1755; four years later he obtained possession of Bhadson, and in 1763, having joined Raja Ala Singh of Pattiala and the other Sikh Chiefs in the great battle of Sirhind, when Zin Khan, the Muhammadan Governor, was slain, he obtained Imloh or Amloh as his share of the spoil. He conquered Rori from Rahimdad Khan in 1776. Hamir Singh was the first Chief of Nabha who established a mint,[1] which may be accepted as a sign of his complete independence. Many of the successes of Nabha at this time were due to the ability of a Muhammadan Diwan of the Raja's, popularly known as "Kubba," or the hump-backed.

The town of Nabha founded, A.D. 1755.

The conquest of Sangrur by the Raja of Jhind.

Hamir Singh was not invariably fortunate, and in Raja Gajpat Singh of Jhind he found more than his match. In 1774, the latter Chief invaded Nabha on a frivolous pretext, took Hamir Singh prisoner by treachery, and seized the strong town of Sangrur, which has never been restored.[2]

The death of Hamir Singh, A.D. 1783, and the Regency of Mai Desu.

When Hamir Singh died in 1783, his son, Jaswant Singh, was only eight years of age, and it was necessary to appoint a Regent to carry on the administration. Rani Desu, one of the late Chief's widows, was selected on account of her capacity for business, in preference to the mother of Jaswant Singh. Desu had held her own bravely against Jhind during the imprisonment of her husband, recovering most of the territory which had been seized by Gajpat Singh, with the aid of troops lent by her son-in-law, Sirdar Sahib Singh Bhangi of Gujrat.

With these foreign troops she maintained herself as Regent, ruling in the name of her son till 1790, when

[1] *Vide ante*, pp. 288, 289. [2] *Vide ante*, pp. 286-290.

she died suddenly: her enemy and rival Raja Gajpat Singh at Jhind having died in the previous year. The death of Mai Desu, A.D. 1790.

After this, the relations between Nabha and Jhind became more friendly, and a common danger for the time united them in an attempt to destroy the power of George Thomas, the master of Hansi, whose wars and conquests, so far as they concerned the Cis-Satlej States, have been already related.[1] The expedition against George Thomas.

In the arrangements made at Dehli with General Perron, the Commander-in-Chief of the Northern Mahratta army, for the expulsion of Thomas from Hansi, it does not appear that Nabha was concerned.[2] The agents of the Raja of Pattiala, Raja Bhag Singh of Jhind, and Bhai Lal Singh of Kythal, were the contracting parties, but Nabha was included in the conditions finally settled, as that State would benefit as much as any other from the defeat of the common enemy. The revenue and tribute promised to be paid to the Mahrattas by the Sikhs, who were strangely willing to surrender their independence, is given in the following list, which shows fairly the relative power and resources of the several Cis-Satlej States at the close of the last century. The price of Mahratta assistance.

	Revenue. Rs.	Tribute. Rs.
Raja Sahib Singh of Pattiala, .	1,14,750	38,250
Raja Jaswant Singh of Nabha, .	28,500	9,500
Raja Bhag Singh of Jhind, . .	21,750	7,250
The Chiefs of Maler Kotla, . .	15,000	5,000
The Chiefs of Rai Kot, . .	60,000	20,000
The Chiefs of Raipur and Gujarwal,	15,000	5,000
Bhai Lal Singh of Kythal, . .	45,000	15,000
Total, ...	3,00,000	1,00,000

[1] *Vide ante*, p. 75.

[2] *Vide ante*, p. 82.

The Raja makes friends with the English.

Raja Jaswant Singh of Nabha was not so ready as the Chiefs of Jhind and Kythal to make friends with the English, but he sent his agents to be present at the interview held at Nanak Toda between General Lake and the Cis-Satlej Chiefs, and was thanked by that officer for the friendly sentiments which his agents were directed to express towards the British Government.[1] The following year, when Holkar, the Mahratta Prince, was advancing northwards to Lahore and halted at Nabha, the Raja refused to assist him in any way, pleading his engagements with the English. Lord Lake assured the Raja that so long as his disposition towards the British Government remained unchanged, his possessions would never be curtailed, nor any demand made upon him for tribute.

The Nabha Chief and Maharaja Ranjit Singh, A.D. 1806.

The history of the first connection of Maharaja Ranjit Singh with the Cis-Satlej States, and his conquests and intrigues, have been related with so much detail in the Pattiala narrative, that it is unnecessary in this place to do more than briefly allude to them. Rani Aus Kour of Pattiala, wife of the imbecile Sahib Singh, had for some time been engaged in hostilities with the Rajas of Nabha and Jhind, and, with the assistance of the Thanesar and Kythal Chiefs, was getting the better in the contest, when the Jhind Chief summoned his kinsman, the Maharaja of Lahore, to his aid.[2] Ranjit Singh arrived speedily with a large force, and, although he did little to heal the dispute which existed between Pattiala and the neighbouring States, he rewarded his friends and adherents by grants from the country which he conquered, Raja Jas-

[1] Letter of Lord Lake to Raja Jaswant Singh, dated 26th May 1804.

[2] Circular of Resident Dehli to all Residents, Magistrates, &c., dated 1st November 1806.

want Singh receiving as his share portions of Kot, Basia, Talwandi, and Jagraon, thirty-one villages, worth Rs. 26,690, and seven villages from the Ghumgrana estate, worth Rs. 3350.[1]

The Maharaja's campaign of 1807, 1808.

During the Cis-Satlej expeditions of Ranjit Singh in 1807–8, the Nabha Chief remained his firm ally, hoping to profit by the weakness and dissensions in Pattiala. In 1807, he received a grant of four villages of the Ghumgrana estate, taken by the Maharaja from Gujar Singh, and, the next year, the district of Kannah, consisting of eighteen villages, taken from Rani Raipuri and Ran Singh. But at length he, with the other Cis-Satlej Chiefs, began to understand that Ranjit Singh's friendship was only one degree less dangerous than his enmity, and that he would be satisfied with nothing less than absolute supremacy over the whole country to the north of the Jamna. With this conviction, he was quite willing to turn to the English, with whom he had always remained on friendly terms, for protection. He received Colonel Ochterlony on his arrival at Nabha with the utmost cordiality,[2] and in May of the same year was taken under the protection of the British Government, with the other Chiefs of Malwa and Sirhind.[3]

Nabha is taken under British protection.

The position of Nabha with respect to other States.

At this time Raja Jaswant Singh ranked third among the Cis-Satlej Chiefs. First was the Maharaja of Pattiala, with a revenue of upwards of six lakhs of rupees; the Bhais of Kythal were second, with a revenue of two lakhs and a quarter; and third was Nabha, with one lakh and

[1] *Vide* Appendix A. Statement of the conquests of Ranjit Singh during the years 1806–9.

[2] Colonel Ochterlony to Secretary to Government, 4th February 1809. A. Seaton, Esq., Resident Dehli, to Secretary to Government, 10th August 1809. Colonel Ochterlony to Raja of Nabha, 6th February 1809.

[3] Proclamation of 3d May 1809.

a half; though the Chiefs of Kalsia and Ladwa had almost as large an income, and certainly could bring more troops into the field.[1] Sir David Ochterlony had formed a high opinion of the Raja's abilities; writing to Government, he observed: "Jaswant Singh is one of the principal Sirdars under our protection, and by far superior in manner, management, and understanding to any of them I have yet seen. I have seen much of his country, which is highly cultivated, and proves him to be mild and unoppressive, a character seldom seen amongst them, and is made more conspicuous by his lands being much mixed with the Raja of Pattiala, where the contrast is very discernible."[2]

Although by the proclamation of the 3d May 1809, the Chiefs taken under British protection were exempted from tribute, and confirmed in the exercise of their ancient rights and authority, yet Jaswant Singh sought and obtained from the Governor-General more explicit and personal assurances on these points, and, later, a sanad was granted to him confirming to him all his possessions under the seal of the Governor-General.[3]

The conduct of the Raja towards Pattiala, and his desire to diminish the power of that State.

In 1810, the Raja received from the Emperor of Dehli, to whom he had sent a present of two guns and four bows, a title of honour, "Barar Bans Sarmour Malwindra Buhadar."[4] From his near connection with the family of Pattiala, the Nabha Chief was naturally one of the advisers of that State, with Raja Bhag Singh of Jhind,

[1] Statement prepared in 1809 by Colonel Ochterlony.

[2] Colonel Ochterlony to J. Moncton, Esq., Secretary, 19th May 1810.

[3] Letter of Raja of Nabha to Governor-General, 7th June 1810. Reply of Governor-General, 20th November 1810.

[4] Murasila from Resident Shahjahanabad to Raja of Nabha, 27th September 1810. Letter from Muhammad Akbar Shah, Emperor of Dehli, dated 23d September 1810, to Raja of Nabha, with firman conferring the title, 26th September 1810.

and Bhai Lal Singh of Kythal.[1] The Raja of Pattiala was almost imbecile, and his wife, Rani Aus Kour, virtually exercised supreme authority, subject in certain matters to the advice of the other Chiefs and the British Political Agent. But the influence of the Nabha Raja was not used for good. Both during the last years of the life of Raja Sahib Singh, and during the minority of his son, his only object was to increase the disorders of Pattiala, and to make the scandal of its mismanagement sufficiently notorious to call for direct interference from without, or possibly to break up the principality altogether, in which case he hoped to share in the spoil, and to increase his own possessions at the expense of his kinsman. The character which Sir David Ochterlony had given of the Raja referred alone to his administrative qualities, and not to his conduct towards the neighbouring States, in which he showed himself as unscrupulous and grasping as any other Chief. He was no worse than others, but, at this time, there was no single Chief in the Cis-Satlej territory who appeared to have any idea of right distinct from his own personal interest, and the consideration that his object could only be attained by violence or fraud, gave him no concern. With Pattiala there had always existed on the part of Nabha a jealousy which had led to constant disputes.

The character of Jaswant Singh.

The grievance against Pattiala.

The Nabha Chiefs, who considered that they were by birth and right the head of the Phulkian family, saw with great dissatisfaction the younger branch growing more wealthy and powerful than themselves, and the influence of this feeling may be traced in almost all the relations between the States till the time of the first Sikh war.

[1] Colonel Ochterlony to Government, 9th March 1811.

The dispute regarding the village of Doladhi.

A boundary dispute regarding the lands of Doladhi, a village close to the walls of Nabha, and the ownership of which was claimed by both States, had been a principal cause of ill-feeling. This was one of the cases which Maharaja Ranjit Singh was summoned to decide in 1807, but which, nevertheless, for more than twenty years afterwards continued to be a fruitful cause of strife.[1]

The dispute regarding the village of Aliki.

Many other disputes arose between these States regarding their respective boundaries. In January 1819, the Maharaja of Pattiala sent troops to take possession of the village of Aliki, which he declared was his, and it was only on the representations of the Political Agent that he consented to withdraw them, and appoint arbitrators to settle the dispute.[2] The following year Pattiala complained of the aggressions of the Nabha Raja. The first grievance was with reference to the villages of Kowlasheri, belonging to Pattiala, and Phulasheri, belonging to Nabha. In the previous year Raja Jaswant Singh had complained of the encroachments of the Kowlasheri zamindars on the Phulasheri lands. Arbitrators were appointed, and a decision given in his favour. The Maharaja of Pattiala then sent troops into Kowlasheri, to protect the inhabitants, as he alleged, from the stronger and hostile neighbouring villages. This action was quite unnecessary, for the Phulasheri villagers had gained all they wanted, and had no wish to continue the quarrel; but the Maharaja was unwilling to relinquish his claim, and the result was much contention and bloodshed.

The dispute regarding Kowlasheri.

Other subjects of dispute.

A second subject of dispute was the boundary between

[1] *Vide ante*, pp. 157-160.

Captain Murray to Sir E. Colebrooke, 12th April, 30th July, 30th September, 2d and 13th October, and 13th December 1828. Sir E. Colebrooke to Captain Murray, 11th and 18th June, 25th and 30th July, 30th September, 2d and 13th October 1828.

[2] From Captain Birch to Sir D. Ochterlony, dated 12th September 1819.

the village of Bhadour, belonging to Sirdars Dip Singh and Bir Singh, relations of the Pattiala Chief, and the village of Kangar, belonging to Nabha, in which case also the Nabha Raja had the right on his side; and, thirdly, the possession of the lands in Harriana to the south of the Gaggar, which had been divided between the States when the boundaries of Harriana and British territory were laid down.[1]

Family dissensions. The rebellion of Prince Ranjit Singh.

Raja Jaswant Singh's troubles were not confined to boundary disputes with Pattiala. His eldest son, Kour Ranjit Singh, in 1818, influenced by evil advisers, and chiefly by the Sirdar of Lidhran, rebelled openly against his authority, and it was only through the personal influence of the Political Agent that he consented to dismiss those of his followers who were obnoxious to the Raja, and to return to his allegiance, when his jagir, which had been confiscated, was restored to him.[2] The reconciliation between father and son was not permanent. In 1822 the Raja again believed that Ranjit Singh was plotting against him, and resumed all the lands which had been assigned for his support; and, in 1824, declared that his son was implicated in a conspiracy against his life. He proposed altogether to disinherit the Prince and his children in favour of his second son, and to add the lands of Raja Singh of Lidhran, the most influential of Ranjit Singh's friends, to the State lands. The evidence which the Raja was able to produce in support of his fears was fanciful in the extreme, and the Prince indignantly denied the truth of the charge; but his supposed accomplices were thrown into prison, heavily ironed,

An alleged conspiracy against the Raja's life.

[1] Captain Birch to Sir D. Ochterlony, dated 22d November 1820.

[2] Captain Birch to Sir D. Ochterlony, dated 19th January and 18th February 1819.

while the case was referred for the orders of the Governor-General, who did not consider the charge to be established, and ordered that no restraint should be placed on Prince Ranjit Singh, and that Sirdar Raja Singh should be at once released from confinement.[1]

The charge against the Prince is disproved.

Raja Jaswant Singh was not satisfied with this decision, and submitted to Government a series of documents which he believed would establish the truth of his assertions. But the Governor-General again agreed with Sir Charles Metcalfe, the Resident at Dehli, that the charge was in no way substantiated, and upheld the order which had before been passed.

There is ample evidence to show that the conduct of the Prince had been wild and extravagant, and that the Raja had some reason to be dissatisfied with him. This is established by the various agreements drawn up at various times by the Prince, and attested by Sir David Ochterlony, but they also prove that the serious crime charged was without foundation.

The conduct of the Prince was disgraceful, but not criminal.

The various orders issued by Captains Ross and Murray, subsequent to those of Sir David Ochterlony, show, indeed, the continued immoral and disorderly conduct of the Prince, but do not contain the smallest direct or circumstantial evidence of any wish or attempt at assassination of the Raja. The only document which at all supported the charge, was the alleged confession of Raja Singh of Lidhran; but on this no reliance whatever could be placed. When it was given, Raja Singh was a prisoner at Nabha, completely in the power of Jaswant

[1] Captain Murray to C. Elliott, Esq., 27th and 30th November 1824.
C. Elliott, Esq., to Captain Murray, 6th May and 21st September 1825. C. Elliott, Esq., to Secretary to Government of India, 9th May 1825.
Secretary to Government of India to C. Elliott, Esq., 26th August 1825.

Singh, who had means of inducing his captive to make any confession he wished. The character of Raja Singh was so infamous, that had he been free no reliance could have been placed on his word; and he was, moreover, the acknowledged instigator of the extravagances of the Prince. On evidence such as this no one could justly be condemned, far less of an attempt to commit so unnatural a crime as parricide, and the Prince was accordingly acquitted.[1]

The death of the Prince, A.D. 1832,

But this acquittal Prince Ranjit Singh did not long survive. On the 17th of June 1832 he died at Patriri, the residence of Sirdar Gulab Singh Shahid, to whose sister-in-law he had been married a short time before.

Which is attributed to foul play.

The sudden death of a person of importance in the Sikh States was rarely considered to be due to natural causes, the more especially when, as in the case of Ranjit Singh, he had been for years pursued by the most bitter and unrelenting enmity of his father. The widows of the deceased at once charged the Raja with their husband's murder, and the body certainly bore marks which seemed to suggest foul play. Only two years before, Prince Santokh Singh, the only son of the Prince, had died as suddenly,[2] and the belief then was general that his grandfather, the Raja, had caused poison to be administered to him. But there was no shadow of evidence to support the charges, and soon afterwards the mother of the Prince, who had joined the widows in accusing the Raja of the murder, wrote to Sir George Clerk, declaring her disbelief in the alleged instrumentality of the Raja in causing her son's death, and no further action was accord-

[1] Sir Charles Metcalfe to Secretary to Government of India, 23d November 1826, and to Captain Murray, 3d May 1827.

Secretary to Government of India to Sir C. Metcalfe, 27th April 1827.

[2] Captain Murray to Acting Resident, 4th October 1830.

ingly taken.[1] Prince Ranjit Singh, though of extravagant and dissolute habits, was a young man of considerable promise, and was extremely popular with the Chiefs on both sides of the Satlej.

Kour Ranjit Singh married three wives, the daughters of Sirdars Jodh Singh of Bamne Kaleki, Jassa Singh of Shahpur, and Dya Singh Bhamna. His son, Santokh Singh, was married to Bhagbari, the daughter of Sirdar Sher Singh of Shahabad, with great pomp, all the Cis-Satlej Chiefs and the British Political Agent being present at the ceremony.

The dispute between Nabha and the Lidhran and Sunti Sikhs, regarding the feudal supremacy of the former.

Notice must now be taken of an important case, which illustrates the nature of the relations which grew up gradually between a powerful State like Nabha and its weaker neighbours—from original independence to a state of feudal vassalage.

The rise of the Nishanwala confederacy.

The Sikhs of Lidhran and Sunti were members of the powerful Nishanwala confederacy, which, under Sirdar Sangat Singh, Dassanda Singh, Jai Singh, and Mohr Singh, took possession, after the battle of Sirhind, in 1763, of Ambala, Serai Lashkar Khan, Shahabad, Doraha, Lidhran, Amloh, and Sunti. In the year 1827, the

The complaints of the Sirdars.

Sirdars of Lidhran and Sunti complained bitterly to the Agent of the Governor-General at Dehli of the tyranny of the Nabha Raja, who treated them as his vassals, demanded constant service—from the former fifty, and from the latter seventy horse—and harassed them with numerous requisitions with which it was most irksome to comply, and which the Raja had no right to make, as they were not his vassals at all. The Political Agent, to

[1] Sir George Clerk to Mr Fraser, Governor-General's Agent, 20th June and 7th September 1832; and letters from the widow and mother of Ranjit Singh to Sir G. Clerk.

whom the question was referred, considered that although the Chiefs should continue to furnish contingents for service to the Raja, yet that they should be protected from his oppression, and that their disputes should be heard and decided by the British Agent at Ambala.[1] The Resident did not consider this practicable, as he held the Lidhran and Sunti Sikhs to be dependants of Nabha, and that any interference on the part of the British Government would weaken the position of the Raja. This vassalage was thenceforth considered as proved, although the Chiefs themselves denied any right over them on the part of Nabha; and the documents which affirmed it, purporting to have been executed by themselves, they declared to be forgeries.

In 1836, the case was taken up by Sir George Clerk, and thoroughly investigated. This officer came to the conclusion that, as regarded the Lidhran Sikhs, the Nabha Raja was only *primus inter pares*, and had continued, with the assistance of the British authorities, to usurp the position of a feudal lord. That, with regard to Sunti, the case was very similar, the Nabha Raja having successfully asserted his supremacy at a time when the co-parcenary rights of the Sikhs were imperfectly understood.

The result of the investigation of Sir George Clerk.

This decision was founded on the undoubted fact that, under Sikhism, as originally understood, no such thing as vassalage or feudal superiority had any existence. The principle of the creed was fraternity, and the Sikhs boasted of being communities of independent soldiers. While the Khalsa was still young and enthusiastic, and the power of no individual Chief was inordinately great,

The original constitution of Sikh society was independence and fraternity.

[1] Captain Murray to Sir E. Colebrooke, 13th September 1827. Acting Resident to Captain Murray, 27th July 1827.

this idea of independence represented a state of things not far removed from the truth; but as the more important Chiefships gradually increased in power, their smaller neighbours were compelled, either for protection against others, or to avoid absorption altogether, to place themselves under the protection of some Chief able to defend them, and, in return, to give service in the field.

The Sikhs of Lidhran and Sunti were not only independent of Nabha, but engaged in hostilities against her.

The Lidhran and Sunti Sikhs were, at the time of the conquest of Sirhind, independent members of the Nishanwala confederacy, and when Sirdar Jai Singh seized Lidhran, with twenty-seven adjacent villages, he was still an independent Chief.[1] When the Phulkians, in 1718, attacked Ambala, a Nishanwala possession, the Lidhran and Sunti Sikhs both came to the assistance of the besieged, and fought against the Nabha troops, proving that at this time, at any rate, they were not vassals of the Nabha Chief. After this time the Lidhran Sikhs were never engaged in active hostilities against Nabha, for an alliance was made and cemented by the marriage of the daughter of Sirdar Jai Singh to Raja Jaswant Singh. But the Sikhs of Sunti on several subsequent occasions fought against Nabha, and, so late as 1810 and 1814, when they were at war with the Chiefs of Kannah and Karar, Nabha gave them no assistance, as she undoubtedly would have done had they been her acknowledged feudatories.

The usurpation of Nabha from the Sunti Sikhs, and the decision of the arbitrators.

Soon after the capture of Sirhind, the Sunti Sikhs seized Amloh and thirty-six adjacent villages; but on the approach of Ahmed Shah Durani, who was invading the Punjab from the north, they, in common with other Manjha Sikhs, crossed the Satlej to oppose him. Nabha took this opportunity to possess herself of Amloh and

[1] *Vide ante*, Note, p. 45.

half of its attached villages, and the rightful owners on their return were only able to establish their head-quarters at Sunti, and carry on hostilities against Nabha, with varying success, until Sirdar Jassa Singh Ahluwalia and Sirdar Himmat Singh of Shahabad, acting as arbitrators, assigned Amloh to Nabha, and the thirty-five villages to be held in co-parcenary or *chaharami* tenure between them. This decision the Sunti Sikhs were compelled to accept, but they remained on very bad terms with Nabha, and systematically opposed that State in every possible way.[1]

In reality, both Lidhran and Sunti had been in the position of subordinates to Nabha for some time before 1836.

Documents were undoubtedly in existence which, if genuine, proved that the supremacy of Nabha, and their liability to furnish contingents for service, had been admitted by the Chiefs; but these they pronounced forgeries, and Sir George Clerk appears to have believed them. It was not, however, easy to prove the fraud, if any existed; and the Chiefs had certainly for some years, under protest it may be, rendered suit and service, and their obligation to do so had been maintained on many occasions by the British Government, although once, in 1834, it had reversed a decision of the Raja of Nabha in a case of disputed inheritance in Lidhran.

The decision of Government in the case, maintaining the superiority of Nabha, but checking its arbitrary exercise.

This being the case, the Government of India did not consider it expedient to declare the Sikhs of Sunti and Lidhran altogether independent of Nabha. The complaints which they had made of harassing and perpetual demands for service were nevertheless regarded, and the Raja of Nabha was directed to dispense with their service

[1] Sir D. Ochterlony to Captain Murray, 11th November 1815. Sir George Clerk to Sir T. Metcalfe, Agent Governor-General, 12th August and 1st September 1836. Original documents containing the agreements of the Chiefs with Nabha. Sir T. Metcalfe to Sir George Clerk, 31st March; and Sir George Clerk to Sir T. Metcalfe, 19th April 1837.

altogether, except on the occasion of the birth of a son, the marriage of one of his sons or daughters, the death of the reigning Prince, or in time of actual war. The dignity of Nabha was thus duly considered, and the Sunti and Lidhran Sikhs relieved from the oppression of which they had so bitterly complained.[1]

The Raja offers his services during the Kabul campaign.

The Raja of Nabha offered his services to the British Government at the commencement of the Kabul campaign, and although they were necessarily declined, the Governor-General thanked him for the friendly spirit which had prompted the offer.[2]

The death of Jaswant Singh, A.D. 1840.

On the 22d of May 1840, Raja Jaswant Singh, who had been for some time in a declining state of health, died, aged sixty-six, and was succeeded by his only surviving son, Devindar Singh, then in his eighteenth year.[3] The character of the Raja has been already described. However grasping and unscrupulous his conduct may have been towards his neighbours and rivals, he had always administered the affairs of his own State justly and well. His police was excellent, and his subjects were contented, and had reason to lament his death.

His marriage.

Raja Jaswant Singh married five wives—Dya Kour, daughter of Sirdar Jai Singh Lidhran; Chand Kour, daughter of Sirdar Ram Singh Dhillon, who has lately died at a great age; Ram Kour, daughter of Sirdar Bagh Singh Rallon; Harkour, daughter of Sirdar Hari

[1] Secretary to Government to Agent Governor-General, 25th August 1838, and to Raja of Nabha of the same date. Agent Governor-General to Sir G. Clerk, 8th September 1838, and to Secretary Government, 1st June and 11th August 1838.

Despatch No. 10 of Court of Directors, 12th March 1840.

[2] Raja of Nabha to Governor-General. Governor-General to Raja, dated 8th November 1838, and to Sir G. Clerk of the same date.

[3] Sir G. Clerk to Mr Thomason, Agent Lieutenant-Governor, 28th May 1840.

Singh of Jodhpur; and, lastly, Dharam Kour, the daughter of Sirdar Sujan Singh of Ghumon. Of these, Rani Dya Kour gave birth to Ranjit Singh, and Rani Harkour to Devindar Singh.

The late Raja had been a faithful ally of the British Government. In 1804 he refused to assist Holkar against the English; he gave assistance in supplies and carriage during the Ghurka campaign of 1810, and in that of Bikanir in 1818;[1] and during the northward march of the British army to Kabul in 1838, he advanced a loan of six lakhs of rupees to the Government.[2]

The installation of Raja Devindar Singh.

Devindar Singh was formally installed as Raja on the 5th of October 1840, the Agent of the Governor-General being present. This was the first installation that had taken place in Nabha since the English connection with the States, and the Khillat conferred on the occasion was similar to that given to Raja Fatah Singh of Jhind in 1822, consisting of an elephant with *jhul* or trappings, a horse with a silver saddle, a Khillat of seven pieces, three rugums, and a sword and shield.[3]

His early training and character.

The new Raja's character, the training he had received, and the circumstances of his succession, did not promise a wise or successful administration. It was only after he had quarrelled with Prince Ranjit Singh that Raja Jaswant Singh married the wife who gave birth to Devindar Singh. As this child grew up, the Raja's hatred for his elder son grew more intense, and his determination to disinherit him and leave the State to his younger and favourite son more confirmed.

[1] Captain Birch to Raja of Nabha, 20th July 1819.

[2] Captain Murray to Raja of Nabha, 6th November 1838.

[3] Sir G. Clerk to Secretary to Government North-Western Provinces, 17th September 1840, and to Secretary to Government of India, 28th September 1840.

This resolution was notorious, and in the dispute between father and son, the neighbouring Chiefs were involved, some taking one side and some the other. Devindar Singh was ten years old when his brother died, and from that time was the recognised heir to the throne. He had thus, from his earliest years, been surrounded by flatterers and parasites who desired to please his father, and, in order to accumulate every pretext for disinheriting Ranjit Singh, the greatest pains were taken with the education of his younger brother. When Devindar Singh became, when still a boy, the reigning Prince, his Brahman tutors, as was natural enough, retained their influence, and filled his mind with an exaggerated estimate of his power, dignity, and importance, till a character, which would otherwise have been distinguished for weakness alone, became repulsive from its arrogance and vanity; while the old feud which had for long existed between the rival houses of Pattiala and Jhind was revived with far greater bitterness than ever.

The ill feeling which existed between Nabha and the States of Pattiala and Jhind.

It has been before explained that Nabha was the eldest branch of the Phulkian family, and held the hereditary title of Chaudhri, which had possessed a real meaning when the Chiefs were subjects of the Delhi Emperors. The title of Maharaja granted to the Pattiala Chief had always excited the greatest jealousy on the part of the Raja of Nabha, who was most anxious to obtain the same honour for himself. With Pattiala he had always been at feud, and the Raja of Jhind had generally taken the Pattiala side of the dispute, and was in consequence equally obnoxious to Nabha. But there was another and more recent cause for the bad feeling between these Chiefs.

The special cause of quarrel with Jhind.

When Raja Sangat Singh of Jhind died without male issue, the principal claimants for the throne were Sirdar

Sarup Singh of Bazidpur and his cousin Sirdar Sukhan Singh of Badrukhan, two distant collaterals. The State might justly have been resumed by the British Government as an escheat—collateral succession to Chiefships not being then admitted—but it was determined to make it over to one of the claimants. The discussion as to their respective rights was of long duration; and the Nabha and Pattiala Chiefs naturally supported the one who bid highest for their influence. Pattiala demanded dependence on herself rather than on Nabha; and the latter demanded the cession of the district of Sangrur, which had been treacherously conquered from Nabha by Raja Gajpat Singh in 1774. Sarup Singh is asserted to have signed a bond agreeing to surrender this district, if his claims were admitted; but, after obtaining an acknowledgment of his claims from Government, he refused to fulfil his promise. Neither party cared to bring such a case before the British authorities, but the existence of the bond was a matter of notoriety, and it was moreover believed that Raja Sarup Singh attempted to destroy it when it was put into his hands at Nabha for perusal.[1]

The etiquette of the Raja's Court.

The only revenge Raja Devindar Singh was able to take for this breach of faith was to deny the Jhind Raja any title of honour, pretending to consider him as of inferior birth, being only related collaterally to the late Rajas, and styling him simply Sarup Singh. The Maharaja of Pattiala he would only style Raja; and he introduced into his Court a rigid and painful etiquette abolishing many customs supposed to be of Muhammadan origin. Devindar Singh was a bigoted Sikh, and was always surrounded with Brahmans, who, after the fashion of their

[1] Major Broadfoot to Secretary to Government of India, dated 26th April 1845.

order, flattered the weak-minded prince for their own interest. Sanscrit *Slokas* were recited every evening before him, and the opportunity was taken to exalt his dignity and depreciate that of his neighbours; while the power of the English was asserted to be on the wane, and the day approaching when they would retire from Northern India, and Nabha assume the foremost place which was justly her due.

The commencement of the Raja's reign promised well.

But these open manifestations of disaffection did not show themselves immediately after the Raja's accession. He was then anxious to obtain the title of Maharaja, and endeavoured to win the esteem of the British Government by making large remissions of revenue. He also, finding the Agent of the Governor-General took an interest in native education, proposed to establish a college in which English, Sanscrit, and Hindi should be taught; but this laudable intention was not carried out.

The disaffection of almost all the Cis-Satlej States in A.D. 1842.

In 1842 occurred the Kabul disasters, the effect of which, on the Cis-Satlej Chiefs, has been already noticed. It is almost impossible to exaggerate the influence which a catastrophe such as this had upon ignorant and selfish Chiefs, to whom gratitude was an unknown virtue, and who had only remained loyal to the British Government, which had loaded them with favours, and had taken nothing from them as the price of these favours, because they believed its power to be invincible. There were in the whole of India no native princes who had such reason to be faithful to the British Government, and who had received such unmixed advantage from their connection with it, as those of the Cis-Satlej; but when, as they believed, the British power was materially shaken by the results of the first Kabul campaign, they almost all, the larger States as well as the smaller, wavered in their allegiance, disregarded the orders of the British Agents, and prepared to take advantage of the new order of things which they imagined was about to arrive. Nabha, to the credit of the Raja's intelligence, was one of the first to understand the significance of the successes of the second Kabul expedition, and returned to his former attitude of friendship.

The resumption of Kythal.

But this change lasted only a short time. The resumption of the larger portion of the Kythal State, held by the Bhaikian family and connections of the Phulkians, created great dissatisfaction, and the Chief of Nabha, with those of Pattiala and Jhind, used their utmost endeavours to obstruct the Government and to obtain the succession to the whole estate for the nearest collateral. When they perceived that the Government was prepared to support its rights by force, and had sent a detachment to Kythal to restore order, which their influence had chiefly been instrumental in disturbing, they pretended to be as eager to assist as before they had been to oppose; but, till the last, they remonstrated against the resumption, seeing in the fate of Kythal the probable fate of their own possessions, for the Sikh Chiefs led lives so debauched that it was a common thing for them to have no children; and unless the right of adoption or the claims of collaterals were admitted, their estates would lapse, sooner or later, to the paramount power.[1]

The Nabha Raja disposed to join Lahore against the English.

The Nabha Raja was thus disposed to transfer his friendship from the British Government to that of Lahore,

[1] Envoy to Court of Lahore to Secretary to Government of India, 27th, 29th, 30th March, and 8th April 1843. From Agent Governor-General to Secretary to Government, dated 15th February 1844. Letter of Raja of Nabha to Agent Governor-General, 7th October 1844. Letter of the Envoy to Mai Sahib Kour of Kythal, 9th April 1843, and from Maharaja of Pattiala to Envoy, 13th April 1843.

which had been careful not to risk a collision with the English when wise and able men presided at its councils, but which now, guided by courtesans and drunkards, was fast drifting into war. The Nabha Raja was, like many other Chiefs, tired of the monotony of the English rule. As they expressed themselves in letters to the Governor-General, "the lion and lamb might, through the benevolence and justice of the British Government, drink out of the same vessel," but this state of things was only agreeable to the lamb. The lion desired confusion and war, in which the strong would be the conqueror and the weak the prey, and in an alliance with Lahore the Raja of Nabha fancied he would more easily obtain the objects of his ambition, than by remaining on good terms with the English.

The case of the village of Mowran, and the dispute with Lahore.

At this time, however, a case occurred which requires notice, as it appeared likely to embroil the Raja with the Lahore Durbar, and certainly was considered by the latter to evince an unfriendly feeling on the part of the British Government, helping to embitter the relations between the two States, which were already becoming uncertain and dangerous. To explain the nature of the case it is necessary to go back some way in Nabha history.

Sirdar Dhanna Singh Malwai.

Dhanna Singh,[1] a zamindar of Mowran, in Nabha territory, left his village about the year 1793, and took service with Sirdar Sahib Singh of Gujrat, who had married Subha Kour, the sister of Raja Jaswant Singh. Later he served under Sirdar Fatah Singh Kalianwala, and, in 1807, entered the service of Maharaja Ranjit Singh of Lahore, and, being a fine soldier, soon rose to favour. In the year 1815, he begged his master to obtain for him

[1] Dhanna Singh Malwai. The history of this Sirdar is given in "The Punjab Chiefs," pp. 192–196.

the grant of his ancestral village of Mowran, and the Maharaja accordingly preferred his request to Jaswant Singh, who objected to the grant. Ranjit Singh then said that unless the village was given he would resume the lands held, Trans-Satlej, by Subha Kour, the widow of Sirdar Sahib Singh Bhangi, who had died a short time before. This argument was not without effect, and after some further delay Jaswant Singh consented to the grant, which was made in 1819, the British Agent, General Ochterlony, knowing nothing about it, although the Nabha authorities declared that he not only was aware of the grant, but insisted that it should be made subject to service to Nabha, of which State Dhanna Singh, and his father Mal Singh before him, had been subjects. This was certainly never done, and no service was ever rendered by Dhanna Singh. He, however, occasionally made to the Raja complimentary presents, till 1830, when he broke off all connection with Nabha, commenced building a fort in Mowran, and acted as an independent Chief. Jaswant Singh was very much irritated, and wished to resume the village; but this, during the life of the Maharaja, he did not dare to do, although his agent affirmed that, at the marriage of Nao Nihal Singh, in 1837, he asked the Maharaja's permission to resume, and, in reply, was directed to wait till the death of Dhanna Singh, who was then a man far advanced in years.

The object of the Nabha Raja was to prove that Mowran was not a grant made by him to Maharaja Ranjit Singh, and given by the latter to Dhanna Singh Malwai, but that it was a mere temporary exchange for the village of Manokah, allowed to Rani Subha Kour, his sister; and that when this was resumed on her death, he had a right to resume Mowran. This lady died in

1839, two months before Maharaja Ranjit Singh, by whose successor, Kharrak Singh, her village was resumed.

The death of Dhanna Singh, and the demand for the village.

Sirdar Dhanna Singh Malwai died in May 1843, and Raja Devindar Singh at once called on Hukm Singh, the son of the deceased Chief, to surrender the property. The circumstances of the grant were quite unknown to Sir G. Clerk, who, in 1839, is said to have sanctioned the resumption, under the impression that the village was merely an exchange for that held by Rani Subha Kour; and, moreover, the Raja produced a letter said to have been written by Maharaja Kharrak Singh, and dated the 6th December 1839, which supported this view of the question, and which ran as follows:—

The letter of Maharaja Kharrak Singh.

"As regards releasing or giving up Mowran, in exchange for which Zahura was granted to Mai Subha Kour in the first instance, and Manokah later, which was resumed by me, Ganda Singh[1] has explained the circumstances. He was told that if any one seized Manokah it should be restored, but he insisted much upon the restoration of Mowran. As there is a friendship between us, be satisfied on this subject, and take possession of the village. The case appears to be as follows:—The Maharaja gave Mowran to Sirdar Dhanna Singh, and, as an exchange, first the village of Zahura, and afterwards that of Manokah, was given to Mai Subha Kour: on her death my officials took possession of Manokah. Your officials can now also take possession of Mowran; if Sirdar Dhanna Singh complains, some other village will be given him."[2]

[1] This Ganda Singh was a relation of Mai Chand Kour, wife of Maharaja Kharrak Singh, and had entered the service of the Raja of Nabha, by whom he was sent to Lahore regarding the Mowran case.

[2] Translation by Captain Cunningham, Assistant Political Agent.

Raja Devindar Singh, on the refusal of Sirdar Hukm Singh to surrender the village, sent a force against it in August 1843, opened fire without delay, and took it by storm, refusing to allow any reference to be made to Hukm Singh or to Lahore. The fort was plundered, and a large quantity of valuables, estimated by Sirdar Hukm Singh at more than two lakhs of rupees, was carried off.[1] The Raja's account of the attack was, of course, different: he asserted that the villagers opened fire upon his troops, and the capture of the fort was in retaliation for this outrage, while no valuables of any description were found or removed.[2]

The Raja of Nabha takes Mowran by storm and plunders it.

Maharaja Sher Singh, who had now succeeded to the unquiet throne of Lahore, pretended to be, or really was, most indignant at the violence done to one of his dependants, and wrote to the British Government for redress. But before any reply could be given, Sher Singh was assassinated, and several months of anarchy succeeded, during which Mowran was forgotten. But, in July 1844, the question was again raised, and the nature of the Lahore demands will be seen from an extract from a letter of Maharaja Dalip Singh:[3]—"All the circumstances connected with the village of Mowran are understood by the English, and it is known to them that it belongs to the Khalsa; and you have also ascertained fully the aggression committed, and the deceit practised by the authorities of Nabha. Rai Kishan Chand (the vakil) informed me that the case would soon be satisfactorily settled; and although it was pleasing to hear this, still,

The Lahore Court are very indignant,

And remonstrate.

The letter of Maharaja Dalip Singh.

[1] Letter of Rai Kishan Chand, Agent of the Lahore Durbar, 16th July 1844. Statement of Sirdar Hukm Singh Malwai, dated 25th April 1844.

[2] Letter from Raja of Nabha to Agent Governor-General, dated 16th July 1844.

[3] Received 10th July 1844.

as there has been much delay, I have thought it good to remind you that the right of the Lahore State to the village is proved, and that aggression and deceit on the part of the Nabha authorities have been fully ascertained. The belief is that, considering the friendship of the two States, the case of Mowran will be satisfactorily settled, and all the plundered property will be restored; and that those who have been proved to have committed aggression and practised deceit will be adequately punished."

The importance attached to the case by the Sikhs.

The Mowran case having thus become, in the excited state of the Sikhs, of great political importance, a full investigation was made into the merits of the case. The points on which the whole question turned were the validity of the letter of Maharaja Kharrak Singh, the nature of the original grant, and the person to whom it was made.

The letter of Maharaja Kharrak Singh, permitting the resumption of Mowran, was at once pronounced a forgery by the Lahore Durbar. The original could not be produced, and the Raja of Nabha stated that it had been lost when the papers of his minister, Sahib Singh, were seized. But this excuse could not be admitted in the face of the denial of the Lahore officials that such a document had ever been issued. The truth probably was that Ganda Singh, who was sent to Lahore as a Nabha Agent in 1839, persuaded his relative, Rani Chand Kour, to induce her weak-minded husband, Maharaja Kharrak Singh, to draft a letter similar to that produced; that Raja Dhyan Singh, the Lahore Minister, refused his consent to the alienation, and the letter consequently was never despatched. Raja Jaswant Singh later procured a copy of the draft, which was produced as genuine

The real truth of the letter of Kharrak Singh.

and valid, although the original letter had never been officially issued at all. This was to all intents and purposes a forgery.

The original grant was discovered, dated May 1819, in favour of Maharaja Ranjit Singh, and on this the Nabha Raja was compelled somewhat to change his ground. He admitted that the grant had originally been so made, and stated that the British Agent had been informed of it at the time, but of this assertion there was no proof. There was evidence, however, to show that the English authorities had no knowledge of the transfer. Mr Clerk had given the Raja, in 1839, permission to resume Mowran, having no idea whatever that the Lahore State had any legitimate claim.[1] Colonel Richmond, equally ignorant of the truth, and accepting, as precedents to follow, the orders of Colonel Ochterlony in 1814, and of Mr Clerk in 1839, told the Raja, when about to march against Mowran, that the village appeared to belong to Nabha, and that if the Raja chose to resume it he was at liberty to do so.[2] The grant to Maharaja Ranjit Singh was not signed by the Raja, but this, which was advanced as a plea against its validity, was of little weight, for Sikh Chiefs did not always affix their signatures to documents of such a nature. In any case, the denial of the grant was as foolish as it was dishonest, since the Raja had virtually admitted the Lahore claim by applying there for leave to resume; while the reason for omitting to sign the document was doubtless that the Raja, when making the grant, had intended some day to deny it, either for his personal advantage or to justify

The Nabha authorities had completely deceived the English Government regarding the true state of the case.

[1] Mr Clerk to Raja of Nabha, 8th April 1839, and to Colonel Richmond, 16th September 1843.

[2] Colonel Richmond to Raja of Nabha, 19th August 1843.

himself to the British Government for an illegal transfer of territory.[1]

Should the village be restored to Lahore, although its original transfer was illegal?

The question remained whether the village should be restored to Lahore, which had held possession for twenty-four years under Raja Jaswant Singh's invalid grant. At any other time the British Government would probably have waived their rights, and allowed Lahore to retain what had been so long possessed, notwithstanding the original acquisition was irregular; but the Sikh Durbar had showed so hostile and arrogant a temper, that any concession might have been misconstrued. That the grant was invalid there can be no possible doubt. The British Government was the paramount power, and no feudatory was competent to transfer territory to another independent power without its consent. It is true that no definite ruling was given on this subject till 1828, in the case of Raja Sangat Singh of Jhind, but the principle was known and acknowledged, and that it was understood is proved by the secrecy attending the transfer of Mowran to Ranjit Singh.[2] The village was consequently resumed by the British Government; the Raja of Nabha receiving a severe reprimand, and being directed to pay Sirdar Hukm Singh the value of the property plundered from the fort.[3]

The right of the British Government clear, and the village resumed.

The indignation caused by this decision at Lahore.

The decision of the British Government excited great ill-feeling at Lahore. There can be no doubt that the decision was correct according to every principle of international law; but the Sikhs did not understand inter-

[1] Colonel Richmond to Secretary to Government of India, dated 18th May 1844, and 28th May.

[2] Resident at Dehli, dated 12th June, to Government of India; and Government of India to Resident Dehli, 3d July 1828.

[3] Agent Governor-General to Secretary to Government, 4th August 1844; and Secretary to Government, No. 1297, dated 11th June 1844, and No. 2480, of 5th October 1844, to Agent Governor-General.

national law. They only saw the Raja of Nabha commit, under the shield of British protection, a gross outrage against the Lahore Government, plunder the property of one of the most distinguished Lahore Generals, and kill, in his wanton aggression, several Lahore subjects. The rights of the British Government, as far as its feudatories were concerned, they did not care to understand. They only knew that the village of Mowran had been held by the Lahore State for twenty-four years; that it was seized by violence from Maharaja Sher Singh; and that the British Government, which had always professed the warmest friendship for the Sikh people, not only did not compel its restoration, but took the opportunity to benefit itself by annexing the subject of dispute. This feeling was strengthened by another case which occurred about the same time, and which has been before referred to—namely, the village of Bains, granted by the Raja of Jhind to Jamadar Khushhal Singh.[1] That the suspicions of the Sikhs were groundless and childish may be true; but it is certain that the unsympathetic action of the British Government at this time did irritate the Lahore Government extremely, and was one of the causes of the war which so shortly followed. It may have been well to insist upon the maintenance of a principle, the correctness of which there was no reason to doubt, and to refuse to surrender it in favour of any considerations of expediency; but governments and individuals who talk of principle are generally about to do something ungenerous or foolish; and statesmanship consists as much in respect for prejudices and tenderness for ignorance, as in the

[1] Agent Governor-General to Secretary to Government of India, 30th July 1844.

Vide ante, p. 349.

assertion of principles, however unimpeachable. This the English Government, not for the first or last time, forgot, satisfying itself with the excuse, unworthy of a powerful administration, that any concessions to justice or generosity might be mistaken for weakness.

The war of 1845, and the conduct of the Raja of Nabha.

The autumn of 1845 saw preparations for war between the British and the Lahore Government in progress, and there was soon little doubt with which side the sympathies of the Raja of Nabha were engaged. The vanity and arrogance of this Chief had increased to such a degree, that the plea of imbecility, which was urged in his favour after the conclusion of the war, was not an extravagant one. The etiquette of his Court became more and more rigid; from his courtiers he required prostrations and the most abject servility in speech and manner; he desired to omit all titles due to British officers, even to the Agent of the Governor-General, and his pride would not allow him to meet the Lieutenant-Governor of the North-Western Provinces beyond his own territories. His subjects had now begun to suffer from his exactions. His father had, on his death-bed, commanded him to remit, in perpetuity, one-fourth of the taxes levied, which were far heavier than those levied in British territory, although Jaswant Singh had not been an oppressive ruler. This order Devindar Singh obeyed in the letter, but disregarded in the spirit, for he increased the fines, presents, and collections to an amount which more than made up the deficiency in direct taxation.

Intrigues with Lahore.

That Raja Devindar Singh was engaged in intrigues with Lahore for some time before the Satlej war there is every reason to believe, although direct and satisfactory proofs of a treasonable correspondence were not found. One reason for this failure of evidence was the death of Major Broadfoot, the Governor-General's Agent, at Firushahr, and the loss of a large number of his papers; and, secondly, that such communications as were carried on were not usually trusted to writing. General Ram Singh of the Lahore army, a man notoriously hostile to the English, visited Nabha when the war was in contemplation, and is believed to have had many private interviews with the Raja. The opinion of Major Broadfoot may be seen from a confidential letter to the Nabha Agent of the 15th of December, in which he wrote as follows:—"In consequence of the receipt of intelligence between the Raja and General Ram Singh, sent by Jowahir Singh,[1] and in consequence of other acts unbecoming his position as a ruler, they had before been desired to remonstrate with and restrain the Raja."

The visit of General Ram Singh to Nabha.

But when the conduct of the Raja during the most critical part of the campaign is considered, it will appear superfluous to look for treasonable correspondence. All the requisitions for supplies, carriage, and information which were issued to the Nabha Chiefs are extant, and from them it appears that the first orders and demands of British Agents were treated with silent contempt. On the 3d, 8th, and 10th of December 1845, stringent orders were issued to the Nabha Agents to provide supplies on the road from Kalka to Khanna, and to make a road from Latalla to Basia. No attention was paid to these directions, and the most serious inconvenience was caused to the troops.

The hostile conduct of the Raja during the campaign.

For this neglect, the estates of Dehraru and Amloh were confiscated on the 13th of December 1845, and two days later Major Broadfoot addressed to the Nabha Agents the letter above referred to, and which concluded

Portion of Nabha Territory confiscated.

[1] Jowahir Singh was at this time *Wazir*, or Prime Minister, at Lahore.

thus :—" At this urgent juncture, much trouble and inconvenience have been caused by the Raja's neglect to provide supplies, which have only been procurable by force ; he, therefore, now, in writing, repeats what he had in the morning verbally expressed to them, that unless the Raja of Nabha come into the British camp on that or the following evening, he will be considered an enemy to the British ; further, that Kanha Mal (the Raja's Agent), who had been sent on in advance to collect supplies and had failed, remain in attendance, under surveillance, and in charge of the supply department ; that the Thannadar who had behaved with disrespect to the Assistant (Mr Cust), and who deserves severe punishment, remain in confinement ; and that Mulvi Zahur-ul-Hak (another Agent of the Raja's) remain in attendance, and be treated with the usual respect; that in punishment of the present offence, Latalla, with its dependencies, be confiscated, and, to this end, the Rai of Kotla and Rahmut Ali Khan are ordered to take possession, who will be paid from the revenues of the district."

The orders of Major Broadfoot disregarded.

That these stringent orders were not unnecessary is proved by the inattention paid to them. The Raja did not come into the British camp, but remained at Nabha under the pretence of collecting supplies ; and the death of the Maharaja of Pattiala occurring a few days afterwards, he took the opportunity to visit Pattiala. After the death of Major Broadfoot, the disinclination of the Raja to join the British camp did not abate. Major F. Mackeson, Commissioner of the Cis-Satlej territories, wrote, on the 5th of January, by direction of the Secretary to Government, to the Raja, reminding him of Major Broadfoot's letter of the 15th December, and begging him to come to Firozpur, where he might explain his failure to attend when first summoned.

To this letter no answer was returned, but, on the 12th January, two letters were received by the Secretary to Government and the Governor-General, purporting to have been written on the 29th December. The former was in some sort an answer to Major Broadfoot's letter, declaring the loyalty of the Raja, expatiating on the services rendered by the Nabha State, and attempting to explain his connection with General Ram Singh. During the operations of Sir H. Smith's column south of the Satlej, the Raja once sent his officials to Major Mackeson with unmeaning messages, but not until the 13th of February, three days after the battle of Subraon, did he leave Nabha, in compliance with a special request of Major Mackeson, and proceed to Ludhiana. Apologies to the Governor General

The conduct of the Nabha authorities, with regard to carriage and supplies, was dilatory and suspicious in the extreme. At the time when they were most needed, nothing whatever was provided, though after the battles of Mudki and Firushahr supplies were sent in abundance; and after the final victory of Subraon the whole resources of the Nabha State were placed at the disposal of the Government. Previous to the battle of Firushahr and Mudki, only 32 camels and 681 maunds of grain were furnished; while 21,807 maunds and 864 camels were supplied after these actions, though the resources of the State were such that, in the opinion of Sir Henry Lawrence,[1] it could have furnished early in January all that was supplied eventually, and at least half before the two first battles. No supplies were provided until the British Army was victorious.

[1] Report on the Raja's conduct to Government of India, 18th September 1846.

The Raja of Nabha excluded from Durbar.

At the close of the war the Raja was not permitted, with the other protected Chiefs, to attend the Durbar of the Governor-General at Ludhiana, and an investigation was directed to be made into his conduct, the result of which confirmed, in every particular, the account which has here been given. A long and elaborate defence was submitted by the Raja, some points of which must be briefly noticed.

The defence of the Raja of Nabha.

He first endeavoured to prove that Major Broadfoot's order, summoning him to the British camp, was illegal, as he was not compelled to visit the Governor-General's Agent beyond his own territory. But, in time of war, all ceremony must be waived; those who do not act with the zeal of friends, must be considered enemies; and, after the battle of Subraon, the Raja made no difficulty about proceeding to Ludhiana at the direction of Major Mackeson.

The services alleged to have been rendered by him.

The services rendered in former years by the Nabha State were then recounted; and it was alleged that, during the Satlej campaign, Sirdar Ganda Singh, a Nabha Chief, was placed at Major Broadfoot's disposal, and supplied him with much valuable information, while his son, Lal Singh, was sent to Lahore on the same service. Sir H. Lawrence, however, who succeeded to the agency, after Major Broadfoot's death, at Firushahr, could find no evidence of any such information having been given; nor did Ganda Singh or Lal Singh ever furnish him with a single item of intelligence that was worth anything, although the latter passed through the Sikh camp at Subraon a week before the battle.

The deputation of General Ram Singh to Nabha was explained as being a visit to his native country, where he desired to fix his home, being disgusted with the Lahore service; that he only paid one complimentary visit to the Raja, presenting his *nazr*, and returning at once to Lahore.[1]

The supplies collected.

Supplies, it was asserted, had been collected as speedily as possible, and the Nabha contingent placed entirely at the service of the English, so that the Raja was compelled to raise fresh troops to provide for the protection of his territory. It is indeed true that a contingent of Nabha troops was present at Mudki and Firushahr, but not a man fought on the side of the English in those or the subsequent actions.

The excuse for not having visited the British Camp.

The excuse for disregarding the direction of Major Broadfoot to join the camp was, that the Raja, on his way to the army headquarters, had reached Maler Kotla, when he heard of the death of Major Broadfoot; that he then returned to Nabha; and the death of the Maharaja of Pattiala happening at the same time, his duties as the head of the Phulkian family compelled him to visit Pattiala and attend the funeral ceremonies. The roads, the Raja moreover stated, were unsafe for travelling.

The truth, however, appeared to be that only the road

[1] The character of General Ram Singh Jallawalia was well known. He was high in favour at Lahore, and whatever his visit to Nabha may have signified, he certainly crossed the Satlej with the object of sounding the protected Chiefs, and discovering how far Lahore might count on their assistance. The information which induced Major Broadfoot to issue the order to the Nabha Chief to attend his camp, was given by a native of position, who had considerable opportunities of knowing the truth, and was, true or false, in considerable detail. He stated that Jowahir Singh of Lahore sent General Ram Singh to Raja Devindar Singh, and that they were closeted together for several hours. Afterwards Munshi Sahib Singh was admitted, and the following plan of operations agreed upon :—They estimated that Nabha, Ladwa, and other disaffected Chiefs in the Cis-Satlej States, could raise 60,000 fighting men, who were to be employed, while the Sikh army was engaged with the British, in intercepting the communications of the latter, plundering baggage, and cutting off their supplies. All this having been arranged, General Ram Singh returned to Lahore. This story was very possibly true, but the decision against the Raja was not influenced by it, but by his own acts and omissions only.

The real truth of the matter.

which led to the British camp was, to the Raja, unsafe. The danger was purely imaginary, the road being covered with hackeries and unarmed camp-followers, and the Raja would have had with him a force amply sufficient to protect him had any danger existed. A mere comparison of dates will be sufficient to show the unwillingness of the Raja to attend the summons to the British camp. Major Broadfoot's order was given on the 15th of December, and might easily have been complied with in forty-eight hours. The Maharaja of Pattiala died on the 23d of December, and it was only necessary, for compliance with Sikh etiquette, that the Raja should attend any time within seventeen days from the death, to pay a visit of condolence to the family, and this too was a mere matter of ceremony, immaterial in comparison with the necessity of proving his devotion and loyalty to the Government. It was moreover necessary for him to be present at the cremation. As Pattiala is only eighteen miles from Nabha, one day was amply sufficient for this visit. But the Raja went three times to Pattiala, remaining there seventeen days—from the 24th to the 27th of December, from the 4th to the 17th of January, and from the 16th to the 24th of January—plainly proving that his object was merely to manufacture an excuse to absent himself from the British camp, which, even after this, he never visited at all.

The Raja was beyond doubt altogether hostile to the English.

After a consideration of the evidence against the Raja, and the explanation urged in his defence, no reasonable doubt can be entertained that he had intrigued with the Court of Lahore previous to the war; that he was thoroughly disaffected, though too timid to actually join the enemy as the Raja of Ladwa had done; that he made no effort to supply carriage or food for the troops; that he disregarded the most direct orders to attend the army in person; that he waited till the very last, after the battles of Firushahr, Mudki, and Aliwal, in the hope that the last battle on the Satlej would be a defeat for the English, in which case he would, without hesitation, have declared against them.[1]

Raja Devindar Singh deposed, and one quarter of the Nabha territory confiscated.

The Government of India came to the same conclusion with regard to the conduct of the Raja of Nabha as the officer who had investigated the case. Raja Devindar Singh was ordered to be deposed, and his eldest son, then a boy of seven, to be placed on the throne under the guardianship of his step-grandmother, Rani Chand Kour, aided by three of the most respectable officers of the Nabha State. These four persons were to be responsible to the British Government for the education and safety of the young Raja; all transit duties, estimated at Rs. 12,200 per annum—the customs of the town of Nabha, amounting to Rs. 4500—excluded, were abolished. One-fourth of the Nabha territory, the districts of Pakowal, Dehraru, and Rori, less a portion worth Rs. 12,200, was confiscated, and territory valued at Rs. 28,766 a year was to be retained by the British Government in lieu of a contingent of 100 horse and 133 foot. The remainder, being lands worth Rs. 71,224, was to be divided equally

[1] The correspondence regarding the conduct of the Raja of Nabha during the war is very voluminous. The documents on which this account is founded are, chiefly: the defence of the Raja prepared by his Diwan, Kahn Chand, and submitted to the Agent Governor-General, 21st April 1846; the original letters, parwanas, and kharitas sent to the Raja and his agents by Mr Currie, Mr R. Cust, Major Broadfood, Major Mackeson, and Major Lawrence, with the replies, and abstract of supplies furnished; the report of Mr R. Cust to the Superintendent Cis-Satlej States, dated 7th March 1846; the reports of Major Mackeson, C.B., to Agent Governor-General, dated 17th and 27th July; the report of Captain Mills, Assistant Agent to Governor-General, to Major Mackeson, dated 1st February 1846; and the final report and recommendation of Major H. Lawrence, dated 18th September 1846.

between the Maharaja of Pattiala and the Raja of Faridkot, in reward for services performed during the war. A pension of Rs. 50,000 was allowed to Raja Devindar Singh for life from the revenues of Nabha, on condition of his residing peacefully at any British station south of Dehli or Mehrut.[1]

The Ex-Raja retires to Mathra.

The Ex-Raja selected Mathra for his residence, where he remained till 1854. But his misfortunes had taught him nothing, even supposing him intellectually capable of profiting by any experience whatever. He gave as much trouble as he could, not only to the English authorities, but to his own family at Nabha, to which he bore an unnatural hatred. Notwithstanding his splendid allowance, he fell deeply into debt, and was supposed to sign bonds in the hope that the Nabha Government would be compelled to pay. At Mathra there were many unscrupulous persons who encouraged him in this reckless course, advancing money at exorbitant rates of interest on such security.

His conduct there, and his removal to Lahore.

His behaviour, at length, became so outrageous, that the authorities of the North-Western Provinces considered that he should be either placed under restraint or removed to some other locality where a more complete watch could be maintained over him; and the Supreme Government, in January 1855, sanctioned his removal to any place not in the neighbourhood of Nabha, where the Magistrate would be able to control, in some measure, his extravagances.[2]

[1] Secretary to Government of India to Agent Governor-General, No. 459, dated 17th November 1846, and Agent Governor-General to Secretary to Government, 18th September 1846.

[2] Commissioner Cis-Satlej States to Government Punjab, Nos. 231 and 281, dated 9th October and 2d December 1854. Commissioner Agra to Commissioner Ambala, No. 724, dated 6th November, with enclosures. Government Punjab to Government of India, No. 1061, dated 13th December 1854. Government of India to Government Punjab, No. 440, dated 26th January 1855.

Thanesar had been suggested as the new residence of Devindar Singh, but the Government considered this place unsuitable, as it was not more than 60 miles from Nabha, whither the Ex-Raja might, without difficulty, find his way, and where his appearance would be the signal for disturbance. Even should he fail in exciting disorder, he would probably be able to form a party at Nabha, and carry on intrigues dangerous to the administration of the State. Jalandhar or Hoshiarpur were then suggested for his residence, but it was finally determined to remove him to Lahore, where he arrived on the 8th December 1855, the palace of Maharaja Kharrak Singh being assigned to him.[1]

Death of Devindar Singh, A.D. 1865.

Raja Devindar Singh died at Lahore in November 1865. He had married four wives: first, the daughter of Raja Ram Singh of Balabgarh; then Man Kour, the daughter of Sirdar Wazir Singh of Rangar-Nangal in the Amritsar district; his third wife was the daughter of Sirdar Gulab Singh Mansaia; and the fourth, daughter of Sirdar Kharrak Singh Dhallon. Rani Man Kour was the mother of two sons, Bharpur Singh and Bhagwan Singh, who became successively Rajas of Nabha. The elder of these was born in 1840, and the second two years later.

The arrangements for carrying on the administration at Nabha.

Major Mackeson, Commissioner of the Cis-Satlej States, visited Nabha in January 1847, to install the new Chief, Bharpur Singh, then an intelligent boy, seven years of age. His step-grandmother, Rani Chand Kour, the sur-

[1] Government North-Western Provinces, No. 293, dated 28th March, with enclosures, to Government Punjab. Commissioner Cis-Satlej States to Government Punjab, No. 195, dated 28th August. Government Punjab to Government of India, No. 206, dated 10th March. Government of India to Government Punjab, No. 1450, dated 20th April 1855. Commissioner Lahore, No. 66, dated 25th April 1857, to Government Punjab.

viving widow of Raja Jaswant Singh, and a lady of great ability, was appointed his guardian, and three of the oldest servants of the Nabha State—Sirdar Gurbaksh Singh, Fatah Singh, and Behali Mal—were selected to form the Council of Regency.[1] Gurbaksh Singh, who was appointed to the duty of superintending the education of the young Prince, had been in the service of Raja Devindar Singh, but, previous to the war, had been banished to Thanesar by his eccentric master. He was in exile when Colonel Mackeson called him to Nabha to assume the presidency of the Council.

Sirdar Gurbaksh Singh President of the Council of Regency.

Munshi Sahib Singh.

Munshi Sahib Singh had been the minister of Devindar Singh at the time of the Cis-Satlej war, and is understood to have advised the Chief to evade compliance with the demands of the British authorities, and wait the progress of events before declaring to which side he would adhere. Major Mackeson excluded him from all interference with the administration of the Nabha State; but he was a favourite with Rani Chand Kour, and in a few years recovered much of his influence in Nabha, and laboured to overthrow his rival Sirdar Gurbaksh Singh. In this attempt, through the haste of the Prime Minister to get rich, he entirely succeeded, and, on complaints being preferred against Gurbaksh Singh in 1857, an investigation was directed by the Chief Commissioner, the result of which was that the Minister was proved to have abused his position to enrich himself, and to have filled all offices of importance with members of his own family. He was dismissed from office, his jagirs were resumed, and both he and his family were prohibited from re-employment in

Rani Chand Kour.

The disgrace of Gurbaksh Singh, and the rise of his rival.

[1] Agent Governor-General to Government of India, No. 184, dated 18th September 1846; and No. 210, dated 17th December 1846, to Major Mackeson.

the Nabha State. Munshi Sahib Singh, then, without any special authorisation from Government, succeeded the exiled Minister as President of the Council.[1]

The case of the village of Bhai Rupa, shared by all the Phulkian Chiefs.

The most important case which occurred during the minority of Raja Bharpur Singh related to the village of Bhai Rupa. It will be remembered that this village was held in shares by the Chiefs of Pattiala, Nabha, Jhind, Bhadour, and Malod, and afforded a fair presumption that these families were originally independent of each other.[2] It is by no means easy to determine the early history of the village, but there is no doubt that the site was first selected by Bhai Rup Chand, the *Guru*, or spiritual adviser, of Tilokha and Rama, the sons of Phul, and that he obtained their permission to found a village. He died, however, before carrying out his project, and some time later, his grandson, Bhai Dhanna Singh, built the village on the selected spot, calling it Bhai Rupa, after the name of the Guru.

The land occupied by the village was taken from the adjacent lands of Phul and Kangar, that taken from the former being allowed to the Bhaikians or descendants of Bhai Rupa, rent free, they making their collections from the zamindars without interference from the Phul Chaudhris. In the Kangar division of the village, the Bhaikians had a smaller share, but, after the death of Rai Bakhtyar, who managed the collections of this patti or share, the Bhaikians obtained more land, for which they paid a small acknowledgment to the Miani Jats, owners of Kangar. Subsequently the village of Kangar came into the possession of Nabha, the tribute to the

[1] Government Punjab to Commissioner Cis-Satlej States, No. 293, dated 28th March, Nos. 412 and 427, dated 27th April and 1st May 1857. Commissioner Cis-Satlej States, No. 88, dated 17th April 1857.

[2] *Vide ante*, p. 263.

Mianis ceased to be paid, and, in 1805, the Raja of Nabha took the administration of the Kangar patti of Bhai Rupa into his own hands. After the death of Tilokha and Rama, the Phulkian patti was held in equal shares by Gurditta, Sukhchen, Ala Singh, Man Singh, and Chuhr Singh, the ancestors of the houses of Nabha, Jhind, Pattiala, Malod, and Bhadour. The police management remained with Nabha, as Bhai Rupa was adjacent to that State. This arrangement was for mutual convenience; and although, in 1841, the other sharers denied the right, Nabha had always exercised police control. This village and the rights therein belonging to the several Chiefs was a fruitful cause of dispute, and gave the greatest trouble to the political officers. Each State considered it a point of honour to maintain its position in the village, supporting its claims by any means, however unscrupulous; and it was not till 1851 that the disputes were finally adjusted, and the boundaries fixed.[1]

The Mutiny of 1857.

Raja Bharpur Singh attained his majority a few months after the breaking out of the mutiny of 1857. At this critical time he acted with the utmost loyalty and intelligence, and his services were as distinguished as those of the other Phulkian Chiefs.

The conduct and services of Raja Bharpur Singh.

At the commencement of the mutiny the Raja was directed to hold himself in readiness for service, and, on the 17th of May, was placed in charge of the important station of Ludhiana, which he occupied with 350 horse, 450 foot, and 2 guns, remaining there for six months,

[1] Voluminous vernacular records of 1834, 1841, 1844. W. Wynyard, Esq., to Commissioner Cis-Satlej States, No. 420, dated 9th September 1848, enclosing report of R. H. Greathed, Esq., of the 6th September. H. Davidson, Esq., Settlement officer, to Commissioner Cis-Satlej States, No. 344, dated 7th November 1851.

and, during his occasional absences, leaving his brother in command. He furnished an escort of 300 men for the siege train ordered from Philor to accompany the Commander-in-Chief to Dehli. The Nusseri battalion had been appointed for this duty, but they refused to march, and Nabha troops were alone available for the duty. When the Jalandhar mutineers reached Philor, the Deputy Commissioner took a detachment of 150 Nabha troops, and, destroying the bridge, opposed the passage of the enemy. The troops behaved well, a great number of the mutineers were killed, and several of the Nabha men were killed and wounded.

Raja Bharpur Singh was anxious himself to march to Dehli at the head of his troops, as the Raja of Jhind had done. This was not allowed. He was very young, and such service was more onerous than could be fairly asked from him. A detachment, however, of his force, about 300 in number, did good service at Dehli under Sirdar Didar Singh throughout the siege.

In addition to this, the Raja enlisted many hundred new troops, he furnished supplies and carriage, arrested mutineers marching through his State, and performed every service required of him with the utmost loyalty and good-will. At a time when money was urgently wanted, he advanced to Government a loan of two and a half lakhs of rupees.[1]

The Commissioner of the Cis-Satlej States, after the disturbances were over, recommended that the following rewards should be conferred upon the Raja:— *The rewards recommended for his services.*

(1.) A grant of territory taken from the Ludhiana or Firozpur districts and not exceeding in value Rs. 30,000

[1] Commissioner Cis-Satlej States, No. 69, dated 4th March 1858, with statement of services of the Raja of Nabha.

per annum, to be given to him and his male heirs in perpetuity.

(2.) That his khillat from the Governor-General should be increased from seven pieces to fifteen, to place him on the same footing as the Raja of Jhind.

(3.) That he should be received with a salute of nine guns on visiting any of the large military stations, or at the Durbar of the Governor-General.

(4.) That his visit to the Governor-General should be returned by the Foreign Secretary.

Those granted him by the Goverument.

The Government, however, on further consideration, bestowed upon Raja Bharpur Singh rewards far more valuable than those originally proposed. The divisions of Bawal and Kanti, in the confiscated Jhajjar territory, were made over to him, worth Rs. 1,06,000 per annum, on condition of good behaviour and service, military and political, in times of general danger and disturbance. His khillat was increased from seven to fifteen pieces, a salute of eleven guns was granted him, his visit to the Governor-General was directed to be returned by the Foreign Secretary, and his honorary titles were increased.[1]

The right of adoption and capital punishment conferred.

In addition to these honours, there were conferred upon him those privileges which he, in common with his kinsmen of Pattiala and Jhind, had asked from Government in their Paper of Requests in 1858—the power of life and death, the right of adoption, and the promise of non-interference of the British Government in the domestic affairs of the family and the internal management of the State.[2]

1 Government Punjab to Government of India, No. 135, of 12th March, and 202, of 13th April 1858. Government of India to Government Punjab, No. 1549 A, dated 2d June, and to Raja of Nabha of the same date.

2 Paper of Requests submitted by the three Phulkian Chiefs. For details, *vide* Pattiala History. Commissioner Cis-Satlej States to Government

A Sanad was granted to Raja Bharpur Singh, in May 1860, confirming to him his estates, ancestral and acquired, and conferring independent powers and privileges, similar to those granted to the Chiefs of Pattiala and Jhind. The right of adoption, which had been so earnestly desired by all these Chiefs, was included in this Sanad.[1] The Sanad of 1860.

On the 18th of January 1860, Lord Canning, Viceroy The Durbar of 1860

Punjab, No. 149, dated 20th May 1858. Government Punjab to Government of India, No. 104, dated 16th June. Government of India to Government Punjab, No. 3047, dated 25th May 1859. Secretary of State to Government of India, No. 64, dated 1st December 1859.

[1] Translation of the Sanad given to the Raja of Nabha by His Excellency the Viceroy and Governor-General :—

SIMLA, *5th May* 1860.

Since the establishment of British supremacy in India, the present Raja of Nabha and his ancestor, Raja Jaswant Singh, have given various proofs of their loyalty to the British Government. More recently, the present Chief of Nabha has surpassed the former achievements of his race, by the constancy and courage he evinced during the mutiny of 1857-58. In memory of this unswerving and conspicuous loyalty, His Excellency the Viceroy and Governor-General of India has conferred additional honours and territory upon the Raja for himself and his heirs for ever, and has graciously acceded to the Raja's desire to receive a Sanad or grant under the hand and seal of the Viceroy, guaranteeing to the Raja the free and unreserved possession of his ancestral territories, as well as of those tracts bestowed on the Raja by the British Government.

Clause 1.—The Raja and his heirs for ever will exercise full sovereignty over his ancestral and acquired dominions, according to the annexed list. All the rights, privileges, and prerogatives which the Raja enjoys in his hereditary territories, he will equally enjoy in his acquired territories. All feudatories and dependants of every degree will be bound to render obedience to him throughout his dominions.

Clause 2.—Except as provided in Clause 3, the British Government will never demand from the Raja, or any of his successors, or from any of his feudatories, relations, or dependants, any tribute on account of revenue, service, or any other plea.

Clause 3.—The British Government cordially desire to see the noble house of Nabha perpetuated, and in this spirit confers upon the Raja and his heirs for ever, whenever male issue may fail, the right of adopting a successor from among the descendants of the Phulkian family. If, however, at any time the Raja of Nabha should die without male issue, and without adopting a successor, it will still be open to the Maharaja of Pattiala and the Raja of Jhind, in concert with the Commissioner or Political

and Governor-General, held a Durbar at Ambala, at which all the Cis-Satlej Chiefs were present, and addressed the Raja of Nabha in the following terms :—

The Viceroy's address to the Raja.

" Raja of Nabha—

" You have been equally forward and equally earnest, with other Chiefs of your ancient race, in your support of the authority of the British Government.

" The assistance which you gave to the Queen's army in the transport of its heavy artillery from the Satlej to Dehli was a signal and valuable service.

" Your loyalty and zeal have, as in the case of your

Agent of the British Government, to select a successor from among the Phulkian family; but in that case a nazarana or fine equal to one-third of the gross annual revenue of the Nabha State shall be paid to the British Government.

Clause 4.—In 1847 the British Government empowered the Raja to inflict capital punishment after reference to the Commissioner. It now removes the restriction imposed by this reference, and invests the Raja with absolute power of life and death over his own subjects. With regard to British subjects committing crime, and apprehended in his territory, the Raja will be guided by the rules contained in the Despatch of the Honourable Court of Directors, to the Madras Government, No. 3, dated 1st June 1836. The Raja will exert himself to execute justice, and to promote the happiness and welfare of his people. He engages to prohibit suttee, slavery, and female infanticide throughout his territories, and to punish with the utmost rigour those who are found guilty of any of these crimes.

Clause 5.—The Raja will never fail in his loyalty and devotion to the Sovereign of Great Britain.

Clause 6.—If any force hostile to the British Government should appear in this neighbourhood, the Raja will co-operate with the British Government and oppose the enemy. He will exert himself to the utmost of his resources in providing carriage and supplies for the British troops, according to requisitions he may receive.

Clause 7.—The British Government will not receive any complaints from any of the subjects of the Raja, whether maafidars, jagirdars, relatives, dependants, servants, or other classes.

Clause 8.—The British Government will respect the household and family arrangements of the Raja, and abstain from any interference therein.

Clause 9.—The Raja, as heretofore, will furnish, at current rates, through the agency of his own officers, the necessary materials required for the construction of railroads, railway stations, and imperial roads and bridges. He will also freely give the land required for the construction of railroads and imperial lines of road.

Clause 10.—The Raja and his successors, &c., will always pursue the same

fellow Chiefs, been marked by rewards and honour, which will assure you of the high esteem in which your conduct is held by the Government.

"Additions have been made to your possessions, and the grant will be formally confirmed to yourself and your descendants. If these should fail you, your adoption of an heir from amongst the members of the Phulkian house will be gladly recognised.

"It is the desire of the Queen's Government that the power and dignity of your loyal family should endure and flourish."[1]

course of fidelity and devotion to the British Government, and the Government will always be ready to uphold the honour and dignity of the Raja and his house.

SCHEDULE OF THE TERRITORIES BELONGING TO THE RAJA OF NABHA.

Ancestral Possessions.

Pargannah Nabha Khas.
" Umloh.
" Bhadsun.
" Kapurgurh.
" Dhunowla.
" Phool, with Dyalpoora.
" Jeylokee.
" Sotbuddee.

Share of Bhai Rupa, with right of jurisdiction, and right over all subordinate rent-freeholders residing therein.

Acquired Possessions.

Pargannah Kantee, } By letter from Secretary, Government of India,
" Bawal, } dated 2d June 1858, No. 1549 A.

Feudatories and Tributaries.

The Sikhs of Sonthee.
The Sikhs of Ram Dass Boongguranwalla.
Sodh Kurreea Goomteewalla.

[1] Government notification, No. 122 A, dated Ambala, 20th January 1860. A Sanad of adoption was granted, conferring the right supplementary to the general Sanad of 1860.

"To Furzund Arujmund Ekeedut Pyebund Dowlut-i-Englisha Burarbinus Surmour Raja Bhurpore Singh Mohender Bahadoor of Nabha :—

"*Dated* 5*th March* 1862.

"Her Majesty being desirous that the Governments of the several Princes and Chiefs of India who now govern their own territories should be perpetuated, and that the representation and dignity of their houses should be continued, I hereby, in fulfilment of this desire, repeat to you the assur-

His expression of thanks to Her Majesty the Queen.

The rewards and honours bestowed upon the young Raja of Nabha were well deserved. His loyalty was hearty and genuine, and his gratitude for the generous recognition of his services by the British Government was sincere. At this time he forwarded an address to Her Majesty the Queen, a translation of which may be recorded here as a specimen of oriental complimentary composition.

"To the sublime presence—brilliant with grace and light—the fountain of munificence and honour—Lord of the Universe—famous as Alexander—puissant as Jamsher—the Queen of England (may her Empire endure for ever),

"Your lowly petitioner, Bharpur Singh, placing the sign of humility on the forehead of submission, and bending his head in dutiful obeisance, ventures to present this humble address.

"At a joyful time when the hearts of men were refreshed and gladdened by the mercy of God, and like a meadow were made green and succulent by the bounteous rain of heaven, the key that unfolds the desired treasure of your tributaries arrived in the charge of your

ance which I communicated to you in the Sanad under my signature, dated 5th May 1860, that on failure of natural heirs, your adoption of an heir from amongst the members of the Phulkian house will be gladly recognised and confirmed ; and if at any time the Raja of Nabha should die without male issue, and without adopting a successor, it will still be open to the Maharaja of Pattiala and the Raja of Jhind, in concert with the Commissioner or Political Agent of the British Government, to select a successor from among the Phulkian family ; but in that case a nazarana or fine equal to one-third of the gross annual revenue of the Nabha State shall be paid to the British Government.

"Be assured that nothing shall disturb the engagement thus made to you so long as your house is loyal to the Crown and faithful to the conditions of the treaties, grants, or engagements which record its obligations to the British Government.

(Signed) "CANNING."

Majesty's gracious Proclamation, accompanied by a letter from his Excellency, lofty in rank, pure in spirit, the Right Honourable the Governor-General, and spread a grateful shade over your petitioner. Your servant was overwhelmed with the mighty honour this missive conferred, and his heart was overjoyed at the pearls of grace which every sentence disclosed, and especially with your Majesty's gracious assurances to the Princes and Chiefs of India, that your Majesty would secure the foundations of their power, and confirm all treaties and obligations made by the Honourable East India Company, and also respect, with generous magnanimity, the rights, privileges, and ancient customs of the natives of this country. Your petitioner, and his ancestors before him, have always been steady in their loyalty to a Government whose fame is as wide as the heavens above.

"In commemoration of the happy news, your servant, to show his boundless joy, convened a special Durbar, and having collected all the ministers and servants of the State, as well as the rich and poor, he announced the gracious terms of the proclamation to all present in an audible voice; constellations of fireworks were let off, the streets of the city were illuminated, and your servant's people were intoxicated with happiness and joy. How great is the goodness of God, and how great is the favour of your Majesty; such was the thought and exclamation of every one at the Durbar, who, on hearing the gracious words of the proclamation, broke forth in praises of the Almighty and of His servant the Queen. As God in His wrath had afflicted the people of this country and crushed them in the press of calamity by raising up rebels and traitors, so now, by means of your Majesty's gracious clemency, He has restored them to peace and favour.

The whole population unites its voice in one hymn of thanksgiving. Among the foremost in gratitude are the Princes of India. Your petitioner has always clung to the skirts of your Majesty's protection, and is well assured that his interests will improve as the fortune and wealth of the British Empire advance. With these reflections your servant blows the trumpet of congratulation on your Majesty's accession with a loud and cheerful blast. If every hair of his body was turned into a tongue, he could never finish the peal of praise at your Majesty's fixed intention to uphold ancient treaties. Your petitioner's ancestors placed themselves under British protection in 1808, and from that time they have never swerved from their loyalty, and have found their reward in ever-increasing treasures of honour and favour. Their fidelity to the State has been proved and confirmed by the letters of Lord Lake and other eminent English officers. Your petitioner will follow reverently in their steps, being assured that his prosperity, both present and future, is inseparably bound up with that of the British Empire. Finally, may God Almighty destroy your Majesty's enemies, as the sun rising with the day drives beasts of prey to their noisome dens; and may the Star of your Empire be always in the ascendant, diffusing light over the world, the symbol of victory."[1]

The Nabha loan paid off by a grant of confiscated territory.

It will be remembered that the Raja of Nabha had, at the commencement of the mutinies, given a loan of two and a half lakhs of rupees to the Government. In addition to this there remained due to Nabha seven

[1] This letter was answered by the Secretary of State by command of Her Majesty, 30th September 1859. The Maharaja of Pattiala and the Raja of Jhind, who had also addressed Her Majesty, received, at the same time, most gracious replies.

lakhs, from the 5 per cent. loan of 1848, making a total of nine and a half lakhs. When Raja Bharpur Singh and the Maharaja of Pattiala understood that the British Government was not anxious to retain the pargannahs of Kanoudh and Budwanah, forming part of the confiscated territory of Jhajjar, they applied for it to be given to them, at twenty years' purchase, proportional to the amount of their respective loans. The proposal was agreed to, and Kanoudh villages, worth about Rs. 48,000 per annum, were given to the Raja of Nabha on the same terms as the ancestral and acquired lands had been confirmed to him a short time before.[1]

Twenty years' purchase of these villages amounted to about Rs. 10,000 in excess of what was due to the Raja,

[1] Translation of a Sanad or Grant of portions of the Pargannahs of Kanoudh and Budwanah, District Jhajjar, bestowed on the Raja of Nabha by His Excellency Earl Canning, G.C.B., Viceroy and Governor-General of India :—

Preamble.—Whereas the devotion and loyalty of the Raja of Nabha, and of his ancestor, Raja Jaswant Singh, have always been conspicuous since the establishment of British supremacy in India, His Excellency the Viceroy and Governor-General being desirous of marking his high appreciation of these qualities, has been pleased to bestow upon the Raja portions of pargannahs Kanoudh and Budwanah, of the district of Jhajjar, containing forty-two (42) villages, according to a vernacular list annexed, assessed at a yearly revenue of forty-seven thousand five hundred and twenty-five rupees (Rs. 47,525), and to accept from the Raja a nazarana of nine lakhs fifty thousand and five hundred rupees (Rs. 9,50,500). It is accordingly ordained as follows :—

Article 1.—The territories above-mentioned are conferred upon the Raja of Nabha and his heirs for ever.

Article 2.—The Raja and his successors will exercise the same rights, privileges, and prerogatives in these newly-acquired territories as he at present enjoys in his ancestral possessions, according to the terms of the Sanad dated 5th May 1860, and signed by His Excellency Earl Canning, Viceroy and Governor-General of India.

Article 3.—The Raja and his successors will continue to maintain the same loyal relations with the British Government, and to fulfil the same obligations with regard to this newly-acquired territory, as were imposed on him by the terms of the Sanad dated 5th May 1860, relating to the Raja's ancestral possessions.

but the surplus was deducted from the interest still due to him.[1]

Reforms inaugurated by Raja Bharpur Singh.

Raja Bharpur Singh, on obtaining his majority, evinced great earnestness in improving the character of his administration. Early in 1859 the Agent of the Lieutenant-Governor had made an investigation, which resulted in the dismissal of some of his Ministers. This beginning the Raja followed up by many reforms, undertaken at the suggestion of the Maharaja of Pattiala or the Commissioner of Ambala. It had been the policy of the Raja's advisers to estrange him from the Maharaja of Pattiala, who, being a Prince of ability and related to Nabha by blood, would be likely to give him good advice and discourage their intrigues; but Bharpur Singh was intelligent enough to perceive that his interest was bound up with that of the Maharaja, and he maintained a friendship with him only terminated by death.[2]

His character, intelligence, and acquirements.

The evils which result from minorities in Native States have been noticed in the history of the Jhind State.[3] Raja Bharpur Singh was a remarkable exception to what is unfortunately a very general rule. The excellence of his disposition and his natural intelligence were such as to enable him to resist the deteriorating influences which surrounded him, and he gave promise of being one of the most liberal Princes in Northern India. A taste for learning is rare among the Sikhs, but the Raja was of a

[1] Commissioner Cis-Satlej States to Government Punjab, No. 87, dated 23d May 1860.

Government Punjab to Commissioner, Nos. 806, 947, dated 2d July and 2d August. Government of India to Government Punjab, No. 1977, dated 14th June 1860. Commissioner Cis-Satlej States to Government Punjab, No. 187, dated 22d September 1860.

[2] Commissioner Cis-Satlej States to Government Punjab, No. 92, dated 24th March 1859. Government Punjab to Commissioner Cis-Satlej States, No. 366, dated 2d April 1859.

[3] *Vide ante*, p. 328.

studious disposition. He had thoroughly mastered the Indian vernaculars, and studied English three or four hours a day, whenever the duties connected with the administration of his State allowed him leisure. The work of all departments he supervised himself, and a private memorandum, drawn up in English and containing rules for the disposition of his time, was a very remarkable document, showing how earnestly he was resolved to neglect no opportunity for self-improvement, and to govern for the good of his people. It concluded with these words :—

The rules draw up for the disposition of his time.

"In conclusion, I invoke a blessing from the Almighty, and from the Durbar Sri Suth Gurdial, to preserve me steadfast in the discharge of these my duties, and to enable me so to pass my life, that, under the Almighty's shadow and protection, I may live to His glory, and be a blessing to others."

In September 1863, Lord Elgin, the Viceroy, offered Raja Bharpur Singh a seat in the Legislative Council, the honour of the Star of India having been assigned to the Raja of Jhind. This honour was gratefully accepted by Bharpur Singh, who looked forward with great pleasure to his visit to Calcutta in the following January. But the Raja was destined never to take his seat in Council.

Nominated a member of the Legislative Council by Lord Elgin.

From June 1863, he had suffered severely from fever. His illness was, in the first instance, brought on by fatigue and excitement at an entertainment, given by his aunt, Sirdarni Mehtab Kour, widow of Sirdar Arjan Singh, Rangar-Nangal, on the occasion of the marriage of her son, Attar Singh. This entertainment took place on the 23d of June, and the Raja, after his return, was attacked with fever, which he was unable to shake off

His illness.

for nearly two months, when his physician, knowing his inveterate dislike to quinine, contrived to conceal this medicine in pills, and administer it to his patient, who became entirely convalescent, and took the bath of health, in accordance with Hindu custom. That same day the Raja's illness returned more severely than ever. He had taken unusual exercise on the day in question, had walked to the Gurdhwara, four hundred yards distant, and from his house to the top of the castle, a building of great height, and had changed his sleeping apartment, of the heat of which he complained. At night the fever returned, and never again left him. From a remittent character with ague, it became continual and acute. The great natural delicacy of his constitution and his nervous temperament increased the difficulty of treatment, and his illness became a rapid decline, from which he died on the 9th of November.[1]

Recovers temporarily, but the illness returns, and ends in rapid decline.

His death.

The heir to the Nabha throne.

Raja Bharpur Singh left no son, and it was for the other Phulkian Rajas, in concert with the Political Agent of Ambala, to select a successor from among the members of the Phulkian family, in accordance with the terms of the Sanads of 1860 and 1862.

A *nazrana* was due from the State, no successor having been adopted.

These documents provided that should the Chief die without male issue, and without adopting a successor, a fine, or *nazrana*, of one-third of the gross annual revenue of the State should be levied on the next succession. The Phulkian Chiefs desired to save Nabha from the payment of this fine, and the Maharaja of Pattiala and the Raja of Jhind, on being addressed by the Political

[1] Agent to Lieutenant-Governor Cis-Satlej States, No. A, dated 10th November 1863, to Government Punjab. Government Punjab to Agent, No. 820, dated 23d November 1863. Depositions taken at Nabha of Ghulam Murtaza, physician to the Maharaja of Pattiala, and Muhammad Baksh, physician to the Raja of Nabha.

Agent, Sir Herbert Edwardes, on the subject of the succession, wrote replies precisely similar in character, to the effect that the proper heir was Prince Bhagwan Singh, the younger brother of the late Raja; that it was well known that Raja Bharpur Singh, having no children, had always recognised his brother as his heir, and had always treated him with the greatest confidence and affection; that on the night of the Raja's death, according to the statement of the Nabha officials, he sent for his brother, and, in full possession of his senses, confirmed the Prince as his successor, exhorted him to follow his example of loyalty to the British Government, to carry on the administration of the State for the good of the people, and to heed the counsels of the trusted officials, whom, moreover, he commanded to obey and serve his brother as they had served him.

The other Phulkian Rajas tried to assert that there was an adoption,

This confirmation the Phulkian Rajas stated they considered as proof that Bhagwan Singh had been regularly adopted; that the intention of the Raja, previous to his illness, that his brother should succeed him, was acknowledged; and that, under the circumstances, it would be in accordance with the dignity of the British Government to consider the Prince as the regularly adopted successor, and to waive the right to the fine conferred by the third clause of the treaty of 1860.

Of a sufficiently formal character to excuse the payment of the stipulated *nazrana*.

The request of the Chiefs, though prompted by kindly feeling towards Nabha, and possibly by a hope that their good offices would be, at some future time, returned under similar circumstances, was nevertheless absurd. The British Government had yielded everything to the Phulkian Chiefs except the right, as paramount and sovereign, to a fine in case of death without heirs or without adopting a successor. No Government in the

The request to excuse the *nazrana* was irrational.

world has ever been so generous before to its feudatories; but the concessions granted only induced the Chiefs to endeavour to evade compliance with the only condition by which they were still bound.

Prince Bhagwan Singh had never been acknowledged as successor previous to the Raja's illness.

The story of the acknowledgment of the Prince, previous to the Raja's last illness, was a pleasing fiction. Raja Bharpur Singh was a very young man, and there was every reason to hope that he would have children of his own to succeed him; at any rate, the adoption or acknowledgment of his brother as heir had never been notified to the Political Agent or to Government, and, consequently, had not received such confirmation and recognition on the part of the British Government as, under the terms of the Sanad of the 5th of March 1862, were necessary to its validity.[1]

The story of the confirmation on the Raja's death-bed was an invention.

The story of the death-bed scene, the confirmation of the succession to his brother, and the commitment of the officials and the State to his care, was a pure fiction, invented by the Nabha officials to save their State from payment of the fine. The Prince was present certainly for a short time while his brother was dying, but no conversation whatever passed between them, nor was a word spoken to the officials regarding the succession.[2]

[1] Letters of the Maharaja of Pattiala and Raja of Jhind to Sir Herbert Edwardes, dated 12th December 1863. Commissioner Cis-Satlej States to Government Punjab, No. 309, dated 16th December 1863. Government Punjab to Government of India, No. 478, dated 19th December 1863.

[2] There was no means of proving this statement false at the time; but the following year an investigation was conducted at Nabha regarding the death of Raja Bharpur Singh. The depositions of every one connected with the Court, of opposite parties, were taken, but there is no mention whatever of the circumstances detailed in the letters of the Maharaja and Raja of Jhind, although every word spoken and the minutest details connected with the Raja's death were all scrupulously recorded. The following are extracts from the depositions bearing on the only interview the Prince had with his brother on the night of his death:—

Sirdar Gurbaksh Singh, Prime Minister.—"All time the Raja complained

In the opinion of the Phulkian Rajas that Prince Bhagwan Singh should succeed his brother, the Government entirely concurred. But they rejected altogether the assumption that the nomination of Bhagwan Singh as heir was in any sense an adoption, and the claim to exemption from payment of *nazrana*, as one of right, consequent on that alleged adoption. The construction

The Government allow Bhagwan Singh's claim, but deny his adoption.

of no pain, but complained of being very dry in the throat. I thought it necessary to have him removed to the lower story. He was carried down, and offered an elephant and other offerings. Raja Bhagwan Singh and Behali Mal, Munshi Narayan Singh and Mahammad Hussain Khan, then came on being summoned. I saw no one else. No one expected the event. It was at night, and only a few could attend. The Mai Sahiba, his mother, then asked to come. At first he objected, as she would weep and distress him; but she came at last, and every one went out and left them alone. The Mai Sahiba remained with her son about half an hour. The present Raja was not present at the interview; he was in another room. Bhagwan Singh had no private interview with his brother before the latter's death; but he was with us. *The brothers did not speak to each other. When told the Kour Sahib (Bhagwan Singh) was there, he said, 'Well, let him comfort himself' (tasalli rakha), and the Bhagwan Singh was crying or shedding tears.* After this nothing more passed, and the Raja soon became insensible."

Jiun Singh, Nafar or House Servant.—"They took him (the Raja) down-stairs. I went to inform the Kour Sahib (Bhagwan Singh), and he came and met his brother coming down-stairs. He got worse every moment. I went to the Mai Sahiba's ante-chamber (deorhi) and gave the news; she came to her son. After she left he became worse. He was senseless for two hours before death."

Bukshish Singh, Servant of the Raja.—"They brought him (the Raja) down at about midnight, but I don't recollect. The Kour Sahib met us at the bottom of the stairs. He remained in the janpan in which he was brought down. He did not speak to the Kour Sahib, who was crying; and people put him aside, lest he should disturb the Raja."

Many other depositions might be quoted containing proof, direct or implied, that the Raja held no conversation with his brother at all on the night of his death; that the question of the succession was not even mentioned; and that the story of the Nabha Ministers, related to the Maharaja of Pattiala and the Raja of Jhind, and repeated in their letters, was a fiction from beginning to end. Sirdar Gurbaksh Singh, the Prime Minister, and Manowar Ali Khan, another Minister, calling on the Political Agent on the 17th December, repeated to him the story of the Raja formally nominating his brother on the night of his death in the presence of the Ministers; but at the subsequent investigation at Nabha, the account of Gurbaksh Singh was quite different, as has been shown; while it is certain that Manowar Ali Khan was never present at all on the night of the Raja's death.

of the Sanad of the 5th May 1860 was perfectly clear, and the State was liable to the payment of *nazrana*—"if at any time the Raja of Nabha should die without male issue, and without adopting a successor." Prince Bhagwan Singh was, it is true, the legitimate successor of his brother, but this right did not in any way lessen the obligation which the late Raja imposed upon the Nabha State to pay a fine under certain circumstances, and in return for the privilege of adoption which the British Government conferred upon him, but which he failed to exercise.

The installation of Raja Bhagwan Singh, A.D. 1864. The payment of the *nazrana* was consequently demanded,[1] and the installation of the new Chief took place on the 17th of February 1864, in presence of the Maharaja of Pattiala, the Raja of Jhind, the Nawab of Maler Kotla, and a great number of the Cis-Satlej Chiefs. The Raja of Faridkot arrived after the enthronement. In addition to Sir Herbert Edwardes, Agent of the Lieutenant-Governor, Lord George Paget, C.B., commanding the Division, and a number of English officers, were present, and the ceremony was conducted with great splendour. On the part of the British Government, a *Khillat* was presented, consisting of fifteen trays, three jewels, two arms, a horse, and an elephant.[2]

Troubles at Nabha. Troubles of the most terrible kind soon surrounded the new Chief. His Court was divided between two parties: one favouring the interests of Sirdar Gurbaksh

[1] Commissioner Cis-Satlej States to Government Punjab, No. 312, dated 17th December 1863. Government Punjab to Government of India, No. 480, dated 21st December 1863. Government of India to Government Punjab, No. 54, dated 15th January 1864.

[2] Commissioner Cis-Satlej States to Government Punjab, Nos. 26 and 36, dated 1st and 19th February. Government Punjab to Government of India, No. 106, dated 4th March 1864. Letter of the Viceroy to Raja of Nabha, dated 30th March 1864.

Singh, and the other those of Munshi Sahib Singh; and their intrigues for power resulted in the gravest consequences for Nabha, involving the Court and even the Raja in the suspicion of a great crime.

Suspicions as to the manner of Raja Bharpur Singh's death.

The circumstances of the death of Raja Bharpur Singh were not in themselves such as to raise any doubt but that it was due to natural causes. He had always been delicate, and his death was the result of long continued illness which had thoroughly exhausted his feeble constitution, and induced the rapid decline which terminated his life. He was, moreover, much loved by his people and servants, and it was difficult to say that any party would obtain a direct advantage from his death. But the violent party feeling which prevailed in Nabha, as in most other Native States, was in itself sufficient to account for circulation of rumours that the death of Bharpur Singh was suspicious, and these rumours at length took shape in the assertion that the Raja had died of poison.

Another case confirms these suspicions.

Another case, which tended to confirm in some sort these suspicions, had occurred shortly after the death of Raja Bharpur Singh.

The murder of Sirdarni Mehtab Kour.

On the fourth of January 1864, Sirdarni Mehtab Kour, one of the widows of Sirdar Arjan Singh, and aunt of the Raja of Nabha, after whose entertainment, it will be remembered, Bharpur Singh first fell ill, from the effects, it was asserted, of a magical potion which had been administered to him, was murdered in the court-yard of her private residence at Rangar-Nangal, in the Amritsar district, by men who made no attempt to rob the lady of her jewels, but who, having killed her with blows of a sword, immediately absconded. No trace could for some time be found of them, though popular rumour declared that the murderers were men from the south of the Satlej, who had been seen lurking about the village of Rangar-Nangal, and that the crime had been prompted by powerful parties at the Nabha Court.

The murderers are traced to Nabha, and one confesses.

The police at length succeeded in tracing the murderers to Nabha, and four men were arrested, one of whom, Hira Singh, turned Queen's evidence and confessed; and it appeared clear that the crime had been actually committed by a man named Mehtaba, a resident of Jyton, in Nabha territory, who had been released from jail, where he was undergoing imprisonment for theft, before the term of his sentence had expired. This circumstance was in itself very suspicious, and Raja Bhagwan Singh was directed to use his best endeavours to clear up the mystery, to bring the real criminals to justice, and to remove, in this manner, the stigma which attached to his Court.

The Raja investigates the case, and accuses Sirdar Gurbaksh Singh.

In the month of April following, the Raja held a judicial inquiry, the result of which was to fix the release of the prisoner Mehtaba and the instigation of the murder of Sirdarni Mehtab Kour upon the Prime Minister, Sirdar Gurbaksh Singh.

His counter-charge.

This man was not, however, disposed to fall without dragging down his rivals with him, and protested his absolute innocence, asserting that the trial, which had pronounced him the instigator of the murder, was a mock one, conducted and prompted by his enemies, who had determined to ruin him; that the opposite party at Court, headed by Munshi Sahib Singh, had committed the murder in order to silence a dangerous accomplice, of whose discretion they could not be certain, on the subject of the murder, by poison and necromancy, of the late Raja Bharpur Singh.

These accusations, so circumstantial and grave, could not be allowed to pass unnoticed, although they were but the despairing efforts of a desperate man to escape the consequences of his own actions, and an investigation was directed to be held into their truth at Nabha by an English officer. The question to be determined was whether the death of Raja Bharpur Singh was due to poison, and, if so, by whose instrumentality and instigation administered; and, secondly, who were the persons implicated in the murder of Mehtab Kour.

An inquiry directed at Nabha into the charges.

The inquiry commenced on the 3d November 1864, and lasted three weeks. The Maharaja of Pattiala and the Raja of Jhind were present throughout the whole investigation, and every person connected with the Nabha Court, or who could be supposed to be possessed of any information, was examined on oath and with the utmost care.

The Nabha investigation.

The conclusion at which Major Cracroft, the officer appointed by Government to investigate the case, arrived, was that there was no reason to believe that Raja Bharpur Singh had died of other than natural causes; and that Sirdar Gurbaksh Singh was justly accused of having, with other officials at Nabha, instigated the murder of Mehtab Kour.

The conclusion of the Commission.

With regard to Raja Bharpur Singh, the story of death from poison was shown beyond all doubt to be absolutely without foundation.

The death of Raja Bharpur Singh, by poison, disproved.

No insinuation is more commonly made in Native States than that the death of a Chief is due to poison; for the simple reason that the charge is most difficult to disprove. With Hindus, cremation follows shortly after death, and however grave the suspicions of foul play that might exist, a *post mortem* examination would be objected

The frequency of the assertion that Chiefs have died of poison, and the reasons for its frequency

to by the whole Durbar on religious grounds; so that the danger of detection which is, in the present state of chemical science, almost certain for European poisoners, if suspicion of foul play be once aroused, has little weight among Hindus. This consideration, which might be supposed to make crime more safe, also encourages false and malicious accusations, which a great part of the world would believe to be true simply because it was impossible to prove them false. The charge of the poisoning of a Chief is, moreover, one which can be used with fatal effect against any party which may be supposed to have an interest in the Chief's death. Even if unsupported by a shadow of evidence, and opposed to all the probabilities of the case, the charge still has its effect. It clings to those against whom it is made, and benefits those who are unscrupulous enough to make it. These considerations will explain the frequency of the charge in Native States; but there is no reason whatever to believe that the crime is one frequently perpetrated. On the contrary, it would be easy to adduce instances in which the charge has been loudly asserted, while it has been known to be absolutely without foundation, the cause of death being undoubted and certain.

There was no doubt that Raja Bharpur Singh had died from natural causes.

In the case of Raja Bharpur Singh there is no manner of doubt whatever that he died from natural causes alone —consumption, induced by great natural delicacy of constitution, and a long and wearing illness; and the story of poison may be pronounced an unmitigated falsehood, unsupported by a particle of evidence. The symptoms which were noticed at the death of the Raja forbid absolutely the supposition that he died from the effects of arsenic, which was the poison the accusers declared had been used. But there is also no doubt that Raja Bharpur Singh, who was of a very superstitious disposition, was worked upon by some of those about him to believe that he was suffering from the magical arts of Sirdarni Mehtab Kour and others. The part which magic plays in the investigation at Nabha is a very important one. The belief in the power of magic is universal in India, and the idea that he was the object of unholy arts, may, probably enough, have had a very injurious influence upon a man so nervous and excitable as Bharpur Singh. The imagination has much to do with the health or illness of persons of a highly susceptible temperament, and it would be rash to assert that the belief that he had been bewitched did not have a most unfavourable influence on the recovery of the Raja; but the idea of poison must be altogether rejected.

Magic employed against the Raja.

With regard to the murder of Sirdarni Mehtab Kour, there was little doubt that Gurbaksh Singh had been the instigator of the murder, and that other members of the Court had either actively assisted or had been cognisant of the crime. He appears to have believed, with the Raja, that the magical arts of Mehtab Kour had caused the illness and death of Bharpur Singh, and determined to avenge both it and some private grievances of his own against the lady, who was of a notoriously bad character. He was responsible for the release, in an informal manner, and before the term of his sentence had expired, of the murderer Mehtaba; and his turning upon his rivals and enemies in the State, and endeavouring to implicate them in the double crime of the murder of the Raja and Mehtab Kour, was not only natural, but what might have been predicted with almost absolute certainty beforehand.

The instigator of Mehtab Kour's murder.

The Government of the Punjab and the Government of India considered the conclusions at which the Nabha

The Government accept the conclusions of the Commission.

Commission had arrived to be correct, and directed the prosecution of Mehtaba for murder, and of Sirdar Gurbaksh Singh for instigating the same. The former was tried, convicted, and sentenced to death, though this was later commuted to transportation for life. Sirdar Gurbaksh Singh was placed before the Magistrate of Ludhiana, on the 25th July 1865, on the charge of having abetted the murder of Sirdarni Mehtab Kour, and, after an investigation which lasted seven days, was committed to take his trial before the Sessions Judge of Ambala. The trial commenced on the 5th of September and closed on the 18th, when Sirdar Gurbaksh Singh was acquitted. This result was only to be expected. The great length of time that had elapsed since the commission of the crime; the doubtful nature, from a judicial point of view, of much of the evidence; the position and influence of Sirdar Gurbaksh Singh, and his friends and relatives, combined to render his conviction all but impossible.

Mehtaba, the murderer, sentenced to death.

Sirdar Gurbaksh Singh acquitted,

The Indian and Home Governments found, however, no reason to doubt the correctness of the conclusions of the Court of Inquiry. Sirdar Gurbaksh Singh, Ausaf Ali, Minister of Justice, and Bulwant Singh, stepson of the murdered Mehtab Kour, were banished from Nabha territory; and Raja Bhagwan Singh, acquitted of all complicity in the crimes which had been attributed to or committed by his intriguing officials, was restored to his position among the Princes of India, which he had temporarily lost, while charges so grave were under investigation.

But is banished from Nabha, with others of the Court.

These painful cases, which formed the subject of both political and judicial inquiry, have been recorded as briefly as possible, with the desire to wound as little as possible the feelings of persons, however innocent, who

Justice to the Raja and the Nabha State required some notice of these painful cases.

were implicated in them; but it would have been an injustice both to the present Raja of Nabha and to his Court to have failed to notice what may be called the most remarkable inquiry which has taken place in the Cis-Satlej States since their connection with the British Government, seeing that the investigation entirely exculpated the Raja, while the infamous charges advanced recoiled upon those who first gave them existence.[1]

[1] It cannot be said that the investigation at Nabha arrived at the whole truth of the story connected with the murder of Sirdarni Mehtab Kour. The intrigues, the plots, and counterplots which were then discovered, implicating, in a greater or less degree, almost every one at the Nabha Court, would fill a volume; and all the motives for the murder, and the persons concerned in it or cognisant of it, will never be known in this world. But that the conclusions reached may be accepted as generally correct, may safely be inferred. The writer of the present work, then personal Assistant to the Judicial Commissioner of the Punjab, was deputed to Nabha to assist Major Cracroft in the investigation of the case. He can testify to the painful care and minuteness of the inquiry. Every possible hypothesis was examined, and nothing but the conclusion at which the Commission arrived would agree with the evidence recorded, and with the probabilities of the case. The acquittal of Gurbaksh Singh, in a judicial trial, was expected; and was, indeed, unavoidable. But nothing in that trial in the smallest degree shook the correctness of the conclusion of the Commission of Inquiry. If those conclusions were wrong, then Sirdarni Mehtab Kour was never murdered at all; that the Government of the Punjab, the Government of India, and the Secretary of State accepted those conclusions as correct, after most careful consideration, is at least a guarantee that they were reasonable.

With Sirdar Gurbaksh Singh it was impossible not to feel some sympathy. He was a very fine specimen of an old Sikh gentleman, with commanding presence and irreproachable manners; and although his previous history shows him to have been both avaricious and greedy of power, yet he had undoubtedly a strong affection for Raja Bharpur Singh; and his actions, however reprehensible or criminal, were prompted more by love for his master than by any personal feelings, which still were not without their influence.

The correspondence in this case is so voluminous that it is only necessary to note the principal papers as a clue to the remainder.

Report of Major J. E. Cracroft to Government Punjab, dated 16th December 1864. Government Punjab to Government of India, Nos. 11 and 16, dated 4th January 1865; No. 291, dated 8th June; No. 497, dated 19th October 1865. Government of India to Government Punjab, Nos. 257 and 926, dated 30th June and 4th November 1865.

Despatch of Lord De Grey and Ripon, Secretary of State for India, No. 44, dated 30th June 1866.

The case of the Sunti Chiefs.

Since the investigation of 1864, few cases of any political importance have arisen with regard to the Nabha State. The chief refers to the Lidhran and Sunti Sikhs, whose relations with Nabha were determined, it will be remembered, by the Government of India in August 1838. That decision was not altogether satisfactory. The Raja did not cease his endeavour to coerce the Sikhs; and they, having obtained greater consideration for their grievance than they perhaps deserved, did not cease to complain of his encroachments.

The dispute between them and Nabha referred to the Commissioner by Lord Canning.

The dispute with the Sunti Sikhs referred to the division of the revenue of certain villages shared between them and the Nabha State. A long discussion had been carried on with regard to this point, and at length the quarrel assumed such dimensions, that, after every Political Officer in the Cis-Satlej States had attempted vainly to settle it by compromise, Lord Canning, Viceroy and Governor-General, directed that an authoritative settlement should be, if possible, made. The points to be determined were the value of the shared villages, the amount to be deducted from the Sunti share on account of the Nabha right to escheats, commutation for loss of service, and deductions on account of confiscated and restored territory.

The decision arrived at was rejected by the Sikhs, who appeal to England.

An arrangement was effected by the Commissioner of the Cis-Satlej States, in communication with the Maharaja of Pattiala and the Raja of Jhind, and approved by the Government of India,[1] by which Rs. 5000 a year were allowed to the Sunti Sikhs from the Nabha treasury, free of all deductions; but this award the Sunti Sikhs refused to accept, and appealed their case to the Secretary of State, who accepted the appeal, pointed out that the arrangement was unjust to the Sikhs, who would,

[1] Government of India's letter, dated 8th April 1861.

under a fair estimation of the value of the villages, be entitled to Rs. 10,641, or more than double what they had received. The case was consequently re-opened, and after a long investigation, extending over some years, General Taylor, Commissioner Cis-Satlej States, submitted a final report, the conclusions of which were accepted by the Government of India.

The case re-opened, and decided by General Taylor in 1868.

His award.

The Commissioner found that the value of the shared villages was Rs. 46,085 2 a. 9 p., of which, however, the Nabha Government only collected Rs. 36,638 1 a. 9 p., the balance having been remitted as a charitable grant by Raja Jaswant Singh. The Sunti Sikhs objected to this remission being calculated as against their share, and the point was eventually yielded by the Nabha Government, and a share in other cesses collected was also allowed them, making the total value of the thirty-seven shared villages Rs. 47,000. The value of new villages was in the same manner fixed at Rs. 9000, and the total value of both was thus Rs. 56,000 per annum.

The Sunti share of this was admittedly seven annas or seven-sixteenths, and the Nabha share nine annas or nine-sixteenths. The amount due to the Suntis would thus be Rs. 24,500.

But from this the Nabha State claimed certain deductions:—

Escheats of the shares of $9\frac{3}{8}$ths horsemen, . .	Rs. 3,368	11	0
Compensation for the loss of service of $60\frac{3}{8}$ths horsemen, at 5 annas per diem, ...	6,792	3	0
Deduction of $\frac{1}{4}$th on account of confiscation of $\frac{1}{4}$th of the Nabha territory by the British Government,	6,125	0	0
Total, ...	Rs. 16,285	14	0
Leaving balance due to the Sunti Sikhs, . . .	Rs. 8,214	2	0

With reference to the two first items, it has before

been stated that the Sunti Sikhs were bound to render service of seventy horsemen to the Nabha State, though, in the year 1838, the amount of this service had been considerably reduced, while the third item had reference to the confiscation of Nabha territory after the first Sikh war, a portion of which loss the Sunti Sikhs were justly bound to bear as well as their co-sharers.

It would be tedious to relate the methods employed by the Commissioner to reach a satisfactory decision. His final proposals were that from the Sunti share of Rs. 24,500, the following items might be justly deducted:—

Escheats of 9⅝ths horsemen, ...	Rs. 3,368	11	0
Commutation for loss of service of 60⅝ths horsemen at Rs. 7 per mensem, ...	5,071	8	0
Deduction of ⅛th on account of confiscated territory,	3,062	8	0
Total, ...	Rs. 11,502	11	0
Balance due to the Sunti Sikhs, ...	Rs. 12,997	5	0

Accepted by Government, and the case finally settled.

This decision was accepted by the Government of India. It is true that it was but a compromise at the best; but every effort had been made to arrive at the truth, and it was hopeless to expect that any further investigation would arrive at results more just or more satisfactory.

The Lidhran Sikhs not included in the decision.

The Lidhran Sikhs were not included in this decision. Their position was very different from the Sikhs of Sunti: their district was not included, at the time of confiscation, in the Nabha territory, and Nabha had never exercised police jurisdiction there.[1]

[1] Report of General Taylor, Commissioner Cis-Satlej States, No. 438, dated 11th December 1868, with very voluminous annexures. Secretary to Government Punjab, Nos. 2-6, dated 2d January 1869, to Government of India. Secretary Government of India to Government Punjab, No. 302, dated 2d March 1869.

The Nabha territory has an area of 863 square miles, and a population of about 300,000 souls. The revenue is nearly the same as that of Jhind, between Rs. 6,00,000 and Rs. 7,00,000 per annum. A military force of 1500 men is maintained, of which a contingent of 50 horsemen is due for service to the British Government. Nabha is the only town of importance in the State.

THE HISTORY

OF THE

KAPURTHALLA STATE.

The founding of the town of Kapurthalla.

THE town of Kapurthalla, situated between Jalandhar and the Bias river, is said to have been founded by Rana Kapur, a Rajput immigrant from Jesalmir, about the time of the invasion of India by Sultan Muhmud Ghazni, at the beginning of the eleventh century. The truth of this is, however, quite uncertain, and Rana Kapur has been probably created to provide a sufficiently illustrious founder for the capital of the Ahluwalias.

Rana Kapur a mythical ancestor of the Ahluwalias.

The existence of Rana Kapur being mythical, the claim of the Ahluwalias to descent from him is not likely to be less of a fabulous nature; and, in the same way as every Muhammadan family of respectability claims to be Syad, so that the descendants of Husain would seem to include a large proportion of the professors of Muhammadanism, so every Jat family which has risen to importance is not satisfied until a Rajput ancestor of pure blood has been discovered for them by the bards, who fill, in

India, the place which in European countries has been taken by the Heralds' Office.

It is always difficult to assert that an Indian genealogy is false, or that any given name may not truly represent an ancestor of a particular family; for India, singularly barren of authentic historical records, at any rate until the Muhammadan era, has preserved, by oral tradition and with scrupulous care, the genealogies of even obscure families. In every village the *mirasi* or bard can repeat the names of every proprietor who has held land in the village since its founding, hundreds of years before, and the proof of the correctness of the genealogy is shown in the fact that the village lands are to-day held in the very shares which the descendants of the original founders represent.

The singular accuracy of Indian genealogies.

In the Himalayan mountains there exist ancient Rajput States—Chamba, Mandi, Suket, and, most venerable of all, Katoch in the Kangra Hills, which fell before the united efforts of Gurkhas and Sikhs—counting, without a break, a line of four hundred and seventy Kings. Antecedent to what are called historic times, conjecture must take the place of truth; but it is not difficult to imagine that these long genealogies, by the side of which the noblest names of Europe seem but as of yesterday, contain some semblance of the truth. These quiet mountain valleys, guarded by difficult passes, by ice and by snow, lay altogether out of the path of the invading armies which, one after another, in quick succession, poured down upon the plains of Hindustan from the north-west. Here a peaceful race, with no ambition urging them to try their strength against their neighbours, and with little wealth to tempt invasion, may have quietly lived for thousands of years, and their royal dynasties may

The long dynasties of the Rajput Kings.

have been already ancient when Moses was leading the Israelites out of Egypt, and the Greeks were steering their swift ships to Troy.

The Jat Sikhs are generally of Rajput descent.

If, then, the precision of Indian genealogy will allow the Chiefs of Kapurthalla to claim Rana Kapur for their ancestor, although the assertion is its only proof, they may generally assert Rajput origin without any dispute. The traditions of almost every Jat tribe in the Punjab point to a Rajput descent. The unanimity of these traditions is such that it is impossible to doubt that they are in a great measure founded upon truth. Jats and Rajputs had probably a common origin; but many hundred years after the first waves of Aryan immigration from the north had swept over India, and the Hindus had organised that society the shadow of which is still visible, three or more Rajput immigrations from the south northwards took place, the effects of which can yet be traced in the Punjab. Many Rajputs married into Jat families, losing rank, indeed, but claimed in after years as the true founders of the house; some tribes kept pure their Rajput blood, taking wives of their own race alone, and refusing to degrade themselves by the cultivation of the soil; while others, in the early days of Muhammadanism, when the Jihad was preached by kings with sword in hand, and not, as to-day, by the scum of the gambling-houses and the brothels, abandoned their own faith for one which suited better their warlike instincts, and are now known as Sials, Tiwanas, Ghebas, and Jodrahs, some of the finest men and the best soldiers in the Punjab.

The Rajput immigrations from the south to the Punjab.

The Kapurthalla family of the Kalal or Distiller caste.

But whatever the real origin of the Kapurthalla family, it appears first in history as of the Jat Kalal or Distiller caste, to which Sadao Singh belonged, the founder of the villages of Ahlu (from which the Kapurthalla family takes its name of Ahluwalia), Hallu-Sadho, Tor, and Chak, in the neighbourhood of Lahore.

The story is told, indeed, that Sadawa, the younger brother of Sadao Singh, fell violently in love with a girl of the Kalal or Distiller caste, and the sanction of his relatives being refused to so unequal a match, became so dangerously ill that the marriage was allowed; the parents of the bride, however, stipulating that the whole family of the bridegroom should adopt the disagreeable cognomen of Kalal. This was agreed to, the marriage was celebrated, and the Ahluwalias have ever since been known as Kalals, and marry into that tribe only.

The story is, on the face of it, improbable, and may without any danger be classed with those pleasing and harmless fictions which have been common in every age among those who would vainly try to persuade the world that they had a grandfather. But the Rajas of Kapurthalla have no need of fiction to make them illustrious. Bravery, loyalty, and devotion, wise and just administration, and an example of liberality and enlightenment set to all Princes of India, would have allowed the late Raja of Kapurthalla to dispense with an ancestor altogether without disgrace, had not the true founder of the family, Sirdar Jassa Singh, been the leader of the Khalsa, and the most distinguished of all the Sikh Chiefs north of the Satlej.

Sadawa died without issue; but his brother, Sadao Singh, had four sons—Gopal Singh, Hammu, Sikandar, and Chaka—the younger of whom lived at Lahore, where Chaka built a street which still exists. Little is known of the eldest, Gopal Singh, or of his son Dewa Singh, and they were probably men of no importance.

The genealogy.

The genealogy of the family is as follows :—

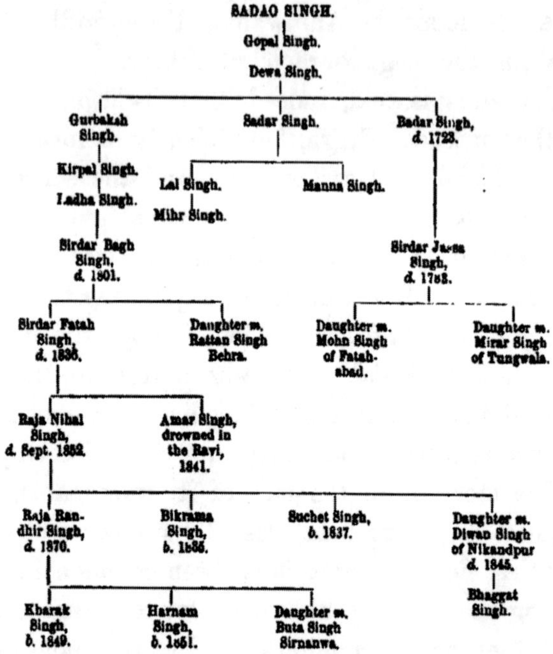

Badar Singh Ahluwalia, and the promise of the Guru.

Badar Singh, the youngest son of Dewa Singh, married the sister of Bagh Singh, a petty chieftain of the Lahore district, but for many years he had no children, and at last sought the blessing of Guru Govind Singh, who promised him a son, on condition that the child should become his disciple; and to this Badar Singh readily agreed. The blessing of the Guru did not take effect at once, and it was not till 1718, ten years after the death of Govind Singh, that a son was born and named Jassa Singh. Badar Singh had then forgotten his promise, and at his death, five years later, the widow, thinking her loss a judgment upon the family for its forgotten vow, set out with her child to Dehli, where Mai Sandri, widow of the Guru, was then living. She was well received, and remained there for several years, serving with every attention Mai Sandri, who became much attached to both mother and son.

The early days of Jassa Singh.

When Jassa Singh was twelve years old, his uncle, Bagh Singh, urged his return to the Punjab. At his departure Mai Sandri blessed him, predicted his future greatness, and gave him a silver mace, saying that he and his descendants would have mace-bearers to attend them. Sirdar Kapur Singh Faizullahpuria was at Jalandhar when the little party arrived there, and to this Chief's protection Jassa Singh's mother commended her son.[1] They then returned to Hallu-Sadho; and Jassa Singh, who was a clever boy, was soon able to conduct business for his uncle, Bagh Singh, who was killed four years later in a skirmish with the imperial troops at Harian.

He becomes himself a Chief.

Jassa Singh now became a Sirdar himself, and soon acquired a great reputation. The Sikhs, since the defeat and execution of Banda, the successor and avenger of Guru Govind Singh, had been a persecuted sect, and it was only after the death of Abdul Samad Khan, Governor of Lahore, and the invasion of Nadir Shah in 1739, that they began to feel themselves strong. On the approach of Nadir Shah, Jassa Singh had left his village, and, with many other Chiefs, had taken refuge at Muktsar, or as it is generally known, Mokatsar, in the Firozpur district, a place sacred to the Sikhs as being the scene of the last great battle and defeat of Guru Govind Singh. When Nadir Shah had left the Punjab, Jassa Singh returned home, and built the fort of Daliwal, on the banks of the Ravi, where he set up his headquarters. He took care

[1] The story of the visit to Dehli and the affection of Mai Sandri for the young Jassa Singh is a tradition in the Ahluwalia family, though there is every reason to doubt its truth.

to maintain friendship with the Faizullahpuria Chief, whose possessions were to the south of the Bias, and joined him in many expeditions.

Hostilities with the Muhammadans.

In 1743, when Zakria Khan, son of Abdul Samad Khan, commonly known as Nowab Khan, or Khan Bahadur, was Governor of Lahore, Jassa Singh, with a large body of horse, attacked Diwan Lakhpat Rai, who was escorting treasure from Imanabad to Lahore, and killed him, carrying off the spoil. This was more than the Muhammadans could bear, and Adina Beg, afterwards Governor of the Jalandhar Doab, was sent against the Sikhs, whom he defeated with great slaughter. The prisoners taken in this battle were executed in Lahore, where the Shahidganj or martyrs' memorial is still pointed out.[1] Jassa Singh escaped to the Satlej, where he seized Lakhumalanwala, Baggoki, Hicharwal, and other Dogar villages. Here another force was sent against him, under Lachmi Narayan, one of the officers of Abdul Samad Khan; and he and his allies, Hari Singh and Jhanda Singh Bhangis, were again defeated, Jassa Singh being forced to take refuge in the hilly country to the north of the Satlej. This happened in 1745, in which year Zakria Khan died, and after a lengthened struggle for the viceroyalty between his sons Yahia Khan[2] and Shah Nawaz Khan, the latter, although the younger, succeeded in obtaining power.

Conquest beyond the Satlej.

The expedition against Kassur, and Ahmad Shah's invasion.

In the cold season of 1747, Jassa Singh, with other Chiefs, made an excursion into the district of Kassur, and almost succeeded in getting possession of the town by

[1] This institution is now in the hands of Akalis. The scriptures (Granth) are read there and the poor relieved. The British Government allow it a small endowment.

[2] Yahia Khan acted for his father Zakria Khan for some time as Viceroy; but it does not appear, as has been often stated, that he was ever Governor himself.—*Vide* Cunningham, p. 99; Murray, p. 4.

surprise, but it was fortified and sufficiently strong to resist assault; and a little later he joined the Bhangi, Kanheya, and Ramgharia Chiefs, and his old enemy, Adina Beg, in opposing the advance of Ahmad Shah Durani, who, on the invitation of Shah Nawaz Khan, had invaded India. The Sikhs at this time were very indifferent as regular troops, and although they harassed Ahmad Shah's march as guerillas, and captured some of his baggage at the Chenab, yet the only time they tried their strength with him in a regular engagement, near Sirhind, they were defeated with considerable loss.

Hostilities with Mir Manu of Lahore.

After the departure of Ahmad Shah, Jassa Singh continued to carry on hostilities with the Governor of Lahore, Mir Manu, better known as Moyan ul Mulk, and his Deputy, Raja Gurdit Mal, who had charge of the Hoshiarpur and Sialkot districts. Adina Beg Khan, who was always intriguing with the Sikhs—now their enemy, now their friend—was attacked by Jassa Singh near Hoshiarpur; but the action was not decisive, and the Ahluwalia Chief then turned upon Salabat Khan, Governor of Amritsar, killed him, and took possession of a large part of his district.

Jassa Singh helps Kowra Mal to seize Multan.

In 1749, Jassa Singh, whose reputation had now become great for bravery and ability, was invited by Kowra Mal to assist him in expelling Shah Nawaz Khan, the late ruler of Lahore, who had been appointed Viceroy of Multan by Ahmad Shah. Mir Manu did not desire any rival in the Punjab, and supported the claims of Kowra Mal to the Governorship of Multan. The latter, who was a man of great energy, being thus powerfully supported, defeated his rival, who was slain in the battle; and Jassa Singh, who had been of great assistance, was dismissed with a share of the booty and a title of honour.

Adina Beg defeats Jassa Singh and his allies.

After the third invasion of Ahmad Shah, Adina Beg Khan determined to make some effort to recover the power he was fast losing. He induced Sirdars Jassa Singh, Jai Singh, and Khushal Singh, Ramgharia, to join him, and attacked the Ahluwalia, Kaneya, and Sukarchakia forces at Makhowal, inflicting upon them a severe defeat. Of all the Ramgharia Chiefs Tara Singh was the only one who stood by the Sikh cause; and this defection of the clan was terribly avenged by Jassa Singh on the Ramgharias a few years later. The next year, 1753, he defeated Aziz Khan, commanding the Lahore forces, plundered Rao Jagraon and Raikot, carrying off at Nadown the tribute of the hill Chiefs, which had been collected for despatch to Lahore. During this and the following year he was engaged in perpetual contests with Adina Beg Khan, with varying success; but in November 1755, he gained a decided advantage at Kaddur, and compelled the Khan to cede to him Fatahabad on the Bias. He attacked and killed Umed Khan, a eunuch high in favour with the Lahore Court, and again defeated Aziz Beg Khan, whom Adina Beg had sent against him. The latter now made peace, believing that friendship was better than enmity with so powerful a Chief; and together, in 1756, they defeated Sarbuland Khan, one of the Afghan generals whom Ahmad Shah Durani had left behind him in charge of Jalandhar, of which place the allies took possession.

Continual conflicts with the Muhammadans of Lahore, A.D. 1754.

Sarbuland Khan, Afghan Governor of Jalandhar, defeated, A.D. 1756.

Adina Beg invites the Mahrattas to his aid.

Adina Beg had little confidence in his new friends, and did not believe that they had the power, even if they had the inclination, to give him effectual assistance in opposing the annual invasions of the Durani monarch, and he accordingly invited Mala Rao and Ragho Rao, two famous Mahratta Chiefs, to join him. These men, ever ready for plunder, marched to the Punjab with a large force, and were joined by Adina Beg and the Sikhs. Prince Timur and Jahan Khan, his minister, fled to Afghanistan, and the conquests of Ahmad Shah seemed for ever lost. But that monarch quickly collected a new army, and marched for the fifth time into India in the winter of 1759. In the Punjab no stand was made against him; Lahore was abandoned by its new masters; Adina Beg, the ablest of his enemies, had just died, and there was little or no sympathy between the Sikhs and the Mahrattas. Ahmad Shah remained in India about fifteen months, and after the victory of Panipat, in which the Mahratta power was completely shattered, he returned to Kabul, leaving Ubed Khan Governor of Lahore; Hingan Khan, of the country about Maler Kotla; and Zin Khan, of Sirhind. During the whole year of 1760, whilst Ahmad Shah was engaged in his campaign against the Mahrattas in the Dehli country, Jassa Singh and the Sikhs had not been idle. He temporarily captured Jandialah from Sarran Das, and plundered Sirhind and Dialpur, which was in the possession of Gajja Singh, giving a half share to the Sodhis of Kurtarpur. He then marched into the Firozpur district, and seized the Dogar[1] ilaqua of Mullanwala, and the Nypal[2] ilaqua of Mukku, in both of which he built fortified posts, and they were held by the Ahluwalia Chief till the Satlej campaign, when they were confiscated by the British Government. He then seized the neighbouring estate of Kot Isai Khan

Prince Timur Shah flees from the Punjab.

The fifth invasion of Ahmad Shah.

The victory of Panipat, 7th January 1761.

Jassa Singh's conquests

[1] The Dogars are a pastoral tribe, resident in the neighbourhood of Kussur, Firozpur, and along the south bank of the Satlej. They are now Muhammadans, but are supposed to have been originally Chouhan Rajputs, emigrants from Dehli.

[2] The Nypals are a tribe inhabiting the Firozpur district, great thieves and vagabonds. They are a sub-caste of the Bhattis, who were originally Rajputs.

from Kadir Baksh Khan, leaving him, however, a few villages. In June of the same year he seized Hoshiarpur,[1] Bhirog, and Naraingbar in Ambala, and exacted tribute from Rai Ibrahim, the Jagirdar of Kapurthalla. He then made an expedition to the south of Lahore, as far as Jhang; but Inayatullah Khan, the Sial Chief of that place, was quite strong enough to hold his own against all comers.

In February 1761, Ahmad Shah left the Punjab, and the Sikhs immediately recovered more than their lost power, for the Dehli empire was completely disorganised, and Kabul was so distant as to be hardly a cause of fear. Jassa Singh, with the Phulkian, Faizullahpuria, and other Sirdars, again ravaged Sirhind, and the Governor of Lahore, Ubed Khan, was shut up within the walls of the city. The expedition which he led against Charrak Singh Sukarchakia, grandfather of Maharaja Ranjit Singh, was unsuccessful, and he was compelled to retire from Gujranwala, with the loss of his guns and baggage.

The position of Jassa Singh among the Sikhs in 1761.

In 1761, Jassa Singh was undoubtedly the chief leader among the Sikhs north of the Satlej, and the equal of any Chief south of that river. He is said to have struck the first Sikh coin, with the following distich: [2]"Coin struck in the world by the grace of the Immortal. In

The first Sikh coin.

[1] Both Bhirog and Naraingbar were, in 1760, held by Muhammad Bakr, the Rais of Kotaha. On the approach of the royal army, Mirza Singh, the Lieutenant of Muhammad Bakr, took fright and abandoned Naraingbar, of which the Raja of Pattiala took possession and made it over to Jassa Singh, who reappointed Mirza Singh as his deputy. When Ahmad Shah again marched southwards, Mirza Singh a second time abandoned Naraingbar, which fell into the hands of the Punjilassa Rajputs, and afterwards of the Nahan Raja, the Ahluwalia Chief only recovering half the estate in 1807, and the remainder in 1832.

Bhirog remained a fief of the Ahluwalias till the first Sikh war, though their supremacy was often questioned, and was the subject of many disputes.

[2] The inscription is given by Cunningham, page 105, "By the grace of

the country of Ahmad, which Jassa Kalal seized," though this is more than doubtful; and he certainly did much to organise the Sikh military system.

Sirdar Kapur Singh Faizullah-puria.

It was only on the death of Kapur Singh Faizullah-puria in 1753 that Jassa Singh obtained any considerable influence beyond his own confederacy or misl. Kapur Singh was, as long as he lived, the first of the Sikh Sirdars, and he it was who truly organised the Dal Khalsa, though Jassa Singh has obtained more than the lion's share of the fame. When Kapur Singh was dying he made over to Jassa Singh the steel mace of the last great Guru,[1] thus appointing him, as it were, the successor to his influence, which Jassa Singh, by his ability and courage, considerably increased.[2]

The return of Ahmad Shah.

After assisting the Bhangis and Sukarchakias to repulse Ubed Khan from Gujranwala, Jassa Singh crossed the Satlej, and made a raid as far south as Shikarpur, Mahammadpur, and Raipur to the south of the Jamna, when he was recalled by the news that Ahmad Shah had returned in force and had recovered

the *Khalsa*," but the word is *Akal*, immortal, referring to God, and rhyming with *Kalal*.

سکہ زد در جہان بفضل اکال
ملک احمد گرفت جسا کلال

Nor were these coins struck before 1762; not in 1757-58, as stated by Cunningham; and it is very doubtful whether they were ever struck in large numbers at all. The Raja of Kapurthalla has none in his possession, nor do I know any one who has seen one. The *Tawarikh-i-Punjab*, of Ganesh Dass, states that the Sikhs did not strike this coin, but that the Kazis and Mullahs in 1764, after the famous Nanakshahi rupee had been struck, and desiring to anger Ahmad Shah against the Sikhs, coined twenty-one rupees, with this inscription, themselves, and sent them to the Shah at Kabul, who was as indignant as they anticipated at the insolence of the Distiller, "Kalal," who claimed to have seized his country "*Mulk-i-Ahmad*."

[1] This is now to be seen in the Akal Bungah at Amritsar.

[2] *Vide ante*, p. 57, Note, the history of Kapur Singh.

Multan and Lahore without a struggle. The confederacies were now collected, and it was at first proposed to give battle at Jandiala, but the swift advance of the Afghans alarmed the Sikhs, who crossed the Satlej near Barnala; they were overtaken, and defeated on the 10th February 1762, with the loss of many thousands killed and wounded. The battle was named the Ghalu Ghara, or great defeat, and was the most terrible blow the Sikhs had yet received. Ahmad Shah, after his victory, remained ten months at Lahore making arrangements for the good government of the province. One expedition he made against Jassa Singh, who, with the Phulkians and Nishanwala Sikhs, was ravaging Sirhind and expelling his garrisons. The Sikhs were again utterly routed, their forces were dispersed, and Jassa Singh, with his brother Chiefs, took refuge in the Kangra hills. Ahmad Shah then confirmed Zin Khan as Governor of Sirhind, Saadat Khan he nominated to Jalandhar, Sarbuland Khan to Kashmir, and Kabuli Mal to Lahore, and then returned to Kabul.

The great defeat of the Sikhs at Barnala, A.D. 1762.

Jassa Singh protects Ala Singh of Pattiala from the wrath of the Sikhs.

When their terrible enemy had departed, the Sikhs wished to turn upon Ala Singh, the Pattiala Chief, who had been taken prisoner early in the year by the Afghans, but who had pleased the conqueror so much that he had been created a Raja and dismissed with rich presents. But Jassa Singh's influence prevented an open quarrel, and he tried to persuade his fanatical co-religionists that Ala Singh had no option as to his acceptance of the obnoxious title, which had not till then been known among the Sikhs; the greatest of them being known only as "Sirdar" or Baron. It is true that Jassa Singh among his own followers was known as "Sultan-ul-Kaum;" but this title was not acknowledged by the

Sikh nation, and there is no proof that he was ever generally acknowledged as *Padshah* or King, which his descendants allege to have been the case.

The Sikhs pre-pare for revenge.

The Sikhs now prepared to attack the Afghan garrisons which Ahmad Shah had left behind him, but they first determined to try their strength against Kassur,[1] a rich Pathan colony and a very strongly fortified town, which had long been the object of desire to the Sikhs, and which they had two or three times attacked with but little success. They now, however, assembled in force for a regular attack. There were Jassa Singh, Ahluwalia; Hari Singh, Jhandha Singh, and Ganda Singh, Bhangis; Jai Singh, Kanheya; Jassa Singh, Ramgharia; and many more Sirdars from either side of the Satlej. Kassur was regularly invested, and it might have held out successfully had not Alif Khan, the Pathan leader, made an unwise and unsupported attack on the Sikh lines. He was beaten back with great loss, two of the Pathan Chiefs, Kamaluddin Khan and Hassan Khan, being slain; and the Sikhs entered the town with the flying Pathans, and completely sacked it. The fort held out some days longer, but eventually fell, and the Kassur territory was made over to the Bhangi Chiefs, who held it till 1794.[2] Preparations were then made for an expedition to Sirhind, which, although it had been twice sacked, was still a rich town, half-way between Ambala and Ludhiana.

The sack of Kassur.

Jassa Singh was Chief among the Sikh leaders on this

[1] Kassur was settled, in the reign of the Emperor Akbar, by a colony of between three and four thousand Pathans.

[2] In 1794, Nizamuddin Khan drove out the Sikhs; and Kassur was again captured by Ranjit Singh in 1807. The present representative of the old Chiefs of Kassur is Malik Khairuddin Khan, who did good service in 1845 and 1857. His mother was a Pathan, niece of Nizamuddin Khan; his own ancestors were Bhatti Rajputs, and settled at Kassur in 1520.

The expedition against Sirhind, and the defeat and death of the Imperial Governor.

occasion, but each misl fought under its own Sirdars, and there was no one who had sufficient influence to assume the sole command. The Krora Singhias, Bhangis, Shahids, Kanheyas, Nihangs, Phulkians, and Ahluwalias joined in the expedition, and the Sikh force numbered 23,000 men. Zin Khan, the Governor of Sirhind, gave them battle under the walls of the city, but was totally defeated and slain with his second in command, Lachmi Narain, commandant of the Buria fort.[1] Sirhind was razed to the ground, for it was hated by the Sikhs as the place where Fatah Singh and Zorawar Singh, the sons of their last and greatest Guru, had been murdered, and the whole surrounding country fell into their hands.[2]

In the Ambala district Jassa Singh seized twenty-four villages, forming the ilaqua of Suhoran; of these he retained eight himself, and gave twelve to the Bundalia Sikhs, who were in his train, and four to the Sirdars of Rurki. But no sooner had he recrossed the Satlej than his own eight villages—Suhoran, Pir Suhanah, Khanpur, Bhagu Mazrah, Simbal Mazrah, Dadu Mazrah, Orijlan, and Bhukri—were seized by the Raja of Pattiala, and it was only by the assistance of Ranjit Singh that they were recovered many years later.

Jassa Singh then returned to Amritsar, where he paid his share towards rebuilding the Golden Temple, or *Darbar Sahib*, which Ahmad Shah, before his departure, had defiled with the blood of cows and then blown up

[1] At Sirhind the Sikhs built, immediately after the victory, a *Shahidganj* or martyrs' memorial, to mark the spot where the sons of the Guru had been buried alive. The Sikhs still hold the place accursed, and as they pass, take a brick from the ruins and throw it into the Satlej.

[2] The Phulkians and Krora Singhias were the chief gainers by this victory. Sirhind fell to the share of the Pattiala Chief, while the two divisions of the Krora Singhias, the Sham Singhias and the Kalsias, took a large territory, much of which they still hold.

with gunpowder; and he also built the Ahluwalia bazaar, which is to this day the handsomest quarter of the city.

The actual Minister at this time at Dehli was Najibuddoulah, commonly known as Najib Khan, or Najibullah, a Rohilla Chief, who had been stationed there by Ahmad Shah in 1756, and who had gradually taken the power into his own hands. Jassa Singh had for some time entertained a strict alliance with Suraj Mal, the Jat ruler of Bhurtpur, and when this Chief was killed in a skirmish on the banks of the Hindan, in 1764, his son Jowahir Singh invited Jassa Singh to join him and take vengeance on Sher Khan, the slayer of his father, who had found an asylum with Najib Khan. Jassa Singh and a large body of Mahratta horse marched against the common enemy, who refused to give up Sher Khan, and the allies gained a victory near Shahjehanabad. Najib Khan then took refuge in Dehli, which was invested by the Sikhs and Mahrattas, and it would probably have fallen had not the besiegers heard that Ahmad Shah was approaching, and this induced them to accept a large sum of money and raise the siege. The Durani monarch, who was now growing old, and whose troops were mutinous, came no further than Sirhind, and then retired to Kabul, not without molestation from the Sikhs, who captured almost the whole of his baggage at the passage of the Chenab.

Najib Khan the Minister at Dehli, and his quarrels with the Sikhs.

The siege of Dehli.

The approach of Ahmad Shah.

The Sikhs now gained possession of all the country between the Satlej and the Chenab; Lahore was captured by the Bhangi Chiefs; and the next year, 1765, Gujrat and the whole country between the Chenab and the Jhelam fell into their hands.[1] Amritsar was much

The conquests of the Sikhs, A.D. 1765.

[1] *Vide* "Punjab Chiefs," pp. 392–394.

The Nanakshahi rupee struck.

enlarged and beautified, and the first national coin was struck with the following inscription :—

"Deg, wa Tegh, wa Fatah, wa Nusrat be Dirang Yaft az Nanak Guru Govind Singh."

Meaning—Hospitality, the sword, and victory, and conquest unfailing to Guru Govind Singh from Nanak.[1]

The expedition of 1766.

In 1766, Jassa Singh marched southwards with the Chiefs of Pattiala and Jhind, and ravaged Jhajjar, Rewari, Bhagpat, and captured Payal and Isru from the Kotla Afghans. The next year Ahmad Shah invaded India for the last time, but uncertain of the loyalty of his troops, he endeavoured to recover the country rather by intrigue than by force, and was so far successful that he sowed jealousy and suspicion between the Sikh Chiefs, which bore fruit later. But he found that it was hopeless to reconquer the country, and retired after having marched as far as the Satlej.

The last invasion of Ahmad Shah, A.D. 1767.

Jassa Singh overruns the country in the neighbourhood of Dehli.

In 1768, Jassa Singh overran the neighbourhood of Dehli, Ghaziuddin, and Anupshahr, defeating Mirza Sukhan, who was sent against him by the Emperor, and capturing the fort of Mehtab. He was not, however, able to retain any country so far south as this, for Amar Singh,

[1] This coin, known sometimes as "Nanaki" or "Nanakshahi," is still current in the Punjab. The inscription was in Persian character, as is the case with all Sikh coins, with the exception of an extremely rare rupee, struck by the mint-master of Amritsar during the reign of Ranjit Singh, on which the one word "Ung" or God, was inscribed in Sanscrit character. The meaning of "Deg" on the Nanakshahi rupee has been generally misinterpreted. Colonel Sleeman translates it in connection with "fatah" as the *pot* victory ("Rambles of an Indian Official," ii. 233), which conveys no meaning; Cunningham, p. 111, renders it *grace*, which is inadequate. Deg is literally a cooking vessel, and the inscription signifies that one of the injunctions received by Govind from Nanak was hospitality to the poor and strangers. When this coin was struck, every Sikh Sirdar, great or small, maintained a "langar" or public kitchen, at which all comers were daily fed. Poverty has compelled the general abandonment of this custom, but it is by some still kept up, among others by Sirdar Nihal Singh Chhachhi, also by Ram Singh Kuka, the newly-arisen Guru.

head of the Phulkian families of Pattiala, Jhind, and Nabha, had now become very powerful, and viewed the increasing influence of Jassa Singh with the greatest suspicion.

Kapurthalla seized and made the headquarters of Jassa Singh.

In 1771, he captured Rai Kot from the Pathans and Rajputs of Berowal, and attacked Kassur without success. The next year he marched against Kapurthalla. held by Rai Ibrahim, who had engaged to pay an annual tribute. But this it was very difficult to realise, and it was only after reducing thirteen forts in the neighbourhood of Kapurthalla, and investing the town itself, that the Rai paid what was due. But Jassa Singh's authority was not really restored, and, in 1777, his son-in-law, Mohr Singh, was shot at from the fort and killed. It was pretended that this was an accident, and Jassa Singh was compelled to accept the explanations offered; but, in 1780, he took advantage of the tribute again falling into arrears to seize the town, where he continued to reside till his death.

He joins a coalition to drive the Ramgharia Chiefs from the Punjab.

In 1776, to avenge an attack made upon him by three of the Ramgharia Sirdars, he formed a coalition with several powerful confederacies, the Bhangis, Kanheyas, Sukarchakias, and others, to expel Sirdar Jassa Singh Ramgharia from the Punjab, and seize his possessions. The expedition was a complete success; the Ramgharias were utterly defeated, and the head of the confederacy forced to fly into Harriana, where he remained in great poverty, and maintained himself by plunder till the death of his enemy in 1783, when he returned to the Punjab, and, with the assistance of Mahan Singh Sukarchakia and the Katoch Rajputs, recovered a considerable portion of his possessions.

Sirdar Jassa Singh died in 1783 at Amritsar, where

The death of Sirdar Jassa Singh, A.D. 1783.

a monument to his memory is still to be seen in the Derah of Baba Attal, near that of Nawab Kapur Singh. Although the influence of the Sirdar has been much exaggerated by his descendants, yet there can be no doubt that he was a man of the greatest ability, and much respected by the Sikhs.

His personal appearance.

In person he was tall, with a fair complexion, overhanging eyebrows, and piercing eyes. His arms are said to have been of unusual length, and he was famous as a marksman, both with the matchlock and the bow.

The reasons of Sirdar Jassa Singh's influence.

Although a most successful general in the field, it was rather as the most saintly and orthodox of their leaders that the Sikhs respected him, and the most powerful Sirdars, Amar Singh Pattiala included, received the Pahal or Sikh baptism from his hand.[1] Nor had he, as has been asserted, any acknowledged command of the Sikh forces.

The Sikh confederacies independent of each other.

The confederacies were, in his time, independent and hostile to each other, although they occasionally combined to attack some common enemy; and the Ahluwalia misl, which did not number more than 4000 fighting men, could never have stood alone in the field against the Krorasinghias, the Bhangis, the Kanheyas, or even the Phulkians. Yet the influence of Jassa Singh was great, and when any combination of the confederacies took place he was allowed a nominal command, though each body of troops fought under its own leaders, and seized whatever territory or plunder it could for itself.

Their manner of fighting.

The Sikh army, or the Dal Khalsa.

Jassa Singh did more than any other Chief to consolidate the Sikh power, which after his death grew more and more disorganised, until the strong hand of Maharaja Ranjit Singh again forced it into cohesion. The Sikh

[1] *Vide ante*, p. 31.

army was known as the *Dal Khalsa*,[1] or army of God. It consisted for the most part of cavalry, called *Kathiwand*, who found their own horses, and received a double share of all prize-money. Each Chief, in proportion to his means, furnished horses and arms to his retainers, who were called *Bargirs*, and as the first tribute exacted from a conquered district was horses, the infantry soldier was, after a successful campaign, generally transformed into a trooper. The infantry were considered an inferior branch of the service, and were only used for garrison and sentry duty, as the battles of the Sikhs were invariably cavalry actions. The only infantry which enjoyed any respect were the Akalis.[2] These were a fanatical body of devotees, who dressed in dark blue, and wore round their turbans steel quoits, partly for show and partly as weapons, though they were not very effective. Their other distinctive signs were a knife stuck in the turban, a sword slung round their neck, and a wooden club. These men, excited with a decoction of hemp, were generally the first to storm a town, and often did excellent service, but they were lawless and uncertain, and, in peaceful times, enjoyed almost boundless licence.

Its composition. The cavalry.

The infantry.

The Akalis.

The Sikh weapon was the sword, with which the cavalry were very skilful. Bows and arrows were used by the infantry, and a few matchlocks, but powder was scarce, and its use little loved by the Sikhs, who were never at ease with a musket in their hands. For the same reasons

The national weapon.

[1] The army was also known as Budha Dal, or the army of old men, though the reason of the young men remaining at home while their fathers were fighting is not known.

[2] The Akalis, or Followers of the Immortal, derive the name from *Akal*, immortal, an attribute of God. They were always a turbulent race; and Ranjit Singh, finding that he was unable to control them, used to employ them on the most desperate undertakings, in which they were successful or killed, either result being satisfactory to the Maharaja.

The artillery. they possessed scarcely any artillery, and although Ranjit Singh, with the aid of French and Italian officers, formed a very powerful and well-appointed artillery, it was, to the last, a branch of the service hated by every true Sikh, and principally filled by Muhammadans. Nor were the Sikhs fond of fighting behind walls; and Sirdar Jassa Singh only maintained the two forts of Daliwal and Werowal.[1]

[1] Under Maharaja Ranjit Singh the character, as well as the constitution, of the Sikh army almost entirely changed. The cavalry ceased to be the chief part of the force, and the infantry became the favourite service. This was in part owing to the labours of some European officers whom the Maharaja took into his service, and who introduced the teaching which had become general in Europe, the value of infantry as against cavalry being everywhere acknowledged. Some of these officers, Allard, Ventura, Avitabile, and Court, were men of considerable ability, and quite competent to perform all they promised in increasing the efficiency of the Lahore army. The infantry under their instruction became a most formidable body of troops, well-disciplined and steady, though slow in manœuvring. Their endurance was, moreover, very great, and a whole regiment would march thirty miles a day for many days together. The enlistment in the regular army during the great Maharaja's reign was entirely voluntary, but there was no difficulty in obtaining recruits, for the service was exceedingly popular.

The cavalry was constructed much in the same manner as it had been in the time of Sirdar Jassa Singh, when clouds of horsemen hung on the skirts of the army of Ahmad Shah Durani, afraid to venture an attack upon regular troops, but cutting off convoys and endangering the communications of the enemy. This is, no doubt, one of the principal duties of light cavalry; but the Sikh cavalry in the time of Ranjit Singh were, as a rule, miserably mounted and armed, and were more celebrated for taking to flight when attacked than for any display of valour.

On foot the Sikh is one of the bravest and most steady of soldiers, and, well led, would probably hold his own against the best European troops. He is unhappy on horseback, and is surpassed by Afghans and Hindustanis, troops far inferior as infantry soldiers. In the time of Ranjit Singh the infantry were the pick of the youth of the country: only the handsomest and strongest men were selected; while the cavalry were irregular troops, the contingents of the different Sirdars, and not appointed for any considerations of bravery or strength. The horses were small, weak, and ill-bred, and the accoutrements were of the roughest and coarsest kind.

The "Akalis," or immortals, towards the end of the reign of Ranjit Singh, lost their old reputation for sanctity, and were only an undisciplined rabble of lawless, drunken savages. They served nominally as irregular cavalry, having been formed into a corps by Ranjit Singh. Before this they had

The prize-money taken in a campaign was equally shared among the combatants. If a soldier was wounded, he invariably received compensation; and if he was killed, his son, or nearest male relative, was entertained in his place. **Plunder and prize-money.**

Sirdar Jassa Singh was an enlightened and liberal-minded man. He did not practise entire religious toleration, yet was far in advance of the majority of his countrymen. A very large number of Muhammadans were employed in his service, and they were allowed to follow their own religious observances without molestation. The call to prayer of the "Muwazzin" was, however, forbidden, as it roused the excitable Akalis to fury, and the slaughter of kine was strictly prohibited. On this point Jassa Singh was a thorough bigot, and twice he made expeditions to punish contumacious cow-killers, once at Kassur and once at Lahore. The Kassur offenders escaped, for the whole town was inhabited by Muhammadans, but the unfortunate butchers of Lahore were almost all massacred. **Jassa Singh a liberal-minded man.** **The killing of cows an unpardonable offence.**

The liberality of the Sirdar was very great. The city of Amritsar was in a great measure rebuilt and beautified by him. After the great temple, the Darbar Sahib, had been for the second time destroyed by Ahmad Shah, the Bhangis and Akalis were compelled to assign the whole income of the shrine to Sahib Rai Chaudhri, who consented to rebuild it. Jassa Singh paid off the whole of **The generosity of Jassa Singh, who rebuilds the Darbar Sahib.**

served on foot, and to the last they generally dismounted for a charge. They numbered about three thousand. The Akalis generally were armed with two or three swords, a matchlock, and steel rings or quoits with sharp edges, which they were supposed to throw with the most deadly effect. The weapon was, however, utterly worthless, and the person in the least danger from it was he at whom it was aimed. An account of the Sikh army under the successive rulers of Lahore is given in "The Punjab Chiefs," pp. 128, 129.

the mortgage himself, and completed the restoration of the temple. He also, at great expense, constructed a large reservoir at Anandpur, and gave largely to the Sodhis resident there. His hospitality was extended to all who asked it, and hundreds were fed daily at his *Langar*, or public kitchen.[1]

Sirdar Bhag Singh succeeds.

Sirdar Jassa Singh had neither son nor nephew, and Bagh Singh, a second cousin, then in his thirty-sixth year, succeeded to the estate, although there was a daughter married to Sirdar Mohr Singh of Fatahabad; but among the Jats a daughter and a daughter's son are not reckoned among the legal heirs. The first quarrel he found on his hands was one bequeathed to him by the late Chief, who had joined Hakikat Singh Kanheya in attacking Jummu, then ruled by Raja Brij Raj Deo. This Prince was so unfortunate as to possess a country coveted by all the powerful Sikh Chiefs, who at one time made alliance with him, exchanging turbans in token of perpetual friendship, and at another attacked him and joined his professed enemies. When the Kanheya Chief played the Raja false, in the usual manner, and joined the Bhangis in attacking Jummu, Jassa Singh broke off alliance with him, and would no doubt have assisted Sirdar Mahan Singh Sukarchakia in his struggle with the Kanheyas in 1783, had not death interrupted his revenge. His successor renewed the alliance with the Kanheya

His wars.

[1] The life of a Sikh Sirdar, in the days of Jassa Singh, was very simple. At daybreak he would rise, perform his ablutions, and dress, repeating the morning prayer or "Sukhmani." He then took his morning meal, which consisted, in Jassa Singh's case, of two pounds of flour and half a pound of sugar candy, and it is not surprising to hear that he grew very fat. He then set about the business of the day, and at 3 P.M. held a Durbar or assembly for all who chose to attend, where all matters of general interest were discussed. After the evening meal, musicians played and sung hymns called "Sabdh Rahras," and an hour after sunset all retired to rest, having repeated the "Ardas," or evening prayer.

Chief, and his first expedition was in company with Sirdar Jai Singh Kanheya against Wazir Singh and Bhagwan Singh, Chiefs of the Nakka country, between Lahore and Gogaira, and connections of Mahan Singh Sukarchakia. The next year he went to the assistance of Jai Singh, when Mahan Singh Sukarchakia, Jassa Singh Ramgharia, and Raja Sansar Chand of Kangra had united to destroy him. His aid, however, was of no avail; Jai Singh was defeated with great loss, near Battala, and never recovered the effect of the defeat. Sirdar Bagh Singh, who was not engaged in the action, retired across the Bias, and, after reinstating the Bedis in their possessions at Chamkour, from which they had been expelled by Sirdar Hari Singh Dallehwala, returned to Kapurthalla. Shortly after this he allied himself with Raja Sansar Chand; and their infant sons, Fatah Singh, who had been born during the Nakkai expedition, and Anrodh Chand, exchanged turbans in token of brotherhood. He then quarrelled with Sirdar Gulab Singh Bhangi, who owned Amritsar and the neighbouring country, and whose people had put to death an Ahluwalia agent at Chabal. He seized Jandiala and Taran Taran, but made no effort to retain these acquisitions, and returned to Kapurthalla satisfied with his success. This was in 1793.

The alliance with Raja Sansar Chand.

Overran part of the Amritsar district.

In 1796, he joined the Kanheyas, who were then led by Sadda Kour, the mother-in-law of Maharaja Ranjit Singh, and one of the most remarkable women in Punjab history, in their attack upon Sirdar Jassa Singh Ramgharia, the old enemy of his house, who had intrenched himself at Miani. But a sudden rise of the river Ravi compelled the allies to retreat in all haste with the loss of their baggage.[1] Nor was he more successful in 1801,

A second attack upon the Ramgharias, A.D. 1796.

Which was unsuccessful.

[1] *Vide* "Punjab Chiefs," vol. i. p. 173.

when he sent a force under Hamir Singh against the Ramgharias, who had been joined by Raja Sansar Chand of Kangra, and who completely routed the Ahluwalias, Hamir Singh being severely wounded. Hearing of this reverse, Sirdar Bagh Singh collected his remaining forces and marched as far as Phagwara against the enemy, but he there fell ill, and growing daily worse, was carried back to Kapurthalla, where he died.

The death of Bagh Singh, A.D. 1801.

Sirdar Fatah Singh succeeds.

Fatah Singh, only son of the late Chief, succeeded to the estate, and one of his first acts was to form an alliance offensive and defensive with Ranjit Singh, who had just gained possession of Amritsar. The young Chiefs exchanged turbans, and swore on the Granth to remain for ever friends. He then marched with his new ally against Kassur, but this Pathan colony was, at this time (1802-3), able to hold its own, and the Sikhs were compelled to retire. Fatah Singh recrossed the Bias, and the next two years employed himself in consolidating his power in the Jalandhar Doab.

His alliance with Maharaja Ranjit Singh.

The expedition of Holkar to the Punjab.

In the autumn of 1805, the Mahratta Chief, Jaswant Rao Holkar, came to the Punjab. Since his repulse before Dehli by Colonel Burn, in October 1804, he had met nothing but reverses. Twice during the following month had he been defeated with great loss by Lord Lake, and was compelled to fly across the Jamna, closely followed by the victor, while Colonel Murray, advancing from Guzerat, took possession of all his territories about Ujain, including his capital of Indore; and Colonel Wallace, advancing with a column from Poona, occupied Chandore and all the forts which commanded his territory south of the Taptee. He coalesced with Sindhia, whose hatred to the English was as bitter as his own, and endeavoured to win the Cis-Satlej Chiefs to his side. But these perceived that his cause was hopeless, and refused to join him, though several gave him assistance in money. He then marched to Amritsar, where he met Ranjit Singh (afterwards Maharaja) and Sirdar Fatah Singh Ahluwalia. The former was at first disposed to aid the Mahratta, and it was through the influence of Raja Bhag Singh of Jhind and Sirdar Fatah Singh that he did not do so. Lord Lake pursued Holkar as far as the Bias, and had not the only thought of the Governor-General been to conclude a speedy peace, one of the most inveterate enemies the English have ever had in India would have been utterly destroyed. But conciliation was considered the better policy: a treaty was made with Holkar, which restored to him the greater portion of the territory which had been wrested from him,[1] and a supplementary treaty was made with Ranjit Singh and Fatah Singh, by which they agreed to cause Holkar to leave Amritsar, pledging themselves to maintain no connection or friendship with him, while, on the other hand, the British Government promised to them a peaceful possession of their territories so long as their conduct remained friendly.[2] Fatah Singh,

The interview with Holkar and the Maharaja at Amritsar.

The treaty with Holkar and the Sikh Chiefs.

[1] This treaty was signed on the 24th December 1805, and by it Holkar renounced all right to the districts of Tonk, Rampura, Bhundi, and territory north of the Chambal. The Company agreed not to interfere south of that river, and to restore at the end of a specified time forts and districts in the Deccan.—*Vide* Aitchison's "Treaties."

[2] Treaty of friendship and amity between the Honourable East India Company and the Sirdars Ranjit Singh and Fatah Singh:—

"Sirdar Ranjit Singh and Sirdar Fatah Singh have consented to the following articles of agreement concluded by Lieutenant-Colonel John Malcolm, under the special authority of the Right Honourable Lord Lake, himself duly authorised by the Honourable Sir George Hilaro Barlow, Baronet, Governor-General, and Sirdar Fatah Singh, as principal on the part of himself, and plenipotentiary on the part of Ranjit Singh.

"*Article I.*—Sirdar Ranjit Singh and Sirdar Fatah Singh Ahluwalia hereby agree that they will cause Jaswant Rao Holkar to remove with his army to the distance of thirty kos from Amritsar immediately, and will never hereafter hold any further connection with him, or aid or assist him with

who had acted as the Agent of Ranjit Singh in the arrangement of this treaty, was presented by Lord Lake with a leopard as a mark of friendship, while he presented the English General with a hawk.

After the execution of these treaties, Holkar left the Punjab, though his intrigues with Lahore by no means ceased.[1]

Sirdar Fatah Singh accompanied Maharaja Ranjit

troops, or in any other manner whatever; and they further agree that they will not in any way molest such of Jaswant Rao Holkar's followers or troops as are desirous of returning to their homes in the Deccan, but, on the contrary, will render them every assistance for carrying such intention into execution.

"*Article II.*—The British Government hereby agrees that in case a pacification should not be effected between that Government and Jaswant Rao Holkar, the British army shall move from its present encampment on the banks of the river Bias, as soon as Jaswant Rao Holkar aforesaid shall have marched, with his army, to the distance of thirty kos from Amritsar; and that in any treaty which may hereafter be concluded between the British Government and Jaswant Rao Holkar, it shall be stipulated that, immediately after the conclusion of the said treaty, Holkar shall evacuate the territories of the Sikhs or march towards his own, and that he shall in no way injure or destroy such parts of the Sikh country as may lie in his route. The British Government further agrees that as long as the said Chieftains, Ranjit Singh and Fatah Singh, abstain from holding any friendly connection with the enemies of that Government, or from committing any act of hostility on their own parts against the said Government, the British armies shall never enter the territories of the said Chieftains, nor will the British Government form any plans for the seizure or sequestration of their possessions or property."

Dated 1st January 1806, corresponding with 10th Shawal, 1220 H. S.

[1] Ranjit Singh told Mr Metcalfe, in 1808, a characteristic story of the Mahratta Chief. When Holkar was encamped in the neighbourhood of Amritsar, news was brought that Lord Lake had crossed the Bias in pursuit of him. He immediately mounted his horse, and the alarm spreading through the whole army, all the troops fled to a considerable distance, leaving their tents standing.—Letter dated 17th September 1808, from Mr. C. T. Metcalfe to Secretary Government of India.

Holkar's reason for alarm was a sufficient one. On the 17th of November 1804, Lord Lake, after a march of fifty-eight miles in twenty-four hours, made a night attack on Holkar's camp. It was a complete surprise, and the enemy were only awoke by showers of grape from the English artillery. The cavalry then charged through the camp, which broke up in the utmost confusion—Holkar himself escaping with great difficulty, and losing more than 3000 men killed and wounded.

Singh in his expedition to the south of the Satlej in October 1806. The Ahluwalia Chief did not wish to join the expedition,[1] but his position in the Jalandhar Doab was critical and he was afraid to refuse.[2] The next year, 1807, he accompanied the Maharaja to Jhang, when the fort was captured, and the Sial Chief, Ahmad Khan, expelled.[3] This expedition occupied several months, and on his return to Kapurthalla he sent a force to Talwandi, a possession of the Sodhis, but which had been seized by the Sikhs of Kung. With the Ahluwalia force troops of Ranjit Singh under Sirdar Mith Singh Padhania were also sent, and the fact of the Lahore contingent having been employed in the expedition, determined the question of supremacy over the Sodhi villages some twenty-four years later.[4] Fatah Singh accompanied the Maharaja on his campaign against Kassur, which was captured after an obstinate resistance, and with the adjoining district annexed to the Lahore State.

Fatah Singh accompanies the Maharaja in his expedition of 1806.

The expedition to Jhang.

When Mr Metcalfe reached Kassur in September 1808, on a mission to Ranjit Singh, the Ahluwalia Sirdar was deputed to meet him, with Diwan Mokam Chand and two thousand cavalry, at a distance of four miles from camp, and escort him to his tents.[5] With the negotiations that followed Fatah Singh had little to do; for the Maharaja had ceased to trust a man whose interests were necessarily opposed to his own, though he appears always to have maintained some personal affection for him. An

Mr Metcalfe's mission to Lahore.

[1] *Vide* Pattiala Statement for an account of this expedition.

[2] Circular of the Resident of Dehli, dated 1st November 1806.

[3] "Punjab Chiefs," p. 505.

[4] Letter from Political Assistant at Ludhiana to Resident Dehli, dated 11th September 1831; with Statement of Sirdar Fatah Singh, dated 18th January 1826.

[5] Letter, dated 13th September 1808, from Mr C. T. Metcalfe to Government of India, from Kassur.

extract from a letter of Mr Metcalfe's will show the opinion entertained by that officer of Fatah Singh's character and position; and that the estimate was a singularly just one later events proved.[1]

Fatah Singh's character and position in A.D. 1808.

"Sirdar Fatah Singh of Ahlu has been supposed to be particularly attached to the Raja, but he is in reality particularly discontented with him. Ranjit Singh and Fatah Singh entered into alliance in early life, and to this alliance the former is principally indebted for his extraordinary rise. The quiet character of Fatah Singh, who was the equal, if not the superior, in rank and power of Ranjit Singh, has yielded to the bold commanding spirit of the other, and he has been the ladder by which Ranjit Singh has mounted to greatness. He now finds himself, not companion and friend of an equal, as formerly, but the nominal favourite of a master. The outward show of intimacy and friendship is preserved, but there is no confidence. He is not of the Raja's councils, nor is he intrusted with his secrets, but marches with a considerable force in the train of Ranjit Singh, without knowing whither or for what purpose. Fatah Singh, in rank and consideration, in military force and territorial possessions, is the first of the Chiefs of Ranjit Singh's army. He possesses the country east of the Satlej, from Jagraon to that river, the country generally between the Satlej and the Bias, and the country to the west of the Bias as far as Amritsar. He has a very fair reputation, and is looked up to by the disaffected as the fit person to be put at the head of a confederacy to throw off the yoke; but he is evidently not a revolutionist; he is mild and good-natured, seemingly simple, and

[1] Letter, dated 8th November 1808, from Mr C. T. Metcalfe to Government of India, from Gougrana, Cis-Satlej States.

undoubtedly wanting energy. This is the Chief who was in Lord Lake's camp on the banks of the Bias. He there acquired a respect for the British character, which causes him to look to the British Government with the hope of obtaining from it a release from the overbearing tyranny of Ranjit Singh."

Fatah Singh joins the expedition of 1809 in the Cis-Satlej States.

Until the departure of Mr Metcalfe, in April 1809, Sirdar Fatah Singh remained with the Maharaja. He joined the expedition south of the Satlej, made in opposition to the wishes and advice of the Envoy, and which nearly occasioned a rupture between the British and Lahore Governments; and he was present at the signing of the treaty of Amritsar, of the 25th April, by which the long and troublesome negotiations were brought to a satisfactory conclusion, the British Government engaging not to interfere in the Maharaja's territories north of the Satlej, while he agreed to attempt no further encroachments to the south of that river.[1]

Rumours of a new alliance of Fatah Singh and the Maharaja against the English.

The Maharaja nevertheless chafed inwardly against this treaty; and if the news which the native agents at Lahore sent later in the year to the British Resident was correct, Sirdar Fatah Singh was not so sincere a well-wisher of the Government as Mr Metcalfe had fancied. These reports were to the effect that the alliance between Ranjit Singh and Fatah Singh had been strengthened by vows upon the Granth, the Sikh scriptures; and that the Maharaja had declared that it would be an eternal disgrace to him and the Khalsa should the British army continue to occupy Ludhiana, and the slaughter of kine be permitted in territory which of right belonged to the followers of Guru Govind Singh. Not only must the British be driven back from the Satlej, but Delhi must

[1] Aitchison's "Treaties," vol. ii. p. 237, No. LVII.

be conquered; and Fatah Singh was directed to supply thirty thousand horse and ten guns, and to post his force conveniently at Phagwara, Kapurthalla, Jandialah, and Koli, ready to join the contingents of the Rajput Chiefs when they arrived from the hills.[1] Fatah Singh promised compliance, but he had in his heart no intention of fighting against the English, whose power he had learned to respect; and, two months later, the arrival of the Kabul monarch, Shah Shuja, in the Punjab, and a projected expedition against Multan, diverted the attention of Ranjit Singh from any operations to the south of the Satlej, which he had probably never seriously meditated.

Fatah Singh accompanies the Kangra expedition, A.D. 1809.

Fatah Singh was present in the Kangra expedition of 1809, when the Maharaja gained by treachery the celebrated fort of Raja Sansar Chand, which had been long besieged by the Gurkhas, under Amar Singh Thappa. In the spring of the next year, when Ranjit Singh marched to Multan, Fatah Singh was left in charge of Lahore and Amritsar; and in February 1811 he accompanied the Maharaja to Rawul Pindee to meet Shah Mahmud, the brother of Shah Shuja, who was on his way to Kashmir, then a province of Kabul.

He aids the Maharaja to ruin Budh Singh of Jalandhar.

In October 1811, he marched against Sirdar Budh Singh of Jalandhar, with Diwan Mokham Chand and Jodh Singh Ramgharia. Budh Singh held territory in the Jalandhar Doab worth Rs. 3,00,000 a year, and the ostensible excuse for the expedition against him was his persistent refusal to attend Ranjit Singh with a contingent in the field. The unfortunate Chief made no resistance, but fled across the Satlej, and all his estates

[1] Translation of a news-letter from Lahore, dated 19th December 1809, to Resident at Dehli. Letter from A. Seton, Resident, to Government of India, dated 28th December 1809.

were confiscated to Lahore. The reasons that induced Fatah Singh and Jodh Singh to aid in the reduction of the Jalandhar Chief are not easy to divine. They were supposed themselves to have formed a secret alliance, offensive and defensive, against the Maharaja, and they must have known that by destroying one of the few nobles of importance whom Ranjit Singh's rapacity had yet spared they were building up his power, and hastening the time, which was fast approaching, when they themselves would share the fate of the man whom they had so basely assisted to ruin. They may, indeed, have hoped that their submission to Ranjit Singh would secure their own safety, but the fate which attends on vacillation and weakness was not long in overtaking the Ramgharia Chief, while English influence barely sufficed to save Sirdar Fatah Singh.[1]

His war service in the Punjab proper.

In the majority of Ranjit Singh's annual campaigns Fatah Singh served with his contingent. He fought at the battle of Haidera, on the 13th July 1813, when Fatah Khan, the Kabul Minister and General, was utterly defeated and driven from the Punjab; he held a command in the Bhimbar, Rajaori, and Bahawalpur campaigns, and when the territory of his old friend Jodh Singh Ramgharia was seized he was not too proud to accept a share of the plunder. He was at the last famous siege of Multan, in 1818, when the whole province fell into the hands of the Maharaja, and Nawab Muzaffar Khan was slain; and established a military post of his own at Talambah, forty-five miles north-east of the city. During the Kashmir campaign of 1819 he

[1] Letter, dated 15th October 1811, from Sir D. Ochterlony to Government of India.

The Ramgharia estates were all annexed by Ranjit Singh in 1816. Letter, dated 2d January 1817, from Sir D. Ochterlony to Government of India.

remained in charge of the capital; and, in 1821, assisted at the reduction of the fort of Mankera, in the desert of the Sind Sagar Doab.

The relations of Fatah Singh with the British Government.

The possessions of Sirdar Fatah Singh being situated for the most part in the Jalandhar Doab north of the Satlej, his relations with the British Government were, previous to 1825, not very intimate, though he would gladly have accepted the protection which assured their territories to the Cis-Satlej Chiefs. On a few occasions, however, he was brought into direct communication with the British.

The Chiefship of Bhirog.

The first time was in connection with the Chiefship of Bhirog. This estate, consisting of about one hundred villages, was conferred by Sirdar Jassa Singh Ahluwalia on a dependant named Mirza Singh, whose son Jowahir Singh fought and died under the Ahluwalia standard. When Maha Singh, the son of Jowahir Singh, was directed, in 1810 and 1814, by the British representative to fulfil his engagements as a Chief under the protection of the Government, he declared himself to be a vassal of Sirdar Fatah Singh Ahluwalia.

Taken possession of by Fatah Singh.

In 1817, Sir David Ochterlony, in consequence of the outrageous conduct of the Bhirogia Chief, called upon Fatah Singh to confiscate the territory. The latter accordingly sent a force across the Satlej, under command of Mir Nizamuddin, who repulsed the Bhirogia force, with a loss on both sides of a hundred and fifty men, and took possession of the whole estate.[1]

But restored to Maha Singh,

Maha Singh was at this time a boy of thirteen years of age, and the mismanagement of his estate was owing to the evil influence of his mother, whose favourites,

[1] Letter, dated 12th March 1817, from Captain Birch to Sir D. Ochterlony.

Bassawa Singh and Rai Singh, committed every sort of oppression. In consideration of his youth, Maha Singh was pardoned by Sir David Ochterlony, and the Ahluwalia Sirdar was directed to withdraw his troops from Bhirog, and reinstate Maha Singh.[1] Fatah Singh was disinclined to restore the estate, and the case was somewhat a hard one; as Sir Charles Metcalfe, the Resident, justly observed: "Sirdar Fatah Singh has already been a sufferer by the restitution of Maha Singh's lands, after permission had been given for their confiscation. The act was generous and considerate towards Maha Singh, but with respect to Sirdar Fatah Singh, it does, I confess, appear to me to have been a hardship, though justified by circumstances."[2] It was only when the Sirdar was informed, in the plainest language, that unless he restored the estate without delay a British force would be sent to dispossess him, that he reinstated his vassal, and withdrew his troops across the Satlej.[3]

Who remains contumacious.

The consideration shown to Maha Singh was not appreciated by that Chief; and, in 1825, he positively refused to acknowledge the supremacy of the Ahluwalia Chief, and paid no attention to the remonstrances of the British Agent, who was compelled to recommend the attachment of the whole or a portion of the jagir until he should obey the orders conveyed to him.[4] The Resident tried to induce Maha Singh to listen to reason, but he had abandoned himself to the guidance of a common courtesan, and would accept no advice, however wise, declaring that

[1] Letter, dated 1st November 1817, from Captain Birch to Sir D. Ochterlony.

[2] Sir Charles Metcalfe to Captain Birch, dated 29th August 1818.

[3] Captain Birch to Sir D. Ochterlony, dated 11th November 1817.

[4] Captain Murray to Agent Governor-General, at Dehli, dated 28th July 1825.

he would rather beg his bread than acknowledge the supremacy of Fatah Singh.[1]

The Government insist upon Maha Singh's submission.

The Government of India, to whom the question was referred, held that the supremacy of Fatah Singh was undoubted, and desired to know whether, by the custom of the tenure, he was entitled to require the services of Maha Singh and his contingent beyond the Satlej.[2] The Resident saw no reason why the authority of the lord paramount should be questioned in this matter, as the treaty with Maharaja Ranjit Singh of 1809 did not absolve any of the old dependants of that Prince or his subordinate Chiefs from their allegiance; and it was undoubted that before that time neither Maha Singh nor his ancestors would have questioned the right of Fatah Singh or his predecessors to claim service beyond the Satlej. The Government of India approved of this view, and allowed Fatah Singh to enforce his supremacy by any measures he might see fit to employ.[3] Fatah Singh was himself in difficulties at this time, and it was not till July 1826 that he took action, sending troops for the punishment of his vassal and summoning him to submit. But the jealousy of the Maharaja was aroused. He peremptorily directed the Sirdar to desist from all hostile proceedings against Maha Singh until he should sanction them, demanding that in any expedition against Bhirog, Lahore troops should co-operate with those of Kapurthalla. The effect of this interference on the part of the Maharaja was to paralyse the movements of Sirdar Fatah Singh,

Maharaja Ranjit Singh interferes.

[1] From Agent Governor-General to Captain Murray, dated 1st and 11th of August 1825; and letters, dated 13th and 16th August, from Captain Murray to Agent Governor-General.

Sir D. Ochterlony's letter to Captain Birch, dated 28th March 1819.

[2] Government of India, dated 9th December 1825, to Sir C. Metcalfe.

[3] Sir C. Metcalfe, dated 31st December 1825, to Government of India; and Government of India, dated 13th January 1826, to Sir C. Metcalfe.

and complete the defection of his vassal. But the Government did not consider it necessary to interfere so long as the action of the Maharaja was confined to prohibiting Sirdar Fatah Singh from proceeding against Bhirog, though it was notified that no permission would be given for Lahore troops to cross the Satlej with those of Kapurthalla.[1]

The building of the fort of Isru. The English Government had, in 1818, to interfere with regard to the erection of a fort at Isru, in protected territory. This fort was designed on the plan of that of Govindgarh at Amritsar, and was far larger and stronger than was necessary for simple defence. Its construction excited the alarm of the Raja of Pattiala, whose ancestor had originally conquered the district, in company with Jassa Singh, and whose territory lay all around it. The Sirdar was unwilling to abandon his design, and it was not till three years later, after several injunctions, that the building was discontinued.[2]

The Kotila case. In 1822, a question of great importance with reference to the different grades of dependence in the protected Sikh States, and the degree of interference between Chiefs and their vassals on the part of the British Government arose, which requires a brief notice. The small fort of Kotila was situated in the centre of Sirdar Fatah Singh's Cis-Satlej territories, and was owned by a Patan family, the eldest representative of which was Nihang Khan. His ancestors had acquired the estate by the sword at a very remote period, and had, previous to the English connection with the Cis-Satlej States, been in a

[1] Letters of the 2d August 1828, from Captain Murray to Sir E. Colebrooke; and letter of the 7th August, from Sir E. Colebrooke to Captain Murray.

[2] Letters from Captain Birch to the Resident at Dehli, of the 10th March 1818, the 22d June 1818, and the 14th November 1820.

certain degree dependent on Sirdar Fatah Singh. This dependence was not absolute, but was similar to that which they, at other times, had incurred to the Pattiala, Rupur, and Bilaspur Chiefs; such dependence, indeed, as in times of great disturbance and reaction, all small Chiefs were necessarily compelled to incur. The Ahluwalia Sirdar was determined to assert his supremacy, and, in the summer of 1822, forcibly occupied the fort of Kotila, and persisted in retaining it in spite of the repeated orders of the British Officer at Ambala. The ostensible reason for this proceeding was found in the quarrels of the Kotila family. Balwant Khan, one of the younger brothers, had long disagreed with his family, and had on two former occasions sought and obtained the assistance of Sirdar Fatah Singh, given on condition of feudal service and full acknowledgment of Ahluwalia supremacy. On neither of these occasions did he go the length of occupying Kotila, and was induced to refrain from interference in 1813, by a letter from Sir David Ochterlony threatening to send a force against him if he did not cease molesting Nihang Khan; and in 1819, by a letter from Captain Birch.[1] From this time Balwant Khan resided at Kapurthalla in the service of the Ahluwalia Chief, till June 1822, when he returned to Kotila, and with the aid of Ahluwalia troops expelled his three brothers and took possession of the fort.

The Kapurthalla Chief asserts his authority over Kotila.

The excuse for his conduct.

The officer at Ambala requested permission to call on the Pattiala Raja for troops to expel Balwant Khan and reinstate his brother, but further information was required as to Sirdar Fatah Singh's claim to supremacy over

[1] These letters accompany Captain Ross's letter, of the 26th August 1822, to A. Ross, Agent Governor-General Dehli.

Kotila.[1] It appeared that Fatah Singh had asserted, in 1813, a claim to a fourth share in Kotila; and on this claim he founded his repeated interference with Nihang Khan; yet this right, if it ever did exist, had certainly been dormant for sixteen years—that is, for more than two years previous to Mr Metcalfe's mission to Lahore—the *status quo* of which period had been formally recognised by Government for the adjustment of all questions of right in property in the protected Sikh States. The Kotila Chiefs had not been formally declared independent Chiefs under British protection, but then none of the protected Chiefs were so declared, the documents announcing the guarantee having only general allusion to the Chiefs to the southward of the Satlej, without any detailed enumeration of them. Besides this, Fatah Singh, in a letter to Captain Birch, in June 1815, had waived his claim altogether, which was a sufficiently good proof that it had never been founded in right.[2]

One passage in a letter of Sir D. Ochterlony to the address of Sirdar Fatah Singh, seemed to give some colour to his claim; but that officer, then Resident in Rajputana, explained that his own opinion was absolutely against any supremacy whatever on the part of Kapurthalla, and that if at any time he had been induced to employ the Ahluwalia authority in the adjustment of Kotila differences, it was only in accordance with his usual practice of employing the more considerable powers on

[1] Letters, dated 9th August 1822, from Deputy Superintendent Ambala to Agent Governor-General, Dehli; and of Agent Governor-General to Deputy Superintendent, dated 20th August 1822.

[2] Letters from Captain Ross, dated 26th August and 29th September, to Agent Governor-General; and from Agent Governor-General to Captain Ross, dated 26th August and 21st September. Also five Persian letters from Sir D. Ochterlony to Sirdar Fatah Singh.

services of such a nature, without the most remote intention of allowing such services to imply any supremacy on the part of the Chiefs employed.[1]

The decision of the Government as to Ahluwalia supremacy in Kotila.

The Government of India, to whom the case was referred for decision, ruled that although Fatah Singh had once had supremacy over Kotila, yet that his right had become obsolete previous to the introduction of the British authority; partly by his own voluntary act, in excusing tribute to the Kotila Afghans as a reward for their gallant services, and partly from his failure to afford them protection against the exactions and encroachments of other Sikh Chiefs. Fatah Singh was, accordingly, warned against attempting to exercise any intervention whatever in the affairs of the Kotila Chiefship: Nihang Khan was reinstated in his rights, and the half share of Balwant Khan in the Kotila fort was forfeited to his elder brother.[2]

Sirdar Fatah Singh crosses the Satlej, abandoning his Trans-Satlej territory.

On the 27th December 1825, Sirdar Fatah Singh, alarmed by the advance of two battalions of the Lahore army towards his territory, fled across the Satlej with the whole of his army, and took refuge at Jagraon in the Protected States, abandoning all his estates Trans-Satlej to the Maharaja.[3] He had for long been suspicious of his former friend and adopted brother, believing that his own fate would resemble that of the Ramgharia Chief, with whom the Maharaja had also sworn eternal friendship, but whose possessions he had seized on the

[1] Letter, dated 1st June 1823, from Sir D. Ochterlony to Deputy Superintendent Sikh States.

[2] Letter, dated 10th March 1824, from Agent Governor-General to Government of India; and reply, dated 30th April 1824, to Agent Governor-General.

[3] Captain Wade to Lieutenant Murray, Deputy Superintendent, dated 28th March 1825; Lieutenant Murray to Sir C. Metcalfe, dated 29th December 1825; and Captain Wade to Sir C. Metcalfe, dated 8th February 1826.

first convenient opportunity. It is true that no considerations of friendship or good faith appeared to have any weight with the Maharaja when opposed to his own interest, but there is some reason to believe that, on this occasion, the fears of Fatah Singh were exaggerated, and that he was one of the few men for whom the Maharaja had any sincere feeling of regard. The Sirdar then attempted to obtain from the British Government some sort of guarantee for the security of his Trans-Satlej possessions. He urged that the intentions of the Maharaja towards him were unequivocal, and that neither his person nor his property were safe; that, since 1805, when the treaty with Lord Lake was concluded, he had been a well-wisher of the British Government; and now claimed the support due to an ally in the preservation of his position and territory north of the Satlej.[1]

Fatah Singh attempts to obtain British guarantee for the safety of his Trans-Satlej estates.

What the Sirdar desired was of course impossible to grant, and the British Government had neither wish nor excuse, under the treaty of 1809, to interfere with the Maharaja's proceedings north of the Satlej; nor, indeed, were the whole of his Cis-Satlej estates under British protection. These consisted, at this time, of 454 villages, of which 291 were held by Fatah Singh in sovereignty, and 163 were in possession of jagirdars. Naraingarh and Jagraon, consisting respectively of 46 and 66 villages, had been received by grant from the Maharaja in 1807, on payment of *nazrana*, or tribute, and over these two estates the supremacy of Lahore was admitted by the Government. The rule adhered to was thus expressed by Sir Charles Metcalfe in his letter of the 14th January 1826: "Whatever possessions on the left bank of the Satlej were held by Sirdar Fatah Singh or his

This the Government could not give.

Some of the Cis-Satlej estates were Lahore grants.

[1] Lieutenant Murray to Sir C. Metcalfe, dated 10th January 1826.

ancestors previously to his alliance with Raja Ranjit Singh, and, of consequence, independently with regard to that Chieftain, should be confirmed to him under our protection, and this might be extended to acquisitions on the same bank of the river made in co-operation with Ranjit Singh at a time when their conquests were portioned on a footing of equality. But with respect to any there should be held under a grant of Ranjit Singh, which would imply sovereignty on his part, and subordination on that of Fatah Singh, the claim of the Raja must be admitted."[1]

His Trans-Satlej estates seized by the Maharaja,

On the flight of Fatah Singh, the Maharaja occupied his Trans-Satlej territory and expelled his garrisons; but, at the same time, he expressed his earnest desire for a reconciliation, promising to give any assurances that might be desired for the security of his person and possessions.[2] The Sirdar, though he did not believe in the assurances of the Maharaja, yet thought it politic to return to Kapurthalla in 1827, the rather as the British Government had declined any interference on behalf of his Trans-Satlej lands. The claim to British protection for his ancestral Cis-Satlej estates was admitted, and this claim Fatah Singh was anxious to assert, as he considered it probable that he might again have to seek an asylum to the south of the Satlej.[3] Whether the fears of Fatah Singh in his flight were exaggerated or not, it is certain that they were shared by others; and in October 1829, one of the principal Trans-Satlej Chiefs, Sirdar Dewa

But restored on Fatah Singh's return to Kapurthalla.

[1] Letters of the 8th and 21st January 1826, from Lieutenant Murray, Deputy Superintendent, to Sir Charles Metcalfe; Government of India to Sir C. Metcalfe, of the 17th February 1826; and Sir E. Colebrooke to Captain Murray, of the 21st March 1828.

[2] From Captain Wade to Sir C. Metcalfe, of 5th January 1826.

[3] Resident to Government of India, dated 17th June 1828; and Sir E. Colebrooke to Captain Murray, of 19th December 1828.

Singh, holding estates in the Jalandhar Doab worth Rs. 1,25,000, and in the Cis-Satlej States worth Rs. 35,000, abandoned all his territory on the right bank of the Satlej, and retired to Sialba.[1]

Although the Government declined active interference, yet their expressed sympathy secured Fatah Singh's possessions to him, both Trans- and Cis-Satlej, and when, in 1836, the Maharaja confiscated Phagwara, which had been one of his earliest grants to the Sirdar, he restored it almost immediately, believing that the Government would interfere in favour of the Chief. During the latter years of his life, Fatah Singh remained at Kapurthalla in comparative retirement.

The death of Sirdar Fatah Singh, A.D. 1837, and succession of Nihal Singh.

Sirdar Fatah Singh died in October 1837, and his son Nihal Singh succeeded to his estates, and was acknowledged by the British Government as Chief.[2] But the Maharaja of Lahore and his unscrupulous Minister, Raja Dhyan Singh, had no intention of allowing the Ahluwalia territory to change hands without gaining something for themselves. Amar Singh, the younger brother of Nihal Singh, was encouraged to hope that his brother would be set aside in favour of himself; but he was too impatient to wait the progress of events, which could only be hastened by most lavish presents to the Lahore Court, and he conspired with some of the Ahluwalia officials against his brother's life. As Nihal Singh was leaving the female apartments, with only one attendant, he was attacked by assassins, but he defended himself gallantly, and escaped with some slight wounds. His servant, who, with true devotion, threw himself before his master to

The intrigues of Amar Singh.

The life of Nihal Singh attempted.

[1] Captain Wade to Officiating Resident Dehli, dated 14th October 1829.

[2] Secretary to Government North-Western Provinces to Sirdar Nihal Singh, dated 27th February 1837.

receive the blows intended for him, was cut to pieces. When the Maharaja of Lahore heard of this tragedy, he summoned both brothers to his presence, and, professing to sympathise with the elder, directed him to allow Amar Singh a separate maintenance of Rs. 30,000 a year, instead of a lakh which he had demanded, and to return home, while he, the Maharaja, would visit the conspirators with exemplary punishment. No sooner, however, had Nihal Singh left court than Amar Singh was admitted to favour, and, on his promise to pay a liberal *nazrana*, was encouraged to attempt to wrest territory worth a lakh of rupees from his brother.[1] This he succeeded in doing. He captured Nihal Singh by surprise, and would not release him until he had consented to assign for his maintenance the district of Sultanpur.

The quarrel between the brothers.

Throughout the remainder of the reign of Ranjit Singh, and that of his successor, Kharrak Singh, the brothers were in a constant state of feud; and Nihal Singh was scarcely able to maintain himself in the Chiefship by even extravagant bribes to the Lahore authorities. When Sher Singh advanced his claims to the throne, Nihal Singh supported him, believing that in him he would find powerful support against both his brother and Raja Dhyan Singh, the Minister, whom Sher Singh hated, although he was unable to stand without him.[2] But the new Maharaja was of a weak disposition, and Amar Singh soon became a favourite at Lahore; and there can be little doubt that his claims would have been admitted, and Sirdar Nihal Singh dispossessed, but for his premature death. On the 28th of March, Maharaja Sher Singh went on a boating excursion on the Ravi, attended by

[1] Captain Wade to Government of India, dated 4th October 1837.

[2] Mr Clerk to Government of India, 5th December 1840.

The death of Amar Singh.

Rajas Dhyan Singh and Hira Singh, Jamadar Khushhal Singh, Bhai Gurmukh Singh, Rai Kesra Singh, Sirdars Attar Singh Kalianwala and Amar Singh Ahluwalia. The weather was fine, but the boat suddenly filled with water and went down. Sirdar Amar Singh was drowned, and the rest of the party escaped with difficulty by means of their riding elephants, which were waiting on the bank, and which were driven into the river to their assistance.[1]

The boating excursion on the Ravi, and its results.

It was generally believed in Lahore that this accident had in it nothing accidental, but that the Maharaja had directed the boat to be sunk, hoping that Jamadar Khushhal Singh, whom he hated for his adherence to the party of Rani Chand Kour, would be drowned. The story was probable enough, but there is no proof to sustain it, and the only person to gain by the catastrophe was Sirdar Nihal Singh, who was rid for ever of a bitter enemy, and who forthwith made friends with Raja Dhyan Singh, receiving a grant of his brother's jagir of Sultanpur, on payment of a large *nazrana.*[2]

The cause of the enmity of Maharaja Sher Singh as alleged by Kapurthalla.

The reasons the Ahluwalia Chiefs have always assigned for the enmity of Maharaja Sher Singh are somewhat remarkable. On the death of Maharaja Kharrak Singh and his son, on the 5th November 1840, Sher Singh, finding the whole Court opposed to his pretensions to the succession, sent a message from Battala, where he resided, to Mr Clerk, the Agent of the Governor-General, through Mulvi Rajib Ali and Mulvi Ghulam Muhammad Khan, a servant of the Ahluwalia Chief, begging for the assistance of the British Government to gain the throne, and promising, as the price of such assistance, to cede

[1] Mr Clerk to Government of India, dated 29th March 1841.

[2] Mr Clerk to Government of India, dated 29th June 1841.

Kashmir to them. In the meantime, Sher Singh, with the aid of the Jammu party, became Maharaja; but still doubtful of his power to hold the position he had gained, without the knowledge or approval of the British Government, he sent Colonel Mohan Lal on a second mission to Mr Clerk, begging that he might be recognised, and the usual letters of congratulation addressed to him. Mr Clerk reminded the Colonel of the promise regarding Kashmir, of which he did not pretend to be ignorant, and returned with the desired letters. But Sher Singh had now established himself securely, and denied altogether that he had ever made any promise regarding Kashmir; and Fakir Azizuddin was sent to discuss the question with Mr Clerk. No written document was producible, and the Ahluwalia Agent, Mulvi Ghulam Muhammad Khan, was summoned to give his evidence in the matter. He was afraid to tell the whole truth, but he told so much of it as to demonstrate the bad faith of Maharaja Sher Singh, and to rouse against Sirdar Nihal Singh his lasting enmity.

The Sirdar had several opportunities of showing his good-will to the British Government, of which he took advantage. On the visit of Lord Auckland to the Punjab in 1838, he rendered good service in collecting supplies, and assisted in the same way the British troops marching to Kabul. He built a bridge at Hari for the use of the Governor-General on his return, and had an interview with him at Makku. Some of the troops under Hyder Ali Khan took part in the Kabul expedition of 1842, marching as far as Jalalabad.

The murder of Sher Singh, A.D. 1843.

Maharaja Sher Singh was assassinated on the 15th September 1843, and Dalip Singh proclaimed his successor. Had Sirdar Nihal Singh possessed any energy or character, he might, at this time, have become the foremost man in the Punjab. Raja Dhyan Singh was dead, the Sindhanwalia Chiefs were scattered, and the new Minister, Hira Singh, was held in contempt by the army. But the Ahluwalia Chief did not care to interfere at Lahore, and would not even attend, as was usual, at the feast of the Dasserah in October.[1] He excused his non-attendance by the plea of ill health, and of the arrival of the ashes of the late Maharaja and Raja Dhyan Singh at Kapurthalla; and although he did not send the customary presents, he offered his congratulations to Dalip Singh on his accession, and professed his intention of proceeding shortly to Lahore.[2] But he delayed his visit from month to month on some excuse or another, the true reason being that he was of a timid and unenterprising disposition, and his ambition was not even excited by the prospect of obtaining the leadership in the Punjab, which might have been his had he come forward to head the Khalsa in opposition to the Jammu Raja, Gulab Singh, who was universally and justly hated. The only other Sikh Chief of considerable influence at Lahore, and whom the army would have been content to follow, was Lehna Singh Majithia, but he was as timid as Nihal Singh, and deserted his country when most it needed his counsel and assistance.[3]

Nihal Singh refuses to visit Lahore.

His unenterprising disposition.

Sirdar Lehna Singh Majithia.

To the Dasserah of 1844, celebrated on the 21st October, Nihal Singh sent a contingent, for it had always been customary at this festival for the Lahore ruler to hold a

[1] Lieut.-Colonel Richmond to Government of India, dated 6th October 1843.

[2] Lieut.-Colonel Richmond to Government of India, dated 16th October 1843.

[3] Lieut.-Colonel Richmond to Government of India, dated 1st November 1813.

review of the whole army, and receive the congratulations and offerings of the commanders of all ranks; but he did not attend in person, pretending that he was under the necessity of performing a vow by a pilgrimage to Jowala Mukhi.[1]

The conduct of Nihal Singh during the Sikh war of 1845.

The weakness of the Sirdar, and his desire to stand well with all parties, brought him well nigh to ruin in 1845, when the Sikh war made it imperative on every Chief in the Protected States to show his loyalty to the British Government by active good-will, or to be accounted a traitor. His obligations were the following:—By the treaty of the 25th April 1809, and by article 4 of the subsequent declaration of the 6th May 1809, the Ahluwalia Chief was bound to furnish supplies to the British troops passing through or stationed within the Cis-Satlej territories. By the declaration of Government in 1828, before referred to, the Sirdar was considered to be "under British protection in respect of his ancestral possessions east of the Satlej, but dependent on Lahore for places conferred by the Lahore Government prior to September 1808."[2] This declaration, made at a time when the Sirdar was, or considered himself to be, in danger of losing every possession through the rapacity of the Maharaja, should have bound him to the British Government through gratitude; but this feeling has never been common among the protected Chiefs.

His obligations.

The manner in which he fulfilled them.

With regard to supplies, Colonel Mackeson proves that, in spite of repeated orders, the Ahluwalia agents failed to supply grain, and Captain Mills wrote that "the Ahluwalia Chief afforded no assistance of any kind in supplies

[1] Lieut.-Colonel Richmond to Government of India, dated 16th October and 30th October 1844.

[2] Government of India to Sir E. Colebrooke, 14th November 1828.

till after the defeat of the Sikh army." Nor was this from inability, for his territory was rich in corn, and Jagraon was the best grain country between the Jamna and the Satlej. Yet the fact was, that practically no supplies[1] were furnished before the two early battles of the campaign, and very little until the final defeat of the Sikhs, after which there were no bounds to the zeal of the Sirdar, who wrote to Major Lawrence that, in the face of 40,000 enemies, he had collected one hundred thousand maunds of grain for the English in the Jalandhar Doab, and he actually unroofed the houses of his subjects to furnish fuel to the British troops returning from Lahore.

With regard to the personal demeanour of the Chief, he stated in his defence that he had not such sufficient warning as enabled him to join the British standard. But the following facts will show that he had warning not only sufficient, but more than he had a right to expect under the circumstances. On the 24th November 1845, Major Broadfoot addressed him a letter, which, under Persian imagery, conveyed a serious warning, the import of which the confidential agent was instructed to explain. "It is great wisdom," wrote Major Broadfoot, "to know how to increase friendship, and its fruits are always good. In any government or country at such times as the bazaar of foolishness is warm, and the eye of reflection is not fixed on the probable result, it behoves the wise and far-seeing who are real friends to take counsel from futurity. This is forethought. The meaning of this letter I have explained to your confidential agent, Basti Ram, to the messenger who carries it."

He fails to attend the British camp,

In spite of friendly warning,

On the 30th November, Major Broadfoot again wrote urging the Chief to cross the Satlej, which letter was

And direct orders.

[1] Literally only fifty-four maunds of grain.—Colonel Mackeson's Report.

answered in the same spirit by him on the 7th December. On the 13th, the proclamation which guaranteed their possessions, Cis- and Trans-Satlej, to all the loyal, and distinctly pointed out the penalty of disobedience, was issued; and the next day news was received that the Ahluwalia subjects and agents had joined the enemy. Major Broadfoot again wrote showing the Raja the folly of his vacillating conduct, and telling him that within five days he must prove his friendship or enmity. On the 19th, the confidential agent returned with a verbal message that all was ready, and "the Sirdar's foot was in the stirrup." On the same day Major Broadfoot again addressed the Sirdar, urging him to join the British without delay; and, on the 2d January, Mr Currie wrote to the same effect. This must have been held to have been ample warning. Major H. Lawrence thus sums up against the Sirdar: "Up to the 13th December, the Sirdar might have done as he liked, and even up to the middle of January, or indeed, the end of the war, it seems to me that at very little personal hazard the Sirdar could have joined the British army. But to run any risk was not his game. When Kirpa Ram[1] started, the battle of Mudki had not been fought. On his return, the report that he wrote of that battle excited the Agent's suspicions, and he, for a short time, was placed under restraint. It appears to me that the rumours of the results of the battles of Mudki and Firoshahr deterred the Sirdar from crossing the river, after he had placed his 'foot in the stirrup.' After the battle of Sobraon his protestations were many and warm, but though, on the 19th February, on his own suggestion, I told him to join me at Lahore, he

The opinion of Major Lawrence of the Chief's conduct.

[1] Kirpa Ram was grandson of Lala Basti Ram, the Sirdar's confidential agent, and bearer of the letter of the 14th December.

even then thought the danger too great, and said he would send his son, and himself attend the British camp in Jalandhar. All this was quite in character. He bore the British Government no ill-will, he bore the Lahore Durbar no good-will; his hopes were all from us, his fears from them; we had heaped favours and kindness upon him, they had plundered him; but to the last he would incur no risk, and trusted, at the worst, to our clemency rather than to the justice of his own countrymen. He therefore gave us empty words, and furnished them with guns and soldiers."

The troops of Kapurthalla fought against the British.

The Ahluwalia troops—cavalry, infantry, and artillery—fought against the English at Aliwal, under the command of Hyder Ali, and also at Buddowal. Nihal Singh alleged, in his defence, that he was unable to restrain his troops, who, on hearing of his intention to join the British, broke into open mutiny, and murdered his Minister. But there is no proof whatever of this, and the mutiny was probably caused by the unpopularity of the Minister, and the difficulty experienced by the troops in obtaining their arrears of pay. Even supposing his troops to have deserted him, it was the duty of the Sirdar to have, alone, joined the English; and the fact that an elephant and nine or ten cavalry horses, plundered from Sir Harry Smith's division by the Ahluwalia troops, were sent as trophies to Kapurthalla, proves, that instead of the Sirdar being at that time kept a prisoner in his palace by his troops, as he asserted, he was an actual sharer in their spoils.

Information withheld.

Nor did the Sirdar even supply information, which his agents, who held the chief places on the line of the Satlej, as well as Jagraon, were well able to procure. No attempt was voluntarily made to furnish intelligence, and when the British authorities sent out messengers, they either never returned, or remained away so long as to render their information useless. Regarding this, Major H. Lawrence writes: "I have never heard of a single item of useful intelligence having been given, nor indeed of any until it had been received from other sources. During the week preceding the battle of Aliwal, when for five days the Governor-General had not a word of intelligence from Sir Harry Smith, though I wrote five or six times a day to Major Mackeson and Lieutenant Cunningham, and daily sent some of the letters by Ahluwalia messengers, with promises of large reward for answers, on no single occasion did I get a reply until the affair was over, although the distance from Firozpur to Aliwal and Buddowal is scarcely above sixty miles, and almost entirely through Ahlu lands."

The defence of Nihal Singh.

The defence made by the Sirdar for his conduct during the war, called for by the Governor-General's Agent, was long and elaborate, but none of the facts alleged by Major Mackeson were attempted to be disproved; and Nihal Singh only endeavoured to give a different colour to his conduct, trusting to the clemency of the British Government. He declared that his intentions had always been friendly, and that it was only the mutiny of his troops, and the restraint under which they placed him, that prevented his joining the English when directed; that Raja Lal Singh and Sirdar Ranjodh Singh would not give him any command, knowing his fidelity to the British Government, and that it was at Ranjodh Singh's instigation that the Ahluwalia troops revolted; that, in spite of the attitude of his troops, he still did all in his power to aid the English with supplies and information; and the defence concluded with a lengthy recital of all the services ever performed by the Ahluwalia Chiefs for the English, from the treaty of 1804 to the Satlej campaign.

The truth regarding the conduct of the Chief. His ingratitude to the British Government.

The Political Agent, Major Lawrence, to whom the Sirdar's defence and Major Mackeson's report had been submitted for opinion by the Government, found no excuse for Nihal Singh's conduct. He was not actuated by patriotism, by relationship, or friendship in the course he had pursued. He simply calculated the chances and followed the policy which, in his opinion, would bring with it the least risk, whatever the result of the war. With the greatest pusillanimity he leagued with his enemies and betrayed his friends. With his eyes open, and duly warned by the proclamation of the rewards which would attend loyalty, and the punishments that would follow disobedience, he turned against those who for forty years had gratuitously protected him, and without whose protection he would undoubtedly have lost all his possessions, Cis- and Trans-Satlej.

The recommendations of the Political Agent,

Major Lawrence recommended that, as a signal punishment, all the territories of the Sirdar south of the Satlej, estimated at Rs. 5,65,000 a year, should be forfeited and declared an escheat to the British Government. Further, that the estates in the Jalandhar Doab, estimated at Rs. 5,77,763 a year, and for which he was bound to furnish four hundred horsemen and five hundred infantry, should be confirmed to him and his heirs on condition of good conduct; that no customs should be levied in his estate, and that lands should be taken from the detached portions of his estate in commutation of the contingent, at the rate of Rs. 16 a month for each horseman, and Rs. 6 for each foot soldier, being Rs. 1,12,800. The Sirdar would thus have an estate in clear sovereignty of Rs. 4,64,960 a year, on terms of general good conduct and management, and of joining the British army during war with all his means, and keeping in repair all highways through his lands.[1]

Which are approved by the Government of India.

The Government of India considered the proofs of Sirdar Nihal Singh's misconduct and disaffection most conclusive, and could find, in his elaborate defence, no excuse for the course pursued by him. The recommendations of Major Lawrence were generally approved; the Cis-Satlej estates were confiscated; the Jalandhar Doab estates were maintained "in the independent possession of the Sirdar, his service engagements, as the conditions of his tenure to the Lahore State, being commuted to a money payment on the same terms as those of the other jagirdars."[2]

The conduct of Nihal Singh during the second Sikh war satisfactory.

This severe lesson had a salutary effect on Sirdar Nihal Singh, and when the second Sikh war broke out he did his best to render assistance to the British Government. He collected supplies for the troops proceeding to Multan, and volunteered to send a contingent of his own, but this was not considered necessary; and at the close of the campaign the Governor-General paid him a visit at Kapurthalla, and created him a Raja.

He is created a Raja.

From this time till his death, Nihal Singh led a quiet life, and did not meddle with politics. He managed his

[1] Letter, dated 21st September 1846, from Major H. M. Lawrence, Agent Governor-General, to Secretary to Government of India.

Letter Government of India to Agent Governor-General, dated 24th March 1846, calling for a report; and ditto, dated 1st June 1846, forwarding Major Mackeson's Report for further comment.

Report of Major Mackeson, No. 69, dated 30th April 1846, with enclosures. Defence of the Ahluwalia Sirdar, with Supplement; and Letter No. 25, dated 27th March 1846, from Captain Cunningham to Secretary Government.

[2] Government of India to Agent Governor-General, North-Western Frontier, dated 17th November 1846.

Letter from Agent Governor-General to Major Mackeson, dated 21st December 1846, and to Sirdar Nihal Singh of the same date.

estates well, and established law courts on something of the English system. When the cantonments were formed at Jalandhar, he received the district of Uchh, in exchange for Surajpur and other villages taken by Government.

Raja Nihal Singh died on the 13th of September 1852. **The death of Nihal Singh. His character.** Popular with his subjects, and of benevolent disposition, he had little strength of character, and was completely in the hands of favourites, whose influence was rarely for good. His apathy and vacillation were such that he was unable to carry out measures which he acknowledged to be advantageous, and he brought on himself and his State troubles which the most ordinary energy and courage might have averted. It is now possible to look back dispassionately on the events of the first Sikh war and the conduct of the different Chiefs who fought on our side, who turned against us, or who remained neutral, doubtful whether the Sikhs or the British would win the day, and undecided whom to join. It is now more easy than it was immediately after the triumphant campaign on the Satlej to acknowledge the difficulty of the position **The position of Nihal Singh in 1845 a very difficult one.** of a Chief like Raja Nihal Singh, with his duty inclining him on one side, and his sympathies and the universal desire of his people and troops drawing him towards the other. A powerful will exposed to so fierce a trial might well have wavered, and a weak one would inevitably yield. It is right for the British Government to punish ingratitude and treason with all severity, and to reward devotion and loyalty with the utmost generosity; but for those who have neither to reward nor punish it is enough to know that treason wears all complexions, from the highest virtue to the darkest crime; and that, if Nihal Singh prayed in his heart for the triumph of the Sikhs, they were still his brothers and his countrymen, their army was still the holy army of the Khalsa, which, in the name of God and the Guru, was ever to march on to victory, and that in all its battles, for a hundred years, the Ahluwalia flag had been carried in its foremost ranks.

Raja Randhir Singh.

Randhir Singh, the eldest son of Raja Nihal Singh, was born in March 1831, and was in his twenty-second year when he succeeded his father. By his first wife,

His family.

who died in 1853, he had two sons, Kour Kharrak Singh, born in August 1850, and Harnam Singh, born in November 1852. His only daughter, born in 1851, married Buta Singh, son of Ram Singh, jagirdar of Sirnanwi, in 1863.

Raja Randhir Singh's second wife died in 1857. She bore one son, who died two months after his birth. Soon after his accession the Raja was requested to state whether he had any objection to make over a portion of his territory in lieu of the tribute, that had been till that time paid, the Supreme Government having, as has been before stated, ruled that such an arrangement was desirable, but that it could not be carried out without the consent of the Raja. He, however, was strongly opposed to any relinquishment of lands which had been owned by his ancestors, and preferred paying the tribute as before.[1]

The will of Raja Nihal Singh.

Two months previous to his death, Raja Nihal Singh had executed a will, which he had sent for approval to the Board of Administration, and which the Board,

[1] Letter of 16th April 1853, from Commissioner Trans-Satlej States to Raja Randhir Singh. Two letters, of 17th April 1853 and 27th October 1854, from Raja Randhir Singh to Commissioner Trans-Satlej States; and Letter No. 387, dated 26th December 1854, from Commissioner Trans-Satlej States to Chief Commissioner; No. 310, dated 7th April 1868, from Government Punjab to Commissioner Jalandhar.

believing the Raja's illness to be of no serious nature, had recommended to the Government of India for confirmation.[1] But the Raja's sudden death altered the position of affairs, and it became necessary to consider the whole question afresh, and the Board requested the Supreme Government to issue no orders regarding the will until a further report should have been submitted by them.[2] For sixteen years the question of Raja Nihal Singh's will was in dispute, and, as the case is of great importance, it will be most convenient to give in this place a *resumé* of the proceedings.

The will was dated 11th July 1852, or 30th Har 1909, and being translated, is as follows :— **Its translation.**

"As in this uncertain world the life of a man is like a bubble, and every living creature must leave this world behind him, agreeably to the old saying, 'Every life will taste death,' it is necessary for a man of sense to look on life as a thing borrowed, and to make such arrangement as will ensure good management among his survivors. He therefore, while in the enjoyment of his senses, with his own consent and will, and without any sort of instigation or force, writes the following :—

"It may be known that through the blessing of God he has three sons, Kour Randhir Singh, the eldest, born from the first wife; Kour Bikrama Singh, and Kour Suchet Singh, from the second wife. As he wishes that these three brothers should live together after his death on good terms and in peace, with friendship and love for

[1] Commissioner to Board of Administration, No. 350, dated 18th September 1852.

Board of Administration to Government of India, No. 903, dated 7th September 1852.

[2] Board of Administration to Government of India, No. 939, dated 20th September 1852.

each other, and that no sign of disagreement or hostility should appear amongst them, as is generally the case in this changeable world, especially in matters relating to governments and estates, wherein even brothers become desperate enemies, and fight with each other with intent to kill (as was the case with him and his own brother, Amar Singh, whom he had nourished and supported as a son, but whose subsequent conduct to himself is notorious); such being generally the case, he cannot expect that these three brothers will remain on good terms and in mutual love; and if (God forbid) hostility should appear among them, it will produce bloodshed, the ruin of the estate, and give them a bad name among the people. He therefore has been deeply meditating a contrivance by which such calamities may be averted, and has come at last to the following conclusion, which appears to effect the desired result.

"That an estate of one lakh of rupees may be allotted to Kour Bikrama Singh, and an estate of the same value to Kour Suchet Singh, without paying any sort of Government *nazrana;* that these two brothers having their estates separate may have nothing to dispute upon, and may live uninterfered with by each other; and that the rest of the country remain in possession of the eldest son, Kour Randhir Singh, the heir apparent, who will have to manage the country, to maintain the allowances now enjoyed by the people, to honour relatives and servants as they deserve, and pay *nazrana* to Government for his and his brothers' shares of the estate. If, however, Government wish to realise the *nazrana* separately from each of them, then the two brothers shall get a proportionate increase to their shares—*i.e.*, more land equal to the amount of the Government *nazrana* shall be added to the share of each brother from the estate of the elder. In short, they shall have each a nett share of one lakh of rupees for their own private use, independent of the Government *nazrana*. And as the heir apparent shall have the management of the criminal cases in the whole three shares, he should conduct the administration impartially and with justice, without any feeling of hostility or opposition towards his brothers; and in case that the two brothers be dissatisfied with the management of Foujdari affairs in their jagirs, the British Government will take it into their own hands, leaving the heir apparent to manage his own share of the estate without having anything to do with the Foujdari of the other two shares. Every one of them should serve the British Government to the utmost of his power, and should consider it a cause of great honour and benefit to him, and should continue to be thankful to Government. When everything has been settled in the above-mentioned manner, they should strive to honour their respective attendants and relations, and give justice to the people and their dues to the poor. They should live in friendship and unity with each other.

"This paper does not contain a detail of the shares of each, being a general proposal for the sanction of the Board. In case of its being approved, he will submit another paper, which will contain a detail of all the districts, property, cash, and houses, and a list of the people who deserve protection. Begs that an authenticated copy of this document be kept in the Board's office, and another forwarded to him bearing the approval and signature of the Board. The British Government is well aware of the services himself and his father have performed, and for which they have been allowed the perpetual possession of their country. He hopes that, in the same manner, his sons will be honoured and allowed to remain under its protection, and that they will try their utmost to serve and please the Government, as their continuance in rule depends upon the blessing of God and the protection of the British Government."

The legitimacy of the younger sons of Raja Nihal Singh.

Raja Nihal Singh, although he declares in this will that he writes without any instigation, was at the time completely under the influence of his second wife, the mother of his two younger sons. She had instilled into his mind a dislike to his eldest son, and it was only the attitude of the British Government which compelled him, much against his will, to leave the State and power to Randhir Singh, who asserted that his brothers were illegitimate, and their mother, who was undoubtedly of low caste, a concubine of the Raja and not his wife. But it is to be observed that the Raja's caste was itself low; that the ceremony of marriage among such castes is but lightly regarded; and that the ordinary *chadar dalna*, throwing a sheet over the woman, is amply sufficient. The Raja, too, in his will distinctly calls her his wife, and this admission is sufficient to dispose of the question of the younger sons' disability to inherit.

The Agent of Randhir Singh addressed the Board of Administration on the death of the Raja, stating that the three brothers did not approve of the will, and had no desire to divide the estate. They wished to live in harmony among themselves; and to carry out the provisions of the will would only ensure the ruin of the State, which had never been divided.[1] Letters were

[1] Letters, dated 14th and 22d September 1852, from Hyder Ali Khan to Sir H. Lawrence.

also received from the Raja and his brothers to the same effect, the latter stating that they had determined to obey their brother in everything, and be guided by his counsels.[1]

The Board of Administration were doubtful how to proceed with regard to Kapurthalla. One member proposed to resume lands in lieu of the *nazrana*, or at any rate to take the outlying lands, such as Phagwara, giving a reduction of the commutation; also to resume the police and criminal powers exercised by the late Raja. The two other members of the Board opposed all these proposals, on grounds of policy and good faith; and being unable to come to a decision, the numerous minutes written on the subject by the members of the Board were forwarded to the Government of India for a final decision upon the points on which the Board could not agree.[2]

The will is approved by the Government of India.

The Government of India,[3] with regard to the first point submitted for its decision—viz., whether the will should be carried into effect, or the estate continued in the hands of the then Raja, as desired by him and his brothers—ruled that the raj should remain undivided in the hands of the Raja "so long as the brothers remain in concord regarding this agreement." "If discord should arise among them hereafter, as is very probable, the will of the late Raja should have effect given to it. In that

[1] Kharitas, dated 19th and 20th September, from Raja Randhir Singh and Kours Bikrama and Suchet Singh.

[2] Letter No. 83, dated 24th January 1853, from Board of Administration to Government of India, inclosing Minute of Mr J. Lawrence of 11th October 1852; ditto of Sir H. Lawrence of 16th October; ditto of Mr J. Lawrence of 1st December; ditto of Mr Montgomery of 2d December; ditto of Sir H. Lawrence, dated 8th December; ditto of Mr J. Lawrence of 13th January 1853; ditto of Sir H. Lawrence, dated 15th January 1853.

[3] No. 907 of Government of India to Chief Commissioner, dated 21st February 1853.

case the shares of the two younger brothers, thus broken off from the Raja's share, would become ordinary jagirs, into which our administration would enter."

The tribute was not to be commuted for land without the consent of the Chief.

The second point, as to whether the Raja should be compelled to commute the *nazrana* for land, the Government of India held to be a question only of good faith. The transfer of outlying lands to Government would, doubtless, be convenient, but it was not competent for the Government, in good faith, to compel such transfer. "From the official documents of 1846 it is clear that it was the intention of Government to make the settlement then pronounced essentially a final one. Lieutenant-Colonel Sir H. Lawrence had recommended that the Raja should pay an annual *nazrana*." The Governor-General, on full consideration, rejected this recommendation, and ruled that his service engagements should be commuted to a money payment.[1] This plan had been deliberately adopted, and it was not possible to change it with justice. The Raja had not only behaved well since 1846, but the Governor-General had, at the recommendation of the local authorities, made him a Raja in 1849, and paid him a personal visit at Kapurthalla. The decision of the Supreme Government had been not for life of the Raja but for perpetuity, and it would not be just to reopen the question of the Raja's position, which had been finally disposed of.

The nature of Kapurthalla independence.

With regard to the resumption of the powers of police, the Government of India held that it was virtually included in the last question. The position of the Ahluwalia Chief, although not strictly sovereign, had yet independent power, which had been confirmed to him by the Government letter before referred to—the districts in

[1] No. 460, dated 17th November 1846, of Government of India.

the Jalandhar Doab "will be maintained in the independent possession of the Sirdar."[1] This was in perpetuity, and the Government had no right to take away the police jurisdiction from the Raja. Orders were given to invest the young Raja with the customary khillat, which was done by the Commissioner in April 1853.[2]

Raja Randhir Singh installed.

Kour Suchet Singh desires the separation of his share.

It was not long, however, before the youngest brother, Suchet Singh, began to desire a division of his share, and the Chief Commissioner directed this division to be made in accordance with the terms of the will.[3] The Raja, however, wished Suchet Singh to abandon his claim altogether, and petitioned against the order of the Supreme Government.[4] The Chief Commissioner addressed the Government of India, and referred to the letter of the 21st February, which affirmed the will, and directed its provisions to be enforced should the brothers not agree. Suchet Singh now desired division, and it should be effected, giving him as far as possible outlying lands, so as not to break up the estate more than necessary. The Raja only wished to allow Suchet Singh Rs. 25,000 a year, with which allowance the second brother, Bikrama Singh, was at this time content.[5] The Government of India agreed to this proposal. The will had been affirmed by the Governor-General, and nothing was left but to carry it into effect.[6]

[1] No. 460, of 17th November 1846, of Government of India.

[2] No. 296, of 15th April 1853, from Commissioner Trans-Satlej States to Chief Commissioner.

[3] No. 577, of 23d July 1853, from Chief Commissioner to Commissioner Trans-Satlej States.

[4] No. 57, of 30th July 1853, from Commissioner Trans-Satlej States to Chief Commissioner.

[5] No. 575, of 12th August 1853, from Chief Commissioner to Government of India.

[6] No. 3979, of 9th September 1853, from Government of India to Chief Commissioner.

Which is sanctioned,

The Commissioner of the Trans-Satlej States was accordingly called upon to carry out the orders of Government, and report on the arrangements made, but the Raja was unwilling to allow any dismemberment of his State.[1]

And carried into effect.

No arrangement could be come to between the brothers as to the value of the lands to be divided off, so that the Commissioner himself had the assessments ascertained, and finding that the two Talukas of Wayan and Bunga were certainly within the amount due, made them over to Suchet Singh in April 1854. In this month a reconciliation was effected between the brothers, and Suchet Singh presented to the Commissioner an agreement by which he consented to accept a smaller jagir with subordinate judicial powers. The clause relating to police jurisdiction in small matters could with difficulty be allowed so as to relieve the Raja of responsibility. The chief reason which induced Suchet Singh to seek a compromise was his objection to reside at Bunga. There were only three large towns in the State: Kapurthalla, where the Raja himself resided, Sultanpur, and Phagwara. Of the two outlying districts which might most conveniently be divided off, Phagwara should, in justice, be reserved for Bikrama Singh, the second brother, should he at a future time require partition. Bunga was the only outlying district available for Suchet Singh, with which Sultanpur could not be joined, as it was at the other extremity of the Kapurthalla estate, and was the favourite shooting-ground of the Raja, who would rather have given up Kapurthalla itself. Wayan was added to the share of Suchet Singh, as being adjacent to Bunga. When this

Suchet Singh is willing to accept a compromise.

[1] No 787, of 26th September, to Commissioner Trans-Satlej States; and No. 114, of 13th December, from Commissioner Trans-Satlej States to Chief Commissioner.

report was made some months after the agreement, Suchet Singh was living at Kapurthalla, but was on bad terms with both his brothers, and especially with Bikrama Singh, who had then no wish to take the share to which he was entitled under his father's will. The Raja wished that at any rate the jagir assigned to Suchet Singh should be subject to some of the charges, religious and personal grants, which weighed so heavily on the whole estate; and the Commissioner considered that the full rates at which the lands had hitherto been assessed, and which were higher than would be possible under English re-assessment, should be the estimate in allowing Suchet Singh's share, and in this case Bunga and Wayan would be quite sufficient for him.[1]

In forwarding this report of his predecessor, Mr Edgeworth, the then Commissioner Trans-Satlej States, strongly recommended that Suchet Singh's request to withdraw his application for partition should be favourably considered. The Raja would allow his brother an estate of Rs. 50,000 a year, with subordinate judicial powers, and this Suchet Singh was willing to accept in lieu of an estate of Rs. 100,000 without such powers. Even supposing the proposal of Suchet Singh to be rejected, the Government had full power to modify the provisions of the late Raja's will should it think fit, and it was to be considered that if the two shares of the brothers were deducted, the Raja would have barely sufficient to carry on the administration, and the *nazrana* might fall into arrears.

The Raja's revenue.

The actual revenue, with its charges, was asserted by the Raja to be as follows:[2]—

[1] Two memos. by Mr D. McLeod, Commissioner Trans-Satlej States, of 29th December 1854.

[2] Letter No. 12, of 16th January 1855, from Commissioner Trans-Satlej States to Chief Commissioner.

Total value of estate, . .	Rs. 5,77,763
Jagirs and Dharamarth, . .	Rs. 53,332
Shares under will, ...	2,00,000
Nazrana, ...	1,38,000
Dharamarths, ...	96,976
Dependants, ...	69,124
TOTAL, .	Rs. 5,57,432
Balance for State and personal expenses,	20,331
	Rs. 5,77,763

The Government do not agree to reconsider the case.

The Chief Commissioner agreed to neither proposal. With regard to Suchet Singh's withdrawal of his application and willingness to accept a smaller allowance from his brother, it was observed that the brothers had been allowed ample time to settle their disputes amicably. This they did not do, and the districts of Bunga and Wayan had been divided off and made over to Suchet Singh in April 1854, the first being annexed to the Hoshiarpur, the second to the Jalandhar district. With reference to this partition, the Government had directed the will to be carried out, and there was no possible reason for objecting to the arrangement. The British Government had no cause to be more anxious that the estate should remain intact than the late Raja had been, and if these arrangements were set aside, there could be no doubt but that new difficulties would again speedily arise.

With reference to the second point, it was inexpedient to modify the terms of the will, which was not an unjust one; and but for the interference of the British Government, the elder brother would never have been Raja at all. The estates left would be ample if only the large expenses for jagirs, dharamarths, and dependants were reduced within moderate limits. The districts of Bunga and Wayan were directed to be taken over at their assessment of Rs. 85,000, and the balance (Rs. 15,000) was to be made up from adjacent villages.[1]

The Commissioner submitted a list of villages which might most appropriately be given to Suchet Singh, but urged as an additional reason against the arrangement that Suchet Singh was a minor when he asked for partition, and since his majority[2] had desired a compromise, and that the will might now be modified as well as formerly, when the Government only upheld a part, and did not sanction the supremacy of the elder brother.[3]

The Punjab Government sanctioned the villages detailed being made over to Suchet Singh, but refused to reopen the general question, which had been definitely settled. Suchet Singh's majority was absolutely immaterial in a political case, since he was of full discretion when he made his application, and the British Government, as paramount, had full right to uphold just so much of the will as it thought proper.[4]

The question is reopened in 1860,

In 1860 the question of Suchet Singh's separate jagir was again revived. Colonel Lake, Commissioner Trans-Satlej States, wrote that the brothers were reconciled, and both wished the separated jagir to be restored. "They have interchanged formal agreements, by which, in the event of Government sanctioning the agreement, the Kour Suchet Singh promises on the one hand fealty

[1] No. 79, dated 31st January 1855, from Chief Commissioner to Commissioner Trans-Satlej States.

[2] Suchet Singh attained his majority 25th December 1854.

[3] No. 89, from Commissioner Trans-Satlej States to Chief Commissioner, dated 5th May 1855.

[4] No. 533, from Chief Commissioner to Commissioner Trans-Satlej States, dated 8th June 1855.

and obedience, while on the other hand Raja Randhir Singh binds himself to leave Kour Suchet Singh in possession of the lands made over to him by the British Government, and to continue the grant to him and his heirs on certain conditions specified in the agreement." The popular feeling was against the will of the late Raja, and the precedent might lead to the dismemberment of all independent principalities. The will would be in no way set aside, the only change being that Suchet Singh would become a dependent of his brother instead of an ordinary jagirdar.[1]

And the divided share of Suchet Singh is again included in his brother's estate.

The Government of the Punjab strongly supported this recommendation, urging the great services of the Raja during the mutiny, and the fact that no loss would accrue to Government, nor would the will be set aside. The Supreme Government sanctioned the arrangement, and the transfer was accordingly made.[2]

Sirdar Bikrama Singh desires his share under the will.

In 1866 the brothers again quarrelled, and the Commissioner of Jalandhar wrote to Government: "On the 20th April, Sirdar Bikrama Singh formally announced to me that he had come to a complete rupture with his brother the Raja of Kapurthalla, and requested that the provisions of his father's will might be put in force as directed by the Government of India."[3]

His right is disputed.

The Punjab Government replied that the existing arrangements could not be disturbed. The Sirdar again urged his case, pleading the provisions of the will and the sanction of the Government, which only allowed it

[1] No. 209, of 27th December 1859, from Commissioner Cis-Satlej States to Government Punjab.

[2] No. 17, of 7th January 1860, from Government Punjab to Government of India; and Government of India, No. 243, of 28th January 1860.

[3] No. 130, of 15th May 1866, from Commissioner Jalandhar to Government Punjab.

to remain in abeyance while the brothers lived together amicably.[1]

Sirdar Bikrama Singh then applied directly to the Government of the Punjab, but was informed that he must now abide by his first decision of waiving the right to enforce the provisions of the will.[2]

The Government were not bound under altered circumstances to maintain the will.

Bikrama Singh then desired to be informed of his exact position, and of the decision of the Punjab Government, not as to the expediency of the separation, but on his absolute and indefeasible right to claim it. In reply, the Government declined to reopen the question. The rule of primogeniture was that which, by Hindu law, as well as usage, had always applied to such holdings ; and when, under native rule, it had been set aside, it was only the result of an arbitrary exercise of power. In 1852 the Kapurthalla territory had been exceptionally treated. The Raja had been entitled to consideration, and the rule of primogeniture had been for some years disregarded. The will was consequently sanctioned, but in Sirdar Bikrama Singh's case it was not carried out, and the subsequent course of events had absolved the Government from any obligation to carry it out, after a lapse of sixteen years, and after the rule of primogeniture had been authoritatively laid down as the ordinary rule of procedure.[3]

Suchet Singh joins his brother in desiring his share to be restored to him.

Sirdar Suchet Singh now again came forward. He desired that his jagir, which had been reunited with Kapurthalla, might be again separated, as the terms of

[1] Sirdar Bikrama Singh's letter, of 20th April 1866, to Commissioner Jalandhar.

[2] Sirdar Bikrama Singh's letters, of 29th May and 9th June 1860 ; and reply of Government Punjab, Nos. 487 and 502, of 9th and 12th June.

[3] Agent of Bikrama Singh to Punjab Government, of 26th October 1866 ; and reply of Punjab Government, No. 837, of 10th November 1866.

the agreement had not been carried out. The points in the agreement to which he especially referred were—"(1) Suchet Singh is vested with authority to raise the assessment; (2) he is to exercise all the powers of the Collectorate." As regards assessment, he had found after the agreement was signed that no enhancement of the Government assessment was permissible until the term had expired; and with regard to collectorate powers, the Raja had only allowed him to try summary suits.

The Government of the Punjab declined to discuss a question which could only tend to bring both parties to ruin; its opinion of the Raja's conduct differed materially from that of Suchet Singh, and the younger sons had already obtained more than they could legally have claimed.[1]

A few months later the Commissioner reported that there was little chance of a reconciliation between the Raja and Bikrama Singh. The Raja was willing to allow his second brother the same provision that he had made to the youngest—namely, Rs. 54,000 a year, including a life jagir of Rs. 25,000 or Rs. 30,000, and a cash pension of Rs. 25,000 in perpetuity.[2] The Punjab Government requested a final decision from the Government of India, which alone could induce Bikrama Singh to agree to anything but a permanent transfer of territory yielding a lakh of rupees per annum. Suchet Singh was not so anxious to press his claim as Bikrama Singh, who was much better off than his younger brother, for besides his allowance of Rs. 50,000, he had an estate of at least equal value in Oude, which, although gained, in his

The question is referred to the Government of India for decision.

[1] Suchet Singh to Government Punjab, of 12th November 1866; and reply of Government Punjab, No. 919, of 15th December.

[2] No. 130, of 12th April 1867, from Commissioner Jalandhar to Government Punjab.

opinion, by his own personal services alone, must justly be considered as in part owing to his position with his brother the Raja, which allowed him opportunity of rendering these services.[1]

The final orders of the Government of India were given in February 1868 to the following effect:— The final orders of Government

The will was sanctioned and approved by the British Government in 1852. Though partition was not actually demanded, yet the liability to partition was affirmed. Against this decision the Raja appealed, but it was distinctly ruled that partition must take place. Since then nothing had occurred to cause the Government of India to form a different decision, nor had there been any surrender on the part of either brother of this right in case of disagreement. The reply given by Lord Canning at the Durbar in 1860 clearly appears to have related only to a fact—namely, that the execution of the will was held in abeyance, and conveyed no promise that the will never would be carried out.[2]

The case was one of equity only, which was clear. The rule of primogeniture was not absolute in the lesser States of the Punjab. But, in any case, the arrangement had been solemnly sanctioned by the Government, and could not now be set aside. The application of the will must accordingly take effect as regarded both brothers.

Suchet Singh obtained partition of an estimated lakh's worth of territory, under the terms of the will, and

[1] No. 204, of 20th May 1867, from Government Punjab to Government of India.

[2] Lord Canning spoke at the Durbar at Phagwara, on the 31st January 1860, to the following effect, as reported by Kirpa Ram, the Raja's Vakil, whose memorandum was attested by the Commissioner :—"In consideration of your loyalty, I bestow upon you your old estate in the Bari Doab, in perpetuity ; and the will of your late father being set aside, your authority is restored in your principality as before, including the ilaquas of Wayan and Bunga."

became a British jagirdar. The new assessment reduced his revenue below the lakh, but this, it was observed, must be adhered to, nor could he claim more from the Raja, nor raise the assessment till the term of settlement had expired.

Bikrama Singh, it was ordered, should have a lakh's worth of territory divided off the amount calculated according to existing revenues, it not being, under the circumstances, desirable to enforce British assessments.

By the will, in case of partition, the jurisdiction—fiscal, criminal, and civil—might be transferred to the British Government, or be exercised by the brothers under the suzerainty of the British Government. The brothers were therefore permitted to exercise all original jurisdiction—fiscal, criminal, and civil—within their respective shares.

Each brother had, under the will, the right to come under the suzerainty of the British Government. But if either should consent to remain under the suzerainty of the Raja, while still retaining his or their original jurisdiction, so much the better, as thus the unity of the Kapurthalla State would be adequately preserved. "Lastly, the appanage of the two brothers Bikrama Singh and Suchet Singh, both in respect of separate revenue and of jurisdiction, must descend to their lineal male issue according to the rule of primogeniture, the elder son inheriting the appanage and providing a moderate maintenance for the younger sons, if any; on failure of male issue lawfully begotten, the appanage would revert to the Raja, or the representative of the Kapurthalla Ahluwalia family for the time being."[1]

The Raja was not satisfied with this decision of the

[1] No. 123, of 1st February 1868, from Government of India to Government Punjab.

Viceroy, and appealed to the Secretary of State for India, who modified, to a considerable extent, the terms of the decision, although the validity of the will was maintained. The following is his despatch to the Viceroy, dated 12th February 1869 :— The order modified by the Home Government.

"1. I have received and considered in Council, with all the attention which the importance of the subject demands, the letters of your Excellency's Government, noted in the margin, with accompanying correspondence, relating to the affairs of the Raja of Kapurthalla and his brothers. Foreign letters, 26th Oct. 1868, No. 190; 9th Dec., No. 215; 11th Dec., No. 219; 21st Dec., No. 234.

"2. It is unnecessary to refer in detail to the circumstances of the late Raja's will, and the subsequent action of the brothers, so fully set forth in the correspondence before me. It is officially announced that on the 31st of January 1860, Lord Canning, Viceroy of India, after thanking the Raja of Kapurthalla for his good services in the field, assured him, in open Durbar, that his territory was given to him in perpetuity, as it existed before his father's death. The words employed by the Governor-General were these :—'In consideration of these loyal and faithful services, we have given you in perpetuity your ancient territory, the ilaqua Bari Doab. The will of your late father has been annulled, and your dominion has in all respects been restored to you in your principality, including Wayan and Bunga, on the same footing as it existed in former times.' In reference to this speech, your Excellency's Government has observed that the reply given by Lord Canning at the Durbar in 1860 clearly appears to have related only to a fact—namely, that the execution of the will was held in abeyance, and conveyed no promise that the will never would be carried out.

"3. I am unable to concur in this view of the meaning

of Lord Canning's words, and am compelled to put upon them a different interpretation. That interpretation does not depend upon the precise accuracy of the English equivalent for the expression used by the Viceroy with reference to the late Raja's will, whether it be 'cancelled' or 'annulled,' or simply 'set aside.' It depends on the whole context of the passage. Lord Canning associated his announcement with an emphatic reference to the political services of the Raja. It was clearly intended to convey a reward for those services. If it had been the mere intimation of an existing arrangement, which depended, and was to continue to depend, upon the pleasure of his younger brothers, it would have been no reward, and the reference to political services would have been altogether unmeaning. But, evidently intended as a reward, it assumed necessarily the character of a promise. This reference, deducible from the whole context of the speech, is confirmed also by the general tenor of previous transactions in the case. The will of the late Raja had involved the danger of an eventual division and dismemberment of the raj. This had previously been prevented by voluntary agreement among the brothers. The nature of that agreement and the circumstances under which it was brought about, indicated how great was the anxiety of the Raja to prevent the dismemberment of his State, and what a calamity he regarded its possible occurrence. No fitter reward, therefore, could be given by the Viceroy for very great and for very timely service, than to assure the Raja that the Government of India would remove this fear for ever from his mind. I cannot doubt that this was Lord Canning's meaning, and that this was the reward to which he pledged the faith and authority of the British Government.

"4. In these circumstances, Her Majesty's Government are of opinion that it is their duty to uphold the decision of Lord Canning, and to decree that nothing shall be done to lower the dignity and authority of a Chief who has been among the most faithful of our allies, and who, when his services were fresh in the memory of the Viceroy, received such assurances from him in open Durbar.

"5. It is my wish, therefore, that the Raja Randhir Singh should remain as now in full possession of the sovereignty of the entire State. I well understand, however, the feeling which appears to have influenced the judgment of your Government in the case—namely, a feeling that every consideration should be shown, and that full justice should be done to the younger brothers, in whose favour certain testamentary dispositions had been made by the late Raja, which dispositions had been treated as valid by the Government of India. But no injustice will be done to the brothers if that arrangement be made permanent to which they had themselves voluntarily assented, and which has been held binding during a course of years. They should receive in money, or in a life tenure of lands, as you may determine, the full value of the shares assigned to them in their father's will. But it is to be thoroughly understood that in the case of the younger brothers holding lands in the Kapurthalla State, they are, so far as criminal jurisdiction is concerned, to be held in entire subordination to the Raja, and that at the death of each, the revenue of the lands held by him shall revert to the Raja, a sufficient provision, to be approved by your Government, for the family of the deceased being made a first charge on the revenues of the estate.

"6. It is to be hoped that, after this distinct announcement of Her Majesty's Government, the Lieutenant-

Governor of the Punjab will be able to make, under your instructions, such an arrangement as will give satisfaction to all parties concerned. Kour Suchet Singh having demanded a separation of his jagir from the principality, has no claim to bind the Raja to the agreement entered into with him in 1859."

All that remained was to arrange the measures for carrying into effect the instructions of the Home Government in such a manner as to leave the Raja and his brothers no just cause of complaint.

Summary of the Secretary of State's orders.

The conclusions and orders of the Secretary of State were simply that Lord Canning's declaration of the annulment of the will was upheld; that Raja Randhir Singh was to hold the State in full sovereignty; that the younger brothers were, for life, to enjoy the whole share in money or lands allotted them under the will; but if the share was given in lands, they were to be subordinate to the Raja in criminal jurisdiction.

The difficulty of carrying out satisfactory arrangements.

The younger brothers were not disposed to accept the decision of the Government without further appeal, and refused all reconciliation with the Raja, who was quite willing to consider the dispute finally settled. It thus became impossible to assign them their share in Kapurthalla lands, and the Government of the Punjab was only able to recommend that a cash allowance to the amount of their shares should be granted.

The amount to which the younger brothers were entitled.

This amount had then to be determined, for under the will of Raja Nihal Singh the younger brothers were entitled to land worth a lakh a year. But it was clearly just that the land thus made over to the Sirdars should be valued at the assessment levied by the Kapurthalla Chiefs, although when severed from that State it would become liable to reassessment on the principles which guided the British Government in revenue matters. It has been seen, in the case of Kour Suchet Singh, that separated lands which yielded under Raja Nihal Singh a lakh of rupees per annum, under the light and liberal assessments of the Government only yielded Rs. 52,014 a year. This, then, was all the brothers were entitled to under the will, for if they elected to become British jagirdars, they must also accept the loss of reassessment of their lands; and should cash be allowed instead of land, they could only fairly claim a pension equivalent to the revenue of the lands as reassessed—viz., Rs. 52,000. But the Punjab Government, unwilling to give Kours Bikrama Singh and Suchet Singh any cause for complaint, recommended that a cash allowance of Rs. 60,000 should be paid to each of them in half-yearly instalments. The districts of Bunga and Wayan were taken over from the youngest of the brothers, and he was permitted to claim compensation for any permanent improvements he might have effected.[1]

This voluminous and lengthy case, which has given rise to a vast amount of ill feeling, and the annoyance and trouble connected with which may be reasonably assumed to have broken the health and shortened the life of Raja Randhir Singh, is now finally settled. That the younger brothers will acquiesce in the decision is hardly to be expected; but they must at least know that the British Government, as paramount, possessed the fullest power to uphold or annul the will of their father; that if this annulment was made after the mutiny of 1857, it was to preserve the integrity of the Kapurthalla State, and to The termination of the case.

[1] Commissioner Jalandhar to Government Punjab, No. 171-1094, dated 4th May 1869; Government Punjab to Government of India, No. 223, dated 16th July; Government of India to Government Punjab, Nos. 921 and 1272, dated 6th July and 9th September 1869.

reward the brilliant and devoted services of the Raja; and, lastly, that if they have not received everything which their father intended for them, they have, at any rate, obtained more than they had any legal or moral right to claim.

The mutiny of 1857, and the active loyalty of Raja Randhir Singh.

It is now necessary to go back a few years in the history of the family, to the time when the mutiny of the Bengal army broke out in May 1857. Raja Randhir Singh took the earliest opportunity of evincing his loyalty towards the British Government. He was, as a vassal of the Crown, bound to render all possible aid to the Government in times of difficulty, and military service could not have been demanded from him, as he paid annually a tribute of Rs. 1,32,000 in commutation of such service. But at the first intimation of the outbreak at Dehli and Meerat, the Raja marched into Jalandhar with every available soldier, accompanied by his brother, Bikrama Singh, and his chief advisers, and remained there throughout the hot season at the head of his troops, a portion of which he volunteered to send to Dehli, and this offer was only not accepted as their presence was absolutely required at Jalandhar. On the night of the mutiny at this town, his troops guarded the civil station, the jail, and the treasury, and he detached the whole of his cavalry, under General Johnstone, for the pursuit of the mutineers.

His services at Jalandhar.

At Hoshiarpur.

In July, when the mutiny at Sialkot rendered it advisable to strengthen the station of Hoshiarpur, the Raja, at the request of the authorities, despatched there 200 infantry, 100 cavalry, and 2 light guns, and this force remained there till the following November. Prince Bikrama Singh was as loyal and energetic as his brother, and their example was so well followed by the Raja's officers and troops, that although encamped for six months in the neighbourhood of a large town, and with the example before them of the mutiny of the Government troops, no breach of discipline occurred, and their conduct was most exemplary.

His decided action has a good effect.

The effect of the Raja's decided action was no doubt important. The Jalandhar Doab was, it is true, the best affected of any portion of the Punjab, and its inhabitants, prosperous, and chiefly agriculturists, had never any desire to rise; yet the Government was nevertheless much strengthened both in the Jalandhar Doab and in the Cis-Satlej by the Raja's conduct. Nor did he withhold the tribute which he might fairly have deducted for the pay of troops which he was not legally compelled to supply, but paid it punctually, preferring to involve himself deeply in debt rather than increase the difficulties of the Government.

The number of Kapurthalla troops employed in 1857.

The force of the Raja employed during this time consisted of 1200 infantry, 200 cavalry, and 5 guns. To this force the Supreme Government sanctioned, in November 1857, a gratuity of Rs. 12,000, equivalent to a month's pay to each officer and soldier.[1]

It should be remembered that the Raja took the side of Government without hesitation, and without having had time or opportunity to ascertain what were the intentions of the great Cis-Satlej Chiefs. After the movable column had marched to Dehli, the only reliable force in the Jalandhar Doab was that of the Raja, with the exception of one hundred Europeans, forming the garrison of Philor fort; the same number of individuals

[1] Letters—Commissioner's No. 189, dated 17th October 1857, to Secretary Chief Commissioner; Government's No. 4750, dated 24th November 1857; with Chief Commissioner's No. 8, dated 8th January 1858.

at Jalandhar; nine hundred Tiwana horse, and a newly raised regiment of Punjab infantry. The Raja did not waver in his loyalty when Dehli continued to hold out against the British, and when so many lukewarm friends despaired of their cause; but he was eager himself to lead his men on active service; and that this was no idle offer, intended to be declined, is proved by his subsequent conduct in Oude.

The Kapurthalla disarmament.

After the fall of Dehli it was determined to disarm the population of the Jalandhar Doab, and this measure the Raja carried out in his own territories with the utmost readiness.[1]

The rewards for service.

The services of the Raja Randhir Singh were most cordially acknowledged by the Government of India. The tribute due from him was reduced by Rs. 25,000 a year; one year's tribute was altogether remitted, and khillats of Rs. 15,000 and Rs. 5000 respectively were conferred upon him and his brother. A salute of eleven guns was assigned to him, and the honorary title of Farzand-dilband Rasikh ul Itikad, while Bikrama Singh received the title of Buhadar.[2]

The services of Raja Randhir Singh in Oude during 1858.

Early in May 1858, the Raja of Kapurthalla, with the approval of the Supreme Government, led a contingent to Oude, Sirdar Bikrama Singh accompanying his brother. For ten months the Raja's force did admirable service in the field. Six times they were engaged with the enemy, and captured nine guns: the Raja and his brother avoided neither fatigue nor danger, but were always to be seen at

[1] Letters—No. 188, Commissioner Trans-Satlej States to Secretary Chief Commissioner, dated 30th January 1858, and No. 962, of 30th November 1858; No. 188 of Secretary to Chief Commissioner to Government of India, dated 8th April; No. 962, Chief Commissioner to Commissioner Trans-Satlej States, dated 11th December 1858.

[2] Letter No. 1549 of Government of India to Chief Commissioner, dated 2d June 1858.

the head of their men in action, where they fought with conspicuous bravery.[1] The presence of the Raja had the very best effect upon the troops, who not only fought gallantly, but gained the highest character for discipline and good conduct.[2] About the end of March 1859, the Raja's force was released from service, and returned to the Punjab.

For the services of his troops the Raja received two lakhs of rupees, as had been previously arranged by the Chief Commissioner of Oude.[3] The native officers of the contingent received khillats of Rs. 500 each, and the English officers attached to it received the thanks of Government. To the Raja was assigned a khillat of Rs. 5000. **The Government rewards these services.**

The two estates of Boundi and Bithouli, confiscated by the rebellion of their owners, were granted to the Raja on *istimrari* tenure, at half rates, he assuming all those rights and privileges, and none other, enjoyed by the former owners. The Government demand on these estates was, in 1858, one lakh of rupees. They are situated on the river Gogra; Boundi on the northern bank, and Bithouli between the rivers Gogra and Chouka. **The grant of estates.**

To Sirdar Bikrama Singh a portion of the Akaona estate in the Baraitch district, worth Rs. 45,000 a year, was granted at full Government rates; and others of the Raja's followers received portions of the same estate.[4] **The estate of Sirdar Bikrama Singh.**

[1] Letter No. 23, of 12th July 1858, and No. 40, of 1st October 1858, from Governor-General to Court of Directors.

[2] From Lieutenant Chamier to Military Secretary Chief Commissioner of Oude, of 29th January 1859.

[3] Chief Commissioner's No. 89, of 1st July 1858, to Government of India; and Government of India Nos. 5212 and 5357, of 13th July and 21st December 1858.

[4] Letter No. 88, of 10th February 1859, from Chief Commissioner Oude to Government of India; No. 2008, of 15th April 1859, from Government

This property has lately formed the subject of a civil suit, which is still in the Courts, and cannot be here discussed, the subject being the terms on which the estate is held, and the future right of the Raja therein. One Court has lately decided in favour of the Raja, and against Sirdar Bikrama Singh, but the latter is understood to have appealed against the decision.

A garden, valued at Rs. 1300, at Naraingbar, in the Ambala district, which had been resumed by the British Government on the confiscation of the Cis-Satlej estates of the Ahluwalia Chief after the first Sikh war, was also granted to the Raja, rent free, in perpetuity, as a further acknowledgment of his services in the Punjab in 1857.[1]

The Sanad of adoption.

The last and the most highly-valued of the privileges conferred upon Raja Randhir Singh was the right of adoption, granted by the following Sanad of Lord Canning, Viceroy and Governor-General:—

of India to Chief Commissioner Oude; No. 54, of November 9th, 1859, from Secretary of State for India to Governor-General; No. 115, of 16th July 1859, from Governor-General to Secretary of State; Letter, of 22d January 1859, from Commissioner Lucknow to Deputy Commissioner Baraitch.

[1] No. 207, of 16th August 1858, from Chief Commissioner Punjab to Government of India; No. 382, of 11th August 1858, from Judicial Commissioner Punjab to Chief Commissioner; No. 215, of 5th August 1858, from Commissioner Trans-Satlej States to Judicial Commissioner; No. 3631, of 9th October 1858, from Government of India to Chief Commissioner Punjab.

The Sanad granting the estates of Boundi and Bithouli to the Raja was dated 15th April 1859, and is in the following terms:—

"Whereas it appears from the report of the Chief Commissioner of Oude that during the disturbances Raja Randhir Singh Buhadoor Ahluwalia, from loyalty to the British Government, came in person to Lucknow at the head of his troops and rendered valuable service: as a mark of satisfaction, I hereby confer upon Raja Randhir Singh Buhadoor the zemindari of Boundi and Bithouli at half revenue in *istimrari* tenure, on the condition that in time of difficulty and danger the Raja shall render military and political service. It is understood that this grant confers on the Raja only the rights enjoyed by the former proprietors of the above zemindari, and nothing more.

"A khillat of the value of ten thousand rupees (Rs. 10,000) is bestowed upon the Raja."

"To Farzand Dilband Rasikool Itiqad Rajegan Raja Randhir Singh Buhadoor of Kapurthalla.

"Her Majesty being desirous that the Governments of the several Princes and Chiefs of India who now govern their own territories should be perpetuated, and that the representation and dignity of their houses should be continued, I hereby, in fulfilment of this desire, convey to you the assurance that, on failure of natural heirs, the adoption by yourself and future rulers of your State of a successor, according to Hindu law and to the customs of your race, will be recognised and confirmed.

"Be assured that nothing shall disturb the engagement thus made to you, so long as your house is loyal to the Crown and faithful to the conditions of the treaties, grants, or engagements which record its obligations to the British Government."

The estates in the Bari Doab. The Raja's desire to recover them.

Raja Randhir Singh had always been desirous of regaining those estates in the Bari Doab which had been resumed on the death of Raja Nihal Singh in September 1852, for they had been the first conquests of Sirdar Jassa Singh, and included the village of Ahlu, which had been the original home of the family, and from which their name had been derived. For three generations they had been held by the Kapurthalla Chiefs, and their resumption was not occasioned by any bad conduct on the part of Raja Nihal Singh, who had performed loyal service in 1849, but simply in accordance with the rules applied to the cases of all conquest-tenure jagirdars. The whole estate was estimated by Colonel Lawrence at Rs. 26,300 per annum,[1] and included eighteen villages in the Lahore district, twenty-one in the Amritsar, and a

[1] Letter of Colonel Lawrence to Raja Nihal Singh, dated 3d January 1850.

garden at Multan. The Regular Settlement had much diminished the value of the estate, which, in 1859, was only estimated at Rs. 15,910 a year, exclusive of the Multan garden.[1] The argument for the restoration of these lands was that the Home Government had directed a reconsideration of all the cases of the conquest-tenure jagirdars,[2] and that, under the operation of these orders, numerous petty chiefs in the Jalandhar and Hoshiarpur districts had regained their estates with some fraction of each granted in perpetuity.[3]

The argument for restoration.

It was urged that if these Chiefs, who had done little or nothing for the British Government, were treated with such consideration, the Raja of Kapurthalla, whose service had been most distinguished, was entitled to more consideration; that the Government would incur no loss, but a possible gain of Rs. 9000 a year, as the Raja was willing to take these estates, which, by the Government Settlement, were only worth Rs. 15,910 a year, in exchange for the remission of tribute of Rs. 25,000, which had been granted to him in 1858.

The wishes of the Raja acceded to, and the villages restored.

The Government of the Punjab strongly recommended that the wishes of the Raja should be complied with, and these estates were accordingly granted in perpetuity, in exchange for the remission of tribute, the jagir villages

[1] This was below the real value as assessed in 1861, and the number of villages was incorrect. There were twenty-five in the Amritsar district, twelve in Lahore. The total value was Rs. 17,532 1 a. 10 p. per annum, of which the Raja drew Rs. 16,742, while Rs. 104 4 a. 8 p. was rent free in perpetuity, and Rs. 685 6 a. 2 p. rent free for life.—Commissioner Jalandhar, No. 178, dated 13th December 1861, to Government Punjab.

[2] Despatch of Court of Directors, No. 20, dated 17th July 1850.

[3] Supreme Government, No. 1993, dated 1st May 1857, to Chief Commissioner; ditto, No. 2674, dated 6th August 1858, to Chief Commissioner; with Chief Commissioner's No. 445, dated 14th May 1857, and 796, dated 6th September 1858.

remaining subject to the civil and police jurisdiction of the British Government.[1]

The Raja was not, however, quite satisfied. He desired to have the same full and sovereign power in his Bari Doab estates as he enjoyed in his Jalandhar territory, and he also wished to consolidate his estates on both sides of the Bias, by giving up certain isolated villages in the Lahore and Amritsar districts and receiving others of equal rental adjoining his territory. But this proposition the Government was not prepared then to entertain, and the Raja was informed that if the estate could be conveniently consolidated, he might hereafter receive the magisterial powers which it was proposed to confer on jagirdars in the Punjab.[2] The Raja had no wish for the consolidation of the jagir unless he could also obtain sovereign powers; but the Government, after further consideration, maintained its opinion that it was unadvisable to change the jurisdiction of villages which had been for fifteen years under British administration.[3]

He desires full sovereignty in these villages.

Which the Government are indisposed to grant.

[1] Letters—No. 204, dated 23d December 1859, from Commissioner Trans-Satlej States to Secretary Government Punjab; letter of Raja Randhir Singh to Major Lake, dated 16th December 1859; No. 18, dated 7th January 1860, from Secretary Government Punjab to Government of India; No. 245, dated 28th January 1860, from Government of India to Secretary Government Punjab.

[2] Letter of Raja Randhir Singh to Commissioner Trans-Satlej States, dated 10th March 1860; No. 56, dated 17th April 1860, from Commissioner Trans-Satlej States to Government Punjab; No. 491, of Government Punjab to Commissioner Trans-Satlej States, dated 25th April 1860.

[3] Letters No. 178, of Commissioner Trans-Satlej States to Government Punjab, dated 13th December 1861; No. 683, of Government Punjab to Government of India, dated 12th December 1862; No. 92, of Government of India to Government Punjab, dated 26th January 1863; No. 21, of Commissioner Amritsar to Government Punjab, dated 27th February 1863; No. 442, of Government of India to Government Punjab, dated 31st August 1864.

A case may here be alluded to as affording a precedent for the determination of claims to lands belonging to States situated on different banks of a river and affected by changes in the river's channel. In 1860, two

New title given to the Raja of Kapurthalla as an Oude Talukdar.

In 1861, the Chief Commissioner of Oude addressed the Supreme Government to the effect that the Raja of Kapurthalla, though of far higher position than Maharajas Man Singh and Dirg Bijai Singh of Bulrampur, being an independent ruler in his hereditary estates, was yet, in Oude, in an inferior position, and requested that some honorary title might be accorded to him which would place him above the ordinary Oude Talukdars. The Government accordingly sanctioned the Raja of Kapurthalla being addressed as Raja Rajagan, or Raja of Rajas.[1] This title is only in force in Oude, and not in the Punjab, to which it was never intended to apply.

Sovereign powers in Oude refused, and exchange of estates.

The Raja desired to be invested with the same powers in his Oude estates as he exercised in his estate in the Punjab; or that estates and full powers within them should be given to him in the Punjab in exchange for

villages, Jhugian Raian and Jhugian Dogaran, were cut from the Kapurthalla side of the Bias river by a sudden change in the stream, and added to the British bank. The question of the right of the Kapurthalla State to claim separated lands was long discussed, and in 1869 it was ruled by the Supreme Government that the villages should continue to be owned by the Raja, the principle in such cases being that if the change in the bed of the river was so gradual as to escape observation, the villages and their revenue would belong to the British Government, but that if the change was sudden, then rights of all kinds, whether of jurisdiction, administration, or revenue, remain as before. This was the principle laid down in the letter of the Government of India, No. 3631, dated 24th August 1860, and approved by the Secretary of State in his despatch, No. 3, dated 16th January 1861.

Letter of Government Punjab to Government of India, 275-1055, dated 1st September 1869; Government of India to Government Punjab, dated 21st October 1869; and Government Punjab to Financial Commissioner, No. 1315, dated 12th November 1869.

A similar case had occurred in 1857, when under orders conveyed in Supreme Government letter No. 2551, dated 12th June, eight villages, which by the action of the river Satlej had been cut off from the Firozpur district, and transferred to the Kapurthalla side of the river, were allowed to remain under the administration of the Raja.

[1] Secretary Chief Commissioner of Oude to Government of India, No. 312, dated 20th February 1861; and Government of India to Secretary Chief Commissioner of Oude, No. 1096, of 12th March 1861.

those in Oude. The Government held out no hopes whatever that this request would ever be granted.[1]

The Star of India conferred on the Raja.

At Lahore, on the 17th October 1864, His Excellency the Viceroy and Governor-General invested the Raja with the insignia of the Most Exalted Order of the Star of India. The Raja was attended by eight of his principal relatives and Sirdars. The following Chiefs were present at the ceremony: the Maharajas of Kashmir and Pattiala, the Rajas of Jhind, Mandi, Faridkot, Chamba, Suket, and Goleria; the Nawabs of Maler Kotla, Patowdi, Loharu, and Dojana; and the Sirdar of Kalsia. The Raja, who received a salute of eleven guns on his arrival and departure, was conducted to the Viceroy by the Maharaja of Kashmir, the only knight of the order present, and by the Secretary of the order.

The Viceroy's speech.

The Viceroy addressed the Raja in Hindostani to the following effect:—

"Raja Randhir Singh, Raja of Kapurthalla, it is with much satisfaction that I find myself empowered by Her Most Gracious Majesty the Queen of England to confer on you so great a mark of her favour as that of the Star of India. This honour has only been granted to those Princes and Chiefs who unite high rank with great personal merit. It rejoices me to install you among the chosen number.

"Your grandfather, Sirdar Fatah Singh, was a Chief of considerable renown. He was the well-known leader of the Ahluwalia confederacy, and the companion in arms of the great Maharaja Ranjit Singh. Your father, Raja Nihal Singh, was an old friend of mine when you were

[1] Extract from Proceedings of Government of India in the Foreign Department of 6th March 1862.

yet a youth. When he passed away, your Highness succeeded to his duties and responsibilities, and have worthily discharged them. When the mutiny of 1857 broke out, you were one of the foremost Chiefs of this country to do your duty and range yourself on the side of the British Government. After the fall of Dehli your Highness headed your troops, conducted them to Oude, and there assisted in recovering that province. For these services you received at the time much praise and liberal rewards; and now, to crown all, you are about to obtain a most signal mark of honour from Her Majesty the Queen of England and India. In the name, then, of the Queen, and by Her Majesty's commands, I now invest you with the Honourable Insignia of the Star of India, of which Most Exalted Order Her Majesty has been graciously pleased to appoint you to be a Knight. I have addressed you in Hindostani, in order that the Princes and Chiefs now present may the more readily participate in this ceremony, and that your relatives and friends may be more highly gratified, otherwise I should have spoken in English, for I know that you thoroughly understand my language. This circumstance, no doubt, has operated as a bond of union between your Highness and my countrymen."

At the conclusion of the address, the Viceroy placed the ribbon and collar of the Order round the Raja's neck, and delivered to him the star.[1]

Family troubles and the dispute regarding the partition of the Kapurthalla estates between himself and his younger brothers much embittered the last years of Raja Randhir Singh's life, and for some time he almost abandoned the Punjab and resided upon his Oude property,

[1] Notification of Supreme Government, No. 600, of 18th October 1864.

till the news that his territory was not to be divided allowed him to return with honour.

The visit of the Raja to England determined on.

The Raja had for long been desirous of paying a visit to England, and his satisfaction at the successful result of his appeal to the Secretary of State in the matter of the division of territory was so great, that he decided to leave for England early in 1870, and remain there for a year if the climate should agree with him.[1] He made arrangements for the proper administration of his State during his absence, leaving his son, Kharak Singh, in charge with responsible ministers, every matter of importance being directed to be reported to him in England. The Raja left Kapurthalla for Bombay on the 15th of March. He had long been in a very delicate state of health from an affection of the liver, and was urged by many of his friends to abandon his intention for the present. But all his arrangements had been made, and he was most unwilling to delay the visit to England, upon which he had set his heart, and from which he anticipated so much pleasure. But this was not to be. Scarcely had he left Bombay when he became seriously ill, and when the ship reached Aden, there was no hope of his life. A committee of medical officers was called, but they declared the Raja could only live a few hours, and advised his being taken on board the mail steamer just leaving Aden for Bombay. This was done, and soon after his removal he died, on the 2d of April.[2] His body was conveyed to Bombay, where it was received by his son Prince Kharak

His illness and death.

[1] Government of India, dated 18th February, and 7th, 14th, and 19th March, 1870. Government Punjab, No. 292, dated 13th September 1869. Government of India, No. 1389, dated 29th September 1869.

[2] Letter of Colonel Lees, dated Aden, April 2, to Secretary Government of India. Report of Medical Board, dated April 2, 1870, Aden. Letter from Prince Kharak Singh to the Viceroy, dated 18th April 1870, and 29th.

Singh, who had hurried from Kapurthalla on hearing of his father's illness. He took the body to the sacred city of Nasik, where the ceremony of cremation was performed, and a fortnight later the ashes of Raja Randhir Singh were conveyed to Hardwar.

The sanction of the Viceroy was at once solicited to the recognition of Prince Kharak Singh to the estates and titles of his father,[1] and this sanction was at once granted, with an expression of deep and sincere regret at the news of the Raja's death. "The British Government," said the Viceroy, "has lost in him an attached and valued friend, and a Chief who, by a vigorous and progressive administration, set an excellent example to other native rulers. The valuable services which he rendered to the British Government in time of trouble and danger will not be forgotten."[2]

The installation of Raja Kharak Singh.

The installation of Prince Kharak Singh took place on the 12th of May. Colonel Coxe, Commissioner of Jalandhar, attended on the part of Government, and a large number of visitors were present, English and native. The customary ceremonies were performed, and khillats were presented on the part of the British Government and the independent Chiefs.[3] During the ceremony of the installation, an address was presented from the subjects of the Kapurthalla State, congratulating Prince Kharak Singh on his accession, and offering large contributions towards a memorial in honour of the late Raja. This address, and the reply of the Raja, showing so

[1] Government Punjab to Government of India, No. 128½, 21st April 1870.

[2] Government of India to Government Punjab, No. 14, A. P., dated 5th May 1870. Government Punjab to Commissioner Jalandhar, No. 517, dated 7th May 1870. Commissioner Jalandhar to Government Punjab, No. 191, 1196, dated 26th April.

[3] Commissioner Jalandhar to Government Punjab, 13th May 1870.

much liberality on the part of the people, and so much enlightenment on the part of the young Prince, cannot be omitted here. They may well be accepted as a good omen for the new reign, and a promise that the liberal opinions of Raja Randhir Singh are shared by his son.

ADDRESS TO H. H. THE RAJA OF KAPURTHALLA BY HIS SUBJECTS.

[*Translation.*]

"YOUR HIGHNESS,—We, the servants and subjects of Kapurthalla State, and of your Highness's Oude estates, bow down our heads with reverent thanks to the Almighty God for His grace in giving us this auspicious opportunity, through the royal protection and favour of the British Government, of witnessing these entertainments of your installation to the throne vacated by the lamented death of your renowned and much esteemed father. Our past experience of your Highness's benevolent and just rule during the late Maharaja's lifetime confirms our hopes that you will inherit all the noble qualities of your father, and will soon remove from our hearts the heavy grief sustained by the loss of our late beloved master, now that you are given scope of displaying your hitherto latent virtues.

"Almost all your illustrious ancestors, since they grew into power, have been remarkable for their meritorious exploits; but when we consider the noble deeds of your father, our grief for his decease takes a permanent shape. The little space at our command forbids our entering into the details of his works; we would, however, cursorily run over them. Previous to the accession of the late Maharaja to the musnud, the Government revenue was in an anomalous state, as in other native principalities. The product of the fields was attached to make it good, which naturally resulted in the ruin of the ryot, and the usurpation of his property by a stronger party. But His Highness seeing the evils of this system fixed the State jumma according to the capabilities of the soil, and regulated the rights of the tenants and the proprietors, by which all enjoyed the fruits of their labour, and in a short time grew so rich as not to stand in need of the village 'Shahokars' under whose heavy debts they ever before groaned.

"In judicial affairs the administration has been so consolidated that all classes of the subjects have been prosperous and secure, and might no longer triumphs over right.

"The police establishment and the police stations have been appointed after the fashion of the British territory. The following short account of the reigning members of the Ahluwalia family would place his late Highness's career in contrast with his predecessors.

"Nawab Jassa Singh, the first Chief of the family, obtained so much power and influence in the Khalsa army as to be unanimously recognised by them as their King. His next successor, Bhag Singh, was also just and wise, but as he was too merciful and mild a ruler, the managers of his estates rose into insurrection against him, which diminished the size of his dominions. He was succeeded by his renowned son Maharaja Fatah Singh, who reduced his insubordinate deputies into subjection, and greatly enlarged his estates. He exchanged turbans with Maharaja Ranjit Singh, at Fatahabad, in token of fraternity, and it was in his reign that the first treaty of alliance of the British Government with the

Punjab was entered into in 1806, between himself personally on his own part and plenipotentiary on the part of Ranjit Singh, and Lord Lake on the part of the British Government. The Sirdars Ranjit Singh and Fatah Singh are mentioned there in terms of equality. But subsequently Maharaja Ranjit Singh not remaining true to his promise, taking advantage of his residence in his Cis-Satlej estates, took possession of a greater portion of his territory in the Jalandhar and Bari Doabs, with a part of the Amritsar city called Kattra Ahluwalia after the name of the family. His son Raja Nihal Singh followed him to the raj. During his reign the administration was peaceful and prosperous. But by the rebellious conduct of his mutinous army against the British troops he lost his hereditary Cis-Satlej estates, which deprived the State of half of its size. His Highness Raja Randhir Singh came next on the stage. Like his great grandfather Raja Jassa Singh, his reign was marked with daily aggrandisement of his power and influence and of his very attractive qualities. The estates of Fatahabad, which were the ancestral patrimony of the Ahluwalia dynasty, were resumed by Government after the demise of Raja Nihal Singh, like similar life-tenure jagirs of other Sirdars. But Maharaja Randhir Singh received them back from the British Government after his meritorious conduct in the Sepoy War of 1857 and 1858. He also received valuable estates in Oude, in recognition of his eminent services in the mutiny. He protected his patrimonial state from two different blows, first, in 1853, from the contemplated partition of the ilaquas Wayan and Bunga, and subsequently, in 1868, from the proposed division of the territory, the latter by appealing to Her Majesty's Secretary of State for India. He received the honorary titles Farzand Dilband Razikul Itikad Doulat Englishia and Raja-i-Rajgan, the President of the Talukdars of Oude, and was honoured with the highest mark of Her Majesty's favour, viz., Knight of the Grand Commander of the Most Exalted Order of the Star of India. He received the Mutiny medal, which though of a lower order as a decoration than the Star of India, His Highness gloried in wearing, in remembrance of having led his forces personally in combat against the enemies of the Queen. His Royal Highness the Duke of Edinburgh in the Calcutta Durbar remarked that such a medal did not adorn the breast of any other Chief present on the occasion, which shows that his late Highness was justified in attaching a peculiar value to the medal. The town of Kapurthalla previous to the time of the late Maharaja was a mere collection of hamlets; but in his administration buildings grew up in it. The bazaars and streets have been properly built; on the principal public streets trees have been planted on both sides of the way, and shops of different manufactures have been opened by firms from Kashmir, Amritsar, and other large towns. The towns of Phagwara and Sultanpur have similarly been improved, and gardens and houses, and beautiful houses, have been erected in various places in the Kapurthalla State and elsewhere. Schools have been established here on the model of those in the British dominions. A canal His Highness had proposed to excavate in Kapurthalla, and establish a great hospital here. But alas! his benevolent aims remained uncompleted. His Highness's dealings with the British Government were equally creditable to him, and won for him the esteem and respect of the authorities. His heroic deeds in the eventful year of 1857-58, performed in his own person, first in the Jalandhar Doab and afterwards in Oude, are too well known to require any mention of them.

"More recently, in the late disturbances on the north-western frontier, and at the beginning of the Abyssinian Expedition, His Highness volunteered his aid, and on both occasions received the thanks of the Punjab Government. His Highness had a very earnest desire of personally paying his homage to his sovereign the Queen, for which he undertook his last disastrous journey to England. Seeing symptoms of ailment in his features, his officials long prevented him from commencing this journey, but nothing could shake his ardent desire of presenting himself to Her Majesty, with besides the hopes of returning, restored in health, from his voyage. We greatly lament that he was not allowed to carry out his energetic aims; and when we consider the benign effects of his rule, we reverentially raise our eyes to heaven and trust that the Almighty Monarch has given his soul the same peace which we enjoyed under him. In order to evince our gratitude to the late Maharaja for his paternal kindness to us, and for the happiness we enjoyed under him, we, the servants and subjects of his Kapurthalla and Oude estates, have raised the sum of Rs. 1,25,000 by voluntary contribution, which we present to His Highness Maharaja Kharak Singh, and ask him to spend it on the erection of a memorial at Kapurthalla in commemoration of the much lamented Maharaja Randhir Singh's merciful and just rule, by which our posterity may feel themselves proud of being under the sway of the representative of such an illustrious prince.

"We conclude this address with our heartfelt prayer to God that He may ever protect this State from all dangers, and ever keep it prosperous under the protection of the British Government.

"May our young Mahawuzer be long spared to rule over us as his honoured father did, and carry us still further in the foremost ranks of progress and civilisation in India."

REPLY TO THE ABOVE.

[*Translation.*]

"GENTLEMEN,—Indeed, as you have described, my late lamented father's death must have caused you deep grief. His loss has been felt by me with a greater sorrow. But as we are all destined to this common lot, and our existence in this world is only transient, we cannot but patiently bear such misfortunes. I feel myself very thankful to you for the large sum of Rs. 1,25,000 which you have collected for the erection of a memorial in honour of my deceased father, which shows your hearts' attachment for him. It delights me the more to find that out of this Rs. 25,000 have been contributed by the people of our Oude estates, which are but recent acquisitions of the late Maharaja. I remember His Highness said on several occasions that the subjects of his Oude estates were dearer to him than those of Kapurthalla, inasmuch as they were acquired by him in person : their present doings, then, verify the above remark of His Highness.

"To dispose of the amount you have advanced for this noble object, I have to remind you that nothing received my father's greater consideration than your enlightenment in sciences and civilisation. It was for this reason that he devoted so much attention towards the establishment of schools, hospitals, &c., &c. Nothing then do I think would be a better memorial in my father's honour than to carry out the inmost design of his heart. I should therefore propose that a college should be started at Kapurthalla to be called Randhir College, which may be of perpetual benefit to yourselves and your posterity for your mental culture and civilisation. Of the amount subscribed Rs. 20,000 can be laid out on the improvement of the old school building, and Rs. 5000 on the erection of a building for a hospital. The rest, one lakh of rupees should be deposited in a Government security of promissory-notes, the interest on which will be Rs. 5000 per annum. I willingly add rupees one lakh more, to be similarly deposited, to increase the interest to Rs. 10,000 per annum. Rs. 10,000 more a year I offer you, to make the aggregate amount of the yearly income of Rs. 20,000, which can be very adequately expended on the establishment of a college and a hospital.

"But I think if Colonel Coxe, our Commissioner, who is present here, will give his kind assistance by reference to Government for the supply of a Principal and a staff of good teachers, then there will be great hope of our succeeding in carrying out these objects."

Raja Kharak Singh has already given another proof of his liberality in the gift of Rs. 25,000, to be so invested as to connect the name of Sir Donald McLeod, the late Lieutenant-Governor of the Punjab, with the province. It has been determined by Sir Donald McLeod to devote this money to the foundation of an annual prize for the best vernacular work, original, compiled, or translated, on Natural Science, the competition to be open to all India. The founding of a Natural Science Prize.

THE HISTORY

OF THE

FARIDKOT STATE.

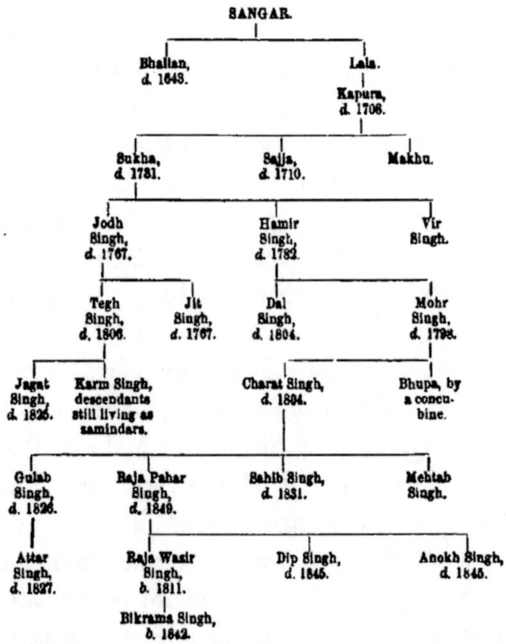

The origin of the Faridkot family. THE Burar Jat family of Faridkot has sprung from the same stock as the Phulkian and Kythal Chiefs, claiming to descend from Burar, the seventeenth in descent from

Jesal the founder of the Jesalmir State, and the reputed ancestor of the Sidhu, Burar, and many other Jat clans.

The Burar Jats were thus originally Bhatti Rajputs; and although, in their own traditions, there is a record of an emigration from Sialkot in the Rechna Doab to the Malwa many centuries ago, yet it is altogether certain that they never travelled to the north of the Satlej at all, but settled in the country in which they are at present found on their first emigration from Rajputana, which was synchronous with that of the Phulkian branch of the tribe. **The Burar Jats.**

The Burars are the most important Jat tribe in the Firozpur district, where they inhabit the whole of the country of Mari, Mehraj, Muktsar or Mokatsar, Mudki, Buchon, Bhadour, Sultan Khan and Faridkot, holding besides many villages in Pattiala, Nabha, and Malod. They are not good agriculturists, and in former days were a wild and unruly race, addicted to cattle-stealing and dacoity, while female infanticide was universally practised, and, among the Maharajkian Burars, was only given up in the year 1836, through the exertions of Mr Clerk, the Political Agent of the British Government.[1] **Their country and character.**

The Raja of Faridkot is the head of the Burar tribe, and rules a territory 643 square miles in extent, with a revenue of about Rs. 80,000. Of the ancestor who gave this name to the tribe mention has already been made,[2] and Sangar was the next of the family of whom tradition takes any notice, the founder of Chakran, now a deserted village in the district of Kot Kapura. The story is told that in the reign of the Emperor Akbar, the **Sangar and Bhallan.**

[1] Agent Governor-General to Political Agent, 28th April 1836; Political Agent to Agent Governor-General, 31st August 1836.

[2] *Vide ante*, p. 4.

Muhammadan Bhattis of Sirsa and the Burars quarrelled about their boundaries, and both parties went to Dehli to ask the Emperor to adjudicate between them. Bhallan, the son of Sangar, represented the Burar clan, and Mansur, who was supposed to have influence at Court, one of his daughters being in the royal harem, was the champion of the Bhattis. The Emperor gave them an audience in open Durbar, and, as was customary, presented them with turbans and a dress of honour. Mansur at once began to wind the muslin round his head, when Sangar snatched it from him. A scuffle ensued in which the turban was torn in two. The Emperor was amused at the quarrel, and said that his decision would correspond with the length of the pieces of muslin which each had managed to retain. On being measured, the fragments were found exactly equal in length, and the Bhattiana and Burar boundary was accordingly laid down on a principle of equality, half the disputed country being given to either claimant. This tradition is preserved by the Burars in a well-known line, "Bhallan chira phari Akbar ka Darbar."[1]

The acquisitions of the tribe.

In the days of Bhallan the Burars held Kot Kapura, Faridkot, Mari, Mudki, and Muktsar, and he was appointed by the Dehli Government Chaudhri or headman of the tribe. On his death, without male issue, Kapura, the son of his brother Lala, succeeded him as Chaudhri. Kapura was born in 1628, and succeeded his uncle in 1643. He was a brave and able man, and consolidated the Burar possessions, winning many victories over his neighbours the Bhattis and others.

The founding of Kot Kapura.

He founded Sirianwala, now in ruins, but abandoned it for a new residence, Kot Kapura, named after himself,

[1] Bhallan tore the turban in Akbar's Durbar.

and which he is reported to have founded at the suggestion of Bhai Bhagtu, a famous Hindu ascetic. This town was peopled by traders and others from Kot Isa Khan, and the reputation which Kapura enjoyed, for justice and benevolence, induced many emigrants to settle in the new town, which soon became a place of considerable importance.

Kapura was a *malguzar*, or tributary of the Dehli Empire, and appears to have served it with some fidelity, for when Guru Govind Singh visited him in 1704, and begged for his assistance against the Muhammadans, Kapura refused to help him, possibly believing, with many others at that time, that the cause of the new faith was altogether hopeless.[1] **His relations with the Imperial Government.**

Isa Khan, the owner of the fort and village of that name, was Kapura's great rival and enemy, and watched his growing importance with the utmost jealousy. The two Chiefs had constant quarrels, resulting in much bloodshed, but Isa Khan, finding that he was unable to conquer Kapura by force, determined to subdue him by gentler means, and concluded with him an agreement of perpetual friendship. Then, inviting him to his house, he feasted him in chivalrous fashion, and assassinated him at the close of the banquet. **His enemy Isa Khan.** **The assassination of Kapura, A.D. 1708.**

Kapura, who was eighty years old at his death, in

[1] There is, however, in the Granth of Govind, Hikayat I: Bet 59: the following Persian couplet—

"Na zarra daren rah khatra tarast
Hamah Kaum-i-Burar hukm-i-marast."

The meaning of which is—

"There is not the slightest danger for thee on this road, for the whole Burar race is under my command."

It is very doubtful whether this couplet is not of later origin, and an interpolation into the text of the Granth Sahib. It is quite certain that, in 1704, when the Granth of Govind Singh was written, the Burars had not generally embraced Sikhism.

1708, left three sons, Sukha, Sajja, and Makhu, who determined to avenge their father's murder, and, assembling the clan and obtaining the aid of a strong Imperial force, they attacked Isa Khan, defeated and killed him, and plundered his fort.

The murder avenged.

Sajja, though the second son,[1] succeeded his father as head of the family, but only survived him twelve years, when his brother, Sukha Singh, became Chief. He added to his possessions the estates of Ranadatta, Behkbodla, Dharamkot, Karman, and Mamdot, and founded the new village of Kot Sukha. To his younger brother, Makhu, the villages Rori and Matta were assigned from the patrimony, and these are still in the possession of Makhu's descendants.

The death of Sukha, and the quarrels among his sons.

Sukha died, in 1731, aged fifty, leaving three sons, Jodh, Hamir, and Vir, who for some time lived together in peace, but at length they quarrelled, and the two younger wished to divide the estate. To this Jodh, the eldest, would not agree, and Hamir and Vir then asked assistance from some of the Sikh Chiefs then rising to power, Sirdars Jassa Singh Ahluwalia, Kapur Singh Faizullapuria, Jhanda Singh Bhangi, and Krora Singh, founder of the misl of that name. These were ready enough to interfere, and, crossing the Satlej in force, compelled Jodh to assign the district of Mari Mustafa to Vir, and Faridkot to Hamir, retaining for himself Kot Kapura, with five villages, known as the "*Kharch Sirdari,*" the excess usually allowed the eldest son, to support the honour of the Chiefship, in families in which the rule of equal partition ordinarily prevails. The con-

The Sikh Chiefs called in and the estate divided.

[1] Sirdar Attar Singh Bhadour, one of the best authorities on early Cis-Satlej history, considers Sukha Singh to have been the second son, and Sajja or Lena Singh the elder. Also that the latter was Chaudhri for only two years, dying in 1710.

federate Chiefs then induced the brothers to embrace Sikhism, and having caused them to receive the "pahal" or Sikh baptism, recrossed the river.

Sirdar Hamir Singh was thus the first independent Chief of Faridkot. His brother, Jodh Singh, in 1766, erected a new fort at Kot Kapura, and almost rebuilt the town; but his oppression was so great that the inhabitants left it, and the artisans, who had been renowned for their skill and industry, emigrated to Lahore, Amritsar, and Pattiala. With Raja Amar Singh, of this last named State, he was constantly engaged in hostilities; and, in 1767, the Raja having found, at the suggestion of the Chief's brother, a satisfactory pretext for a quarrel, marched to Kot Kapura, with a strong force, and prepared to invest the fort, when Jodh Singh and his son, advancing too far beyond the walls, fell into an ambuscade laid by the Pattiala troops and was killed, fighting gallantly to the last, his son, Jit Singh, being mortally wounded.[1]

Sirdar Hamir Singh of Faridkot.

Jodh Singh is attacked by the Raja of Pattiala and killed, A.D. 1767.

Jodh Singh was succeeded by his son, Tegh Singh, who appears to have been a man of very small intelligence. He continued the family feud with Pattiala, and avenged his father's death by massacring all the inhabitants, men, women, and children of the four Jalal villages who were in the pay of Pattiala, and by whom Jodh Singh had been slain. Hamir Singh of Faridkot joined in this expedition, but shortly afterwards quarrelled with his nephew, who refused submission to him, and, taking him prisoner, confined him in the Faridkot fort. The Phulkian Chiefs, however, used all their interest to get him set at liberty, which Hamir Singh only consented to do on condition that he would never leave his town of Kot

Tegh Singh.

Captured by Hamir Singh of Faridkot.

[1] *Vide ante*, pp. 33, 34.

Kapura. The result was the utter disorganisation of the estate. The zamindars, unable to obtain justice, refused to pay revenue, and robbery and violence were everywhere prevalent, while Maha Singh Sarai, brother-in-law of the Pattiala Chief, seized Mudki and eighteen neighbouring villages.

Murdered by his sons,

The end of Tegh Singh was very tragical. He had been for long on the worst of terms with his son Jaggat Singh, who, in 1806, set fire to the house in which his father was residing, and a large quantity of powder having been stored in the vaults beneath, the house was utterly destroyed and the Chief killed by the explosion.

Whose estates are seized by Diwan Mohkam Chand.

The guilty son did not long enjoy the lands of which he thus became possessed. The next year, 1807, his elder brother, Karam Singh, calling Diwan Mohkam Chand to his assistance, defeated him and took possession of the district, but the Diwan and his master, Maharaja Ranjit Singh, had no intention of restoring it to the rightful owner, and Kot Kapura the Maharaja kept for himself, giving five Jalal villages to the Raja of Nabha. The villages of Mudki, which Maha Singh had seized, Ranjit Singh also retained, leaving to Maha Singh shares in two only, Patli and Hukumatwala.

In 1824, Jaggat Singh made an attempt to recover the estate, and drove the Lahore garrison out of Kot Kapura, but he was unable to hold it, and was compelled to surrender it after twenty days. He then endeavoured to make his peace with Lahore, and gave his elder daughter in marriage to Sher Singh, the Maharaja's reputed son; but the following year, 1825, he died without male issue. The descendants of Karam Singh, the elder brother, are still living, but are of no political importance.

It is now necessary to return to the younger branch of

Faridkot, represented by Hamir Singh, who, in 1763, received that estate as his share of the patrimony. The town had been founded some time before, and named after a celebrated saint, Baba Farid, but Hamir Singh enlarged it, inducing traders and artisans to people it, and built a brick fort for its protection. He had two sons, Dal Singh and Mohr Singh, the former of whom was of an intractable disposition, and rebelled against his father, who suspected that Mohr Singh, the younger brother, was also concerned in the plot. He accordingly called them both before him, and, to test their temper, directed each to fire at the leg of the bed on which he was reclining with their muskets, or, according to other accounts, to shoot an arrow at it. Dal Singh fired without hesitation, and split the leg of the bed; but Mohr Singh refused, saying that guns were fired at enemies and not at friends. This conduct so pleased the Chief that he declared Mohr Singh his heir, and banished Dal Singh altogether from Faridkot, assigning for his support the villages of Dhodeki, Malloh, and Bhalur.[1] This selection of Mohr Singh as his successor created a deadly feud between the brothers, and Mohr Singh besieged his rival in Dhodeki. But the latter managed to hold his own, and, calling to his assistance the Nishanwala Chief, defeated his brother, and compelled him to return to Faridkot.

The Faridkot branch.

The disinheriting of Dal Singh, and the feud between the brothers.

Sirdar Hamir Singh died in 1782, and Mohr Singh succeeded him. The new Chief was an incapable, debauched man, and paid no attention to the administra-

Death of Sirdar Hamir Singh, A.D. 1782.

[1] According to the Faridkot Chief, Dal Singh was the second son, Mohr Singh the elder; but this is contradicted by the Bhadour Chief, the "Barah Misl," and other records, who make Mohr Singh the younger. In 1827, Sirdar Pahar Singh declared primogeniture always had prevailed in the family. This was, however, a case of disinheritance.

tion of his estates, several of which, Akuhar, Karmi, and Behkbodla, were seized by his neighbours. He married a daughter of Sirdar Sobba Singh, of Man in Jhind, by whom he had a son, Char Singh, or, as he is generally known, Charat Singh, and who, according to the almost invariable practice of the family, rebelled against his father. The origin of the quarrel was as follows.

Mohr Singh and his sons.

Mohr Singh had another son, Bhupa, born of a Muhammadan concubine, Teji, of whom he was passionately fond, and this boy had a far larger share of his father's love and attention than the legitimate son, who regarded his rival with the greatest jealousy and dislike. On one occasion the Chief was setting out on an expedition towards Philor, and told Bhupa to accompany him. The spoiled child refused unless his father allowed him to ride the horse on which his brother always rode, and on which he was then mounted. Mohr Singh ordered Charat Singh to dismount and give Bhupa the horse. This insult, though an unintentional one, sank deep into the heart of Charat Singh. He could not endure that he, the legitimate son, should be slighted for the son of a slave girl, and determined on revenge. With Kalha and Diwan Singh, his advisers, he formed a conspiracy to dethrone his father; and during Mohr Singh's absence, he surprised the Faridkot Fort, and put Teji, his father's mistress, to death. Sirdar Mohr Singh, hearing of what had happened, hastily collected a large body of peasants, and attempted to recover the fort, but he was repulsed with loss, and retired to the village of Pakka, some four miles distant. Here he was surrounded by the troops of his rebel son, and, after a fruitless resistance, was taken prisoner and sent to Sher Singhwala, a village belonging to the father-in-law of Charat Singh, in which he was confined for a considerable

Charat Singh rebels against his father,

And imprisons him.

time. At length, Sirdar Tara Singh Gheba, a powerful Chief, interfered in his behalf, and induced Charat Singh to set him at liberty, although he refused to aid Mohr Singh against his son. After this, Mohr Singh made more than one attempt to recover his authority in Faridkot, but without success, and he died an exile in 1798.

The fortunes of Sirdar Charat Singh.

Sirdar Charat Singh now considered himself safe from attack, and reduced the number of his troops. The Pattiala State, his old enemy, was not likely to attack him, for he had repulsed an attack of the famous Diwan Nanun Mal, Minister of Pattiala, during the minority of Raja Sahib Singh, with some loss, and had acquired a great name for courage. But he had forgotten to number among his enemies his disinherited uncle, Dal Singh, who was only waiting an opportunity to regain his lost possessions; and, in 1804, having collected a small body of followers, he attacked the Faridkot fort by night and obtained possession. Charat Singh was surprised and killed, and his wife and three children, Gulab Singh, Pahar Singh, and Sahib Singh, barely escaped with their lives. Sirdar Dal Singh only enjoyed his success for a single month. The children of the murdered Chief were very young, the eldest being no more than seven years of age; but they had many friends, the most able of whom was their maternal uncle, Fouju Singh, one of the Sirdars of Sher Singhwala, and, moreover, Dal Singh was generally hated for his tyranny. A plot to assassinate him was formed, and Fouju Singh, with a few armed men, penetrated at night to the apartment of Dal Singh, where he was sleeping with two or three attendants, and killed him. Then they beat a drum, which was the signal for the friends of the young Gulab Singh to bring him into the fort. There he was declared Chief without opposition, and his uncle,

Sirdar Dal Singh assassinated.

Fouju Singh, was appointed Diwan or Minister. The affairs of the little State were conducted with tolerable efficiency for some time, until Diwan Mohkam Chand, the Lahore General, invaded the Cis-Satlej territory in the cold season of 1806-7. He seized Zira, Buria, Mokatsar, Kot Kapura, and Mari, which had been assigned to Vir, the youngest son of Sukha, but which had fallen into the hands of the brother-in-law of Tara Singh Gheba. The Diwan then marched against Faridkot, summoning the garrison to surrender, and, on their refusal, besieged the fort. The garrison trusted more to their position than to their numerical strength. Faridkot was situated in the true desert, and the only water for a besieging army was to be found in a few pools filled with rain water, and scattered round the place, and these the besieged filled with the branches of a poisonous shrub, which so affected the water as to give the Lahore troops the most violent purging, and the General had no other resource than to raise the siege. He contrived, however, to exact a tribute of Rs. 7000 from Fouju Singh, and in his heart resolved to conquer Faridkot on the first favourable opportunity. This opportunity was not long in arriving.[1] While Mr Metcalfe, the Agent of the British Government, who had been sent to the Maharaja to conclude a treaty, offensive and defensive, against France, was in his camp, Ranjit Singh crossed the Satlej with his whole army, on the 26th September 1808, and marched against Faridkot. He himself halted at Khai, and sent forward an advanced guard, to which the fort surrendered without resistance, for the garrison knew that the Maharaja was present in person with the army, and his reputation for uninterrupted success was at this time so great,

Mohkam Chand besieges Faridkot.

But is compelled to retire.

Ranjit Singh of Lahore captures the town.

[1] *Vide ante*, p. 101.

that he rarely met with direct opposition. A few days afterwards he himself marched to Faridkot, much elated at finding himself in possession of so fine a fort with so little difficulty. Mr Metcalfe accompanied him; for the Maharaja, under pretence of signing the treaty, drew the British Agent from one place to another, forcing him to be an unwilling spectator of all his Cis-Satlej acquisitions; and although Mr Metcalfe's diplomacy was much commended by the Government of the day, there can be little doubt that he was outwitted by the Maharaja, who would have been permitted to retain all his conquests to the south of the Satlej had not the policy of the British Government suddenly undergone a change by the removal of all apprehension of a French invasion.[1]

The estate is given in jagir to Diwan Mohkam Chand.

Before abandoning the fort, Fouju Singh made as good terms for his nephews as were possible, obtaining a grant of five villages, to which they retired. The Phulkian Chiefs each tried to obtain the district of Faridkot from the Maharaja. Pattiala had the best claim, for it had once been subject to her authority; but Raja Jaswant Singh of Nabha and Raja Bhag Singh of Jhind both bid high. But Diwan Mohkam Chand, who had set his heart on possessing Faridkot ever since his repulse in 1807, was the fortunate grantee, although he had to pay for it a large *nazrana*, or fine.

Its restitution demanded by the British Government.

When the British Government demanded from the Maharaja the restitution of all his conquests on the left bank of the Satlej, made during 1808 and 1809, Faridkot was the place he surrendered most unwillingly. To it he pretended to have a special right—firstly, from its being

The Maharaja maintains his right to it.

[1] Mr C. Metcalfe to Government, 30th September, 1st October, 5th October, 10th October 1808; Raja Sahib Singh of Pattiala to Resident Dehli, 3d December 1808; Resident Dehli to Captain Close, Acting Resident with Sindiah, 16th January 1809.

a dependency of Kot Kapura, which he had previously conquered; and secondly, from an alleged promise made by the owners when it was besieged in 1807, that they would, within one month, put themselves under his authority, and that, should they fail to do so, they would consent to undergo any punishment which he might think fit to impose upon them. With regard to the first claim advanced, it is manifest that no right could be maintained on account of any connection between Kot Kapura and Faridkot. Ever since the division of the territory among the sons of Sukha, Faridkot had been independent, more powerful than Kot Kapura, and in no way subject to it. Even had there been any connection such as that alleged, the Maharaja's case would have been no stronger, for his seizure of Kot Kapura, before he had requested the assent of the British Government to the extension of his conquests beyond the Satlej, could not warrant his seizure of Faridkot after he had made such a request.

The second ground on which the Raja based his right was in some degree more valid, except that its truth could not be ascertained, and the conduct of the garrison and the sudden and forced retreat of Diwan Mohkam Chand seemed to contradict it; nevertheless, the British Envoy consented to refer the claim of Faridkot, being an old conquest, for the decision of Government. This proposal did not at all please the Maharaja, who told Mr Metcalfe that he must consult with the Chiefs of his army on the Satlej respecting the propriety of restoring Faridkot. The Envoy replied that he should consider the Maharaja's moving to join his army on the Satlej as a declaration of war, and quit his Court accordingly.[1]

[1] Mr C. Metcalfe to Secretary to Government, 22d December 1808, and 12th January 1809.

Diwan Mohkam Chand at this very time returned from Kangra, where he had been negotiating with Raja Sansar Chand for the expulsion of the Gurkhas; and took up his position at Philor, commanding the passage of the Satlej at its most important part, opposite the town of Ludhiana. His inclination was for war with the English, whom he hated and suspected, and he did not wish his master to surrender Faridkot, which had been made over to him in jagir. His influence, from his experience and ability, was very great with the Maharaja, and it was Mr Metcalfe's firmness alone which, at this time, prevented a rupture with the English.

The surrender of Faridkot almost made a *causus belli* between Lahore and the English.

Ranjit Singh at length, and with great unwillingness, gave orders for the evacuation of Faridkot. But Diwan Mohkam Chand evaded compliance as long as possible. He wrote to the Maharaja that a British officer had been appointed to proceed to Faridkot, and that it was intended to occupy the place with a British garrison, and urged his master to suspend his order until such time as he could verify the information sent him.[1] The British Government had no intention of garrisoning the town, but they had determined that it should be surrendered to its original owners, and it was resolved by the Resident of Dehli to compel the restitution by force of arms. The hot weather was approaching, when the British army could not act in the field without great inconvenience, and the immediate march of troops on Faridkot would hasten its surrender, if Ranjit Singh really intended it; or, in case the evil counsels of Diwan Mohkam Chand should prevail, would only precipitate a contest which would sooner or later be inevitable.[2]

Every means of evading compliance tried.

[1] Mr C. Metcalfe to Government, 4th and 22d March 1809.

[2] Resident at Dehli to Military Secretary to Commander-in-Chief, 1st

But it is finally restored.

At the last moment, however, the Maharaja shrank from a collision with the English, and, on the 3d of April 1809, restored Faridkot to Sirdar Gulab Singh and his brothers.[1] All obstacles to the completion of the treaty between Lahore and the British Government were now removed, and it was signed shortly afterwards.

The minority of Gulab Singh.

Fouju Singh ably administered the affairs of the State until Gulab Singh became adult. No further attempts were made by Lahore to obtain possession, and Faridkot was so far distant from the stations of the British Political Agents, and was so insignificant in size and importance, that for many years its very existence seemed almost forgotten.

The revenue of Faridkot.

The revenue of Faridkot was at this time very small, and always fluctuating. The country was entirely dependent on rain for cultivation, and this fell in small quantities, and some years not at all. Wells were difficult to sink, and hardly repaid the labour of making them, as the water was from 90 to 120 feet below the surface. In a favourable season the estate yielded Rs. 14,000 or Rs. 12,000, in a bad season Rs. 6,000, and sometimes nothing whatever. The number of villages in the estate, principally new ones, was about sixty.

Gulab Singh married two wives, one the daughter of Sirdar Jodh Singh Kaleka, of Jamma in Pattiala, and the second, the daughter of Sirdar Sher Singh Gil, of Gholia in the Moga district.

The assassination of Gulab Singh.

On the 5th of November 1826, Sirdar Gulab Singh was assassinated when walking alone outside the town of Faridkot. The persons who were last seen with him

April 1809. Resident Dehli to Government, 5th February 1809. General Ochterlony to Adjutant-General, 5th February 1809.

[1] Resident at Dehli to Government, 9th April; General Ochterlony to Government, 28th March and 5th April 1809.

before his death were Jaideo, a Jat, and Buhadar, a silversmith, and their flight seemed to connect them with the crime. But if these men were the actual assassins, it was generally believed that the instigators of the crime were Fouju Singh, the Manager, and Sahib Singh, the youngest brother, of the Chief. No shadow of evidence could be procured against the former, who had served the family faithfully for twenty-five years, but the discovery of Sahib Singh's sword as one of those with which his brother met his death, the concealment of the scabbard, and his contradictory replies when Captain Murray, the Political Agent, questioned him, were suspicious in the extreme; but, in the absence of all direct proof, he was acquitted.[1]

His younger brother suspected of the crime.

Gulab Singh had left one son, a boy named Attar Singh, nearly four years old, and, as the custom of primogeniture seemed to prevail in the Faridkot family, this child was acknowledged as Chief by the British Government, the administration of affairs remaining, until he should reach his majority, in the hands of Fouju Singh and Sirdarni Dharam Kour, the widow. Pahar Singh and Sahib Singh had, during the lifetime of their brother, lived with him and enjoyed the estate in common, and it was decided that they were at liberty to remain thus, an undivided family, or, should they desire it, to receive separate jagirs.[2] Another brother of the late Chief, Mehtab Singh, was living, but his mother had been divorced by Sirdar Mohr Singh, and he was not entitled to inherit.

Attar Singh acknowledged Chief.

[1] Captain Murray to Sir C. Metcalfe, 13th November and 21st December 1826. Mr E. Brandreth, in his Settlement Report of Firozpur, notes that Pahar Singh was suspected of his brother's murder. No such suspicion ever attached to him.

[2] Investigation at Faridkot, 22d November 1826. Resident Dehli to Captain Murray, 4th January 1827.

His sudden death.

The young Chief, Attar Singh, died suddenly in August 1827. It was generally believed that he had been murdered, for in this unhappy family it was the exception and not the rule for death to result from natural causes; but the crime, if such it were, could not be brought home to any individual. The child was of so tender an age that he lived in the women's apartments, and no satisfactory investigation was possible.[1] Sirdar Pahar Singh was now the legitimate heir, supposing the right of collateral succession to be admitted, and was acknowledged as such by the British Government, being required to make such provision for his younger brother and sister-in-law as the custom of the family might justify.[2]

Sirdar Pahar Singh. His character and administration.

The new Chief was a liberal-minded and able man, and immensely improved his territory, more than doubling the revenue in twenty years. He founded many new villages, and the lightness of the assessment, and his reputation for justice and liberality, induced large numbers of cultivators to emigrate from Lahore and Pattiala to his territory. The larger portion of the State was desert when he acquired it, and the journal of Captain Murray, written in 1823, describes the country at sunrise as presenting the appearance of a vast sea of sand, with no vegetation except pilu, or other desert shrubs, which added little to the life of the landscape. But the soil, although sandy, only required water to produce magnificent crops of wheat. In old days a canal from the Satlej had been dug by one Firu Shah, from near Dharamkot, half way between Firozpur and Ludhiana, and, passing by Kot Isa Khan at Mudki, had irrigated

[1] Captain Murray to Resident Dehli, 2d September 1827.

[2] Resident Dehli to Captain Murray, 6th and 20th September 1827. Captain Murray to Resident Dehli, 16th September 1827.

the country to some distance south of Faridkot, where it was lost in the sand.[1] Sirdar Pahar Singh was not rich enough to make canals, but he dug many wells, and induced the peasants to dig others; and set an example of moderation and benevolence which might have been followed with great advantage by other and more powerful Chiefs.

Sahib Singh, his second brother, died soon after he assumed the Chiefship; and to Mehtab Singh, the son of Mohr Singh's divorced wife, he gave a village for his maintenance. He married four wives, the first of whom, Chand Kour, was the daughter of Samand Singh Dhalwal of Dina, and became the mother of Wazir Singh, the present Raja. His second wife, Desu, was the daughter of a Gil zamindar of Mudki, and bore him two sons, Dip Singh and Anokh Singh, who both died young. He married the third time, by *chaddar dalna*, the widow of his brother Sahib Singh; and, lastly, Jas Kour, daughter of Rai Singh of Kaleka, in the Pattiala territory. His family.

The first years of Pahar Singh's Chiefship were not by any means peaceful, and, according to the custom of the family, his brother Sahib Singh took up arms against him, and gave him so much trouble that the Chief begged for the assistance of English troops to restore order, and, failing to obtain these, was compelled to accept assistance from the Raja of Jhind, although such procedure was His quarrels with Sahib Singh, his brother.

[1] Traces of this canal are still to be seen. The tradition in the country is that an ancient Chief of Faridkot had a daughter of great beauty, whom he declared he would only give to a man who should come to Faridkot riding on a wooden horse. This Firu Shah accomplished by digging a canal and coming to win the beauty in a boat. On his return journey with the lady, he asked her for a needle, which she was unable to give him, and suspecting that she would not prove a good housewife, he left her at Mudki, on the banks of the canal, where a large mound of earth is supposed to convince the sceptical of the truth of the story.

highly irregular, one of the conditions of British protection being that no State should interfere in the internal affairs of another.[1] However, on the death of Sahib Singh, everything went on well, and the Sirdar was able to carry out his reforms without any further interruption, excepting occasional quarrels with the officer of the Lahore Government commanding at Kot Kapura, which was only six or seven miles to the south of Faridkot, and which, as the ancestral possession of his family, Pahar Singh would have been very glad to obtain.[2]

The good service of Pahar Singh during the Satlej campaign.

An opportunity for attaining this, the great desire of his heart, at last arrived, and Pahar Singh, like a wise man, seized it without hesitation. When the war with Lahore broke out in 1845, and so many of the Cis-Satlej Chiefs were indifferent or hostile, he attached himself to the English, and used his utmost exertions to collect supplies and carriage, and furnish guides for the army. On the eve of the battle of Firushahr he may have shown some little vacillation, but that was a critical time, when even the best friends of the English might be excused for a little over-caution; and after it was fought, though neither side could claim it as a victory, and the position of the English was more critical than ever, he remained loyal and did excellent service.[3] He was rewarded by a grant of half the territory confiscated from the Raja of Nabha, his share, as estimated in 1846, being worth Rs. 35,612 per annum.

He is created a Raja.

The ancestral estate of Kot Kapura was restored to him; and he received the title of Raja. In lieu of customs

[1] Mr F. Hawkins, Agent Resident Dehli, to Captain Murray, 22d September 1829. Captain Murray to Mr Hawkins, 27th September 1829.

[2] Captain Murray to Resident Dehli, 26th December 1829.

[3] Report of Colonel Mackeson to Government, 27th July 1846, and of Mr R. Cust, 7th March 1846.

duties, which were abolished, he was allowed Rs. 2000 a year; and an arrangement was made by which the rent-free holdings in the Kot Kapura ilaqua should lapse to the Raja instead of the British Government, a corresponding reduction being made in the commutation allowance.[1]

Raja Pahar Singh died in April 1849, in his fiftieth year, and was succeeded by his only surviving son, Wazir Singh, then twenty-one years of age. His death, A.D. 1849.

This young man, during the second Sikh war of 1849, served on the side of the English. During the mutiny of 1857, he seized several mutineers and made them over to the English authorities. He placed himself and his troops under the orders of the Deputy-Commissioner of Firozpur, and guarded the ferries of the Satlej against the passage of the mutineers. Raja Wazir Singh.

His troops also served under General Van Cortlandt with credit in Sirsa and elsewhere; and he, in person, with a body of horse and two guns, attacked a notorious rebel, Sham Das, and destroyed his village.[2] For his services during 1857–58, Raja Wazir Singh received the honorary title of "Burar Bans Raja Sahib Buhadar," a khillat of eleven pieces, instead of seven as before, and a salute of eleven guns. He was also exempted from the service of ten sowars which he had been previously obliged to furnish.[3] His services, And rewards.

On the 11th March 1862, the right of adoption was

[1] Report of Sir Henry Lawrence to Government, 18th September 1846; and Government to Sir Henry Lawrence, 17th November 1846. Sanad, dated 4th April 1846, from Governor-General creating Pahar Singh Raja, and conferring on him a valuable khillat.

[2] Letters from Deputy-Commissioner Firozpur, 14th, 16th, 20th, and 27th May, 12th July, 7th and 20th August, to Raja Wazir Singh.

[3] Commissioner Lahore to Raja Wazir Singh, 2d August 1858, enclosing letter from Governor-General.

His family.

granted him, with the annexed Sanad.[1] His son and heir is Bikrama Singh, born in January 1842, and married to the daughter of Raja Nahr Singh of Balabgarh.

The Raja himself has married four wives—Ind Kour, the daughter of Sham Singh Man of Munsab and mother of Bikrama Singh; the daughters of Basawa Singh of Raipur and Sirdar Gajja Singh of Lahore; and the widow of his brother Anokh Singh, who died of cholera in 1845.

[1] "Her Majesty being desirous that the Governments of the several Princes and Chiefs of India who now govern their own territories should be perpetuated, and that the representation and dignity of their houses should be continued, in fulfilment of this desire this Sanad is given to you to convey to you the assurance that, on failure of natural heirs, the British Government will recognise and confirm any adoption of a successor made by yourself or by any future Chief of your State that may be in accordance with Hindoo law and the customs of your race.

"Be assured that nothing shall disturb the engagement thus made to you so long as your house is loyal to the Crown, and faithful to the conditions of the treaties, grants, or engagements which record its obligations to the British Government."

THE HISTORY

OF THE

MANDI STATE.

MANDI is a compact State 1200 square miles in extent, bounded on the north and east by Kulu, on the south by Suket, and on the west by Kangra. Its extreme length, from Baijnath to the foot of Teon and Seon in Kehlor, is about sixty miles, and its breadth from Kamlagarh to the Dorechi Pass, near Bajoura, on the Kulu border, is forty-eight miles. Mandi is a very mountainous country, and looking southward from the Kulu range, which forms its northern boundary, it appears a sea of mountains without any arrangement whatever. Yet there are two distinct and almost parallel ranges which intersect the country, and from which numerous smaller hills and ranges diverge. The higher of these is known as the Goghar ka Dhar, rising from Haribagh to a height of about 7000 feet, near Putakal, then rapidly diminishing in altitude to a point a few miles south of Dirang, where the Bias has forced its way through, it again rises into the high lands of Suket. This range is well wooded and fertile, and abounds in game. Here are situated the salt mines which furnish so large a portion of the Mandi revenue.

Description of the country.

The mountain ranges.

The Goghar ka Dhar.

This range has a reputation similar to that of the Brocken in the Hartz Mountains on Walpurgis night. On the 3d September the demons, witches, and magicians from the most distant parts of India assemble here and hold their revels, during which time it is dangerous for men to cross the mountain. The spirits of the Kulu range are also said to wage war with those inhabiting the Goghar, and after a violent storm the peasants will show travellers the stones which have been hurled from range to range.

The Sikandar ka Dhar.

The second Mandi range, known as the Sikandar ka Dhar, or range of Alexander, runs south-west from Baijnath. Its name may possibly refer to some lost tradition of Alexander the Great; and Mr Vigne, who crossed it in 1839, believed that in the ruins of an old Rajput fort he had discovered the famous altars of Alexander, the site of which has been so often in dispute. The Sikandar range rises at one point to 6350 feet in height, but its average altitude is about 5000 feet. The valleys between the ranges are very fertile, and produce all the ordinary grains, with the more valuable crops of rice, sugar-cane, maize, poppy, and tobacco.

The Kulu range.

On the northern boundary rises the Kulu range, portions of which are in the Mandi State, from 9000 to 12,000 feet in height. This line of mountains is beautifully wooded with every species of pine, cedar, walnut, chestnut, and sycamore, and contains iron mines, which would be most valuable were they more accessible.

The salt mines.

The salt mines are situated at Gumah and Dirang, though there is at neither place such excavations as in Europe would be called mines, the salt being dug out of the face of the cliff, or from shallow open cuttings. The ascent to Gumah, which is about 5400 feet in elevation, is difficult and steep, but a new road has been lately constructed, which renders it far more approachable. At Gumah the salt is dug from a gorge some 500 feet below the village, to which it is carried to be weighed and sold. Dirang is at the foot of the same range, about twenty miles nearer Mandi, and only four miles from the Bias, which is, however, at this part of its course so violent a current as to be useless for navigation. The mines are not farmed to contractors, but worked by the Raja, who sells the salt to purchasers at the mines. About 150 labourers are employed at Gumah, and the same number at Dirang, and the cost of establishment and working is about 20 per cent. on the amount of salt sold. The Gumah salt is considered purer than that of Dirang, but both contain a large percentage, from 25 to 38 per cent., of foreign matter. This salt is, however, almost exclusively used in the higher hills as far as Lahoul, that of Gumah finds its way westward into British territory as far as Nurpur and Pathankot, and that of Dirang to Nadown, Bilaspur, and even Ludhiana.

The price of Mandi salt.

In 1820, the price of salt at the mines was seven annas, in 1846, eight annas, and in 1868, twelve annas per maund. In 1845, the revenue from salt was about Rs. 60,000; in 1850, it had risen to Rs. 83,000; and in 1862, to Rs. 1,00,545. There was a decrease in 1867-68, on account of the great quantity of rain that had fallen during the year, which hindered the working.

Iron mines.

Iron is found at Sunor, Budar, Natchni, Suraj, and Chuari, generally in such small particles as hardly to be called ore. It is smelted at the places where it is found, and brought to Mandi to be stamped and taxed. Its selling price at Mandi is about two rupees four annas a maund. In 1830, according to Mr Trebeck's journal, it was three rupees eight annas a maund. The income from iron, in 1845, was Rs. 14,000; in 1850, Rs. 27,300; and in 1862, Rs. 26,261. In many parts of Mandi, especially in the Sona Khad, lignite is found in considerable quantities, but too impure to be of any commercial value, and the geological formation of the country forbids the hope of the discovery of coal. The Sona Khad takes its name from gold which is obtained there, by washing, in small quantities.

The climate.

The climate of Mandi is cool, with the exception of the capital, which is shut in by hills, and the western portion of the country, which does not rise more than 2000 feet above the plains.

The capital of the State.

The town of Mandi, which contains 7300 inhabitants, is said to take its name from a remote ancestor of the present Raja; but as it is in a favourable situation for trade, Mandi, which signifies a market, is probably the more simple derivation. It stands most picturesquely on the banks of the Bias, here a swift torrent, 2557 feet above the sea. The banks are high and rocky, and the width of the stream is about one hundred and sixty yards. The effect of the melting of the snow in the neighbouring mountains is seen each day in the river, which during the hot season rises every evening, continues to increase in volume during the night, and declines again towards morning, when the amount of water in its bed is perhaps one-third less than at midnight. The palace of the Raja is a large white building, roofed with slate, and stands in the southern part of the town, in which there are no other buildings of importance. A famous temple, containing an idol brought from Jagarnath, some two hundred and fifty years ago, by an ancestor of the present Raja, stands on the banks of the Sukheti river, which joins the Bias just below the town; and twelve miles distant, on the crest of the Sikandar range, is the lake of Rewalsar, celebrated for its floating islands and a sacred place of pilgrimage. To the Buddhists of Thibet, Rewalsar is especially sacred. They resort to it in great numbers during the cold season, generally under the guidance of a Llama. They approach the lake from a considerable distance on their hands and knees, and it is considered a meritorious action to carve their names on the surrounding rocks, which are thus covered with inscriptions, some of them exceedingly curious. The lake is about 6000 feet above the sea. Mandi was supposed in ancient times to have contained 360 forts, but of these only ten are now in any preservation—Kamlagarh, Shahpur, Madhopur, Beira, Kalipuri, Tungal, Bajarkot, Dangri, Bagra, and Karnpur, while the first five only are garrisoned. Kamlagarh is one of the most celebrated forts in all the hill country, and a short description of it may be given, as the independence of Mandi has often depended upon the impregnability of its chief fortress, and as no description of the fort is known to have been published, with the exception of that by Mr Vigne, which is very incorrect.[1]

The forts of Mandi.

The fortress of Kamlagarh.

The hill upon which the fortress is situated extends nearly north and south for six or eight miles, running parallel to and about ten miles from the Janetri Devi on the east, and about four miles from the Bakar Khad on the west. The hill is formed of conglomerate sandstone, from 150 to 200 feet in height, while the ridge is narrow and serrated, and in several places intersected with deep ravines, the eastern and western side presenting an uninterrupted scarp of from 40 to 150 feet along the

[1] Vigne's "Travels in Kashmir," &c., vol. i. p. 111.

whole length of the hill, except at the two approaches to the positions of Nantpur and Kamla, which are guarded by forts difficult of access, the ground for several miles round the hill-side being intersected with tremendous ravines, which carry off the water either into the Sona or Bakar Khads, thus forming a most difficult country for the transport of artillery, and a most favourable one for defence by a determined body of men.

The position of Nantpur contains five distinct forts, built in the irregular style usual to these hills, to suit the ground intended to be occupied and protected—viz., Nantpur, Samirpur, Bakhtpur, Partabpur, and Nyakila, the last built by the Sikhs though never completed, besides many smaller outworks. Within this position there is abundance of good water in two or three different springs, besides grass and wood. Although on two sides entirely impregnable, and on the third extremely strong, Nantpur is commanded from a hill about 800 yards distant, and could certainly be scaled with ease under cover of guns from the neighbouring hill.

Kamla contains six distinct forts—viz., Kamla, Choki, Chiburrah, Padampur, Shamsherpur, and Narsinghpur; and although, like Nantpur, impregnable on two sides and nearly so on the third, where the gateway is reached by a ladder of about forty steps, yet the eastern side might be easily occupied by an enemy if once in possession of Padampur. There is no spring of water in Kamla itself, the spring for the supply of the place being some distance below; but, like all hill forts, it contains excellent tanks, in which sufficient water for the supply of a small garrison for several months might easily be stored.[1]

[1] Hon. J. C. Erskine to Secretary Government of India, No. 44, dated 28th March 1846.

A large number of troops would be necessary to garrison Kamlaghar effectively, but at present the garrison only consists of a hundred men, with a battery of six guns, which are unserviceable.

The reigning family in Mandi is Rajput of the Chanda Bansi tribe, and is known as Mandial. The origin of this tribe and its ancient history will more appropriately be given elsewhere, and it is only necessary to trace the family from the date of its separation from that of Suket, which happened about the year 1200 A.D. Up to that time the two States had been united, but the reigning Chief, Sahu Sen, having quarrelled with his younger brother Bahu Sen, the latter left Suket to seek his fortune elsewhere. The following list gives the first twenty-five Chiefs of Mandi:— The reigning family of Mandi.

1. Bahu Sen.[1]
2. Nim Sen.
3. Nirhabat Sen.
4. Kahabat Sen.
5. Sammat Sen.
6. Bir Sen.
7. Samodar Sen.
8. Kesab Sen.
9. Malab Sen.
10. Jai Sen.
11. Kranchan Sen.
12. Ban Sen.
13. Kalian Sen.
14. Hira Sen.
15. Dharitri Sen.
16. Narindar Sen.
17. Prajar Sen.
18. Dilawar Sen.
19. Ajbar Sen.
20. Chattar Sen.
21. Sahib Sen.
22. Narayan Sen.
23. Keshab Sen.
24. Hari Sen.
25. Suraj Sen.

[1] Sen is the name borne by the reigning Chief of Mandi, the younger members of the family being known as Singh. In consequence of the original blood connection between Mandi and Suket, no marriage is held to be valid between the families. This rule has, however, been broken through twice if not oftener. Three generations back Surma Singh of Mandi married a daughter of Mian Buhadar Singh of Suket; and Jowala Singh, illegitimate son of the present Raja of Suket, married the natural daughter of Raja Balbir Sen of Mandi.

The genealogy.

From Raja Hari Sen to the present day the genealogy of the Mandi family is as follows :—

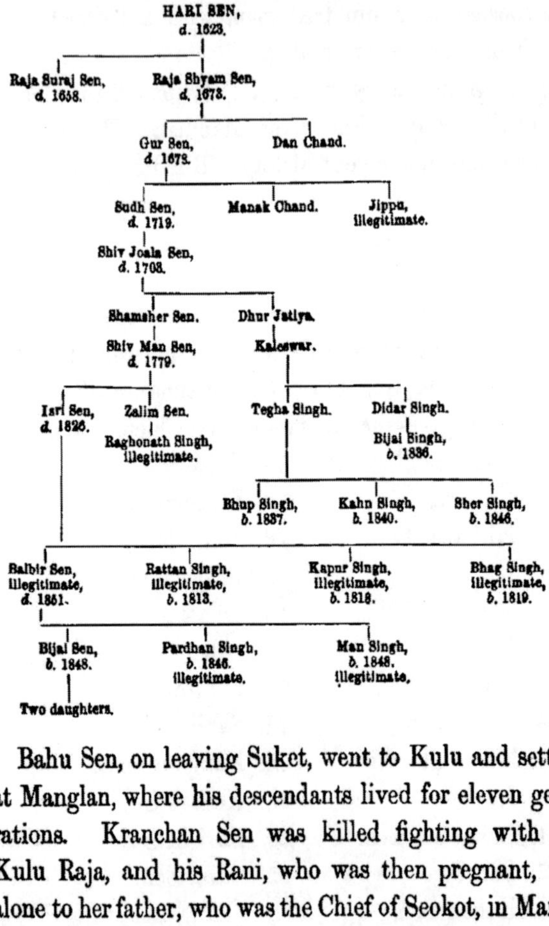

Raja Bahu Sen, and his successors.

Bahu Sen, on leaving Suket, went to Kulu and settled at Manglan, where his descendants lived for eleven generations. Kranchan Sen was killed fighting with the Kulu Raja, and his Rani, who was then pregnant, fled alone to her father, who was the Chief of Seokot, in Mandi. She had nearly reached her home when she lost her way, and, night coming on, fell exhausted under a ban tree, where her child was born. In the morning some followers of the Rana of Seokot found her insensible and carried her to the Chief's house. He had no son, and brought up his daughter's child as his own, giving him the name of Ban or Bano, from the tree under which he was born. The boy was only about fifteen years old when he distinguished himself by attacking a rapacious Chief, the Rana of Kilti, who used to descend from his fort and plunder travellers. At a fair held near Seokot, Bano, with a small force, attacked and defeated him, killing a number of the band. At this time, and for many years afterwards, Mandi was not under one rule, but was covered with forts, one on almost every hill, the stronghold of a Rana or Thakur, who was practically independent, and who obeyed no authority whatever. On the death of his grandfather, Bano succeeded to the little chiefship of Seokot, under the title of Ban Sen. He somewhat enlarged his possessions, and, killing the Rana of Sakor in battle, took possession of his lands, living at Sakor for some years. He then changed his residence to Bhiu, some four miles above Mandi on the Bias. His son, Kalian Sen, bought Batahu, on the opposite side of the river to the present town of Mandi, and the ruins of his old house are still to be seen. His son, Hira Sen, was killed fighting with the Rana of Tilli, and, being without male issue, was succeeded by his brother, Daritri Sen. He, too, left no heirs, and Narindar Sen, brother of Kalian Sen, succeeded. Nothing is known of this Chief or of his immediate successors, and Ajbar Sen, nineteenth in descent from Bahu Sen, may be called the first Raja of Mandi. He founded the town and built the old palace with four towers, now almost in ruins, known as Chowki. On succeeding his father in 1527, he at once determined to reduce to submission the four Ranas of Maratu, Sadiana, Kunhal, and Gandharba, who refused to acknowledge his supremacy. They united their forces, amounting to about 1300 men, of whom

Raja Ajbar Sen founded the town of Mandi in 1527, A.D.

more than half were archers, and came down into the Bal plain to meet Ajbar Sen, who defeated them with some loss. He then pursued them into the hills, and another skirmish took place, in which Goluk, the Chief of Gandharba, was killed. Chattar Sen, the eldest son of Ajbar Sen, then marched against Achab, Rana of Maratu, but was defeated, wounded in the thigh, and three of the chief men of Mandi were slain. These men were brothers, members of a Khatri family, and acted as councillors to the Raja, who granted to Madsudhan, the fourth and surviving brother, the lands conquered from the Ranas. The family still reside in Mandi, though now of no importance, and they possess the original grant of Ajbar Sen, engraved on copper, dated Samat, 1584 (A.D. 1527). It was not, however, till some time later that the power of Maratu and Kanhal was finally broken.

Raja Ajbar Sen died in 1534, and of his son and successor, Chattar Sen, little is recorded worthy of record. His grandson, Sahib Sen, formed an alliance with Raja Jaggat Singh, the famous Chief of Kulu, and they together attacked Jai Chand, the Raja of Vaziri Laksari, and took possession of a great part of his territory, the portion now known as Saraj Mandi falling to the share of Mandi, while the Kulu Raja obtained the portion now known as Saraj Kulu, including Bokla, Palaham, Talokpur, and Fatahpur. A second joint expedition against the same Chief won, for Mandi, Sanor and Badai; while Raja Jaggat Singh of Kulu obtained Birkot, Madanpur, with twelve neighbouring villages.

Raja Narayan Singh, the next Chief of Mandi, conquered the Ranas of Ner, Bandoh, and Chuhar. He became paralytic, but is said to have been cured by a pir, or gosaon, whose descendants still receive an allowance from the Mandi treasury. Of Keshab Sen and Hari Sen tradition says nothing save that the latter was a famous hawker.

Raja Suraj Sen was a good soldier, but his ambition brought great disasters upon Mandi. He attacked the Raja of Nabgal; brother-in-law of Raja Man Singh of Kulu, bringing down upon him the wrath of the latter Chief, who marched to the assistance of his relative, and defeated the Mandi force, seizing, after the battle, the forts of Karnpur, Shahpur, and Shamsherpur, and taking from the Raja of Nabgal, as the price of his assistance, Dewal, Sansal, and Ber. The boundary line between Mandi and Kulu was fixed at the villages of Ber and Apju. **Raja Suraj Sen and his wars with Kulu**

Raja Suraj Sen soon afterwards made an effort to recover his position, and invaded Kulu territory, seizing the villages of Madanpur, Sapari, and Tarapurand, but he was driven out of them with loss; the Kulu army overran the whole of the Mandi State, and the salt mines of Gumah and Dirang fell into the hands of the enemy. So large a portion of the Mandi revenue was derived from salt that Suraj Sen was now compelled to ask for peace, which was granted on his paying the whole expenses of the war, the boundary between the States being fixed as before.

Nor was Suraj Sen more successful in his quarrels with Man Singh Goleria, who twice sacked Mandi, and held possession for some time of the district of Kala, in which the Raja had built the fort of Kamlagarh in 1625, having two years previously seized Nantpur. In 1653, Suraj Sen took Patri and Sulani from Suket, the last held by Mian Ram Chand, who lost 700 men in its defence. He built the second palace at Mandi, known as Damdama. His eighteen sons all died in his lifetime, and in despair of an heir he caused to be made a silver image, which he named Madho Rai,[1] and to which he assigned the kingdom. This silver image is still carried in sacred procession, in Mandi, on festival days, and bears a Sanscrit inscription, of which the following is a fac-simile and translation:—

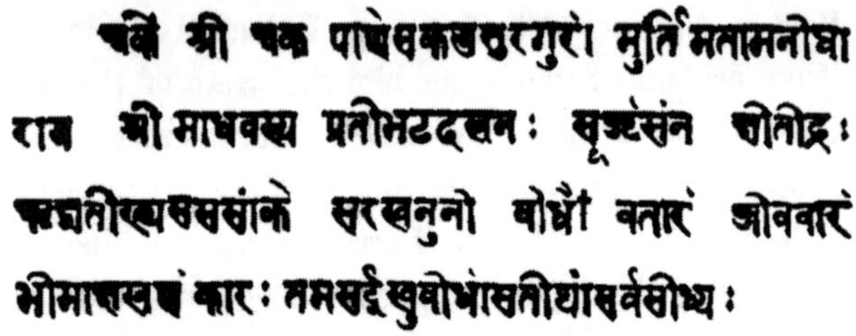

"The image of Vishnu was made by order of Raja Suraj Sen, who named it Madho Rai. Bhima, goldsmith, made the image in the month of Magh, Jik Nachattar.

"Virwar, Samat, 1705 (A.D. 1648)."

The only daughter of Suraj Sen married Raja Hari Dev of Jammu.

Raja Shyam Sen, A.D. 1658.

Shyam Sen, his brother, succeeded in 1658, and reigned fifteen years. He had been, for those days, a great traveller, having visited Nepal, Benares, and Jaganath, sometimes for adventure, sometimes for devotion. He took the territory of Dhunjugarh from Kulu in 1659, and later in the same year conquered Lohara from Suket. He built the Shama Kali temple on the Dhar Taran above the town, and a tank in the suburb beyond the Bias, to which all the children of the royal family are carried for the ceremonies which are performed eight days after birth, and he also added largely to the palace.

Raja Gur Sen.

Gur Sen only reigned five years. He was something of a soldier, but more of a devotee, and brought himself

[1] Madho is a name of Vishnu, and Rai signifies heir-apparent, or Tika Sahib.

from Jaganath the famous image which is preserved in the temple on the plain above the town. He made an alliance with Kehlor against the Katoch Rajputs of Kangra, and a battle took place at Hatali, between the rival forces, with doubtful result. In 1675 he captured Dhanyara from Suket, and the next year Baira and Patri, which had been several times won and lost.

The wars and rivalries between Suket and Mandi.

Mandi and Suket have always been rivals and generally enemies, but there was no great result of their warfare. When a powerful Raja ruled at Suket he won back all the territory which his predecessors had lost and gained anew; and at one time the Suket possessions extended to the very walls of Mandi. In the same manner, when a powerful Chief, like Ajbar Sen, or Sidh Sen, ruled in Mandi, the borders of Suket were much reduced, and its outlying forts and districts fell into the hands of its rival. The plain of Bal was common ground of desire and dispute.

The Bal plain.

This little valley, which somewhat approaches level ground, and is rich and fertile, stretches from within five miles of Mandi to the town of Suket, a distance of some ten miles, with an average width of perhaps two miles. Here was the scene of many a fight, and the story of one, which sounds like a repetition of Chevy Chase, is still sung in Mandi ballads. The Suket Prince had gone to hunt on the Bal plain, with a large following, and Gohur Sen of Mandi, then heir apparent, set out to oppose him, resolved to spoil his sport. The result was a fight, in which many on both sides fell, the Suket Prince himself having a narrow escape. He was pursued by a Katoch Mian who was in the service of Mandi, and being overtaken would have been slain had he not adjured his enemy to spare a god-descended Prince.

The Katoch, who himself traced back his family some four hundred and fifty generations, dropped his sword, but he snatched from the head of the Suket Chief his insignia of royalty, which he carried back to his master, who assigned him and his descendants for ever a certain quantity of salt from the Dirang mines, which is still duly paid.

Raja Sidh Sen, his administration and his conquests.

Jippu, the illegitimate brother of Gur Sen, was a man of considerable ability. The whole administration of Mandi was in his hands, and he inaugurated the revenue system which is still in force. He remained Minister during the first part of the reign of Sidh Sen, who came to the throne in 1678. This Chief was a great warrior, and Mandi, under his rule, was more powerful than ever before or since. In 1688, he conquered the districts of Nachan, Hatal, Dalel, and in this same year a terrible famine occurred, from which very many people died. In 1690, he captured Dhanesargarh, and five years later, built the fort of Sarakhpur. In 1698 he took Raipur from Suket, and the next year Madhopur. In 1705 he built Shirapuri; and, in 1706, recaptured Hatali, and ravaged the Ladh district belonging to Hamir Chand Katoch.

The visit of Guru Govind Singh to Mandi.

Towards the end of the seventeenth century Govind Singh, the tenth Sikh Guru, is said to have visited Mandi. He had been imprisoned at Sultanpur by Raj Singh, the Chief of Kulu, from whom he had sought assistance against the Muhammadan troops; and his followers believed that by an exercise of miraculous power the iron cage in which the Guru was confined rose with him in the air, and conveyed him without accident to Mandi. There he was hospitably entertained by Sidh Sen, and on his departure he told the Raja to ask anything he might desire and it should be granted. Sidh Sen begged that his capital might never fall into the hands of an enemy; and this was promised in a couplet still current in Mandi—

The prophecy of the saint.

> "Mandi ko jab lutenge,
> Asmani guli chutenge."

But the prophecy was not very successful, as the later history of Mandi will show.[1]

Miraculous powers of Sidh Sen.

Tradition asserts that Sidh Sen possessed powers no less miraculous than Guru Govind Singh, and that he had a little book, which, like that of Michael Scott, contained charms and spells which demons were compelled to obey: when he placed it in his mouth he was instantly transported whither he wished, through the air. When he felt himself about to die, unwilling to transmit a power which might be used more probably for evil than for good, he threw his book into the Bias, where it runs deepest and swiftest, and it was lost for ever.

The truth seems to have been that Sidh Sen was far more intelligent than his countrymen, and his uniform success was attributed to supernatural agency. He was also of enormous stature, and some clothes, said to have been his, are still preserved in the Mandi palace, which could only have been worn by a giant.[2]

The temples built by Sidh Sen.

Sidh Sen built the great tank before the palace, and a lamp is kept burning to his memory on a pedestal in the midst of what should be the water, but the tank has fallen out of repair, and has been dry for many years. He also built the temple to the god Ganesha, two miles from

[1] This promise is said by some to have been made by Banda, the follower of Govind, but there is no evidence to prove that he ever visited Mandi.

[2] They are, at any rate, said to be preserved. The Raja offered to show them to the author on one occasion, but they could not be found at the moment.

Mandi, and known as Sidh Ganesh; also Tiloknath, near the river. His reign lasted forty-one years, and he was a hundred years old when he died. His only son, Joala Sen, had died during his lifetime, and he was succeeded by his grandson, Shamsher Sen, who married the daughter of Agar Sen, Raja of Chamba. This Chief reconquered Madhopur from Kulu, and was constantly at war with his neighbours on all sides, with very indifferent success, though he conquered Chuboroi, Ramgarh, Deogarh, Hashtpur, and Sarni from Kulu, taking advantage of the absence of Raja Jai Singh at Lahore.

Raja Shamsher Sen.

Mandi is conquered by the Katoch Raja, and the Chief made prisoner.

Isri Sen was only five years old when his father died in 1779, and Raja Sansar Chand, Katoch, who was becoming supreme in the hills, lost no time in taking advantage of this circumstance. He invaded Mandi and plundered the town; the district of Hatali, which had been often won and lost, he made over to Suket; Chuhari he gave to Kulu, and kept himself the district of Nantpur. He carried off Isri Sen to Kangra, and kept him there a prisoner for twelve years, leaving the administration of Mandi in the hands of its Ministers, but demanding an annual tribute of a lakh of rupees. When the Gurkhas, on the invitation of the Kehlor Raja Mahan Singh, invaded Kangra, Isri Sen, like most of the Rajput Chiefs, gave in his submission to Amar Singh Thappa, the Gurkha general, on condition of being left in unmolested possession of his territories, and promising on his part to make no opposition to their occupation of Kangra.

Intrigues with Lahore.

On the retreat of the Gurkhas in 1810, and the occupation of the fort of Kangra by Maharaja Ranjit Singh of Lahore, Sirdar Desa Singh Majithia was appointed *Nazim* or Superintendent of all the Hill States, including

Mandi. Raja Isri Singh was compelled to pay a *nazrana* or tribute of Rs. 30,000, and this was levied annually till 1815, when Zalim Sen, brother of the Raja, and who hated him with a true brotherly hatred, went to Lahore to see whether he might not be able to obtain the throne for himself. Maharaja Ranjit Singh, always delighted to sow dissensions between Chiefs who might be dangerous united, and mean enough to make every intrigue an opportunity of exaction, warmly espoused the cause of Zalim Sen, who had no right whatever on his side, and Isri Sen was compelled to pay a tribute of one lakh of rupees to retain his throne. The next year, 1816, Jamadar Khushhal Singh, who had lately risen to favour at the Court of Lahore, was sent to Mandi to collect the tribute.[1] The Raja retired to Kulu, accompanied by a large force, and thought, by combining with the Kulu Wazir, who had no less than 18,000 troops, to oppose the Sikhs successfully, but his resolution gave way, and returning to Mandi he contrived, by heavily bribing Khushhal Singh, to obtain a reduction of the annual tribute to Rs. 50,000, and thus it remained till the death of the Raja in 1826.

In the time of Isri Sen, Mandi was an asylum for several wandering Princes. The ex-Raja of Bussahir lived there for long, and was liberally supported with his followers,[2] and the ex-Raja of Nagpur[3] resided there for four years after his expulsion from his country, receiving support from Isri Sen and intriguing with Lahore, in

[1] Captain Ross to Sir D. Ochterlony, 1st December 1816.

[2] Officer Commanding at Kotghar to Captain Kennedy, 18th and 31st August 1825.

[3] Officer Commanding at Kotghar to Captain Kennedy, 5th August and 6th November 1824; and Captain Murray to Resident Dehli, dated 16th June and 13th July 1824.

which territory he desired to be allowed to raise troops, till Zalim Sen came to the throne in 1826, when he found it expedient to seek an asylum elsewhere.[1]

Zalim Sen had always quarrelled with his brother and intrigued against him, and during the latter years of Isri Sen's life had been compelled to leave Mandi, and take refuge with Raja Sansar Chand, of Kangra. He succeeded to the throne, as his brother had left only illegitimate sons—Mians Rattan Singh, Kapur Singh, Balbir Singh, and Bhag Singh. Zalim Sen paid a lakh of rupees, as succession duty, to Lahore, and in following years, until his death in 1839, a tribute of Rs. 75,000 was levied. Some years before his death the Raja made over the administration of the State to his nephew, Balbir Sen, who was not only illegitimate but one of the younger sons of the late Chief, but, by payment of a large sum of money, the succession was confirmed to this young man by the Lahore Court, which conferred upon him all the usual insignia of royalty. Zalim Sen disgraced himself by beheading his prime minister, Dhari, who had served the State well and faithfully, and whose interest with Maharaja Ranjit Singh had saved it from annexation.

Balbir Sen was twenty-two years old when he became Raja, much to the disgust of his elder brothers, and of the younger branch of the family descended from Mian Dhurjatiya, brother of Raja Shamsher Sen, who considered the throne disgraced by the son of a concubine.

After the death of Maharaja Ranjit Singh, in June 1839, the Sikh army, which had for long been difficult to manage, grew more powerful every day, and Prince Nao Nihal Singh, who really ruled the Punjab, of which

[1] Captain Kennedy to Lieutenant Murray, Deputy-Superintendent, 2d January 1827.

his father, Maharaja Kharrak Singh, was the nominal King, felt that some employment must be found for troops who would otherwise quickly get beyond his control.

The hill country, Trans-Satlej, Suket, Mandi, and Kulu, had been virtually conquered, though not occupied, by Sikh troops, and the last acquisition, Ladak, was only considered as a step to the conquest of a portion of Chinese Tartary, which was now much talked of at Lahore, although Sikh ambition, in this instance, was no more than the personal ambition of Raja Gulab Singh, of Jammu, and his brother, Dhyan Singh, the Minister at Lahore. But, before such an expedition, it was thought necessary to reduce Mandi completely, and, at all events, not to leave so strong a fort as Kamlagarh in the rear of the Sikh army. Accordingly, in June 1840, a large force, under General Ventura,[1] was sent to Mandi. He crossed the Sikandar range, encamped seven miles from the capital, sending to demand the immediate payment of certain arrears of the tribute, which formed the excuse for the expedition. Raja Balbir Sen paid instantly the money claimed, and wrote off to Colonel Tapp, Political Agent at Subathu, begging for an asylum for himself and his family in British territory. He saw pretty clearly that the total subjugation of his country was intended, and he hinted that he would be delighted to exchange Sikh tyranny for British protection.[2] But the Govern-

The Sikh invasion of Mand under General Ventura, in 1840.

Raja Balbir Sen looks to the English for assistance.

[1] The reason for the selection of General Ventura was that Prince Nao Nihal Singh, at this time, was trying to rid himself of his father's powerful minister, Dhyan Singh, who hated and feared the French party at court, headed by General Ventura, and the Prince hoped to strengthen himself, by giving the General a command.

[2] Letter from Raja of Mandi to Political Agent Subathu, 12th June 1840. Letter of Political Agent Subathu to T. Metcalfe, Esq., Agent Lieutenant-Governor of the North-Western Provinces, 3d July 1840.

ment, while offering an asylum to the Raja's family, did not at this time think it advisable to receive the fugitives as political characters, or to give the Raja any assurance of aid against the invaders.[1]

The Sikhs take possession of the capital.

Balbir Sen, having paid his tribute, was ordered to attend the Sikh general in his camp. On his arrival there he was surrounded and made prisoner, his own people, according to the Rana of Bhajji,[2] playing him false, and he was told that he could not be released until he had made over to the Sikhs all the forts of Mandi. Whether his officials betrayed him or not is doubtful, but Suket, delighted to pay off many an old grudge, assisted General Ventura, and this conduct has strengthened the ill feeling between the two States. The Raja was helpless, and consented to everything demanded, and the Sikh troops took possession, for the first time since the prophecy of Guru Govind Singh, of the capital of Mandi.[3] The Raja was sent a prisoner to Amritsar, and was confined in the fort of Govindgarh, whilst General Ventura took possession of the numerous forts, without much resistance from the Mandi troops. Kamlagarh, however, which had for some time been almost independent of the Raja's authority, refused submission, and the Sikh army invested it in the month of September. The task of its reduction was a difficult one, and additional troops were sent under the command of Sirdar Ajit Singh Sindhanwalia, but great sickness broke out amongst them, and

The siege of Kamlagarh.

[1] No. 132, Mr Thomason, Secretary to Government North-Western Provinces, to T. Metcalfe, Agent at Dehli, 16th July 1840.

[2] Letter of the Rana of Bhajji to Political Agent Subathu, 8th July 1840.

[3] Though the Sikhs had for many years taken tribute from Mandi, they had never entered the capital, and the tribute was paid outside the town. Vigne mentions, in his travels, that the officer of the Maharaja in attendance upon him did not enter the town.—Vigne, vol. i. p. 100.

the mortality was increased by the great cold which came on later.[1] But the siege was pressed with great vigour: early in November the garrison were driven from some of the outworks, and although the news of the death of Prince Nao Nihal Singh, on the 5th November, raised the hopes of the garrison, it also strengthened the determination of General Ventura to capture the place. At length, on the 29th November, it capitulated, and the General, leaving Sikh troops in possession, marched with the remainder of his force to Kulu.[2]

The Raja of Mandi released from prison.

In January 1841, Sher Singh became Maharaja of Lahore, and, some months later, the Raja of Mandi was released from confinement, and permitted to return to his country, taking with him the silver image of the goddess Devi, which was the object of general veneration in the hills, and which the Sikhs had carried away from her temple at Kamlagarh.[3] The release of the Raja was a spontaneous act of Maharaja Sher Singh, who was of a kindly disposition, and was exceedingly displeasing to the Minister, Dhyan Singh, who found himself disappointed of a very large present to himself and a *nazrana* to the State treasury, that had for months past formed the subject of a secret negotiation between him and certain Gosaon bankers of Mandi.[4]

When the Raja was sent to Amritsar, Shaikh Ghulam Mohiuddin, the most grasping of all the Sikh revenue officers, was directed to make a settlement of the territory

[1] Agent Governor-General to Officiating Secretary Government of India, 20th October 1840.

[2] Agent Governor-General to Secretary Government of India, of the 14th November, 17th November, and 11th December 1840.

[3] Mr Clerk to Secretary Government of India, 10th August 1841.

[4] Mr Clerk to Secretary Government of India, 18th August 1841.

for Rs. 2,35,000. This he contrived to raise before April 1841, when he was sent as Governor to Kashmir. The Raja, on his release, was ordered to increase the revenue to four lakhs of rupees, an amount which the territory could not yield without oppressing the people, and of this, one lakh was to be retained by the Raja for his own use, Rs. 90,000 for the expenses of the Sikh garrison, Rs. 12,000 as jagirs to Sikh Sirdars, Rs. 45,000 for religious and miscellaneous expenses, and the balance was to be sent to the Sikh treasury. The Raja never succeeded in raising four lakhs of revenue, but, as no precise amount of tribute was fixed, he was able, with the connivance of the Majithia Sirdars, Lehna Singh and Ranjodh Singh, to retain considerably more than the one lakh assigned for his own use.

Balbir Sen again addresses the English Government.

Shortly before the Sikh war, in 1845, the Raja sent several messages to Mr Erskine, Superintendent of the Hill States, expressing his anxiety to obtain British protection, and to act in concert with the Government against the enemy. Mr Erskine entered into secret communication with the Raja, for the purpose of securing his neutrality whenever a rising in Kulu should take place, for the management of Saraj, a Kulu province, had been entrusted to him by the Durbar; and he was also directed to expel, if possible, the Sikh garrison from his forts.[1]

His advances are well received.

His action during the Satlej campaign.

But, although Balbir Sen was well disposed towards the British, he was compelled to send a contingent of 300 men, under Wazir Gosaon, to join the brigade of Sirdar Ranjodh Singh Majithia, under whom the Mandi troops fought at the battle of Aliwal. In this manner, and by the payment of considerable sums towards the

[1] Mr Erskine to Secretary Government of India, 24th February 1846.

expenses of the campaign, the Raja was able to avoid taking part personally against the English, although he was repeatedly ordered to join the Sikh camp; and immediately after the battle of Sobraon he, with his neighbour of Suket, sent a confidential agent, Sibu Pandit, to the Superintendent of the Hill States, tendering his allegiance to the British Government, and requesting an interview. This was readily granted, and on the 21st February 1846, the Rajas of Suket and Mandi visited Mr Erskine at Bilaspur, and formally tendered their allegiance to the British Government.[1]

He tenders his allegiance to the British Government.

The Raja had not however waited for the decisive victory of Sobraon to declare himself on the side of the English, or rather opposed to his natural enemies the Sikhs. On the 4th February he surrounded Sirdar Mangal Singh Ramgharia, who was stationed at the town of Mandi, and the Lahore detachment would most certainly have been utterly destroyed, had not the Sirdar begged hard for the lives of himself and his men. This request was granted, and they were escorted to the Kangra frontier, about seventy-five miles distant. Thence, contrary to the solemn assurances of Mangal Singh and his followers, they returned by a double march, burnt a number of villages round Kamlagarh, and threw themselves into one of the forts, while the Mandi troops were employed elsewhere. At the same time that the rising in the capital took place, the twelve forts, garrisoned by Sikhs, were attacked and captured in a few days, except at Kamlagarh, which was regularly invested by 6000 men, and only surrendered after the conclusion of the war.

The rising in Mandi against the Sikhs,

Who are everywhere expelled.

By the treaty of Lahore of the 9th March 1846, all

[1] Mr Erskine to Secretary Government of India, No. 16, dated 15th February 1846; and No. 24, dated 23d February 1846.

the rights, forts, and territories of the Maharaja in the Jalandhar Doab were ceded to the British Government.

Raja Balbir Sen confirmed in his possessions.

A claim to the throne of Mandi was immediately instituted by Rana Bhup Singh, who was the representative of the legitimate branch of the family; but the Supreme Government, on the ground that for four generations this branch had been excluded, and that it was unadvisable to revive obsolete claims, refused to entertain it, and the Raja was confirmed in his possessions;[1] and, on the 24th October, a Sanad was granted to him defining his rights and obligations.[2]

A Sanad granted him.

Rana Bhup Singh was at this time only ten years of

[1] Letter No. 2047, from Secretary to Government of India to Major Lawrence, Agent Governor-General, dated 6th October 1846, enclosing petition from Rana Bhup Singh; and No. 237, from Agent Governor-General to Secretary Government of India, dated 14th October 1846.

[2] Translation of Sanad from the Governor-General, dated 24th October 1846:—

Whereas, by the treaty concluded between the British and Sikh Governments, on the 9th March 1846, the hill country has come into the possession of the Honourable Company, and whereas Raja Balbir Sen, Chief of Mandi, the highly dignified, evinced his sincere attachment and devotion to the British Government: the State of Mandi, comprised within the same boundaries as at the commencement of the British occupation, together with full administrative powers within the same, is now granted by the British Government to him and the heirs male of his body by his Rani from generation to generation. On failure of such heirs, any other male heir who may be proved to the British Government to be next of kin to the Raja, shall obtain the above State with administrative powers.

Be it known to the Raja that the British Government shall be at liberty to remove any one from the Gaddi of Mandi who may prove to be of worthless character and incapable of properly conducting the administration of his State, and to appoint such other nearest heir of the Raja to succeed him as may be capable of the administration of the State and entitled to succeed. The Raja, or any one as above described, who may succeed him, shall abide by the following terms entered in this Sanad, viz.:—

1. The Raja shall pay annually, into the treasury of Simla and Subathu, one lakh of Company's rupees as *nazrana*, by two instalments; the first instalment on the 1st June, and the second instalment on the 1st November.

2. He shall not levy tolls and duties on goods imported and exported, but shall consider it incumbent on him to protect bankers and traders within his State.

age, and was entirely in the hands of designing persons who were determined to make an effort to enforce the recognition of his claims. He was the representative of the legitimate branch of the Mandi family, and, among Rajputs, purity of blood is considered all-important in the reigning Chief. **The claims of Rana Bhup Singh,**

But for five generations, since the time of Shiv Joala Sen, this branch had possessed no power, and had been merely dependants of the Raja, receiving small allowances from him. Tegha Singh, the father of Bhup Singh, left Mandi in 1840 and settled in Suket with his family, remaining in the service of the Prince of that country **Which are unfounded.**

3. He shall construct roads within his territory not less than twelve feet in width, and keep them in repair.

4. He shall pull down and level the forts of Kamlagarh and Nantpur, and never attempt to rebuild them.

5. On the breaking out of disturbances, he shall, together with his troops and hill porters, whenever required, join the British army, and be ready to execute whatever orders may be issued to him by the British authorities, and supply provisions according to his means.

6. He shall refer to the British Courts any dispute which may arise between him and any other Chief.

7. In regard to the duties on the iron and salt mines, &c., in the territory of Mandi, rules shall be laid down after consultation with the Superintendent of the Hill States, and these rules shall not be departed from.

8. The Raja shall not alienate any portion of the lands of the said territory without the knowledge and consent of the British Government, nor transfer it by way of mortgage.

9. He shall so put an end to the practice of slave-dealing, satti, female infanticide, and the burning or drowning of lepers, which are opposed to British laws, that no one in future shall venture to revive them.

It behoves the Raja not to encroach beyond the boundaries of his State or the territory of any other Chief, but to abide by the terms of this Sanad, and adopt such measures as may tend to the welfare of his people, the prosperity of his country, and the improvement of the soil, and ensure the administration of even-handed justice to the aggrieved, the restoration to the people of their just rights, and the security of the roads. He shall not subject his people to extortion, but keep them always contented. The subjects of the State of Mandi shall regard the Raja and his successors as above described to be the sole proprietor of that territory, and never refuse to pay him the revenue due by them, but remain obedient to him and act up to his just orders.

till his death.[1] Nothing therefore could excuse the conduct of Bhup Singh's advisers, who, on the refusal of the British Government to entertain his claim, raised some 3000 men from Kangra and Kehlor, and made a night attack on Mandi, where they destroyed much property, and then plundered the salt factories at Gumah. The Raja complained to the Superintendent of the Hill States, and a small force was sent against the insurgents, who were easily dispersed. Bhup Singh and his brothers were imprisoned for short periods in the Simla jail, but he was soon released on promise of good conduct, though he refused to relinquish his claim to the throne.[2]

He attempts to assert them by force.

The authority of Raja Balbir Sen was now firmly established. But there was a man in Mandi who possessed more real power than the Raja, and this was his Minister Wazir Gosaon. His talents and devotion had been the mainstay of the Raja's party; it was chiefly through his agency that the Raja had obtained his throne from the Sikhs, and by his ability alone its possession had been maintained. The Wazir thus assumed a position in the State which was viewed with jealousy by the Raja, and with envy by a party headed by Parohit Harjas and Wazir Singh, who strove to undermine the Minister's power, to which they hoped themselves to succeed.

Wazir Gosaon of Mandi.

The conduct of the Wazir, at the commencement of the war, had roused the Raja's suspicions. There hardly appears sufficient reason to believe, with the Superintendent of the Hill States, that Wazir Gosaon behaved with treachery towards his master, but he, no doubt,

[1] Statement of Wazir Gosaon of Mandi, received 17th January 1852.

[2] From Deputy-Commissioner Kangra to Commissioner Trans-Satlej, dated 25th August 1851.

intrigued deeply with the Sikhs; he accepted from Sirdar Ranjodh Singh Majithia a very profitable farm of the customs from Jalandhar to Ladak, as well as a considerable revenue charge in the plains; and when the rising at Mandi took place, he remained at Philor with his troops and delayed his return under various pretexts, in spite of the repeated orders of his master.[1] **His conduct during the Satlej war.**

The Raja's power was also much increased by the recognition of the British Government: he felt that he was now able to stand without the assistance of his Minister, and would have been glad had he been able altogether to discard him. But this he could not do, for the Minister was supported by the English authorities, without whose aid and protection his position, his property, and even his life would have been in danger.[2]

The death of Raja Balbir Sen, 1851.

Raja Balbir Sen died on the 26th January 1851, leaving a son, Bijai Singh, four years of age. Shortly before his death, feeling that Wazir Gosaon was, after all, the only one of his servants whom he could trust, he sent for him and communicated to him his last wishes. But the party hostile to the Wazir had possession of almost all the chief offices of the State, and for a considerable time there appeared small hope of establishing a stable administration. The mother of the late Raja, who was only a concubine of Raja Isri Sen, was an intriguing woman, and had several times during the life of her son endeavoured to obtain some share of power, but had been as often summarily put aside, and had been for a long time forbidden even to enter the palace. On the death of Balbir Sen she at once assumed the management of the **The intrigues which followed.**

[1] Honourable C. Erskine to Secretary Government of India, No. 44, dated 28th March 1846.

[2] From Deputy Commissioner Kangra to Commissioner Trans-Satlej, dated 20th January 1853.

palace, in which was situated the treasury. The accounts were in the hands of Harjas Kayat, who with the Parohit also assumed charge of the Judicial Department. The Sahibni hated Wazir Gosaon, who had always opposed her intrigues, and threw her influence entirely into the hands of his enemies, but they found that they were unable to do without him: he was a man of great financial ability, of great experience, and had a most intimate knowledge of the country. He had retained control of receipts and expenditure, supervised the land revenue, the salt and iron mines, and the general income of Mandi. Accordingly, the Wazir's name was submitted as one of the Council of Regency.

A Council of Regency appointed.

The Board of Administration agreed to the Council, but thought the Wazir too unpopular to be at its head. The arguments of Mr Barnes, the Commissioner of the Trans-Satlej, convinced them, however, that the Wazir's unpopularity was only with an interested party, while he was much liked by the people of Mandi; that Mian Bhag Singh would be unpopular as head of the Council from the fact of his being the next heir of the throne; and that there was no other man who was competent to preside except Wazir Gosaon, who was reputed to be the wisest man in all the hill country. He was accordingly nominated President, and Mian Bhag Singh and the Parohit, the spiritual adviser of the late Raja, the other members.[1]

The party opposed to the Wazir was still powerful, and he did not wish to come to an open breach with them, as

[1] Commissioner to Board of Administration, 27th January 1851.

Deputy Commissioner to Commissioner, 5th February 1851; Secretary to Supreme Government to Board of Administration, 24th February.

Deputy Commissioner to Commissioner, 2d March; Commissioner to Deputy Commissioner, 25th March; Deputy Commissioner to Commissioner 28th March; Board of Administration to Commissioner, 30th April 1851. Deputy Commissioner to Commissioner, 20th January 1853.

The case of Mian Bhup Singh, and the arrangement proposed for him.

he felt his position was somewhat precarious; and should he be displaced his great wealth, which he had acquired by trading, would have been in danger of confiscation. He trusted that his rivals would soon bring themselves into contempt by their incapacity and dishonesty, and that his own services would become more and more necessary to the State; and this proved to be the case. Mian Bhup Singh was one cause of dissension. An allowance of Rs. 3000 per annum had been proposed for him and his two brothers, but this the Government thought too high, and suggested Rs. 840, which the Mian refused to accept, and declared his intention of proceeding to Lahore to urge his claim.[1] His case was certainly a hard one. The Wazir hated him bitterly, and was averse to allowing him any maintenance whatever, while the opposite party had no reason to support a pretender whose intrigues might ruin them, but who could bring them no advantage. An arrangement was at length made, by which Bhup Singh was to receive Rs. 1220 a year, he engaging not to disturb or enter the Mandi State. He would not, however, swear fealty to the reigning prince, or renounce his own claim to the throne, as he imagined that this would bring him into contempt with his clan.[2]

The maladministration of Mandi.

In 1852, the administration of Mandi had fallen into the confusion and disorganisation which Wazir Gosaon had foreseen. The oppression committed by the Courts of Law was perhaps the worst of the grievances of which the people complained. So-called justice was only an

[1] Letters, Board of Administration to Commissioner, of 15th January 1852; ditto, of 23d February; Commissioner to Board of Administration, of 26th April.

[2] Letters, Deputy Commissioner of Kangra to Commissioner, of 27th June 1853; Board of Administration to Commissioner, of 27th September and 19th November 1853.

engine for gratifying private revenge or avarice; the most severe punishments were inflicted for the most trifling offences; and women were publicly sold by order of Court, even for offences committed by their relatives, while it was notorious that these orders were often passed simply to forward the licentious ends of adherents of the Sahibni and her party.[1] The wishes of the British Government, its warnings and injunctions, were alike disregarded, and it became a question whether, in the interest of the country, the direct administration should not be assumed by the British Government until the majority of the youthful Raja. But it was felt that however advantageous such a step might be, it would still be viewed by the neighbouring States with a certain suspicion, and it was resolved to reorganise the Council of Regency, giving almost the entire control of the administration, judicial and financial, to Wazir Gosaon, whose loyalty and integrity were undoubted.[2]

The Regency Council reorganised.

The improvement which resulted.

The beneficial results of this step were soon evident. The revenue increased steadily, the people ceased to complain of the maladministration of justice, and the intrigues among the officers of state were very little heard of. The Parohit, who was a bigoted old priest, much respected by the people, had charge of the palace and the domestic arrangements; while Mian Bhag Singh, who had little or

[1] The sale of women by their parents, guardians, or the Government, had always been a custom in Kulu and Mandi, and the people of the plains looked to obtaining their wives and concubines from the hills. Widows and those women who had no one to claim them, were sold by the Government; and when the Sikhs held Mandi, they rigorously enforced this right, nor did any widow dream of taking a second husband without the permission of the authorities. This custom of the country makes the abuses of the Law Courts, as described above, far less grave than they would otherwise have been.

[2] Letters, Deputy Commissioner Kangra to Commissioner, dated 20th January 1853.

no ability, was master of the horse. All real power—the treasury, finance, and justice—was in the hands of Wazir Gosaon, who, although exacting and severe, yet ruled the little State with the utmost wisdom, which was readily acknowledged by the Government.[1] In 1856, the salaries of the Members of the Council of Regency were doubled, while the State expenditure on administration was considerably reduced, and reforms, such as the reduction of the system of forced labour, were carried out.[2] New regulations were imposed upon the remarriage of widows, if that could be so called at which no ceremony whatever took place, for the Hindu law is opposed to all such remarriages. The widow who took a new protector was considered as a mistress, not as a wife; the connection was only temporary, and she was often passed from one master to another as if she had been a bullock or an article of household furniture. By the new rule a registration fee was levied on the remarriage of widows, a sum so small as not to be felt as a grievance, while it invested the new engagement with a certain solemnity and legal recognition. A man marrying a widow and deserting her, or making her over to another, was to be punished by law.[3]

Reforms introduced.

[1] Letters, No. 154, dated 23d November 1854, from Commissioner to Secretary to Chief Commissioner.

No. 953, dated 23d December 1854, from Secretary to Chief Commissioner to Commissioner.

No. 6, dated 9th January 1855, from Financial Commissioner to Secretary to Chief Commissioner.

No. 92, dated 29th January 1855, from Secretary to Chief Commissioner to Secretary to Supreme Government.

Despatch from Court of Directors to Government of India, dated 24th October 1855.

[2] Report of Major E. Lake, dated 25th September 1856; and No. 84, dated 18th October, from Secretary Chief Commissioner to Commissioner Trans-Satlej States.

[3] No. 182, from Commissioner Trans-Satlej States to Secretary Chief Commissioner, dated 13th December 1856, enclosing petition of Wazir

The marriages of the Raja.

On the 21st of July 1859, Raja Bijai Sen was married to the grand-daughter of the Raja of Datarpur; and on the 25th of the same month to a niece of the Raja of Haripur. Both these families were very poor, but among Hill Rajputs the high birth of the wife is chiefly looked to, and these marriages gave great satisfaction to the people of Mandi.

The Raja was at this time an intelligent boy of thirteen. The superintendence of his education was entrusted to the Parohit, one of the Members of the Council of Regency; but the old man had a bigoted dislike to instruction in English or Persian, and it was necessary to remind him that his position merely depended upon a proper discharge of his duty.[1] This admonition had, however, no effect. Not only was the education of the Raja neglected, but both the Parohit and Wazir Gosaon winked at, even if they did not encourage, excesses which seriously injured the constitution of the young Prince.

Parohit Shibshankar banished from Mandi.

In May 1861, the Commissioner visited Mandi, and finding that the accounts of the Parohit's negligence had been in no way exaggerated, but that his influence over the Raja was only for evil, deported him to Kangra, and fined the Wazir, who had not been less culpable, two thousand rupees. The Government approved of these measures, and further directed that the sons of the Parohit should also be banished from Mandi.[2]

Gosaon; and No. 92, from Secretary Chief Commissioner to Commissioner Trans-Satlej States, dated 14th February 1857.

This enactment was the more necessary, for the immorality of Mandi was a proverb in all the hill country, in which female chastity was everywhere a rare virtue.

[1] Report of Commissioner Trans-Satlej States, dated 20th July 1859; and Letter 889, dated 5th August 1859, from Secretary to Government Punjab to Commissioner Trans-Satlej States.

[2] Letter No. 53, from Commissioner Trans-Satlej States to Secretary to Government Punjab, dated 3d May 1861; and No. 378, dated 15th May 1861, of Secretary to Government Punjab to Commissioner Trans-Satlej States.

No one was appointed to succeed Parohit Shibshankar in the Council of Regency. There was not indeed a man in Mandi competent to perform all the duties which were supposed to be performed by the Parohit, nor was it advisable to place in Council a third member whose influence would, in all probability, have been united with that of the Wazir to diminish the influence of Mian Bhag Singh, the Raja's uncle. After this change in the administration, affairs progressed more smoothly; and, in 1863, Mr Clarke, an officer of the Educational Department, was appointed to superintend the Raja's education.[1]

Salute granted to the Raja.

The Government of India, in 1864, granted the Raja a salute of eleven guns, and the right of being received by an Assistant Commissioner on his arrival at the head-quarters of a district;[2] and, on the 12th of October 1866, the Raja, having attained his majority, was invested in full Durbar with the usual khillats of investiture by the Commissioner of Jalandhar. The influence of Wazir Gosaon was at this time very small, and the Raja wished to place most of the power in the hands of his uncle; but he was induced to abandon this intention, and make friends with the Wazir, whom he confirmed in all his appointments.

Installed as Raja, 1866.

The public works planned by the Raja.

Desirous of marking his sense of the benefits derived from the prudent management of his Ministers, the Raja determined, as an auspicious commencement of his reign, to devote a lakh of rupees from the savings which had accumulated during his minority, to public works most beneficial to his State. These included a post-office, con-

[1] Letters—Government of India, Foreign Department, No. 2656, of 23d May 1861; No. 19, of 10th January 1862; and No. 149, from Commissioner, Trans-Satlej States to Secretary to Government Punjab.

[2] No. 394, Government of India, Foreign Department, dated 13th April 1864.

nected with the Government Postal Department; a large school at Mandi; a dispensary; a good mule road from Baijnath to Sultanpur Kulu, over the Babbu Pass; and serais and travellers' bungalows along the line of road from the Kangra valley, through Mandi, towards Kulu and Simla. These works were at once undertaken; some have been already completed, and others are still in progress.[1]

The promise of the commencement of the Raja's reign not fulfilled.

The promise of the opening of the Raja's reign has not, unfortunately, been realised. It might reasonably have been supposed that in Mandi, a State completely under the control of the British Government, which had not bound itself, as elsewhere, to abstain from all interference with its internal management, the young Chief might have received a training such as would fit him to fulfil the duties of a ruler with honesty and ability, to know the servants whom he might with safety trust, and to study the welfare of the people entrusted to his care. From the time that the Raja had been four years old, his education and training had been conducted under the direction and care of Government officials, and for several years previous to his installation an English tutor had been specially appointed to superintend his studies and complete his education. But the influence of the zanana, and the evil counsels of men who found their interest in the incapacity of the Chief, have made Mandi furnish another example of the almost universal rule which shows a long minority in a Native State to be fatal to the character of the Chief.

[1] Letter of 13th October 1866, from Commissioner Jalandhar to Secretary Government Punjab; and No. 881, dated 3d December 1866, of Government Punjab.

No. 129, of 8th April 1867, from Commissioner Jalandhar to Secretary to Government Punjab.

The administration of Mandi soon fell into the greatest confusion; the Raja would not himself attend to business, and was jealous of the interference and advice of his Minister; all expenditure on useful works was stopped; the revenue was wasted on unworthy objects; and the Viceroy, in 1868, found it necessary to convey to the Raja a most serious warning to the effect that the arrangement concluded with the Mandi State in 1846 gave to the British Government the power of removing from the throne any ruler who might prove himself of worthless character, and incapable of properly conducting the administration; and this power, in the interests of the people and the country, would be exercised if friendly counsel was found unavailing.[1]

The disorder and extravagance at Mandi.

The warning of the Government.

The result of this warning was a temporary improvement in the administration; but matters soon relapsed into their former state, and, in June 1870, Mr Clarke was removed from the position of Councillor to the Raja, which he had occupied since October 1866, when the Chief was installed, and Mr E. Harrison, B.C.S., was appointed in his place, to advise the Raja in all matters of administration in association with Wazir Gosaon, and to endeavour to introduce into Mandi the reforms long promised and long delayed.[2]

A new Councillor appointed.

The population of the Mandi State is about 140,000. The revenue, according to the latest returns, is about Rs. 3,50,000 per annum. The principal sources of

The population and revenue of Mandi.

[1] Report of Commissioner Jalandhar to Punjab Government, Government Punjab to Government of India, No. 481, dated 27th November 1868; Government of India to Government Punjab, No. 1503, dated 18th December 1868; Lieutenant-Governor to Raja of Mandi, dated 29th January 1869; Secretary of State's despatch, No. 50, dated 4th March 1869.

[2] Commissioner Jalandhar to Government Punjab, dated 18th June 1870. Government Punjab to Commissioner Jalandhar, No. 798, dated 9th July 1870.

revenue are the land tax, salt, and iron, the former yielding nearly half the revenue, and salt one-third. The ordinary expenditure can be easily kept down to two lakhs and a half, including the tribute paid to the British Government of one lakh of rupees.

The revenue from salt has somewhat increased of late years, while that from the iron mines has remained nearly stationary. In the financial year 1851–52, the receipts from these sources were Rs. 74,887 and Rs. 25,474 respectively; in 1854–55, Rs. 85,353 and Rs. 29,835; in 1857-58, Rs. 85,378 and Rs. 19,116; and in 1861–62, Rs. 1,00,545 and Rs. 24,772. The land revenue never rises much above Rs. 1,55,000. The Mandi State can scarcely be said to maintain a military force. There are no cavalry, and the artillery consists of four small guns. In the present year, 1870, there are nominally 1750 infantry entertained, armed with swords and matchlocks, but they are quite undisciplined, and their duties are those of rural police. They are paid in grain or by an assignment of land.

APPENDICES.

The following Statements, drawn up in the early years of British administration of the Cis-Satlej territory, are in many cases incorrect, and some of the names are difficult to trace; but they contain much interesting information, and are accordingly published without any attempt at correction.

Appendix A.—STATEMENT of the CONQUESTS and YEARS 1214, 1215,

Villages.	Taluqas.	Parganahs.	From whom Taken.
18	...	Ludhiana	Rani Roy Ilias Rai Alyas
6	...	Do.	Rani Roy Ilias and Rani Luchmy
1	Jhundala	Do.	Rani Roy Ilias
9	Do.	Do.	Do. and do.
14	...	Do.	Do.
2	Kote	Pyub	Do.
2	Jugraon	Tahara	Do.
2	Busia	Do.	Wife of Miah Ghouse
3	Ghungrana	Pyub	Gujur Singh and Jut Mul Singh of Roypoor
27	Moumda	Sirhind	Sons of Durrum Singh of Umborsir
17	Buddowala	Ludhiana	Rani Roy Ilias
8	Do.	Do.	Do. and Sikhs of Khunna
5	Jugraon	Tahara	Do.
2	...	Pyub	Do. and Luchmy
4	Ghungrana	Do.	Gujur Singh and Jate Singh
1	Do.	Do.	Do. and Jut Mul Singh
2	...	Ryhimabad	Rani Luchmy
13	Kote	Pyub	Rani Roy Ilias
8	Do.	Tahara	Do.
1	Do.	Pyub	Do. and Gujur Singh
2	Busia	Tahara	Wife of Miah Ghouse
6	Tulwundee	Do.	Rani Roy Ilias
1	Jugraon	Do.	Do.
2	Ghungrana	Do.	Gujur Singh
5	Do.	Do.	Do. and Kabool Khan
4	Do.	Do.	Do.
2	Kunnah	Pyub	Rani Roypooree
8	Do.	Sirhind	Do.
7	Do.	Pyub	Run Singh and Nadown Singh
1	Do.	Machunwara	Do.
8	Dhaka	Ludhiana	Rani Roy Ilias
3	Do.	Do.	Do. and Sikhs of Kankra
3	Kote	Pyub	Rani Roy Ilias
71	Jugraon	Tahara	Do.
1	Busia	Do.	Wife of Miah Ghouse
19	Tulwundee	Do.	Rani Roy Ilias
41	Narain Gurh	Nahun	Kour Kishin Singh
3	Roypore	Pyub	Jut Mul Singh and Hulla Singh
12	Ghilla	Ludhiana	Rani Roy Ilias and Luchmy
14	Do.	Pyub	Do. and do.
3	Do.	Do.	Do. and Nund Singh
8	Kote	Do.	Do.
25	Jugraon	Tahara	Do.
7	Tulwundee	Do.	Syud Mahomed, Syud Mirza, and Rani Ilias

GRANTS OF RAJA RANJIT SINGH IN THE FALSI AND 1216; 1806, 1807, 1808.

To whom Given.	Estimated Revenue.		Year.
Raja Bhag Singh	Rs. 14,040	Rs.	1214
Do.	1,340		1214
Do.	710		1214
Do.	1,940		1214
Do.	1,720		1214
Do.	600		1214
Do.	1,400		1214
Do.	1,510		1214
Do.	2,255		1215
Do.	17,000		1215
		42,515	
Goordut Singh	15,500		1214
Do.	750		1214
Do.	4,480		1214
Do.	360		1214
Do.	1,805		1214
Do.	550		1214
Do.	250		1216
		23,790	
Raja Jaswant Singh	14,240		1214
Do.	4,000		1214
Do.	810		1214
Do.	1,630		1214
Do.	5,310		1214
Do.	700		1214
Do.	1,950		1214
Do.	1,400		1214
Do.	315		1215
Do.	525		1216
Do.	1,000		1216
Do.	1,502		1216
Do.	800		1216
		34,240	
Futta Singh, Ahluwalia	4,280		1214
Do.	410		1214
Do.	3,620		1214
Do.	26,195		1214
Do.	210		1214
Do.	5,800		1214
Do.	12,580		1215
Do.	1,200		1215
		54,295	
Dewan Mohkum Chund	6,680		1214
Do.	2,075		1214
Do.	640		1214
Do.	5,770		1214
Do.	13,770		1214
Do.	3,000		1214
Carry forward—	31,935	1,54,840	

Statement of the Conquests and Grants

Villages.	Taluqas.	Pargannahs.	From whom Taken.
2	Tulwundee	Tahara	Rani Roy Ilias
12	Durrumkote	Do.	Rani of Sirdar Tara Singh
77	Kotekupoora	Do.	Juggut Singh of Booreea
12	Zeerah	Do.	Wife of Mohur Singh
21	Turrudkote	Do.	Goolab Singh
6	Sanewall	Pyub	Rani Luchmy
8	...	Rahoo	Do.
13	...	...	Do.
10	Jundhur	Ryhimabad	Raho Mahomed Khan
12	Chundpore		
14	Dhraee		
12	Baardpoor		
1	Kote	Pyub	Rani Roy Ilias and Goojur Singh
9	Jugraon	Tahara	Rani Roy Ilias
3	Busia	Do.	Wife of Miah Ghouse
1	Tulwundee	Do.	Rani Roy Ilias
12	Bhurrut Gurh	Pyub	Wife of Tara Singh
17	Do.	Ryhimabad	Do.
1	Do.	Rahoo	Do.
2	Labaun Gurh	Do.	Do.
25	Do.	Ryhimabad	Do.
5	Dhunnour	Do.	Do.
34	Durrumkote	Tahara	Do.
13	Share Gurh	Do.	Do.
1	Ghungrana	Do.	Goojur Singh and Teekosha
27	Khumur	Sirhind	Durrum Singh
9	Chulloudee	Judree	Wife of Sirdar Bangali Singh
9	Kylawur	Boorna	Do.
20	Ghungrana	Pyub	Goojur Singh
7	Do.	Do.	Goojur Singh and Jote Singh
5	Do.	Do.	Do. and Patans of Kote Meler
4	Do.	Do.	Goojur Singh

This list was drawn up in 1809.

OF RAJA RANJIT SINGH.—(*Continued.*)

To whom Given.	Estimated Revenue.		Year.
	Rs.	Rs.	
Brought forward—	31,935	1,54,840	
Dewan Mohkum Chund	2,110		1214
Do.	401		1215
Do.	61,400		1215
Do.	7,500		1215
Do.	19,125		1216
Do.	2,461		1216
Do.	1,778		1216
Do.	2,525		1216
Do.	25,000		
		1,54,235	1216
Busawa Singh	814		1214
Do.	4,900		1214
Do.	1,200		1214
		6,914	
Sirdar Banga Singh	400		1214
		400	
Ghurba Singh	4,370		1215
Do.	6,011		1215
Do.	300		1215
Do.	120		1215
Do.	6,168		1215
Do.	3,665		1215
		22,634	
Atur Singh	3,030		1215
Do.	980	4,010	1216
Dola Singh	70		1215
		70	
Jodh Singh, Runsia	42,000		1216
		42,000	
Jodh Singh, Kulseea	6,000		1216
Do.	4,000		1216
		10,000	
Kurum Singh, of Nugla	13,335		1215
Do.	3,350		1215
Do.	3,410		1215
Do.	3,320		1215
		23,415	
Total,		4,00,518	

(Signed) D. OCHTERLONY,
Lieutenant-Colonel.

APPENDIX B.—STATEMENT OF CHIEFS POSSESSING TERRITORY between the Satlej and Bias or Doab Jalandhar, exclusive of Districts in the Hills, as taken from old documents (privately obtained) in the time of Adina Beg Khan, Hijra 1167-70, or about A.D. 1750.

NAMES OF THE CHIEFS.	PARGANNAH.	REVENUE.	GRAND TOTAL.	FORCES. Cavalry.	FORCES. Infantry.
		Rs.	Rs.		
Succoo Singh,[1]	Tallawun, .	10,000	10,000	40	
Sirdar Futta Singh Ahlu, .	Ditto, . .	1,45,000			
Ditto, ...	Shakoopoor, .	2,65,141			
Ditto, ...	Sultapoor, .	61,105			
Ditto, ...	Badshahpoor,	70,031		7000	
Ditto, ...	Itwarpoor, .	90,195			
Ditto, ...	Hydeabad, .	7,011	6,38,483		
Boodh Singh, Fyzulaporia, .	Jalandhar, .	4,75,504			
Ditto, ...	Puttedanath, .	65,314		400	
Ditto, ...	Sohadurree, .	24,045	5,64,863		
Godh Singh, Ranigurria, .	Meanee, . .	11,901			
Ditto, ...	Ryhimabad, .	4,604			
Ditto, ...	Acberabad, .	91,450			
Ditto, ...	Dysooah, . .	2,21,000			
Ditto, ...	Hajipoor, . .	15,000			
Ditto, ...	Bassyedudeal, .	11,901		3000	2000
Ditto, ...	Sharepoor, .	7,000			
Ditto, ...	Myanee, . .	11,501			
Ditto, ...	Zuhoora, . .	41,101			
Ditto, ...	Naw Nungal,	51,021	4,66,779		
Dewan Mokum Singh, . .	Darduch Rahoo,	6,11,510			
Ditto, ...	Nakodur, . .	31,101	6,42,611		
Son of Durm Singh, of Amritsar, ...	Maulpoor, . .	1,61,901	1,61,901	400	
Godh Singh, Kulsea, . .	Sum Chowlan,	1,85,911	1,85,911	1000	
Raja Sunsar Chund, . .	Budgewara, .	4,391	4,391		
Wife of Bugale Singh, . .	Sheir Gurh, .	3,307			
Ditto, . . .	Hurana, . .	75,122	78,429	1000	
Ganda Kohie, ...	Mullout, . .	2,711	2,711	...	500
Mohur Singh, son of Munsa Singh, ...	Ghurdoombala,	61,525	61,525		
Churrut Singh,[2]	Noormuhal, .	50,111	50,011	150	
Dava Singh, ...	Sakur, . . .	25,000	25,000	1500	
	TOTAL,	. . .	28,92,615	14,490	2500

[1] Dependent on the wife of Bhungel Singh. [2] Dependent on Futta Singh Ahluwalia.

This list was drawn up in the year A.D. 1808, and is incorrect in some particulars, but is given for what it is worth.

Appendix C.—STATEMENT of the Power and Resources of the Sikh Chiefs between the Satlej and Jumna.

Names.	Distinction or Place of Residence.	Force. Cavalry.	Force. Infantry.	Revenue.
				Rs.
Maharaja Sahib Singh,	Pattiala,	2000	1000	6,10,000
Bhais Lal Singh, Busawa Singh, and Kurm Singh,	Kythal Baut,	600	...	2,25,000
Raja Jaswant Singh,	Nabha,	400	...	1,50,000
„ Bhag Singh and dependants,	Jindh,	600	...	1,25,000
Nawab Rehmut Khan,	Koonjpoora,	250	...	50,000
Sirdar Goordut Singh,	Ladwah,	1000	...	1,50,000
„ Dulcha Singh	Rudour,	125	...	60,000
„ Bhugwan Singh, Jymul Singh, and Golab Singh,	Boorea,	600	...	1,00,000
„ Bunga Singh and Goolab Singh,	Thunasir and Dehli,	325	...	75,000
Rani Dya Kour and dependants,	Ambala,	500	...	95,000
Ata-ulla Khan and Pathans,	Maler Kotla,	400	...	40,000
Boodh Singh,	Fyzoolapoor,	200	...	15,000
Jodh Singh and dependants,	Kulseah,	1000	...	1,50,000
Sirdar Futta Singh Ahlu,	Isaroo,	...	...	50,000
Mia Maul Leaoh,	Ramgurh,[1]	150	...	40,000
Jowar Singh,	Baroope,[1]	300	...	1,00,000
Golab Singh, Mehtab Singh, and Dya Singh,	Syheedgurh,	250	...	50,000
Dava Singh,	Bugvaean,	500	...	50,000
Gopaul Singh,	Mansemajra,[1]	200	400	1,00,000
Sodhe Surjun Singh and Dedar Singh,	Mukhowal,[1]	300	...	1,10,000
Sodhe Churut Singh,	Machewara,[1]	70	...	20,000
Nund Singh,	Chumkoor,	40	...	10,000
Goojur Singh,	Nara,	50	...	10,000
Churut Singh,	Luddeah,	100	...	10,000
Shair Singh and Sooja Singh	Sooter,	200	...	15,000
Dubail Singh and Bagh Singh,	Mullowdah,	220	...	35,000
Joy Singh	Gharauk,	25	...	5,000
Beer Singh and Deep Singh,	Buddowree,	150	...	20,000
Mohur Singh,	Tulwande Majooka,	25	...	5,000
Miah Noudah,	Budnee,	150	...	10,000
Baug Singh, Itulgah,	Dakharee,	40	...	4,000
Punjab Singh,	Sadoora,	100	...	10,000
Nutha Singh,	Khooruaneah,	200	...	10,000
Hummeer Singh,	Pukkee,	40	...	5,000
Kootuboodden Khan Kapoor,	Mumdout,	300	...	5,000
Doonah Singh,	Firozpur,	60	...	10,000
Sikhs of Byrar,	Maharajke,	100	...	15,000
Futta Singh and Runjit Singh,	Shahabad,	200	...	40,000
	Total,	11,450	1400	25,84,000

[1] Near the hills.

This list was drawn up about A.D. 1808. It is very far from correct, and much underestimates both the revenue enjoyed by the Chiefs, and the number of men they could put into the field.—L. G.

APPENDIX D.—STATEMENT OF THE POSSESSIONS, MILITARY FORCE, AND REVENUE of the Sikh Chieftains south of the Satlej, drawn up A.D. 1809.

NAMES.	TOWNS, &c.	REVENUE.	MILITARY FORCE.
		Rs.	
Raja Sahib Singh and his dependants,	Duties collected in the town of Pattiala, . . .	27,000	
	Duties collected at the village Rookee, near Pattiala, . .	19,000	
	Duties collected on moligo throughout the Raja's territory, .	25,000	
	Pargannah Ginor and 56 villages,	22,000	
	Burwalah Batter with 36 ,,	19,000	
	Rannee Magra and 32 ,,	15,000	
	Korain with . 30 ,,	14,200	
	Kunheer . 45 ,,	45,000	
	Mardanpur and Harpalpur, . 40 ,,	40,000	
	Kurwanun Krotan with . 30 ,,	19,000	
	Abluwal, . 27 ,,	10,000	
	Jagir Jib, . 25 ,,	10,000	
	Sefabad, . 24 ,,	20,700	
	Sirhind, . 40 ,,	25,000	
	Mundpur Koolomal with . 28 ,,	14,000	
	Himmat Gurh, 260 ,,	10,000	
	Pyj Gurh, . 17-6 ,,	11,000	
	Pihal, . . 70-6 ,,	35,000	
	Dhodi, . . 29-6 ,,	14,000	
	Mansopur, . 27-6 ,,	12,000	
	Umar Garh, . 30-6 ,,	40,000	
	Sherpur Bassawra with 25-6 ,,	16,000	
	Gunam, . 35-6 ,,	17,000	
	Dhurbuh, . 25-6 ,,	15,000	
	Munak, . 29-6 ,,	22,000	
	Utkhiria, . 40-6 ,,	12,000	
	Bathinda, . 50-6 ,,	35,000	
	Hudeauh & Barnalah, 40-6 ,,	17,000	
	Palvih, . 24-6 ,,	10,000	
	Oolniwal, . 7-6 ,,	10,000	
	Balu, . . 20-6 ,,	2,000	
	Banooch, . 45 ,,	40,000	
	Labu, . . 40-6 ,,	24,000	
	Panjaur Dun with 40 ,,	10,000	
	Jhariy, . 18-6 ,,	10,000	
	Tarneh, . 35-6 ,,	9,000	
	Ranniah, . 55-6 ,,	12,000	
	Gamanah, . 30-6 ,,	10,000	
	Badsikhri, . 25-6 ,,	11,200	
	Mohri Tega, . 40-6 ,,	15,000	
	Gamurdgarh, . 20-6 ,,	11,000	
	Mihilari, . 30-6 ,,	10,000	
	Hareg, . 30-6 ,,	11,000	
	Chumaru Shamdi with 12-6 ,,	3,000	
	Maudpur Sahori with 15-6 ,,	7,000	
	Khurali with . 56 ,,	2,000	
	Laungowal, . 11-6 ,,	5,000	Horse, 2500
	Mussingurh, . 35-6 ,,	10,000	Foot, 2200
	Manshuh, . 10-6 ,,	6,000	with a considerable number of guns of various calibre
	Talwandi, . 14-6 ,,	5,000	
	Moripur, . 16-6 ,,	13,000	
	Chiwaltal, . 17-6 ,,	9,000	
	Total, ...	8,36,100	

Appendix D.—(Continued.)

Names.	Towns, &c.	Revenue.	Military Force.
Bhai Lal Singh and his dependants,		Rs.	
	Duties collected at Kythal,	28,500	
	25 villages,	25,000	
	Nibki Taluqa, with 41 „	47,350	
	Murtazapur, . 7-6 „	7,000	
	Dhanitah Barat, . 27-6 „	21,350	
	Gulloh, . . 60-6 „	50,000	
	Miholan, . . 12-6 „	10,500	
	Kular, . .	3,000	
	Dabar Chaboh, . 3 „	1,600	
	Chall Buchon, . 5 „	1,200	
	Fateh Kot, . . 3 „	500	
	Pundri, . . 7 „	11,400	
	Pai, . . . 3 „	7,000	
	Honburg, . . 7 „	1,250	
	Amir, . . 4-6 „	2,000	
	Mahatudi, . . 12-6 „	18,000	
	Churasi, . . 5-6 „	17,000	
	Half of the town of Guhanahaud, . 22-6 „	19,000	
	Faridpur, &c., . 18-6 „	16,000	
	Possessions in the Buranah country, ...	15,000	
	Total	3,02,650	
Karm Singh, . .	Kakralah, Mardirhirah, Sonsoh, Barnoh, Budledah, &c., &c., Number of villages unknown,	27,000	
Bisawa Singh, .	Anauli, . . 14-10 villages,	25,000	
	Given to him by Royit Singh, . 13-6 „	6,914	Horse, 900 Foot, 2000
	Total Revenue of Bhai Lal Singh, &c., . .	3,61,564	
Bhag Singh and his dependants,	Kar Bhodoh, . 20 villages,	50,500	
	Duties collected in Jhind, .	18,000	
	and, . . 72 villages,	52,000	
	Safidon, . . 12 „	10,000	
	Panjgiraun, &c., . 10 „	5,000	
	Lachaneh, . .	45,000	
	Sangrur, . .	25,000	
	Bhuwanoh, . .	14,000	
	Half of Gubana and . 26 „	21,000	
	Barsat, &c., . . 20 „	16,500	
	Bassian and other places in the Buranah country, .	20,000	Horse, 800 Foot, 200
	Dharm Garh, . 5-6 „		
	Total, . . .	2,77,000	

APPENDIX D.—(*Continued.*)

NAMES.	TOWNS, &c.	REVENUE.	MILITARY FORCE.
Juswant Singh, .	Duties collected at Nabha and other places, . . .	Rs. 19,700	
	30 villages,	26,000	
	Pakhowal, . . 25 ,,	32,000	
	Bahadro, . . 25 ,,	15,000	
	Amlah, . . 20 ,,	16,000	
	Phul, . . 22 ,,	10,000	
	Dhanolah, . . 20 ,,	15,000	
	Andlu, . . 17 ,,	19,000	Horse, 600
	Dholah, . . 11 ,,	8,000	Foot, 600
	Baddo, . . 7 ,,	4,000	6 large guns.
	Rori, . . 30 ,,	25,000	8 small ones.
	Kanyya, . . 14 ,,	15,000	
	Total, . . .	2,04,700	
Gurdit Singh and his dependants,	Duties collected at Ludhiana, .	12,200	
	and . . 94 villages,	81,350	
	Baddowal, . . 26 ,,	30,000	
	Paddhi, . . 18 ,,	17,000	
	Shekpoora, . . 9 ,,	9,000	
	Singhor and 20 villages taken from the family of Diwan Singh, .	50,000	
	Total, . . .	1,99,550	
Dal Singh, . .	Half of town of Indri and 2 villages.	4,000	Horse, 1530
Dunna Singh, Mahna Singh, and Sahib Singh,	9 ,,	10,000	Foot, 400 6 small guns.
Ugah Singh, . .	Sikrandah, . . 9 ,,	4,000	2 ten-prs.
	Total Revenue of Gurdit Singh and his dependants, .	2,17,550	
Bhanga Singh and his dependants,	Duties collected in Manassah, .	10,000	
	and . . 35 villages,	30,000	
	Kalsowah and 9 villages near the bank of the river, with ¼ of Biana,	35,000	Horse, 400
	Dhoatambal and 40 villages taken from the family of Diwan Singh,	35,000	Foot, 150 2 eight-prs.
Gulab Singh, . .	Damkouli and 150 villages, .	10,000	4 small guns.
	Total, . . .	1,20,000	
Sher Singh, Khark Singh and Ranjit Singh, the sons of Karm Singh deceased, and their dependants,			
Sher Singh and Khark Singh, . .	Duties collected in the town of Soomalabad and Shahabad, .	5,000	
	14 Villages, . . .	20,000	Horse, 250
Ranjit Singh, .	13 Villages, . . .	10,000	Foot, 150
6 Pattiwalas, or principal Zamindars, related to the family, and possessing between them, . . .	49 Villages, . . .	30,000	
	Total, . . .	65,000	

Appendix D.—(*Continued.*)

Names.	Towns, &c.	Revenue.	Military Force.
Dya Kaur and her dependants,	Duties collected in Ambala, 31 villages,	Rs.	
Rakh Bha Sing, .	Tirooh, . . 29 ,,		
Dya Singh, . .	Baial, . . 15 ,,		
Sukhdas Singh, .	Panjakwah, . 18 ,,		
Desa Singh and Tehl Singh, . .	Bah, . . 9 ,,		
Rajat Singh, . .	Jhandali, . . 8 ,,		Horse, 400
Bagh Singh Giljah	Dukhiri, . .		Foot, 150
	Total, . .	1,00,000	
Petty chieftains of .	Cheloh, Munsauli, Karoh, Mandoh, &c.	3,00,000	
Dulchi Singh and dependants, . .	Duties collected in Ridhor,	1,000	
	and . . 39 villages,	46,000	
Parem Singh, .	Haliahar and villages,	8,000	
Joud Singh Patli,	Patli and . 2 ,,	6,000	
Sudha Singh and Tolyni Singh, . .	Dhinhonah, . .	3,000	
Jay Singh, . .	Jynper, . . .	5,400	Horse, 184
Khushhal Singh and Orewuh Singh,	4 ,,	7,500	Foot, 120
	Total, . .	76,900	
Bhagwan Singh and his dependants,	Duties collected at Buria, .	500	
	—— Jigadri, . . .	11,000	
	—— the ghats of Mikoord, Jittabuh, and Tigru, . .	7,500	
	—— Bughat, . . .	1,000	
	81 villages,	85,000	
	Duties collected, . . .	5,000	
Golab Singh and Zalam Singh, the sons of Sher Singh, deceased,	Chauki Damloh, . . .	3,700	
	Duties collected at Raj Ghat, .	2,000	
	At Buria, . . .	300	
	72 villages,	60,000	
	Duties, .	6,200	
Suba Singh, . .	25 ,, .	30,000	Horse, 330
	Duties, . .	5,000	Foot, 495
	Total, . .	2,17,200	
Gopal Singh, . .	Duties collected at Manimajra,	5,000	
	45 villages,	55,600	
	Mulapur, . . 126 ,,	6,000	Horse, 200
	Duties, . .	2,000	Foot, 300
	Chandikli, and . 6 ,,	5,000	1 twelve-pr.,
	Parbat, . . 7 ,,	6,000	1 eight-pr.,
			1 six-pr., and
	Total, .	79,000	4 guns.

APPENDIX D.—(*Continued.*)

NAMES.	TOWNS, &c.	REVENUE.	MILITARY FORCE.
		Rs.	
Dalel Singh, .	Sinoh, . . 40 villages,	35,000	10 guns.
	Mallaud, . . 25 ,,	15,000	Horse, 150
	Duties, ...	2,000	Foot, 150
	Total, . . .	52,000	
Dharm Singh, .	Khar, . . 256 villages,	20,000	200
Dunna Singh, .	Faridkot, . . .	35,000	200
Ata-ulla Khan and Pathans, . .	Maler Kotla, . . .	40,000	400
Rehmat Khan, .	Koonjproosh, ...	3,000	
	38 villages in Pargannah Karnal, .	50,000	
	20 villages in Pargannah Indri and Badoli, ...	19,058	
Ghulam Muhay-uddin Khan, . .	Baroging, and . 30 villages,	14,050	Horse, 20
Karm Khan, . .	Gir, and . . 30 ,,	2,900	Foot, 600
	Total, . . .	89,008	
Jodh Singh Kalsia,	Chichrauli, . . 45 villages,	40,000	
	Bilaspur, . . 13 ,,		
	Rannipur, Badhi, and 20 ,,	20,000	
	Khizarabad, . . 40 ,,	10,000	
	Kullawah, Chulandu, & 22 ,,	6,000	
	Gudholi, Binjipur, and 28 ,,	10,000	
	Bhirtal, . . 24 ,,	10,000	
	Sidhomah, . . 16 ,,	15,000	
	Burail Koorhan, . 24 ,,	35,000	
	Deroh, Bassi, and . 22 ,,	20,000	
	Chuni, Machli, Kurun Ghin, and . . 21 ,,	15,000	
	Ramgarh, . . 27 ,,	10,000	
	Mustaufabad, Sarund, Jaghdri, and Tuskeh, 59 ,,	39,000	Horse, 1535 Foot, 850
	Duties, ...	27,000	
	Total, . . .	2,57,000	
Fateh Singh, .	Half of Naraingarh, . .	15,000	
	Kahnpur, . . 21 villages,	7,000	
	Fatehpur, . . 7 ,,	8,000	
	Jagrawn and . . 20 ,,	19,000	
	Tehawah and . . 10 ,,	13,000	
	Sidham, . . 25 ,,	20,000	
	Bhosi and . . 35 ,,	22,000	
	Jeui and . . 37 ,,	30,000	
	Hattouh, . . 10 ,,	5,000	
	Khupur Baretah, . 15 ,,	5,000	
	Golia Jhulaiah, . 20 ,,	4,000	
	Isan Ker Kot, and . 25 ,,	22,000	Horse, 1000
	Maknoo, . . .	6,000	Foot, 400
	Total, . . .	1,76,000	

Appendix D.—(*Continued.*)

Names.	Towns, &c.	Revenue.	Military Force.
Sons of Jawahir Singh,	Half of Naraingarh, . .	15,000	
	Fatehgarh, ...	} 55,000	
	Jutwar, ...		
	Bhudi, ...		Guns, 3
	Biragh, ...		Horse, 250
	Duties, ...	7,200	Foot, 400
	Total, . . .	77,200	
Mehtab Singh and Gulab Singh, sons of Karm Singh Shahid	Shahzadpur and 18 villages with Kiri and . . 18 villages,	39,000	
Dya Singh, . .	Fingor, . . 7 „	7,000	
Subu Singh, and Golab Singh Mandpuri, ...	. . . 18 „	26,000	Horse, 130 Foot, 100
	Total, . .	72,000	
Bhup Singh, and Dewa Singh,	Rupar, . . 60 villages,	36,000	
	Khizarabad, and . 32 „	10,000	
	Lalbi Mazara, . 10 „	2,000	
	Mianpur, . . . 13 „	5,000	
	Total, . .	53,000	
Mohkam Chand and other Sirdars, dependent on Ranjit Singh,	Kot Kapurah, . 35 villages,	29,000	
	Jhira, . . 15 „	5,000	
	Rahimbad, . .	} 76,000	
	Talwandi, . .		
	Sunwal, and other places,		
	Gungranah, . .	24,500	
	Gajjarwal, Raepur, .	500	
	Soholi, . . 12 „	10,000	
	Badni, Himmalpura,	5,000	
	Jhito ke Qille, .	6,000	
Garhba Singh, .	Bhart Garh, Salan Garh, with . 78 „	30,000	
		1,86,000	
	Chanolgarh, . 8 villages,	8,000	
	Dhana Sanu Khon and . . 10 „	2,000	
	Balolpur, . . 9 „	10,000	
	Duties, . .	3,200	
Dunna Singh, . .	Firozpur . . 40 „	40,000	
Ottuh Singh, . .	Dharm Kot, .	40,000	
	Total, . .	2,89,200	

APPENDIX D.—(*Continued.*)

NAMES.	TOWNS, &c.	REVENUE.	MILITARY FORCE.
Soojhun Singh and Jeymul Singh,	Chankowah with . 100 villages,		
	Raomajra, . . 8 „		
	Mansowah, . . 5 „		
	Salahpur, . . 5 „		
	Dhawli, . . 18 „	45,000	
Khem Singh, . .	Makhowal, . .	20,000	
	Nandpur, . . 40 „		
	Phulsondah and . 2 „		
Nunel Singh, . .	Khowali, . . 20 „		
	Atalah, . . 15 „	12,000	
Charht Singh .	Bakhmajra and . 2 „	600	
	Total, . . .	77,600	
Gujjar Singh, Khazan Singh, and Muttah Singh, called the Kahar Seeks, . .	Kurana, . . .	25,000	
Ramsarn, son of Gujjar Singh,	Palasian, . . 30 villages,	10,000	
	Gulawaiah, . . 10 „	5,000	
	Badhian, . . 20 „	7,000	
	Macholi, . . .	5,000	
	Sukrai, . . .	5,000	
	Total, . . .	57,000	
Budh Singh Fyzullapuria,	Mator Barial, . .	16,000	
	Kotallah, . . 27 villages,	14,000	
	Amankot, . . 60 „	24,000	
	Total, . . .	54,000	
Charht Singh, .	Machewal, . . .	20,000	
Other petty Chieftains, ...	Ramgarh, &c., &c., . .	1,00,000	
	Total, . . .	1,20,000	

ABSTRACT.

NAMES.	TOWNS, &c.	REVENUE.	MILITARY FORCE.
		Rs.	
Raja Sahib Singh, . .	Pattiala, . .	8,36,500	4,700
Bhai Lal Singh, . .	Kythal, . .	3,91,564	2,900
Bhag Singh, . . .	Jhind, . .	2,89,000	2,000
Jaswant Singh, . . .	Nabha, . .	2,04,700	1,200
Gurdit Singh, . . .	Ladhwa, . .	2,17,550	1,930
Bhanga Singh, . . .	Thanasah, . .	1,20,000	550
The sons of Karm Singh of	Shahabad, . .	65,000	400
Rani Dya Kour, . .	Ambala, . .	1,37,000	550
Dulcha Singh, . . .	Ridhor, . .	76,900	304
Bhagwan Singh, . .	Buria, . .	2,17,200	825
Gopal Singh, . . .	Manimajra, .	79,000	500
Dalel Singh, . . .	Mallaudh, . .	52,000	300
Ata-ullah Khan, . .	Maler Kotla, .	40,000	400
Rehmat Khan, . . .	Kunjpuria, . .	89,008	800
Petty Chieftains, . .	Chelah, Manouli, &c.,	4,00,000	600
The above Chieftains may be considered as under the protection of the British Government.		29,15,472	17,959
The following are subject to Ranjit Singh :—			
Johd Singh, ...	Chichrauli, .	2,57,000	Kalsia.
The sons of Karm Singh, Shahid, ...	Shahzadpur, .	72,000	
Fateh Singh Aluah, . .	Jagrawn, . .	1,76,000	
Jawahar Singh, . . .	Jatwar, . .	77,200	
Mohkam Chand, . .	Rahimadad, .	1,60,500	
Garhbu Singh, . . .	Bhartgarh, . .	53,200	
Budh Singh, ...	Amankot, . .	54,000	
Bhup Singh and Dowa Singh,	Ropar, . .	53,000	
Gajjar Singh and others, .	Makhowal, .	77,600	
Gujjar Singh and others, .	Kamano, . .	25,000	
Dharm Singh, . . .	Khar, . .	20,000	
Ram Sarn Singh, . .	Palasian, . .	32,000	
Atar Singh, ...	Dharm Kot, .	40,000	
Charht Singh and Garhbu Singh, ...	Machiwari, .	20,000	
Dunna Singh, . . .	Firozpur, . .	40,000	
Golab Singh, . . .	Faridkot, . .	35,000	
Petty Chieftains, . .	Ramgarh, &c., .	1,40,000	7,000
		13,32,500	7,000
Total amount of revenue of the country between Dehli and Satlej, exclusive of the British possessions, ...		42,47,922	24,959

(Signed) F. S. WHITE.

This statement is only given for what it is worth, and is not believed to be very accurate. The total of the country under British protection should be Rs. 32,03,422, and not as given, Rs. 29,15,422.—L. G.

Appendix E.—STATEMENT of the Chiefs east of Satlej who are dependent on the Raja of Lahore, and others who have been left undisturbed in their Possessions by him, and have not sent Vakils or maintained any intercourse with the English.

Names of Chiefs.	Destination or Place of Residence.	Distance from Ludhiana. Miles.		Remarks.
Diwan Mohkam Chand				
Ghurla Singh, .	Bhart Garh, .	22	East.	These are dependants of Raja Ranjit Singh, and generally owe their possessions to his bounty, paying a trifling tribute or holding in Jaidad.
Atar Singh, . .	Dharm Kot, .	40	West.	
Dalel Singh, .	Tibba, . .	15	East.	
Fateh Singh Ahluwalia, . .	Kot Jagrawan, .	20	West.	
Karm Singh, .	Gungrana, .	11	East	
Deva Singh and Bhup Singh, .	Ropar, . .	30	”	
Sabar Sargan Singh and Deva Singh,	Makhowal, .	4	”	
Sadu Charht Singh,	Machhiwara, .	15	”	
Nand Singh, .	Khankoia, .	10	South-East.	
Gujjar Singh, .	Narah, . .	40	East.	These distances and bearings are not correct, but the Chiefs may be deemed neutral, or for the most part from selfish motives would probably join the English in case of a rupture with the Raja of Lahore.
Charht Singh, .	Luddeha, . .	15	”	
Dalel Singh and Bhag Singh, .	Malland, . .	15	”	
Jay Singh, . .	Gharank, . .	25	”	
Mohan Singh, .	Talwandi Majoka,	25	South.	
Bhag Singh Giljah,	Dakhari, . .	24	East.	
Nath-tha Singh, .	Khumaneh, .	15	”	
Karm Singh, .	Pikee, . .	70	South.	
Mian Mul Dai, .	Ramgarh, . .	40	East.	
Jawahar Singh, .	Barup, . .	40	”	
Mian Nandah, .	Badni . .	30	West.	
Dunnah Singh, .	Firozpur, . .	70	”	

(Signed) D. OCHTERLONY,
Lieutenant-Colonel.

List drawn up in A.D. 1809.

INDEX.

INDEX.

PRINTED BY BALLANTYNE AND COMPANY
EDINBURGH AND LONDON